GORBACHEV AND HIS REFORMS
1985–1990

GORBACHEV AND HIS REFORMS 1985–1990

RICHARD SAKWA

Keynes College
University of Kent

Prentice Hall

New York   London   Toronto   Sydney   Tokyo   Singapore

First published 1990 by
Philip Allan
66 Wood Lane End, Hemel Hempstead
Hertfordshire HP2 4RG

A division of
Simon & Schuster International Group

This edition published 1991
by Prentice Hall, Inc.
A division of Simon & Schuster
Englewood Cliffs, New Jersey 07632

Printed and bound in Great Britain
at the University Press, Cambridge

ISBN 0–13–362427–7

Library of Congress Cataloging-in-Publication data
are available from the publisher.

1 2 3 4 5   95 94 93 92 91

TO ROZA

CONTENTS

ABBREVIATIONS

A. i F.	*Argumenty i fakty*
G	*Guardian*
Ind.	*Independent*
Iz.	*Izvestiya*
K	*Kommunist*
LF on EE	*Labour Focus on Eastern Europe*
LG	*Literaturnaya gazeta*
MEMO	*Mirovaya ekonomika i mezhdunarodnye otnosheniya*
MN	*Moscow News*
NM	*Novyi mir*
NYR	*New York Review of Books*
Ob.	*Observer*
P	*Pravda*
PZ	*Partiinaya zhizn'*
PSS	*Polnoe Sobranie Sochinenii*
RM	*Russkaya mysl'*
SI	*Sotsialisticheskaya industriya*
SN	*Soviet News*
ST	*Sunday Times*
VI KPSS	*Voprosy istorii KPSS*

PREFACE

This book will assess the nature and significance of the changes in the Soviet Union under the leadership of Mikhail Gorbachev. With his election as General Secretary of the Communist Party in March 1985 the country embarked on the long-delayed modernisation of its political and economic institutions. The USSR once again became accustomed to having a dynamic leader after the long years of stability under Brezhnev, which in its final stages had degenerated into near immobility.

But why do we talk about Gorbachev and *his* reforms? The emphasis on the role of an individual in the momentous changes affecting a whole society may appear misplaced. After all, it might be argued, there were elements of collective leadership in the Soviet political system. Furthermore, with or without Gorbachev the need for change was self-evident and pressing, and a broad constituency was coalescing in favour of new policies. Economic development had created a more educated, urbanised and informed society. Several points can be made in response. The structure of Soviet politics meant that change was inevitably focused on the person of the leader, and leadership change is traditionally an opportunity for policy change. The theme of collective leadership was remarkable for its near absence after 1985, and in its place a presidential system emerged. Furthermore, the recognition of the need for change does not necessarily mean that change will take place. History is littered with examples of nations and empires that failed to respond to developments in time and were fated to pass into oblivion. The Ottoman empire is a case in point, not to mention the autocracy in pre-revolutionary Russia itself. The revolutions of 1989 in Eastern Europe perhaps demonstrated the fate that the Soviet leadership so narrowly averted.

The reforms between 1985 and 1990 in the USSR were stamped at all stages with Gorbachev's personality and character. Valentin Falin, then head of the Novosti news agency, went so far as to argue that

'*Perestroika* (restructuring) is Gorbachev, and Gorbachev is *perestroika*' (Panorama, 23 May 1988). It took an act of political and personal courage to plan and implement the reform programme. The reforms were very much Gorbachev's personal achievement. While impersonal sociological processes, considered by Marxists the main driving force of history, have undoubtedly contributed to *perestroika*, equally indisputably the crucial role of personality in history has been demonstrated over and over again during the whole course of Soviet history, and with particular force since 1985. Clearly the reform process did not spring from Gorbachev's mind like Minerva from the brow of Zeus. Long-term factors and socioeconomic changes played a crucial role, together with changing perceptions of the Soviet leadership as a whole and new ideas taking hold of the intellectual élite and society.

Gorbachev recognised that the problems of the Soviet economy and society lay not just in the shortcomings of Brezhnev's leadership. They were exacerbated by a prolonged period of drift, but ultimately Gorbachev came to the conclusion that the model of socialism adopted in the early years of Soviet power had certain flaws. Stalin himself, it has been admitted more and more openly, only aggravated problems that were already inherent in the Soviet system of government bequeathed by Lenin. The confusion between the party and the state, for instance, the ambivalence towards the rule of law, and the confused constitutional position of the leader provided the conditions for the emergence of Stalinism. The new understanding of the past thus became an essential part of the attempt to change the present.

The use of the word 'reform' still has to be justified. Gorbachev himself avoided using the term in his first year in office, preferring the more neutral concept of *perestroika* under which to promote his changes. The various periphrases of earlier years, such as 'improving the economic mechanism' and 'perfecting socialist construction' only gradually gave way to a new vocabulary. From 1987 the concept of 'radical reform' became dominant. Gorbachev himself, understandably, liked to argue that the changes represented a veritable 'revolution', given the positive connotations of the word in Soviet political culture. While the originality of the reforms should not be minimised, the process up to early 1990 could not be considered a revolution. The elements of continuity with the past could not be ignored. A revolution aims not only to change a government but also to transform the political system and the property relations in society. Gorbachev's reforms were not designed to overthrow the old but to tap the potential of the existing system and to make it work better. Hence the process was indeed a reform, but whose radicalism excuses the use of the term revolutionary reformism. It was indeed a 'revolution within a revolution'.

The Soviet reformist leadership tried to develop a model of socialism that was more dynamic than the state-centred and authoritarian structures of the past. The reforms were launched in the belief that such a socialism could be salvaged from the wreckage of the earlier Utopianism once the 'deformations and deviations' of the past had been overcome. However, the question increasingly arose whether traditional socialism, and in particular Leninism, could be regarded as part of the solution rather than part of the problem, a view which appears to have been dominant in the East European revolutions. The belief of the Gorbachevites was emphatically that a new political and economic model of socialism could be found to satisfy the demands of a great state and the aspirations of a sophisticated people into the twenty-first century. The aim of this book is to examine the features of this new system as they had become apparent by 1990, to evaluate the arguments, debates and actions that accompanied their implementation, and to analyse their limitations.

This book is not an attempt to inflate the personality cult of Gorbachev but rather tries to understand the reform process as the interaction of individuals, institutions, ideas, groups and nations. Nevertheless, *perestroika* was shaped by the role of leadership focused on the person of Gorbachev. He led from the front and each decisive turn in the spiral of reform was achieved by his decisive personal intervention. The limitations of the reforms also reflect the limitations and hesitancies of Gorbachev himself. The course of reform to early 1990 was still a directed process governed by leadership intervention. As the reforms became more spontaneous and penetrated more deeply into society then one could with less justification talk of 'Gorbachev and his reforms'. By the same token, the whole concept of *perestroika* suggested a directed process: when the reforms became spontaneous and self-sustaining the term *perestroika* became redundant. Reform indeed began to give way to a second Russian revolution. This stage was reached in early 1990, and thus provides a convenient point at which to end the book.

The work does not aim to provide a detailed blow-by-blow account of Gorbachev's rule. Such a task would require a much larger volume. My intention is to provide an introduction to the key issues facing the system and to suggest the outlines of an analysis that can begin to place the reforms in their historical and theoretical context. Chapter 9 takes the form of an extended conclusion which meditates on the problems of the reforms, the features of the new model of socialism, and the impact of *perestroika* on the world.

This book developed out of a public lecture with the same title that I gave at the University of California, Santa Cruz, in January 1987. The lecture became a paper, then a chapter, and continued to grow into the present volume. I am pleased to acknowledge the influence and ideas of colleagues at Santa Cruz, Berkeley and Stanford, the Centre for Russian and East European Studies at the University of Birmingham, and the Soviet and East European graduate seminars at the London School of Economics, and the support of colleagues and friends at the University of Kent at Canterbury. The assistance of the University of Kent's research committee in the preparation of this work is gratefully acknowledged. It also gives me great pleasure to recognise the assistance of the British Council. The extremely useful comments of Martin Crouch and Martin McCauley did much to improve the work. I am particularly happy to thank Jeff Gleisner and Howard White for devoting their time and knowledge to make this book better than it might have been. The faults, as usual, remain my own.

1

THE SOVIET POLITY IN THE 1980s

Gorbachev comes to power

Mikhail Sergeevich Gorbachev was elected General Secretary of the Communist Party of the Soviet Union (CPSU) on 11 March 1985. His accession put an end to a decade of weak leadership and policy drift. The choice of a relatively young man of 54 looked set to establish the tone of Soviet politics for the rest of the century.

On Brezhnev's death in November 1982, after a period of rule lasting eighteen years, the Politburo chose the former head of the KGB, Yuri Andropov, to the party leadership. The first few months of his rule were marked by dramatic attempts to shake the country out of the lethargy into which it had sunk in Brezhnev's last years. A spate of policy initiatives was accompanied by leadership renewal. However, from September 1983 Andropov disappeared from view until his death from kidney failure in February 1984. The selection of the 72-year old and infirm Konstantin Chernenko by the Politburo, threatened by Andropov's reforms, was an attempt, if only briefly, to hold back the tide of change. They put their own interests above that of the country and, as Zhores Medvedev (1986a) points out, from the first there was a sense of illegitimacy about Chernenko's rule. However, the reform-minded members of the Politburo ensured that a number of conditions were placed on Chernenko's leadership and that their candidate, Gorbachev, acted as *de facto* deputy leader. Chernenko's health rapidly deteriorated during the course of 1984, and following his death on 10 March 1985 the Soviet Union was faced with its third leadership election in as many years. After only a few hours the long-serving foreign minister, Andrei Gromyko, nominated Gorbachev on 11 March for the party leadership to the Central Committee (CC) with the now notorious phrase: 'This man has a nice smile, but he has iron teeth', a sentence left out of the published version of his nominating speech (*K*, 5/1985).

1

Promoted by Andropov to oversee the economy and in effect sharing power with Chernenko, Gorbachev's election to the leadership of the Communist Party, and thus of the country, was no foregone conclusion. He was opposed by the Brezhnevites Viktor Grishin, First Secretary of the Moscow city party committee, and Grigorii Romanov, formerly leader in Leningrad who had been brought to Moscow as a party secretary by Andropov. A large number of the Central Committee apparently had misgivings. Gorbachev's election was by consensus (*edinodushno*) rather than by unanimous vote (*edinoglasno*), suggesting some divisions (Z. Medvedev, 1986a: 16). Egor Ligachev revealed at the June 1988 party conference that Gorbachev's election had been due to the crucial support of himself, Andrei Gromyko, Mikhail Solomentsev and Viktor Chebrikov (*XIX konf.*, vol. 2: 85). Gromyko's nomination had little to say about Gorbachev's service record, but unusually stressed his personal qualities.

Gorbachev was born into a peasant family on 2 March 1931 in the village of Privolnoe in the Krasnogvardeiskii *raion* (district) of the agricultural Stavropol *krai* (region) of south Russia. His birth coincided with the second year of the storm of the collectivisation drive, in which peasants were driven from their individual plots into collective farms (*kolkhozy*). The local leadership in Stavropol *krai* enthusiastically drove on the pace of collectivisation, and by 1931 some 86 per cent of the area had been collectivised compared with a national average of about half (Tatu, 1987: 22–3). Gorbachev's grandfather was chair of one of the first *kolkhozy*, and his father Sergei was a tractor driver. His mother, Maria Panteleevna, born in 1912, was Sergei's second wife. She is apparently a religious believer and reputedly had her son Mikhail baptised.

Gorbachev's father was serving elsewhere when Privolnoe was briefly occupied by the Germans between August 1942 and January 1943, and thus the family was not tainted by the imputation of collaboration suffered by so many in the post-war years. Mother and son were left to fend for themselves. The Germans retained the *kolkhoz* structure as the most efficient way of obtaining food from the peasants. Following the return of the Soviet Army, Stalin ordered the deportation to Central Asia of some 80,000 of the Karachai population from Stavropol *krai* in November 1943. In December, the neighbouring Kalmyks, only some forty miles from Privolnoe, were deported for their alleged collaboration with the Germans, and they were allowed to return only in the late 1950s. In 1944 the same fate befell other Moslem groups: the Meskhetians, Chechens, Ingush, Kabardins, Balkars and Crimean Tatars.

Between 1946 and 1950 the young Gorbachev continued his

interrupted secondary education. In the summers he worked in the local machine tractor station (MTS) as an assistant combine driver. In later years Gorbachev's career was no doubt advanced by his working peasant background (Tatu, 1987: 32). In 1950 he travelled for the first time to Moscow and witnessed the devastation of the German occupation for himself on his two-day journey. Why he chose to study law at Moscow State University at a time of lawlessness remains a conundrum, though the subject gave him access to such texts as Rousseau and Montesquieu. Gorbachev joined the party in 1952, in the last year of Stalin's rule. He was active in the Komsomol youth organisation, though later refused what could have been a glowing career in the KGB. Khrushchev used the Komsomol as a source of personnel to replace Stalin's henchmen; two of its leaders, A. Shelepin and V. Semichastny, went on to lead the KGB.

Gorbachev's fellow students, above all the future Czech reform Communist Zdeněk Mlynář, bear testimony to his abilities and relative open-mindedness (Hofheinz, 1987b), although more critical views are provided by two other students in the law faculty who later emigrated, Lev Yudovich and Friedrikh Neznansky (Z. Medvedev, 1986a: 38–9). Gorbachev himself, in an interview with *l'Unita*, spoke of his broad range of interests (*P*, 20 May 1987). He graduated with a degree in law in 1955, and his urge to broaden his education (and advance his career) was reflected in his gaining a correspondence degree in agronomy in 1967. At university he met his wife Raisa Maksimovna, whose later sociological doctoral dissertation on social differentiation and the conditions in the local Stavropol collective farms was marked by a frankness untypical of the time, revealing that in 1967 only a small proportion of peasants had central heating or running water. Back in Moscow in the late 1970s, she taught Marxist–Leninist philosophy at Moscow State University. Their only daughter was born in 1956.

Gorbachev spent his early career (1955–78) in his native Stavropol *krai*, rising from Komsomol chief to the party leadership. In 1958 he was appointed Second Secretary of the Stavropol *krai* Komsomol organisation, and in 1960 First Secretary of that body; in 1962 he gained his first major party appointment supervising personnel policy and organisation in the regional party organisation; in 1966 he became First Secretary of the Stavropol city CPSU committee; and in 1968 he became Second Secretary of the *kraikom*, the regional party committee. His career was that of a typical party official, though marked by rapid promotion and a refusal to be trapped in a narrow specialism.

Promotion was assisted by his association with Fedor Kulakov, the First Secretary of the *kraikom* from 1960, and with Mikhail Suslov, who had led the organisation from 1939 to 1944 and who later became the guardian of Brezhnevite ideological orthodoxy. They acted as Gorbachev's patrons. Gorbachev was a member of the Stavropol delegation to the 22nd party congress in October 1961. Apparently inspired by Suslov's fears of instability, the group remained remarkably quiet during the vigorous denunciations of Stalin (Tatu, 1987: 70–2). According to Mlynář, Gorbachev was not opposed to the ousting of Khrushchev in October 1964 because of the latter's constant interference and ill-considered enthusiasms. Kulakov indeed was involved in the plot and was certainly a beneficiary. In December 1964 Kulakov was transferred to Moscow and in September 1965 became the Central Committee Secretary responsible for agriculture. Gorbachev thus found himself with a powerful protector in Moscow (Tatu, 1987: 73–4). Gorbachev replaced Kulakov's successor, Leonid Efremov, as head of the *kraikom* on 17 June 1970 to become the youngest of the group called by J. Hough (1969) the Soviet 'prefects' because of their broad powers in the localities, though perhaps a better comparison is with the *intendants* of pre-revolutionary France. In the same month Gorbachev was elected a deputy to the Supreme Soviet for his home constituency and in the following year at the 24th party congress he became a full member of the Central Committee, missing out the candidate stage. Kulakov at the same congress became a full member of the Politburo while retaining his seat on the Secretariat.

This period was marked by a number of journeys abroad, including visits to Italy, France, Belgium, West Germany, and in 1969 Czechoslovakia. While the majority of the *nomenklatura* office-holding élite were enjoying the consolidation of their privileges at home, Gorbachev continued to broaden his mind and kept himself clear of the 'mafia' around Brezhnev. As a regional party leader he achieved significant successes with his policies of agricultural innovation and support for greater individual initiative. He encouraged the 'autonomous link' (*beznaryadnoe zveno*) system of contract labour whereby a group of *kolkhoz* workers and family members achieve payment by result. The system was extended to all of Stavropol *krai* in 1975–6. However, at that time experimentation turned in the other direction with centralised crop gathering and processing by large fleets of mechanised labour under the control of the local party organisations, first tested with apparent success in 1977 in the Ipatovo *raion* of Stavropol *krai* and then extended to the rest of the country (Weickhardt, 1985: 256–7). Only later did it become clear that the system was flawed, diminishing the autonomy of farm managers and only suitable for certain areas. From 1980 the Ipatovo experiment was no longer lauded as one to be emulated. Gorbachev's own reforms from 1985 tended towards deconcentration, and it may well be that the Ipatovo failure was

Kulakov's, in overall charge of agriculture, rather than Gorbachev's (Tatu, 1987: 82–4).

On Kulakov's death in 1978 Gorbachev, at the youthful age of 47, replaced him in November as Central Committee Secretary responsible for agriculture. With Gorbachev's career untainted by corruption, and given that he was sufficiently removed from the 'Dnepropetrovsk mafia' of gerontocrats surrounding Brezhnev, Suslov may well have been grooming him for the succession against Brezhnev's favoured candidate, Chernenko (Z. Medvedev, 1986a: 90; Tatu, 1987: 91–4). Gorbachev's reputation emerged remarkably unscathed from the series of poor harvests from 1979: he rose to become a candidate member of the Politburo in November 1979 and a full member in October 1980. In addition, from 1979 Gorbachev chaired the legal commission of the Soviet of the Union of the Supreme Soviet, reviewing legislation, a post held after him in turn by those destined for advancement: Egor Ligachev, Nikolai Ryzhkov and Georgii Razumovskii.

Throughout the Brezhnev period Gorbachev, despite his rapid advancement, failed to address a single national party congress, including the 26th in 1981 when, as a Politburo member, he might have been expected to speak. In a period of a mini-cult of the personality Gorbachev was unable to escape the occasional eulogy to the prowess of Brezhnev, but his contribution to inflating the cult was modest. More important for his advancement probably were the contacts he made at the sanatoria in Kislovodsk, Pyatigorsk and Mineralnye Vody in Stavropol *krai*, where as host he welcomed senior figures like Andropov, Suslov, Prime Minister Aleksei Kosygin and Andrei Kirilenko during their vacations. Brezhnev himself preferred to recuperate from his labours at Sochi in Krasnodar *krai*, the territory of his loyal ally Sergei Medunov.

Gorbachev was able not only to distance himself from the poor harvests of 1979–83 but also from the methods advocated by the Brezhnev group: huge financial investments, grandiose irrigation schemes, a surfeit of large-scale machinery, and so on. Brezhnev's 1982 'Food Programme' was a last attempt to use traditional means to solve the growing food crisis. Even though responsible for agriculture, Gorbachev held himself aloof from the proposals.

The death of Suslov in January 1982 signalled the end of the Brezhnev era. The exposure of scandals surrounding Brezhnev's daughter, Galina, claimed victim her husband, Yuri Churbanov, and First Deputy Chair of the KGB, Semën Tsvigun. Andropov took the lead in forcing action, and after a bitter discussion Tsvigun committed suicide and Suslov died of a heart attack. Andropov gave up the leadership of the KGB and in May took over Suslov's party responsibility for ideology, thus placing himself in a strong position to bid for the leadership. Brezhnev's death on 10 November 1982 indeed saw Andropov elected General Secretary two days later in preference to Chernenko.

Under Andropov Gorbachev was clearly favoured, presenting the important speech on the anniversary of Lenin's birth on 22 April 1983 (1987b: 382−401). He spoke of the 'Leninist principle' of taking into account objective economic laws and the intelligent application of market relations, of material and moral incentives. Later Gorbachev was to cite this as an example of his early appreciation of the need for radical change (1987a: 25−6), a view repeated in conversation with American officials in 1988 when he stated that he had been working on a concept of *perestroika* for some six years (Miller, 1989: 122). Gorbachev's claim that his views were warmly received is not borne out by the official report. Romanov also advanced rapidly, being transferred from Leningrad to become a 'supersecretary' (a member of both the Politburo and the Secretariat) together with Gorbachev in June 1983 and taking responsibility for party affairs. His promotion can well be interpreted as a way of cutting Romanov off from his local base (Tatu, 1987: 103−4). During Andropov's final illness from December 1983 Gorbachev acted as his liaison with the rest of the Politburo.

Andropov's death on 9 February 1984 had not allowed time for either of the two younger rivals, Gorbachev and Romanov, to consolidate their positions, and after three days of bitter debate Chernenko was elected leader. His election, apparently, was conditional on his retaining Andropov's policies and personnel changes, and on Gorbachev acting as a 'Second Secretary' and heir apparent (Murarka, 1987: 131). Gorbachev now became a much more visible public personality. To strengthen his experience of foreign policy, hitherto almost negligible, he was appointed chair of the foreign affairs commission of the Soviet of the Union of the Supreme Soviet, a post usually occupied by the ideology chief (Tatu, 1987: 105). He had already led a parliamentary delegation to Canada and had received favourable plaudits. He renewed his acquaintance with Italy in June 1984 when he attended the funeral of the leader of the Italian Communist Party (PCI), Enrico Berlinguer. His visit to Britain in December 1984, again at the head of a parliamentary delegation and accompanied by Raisa, turned into a veritable triumph as Mrs Thatcher learnt that he was a man with whom she could 'do business'. Personal identification with agriculture was now firmly behind him, and Gorbachev began to broaden his appeal. In an important speech to party ideological workers on 10 December 1984 Gorbachev first used the words *glasnost* (openness) and *uskorenie* (acceleration), and stressed the importance of the 'human factor' in social development. He declared war against 'conservatism, indifference and stagnation', the latter word (*zastoi*) becoming the epithet for the later Brezhnev years. He outlined plans for 'profound transformations in the economy and in the entire system of social relations' in order to raise the economy 'to a qualitatively new scientific—technical and organisational level' (1987c: 75—108). The speech, with all its limitations, was the manifesto of the first phase of *perestroika*.

On coming to power in March 1985 Gorbachev was 54 years old, the youngest Soviet party leader since Stalin's rise to power in the 1920s. His adult experiences were of the post-war era, and for him the traumas of collectivisation, purges and war were at most childhood memories. He was the first of the post-Stalin generation of Soviet leaders. Gorbachev was chosen by his peers not only because of his obvious charm and intelligence, but also because of his demonstrated political skills. In the years of his climb to the top he had not needed to dissemble since he had no worked-out alternative vision of Soviet development, but he had kept his reservations about certain policies to himself. While his personal philosophy might well be not to have one, he did 'cultivate a certain idea of the good. . .of the old believers in Marxism of his father's generation' (Tatu, 1987: 11). For him power was not an end in itself, as it had been for Brezhnev, and he clearly has had an evolving vision of a modern, dynamic and, according to his lights, democratic system. The attempt to humanise Soviet socialism through emphasis on the 'human factor' tried to prove wrong the assertion that an inhuman system cannot be humanised.

Traditionally Communist leaders only developed their platforms *after* becoming leaders. Gorbachev was forced to fight for his reforms and to create a constituency in his support. The reservations felt by sections of the party leadership persisted throughout the first five years of Gorbachev's rule. The existence of a bloc of lukewarm reformers, if not outright conservatives, on the Central Committee held back the process of change.

Gorbachev's relative youth, his education and his lively and enquiring mind all marked him out from his predecessors. Within weeks of coming to power he launched some of the themes that were to be extended and deepened in later years. The April 1985 plenum of the Central Committee saw Gorbachev advance a critique of Brezhnev's policies that planted his banner firmly in favour of change, albeit modest at this stage (1987c: 152—73). The policies of *perestroika*, *glasnost* and acceleration of the economy all indicated the advent of a serious reformer. Andropov had understood the need for change but his preferred method appeared to be greater discipline. Gorbachev's reforms from the first took a broader view and yoked political reform to the cause of economic modernisation. Tentatively at first, but with growing confidence, the slogan of democratisation became the watchword of the reforms. Gorbachev insisted that a radical restructuring was the only solution to the country's accumulating problems. His speech to the plenum stressed the objective need for reform since there was 'no alternative'.

The reforms under Gorbachev did not spring from a single act of enlightenment on the part of an individual but are linked to a continuing process of change and development. In their first five years the reforms passed through three broad stages. The first lasted from Gorbachev's accession in March 1985 to mid–1986. In this period the basic outlines of the key policies of *perestroika* and *glasnost* were established, though the way that they would be implemented remained vague. Many of the themes raised by Andropov were continued and so this first period should be seen as a transitional phase into radical reform rather than a sharp break with the earlier period. They continued within the broad framework of the authoritarian *perestroika* launched by Andropov. Personnel changes were used to combat the corruption and cliqueishness that had marked Brezhnev's policy of 'stability of cadres'. An assault against corruption and excessive élite privileges was conducted under the slogan of the restoration of social justice. The declining social cohesion of the 'era of stagnation' challenged the foundations of the political stability that Brezhnev had fought so hard to maintain (Shlapentokh, 1988).

Perestroika was at first envisaged as a long-term economic programme whose benefits – a modernised economy and a society marked by social justice – would be apparent by the year 2000. At the 27th party congress in February–March 1986 Gorbachev defined the aim of *perestroika* as not only improved economic performance but also a qualitatively different type of growth: the intensification of production on the basis of scientific and technological progress, the structural reorganisation of the economy, improved management and better incentives for labour (*P*, 26 February 1986). Andropov's attempt to imbue the Soviet economy with dynamism now became known, with Gorbachev's usual gift of characterising a policy with a vivid term, as acceleration, or intensification, of economic development. The *uskorenie* phase of Gorbachevite economic reform included several traditional features, such as praise for Stakhanovite 'shockwork' and for socialist emulation, and the use of moral exhortation rather than economic mechanisms to improve labour productivity. The first phase was also marked by a clearly unbalanced investment programme which envisaged the diversion of resources to heavy industry (including increased reinvestment to modernise old plant), based on wildly exaggerated hopes for improvements in output and productivity (Rumer, 1986; Aslund, 1989).

The second phase of Gorbachev's reforms from mid–1986 focused much more on *glasnost* and represented an attempt to generate ideas and mechanisms of change. A new understanding of the political conditions required for economic and social modernisation emerged, amounting to an unprecedented break with Soviet traditions (*P*, 5 April 1988: 2). It appeared that Gorbachev himself was shaken by the realisation that the strategy pursued up to that time would not be sufficient to reinvigorate society or the economy. It became clear that economic reform alone or modifications of the existing power structure would not be adequate. The forces dragging *perestroika* towards the fate of so many earlier attempts at reform seemed stronger than had originally been thought.

The resistance to radical reform was translated into persistent rumours about Gorbachev's personal safety. Like President Kennedy, Gorbachev followed an aged leader and promised a new vision of the future which captured the imagination of a generation. The comparison with Kennedy's Camelot and the thousand days, while in most respects exaggerated, does at least serve to highlight the dangers of charismatic leadership. In 1986 the country was rife with rumours that there had been an assassination attempt against Gorbachev while he was holidaying by the Black Sea, possibly fanned by Victor Louis, the long-time source of insider information (*Baltimore Sun*, 17 September 1986). Whatever the truth of the stories, they throw into sharp relief the struggle between the 'innovators' and 'conservatives' in the leadership. The reforms provoked opposition since ultimately they threatened the position of the whole bureaucracy. Rumours, fears and opposition clearly demonstrate that the reform of the Soviet system requires not only great effort but also great personal courage.

Gorbachev's vigorous reappearance in Krasnodar and his important speech there on 18 September 1986 on his way back to Moscow was accompanied by blunt denunciations of those who 'shout louder than all others from all platforms about *perestroika*, but who in fact hold it back' (1987e: 86−103). Already in a speech in Khabarovsk on 31 July Gorbachev had likened *perestroika* to a revolution (1987e: 35−52), and he now broadened the anti-corruption drive into a general assault on bureaucracy. *Perestroika*, he argued, was being held back by bureaucratic resistance, and the only antidote was a radical democratisation of Soviet society and a thorough restructuring of the party (*P*, 20 September 1986). His whole strategy for the renovation of Soviet society was radicalised. On many occasions from then on Gorbachev argued 'We need democracy as we need air.' The very notion of reform was unavoidably expanded from something that could be quantified to a broader concept of qualitative changes to the whole structure of Soviet life. Gorbachev began to call the reforms a 'revolution' as the concept of democratic *perestroika* took the place of the earlier authoritarian approach. Political democratisation was to accompany economic change.

By the time of the thrice-postponed Central Committee plenum of 27 January 1987 Gorbachev insisted that *glasnost* and democracy were inalienable aspects of *perestroika*. Reform was to be based on a profound 'psychological restructuring' of the Soviet character away from the submissiveness and apathy engendered by years of authoritarian leadership. The mass of ordinary Soviet citizens were now called upon to put their shoulders to the wheel of reform. Personnel renewal on its own was seen to be inadequate, and a thorough democratisation of the whole system was advanced as the mechanism to ensure the implementation of *perestroika*. Elections were to be used to dislodge some of the conservatives and as a way of allowing greater popular participation in the management of society. Individual initiative was encouraged to allow the development of the 'human factor' in the economy and society. *Glasnost* was an essential weapon to clear away the suffocating secrecy of the existing structures and to broaden the pores of popular participation in the life of the country. Only in this way could society be democratised and socialist self-management advanced (*P*, 28 January 1987). Gorbachev's speech went far beyond what most CC members were prepared to accept; this was reflected in the fairly modest proposals incorporated in the plenum's final resolution, and Gorbachev did not insist on limited tenure for leadership posts. By the time of the 25–26 June 1987 CC plenum, which adopted a package of radical economic reforms, the economist Gavriil Popov's (1985) characterisation of the old type of socialism as the 'administrative command system' had lodged in the popular consciousness. The old system, the June 1987 CC meeting insisted, had put a brake on development and could only be remedied by promoting democracy (*P*, 26 June 1987).

The third phase of reform began from mid–1988 and was characterised by the attempt to find ways of implementing the democratising reforms outlined in the second phase. The 19th party conference in June–July 1988 sought to find ways of institutionalising a 'state governed by law'. The personnel changes of September 1988 in effect signified the end of the beginning of *perestroika*. Having developed a programme of radical reform, the Gorbachevites vowed to implement it. Gorbachev defined the new phase in his presidential acceptance speech of 1 October 1988 as one in which 'We need practical movement ahead, a genuine improvement of the situation in all directions of our work and especially where the people's living standards are concerned' (*P*, 2 October 1988). The third phase was marked by the creation of the institutions of a reformed Soviet system and was accompanied by a rapid politicisation of society through elections and the growth of a vigorous independent society of groups and associations. *Perestroika* no longer focused on the mistakes of the past but now faced the challenge of actually doing better. This it appeared unable to do, and by early 1990 a fourth phase of open multi-party politics began. *Perestroika*, defined as a Communist Party-directed process of political change, began to give way to a new era of competitive politics.

Consolidating power and authority

On coming to power leaders in the Soviet Union tried to strengthen their position through personnel changes in the key bodies of the party and state. In contrast to liberal democracies, leaders in Communist systems 'campaigned' not in order to achieve power but to consolidate it once installed. The power of a leader derived as much from personality and ability to promote supporters as from the post occupied. The absence of a cabinet system of rule meant that a new team was not automatically created with the accession of a new leader but had to be achieved in the teeth of the resistance of those already in power. It had taken Brezhnev some ten years after 1964 to consolidate his position, while Andropov had begun a rapid process of personnel renewal in his fifteen months in office. Gorbachev had to reckon with the large number of senior officials of the Brezhnev era, as well as the promotions of the Andropov period. These included Geidar Aliev, who became a full member of the Politburo on 22 November 1982, and at the same meeting of the CC Ryzhkov joined the Secretariat. In June 1983 Romanov joined the Secretariat, having been a full member of the Politburo since 1976. In December 1983 Vitalii Vorotnikov and Mikhail Solomentsev became full members of the Politburo, Chebrikov became a candidate member, and Ligachev was appointed to the Secretariat (see Appendices 2 and 3).

Gorbachev constantly tried to focus attention on issues rather than personalities; yet he also, no less than his predecessors, was forced by the very structure of Soviet politics to consolidate his position and that of his supporters. Personnel management is traditionally a source of power, and Gorbachev used it with great vigour. Brezhnev's 'stability of cadres' policy had led to a marked ageing of the political leadership. There was remarkably little turnover of top personnel, with only 5 of the then 156 *oblast* (regional) first secretaries being changed between 1976 and 1981. In certain respects Andropov helped Gorbachev begin the process of consolidating power. Under Andropov 21 per cent, or 33 out of 157, regional party secretaries had been replaced. They represented the single largest cohort on the Central Committee and were thus crucial for the consolidation of the power of a General Secretary. The rate of change slowed under Chernenko, then once again accelerated under Gorbachev. Under Chernenko Gorbachev was able, as 'Second Secretary', to place a moratorium on leadership renewal that might have proved awkward later. The short tenures and poor health of recent leaders all fuelled Gorbachev's relatively rapid consolidation of power. The advanced age of most of the leadership, a spate of deaths, the good fortune of a five-yearly party congress due to be held soon after his accession, and his own relative youth placed Gorbachev in an unusually strong position.

In Gorbachev's first year five plenary sessions of the CC were held and some twenty-three people changed their posts in the Politburo and Secretariat. At the April 1985 CC plenum Chebrikov became a full member of the Politburo, the CC secretaries Ligachev and Ryzhkov became full members without having passed through the candidate stage, and Viktor Nikonov joined the Secretariat with responsibility for agriculture. Ligachev took over responsibility for ideology. At the 1 July plenum Romanov was removed, and Edward Shevardnadze, who had been a candidate member of the Politburo since 1978, became a full member. Lev Zaikov and Boris Eltsin joined the Secretariat. In September 1985, at the age of 80, Nikolai Tikhonov, premier since 1980, resigned from the Politburo and was replaced as Prime Minister by Ryzhkov. In October the chair of Gosplan, Nikolai Baibakov, who had been in the job since 1965, was replaced by Nikolai Talyzin, who at the party congress was granted a non-voting seat on the Politburo.

The 27th party congress met less than a year after Gorbachev's election and yet was stamped by his personality and critical approach to the past. He used the opportunity to consolidate his power by increasing the turnover rate in the Central Committee. Under Brezhnev about 90 per cent of living CC members were re-elected every five years, whereas on 5 March 1986 only 60 per cent of full members were re-elected and twenty-three candidates of 1981 became full members (Gustafson and Mann, 1986; Brown, 1987b). This still meant, however, that the new CC of 307 full members contained a large proportion of Brezhnev appointees who were to act as a brake on the reform process by preventing Gorbachev from commanding a natural majority. The next major opportunity for renewal of the CC would not normally be until the next quinquennial party congress, due to meet in 1991 (later brought forward to 1990), and for this reason it appears that Gorbachev hoped, but in the event failed, to use the 19th party conference in June–July 1988 to change a proportion of the Central Committee.

The seventeen people promoted at the 27th congress made up two-thirds of all Politburo and Secretariat members. On the eve of the congress Grishin was removed from the Politburo and Eltsin, who had taken over his post as head of the Moscow party organisation in December 1985, was promoted to become a candidate member and removed from the Secretariat. Zaikov was made a full member of the Politburo and stayed in the Secretariat, while new candidate members included Nikolai Slyunkov, who had headed the Belorussian party since January 1983, and Yuri Solovëv, head of the Leningrad regional party organisation. The CC Secretariat underwent significant renewal, and indeed became Gorbachev's major institutional base of support. Ivan Kapitonov, Boris Ponamarëv and Konstantin Rusakov of the Brezhnevite old guard lost their seats, though Mikhail Zimyanin survived. Georgii Razumovskii became head of the CC's party organisational department, Anatolii Dobrynin was brought back from the Soviet embassy in Washington to head the international department, Aleksandra Biryukova took over responsibility for light industry, Vadim Medvedev for relations with Eastern Europe, and Aleksandr Yakovlev, one of the main architects of *glasnost* and the political reforms of *perestroika*, was placed in charge of propaganda and academic affairs. By 1986 the average age of the Politburo had fallen to 64, some six years below what it had been at Brezhnev's death in 1982, and the average age of the Secretariat had fallen by eight years. Gorbachev accelerated the renewal of the crucial regional party secretaries that had begun under Andropov. By November 1986, 57 out of the 157 had been changed, a much higher turnover rate than Andropov had achieved. Dozens of lower officials were replaced. The Council of Ministers underwent significant renewal, with 48 of its 134 members being changed between March 1985 and February 1986 alone.

In sum, within a year of coming to power Gorbachev had replaced two-thirds of the top leaders including eight out of the eleven members of the Secretariat, one-third of ministers and one-third of republican and regional leaders. Despite these changes Gorbachev to a degree reversed what R. V. Daniels called the 'circular flow of power'; and instead of starting at the bottom and gradually consolidating power at the top, Gorbachev quickly secured his position in the higher echelons and then set about the transformation of lower-level officials, a process which took several years and which can never be considered completed. As the reforms became more radical earlier appointments in their turn had to give way to new figures.

The replacements differed little from their predecessors. They were, however, slightly younger and represented a generation accustomed to peace. Most gained their experience not in political work but in practical management of the economy. The key difference, however, was their attitude to the problems facing the Soviet Union. The pattern of early appointments showed some continuity with Andropov's, above all the reliance on those who had been associated with Kirilenko's apparent aim of greater investment in the modernisation of the economy in the 1970s. Gorbachev continued Andropov's tendency to rely on this group from the Urals and West Siberia such as Ryzhkov, Eltsin, Zaikov and Vorotnikov. Under Andropov Ligachev had been brought from the Urals to join the Secretariat – responsible for a range of portfolios, including ideology, that made him, once he joined the Politburo in April 1985, the *de facto* Second Secretary. Gorbachev's appointments were not an innovative group of reformers but followed the pattern of their predecessors. There was an engineering flavour to his appointments, but this did not in any way challenge party hegemony. There was no real evidence of any split between 'technocratic' and 'party' approaches to solving the Soviet Union's problems. They were a combination of party officials and technical experts, hence bending the technocracy to the service of the party. The idea that there was an alternative techno-cratic establishment waiting in the wings (Shtromas, 1981) proved exaggerated.

Gorbachev moved cautiously and did not initially push the idea of early retirement on the grounds of age or length in the post, as Khrushchev did. He was more interested in performance than any other criteria. Some of the oldest people were retired, demoted or moved out of crucial leadership positions. On 1 July 1985 the veteran foreign minister Andrei Gromyko was sidetracked into the largely ceremonial position of President. The appointment of the relatively inexperienced Shevardnadze allowed Gorbachev to play a greater personal role in foreign affairs.

Under Brezhnev the Politburo had become more representative of the Soviet leadership, with regional officials balanced by the key functional offices, such as heavy industry, ideology, foreign affairs, defence and the KGB. Under Gorbachev a new pattern of representation on the Politburo emerged, with membership determined more by political rather than functional criteria. The military achieved only a non-voting status, while one of the major modifications was the sharp decline in the representation of non-Russian republics. Out of seventeen full and candidate members of the Politburo in January 1987 only one held a job outside the RSFSR – the long-time leader of the Ukrainian party organisation, Vladimir Shcherbitskii. The leader of the Kazakhstan party organisation, D. Kunaev, was relieved of his post in December 1986 amid a tangle of corruption and gross mismanagement of the affairs of the republic. He was replaced by a Russian, Gennadi Kolbin, leading to protest demonstrations in the capital, Alma Ata. As a relic of Brezhnevite complacency, the lukewarm reformer Shcherbitskii's sur-vival in the Ukraine up to September 1989 appeared anomalous; yet it may have served Gorbachev well to have someone who could keep order in the USSR's second most populous republic. The Russification of the Politburo, however, was achieved not out of any overtly nationalistic impulse but out of expediency and to combat the degeneration of local indigenous leaders. The republican bureaucracies appeared tiresome, complacent and above all corrupt.

One of Gorbachev's means of consolidating his position was the development of a semi-formal group of personal advisers. Here also, as in personnel policy, there was a Siberian air to the group. The Siberian division of the Academy of Sciences based in Novosibirsk had already in Brezhnev's time proved itself the source of some of the most stimulating work, and it now emerged as one of the major sources of intellectual support for reform. The noted economist Abel Aganbegyan moved to Moscow to act as Gorbachev's speech-writer and special adviser on economic affairs. The sociologist Tatyana Zaslavskaya informally advised Gorbachev on social matters. The new head of the Academy of Sciences, replacing the aged Aleksandrov, was the former head of the Novosibirsk Academy of Sciences, G. I. Marchuk.

By the fifth year of his leadership it was clear that Gorbachev's power was strong but that his authority was more precarious than the personnel changes might have suggested. Despite the changes there remained a solid core of resistance, in particular in the CC, the regional party leadership and the middle level of the bureaucracy, to the more radical of Gorbachev's proposals. The major source of Gorbachev's power in the early period was his ability to place a group of supporters in the Secretariat. Ligachev and Gorbachev were joined as dual members of the Politburo and the Secretariat by a group of reformers, including notably Yakovlev and also Medvedev. Only after some five years did Gorbachev create a Politburo that owed its rise to national power solely to himself, and even then he could not be sure of its loyalty.

By 1988 the growing disillusionment with the slow pace of reform and the lack of material benefits for the population seemed to force Gorbachev's hand, despite the lack of a solid majority in favour of radical reform in the Central Committee. Meetings with workers during his visit to Krasnoyarsk in late September 1988 brought home to Gorbachev the gulf that had opened up between the promise of *perestroika* and its meagre benefits. The achievements of *glasnost* had far outstripped the development of economic *perestroika*. People increasingly used the new openness to complain that supplies of food and consumer goods had actually deteriorated since the Brezhnev era. At an emergency one-hour meeting of the Central Committee on 30 September 1988 Gorbachev engineered dramatic personnel and organisational changes in the leadership to neutralise the more cautious of his colleagues and to enhance his own position (*P*, 1 October 1988). Ligachev was effectively demoted by being given the important but no longer central position at the head of the new agriculture commission. He lost his responsibility for ideology and with it the deputy leadership. Gorbachev was thus able to marginalise one of the most important restraining personalities on the Politburo. Another of the more cautious reformers, Chebrikov, lost the leadership of the KGB to Vladimir Kryuchkov and was appointed head of the legal commission. Vadim Medvedev was promoted from the Secretariat to become a full member of the Politburo, without going through the candidate stage, to head the ideology commission and to chair the Politburo in Gorbachev's absence. Yakovlev, closely associated with Gorbachev's reforms, lost his official responsibility for ideology and was placed in charge of the international policy commission (for more details on CC commissions, see pp. 172–3). Among the more significant demotions was Mikhail Solomentsev's loss of his Politburo seat. As head of the party control commission he had been responsible for setting the agenda. The post was taken by Boris Pugo, though without a Politburo seat.

The next day (1 October 1988), at a 45-minute meeting of the Supreme Soviet, the first emergency session for eleven years, Gorbachev replaced Gromyko to become Chair of the Supreme Soviet in anticipation of the conversion of the presidency into a stronger post in May 1989 (*P*, 2 October 1988). The session was reminiscent of the worst days of Brezhnev, with no discussion, no alternative candidates, and complete unanimity of the 1,500 deputies. Brezhnev had waited thirteen years before assuming the presidency in 1977, and by then his health was visibly failing. Andropov and Chernenko had both taken on the post, but were too ill to make much of it.

The more conservative leaders such as Ligachev and Chebrikov were to a degree marginalised, but the views of cautious reform that they represented could not be ignored. The whole drama of the two days illustrated Gorbachev's increasing grasp of the leadership. He became, in formal terms at least, the most powerful Soviet leader since Stalin. His own elevation can be seen as a victory for radical *perestroika* and thus was not simply a process of personal aggrandisement. The consolidation of his power was also a consolidation of the political support necessary to drive through changes. Nevertheless, the methods he employed of a swift counterstroke within the apparatus of power with a minimum of respect for democratic niceties was highly reminiscent of the bad old politics that he so often condemned. His personal dominance, and apparent fear of allowing another major personality to emerge, was at odds with his exhortation for the whole population to become involved in the process of change. He was using old methods to achieve new purposes but, as so often in the tragic history of Soviet politics, the means could well turn out to colour and distort the ends.

Following the June—July 1988 party conference the whole party was drawn into an internal election campaign. The aim was to replace those who, like Ligachev, put a conservative gloss on *perestroika* and to draw in a whole new cohort of 'little Gorbachevs' to drive forward the process of reform. More local, regional and republican leaders lost their jobs, swelling the number of 'dead souls' in the Central Committee, those who had lost the post that had entitled them to membership in the first place. A long-overdue change in generations was set in motion, though once again the conservatives managed to blunt the edge of party renewal.

Continuing frustration at the obstruction posed by the largely unreconstructed Central Committee culminated in the 'plenum of the long knives' of 25 April 1989. The CC under Brezhnev and the early Gorbachev years had become something akin to a Soviet House of Lords, where former worthies could retain their privileges and influence on politics even if they had been effectively demoted or retired. Gorbachev's radical purge of these 'dead souls' was an attempt to restore the CC to its intended purpose as a pool of talent and a high gathering of the party's active élite. In one fell swoop Gorbachev engineered the resignation on grounds of age of seventy-four full members (whose average age was 68.6) and twenty-four candidate members, together with twelve of the eighty-two members of the auditing commission, in what he called 'a serious regrouping of forces in the party'. Total membership of the CC fell from 458 to 360, and full membership from 301 to 251. Eleven survivors of the Brezhnev Politburo retired. Prominent 'personal pensioners' included the 79-year-old Gromyko, Tikhonov, Ponomarëv, Aliev and the former Chief of General Staff General Nikolai Ogarkov. Twenty-four candidate members (average age 52) were promoted to full membership, but no new people were brought in since this is the sole prerogative of party congresses or, partially, conferences. Despite the rhetoric of rejuvenation, the average age of the CC had not declined significantly. Moreover, against the background of growing political tension and social disorders, some of the 30-odd conservative party leaders who had lost in the March elections to the Congress of People's Deputies subjected the whole process of radical *perestroika* to bitter criticism (*P*, 27 April 1989). The impasse fuelled speculation that the 28th congress would be convened in October 1990, and indeed this was decided at the September 1989 CC plenum (subsequently brought forward by the February 1990 plenum to July 1990). The anomaly remained, however, that in a time of rapid personnel change the new leaders of some six republics (Estonia, Latvia,

Lithuania, Armenia, Azerbaidzhan and Georgia), all affected by nationalist movements, remained outside the Central Committee.

The 2,250 members of the newly elected Congress of People's Deputies met on 25 May 1989 to elect a Supreme Soviet of 542 members and a President and Vice-President. No candidate stood against Gorbachev and he was elected by 2,123, with 87 votes against and 11 abstentions. His ally and student friend Anatolii Lukyanov was elected Vice-President. The emergence of the relatively independent legislature allowed Gorbachev to drive through reforms bypassing the Central Committee and gave him an alternative source of institutional support (see Chapter 4).

Personnel changes allowed Gorbachev to consolidate his power in a remarkably short time. However, he was not able to have his own way entirely and had to fight hard for personnel and policy changes. Georgii Razumovskii, for example, failed to gain full membership of the Politburo on 30 September 1988, which his key position responsible for the election of reform-minded officials in the party apparatus might have warranted. Shcherbitskii's position as the only one of Brezhnev's 'old guard' on the Politburo looked increasingly anomalous. The restructuring of the party apparatus was only slowly extended from the top levels in the Central Committee in Moscow to the provincial party apparatus, where Ligachev enjoyed most support. The appointment of Chebrikov and Ligachev to key positions also smacked of compromise. Even after four years of Gorbachev's consolidation of power, Andrei Sakharov felt moved to comment that 'Either they [the conservatives and the apparatus] will overthrow him, or they will dictate what policies he should follow' (*ST*, 29 January 1989).

Further personnel changes took place at the CC plenum of 20 September 1989. Chebrikov, Nikonov and, at last, Shcherbitskii were all removed. The Politburo was all but purged of those whom Gorbachev had not appointed, yet after five years in power this revealed not so much Gorbachev's power but the enormous restrictions on a reforming leader imposed by the Soviet system of government. Each reshuffle of the Politburo had been hailed as a defeat of the conservatives, yet by February 1990 out of twelve full members Gorbachev could count on the wholehearted support of only two, Shevardnadze and Yakovlev. Guarded support could be expected from Kryuchkov and Medvedev. In the centre was a bloc of three people responsible for the economy: Ryzhkov, Slyunkov, chair of the social and economic commission, and Yuri Maslyukov, chair of Gosplan. At the more conservative end of the spectrum were Lev Zaikov, CC Secretary responsible for heavy and defence industry, Vitalii Vorotnikov, President of the Russian federation, and Vladimir Ivashko, new leader of the Ukrainian party organisation.

Above all there was Ligachev, a strong opponent of the introduction of private property and of radical democratisation of the party, and apostle of discipline and order. In addition in February 1990, nearly five years after Gorbachev's coming to power, 51 per cent of the Central Committee had been appointed by his predecessors. Gorbachev realised that only a profound reorganisation of the party and the political system could secure radical reform.

All this yet again illustrates that the consolidation of power is not an irreversible process and on its own is not sufficient to secure a leader's position. The whole concept of 'consolidation' is ambivalent. In the Soviet Union, as elsewhere, power has to be supplemented by authority, and this is achieved by successes in policy initiatives (cf. Breslauer, 1982). It was clear that Gorbachev was full of new ideas designed to modernise the Soviet economy and polity. But it is equally clear that his pattern of policy innovation was not part of a grand strategy but developed in response to his own developing understanding of the bounds of the possible in achieving his aims. Gorbachev rose through the party hierarchy and retained the instincts and beliefs of a party official. However, his considerable political skills and abilities were supplemented by a growing confidence and boldness derived from the consolidation of his power through personnel changes. The Soviet leader gradually gained a certain degree of freedom of manoeuvre and independence from the shackles of the party bureaucracy.

The role of leadership has been redefined by the process of reform, yet major limitations remain (see Chapter 4). While the views of the other members of the leadership have to be weighed in the balance, the addition of the post of Supreme Soviet and then national President allowed the Soviet leader an unprecedented constitutional accumulation of power and authority. Gorbachev was no longer so vulnerable to a vote against him in the CC, of the sort that ousted Khrushchev in 1964, since the President can be removed only by an open vote of the Congress of People's Deputies. No longer was his position the result of *ad hoc* circumstances or of a cult of personality, but the legal expression of a system that formalised the dynamism of an executive leadership to overcome the inherent tendency towards entropy engendered by the old system of constitutional confusion.

The changing nature of politics after 1985 reinforced the need for the leader to cultivate the skills of the politician together with those of the administrator. Gorbachev's favoured approach has been the sudden strategic initiative, the aggressive proposal of policy change or personnel overhaul, rather than the cautious incrementalism of the Brezhnev years. For policy implementation, in keeping with his more open approach to politics, Gorbachev has relied on the 'human factor' and the mobilisation of individual resources. However, while he has been a consummate party politician and a master of bureaucratic procedures, and in international affairs his bold proposals elevated him to a statesperson of world historical rank, success in one major constituency, namely the Soviet people as a mass, was only partial in his first five years. Gorbachev managed to consolidate his position at the head of a party that had not put itself to the test of contested elections since 1917, and thus his leadership lacked national legitimacy. Moreover, support for the institutions of leadership could be achieved only by democratising the state in its entirety. As a General Secretary, elected by the small group in the Central Committee, and as a President elected not by the nation but by an uncontested vote in the Congress of People's Deputies, his leadership lacked a genuine popular mandate.

The legacy of the past

The legacy facing Gorbachev in 1985 was an unenviable one. Not only had Brezhnev's rule witnessed a declining economic growth rate, stagnant if not falling standards of living, and growing corruption, but also the basic principles on which the Soviet system was based appeared in need of a radical overhaul.

Brezhnev's programme had been a radical-sounding one: the modernisation of the Soviet Union into what was called 'developed socialism', accompanied by the 'scientific management of society'. But the implementation of the programme left much to be desired, especially in achieving consistent rises in standards of living and economic efficiency. Brezhnev was perhaps not so much opposed to Khrushchev's attempts to reform the Stalinist system as suspicious of the way that he had tried to achieve the reforms. Brezhnev relied on the party to co-ordinate development and thus eschewed a shift to the market and decentralisation, as proposed by Kosygin's economic reforms of 1965, and avoided greater autonomy for soviets and other mass participatory bodies. In circumstances of weak leadership, however, a devolution of authority took place to institutions like the ministries and the defence sector. 'Developed socialism' as defined by Brezhnev meant a limited degree of deconcentration co-ordinated by a revitalised CPSU acting as the motor for political and economic development. In the light of later events Brezhnev's boasts to the 25th party congress in 1976 take on a sad air:

> We have created a new society, a society the like of which mankind has never known before. It is a society with a crisis-free, steadily growing economy, mature socialist relations and genuine freedom. It is a society governed by the scientific

materialist world outlook. It is a society of firm confidence in the future of radiant communist prospects. Before it lie boundless horizons of further all-round progress. (Brezhnev, 1976: 103)

The self-satisfied intellectual sterility of the middle and later Brezhnev years, the inability to take decisions because of the absence of effective leadership, and the lack of a coherent vision of practical change led to stagnation and in some respects eighteen wasted years.

As former head of the KGB, Andropov was better informed than most about shortcomings, and a mere fortnight after Brezhnev's death he devoted a large part of his speech at the CC plenum of 22 November 1982 to criticising inadequacies and urging improvements in management, planning and the economic system as a whole (Andropov, 1983: 7–19). His health failed before he was able to achieve much, and his successor, Chernenko, barely admitted the problems. Gorbachev's election reflected the view of a section of the leadership that drastic remedial action had to be taken.

The elements making up what Gorbachev in June 1987 called the 'pre-crisis situation' of the early 1980s cover most aspects of Soviet life. The problems included corruption, the decay of the social infrastructure, declining economic dynamism and the growth of the second economy, relative technological slippage and the inability to implement policies despite the centralised controls exerted by the ministries. Lower levels began to operate according to a law of 'survival politics' with conflicting imperatives and orders. The 'leading role' of the Communist Party itself lost dynamism, held as it was in a firm lock of ideological sclerosis by the ageing leadership and institutional arthritis. Too much respect for cadres protected the weak and the infirm, the corrupt and the incompetent.

While major achievements can be credited to Brezhnev's regime, such as the attainment of strategic parity with the United States and improvements in social welfare, housing and so on, equally severe criticisms can be made of its shortcomings, such as the stunted service sector, the deadening bureaucratisation of public life, and increasingly unbalanced budgets. However, an overall assessment cannot be achieved simply by weighing up the successes and failures. One needs to look at the viability of the system as a whole.

This Gorbachev found wanting. He soon realised, as Paul Kennedy put it in the context of the relative decline of Britain as *The Weary Titan* of the late nineteenth century, and America today, that '"National security" in the proper sense of the term involves much more than military security. . .To remain number one, the country concerned needs not only adequate and efficient armed forces; it also needs a flourishing economic base, productive and modern manufacturing, efficient plant and infrastructure, an enormous commitment to education at all levels, and a healthy, properly nourished, and decently housed population whose potential talents and energies are not sapped by deprivation' (1989: 38). For the USSR in 1985, one would have to add a whole range of political factors: honest and efficient government; accurate statistics and the truth about the past and present; effective participatory mechanisms; the rule of law; and the delineation of authority between the Communist Party and the state.

The problem of how the Soviet Union could sustain its global aspirations at a time of profound economic and social difficulties had become ever more acute. In the 1950s the Soviet economy grew at an average annual rate of 6 per cent, but the growth rate has been falling ever since. Between 1980 and 1985 the rate of economic growth appears to have fallen to zero (Aganbegyan, 1988a: 3), and the non-military economy may well have been shrinking for some years. Japan overtook the Soviet Union in GNP terms to become the second largest economy in the world. The *per capita* standard of living of the Soviet people fell from 56th place in 1976 to 70th in 1982. No doubt it has declined since then because for most of the 1980s living standards have remained stable (according to Soviet figures) and in the opinion of most Western experts have fallen. The Soviet economy suffered from decreasing returns on investment, low labour productivity and a relatively backward level of science and technology. The technological gap put the Soviet Union about ten to fifteen years behind the West. Furthermore, *détente* had helped postpone the necessary restructuring of the domestic economy by offering the prospect of increased purchases of technology and consumer goods from abroad. The Soviet Union had, in certain respects, displaced Britain from the dubious honour of being the sick man of Europe.

Infant mortality rates were rising and life expectancy falling. At the 19th party conference in June 1988 Evgenii Chazov, the new Minister of Health, reported that the USSR was in 50th place in the world for infant mortality, after Barbados and Mauritius, and that life expectancy ranked 32nd in the world (*P*, 30 June 1988). The reason was simple: *per capita* expenditure on health was miserly compared with most developed countries. Speaker after speaker highlighted the problems. G. A. Yagodin, chair of the reorganised State Committee for Public Education (Gosobrazovanie), reported that half the schools in the union lacked central heating, running water or sewerage, a quarter of all students attended school in split shifts, and 53 per cent of all schoolchildren were not in good health (*P*, 2 July 1988). A. A. Logunov, rector of Moscow State University, deplored the poor condition of Soviet science (*P*, 1 July 1988). Ivan D. Laptev, editor of *Izvestiya*, pointed the finger at the conference delegates themselves. The system of party rule 'created the astonishing and unique situation whereby the people who take decisions [i.e., party officials] bear no legal or material responsibility for its consequences, whereas the people who bear that responsibility [managers, directors, etc.] do not take the decision' (*P*, 1 July 1988).

The Soviet Union's relative underdevelopment became an increasingly important factor in its international relations. Trade with the West and its Pacific neighbours was stifled by unresponsive structures and the heavy hand of the centralised bureaucracy. Local managers had little scope for domestic, let alone foreign, initiative. The underdevelopment of the Soviet Far East, in particular, inhibited participation in the rapidly growing Pacific economic region. The failure of the Stalinist command economy to achieve a sustainable pattern of growth and prosperity was to a degree caused by excessive diversion of resources into military expenditure. The USSR helped fuel the arms race by an ambitious attempt to match the United States missile for missile, tank for tank, with a generous margin allowed for safety. The decline of the old Soviet economic model undermined the belief that the USSR was a historically ascendant world power, and thus the door was opened for a new relationship with the West.

The Soviet Union has the right to feel itself cheated by history. Stalin set the country the task of 'catching up and overtaking' the West during the early five-year plans. The Soviet Union achieved this — but in the terms of the Western economies of the second industrial revolution. Its own smokestack industries are the largest in the world, while in the West they have turned into rustbelts. The West is transforming itself into what has been called the post-industrial society where service industries and knowledge are the key indicators of economic modernity. In this race the Soviet Union is far behind.

The scale of the problems and the solutions were already being analysed in the years before Gorbachev's accession to power. In 1970 the nuclear physicist Andrei Sakharov, the historian Roy Medvedev and the mathematician Valentin Turchin warned Brezhnev that the economy was stagnating because of the absence of democracy and civil liberties in society. Economic reforms without the dismemberment of the Stalinist political system would be inadequate, they warned. Their proposals read like a prescription for current reformers: *glasnost* in public life, freedom of the Press and information, reviving the soviets, genuine elections with a plurality of candidates (Hosking, 1990: 3). Even if we disagree with the term 'totalitarianism' to describe the Soviet system before 1985, certain features associated with the totalitarian syndrome undoubtedly applied which distinguished the country from more traditional authoritarian systems, namely the dominance of a single mass party, the central role of the leadership principle, the pervasive ideology, state controls over the media and culture, the centralised command economy and the prominent role of the security police. Several leading reformers under Gorbachev had no hesitation in describing the earlier system as totalitarian, and regarded its pernicious legacy as the major stumbling-block for reform.

Under Andropov and in the first phase of Gorbachev's reforms there remained a belief that the Soviet Union could somehow refine the problem of technological backwardness and economic entropy while maintaining the old structure of power. Gorbachev gradually accepted that economic progress required radical modifications to the institutions and practices of government. The historical conjuncture which had arrived in the Soviet Union was the transition from an extensive economy to an intensive one: not more shoes, but better ones, with better use of resources rather than relying on increased inputs of labour and investment (Aganbegyan, 1988a: 7–15). The economic reforms sought to rejuvenate the system and break the cycle of stagnation.

But the problem was not only economic. There was also a perceived decline in the polity. The greatest challenge facing the Gorbachevite reformers was the weakening in the political and social coherence and integrity of the Soviet system as a whole. However, the need for reform, which had been apparent since at least the death of Stalin in 1953, did not necessarily mean that reform would occur. The decline of the great empires of the past demonstrates that a system can survive prolonged relative economic stagnation and decline and fail to find the necessary means or forces to effect reform (Kennedy, 1988).

As we shall see, Gorbachev's first period in office was devoted to overcoming the legacy of Brezhnev's eighteen years in office. He exposed the 'era of stagnation' with unprecedented frankness and acerbity. However, he gradually came to see that the problems had their roots in more than Brezhnev's rule, and that the thirty years of reform and counter-reform since 1953 had been attempts to come to terms with the legacy of Stalin and patterns of power and authority established after the October Revolution. The 'systemic' inadequacies of the Soviet system are deeply rooted and, as Gorbachev learnt with increasing force, are not susceptible to palliatives.

It was clear from the first that Gorbachev was set to break the mould of Soviet politics. It was equally clear from 1987 that Gorbachev would not be an authoritarian reformer in the Andropov mould. Under Gorbachev new patterns of power and authority have emerged that have the potential of radically transforming the Soviet polity. At the same time, the legacy of the past still weighs heavily on the current reform process. The fundamental issues are traditional ones that were unresolved under Lenin and remained to poison and distort the Soviet polity for seventy years. Gorbachev has represented a return to the traditions, so sharply truncated in 1921, of democratic socialist reform that tried to use the initiative of rank-and-file party members and the party's natural constituency among the working class. At the same time, Gorbachev was not able at a stroke to free himself of the necessity to operate in a highly structured political system. It was unrealistic to expect a dramatic and immediate transformation of the system in the Soviet Union. Not only had the legacy of seventy years of 'distortions' to be overcome, but processes that took centuries to mature in the West will now take many years to recover: an active and tolerant society, individual economic initiative and responsibility, the democratic psyche which encompasses pluralism and proceduralism, and the de-ideologisation of political culture. Gorbachev's achievements and failings will be examined in the following chapters.

2

COMMUNISM AND REFORM

Perestroika was one of the most sustained and far-reaching periods of Communist reformism. However, Communist reformism is characterised by a fundamental contradiction: on the one hand, it aims to revive and sustain an existing system of power and property; on the other, it tries to transform the system while remaining true to its initial principles. These two sides of Communist reformism, the system-maintaining and the system-transforming ones, are at odds with each other. These were the two faces of Gorbachevite reformism, and the source of many of its compromises and failings. The revolutions in Eastern Europe in 1989 rapidly moved beyond the contradictions of Communist reformism and heralded the arrival of a post-Communist phase of development. This chapter will begin by presenting a brief comparative survey of some of the major examples of reform processes, both in the Soviet Union and in other Communist countries, and will then examine the nature and limitations of the reform model of Communism.

The history of Communist reform

Soviet history since 1917, and with greater force since the death of Stalin in 1953, has alternated between periods of reform and conservatism (cf Cohen, 1985: 128–57). The nature and meaning of conservatism are not as obvious as may appear. Even during the periods of retrenchment there has been economic development, social modernisation and a degree of political responsiveness. Each reform period, moreover, has been stamped by the preceding phase and has taken its character from the specific circumstances in which it has taken place; thus any cyclical theory of Soviet politics must be rejected. The elements of continuity are as marked as the elements of innovation.

The Gorbachevite reformers have been confronting some of the baleful consequences of the prolonged period of self-satisfied drift of the Brezhnev years (cf. Colton, 1986). This period, especially from 1976 when Brezhnev's health was clearly failing, has now been characterised by the insalubrious epithet of the 'era of stagnation' (*period zastoya*). While these years were not as devoid of achievements as the term might suggest, there were nevertheless factors at work that undermined the developmental prospects of the country and its moral self-esteem. The politics of this time were marked by a self-confidence that soon turned into smugness and widespread corruption.

The Brezhnev years can be understood as the apogee of what has been called the social contract policies of the 'neo-Stalinist compromise'. This was a system that emerged after Stalin's death in 1953 predicated on the continuation of the Stalinist socioeconomic system but stripped of its terroristic features and its most inflexible economic policies. The regime in effect made an unspoken bargain with the population. In return for improved standards of living, job security, subsidised food and housing, stable prices and a reduction in income inequalities, Soviet citizens should not encroach upon the prerogatives of the political élite or the bureaucratic apparatus by demanding civil liberties or personal freedom (Bialer, 1980; Zaslavsky, 1982; Breslauer, 1984: 221; Connor, 1988; Kessler, 1988). The very success of the Brezhnev regime in blunting independent reform initiatives condemned to sterility its own attempts at gradual amelioration of economic and social processes.

Brezhnev's rule provides a number of instances demonstrating how reform processes can be defeated. This is most evident with the reversal of Kosygin's economic reforms of 1965 (Aslund, 1989: 10–13). The political and social stability of the Brezhnev years was achieved at a very high cost, and by the early 1980s it had become clear that the neo-Stalinist compromise was no longer tenable. Sluggish economic growth and agricultural difficulties could no longer sustain rises in consumption; and the absence of a dynamic political interaction between the population and the regime condemned society to stagnation. Even worse, from the Soviet point of view, the great Communist rival China had launched an ambitious reform programme in 1978 that rapidly achieved a revitalisation of the economy, and in particular agriculture.

Andropov realised that the compromise had to be broken in order to stimulate the economy and to tackle the grave social problems. Andropov's fifteen months in power witnessed a vigorous attempt to reform both the economy and what could be called the structure of social relations. In his article in *Kommunist* (3/1983), Andropov presented several themes that were to be developed in Zaslavskaya's famous paper of April that year (Zaslavskaya, 1984). He noted that 'the forms and methods of management are lagging behind the requirements made by the level attained by Soviet society in its material, technological, social and cultural development.' In other words, there was a growing disparity between the organisation of the economy and the demands made by the development of society. He stressed the need to improve the material well-being of the people, and warned that 'One should in general handle with care the so-called fundamental truisms of Marxism', suggesting greater ideological flexibility. The emphasis was to be on a new authoritarianism under the slogan of discipline. The command economy was to be revived shorn of corruption, incompetence and inefficiency. We do not know what the long-term fate of Andropov's reforms might have been since he died before their full impact could be measured.

Economic and political factors propelled Gorbachev to move even further in challenging the social contract policies of the Brezhnev years to achieve a modernisation of the economy and society. In reaction against the comfortable corporatism of the Brezhnev years, *perestroika* represented an attempt to renegotiate the basic relationship between state and society (Hauslohner, 1989). The April 1985 CC plenum, Gorbachev's first as leader, was already marked by an impatience with the existing situation and proposals for change (*P*, 24 April 1985). He insisted that the later Brezhnev years were marked by a 'pre-crisis' which would have become a full-scale crisis if timely action had not been taken. The question was no longer one of how to sustain the compromise but of what to replace it with. While there was a growing consensus over the need for change, there was no agreement over the shape that it should take.

The reform process launched by Gorbachev, however, was not devoted purely to undoing the negative effects of Brezhnev's rule. The second level of reform was concerned with tackling the Stalinist legacy in the broadest sense. Khrushchev until his ousting in 1964 had already modified some of the more catastrophic of Stalin's policies. The vast prison population of the gulags was reduced, and Stalin's cult of personality and the purges were condemned in Khrushchev's Secret Speech of February 1956 at the 20th party congress and again in 1961 at the 22nd party congress. Khrushchev also sought to establish a new balance in the Soviet system between coercion and mass participation. The concept of a 'state of the whole people' in 1961 was predicated on the idea that there were no longer hostile classes in the country and that the whole society could be incorporated in the project of building socialism. Social organisations were gradually to take over as the state apparatus withered away.

Destalinisation under Khrushchev was not limited to political reform but sought to modify the vast concentration of economic power in the hands of the ministries based in Moscow. Following the launching of the first five-year plan in 1928 and the policy of rapid collectivisation of the peasantry in 1929 the whole economic life of the country had become concentrated in a vast bureaucratic machine. The peasant *kolkhozy* and state farms (*sovkhozy*) had almost no control over what they produced, and received almost no payment for their goods. Khrushchev alleviated some of the most onerous burdens on the peasantry, but retained the basic system of state control over agriculture. In industry the five-year plans tried to allocate resources and control the activities of enterprises. Khrushchev retained this system, though in 1958 he abolished the ministries in favour of deconcentrating economic management to local economic councils which he hoped would bring the planning process closer to the needs of the factories. The scheme failed due to the difficulty of co-ordinating policy between the hundred-odd councils. Though Khrushchev initiated some long-overdue reforms, the fundamentals of the hierarchical Stalinist command economy survived in all essentials into the Gorbachev era (Berliner, 1988: 269–97).

Gorbachev's reforms necessarily have shared certain features with Khrushchev's policies since they have dealt with much the same structural problems. Both sought to consolidate the Soviet system through reform. Similar themes once again emerged, such as the need for effective popular participation and initiative, an understanding of the past and a new approach to economic and political organisation. The fundamental principle of both sets of reforms was the theme of returning to an unsullied Leninism by stripping the system of the accumulated layers of distortion and bureaucracy. Moreover, while Khrushchev held his predecessor, Stalin, as primarily responsible, Gorbachev had Brezhnev to blame. Both reform processes reflected the forceful personalities of the two leaders, demonstrating once again the role of leadership in Soviet-type systems.

However, some thirty years separated Gorbachev from Khrushchev and too much had changed in the Communist world, in international relations and in ideology, to permit exaggerated comparisons between the two periods of reform. Each reflects a certain historical conjuncture and has its own distinctive features. Khrushchev's reforms were marked by a revolutionary optimism and fulsome belief in the invincibility of Communist ideas, whereas Gorbachev's reforms have taken place at a time of declining optimism. For Khrushchev Communism was still a cause, a religion to be defended against the infidel, whereas for Gorbachev it had been secularised to offer no more than a pragmatic approach to solving the problems of development and society. Khrushchev believed he had inherited a basically sound system, whereas

Gorbachev began to look for a new model of socialism. Krushchev's reforms remained within the framework of the political ideas of the 1920s. His attitude to civil society, market reforms, reforms in Eastern Europe and his foreign policy all differed from Gorbachev's. Khrushchev's reforms were not a stillborn spring since by their very nature it is unlikely that they could have turned into a summer of political, ideological or social pluralism. In the 1950s and early 1960s the reforms became identified with the personality of Khrushchev, leaving them vulnerable to leadership change, whereas *perestroika* encouraged autonomous mass involvement. The transition from Khrushchev to Gorbachev is the transition from cause to calculation, from an epoch still imbued with revolutionary ideals to pragmatic reform.

The third level of Gorbachevite reform was concerned with modifying the institutional and political patterns of power that took shape under Lenin. While Khrushchev was a Leninist revivalist, Gorbachev sought to find a Lenin more suited to his needs. Before 1917 the social democratic movement was torn by a series of debates over the organisation of the party and its relationship to the working class, and indeed to society as a whole, in which alternatives were put forward to Lenin's ideas by such figures as Yulii Martov, Aleksandr Bogdanov, Leon Trotsky, Karl Kautsky and Rosa Luxemburg. These debates continued in a modified form after the Revolution as well. The Bolshevik Party in its early years in power was wracked by a series of controversies whose resolution established the contours of the Soviet polity. The debates proved that revolutionary socialism was broader than Leninism, and indeed larger than Bolshevism itself.

The first major attempt at reform in a Communist system was the struggle waged within the Bolshevik Party during war Communism from late 1918 to 1921 for the democratisation of the party and the definition of the functions of the various branches of government. The reformers above all sought an active role for the rank-and-file Communist in the party and some limits on the powers of the party's own bureaucratic *apparat*. The Democratic Centralist group, for instance, insisted that a Soviet government should be established with clear lines of authority and a demarcation of functions between its constituent elements. In particular, they argued that the functions of the party and the soviets should be separated in order to avoid the substitution (*podmena*) of the party for the soviets. Another of the groupings of the period, dubbed oppositionists although until 1921 such coalitions of views had every right to exist, was the Workers' Opposition. In the reform debate of 1920–early 1921 they sought some direct method for the working class to participate in economic decision-making. This, they argued, was what the socialist revolution was all about.

The demands of the various groups, which were not always compatible, seemed within grasp of fulfilment at the 9th party conference in September 1920. A range of reforming resolutions were passed, some of which recall themes raised by the 19th party conference in 1988, on the democratisation of inner-party life and of the system as a whole. Soon after, following a bitter debate launched by Trotsky over the role of the trade unions in the Soviet state, the reforms were undermined, and indeed the struggle to defeat the oppositions served to consolidate the powers of the apparatus. The end of effective political reform was symbolised by the famous resolution stipulating a 'ban on factions' in March 1921 at the 10th party congress. Not only were the arguments of the groups rejected, but the very right of Communists to join together to argue a viewpoint was prohibited. Expanded administration took the place of politics. A particularly restrictive form of democratic centralism was consolidated that remained in force until 1990.

Following Lenin's death in January 1924 Stalin thus had the means to consolidate his power in the party bureaucracy and to defeat his rivals in the struggle for the leadership. Later he used the secret police, whose arbitrariness and lack of control had been condemned during Lenin's lifetime, to destroy all sources of actual and imagined opposition. The defeat of the reform proposals sentenced the USSR to seventy years of constitutional confusion and, indeed, political sterility. The exceptionally great powers of the revolutionary regime allowed the unscrupulous Stalin to establish a twenty-five-year personal dictatorship.

The reasons for the failure of this early and in many ways most far-reaching of reform periods help to put Gorbachev's reforms in perspective. The so-called oppositions were divided, and no common programme could be agreed between them. Above all, democracy was to be restricted to party members and their allies, and this exclusive approach meant than no appeal could be made to democracy as an inalienable element of a socialist society as argued, for example, by Rosa Luxemburg (1919) and Karl Kautsky (1919/1964). The powers of the party machine, even at this early stage, could be mobilised to destroy independent currents. The analyses of most of the oppositionists of what was wrong in the Soviet system was flawed. The belief that the overweening power of the apparatus and the distortions of the system were the result of class distortions, the legacy of Tsarism, the influence of 'petty-bourgeois' elements, careerists and former members of moderate socialist parties, all diverted attention from the real *political* sources of the problem. The leadership was able to rally behind a programme of moderate reform, called workers' democracy, that undercut the radical reformers by taking some of their proposals, thereby making themselves the trustees of reform (Sakwa, 1989c). While victory in the civil war was assured, the threatening international situation and the republic's isolation put the premium on unity and were used by the leadership to impose party discipline. Furthermore, the economic catastrophe engendered by years of war and the disastrous economic policies of war Communism led to the belief that the priority should be economic rather than political reform (Sakwa, 1988a). Some of these patterns reasserted themselves in later reform periods.

The major achievement of these early 'reformers', despite their defeat, was to demonstrate that Soviet politics was not marked by the choicelessness that is sometimes assumed. There were alternatives not only to the Stalinist administrative system but also to the conditions that prepared the way for its emergence under Lenin. The consolidation of Soviet authoritarianism was not the result of some primordial Russian problem or even of relative Russian underdevelopment; it was the consequence of political stratagems and beliefs.

To alleviate the dire economic situation Lenin proposed in early 1921 what came to be known as the New Economic Policy (NEP). The struggle waged by Lenin to implement these policies, which included concessions to the peasantry and a degree of marketisation of the economy, is one to which Gorbachev frequently referred. However, the introduction of the NEP was not such a struggle as is sometimes made out. Although the left of the party was never fully reconciled to its practice or consequences, the overwhelming need for a retreat, if only temporarily, from war Communist hypercentralisation of economic life was clear.

Gorbachev's *perestroika*, in contrast to the NEP, did not originate from a sudden tactical shift but was the outcome of some thirty years of episodic reform and came to represent a strategic reorientation of political and economic policy. While NEP policies accepted only to a limited degree the need for negotiation to resolve conflicts of interest between groups, restricted above all to labour relations and strictly curbed in political life, Gorbachev's *perestroika* entailed a much broader, though still limited, revival of political bargaining as part of what Gorbachev hoped would be an expanding democratic socialist consensus. Like the NEP, however, *perestroika* was the result of a decisive shift in leadership positions and arose in response to a similar problem, namely the inadequacy of war Communist commandist political and economic policies.

Lenin's economic policies showed a degree of flexibility, whereas his political policies were more of a piece. Hence when Communist reformers now talk of deleninisation, they have in mind the restoration of democracy within the Communist Party, with an end to its institutionalised leading role in society and its claim to a privileged position in the political system based on its special relationship to socialist ideology. Deleninisation also entails the re-emergence of the state, above all the soviets, from the shadow of the party, and a greater scope for an independent society freed from the administrative apparatus. In short, deleninisation means the restoration of a pluralistic politics in place of Leninist monism.

Gorbachev's reforms did not move with equal speed at the three levels of debrezhnevisation, destalinisation and deleninisation. Indeed, the more radical reform Communists came to believe that the success of the first two required progress in the third. In some areas there was immediate progress, as in the condemnation of Brezhnev's stagnation, but destalinisation only slowly gathered pace (see Chapter 3) while deleninisation lagged far behind. The Spanish and Italian Eurocommunist parties in the late 1970s rejected Leninism and nailed their colours to a programme of democratic socialism. Gorbachev preferred the tactic of reinterpreting Leninism rather than condemning it, although the bolder Soviet reformers advanced ever sharper and more overt critiques of Leninism.

We will now examine the experience of Communist reformism outside the USSR. The export of the Stalinist model of socialism to Eastern Europe following the Second World War imposed its own strains. After the break with Stalin in 1948 the Stalinist Yugoslav leader, Tito, began to edge towards a type of self-managed socialism which allowed considerable scope for the market and regional autonomy. However, destalinisation of the economy was not accompanied by the deleninisation of the political system. Self-management, according to Tito's former associate Milovan Djilas, simply shifted to local officials and regional bureaucracies the patronage rights and privileges elsewhere exercised by central authorities (*Ind.*, 15 October 1988). The problems that Yugoslavia faced after forty years were stark. Rampant regionalism fuelled by virulent nationalism threatened the very unity of the state; lack of economic co-ordination and wasteful investment strategies led to duplication as every republic poured resources into such prestige items as steel mills; excess borrowing led to a vast foreign currency debt of some $21 billion by 1988; growing labour unrest and inflation threatened the viability of the economy. Politically, of course, some of the benefits were a relatively open political system, a degree of freedom for citizens unknown elsewhere in the Communist world and an active intellectual and cultural life.

Following the disastrous bid for independence by the Hungarian leader, Imre Nagy, in 1956 and the crushing by Soviet tanks of the popular destalinising, and indeed desovietising, movement in November of that year, the new leader János Kádár gradually achieved a measure of reconciliation between the regime and society. The New Economic Mechanism introduced by Reszo Nyers in 1968 allowed greater enterprise autonomy and moved towards the marketisation of the economy. 'Kadarism' represented a classic application of the 'neo-Stalinist compromise' in which moderate economic reform and the satisfaction of some consumer demands were to be achieved at the price of the political exclusion of the population. By the mid–1980s, however, it was clear that 'goulash Communism' had gone both too far and not far enough, with the reforms trapped in a limbo of unreconciled contradictions where the market fought with the bureaucracy and the elements of planning. Inflation of 16 per cent by 1989 and a foreign debt of $21 billion (£13 billion) for a population of only 10 million, one of the highest *per capita* debts in the world, constituted a veritable economic crisis. With the changes of May 1988, when Kádár was replaced as party leader by Karoly Grosz, a momentum for change was established in which the leading reformer Imre Pozsgay argued that the Hungarian Socialist Workers Party (HSWP) should place itself at the head of the pressure towards pluralism in order to avoid extinction as a political movement. The period of one-party pluralism, of the type represented by *perestroika* in the Soviet Union, lasted barely a year however. Increasingly pluralistic elections saw the emergence of organised opposition parties with representatives in the revived Hungarian parliament. The HSWP in October 1989 transformed itself into a non-Leninist Socialist Party but failed to keep more than a fraction of its earlier membership. In the elections of March–April 1990 the new Socialist Party gained only 8.5 per cent of the vote and was beaten into fourth place. The centre right Hungarian Democratic Forum won with 42.7 per cent of the vote.

The attempt at political reform in Czechoslovakia in 1968 represented the high point of Communist reformism. There are obvious similarities between what the Czechoslovak reformers tried to achieve in 1968 and Gorbachev's model of economic and political reform during *perestroika*. Indeed, the radical Action Programme of the Czechoslovak Communist Party of April 1968 could have acted as a manifesto for Gorbachev's *perestroika*. The need to achieve authority for the party rather than imposing it, to curtail centralised appointments, to introduce a separation of powers, an independent judiciary, and so on, are part of a common programme. In his first public speech for twenty years at Bologna University on 13 November 1988 Alexander Dubček defended his attempt to 'reconcile human values and socialist aspirations' (*Ind.*, 14 November 1988). He for one was convinced that his own attempts to develop a new model of socialism prefigured those of Gorbachev.

The 'Prague Spring' contained many internal contradictions, but its demise was brought about by the Soviet-led Warsaw Pact intervention of 20–21 August 1968. The invasion preserved a generation of neo-Stalinists and promoted two decades of relative stagnation. What came to be known as the 'Brezhnev doctrine' justified the defence of the old model in these terms:

> There is no doubt that peoples of the socialist countries have and must have freedom to determine their country's path of development. However, any decision of theirs must damage neither socialism in their country nor the fundamental interests of the other socialist countries nor the worldwide workers' movement which is waging a struggle for socialism. This means that every communist party is responsible not only to its own people but also to all socialist countries and to the entire communist movement. (*P.*, 25 September 1968)

Class interests and a Soviet-defined notion of socialism ranked higher than national sovereignty or the independence of individual Communist parties. Narrowly defined Soviet power interests took precedence over attempts to rejuvenate socialist institutions and ideology, and by the same token led to a growing debasement of both which gave rise to Brezhnevite stagnation and culminated in the revolution of 1989.

The suppression of the attempt to achieve 'socialism with a human face' discredited alternatives for a generation and blocked attempts at Soviet domestic reform. Its defeat marked the end of the buoyant phase of Communist reformism and led, in Dubček's words, to 'moral crisis and economic collapse'. In its place the factors which gave rise to Soviet stagnation were once again imposed on the region. Gorbachev noted that allied leaderships 'kept quiet, even when they noticed something of concern' (1987a: 162). The invasion destroyed not only a country but also an idea. It made Gorbachev's attempts to revive popular belief in the reformist model of Communism immeasurably more difficult, and indeed it could be argued, bearing in mind the defeat of reformism after Khrushchev and the NEP, that the corpse of reformism, buried by the Soviet leaders themselves so many times, cannot be brought back to life. In the Czechoslovak revolution of late 1989 supporters of change had moved far beyond the ideas of 1968, and while Dubček was a revered figure, he was also an outdated one.

It is a moot point whether Dubček was twenty years too early or whether Gorbachev, in the light of declining popular belief in Communist reformism, was twenty years too late. However, more than time – the 'twenty years' which Gennadi Gerasimov once identified as the only difference between Gorbachev's and Dubček's reforms – separates the two. The major distinction between the Prague Spring and *perestroika* is ultimately in process rather than in content. *Perestroika*,

Gorbachev has repeatedly argued, is not a spontaneous but a governed process led by the Communist Party. The motive force behind the 1968 reform movement was a mass movement of discontent rallying around the slogan of socialist democracy, and the party struggled to respond to this 'revolution from below'. Vitalii Korotich, editor of the radical journal *Ogonëk*, noted another aspect of this difference. Gorbachev in the first five years remained at the head of the reform process and managed, albeit with increasing difficulty, to control it. Dubček lost control and 'pressure from below ran him over' (Svec, 1988: 997). Moreover, Gorbachev retained a mastery of the main ideas fuelling the reforms and kept a firm control of the agenda, whereas Dubček for long periods seemed to be at a loss. The quality of leadership, though not the quality of the men, was very different in the two reform periods. The popular movement in 1968 quickly began to bypass the official structures of power, whereas under *perestroika* (though not in the Baltic and the Caucasus) the official structures until early 1990 by and large remained intact and in control of the process of change. The fundamental difference between the two reform processes, of course, is that in Czechoslovakia events unrolled in the shadow of the threats and growls of the USSR and its allies, whereas Gorbachev did not need to take into account 'geopolitical realities', other than from his domestic critics, to the same extent. Gorbachev was a much more formidable Soviet Dubček precisely because he was not threatened by external intervention.

History, however, may well judge *perestroika* as a more slowly developing form of the Prague Spring. While in 1968 the principle of political contestation and the pluralistic interaction of autonomous social groupings was rapidly conceded, the leaders of *perestroika* remained loyal to a modified version of commune democracy. This in essence emphasised the principle of social community and the resolution of conflict within a single centre of power rather than through competition between different parties and groups. *Perestroika* initially represented a participatory form of direct democracy which tried to achieve a type of socialist *Gemeinschaft* (community) rather than allowing the unfettered development of the egoism and divisiveness typical of a *bürgerliche Gesellschaft* (civil society) (see Keane (ed.), 1988). While Gorbachev began the process whereby the USSR will ultimately be reintegrated into the mainstream of European politics, *perestroika* was not simply a process of Westernisation. The distinction can be seen as one between the post-Communism from 1989 of Eastern Europe, which gladly embraced Western political and economic policies, and the attempt in the Soviet Union from 1985 to develop a distinctive form of late Communism which would develop in parallel to but not converge with the West.

The Polish reform process since 1956 has dramatically illustrated the sharp struggle between reformism and conservatism, with the distinctive feature that reformism has been promoted above all from outside the political leadership. Civil society in the sense of the development of an 'alternative society' parallel to the Communist power system was the central concept of the Polish independent movement (Michnik, 1985). The Polish impasse was of long duration, with popular forces neutralising leadership initiatives leading to a prolonged period of drift. General Wojciech Jaruzelski's suppression of the Solidarity movement in December 1981 was an attempt at a radical breakthrough, but was condemned to failure against the background of weakening government authority and economic decline. In Poland, more than in any other country, it was Gorbachev's reforms which provided the key to unlock the door to escape from the tragic cycles of history since 1945. By removing the excuse for the prevarications of the leadership, who claimed that 'geopolitical realities' limited their freedom of action, the possibility of genuine change appeared.

The round-table talks of early 1989 opened the door to reconciliation with the undaunted independent movement which, unlike the reformists during the 'normalisation' in Czechoslovakia from 1969, was treated relatively mildly following the imposition of the state of war. The emergence of what Adam Michnik called a 'community of free people', based on the Roman Catholic Church, the Solidarity trade union, the unofficial Press and a host of alternative institutions, meant that a situation emerged in which the government could not win and the alternative society, rooted in the fibre of society, could not be defeated. The assertion of the then Prime Minister, Mieczyslaw Rakowski, during his visit to Vienna in November 1988 that 'democracy can be developed without Solidarity' was proved wrong and his attempts to impose 'democracy from above', bypassing the movement, failed. This vision of *apparat* democracy gave way to the more sober reasoning of the political leadership that some sort of accommodation had to be reached. Relatively free elections in June 1989 saw Solidarity inflict a crushing defeat on official government candidates, including the Prime Minister.

In Eastern Europe destalinisation tended to be accompanied by the rejection of Leninism, both being equally alien to historical traditions and cultures. The tendency of East European reform to breach acceptable limits had prompted Khrushchev and Brezhnev to halt changes early in their tracks. While the first stages of the East European 'new democracy' required Gorbachev's sanction, in the latter stages it became independent of Soviet domestic politics. Gorbachev's assertions in favour of national autonomy (see Chapter 8) were found in 1989 to be genuine as one after another the countries of Eastern Europe dismantled the Leninist power system. The loss of party control in Eastern Europe immediately radicalised the reform process in the USSR. The compromises of *perestroika* appeared all the more intolerable in the light of the rapid moves towards post-Communism in Eastern Europe. Reform had turned into revolution. The process rapidly became irreversible as the horse of undisputed Communist dominance slipped out in Poland, Hungary and Bulgaria, and was chased out in the GDR, Czechoslovakia and Romania.

The Chinese economic reforms under Deng Xiaoping in their early years achieved some dramatic successes, yet they starkly illustrated the relationship between economic reform and political change. The 'four modernisations' launched in 1978 aimed to develop agriculture, industry, science and technology, and defence, yet were circumscribed by the 'four basic political principles': maintenance of the leadership of the Communist Party; the dictatorship of the proletariat; the socialist system; and Marx–Lenin–Mao thought. Dubček's dictum that the key to economic reform 'lies in the political sphere' was rejected (*Ind.*, 14 November 1988). By the late 1980s the Chinese reform process, like Yugoslavia's earlier, had demonstrated the pitfalls of trying to turn a command economy towards the market without corresponding political changes. Rising inflation, growing lawlessness, official corruption, declining production in basic commodities such as grain, a large foreign trade imbalance and regional economic conflicts provoked by decentralisation without democratisation led to economic crisis and ultimately, by May–June 1989, to a thorough crisis of the polity and the discrediting of the leadership and the Communist system as a whole.

The development of what dissident Chinese intellectuals, such as the astrophysicist Fang Lizhi, called the 'fifth modernisation', political democracy, received an early rebuff with the crushing of the 1979–80 'Beijing Spring' democracy movement. The leading figure in the 'democracy wall' movement, Wei Jingsheng, was sentenced to fifteen years' imprisonment for his forceful advocacy of the view that economic reform without political democracy would end in failure. Student demonstrations in December 1986–January 1987 resulted in the demotion of the reformist party leader Hu Yaobang and the launching of yet another 'anti-rightist' campaign against 'bourgeois liberalism' and 'spiritual pollution'. Leading reform intellectuals were dismissed, including the Marxist scholar Su Shaozhi, sacked as director of the Marx–Lenin–Mao Zedong Thought Institute. By early 1989, Su was convinced that China faced 'a total crisis in reform, politics and the economy' (*Ind.*, 17 February 1989). His words were tragically borne out by the seven-week student and worker demonstrations culminating in the 4 June 1989 massacres sanctioned by Deng and the premier, Li Peng. Deng's repeated assertions that he would never tolerate Western-style democratic challenges to party rule were revealed as no idle threats.

Chinese experience lends support to the view of Soviet reform Communists that economic reform without democratisation in a Communist polity, known in Poland as 'Pinochetisation', leads to severe social tensions and political paralysis. Oleg Bogomolov, the director of the Institute of the Economics of the World Socialist System, argued that 'The market requires democracy since it cannot function normally in the absence of the economic independence of producers and consumers, equality between different forms of property, or freedom of choice for buyers and sellers' (1989: 40). The absence of reformed political institutions in China left the economic reforms vulnerable to shifts in leadership policy and defenceless against the onslaughts of the conservatives. In contrast to Khrushchev and Deng, Gorbachev was careful to embed his reforms in revamped institutional structures. Moreover, Gorbachev avoided the goal of economic modernisation becoming a pallid substitute for an all-round revived socialist ideology of human development. He therefore broke with what Fang Lizhi identified as the two cardinal principles of Dengist reform. The first suggested that Chinese culture lacked a tradition of democracy and hence was not suitable for a democratic system. This 'law of conservation of democracy', as Fang put it, asserted that a society's total capacity for democracy is fixed: if a country has never had democracy, then this proves that it can never have democracy. The second law, borrowed from South Korean or Brazilian experience of authoritarian modernisation, argued that economic development does not necessarily require a democratic system. The problem here is that the socialist reform economies have never been 'free market' systems because of the distinctive forms of social ownership; hence the 'political dictatorship plus free economy' formula cannot be applied to Communist systems (Fang Lizhi, 1989; *Ind.*, 18 January 1989).

From the survey above it is clear that, to date, the history of Communist reformism has overwhelmingly been a story of failure. The measurement of success or failure is, of course, problematical and will be discussed below, but for the present we will examine some of the factors that can be identified in the failure or success of reform processes.

Splits in the leadership and leadership struggles weaken reformist drives. This applies particularly to post-Mao and post-Stalin reforms, and to Yugoslavia. Divisions in the ranks of the reformers also have a debilitating effect on reforms, and were particularly evident in the Soviet reform process of 1920–1. The lack of correspondence between political and economic reform, as during the NEP and the Dengist reforms, is a crucial factor. The retention in all essentials of war Communist political systems under conditions of a relatively marketised economy leads to profound tensions that ultimately threaten the existence of the polity and result in the vigorous reassertion of state power. External pressure, which in its extreme form includes invasion, applies to a greater or lesser extent to all of Eastern Europe; even Yugoslavia was not wholly free of the threat of Soviet interference. The entrenched power of bureaucracies and the inertia of existing institutional structures act as one of the most profound inhibiting factors in the development of reforms. In Hungary the power of the ministries continued to stifle economic activity. Brezhnev's ill-fated economic reforms were designed not to challenge the ministerial bureaucracy but to co-opt them, yet neither Khrushchev's frontal assault nor Brezhnev's blandishments proved effective.

The weakness of mass input takes many forms, but all reforms (with the exception of Czechoslovakia) until Gorbachev tended to be 'reforms from above' and thus failed to institutionalise popular support for changes. Polish *odnowa* (renewal) from 1980, indeed, was designed to bypass the mass Solidarity movement. Similarly, the slogans of workers' democracy in 1920–1 drew the teeth of the opposition groupings and allowed the leadership to divert the reform process into safer channels and ultimately to abandon it altogether.

The role of powerful leadership is a critical factor in even the modest success of reform processes. From Tito to Deng Xiaoping, Khrushchev to Gorbachev, the leader is always crucial. But while strong leadership is a necessary condition it is not a sufficient one. After December 1981 Jaruzelski was undoubtedly a powerful figure committed, rhetorically at least, to reform, and yet nearly a decade later the Polish economy was as diseased as ever.

This leads to two general laws of reform. First, to succeed, reforms must have a mechanism which can impart a constant source of dynamism. This does not preclude periods in which the reforms apparently mark time, and indeed they may require periods of consolidation. But they then need yet another impetus to move ahead; otherwise they have a tendency to slide back into the comfortable security of ministerial or party tutelage. This impetus can be provided only by a dynamic leader or mass pressure. The second law suggests that even a strong dynamic force is not sufficient but that some self-sustaining mechanism of reform is required to make them irreversible, and for this they must be open-ended.

A common pattern can be identified in all previous reform attempts.

Reformers decentralise, leading to instability, leading to the reimposition of controls. There is therefore a threshold over which a reform must pass in order to become 'irreversible'; otherwise it will roll back down the original slope of change. This can be called the 'threshold of irreversibility'. At that stage, even if the reform marks time, it is no longer in danger of reverting to something approximating the original position at the outset of reforms.

Attention should be paid to the circumstances of reform. A sense that 'there is no alternative' is essential. This allowed Lenin relatively easily to introduce the NEP, and for Deng to argue that his reforms were essential to overcome the disasters of Maoism. This factor also worked powerfully to stimulate Gorbachev's reforms. Thirty years of stalled economic reforms following Stalin's death led to stagnation. Sixty-five years of stalled political reforms following the failure of the 1920 reforms led to a profound moral, ethical and social stagnation. Gorbachev constantly argued that there was no time to delay and no alternative to *perestroika*. In his acceptance speech for the presidency of the Supreme Soviet on 1 October 1988, for instance, he argued that *perestroika* was 'born through suffering' (*P*, 2 October 1988). However, his position in this respect has been weaker than Deng's since the suffering, while certainly not less than elsewhere, has lost some of its impact. Maoism was indeed catastrophic and largely discredited itself, whereas conservatives of various hues can point to significant successes in the thirty years before Gorbachev's accession. Even Stalin, despite the huge loss of life, has been defended by Ligachev and others as having contributed much to the 'building of socialism' in the Soviet Union.

A further element in all reform processes is the question of their speed and scale. Hurried reforms led to disaster, either by foreign intervention (Hungary 1956, Czechoslovakia 1968) or by the disorganisation they trailed in their wake. As for the question of scale, it appears that small reforms may not generate enough momentum to carry them over the threshold of a new phase; and excessively large reforms may lead to the instability that undermines the reformers and also drags them back to the past. There is, therefore, perhaps an optimal speed and scale of reform, one which can only be discovered in the detailed circumstances of a specific reform process. The Soviet reformers under Gorbachev sought this happy medium.

The general crisis of Communism

The coincidence of crises in the late 1980s from Yugoslavia to China, the USSR and throughout Eastern Europe, led many commentators, such as Djilas (*Ind.*, 15 October 1988), to identify a 'general crisis' of Communism. A report issued in February 1989 by a special four-person party commission of the HSWP, and vigorously endorsed by Pozsgay, argued that the 'entire socialist world' was in crisis and that 'socialism was an obstacle to progress'. The deleninising theme was taken to the limit in arguing that the Bolshevik Revolution itself was a mistake since it tried to build socialism in a 'semi-feudal' and isolated Russia. More traditionally, they insisted that Stalin's contribution to Marxism was heretical in that genuine socialist internationalism was perverted into Soviet imperialism, and that the imposition of the Stalinist model of Communism on Hungary and the rest of Eastern Europe was an unmitigated disaster. 'Post-Stalinism' was only a milder version of the original, and as a result, the report declared, Eastern Europe had been lurching from one crisis to another for forty years (*Tarsadalmi Szemle*, HSWP theoretical journal, 16 February 1989, cited in *ST*, 19 February 1989). This analysis could not have been more scathing, though it located the origins of Stalinism in some primordial Russian problem and thus tended to ignore the indigenous roots of what was in Hungary a particularly virulent form of Stalinism.

The crisis in Communist systems led Eduard Goldstücker, one of the leading reformist intellectuals in the Prague Spring, to argue that the Soviet model of development has exhausted its potential. In apocalyptic terms he has argued that the alternatives are democratisation or destruction: 'After 1968, and after Poland, there is no productive force to be derived from the Soviet system any longer. It is finished, and sooner or later it has to be destroyed.' He went on to insist: 'Either the system will find some sort of path indicated by the democratisation efforts of Hungary in 1956, or Czechoslovakia in 1968, or Poland [in 1980−1], or it will have to be destroyed in a terrible explosion' (cited by McAdams, 1987: 107). Djilas, one of the leaders in Yugoslavia until expelled from the party in 1954, was possibly even more pessimistic about the ability of Communism to survive, certainly in Yugoslavia and possibly elsewhere. The espousal of elements of the market economy from Beijing to Belgrade, he insisted, was simply not compatible with the existing political structures of Communist rule (*Ind.*, 15 October 1988: 10).

Like the debate over the general crisis of the seventeenth century, there was a debate over whether there was such a general crisis of socialism. Did the crisis affect only the unreformed system, or was reform itself part of the problem rather than the solution? What was the scope for some sort of democratic 'late Communist' socialism? Not only Stalinist socialism but even reformed Communism has been condemned. Milan Kucan, the Slovenian Communist party leader, declared in 1989 that the last forty years of Yugoslav reform socialism were a 'complete error' (*ST*, 26 February 1989).

Gorbachev himself has argued that when he came to power in 1985 the Soviet Union was in a pre-crisis condition suggesting that problems were so acute that a failure to take rapid and drastic remedial action would have led to a thorough crisis of the system. The basic intention in using the term was of course to avoid admitting that in 1985 the Soviet Union faced a full-scale crisis—which raises the question of what constitutes a crisis in a socialist system. The debate over the concept of crisis is one which extends to all the cardinal moments of Communist power, from 1920–1 in the USSR and the crisis of war Communism, to Hungary in 1956, Czechoslovakia in 1968 and Poland in 1980–1. Were these moments, and others like them, symptoms of a political crisis in the whole socialist system or were they specific breakdowns caused by conjunctural factors?

The general crisis of Communism was made up of several elements. One feature precipitating change and awareness of problems, of course, was the ripple effect of Gorbachev's own radical *perestroika* and *glasnost*. The authority of Communist governments weakened as social, economic and ideological changes left them increasingly exposed, isolated, and devoid of legitimacy. The old ferocity in destroying opponents was no longer a practicable alternative, and when applied, as in Poland in 1981 and China in 1989, only hastened the disintegration of authority. The growth of Communist liberalism can be seen to be a rational response to challenges rather than a Damascene conversion to a new and more tolerant political practice.

Above all, the crisis lay in declining economic efficiency and the perception that Soviet-type economies could no longer deliver the goods. Seventy years of trying to introduce socialism failed to create a dynamic, effective and just society. Socialist societies, it was argued, no longer offered a credible alternative to free market or welfare capitalism. They could no longer match the dynamism of capitalist economies, or fulfil the socialist promise of full employment, effective health care, housing and the other elements of a programme which prioritised economic security over traditional liberal democratic political values such as individual rights. This prompted the transfer of economic responsibility to various types of market forces. The 'invisible hand of supply and demand', as Adam Smith put it, was to reduce the interference of the 'visible hand' of planning and the bureaucracy. However, in the Soviet Union this approach only exacerbated the crises since the market failed to respond when inserted into the existing structures of the planned economy.

Furthermore, the decline in ideological commitment increasingly led to the belief that Communism itself was an impracticable 'Utopian concept' and, in the words of the much-repeated East European joke, 'merely the longest route from feudalism to capitalism'. From this perspective, the seventy-two years of Bolshevik power from October 1917 to the second Russian revolution of 1990 was merely a long interlude before the liberal democratic promise of the February 1917 revolution was fulfilled. The Communist belief in an alternative modernity to capitalism was increasingly perceived as an expensive mistake. All Communist parties were thrown into theoretical disarray by the collapse of cherished beliefs in progress led by a one-party system.

A major element in the crisis was the re-evaluation of history. As the Communist systems lost control over the interpretation of the past, so they lost control of the present. In Hungary this focused on a debate over the nature of the 1956 uprising. One of the more surprising formulations in 1988 was that the movement was a 'counter-revolution made by revolutionaries', but in 1989 Pozsgay's view that it was a 'popular uprising' triumphed. New thinking about the Soviet past will be examined in Chapter 3, but it should be noted that the debate over the past is equally a debate about the future. In Hungary and Poland historical revisionism did not threaten the existence of the state, but in the Soviet Union (and the GDR) it challenged the very basis on which the systems were built.

There was a social element to the crisis, in that the 'new class' of political bureaucrats, whose rule was based on socialist rhetoric and the promise of economic modernisation, could no longer rule in the old way, and the people would no longer tolerate rule in the old way, the classic Leninist formulation of a revolutionary situation. Brezhnev's coming to power in 1964 can in part be seen as a counter-reform, a class reaction against Khrushchev's challenge to the power and privileges of an entrenched élite. The cohesion of the old ruling class could no longer be taken for granted as the shortcomings of command mechanisms and neo-Stalinism became ever more apparent. Gorbachev by late 1986 was clearly convinced that no economic reform strategy would be worth much if the 'superstructure' of political life remained unreformed. The party apparatus and the state bureaucracy had plenty of resources and years of experience in stifling reforms and debilitating them with a thousand strokes of the pen. Some of Gorbachev's language was reminiscent of Mao's strictures against the bureaucracy, and indeed on occasion the tone of his exhortations for a 'cultural revolution' against bureaucratism was redolent of the Maoist approach although, of course, applied in a very different way.

This approach went beyond the earlier tenet of Communist revisionism that the problems were rooted in 'errors' and 'distortions', and instead suggested that the systems themselves were at fault. In other words, it moved beyond reformism and challenged the very foundations of Soviet-type systems. Radical reformers began to suggest that the whole Bolshevik project was misconceived from the very beginning (Tsipko, 1988–9). *Perestroika* in this light was no longer reform but reflected the terminal crisis of the system born of October 1917 and imposed on Eastern Europe after 1945. Reformism gave way to a revolutionary challenge to the existing structures of power in which no option, including liberal parliamentary democracy on the Western model, was excluded. Scandinavian and Austrian social democracy exerted a special fascination for East European and Soviet reformers. The failure of the socialist economies drove the reformers to adopt what were earlier considered anti-socialist measures.

The impetus for reform in the Soviet Union came about through a combination of social, intellectual and political pressures. Gorbachev's reforms can be seen in part as the outcome of the maturation of socialist society. The modernisation of the polity, it is argued by writers such as Lewin (1988), results from the social process of modernisation that has been accelerating in the post-war period. By 1960 the number of town-dwellers exceeded the rural population, and by 1980 two-thirds of the population were urban. In the 1950s half the population worked on the land, whereas now less than a quarter are engaged in agriculture. The number of people with higher education has grown from 2 per cent in 1959 to 9 per cent in 1988, and 22 million are college graduates (Lewin, 1988: 47). The occupational structure reflected these changes, with a sevenfold growth in administrative and professional occupations since 1940. All this generates a specific set of social needs like housing, transport, welfare facilities and consumer goods. An urban population is much more dependent on state provision than a rural one. Moreover, urbanisation tends to generate a range of political demands, such as a thirst for information and participation. The urban population, in addition, is better informed about conditions in the country and in the world at large.

The politics of reform clearly has a social dimension, both in terms of 'class interests' and general processes of societal change, but there remains a question over the influence that an urbanised, professional and educated society has on a political system. The problem with the view of *perestroika* as the outcome of social change is the absence of a demonstrated mechanism linking social transformation to political change. No simple correlation can be drawn between social develop-ment and the achievement of a pluralistic political system. The point at which quantitative changes can be transformed into qualitative changes must be understood. While social changes undoubtedly generated pressure for political modernisation there is no automatic connection between the two. They are a useful, possibly necessary, but certainly not a sufficient condition for political reform.

Perestroika challenged accepted Marxist and non-Marxist notions of the relationship of politics and economics. Indeed, the revolutions of 1989 can well be seen as the vindication of Hegel's assertion that consciousness determines being. One of the more startling features of *perestroika* was the relative ease with which political structures could be changed, and the stubborn persistence of old forms of economic behaviour and structures. More importantly, to what degree did economic changes or the maturing of development and modernisation precipitate *perestroika*? The concept of modernisation on its own can offer little by way of an explanation for Communist reformism. The idea suggests that political reform had to await the maturing of social and economic relations. Instead, reform has always and everywhere been above all a *political* process, which given the right circumstances could have been achieved in 1921, 1928, 1953, 1964, 1968 or any other date. The movements in Berlin in 1953, in Poland and Hungary in 1956, in Czechoslovakia in 1968, and Poland at any time demonstrate the readiness of populations and their societies for reform. The reasons for the inability of Communist political systems to respond to them in a structured way does not lie in economic but in political factors. Similar economic forces can give rise to very different political responses.

No doubt the maturation of Soviet society facilitated Gorbachev's reforms, but other socialist societies with more advanced social structures, such as the GDR and Czechoslovakia, had until 1989 adopted more conservative positions. Clearly, this difference derives from the specific historical circumstances of each country, but suggests that social changes have no automatic political consequences. Romania and Bulgaria have much more traditional social structures yet they too achieved revolutions of sorts in 1989. Moreover, it would clearly be difficult to argue that Khrushchev's reforms were stifled because of a lack of social development. The bureaucratic class, moreover, found that its interests could be better pursued within the terms of the neo-Stalinist compact than in the harsh environment of marketising and pluralising reforms. The task facing Gorbachev was if anything far more awesome than even that facing Khrushchev. One aspect of this was the consolidation and expansion of the bureaucracy, growing by 60 per cent between 1966 and 1977 alone (Schroeder, 1979: 314). Gorbachev can be seen as an apostle of the enlightened bureaucracy, featuring democratisation, liberalisation and market reforms. However, this would be at best a very partial view of his reforms since their basic drive is to reduce the power of the bureaucracy. Under Brezhnev the sphere of personal autonomy was permitted to grow as long as it did not extend to political demands, whereas under Gorbachev the political activism of the people was specifically encouraged to challenge the power of the bureaucracy. Reform is ultimately a political project, and the problem for reformers is to find a way of converting changes in the structure of society into specific constituencies of social support for political reform.

In addition, while the Soviet population was no doubt better informed in 1985 than in 1955, real understanding has been a consequence of *glasnost* rather than a cause of *perestroika*. For example, until about 1987, as far as we can tell, the great majority of the population still retained a respect for Stalin, for the alleged order, stability and sense of purpose of his rule. Only after the full extent of the corruption and evil of his years became common knowledge did public opinion turn against him. At any point since 1917 there has been a large constituency for some form of democratisation, as much in the 1920s as in the 1950s or 1980s. Further, even a highly sophisticated society, given the right circumstances, can turn towards authoritarianism, as in Nazi Germany. The intellectual climate must be taken into account. As Russia developed into a more modern society in the late nineteenth century those very intellectuals in the vanguard of change turned towards populist or socialist authoritarianism, flushed by the Utopianism of the prospect for total human liberation. While the current intellectual climate in the USSR appears on the whole in favour of toleration and democracy, there is far from a consensus in favour of a pluralistic liberal democratic type of political system. A plethora of alternatives are being proposed, from some sort of theocratic monarchical authoritarianism for the Russians, to the anarchical abolition of the state altogether. The social basis for alternative programmes must clearly be sought (Zaslavskaya, 1990), but the scale and scope of social change alone tell us little about the type of political change and movements that might accompany it. Only after the event can we with any assurance identify particular constituencies with specific political outcomes.

This is not to deny the importance of economic and social change in stimulating political change, but rather to suggest that economics is neither a sufficient nor an exclusive determinant. The methods of political sociology, and indeed the new discipline of economic sociology advanced by Zaslavskaya (Zaslavskaya and Ryvkina (eds.), 1989), which sees economic development as a social process, are crucial but need to be balanced by an understanding of the ideological context for social and political change. Yet another new discipline of philosophical sociology may well be required.

The cardinal relationship in Communist systems was that between society and the party. Society was long in a state of tension with the party-state system, and the social changes exacerbated the tension as its political and economic costs became more apparent. In early years the party-state had the courage of its convictions and used sufficient force to mould society and suppress the inherent tensions. Organic processes of adaptation in party–society relations were inadequate and crises tended to act as the method of achieving major changes. Reform is no more than the mechanism whereby Communist systems adjust economic and political policies.

'The real dilemma facing East European socialism', Silviu Brucan, a former member of the Romanian Politburo, ambassador to the United Nations and a member of the National Salvation Front after the revolution of December 1989, argued, 'is reform or die, and go down as an abortive social experiment' (*G*, 12 November 1988). It could be argued that the crisis was not restricted to socialist countries alone, but reflected a larger crisis in socialist ideology and socialism itself. Its major concerns, it might be argued, speak to a world that is passing and offer no effective response to the actual problems of the 'post-modern' world. The emphasis on large-scale industrial development, for instance, contributed to the global ecological catastrophe. The relationship between nature and society has to be rethought. Large-scale mass production, or Fordist, forms of economic organisation began to change towards more flexible units of production which encourage decentralisation of decision-making, diversity, looser forms of control, and consumer choice (post-Fordism). Moreover, the argument of Eric Hobsbawm that in the 1950s the 'forward march of labour' of the last century or so had come to an end because of changes in economic and social structures challenged the Left to rethink some of the basic principles of traditional socialism (Jacques and Mulhern (eds.), 1981).

These issues have been discussed in the Soviet Union for some years, though not always directly. Leadership is a crucial factor in determining the pace and nature of reform, but it would be quite wrong to see the impetus for change coming from Gorbachev and his associates alone. Gorbachev's reforms underwent a long process of gestation and he has drawn on a wide variety of ideas to justify them. Soviet reformism in the 1980s, both in domestic and foreign policy, emerged from many different strands, some of which were rooted in Soviet officialdom and the Communist Party itself and influenced by currents of world thought.

In an important article Brzezinski (1966) argued that the cumulative policy failures and unregulated leadership struggles meant that the existing party-dominated systems would be unable to legitimate themselves and hence were faced with a dire choice: transformation or degeneration. The leaders would either have to transform the manner and purpose of their rule, including modifying the leading role of the party, or their systems would face the prospect of degeneration. It appeared during the long years of Brezhnevite stagnation that Brzezinski's forecast had proved correct. Gorbachev's reforms, however, at last took up the option of transformation.

Contrary to crude versions of totalitarian theory, we can assume that no system can remain indefinitely static. At the same time, sophisticated theories of the development of Soviet society advanced to replace totalitarianism have also been shown to be inadequate. Occam's razor has been working full time since Gorbachev's accession. Complex theories, such as those examining the role of traditional authoritarian political cultures in generating political legitimacy for Communist regimes, have given way to some fairly basic propositions on the relationship between the unreformed system and society. Up to 1985, while one cannot deny real change, the salient feature of the Soviet system was how little change was institutionalised in political structures or incorporated into the daily processes of what Habermas calls the 'life world' of society. The concept of stagnation is a very real one and is more than the usual attempt of new Communist leaders to discredit their predecessors. It represents the extraordinary degree to which the Soviet polity and similar ones had become insulated from the sources of dynamism (cf. Johnson, 1970: 1–32).

In the Soviet Union the post-Stalin years witnessed considerable political development, but within narrowly circumscribed limits. The ability of the leadership to control social processes ebbed, but the leakage of power to forces beyond the *nomenklatura* élite's immediate purview was kept within strict bounds. The one-party system remained secure, but the power of the leader was limited by the principle of collective leadership. Mass terror gave way to sustained low-level coercion against political deviancy. The economy remained securely in the hands of the planners and the bureaucracy, and several attempts at reform, notably in 1965, remained stillborn.

With the above considerations in mind it is natural that we should have begun our examination of sources of change by a discussion of the historical legacy of relative changelessness and half-hearted reform. Given the scope and radicalism of the reforms under Gorbachev, and indeed in China as far as the economy is concerned, we need to identify the sources and mechanisms of change in Soviet-type societies. This can be examined at three levels: sources of change within the system; forces of change outside the official parameters of tolerated activity; and the winds of change blowing across the borders of the Communist nation-state.

The locus of change within the system appears to be sections of the élite, the specialist institutes, some of the old departments and in the commissions of the Central Committee. Gorbachev argued that the analysis underlying *perestroika* and the public perception of the need for change predated the April 1985 CC plenum and was developed by 'a group of party and state officials' (1987a, pp. 24, 27). Gorbachev's accession as a reforming leader seemed to confirm the hopes of those, like Roy Medvedev, who have long argued that the most realistic perspective for change in the Soviet Union would come from within the system itself, a new leader supported by reforming officials and sections of society (Breslauer, 1978: 75). *Perestroika* can be seen as the attempt of a reformist section of the leadership to impose change not only on society but also on the traditional structures of power. Gorbachev revived the revisionist approach of inner-party renewal last practised in the USSR by Khrushchev and thought to have died with the crushing of the Prague Spring in Czechoslovakia in 1968.

Ideas in favour of *perestroika* were developed in a number of Moscow institutions, including the Central Economical and Mathematical Institute (TsEMI), which elaborated the SOFE (System of the Optimally Functioning Economy) model of optimal socialist planning, the Institute of the Economy of the World Socialist System, headed from the late 1960s by Oleg Bogomolov, and the Institute of State and Law where its researchers, including Boris Kurashvili, proposed many of the policies concerning legal and political reform that have now been implemented. Precursors of *perestroika* could be found at the Institute of Economics and Industrial Organisation of the USSR Academy of Sciences in Novosibirsk. Abel Aganbegyan was appointed director in 1966 and turned it into a centre for debate over the economics of the socialist market. The monthly journal *EKO* proposed radical ideas and in relatively strong terms provided a critique of current inadequacies. This trend culminated in the Novosibirsk report of April 1983 which basically set the tone for current reforms. In this paper, Zaslavskaya (1984) identified a growing gulf between the system of economic management created in the 1930s and the needs of a modern economy.

Unofficial pressure culminated in the development of the independent movement (to be discussed in Chapter 5). Many of the ideas of the so-called dissidents have now been incorporated into the official definition of *perestroika*. The dissident movement acted as a profound mechanism of change by the exertion of pressures from below in the form of resistance and publicity, but perhaps above all through the development of alternative ideas and structures of political and social life.

Pressure from abroad takes many forms. Since the death of Stalin the Soviet Union has closely monitored developments in Eastern Europe in order to glean from its experience aspects that could be of use to the development and modernisation of the Soviet system itself (Höhmann,

1989). To a degree individual East European countries became 'laboratories' where experiments in social and political reform could be monitored, and then applied either in other socialist countries or in the USSR itself (Hazan, 1985: 370). Developments in the world economy and society have been studied by a number of academic institutes.

There were several practical attempts to develop *perestroika*-like policies before 1985. Gorbachev's own agricultural innovations have been noted (see page 4). In Georgia Shevardnadze led the way in the campaign against corruption even before Andropov made it state policy at national level. As the Georgian party First Secretary between 1972 and 1985, following a career in the ministry of the interior (MVD), he arrested 25,000 people for corruption, including 17,000 Communists and 70 KGB officials. His economic reforms prefigured those of Gorbachev, with more flexible agricultural policies encouraging initiative. Food queues disappeared from Tbilisi while they lengthened in Moscow. He also established a Centre for the Study of Public Opinion years before Moscow dared to take the same step.

The discussion above establishes the framework to analyse what is a 'reform' in the Communist context. Since the founding of the first socialist state, later joined by some fifteen more, a recurrent theme of their history has been the launching of various campaigns known by the word reform or some equivalent term. It is important to note also that some countries have failed to institute reform processes, and the very absence itself helps establish the parameters of a definition of reform. Why do some countries launch reform processes and others not? Why, indeed, is the concept of reform an integral part of the development of some Communist systems and not of others?

Thus any study of Communist reformism must try to understand the nature of Communist conservatism. In Czechoslovakia, the 'normalisation' following the invasion reflected the interests of a section of the polity as well as the concerns of the USSR. In Romania, Ceausescu's dictatorship hardened its grip and launched vast projects of social engineering that the post-Stalinist leadership in the Soviet Union had long ago abandoned. In Cuba reform was considered unnecessary and the system under Castro's sclerotic leadership settled down to stagnation as he declined into old age. The suppression of the democracy movement in China in 1989 clearly revealed the logic of Communist conservatism as a reflection of the needs of the power system. The revolutions in Eastern Europe meant that a reappraisal had to be made of the countries that had resisted reform in the early years of Gorbachev's rule. By the end of 1989 none of the countries that Gati (1989) dubbed the 'gang of four' – Bulgaria, Czechoslovakia, the GDR and Romania – could still be so called. A new 'gang of four' emerged made up of Albania, China,

Cuba and North Korea, and even they were not immune to the pressure for democratisation. The neo-Stalinist countries, those that had accepted the post-Stalinist 'contract' to improve standards of living, eschew ideological mobilisation and allow greater personal freedoms as long as these were not translated into demands for political reform, were the first to set out on the path of post-Communism. Now only the Stalinist countries remained, suggesting that neo-Stalinism had not proved a viable system and that there was no middle way of Brezhnevite muddling through.

Communist conservatism is made up of a number of elements, including an attachment to basic dogmas and a belief that basic social compact policies retain scope for development. The 'authoritarian reformist' trend rejects the apocalyptic language of Communist crisis and regards the thinking that prompts it as ideological subversion promoted by the class enemy. Communist conservatives do not recognise the need for the radical restructuring of existing political institutions and argue that the cure can be worse than the illness. The 'party populist' trends are willing to accept the enormity of the USSR's problems, but their solutions would be found within a traditional framework (the trends are identified by Jeff Gleisner, 1989).

It would be an exaggeration to see Ligachev as a full-blooded Brezhnev restorationist, but on a range of policy issues his support was for a more limited form of *perestroika* reminiscent of Andropov's authoritarian version. He was a conservative insofar as his appraisal of the past was more positive than that of most of the radical reformers. His vision of modernisation included the need for economic reform, the campaign against alcohol and the need for the party to lose some of its functions. In a speech in Gorky on 5 August 1988 he inveighed against private property and excessive marketisation of the Soviet economy and its attendant dangers of unemployment and deepened social inequalities. In foreign policy he sought to maintain the class approach and condemned the pragmatism that reduced the importance of Third World liberation struggles and of ideological alliances. He was suspicious of *glasnost* and condemned some of its more radical exponents. He opposed a too thorough exposure of the 'blank pages' in Soviet history and thus sought to portray the Stalin experience, from which his family also had suffered, in its most positive light (Ligachev, 1989: 275–91 and *passim*). In sum, his authoritarian reformism acted as a powerful inhibition on the full-blooded democratisation, pluralisation and mar-ketisation of Soviet society. While he was willing to reform, many orthodox principles of the party's leading role and ideology were to remain sacrosanct.

Reform Communism

The nature and direction of change in Communist systems must be understood in order to come to terms with Gorbachev's reform process. In the long perspective one can characterise Gorbachev's reforms as the third phase of Soviet power. The first was the system-building phase, from 1917 to 1953, in which Lenin and Stalin created the basic institutions and structures; the second was the system-management phase, from 1953 to 1985, in which Khrushchev, Brezhnev and his two successors sought to find a way of making the system work; and the third has been the system-transformation phase under Gorbachev from 1985 that has not only rejected the neo-Stalinist system-management phase as unviable, but has sought qualitatively to transform the basic institutions as forged by the first two Soviet leaders while remaining within the broad framework of their ideas. This was the aim and ambiguity of Gorbachev's reform Communism.

The study of reform in Communist systems must take into account the general question of developmental politics, not only of the so-called Communist Second World but also of the Third World. At issue is the primacy of the developed First World as the goal towards which other societies strive. This is seen at its starkest in the concept of *modernisation*. This inevitably assumes a concept of modernity, but the notion can have very different interpretations depending on historical background and level of socioeconomic development. The idea is often associated with a degree of political freedom, but this may well be an unwarranted assumption. The attainment of a high degree of development and the provision of basic welfare and social well-being may be achieved through very different means. The problem for the Soviet reformers is that ultimately the old administrative model of socialism could neither deliver the basic economic goods and a rising standard of living, nor generate an expanding sphere of individual or sociocultural development.

The notion of modernity is certainly an elusive concept, yet it is worth dwelling on some of its key features. Communism had long proposed itself not only as an alternative form of modernity to that of the West but also, in its Bolshevik guise, as an alternative path towards achieving modernisation. This involved the 'jumping' of stages in Marx's schematic account of development, as practised by Lenin in achieving the October Revolution and Trotsky in his theory of 'combined and uneven development'. One of the leading exponents of the developmental model, John H. Kautsky, pointed out that all modern countries are industrialised, but not all industrialised countries are modern

(Kautsky, 1972). The question remains whether there is one modernity, as suggested by Talcott Parsons, or many, as argued by George Schöpflin (1988b: 127). The fundamental problem is that there may not be an alternative form of modernity, and thus the alternative path to it may be a historical dead end. Hence the search for a late Communist alternative to capitalism, the essence of democratic *perestroika*, may be futile.

Gorbachev's reforms can be interpreted as a modernising revolution, though this depends on how modernity is defined. There is a tendency to see the general crisis of socialism as part of the larger crisis of modernity as a whole. The despair of those who have been disillusioned with traditional alternatives has, for example, prompted the rise of ecologism. It could be argued, however, that there is no crisis of modernity but only a crisis of the socialist attempt to create an alternative to the Western modernity characterised by the market and liberal democracy. In so far as Gorbachev's reforms are a revolt against post-modernist relativism they have been inspirational. Gorbachev has rehabilitated the Victorian idea of progress, the search for real solutions to real problems. This has been achieved by redefining the traditional Soviet view of modernisation away from an obsession with tons of steel produced and number of engineers trained to stressing the political component, individuation and the increased pluralisation of society, all part of the post-modern agenda. Hence *perestroika* tried to fulfil the aspirations of modernity, the metascheme of things as outlined by Marx, while tending at the same time to a post-modern view of the world. However, in so far as Gorbachev remained loyal to the attempt to find an alternative to capitalist modernity it appeared that *perestroika* was only perpetuating the crisis and would be unable to achieve the promise of either.

Gorbachev rejected simplistic solutions to the mystery of human consciousness, history and development. No longer was the solution found in the Lenin–Stalin class or economic dimension alone. Indeed, he returned, albeit unwittingly, to the idea of Max Weber in realising that development entails a psychological and cultural dimension. The emphasis on the human factor under *perestroika* returned to the themes raised by Weber's analysis of the Protestant work ethic in his *The Protestant Ethic and the Spirit of Capitalism*, which demonstrated that complex social processes lie behind self-sustaining economic development. The new Soviet understanding of the 'human factor' rehabilitated the whole sphere of human relations and consciousness that was once seen as malleable and dependent on will and economic factors.

The concept of modernisation and the *developmental model* are associated, yet it seems valid to distinguish between the two. Whereas modernisation has connotations of striving to achieve a given type of modernity, including certain political characteristics, development is a more neutral term and expresses the dynamics of economic and social advancement without imposing any predetermined political pattern. The developmental model in broad terms focuses on the transition from agrarian and peasant societies to industrial, urbanised and educated societies (Almond and Powell, 1966).

Kautsky argued that Communist countries were at very different stages of development and therefore care should be taken to distinguish between them, rather than subsuming them under general catch-all phrases such as totalitarian, or indeed 'Communist'. Countries like Cuba probably had more in common with other Caribbean countries than with, say, Poland. Both Communist and non-Communist developing countries under the aegis of mobilising regimes had more in common with each other than with the more developed Communist or capitalist countries (Kautsky, 1973). Kautsky thus highlighted one of the salient features of most Communist revolutions to date, namely that they have occurred where Marx least expected them, in underdeveloped regions rather than in the advanced metropolitan centres. Hence Communist revolutions have been forced to take upon themselves the task of economic development. The political revolutions came before the economic conditions that were, according to Marx, the precondition for socialism. This already suggests that Kautsky's arguments should be modified in that the very project of socialist development imbued Communist countries with very different ideological perspectives, political organisations and economic structures than non-Communist countries.

In Communist countries what can be called a crisis of development began to make itself apparent from at least the late 1970s. The mere fact that Communist regimes survived revealed more about the tenacity of their élites than their viability as agents of development. The Polish regime survived the challenge of Solidarity in 1980−1, but its victory only plunged the country further into the systemic crisis that had provoked the emergence of Solidarity in the first place. Soviet Communism avoided the more spectacular of Polish-type breakdowns; yet its problems were little less profound.

The achievements of the modernising Communist regimes in fields like social and welfare policy have been increasingly vitiated by their inability to translate them into broad-ranging and sustained improvements in standards of living or the sophistication of political processes. The breakthrough into modernity constantly eluded the Communist leaderships; and Khrushchev's boasts in 1961 of overtaking the US economy by 1970 and achieving Communism by 1980 appear amusing in retrospect. The leaderships under Brezhnev, Eduard Gierek in Poland in the 1970s and others compensated by proclaiming an increasingly hollow 'propaganda of success' and took on the patina of national and patriotic symbolism. This may well have guaranteed their survival for a time, but it further stifled dynamism as development gave way to a mean and incompetent paternalism.

The major question that arises, however, is whether there are intrinsic features in the Marxist–Leninist model that inhibit sustained social development and engender recurring crises. It might be argued that Communism as a model of development is no different from any other path, since all have entailed high costs in terms of social dislocation and human misery. While industrialisation and modernisation have always indeed entailed a high cost, the balance is drawn by results, and this the Communist regimes themselves found wanting. The problems do not lie simply in the past, and the question became ever more insistent whether a restructured USSR could set out boldly towards a 'self-regulating, constantly self-renewing' form of socialism as a 'higher form of civilisation' (Bogomolov, 1989: 34, 37). Is there a non-capitalist high road to civil peace and economic prosperity?

Marketisation is often prescribed, notably by the economist Nikolai Shmelëv in the Soviet Union, as a universal antidote to the inefficiencies of the old state-dominated pattern of development. Moreover, market-isation has a political purpose in that it undermines the logic whereby centralised and authoritarian plans lead to centralised and authoritarian politics. There is a major debate as to whether some sort of democratic planning is feasible, with Alec Nove arguing that such a third way is impossible (Nove, 1983). As we shall see, reform Communists now argue that markets are an independent variable not confined to any specific political system (cf. Harrington, 1989).

How to achieve the marketisation of centralised economies is a problem facing post-Communist and late Communist systems alike (cf. Yasin, 1989). In the first instance, economic liberalisation may bring in train a range of undesirable features and actually provoke a decline in standards of living in the short term as the restructuring starts to bite. Rising prices, the erosion of social services and welfare, increased demands on worktime, loss of job security and so on have to be balanced by a belief that the sacrifices will ultimately be worth while. While the Polish population in 1990 appeared to have this faith, the Soviet population had no confidence that such sacrifices would be worth while within the context of *perestroika*. Seventy years of promises about Communist jam tomorrow eroded popular belief in the authority's ability to deliver socialist jam today.

A further approach to change in the Soviet Union are the twin ideas of *convergence* and *pluralism*. It has often been assumed that as societies develop and their economies become more complex an 'iron law of pluralism' begins to operate, though this has been shown not necessarily to be the case (White, 1978). The differentiation of society suggests that interests become consolidated and begin to seek forms of political expression. In place of the earlier alleged monolithism, or totalitarianism, Communist systems begin to look like modern industrial societies, whatever their political system. Socioeconomic imperatives impel these societies to begin to converge with their capitalist counterparts. There are many different versions of the convergence thesis but they all suggest a link between the economic 'base' and the political 'superstructure'. The validity of this assertion is open to doubt.

The fact that the two major systems, Communism and capitalism, were forced to coexist should not be taken automatically to mean convergence, or so Soviet reform Communists argued. In his inaugural speech as chair of the CC ideology commission entitled 'Contemporary conceptions of socialism' Vadim Medvedev was at pains to stress that while capitalism and socialism could not develop in isolation of each other but would inevitably intersect as part of general human civilisation, this did not entail convergence. Both would develop according to their own dynamics (*P*, 5 October 1988). The editors of *Kommunist*, however, argued that 'the most socially developed capitalist countries in several respects are closer to the "mature model of socialism" than certain socialist countries' (*K*, 13/1989: 7). There remains a tension in reformist thinking about the acceptance of Soviet participation in the 'world civilised society' (*K*, 13/1989: 3) and its attempts to remain distinct (Bogomolov, 1989: 35).

Constitutionalism as expressed in the attempt to create a 'socialist legal state' is a cardinal element of Gorbachev's understanding of reform. Marketising economic reforms, reformists argued from 1987, will not work unless accompanied by a transformation of the political system. From 1989, however, the contrary case was argued with equal conviction, that democratisation of the political system would not work without marketisation of the economy. Communist reforms from Beijing to Budapest have been marked by a common element, namely liberalisation of the economy in order to overcome the consequences of old-style centralisation, and this then led to pressure for the pluralisation of political life. The new emphasis on effective constitutional separation of powers represented a defeat of the original Communist project in that the 'political' state was reprieved from Marx's and Lenin's condemnation. The proceduralism of liberal democracy was accepted, though not yet liberal democracy itself. The post-Marxist era is above all characterised by the demise of the belief in the emancipatory potential of working-class struggle. It now became obvious that a state based on some sort of working-class dictatorship (the dictatorship of the proletariat) by its very nature contained a dreadful potential for the elimination of civil liberties and democracy. The old belief that not only economic life but also political activity could be consciously regulated to achieve a harmonious balance was modified. Democratisation represented a partial retreat from the 'guidance' exercised by the party over society; representative democracy would represent a rout.

Democratisation has been interpreted as a stage in the evolution of the Soviet system from totalitarianism to *authoritarianism*. According to the famous Jeane Kirkpatrick argument, the distinction between an authoritarian regime and a totalitarian one is that while the former can be thrown off, the latter is permanent. She urged the United States to support authoritarian governments but oppose the totalitarian ones (1979). The transition from authoritarian to democratic regimes in Spain, Portugal, Greece and South Korea would suggest that the Kirkpatrick argument has some validity, but the differences lie much deeper and can be found in the totalitarian urge to remould society and to exercise control over all facets of social life. An authoritarian system, on the other hand, allows scope for a degree of independence for sections of civil society as long as they are not overtly hostile to the regime (Migranyan, *LG*, 16 August 1989). The transition from dictatorship to representative democracy in Spain exerted a special fascination for Soviet reformist thinkers. The transition from totalitarianism to democracy appears to require an intermediary stage of authoritarianism of variable length. In Hungary the transition was a long one, signposted by Kádár's assertion in 1962 that 'he who is not against us is for us'. The authoritarianism of Kadarism was rapidly jettisoned after his ouster in May 1988, and attempts to retain a guided democracy shrivelled in the face of popular pressure for the institutions of formal democracy. The revolutions of 1989 suggest that neo-Stalinism is only a transitional stage on the road from totalitarianism to representative democracy.

The majority of observers of Soviet affairs, quite justifiably, would have agreed at the time with Shtromas's observation that there was only a slight possibility of a 'democratic and constitutional Russian state emerging in immediate succession to the present regime' (Shtromas, 1987: 277). While this is still some way off, there is nevertheless movement *within* the regime in this direction. The socialist legal state can be seen as a way of preventing the detotalitarianising process from developing into a general conversion to representative democracy. V. Aksyuchits argued, for example, that even after four years of *perestroika* the Soviet Union had less freedom than Chile: religious freedom, an independent Press and television, a free economy and freedom to leave the country were all restricted (*RM*, 17 February 1989: 3). There was a gulf between what was promised and what was achieved. The dissolution of a totalitarian system from within is unprecedented and no one can prophesy the shape of its successor. A system that has rejected the totalitarian panopoly of power might well evolve into an authoritarianism that will allow the pluralistic expression of interests which in turn may lead to representative democracy.

After the failure of so many reforms in Communist systems it appeared by the early 1980s that *Communist reformism* had lost any chance that it might have had of reviving the Communist project of ruling and developing societies in a more rational and effective way than its non-socialist alternatives. Gorbachev's great achievement was to revive earlier hopes for Communist self-reform. His reforms tapped the alleged latent possibilities of Communist-type systems and tried to prove, up to 1990 at least, that there was no incompatibility between the goals of modernisation and the retention of Communist Party control. The caution that characterised Gorbachev's reforms was the result of both his acute awareness of what was politically feasible and the limitations of his own thinking. The process of his own enlightenment, though, reflected the broadening parameters of political change as the reforms achieved a dynamic of their own.

In contrast to the dissolution of the Communist regimes in Eastern Europe and the emergence of post-Communist systems, Gorbachev tried to achieve what could be called 'late Communism' in the USSR, a term used in an analogous way to describe the idea of late capitalism developed by Claus Offe and used by Ernest Mandel (see Keane, 1984). Late Communism, like late capitalism, is concerned with welfarism and is relatively de-ideologised. It is marked by pluralistic economic and political relations, and by structures of power bound by constitutions and the rule of law. The difference between a late Communist and a late capitalist system lies in the continued 'leading role' of the party, whether constitutionally guaranteed or not, with all that this entails for political interactions and economic life, and an emphasis on community and non-competitive democracy. The danger for reformers, however, is that late Communism can set up a momentum for the transition to post-Communism where the Communist Party loses its monopoly on effective political power.

Communist reformism is based on the belief that the system of Communist power can be humanised and democratised to allow the flowering of human endeavour in the arts, sciences and economy. *Perestroika* was predicated on the reformability of Communist systems, the belief that they contain within themselves the capacity for flexible adaptation to changing circumstances. Gorbachev's reforms amounted to the promise of reactivating the assumed potential of the Revolution itself, bringing to life the promises and principles of the Soviet regime that had been neglected or distorted over the years. Dubček in Bologna insisted that 'The whole democratic world should care about what Gorbachev is doing because it is an attempt to reform socialism on the basis of its original ideals' (*Ind.*, 15 November 1988). Deutscher (1967) talked of the 'unfinished revolution' in the Soviet Union. Gorbachev can be seen as 'finishing' the revolution, modernising the economy and the polity, and redefining the role of the state and the party to allow the alleged potential of the October 1917 Revolution to blossom. However, such a view is excessively mechanistic, and indeed historicist, in suggesting that there are necessary stages through which a socialist country, and the USSR in particular, had to pass. The application of chaos theory to Soviet politics has equal validity: the view that even in the midst of disorder chaotic systems are governed by relatively simple and strict rules, though sheer complexity does not allow predictions to be made very far into the future. Such an interpretation of Soviet politics, indeed of world history in its entirety, may actually yield more insights into their development than the imposition of certain patterns which have their origin in normative thinking. Gorbachev's reforms have represented not only a reconstruction of Soviet politics but also their transformation; however, the trajectory of this cannot be predicted.

One of the circumstances forcing *perestroika* to make such heavy weather was that the economic problems had grown so much worse since the glad days of the 1950s. Confidence in the viability of Communist reformism had been severely eroded under the impact of successive failed or aborted reforms. The question facing Communist reformism was whether it had missed its historic chance and that not only was it unable to muster popular support but that it was also irrelevant, and was indeed retarding the development of society. Fukuyama (1989) argued that some sort of liberalism is in the ascendant together with a civil society independent of the state. The half measures of Communist reformism associated with late Communism were simply not compatible with such a programme. From this perspective the East European revolutions of 1989 were the fulfilment of the ideals of the French Revolution of 1789.

The task of Soviet reformers was, if anything, harder than for comparable reformers elsewhere for the simple reason that the Soviet Union had existed far longer. In its seventy years it had been able to root out more thoroughly the foundations on which a possible regeneration could be based. Peasant initiative, for example, will be very hard to revive after the ravages of fifty years of collectivisation. The loss of skills in all areas of life and the debilitating legacy of the past was noted by Shmelëv. He argued that Soviet society was like 'a seriously ill person who, after a long time in bed, takes the first steps with great difficulty and discovers to their horror that they have almost forgotten how to walk' (Shmelëv, 1988). There is a fundamental problem about Communist reformism's belief that Communist development is a stage towards something else, an end state of Communist maturity. As Alain Besançon put it: 'If the absence of socialism is caused not by technical but by ontological reasons, if it does not exist simply because it cannot exist, then its introduction will lead only to the destruction of what already does exist' (cited in *Glasnost*, 13/1988: 19). Hence *perestroika* was faced by what can be called an 'ontological block': it could not go anywhere because there was nowhere for it to go.

Gorbachev's reform Communist position has been challenged from two main directions, leaving aside for the moment non-socialist challenges. The first is represented by a broad spectrum of 'conservative' thought, ranging from the *apparat* of party and state bureaucrats to Russian nationalist traditionalists (see page 252ff). The second has been from the 'radicals' who have argued that the existing system must be thoroughly transformed to allow a completely new model of socialism to emerge (cf. Igor Klyamkin, *MN*, 27/1989: 12). They have argued the necessity of moving beyond the system in order to achieve viable patterns of political authority, legitimacy and economic dynamism. For them the notion of 'reform or die' is becoming 'reform and die', that which has to die being the old system, not reformed but transcended in order to release the creative potential of society.

Under the pressure of the multiple failures of the reform process itself Communist reformism has begun to take a stronger form in the shape of *revolutionary reformism*. Gorbachev has described the reform process in the Soviet Union as a 'revolution without shots'. The ambivalence over terms is reflected in Gorbachev's own characterisation of the changes. When asked in an interview in February 1986 with *L'Humanité* if the policies made up a new revolution, Gorbachev answered emphatically in the negative. However, during his visit to Khabarovsk on 31 July 1986 he argued that reform 'is a term with wide-ranging implications' encompassing 'not only the economy but also all other spheres in our social life' including the political system (*P*, 2 August 1986). The concept of reform deepened, and he insisted that the changes were no less significant than the most fundamental periods under Lenin in the early 1920s and of the first five-year plans for the rapid industrialisation of the country under Stalin. He called the changes by the usual name of 'restructuring' but he also categorised them as a revolution. The word 'reform' seemed to disturb some of the more conservative in the leadership with its echoes of the great reforms of Aleksandr II from 1861.

The dilemma facing Gorbachev was the one which faced the original socialist revolutionaries – reform or revolution: to what extent can the existing system be utilised to achieve the desired changes, or does it have to be smashed? Can the bureaucratic apparatus be transformed or would any attempt to use the existing system be caught in the snares of bureaucratic formalism and gutted of meaning? As Lenin argued in 1917 in *State and Revolution*, the Bolsheviks could not simply lay hold of the old state machinery from the bourgeoisie and turn it to socialist ends. A reformer, as opposed to a revolutionary, seeks legitimacy in the existing social order and focuses on the realisation of unfulfilled potential or promise. Gorbachev in this respect began as a genuine reformist in the tradition of the Second International, which took a gradualist approach to political change within the existing institutions, but has bit by bit been radicalised.

As noted at the beginning of the chapter, the nature of *perestroika* is ambiguous and its two sides are reflected in the debate of whether it should be called a reform or a revolution. *Perestroika* was more than a political revolution led by the Gorbachev group. It represented the culmination of long-term trends of economic and social change, and the evolution of ideas and political institutions. The distinctive feature of *perestroika* is that it is, in Gorbachev's words, a revolution *within* a revolution. Hence while it retained many of the old building blocks, *perestroika* began to endow them with radically new meaning. The party, the soviets, the ministries, the planning agencies, all remained in place, but the cement that held them in place was changing. The rise of mixed forms of property (even though in 1990 80 per cent still remained in state hands), the shift to the market, the new honesty signalled by *glasnost* and the rise of the new democracy, all heralded a qualitative transformation of the system. Much of this remains tenuous, however, and could be reversed by a decisive shift at the centre. The peculiar nature of a revolution within a revolution is that it remains a reform, though contains the potential to become a revolution, defined as a change in the nature of power and property. System-transformation can thus become system-termination.

The debate over reform or revolution to describe the changes expresses a profound truth on several levels. If we accept Marx's definition of a revolution as a radical adjustment of the political superstructure to take into account changes in the economy, then this is a revolution. If we accept Lenin's definition of a revolutionary situation as one in which the ruling class can no longer rule in the old way, and the masses will no longer tolerate rule in the old way, then once again this is a revolutionary situation. The Gorbachevite transformation was indeed revolutionary in its implications in that it came to challenge the old structures of power and property. However, as long as the reforms were contained within the terms of the notion of late Communism it would probably be more accurate to describe them as a revolutionary reform rather than as a revolution *per se*. Political reform differs from revolution in this crucial respect: whereas revolution is designed to open up or destroy hierarchies of power to allow a system to institute rapid changes, Communist reform is above all a process of restructuring political relationships within an existing system to permit each greater autonomy and a valid sphere of activity. Hence Communist reform is first and foremost the constitutionalising of social and political relations within a given polity. Reform Communism is by its nature 'conservative', remaining within the basic political framework established in the early years of Soviet power. Gorbachev's aim has been to modernise Soviet socialism and to strip it of its alleged distortions rather than to revolutionise Communism out of existence. This may be the result, but was certainly not the intention.

In an epistemological sense, however, neither the term reform nor the term revolution are applicable: the Gorbachevites' own self-description of the process as *perestroika* is correct. It denotes the self-limiting nature of the changes up to 1990. Jadwiga Staniszkis (1984) described the stalemate in Poland as a self-limiting revolution. Gorbachev's reforms are a good example of one in that they remained within the existing power system. Transformation of economic mechanisms was accompanied by challenges to the political system, but always limited by the attempt to retain political control. When this broke down in 1990 then self-limiting reform had indeed become a genuine revolution and the whole notion of *perestroika* became increasingly redundant.

The concept of reform, once a term of abuse and held to be symptomatic only of bourgeois systems, became the favourite term in the lexicon of Soviet leaders. Reform is a moment of truth, and an effective strategy for the future could only be derived from an honest evaluation of the present and the past. In this context gradualists came into conflict with those who saw the need for a sudden, sharp transformation of the economy. A number of graphic images reflect this thought: one cannot be a little pregnant; one cannot jump a canyon in two steps; it would be foolish to have a staged shift from driving on the left to the right. One chance is all that is vouchsafed the reformers. The debate over the process of reform has also been one about its ends. The alternative to radical maximalism is the gradualist position based on the argument that a system built up over seventy years cannot be reformed in five. Gradualists argue that many of the problems stem in the first instance from an impatience with incremental change. The attempt to jump over stages, to storm all fortresses in the face of an imperious will, led to the elimination of rational argumentation and opened the way to the excesses of Stalin. Gradualists argue that the best way forward is to win people over to the cause of reform, to build alliances and develop hegemony, and thus to allow reform to proceed on the basis of consensus rather than in the teeth of opposition and the storm of conflict.

Perestroika under Gorbachev was clearly a radical type of Communist reformism, moving far beyond the constraints imposed by the neo-Stalinist compromise. In 1985 the Soviet Union faced a dilemma: if the country stayed as it was it would encounter economic and social crisis; but if it did something it would provoke a political crisis. Alexis de Tocqueville's dictum that 'the most dangerous moment for a bad government is when it seeks to mend its ways' is applicable to the process of change under Gorbachev. As in France in the 1780s, reforms have a habit of turning into revolutions.

3

IDEOLOGY AND REFORM

One of the major features of the unreformed Soviet system was the party's claim to a monopoly of wisdom which gave it a moral right to rule. The onset of *glasnost* weakened the view that there was a single truth vouchsafed to the party, and thus the bounds of debate were significantly extended. This was accompanied by radical analyses of past mistakes and a broadening of permitted political activity described by the concept of the socialist pluralism of opinions. The very idea of socialism is being reinterpreted. The party itself has been forced to justify its leadership in new ways and its role has been modified.

Glasnost and the intelligentsia

Glasnost became the word to describe a broad range of policies designed to expose Soviet society to criticism and self-criticism. *Glasnost* represented the cleansing, in Vasil Bykov's words, of the 'ecology of the soul' (*MN*, 1/1989 :1). As Solzhenitsyn argued in his letter of 12 November 1969 to the board of the Union of Soviet Writers, '*Glasnost*, honest and full *glasnost*, is the basic condition for the health of any society, and ours as well. The person who doesn't want *glasnost* in our country is indifferent to the fate of our homeland.' Gorbachev abandoned the 'newspeak' 'propaganda of success' style of earlier years to allow discussion of problems in the economy and society. These are now accepted to have arisen within the system rather than having been imposed from outside by malevolent imperialists or by the legacy of the past. No longer was reform couched in the language of 'perfecting socialist relations' or 'further strengthening the economic mechanism'. *Glasnost* exposed the extent of the crimes of the past and revealed the shortcomings of the present.

In his first speech as leader on 11 March 1985 Gorbachev called for more *glasnost* in the work of party and state organs (*P*, 12 March 1985). At the 27th congress he argued that *glasnost* was 'the starting point for the psychological restructuring of our cadres' and dismissed arguments in favour of caution by insisting that 'There can only be one answer to this, a Leninist answer: under all circumstances, Communists need the truth' (*P*, 26 February 1986). On 11 February 1987 at a meeting with media figures he announced what was in effect a manifesto for *glasnost*, declaring that 'there should not be any blank pages in either our history or our literature', but warned that 'criticism should always be from a party point of view' (*P*, 14 February 1987). Lenin's insistence that 'The people must know the whole truth (*PSS*, 45: 396) is frequently cited in support. In the same spirit Gorbachev accepted Lenin's view that '*Glasnost* is a sword that heals its own wounds' (*Ibid.*, 45: 403). Moreover, *glasnost* is a feedback mechanism (Solodukhin, 1989: 14). It is the essential way of achieving a 'socialist pluralism of opinions'. *Glasnost* became an inseparable part of *perestroika* and consists of three main processes: information, discussion and participation.

Information

The major feature of *glasnost* is the lifting of most restrictions on the circulation of information. Censorship has been relaxed though not abolished. The Soviet population was to know about 'life with all its contradictions and complexity' (*PZ*, 4/1987: 19). The 'blank pages' in history and literature indeed began to be filled in. Statistics on economic, social and party affairs became much fuller and lost some of the distortions of the past. Under Stalin even topographical information had become a state secret, and *glasnost* at last allowed new maps to be published which made it possible for Soviet citizens and visitors to find their way about. Details were revealed of past disasters, like the nuclear explosion in the Urals in 1957, and reporting about current accidents became increasingly swift and full. The gulf between leadership assertions and popular knowledge in the later years of Brezhnev and under Chernenko had grown so large as to constitute a veritable crisis of authority. *Glasnost* helped bridge the credibility gap. The leadership under Gorbachev realised that secrecy itself was a major force holding back the development of society, undermining efficiency, isolating individuals and eroding the morale of society.

The new technology of personal computers, international communications, photocopiers and fax machines has been transforming the political possibilities of independent groupings. Only with great difficulty, and at great cost to itself, could the state now attempt to restrict the flow of information.

Censorship was relaxed with the abolition of the censorship functions of Glavlit (Main Administration of Literature and State Publishing Houses) in June 1986, thus limiting the functions of a body which had survived in one form or another since 1918. Materials for publication no longer have to be submitted for its approval, though there remains an office to monitor security matters. Glavlit's judgements had been regulated by no proclaimed laws or procedures, and its decisions had been arbitrary. Prior censorship disappeared and editors and publishers were no longer directly answerable to the propaganda department of the Central Committee. In September 1988 this department became part of the ideology commission of the CC, and Vadim Medvedev took over control of the Press, which he exercised by regular briefings to editors.

Glasnost opened up the workings of the Soviet party and government in a way unprecedented since the 1920s. As part of Khrushchev's attempts to restore inner-party democracy full reports of Central Committee plenary meetings had been published, a practice dropped by Brezhnev and replaced by brief summaries and the text of main speeches. Now once again full reports were published, and indeed meetings of the CC are occasionally televised. *Glasnost* also shed more light on the workings of the Politburo. Andropov in 1982 had instituted the publication of short reports on matters discussed, and this was continued by Gorbachev. The 19th party conference pledged to report more fully on the operation of the party and government, and this was implemented with the publication of *Central Committee News* and *Government Herald* from early 1989.

Changes in the ideology and the obvious discrepancy between official statements and everyday reality led to the attempt, begun by Andropov, to modernise the ideological apparatus itself. From 1985 the party's ideological departments and journals were reorganised to allow them to become the generators of ideas rather than the purveyors of stale dogmas. A Central Committee resolution of 16 August 1986 spoke of the need to upgrade ideological work to keep up with world social, economic and political developments. This was to be achieved specifically through improving the CPSU's theoretical journal *Kommunist* (*KPSS o perestroike*: 147–58). Changes in personnel allowed the journal to become the intellectual muse of the Gorbachev regime and the forum for vigorous debate. In 1989, for example, an unsigned editorial developed a broad-ranging and stimulating analysis of the new model of socialism with the concept of civil society at its centre (*K*, 13/1989: 3–24). *Pravda* itself, the 'Organ of the Central Committee of the CPSU' and thus not of the party as a whole, dismissed its relatively conservative editor, Viktor Afanasev, in late 1989 and under Ivan Frolov, formerly one of the advisers to Gorbachev, reintroduced a 'discussion page', last seen in 1921.

Glasnost allowed the Press to look at Soviet reality in a new and more critical manner. Leading the way in boldness was the journal *Ogonëk* under the editorship of Vitalii Korotich. Newspapers such as *Socialist Industry*, a radical reforming paper of the Central Committee of the party, vented far-ranging debates over economic reform. *Novyi mir* once again, as under Khrushchev, became the tribune of critical intellectuals and published literature that had been kept under lock and key under Brezhnev. The broadsheet *Argumenty i fakty*, officially the bulletin of the *Znanie* (Knowledge) society, reached sales of some 33 million by early 1990 with its probing and factual analysis of Soviet reality. *Moscow News* was transformed under the editorship of Egor Yakovlev into one of the most daring forums for discussion of the progress of *perestroika*. Another of the leading journals at the frontier of *glasnost* was *XX Century and Peace*, published by the Soviet Peace Committee. Under the editorship of A. Belyaev and with Gleb Pavlovskii what used to be a staid organ of official propaganda became one of the most outspoken journals, being the first in early 1989 to publish a work by Solzhenitsyn, *Live Not by Lies*, prefaced by the comment by Igor Vinogradov that his exile was 'shameful'. A number of central papers were reorganised from 1 January 1990. *Socialist Industry* was merged with a smaller paper and renamed *Workers' Tribune*, with the brief to give voice to working-class interests. Two Communist ideological journals were merged to create the new party theoretical journal *Dialog*, which rapidly established itself as a stimulating discussion journal.

In 1989 there was an appreciable fall in subscriptions to most major mass circulation papers. The circulation of *Pravda*, despite its new editor, fell in the space of a year from 9.5 to 6.5 million in early 1990. Frolov's brand of reformist Marxism mirrored Gorbachev's own, yet what would have been revolutionary five years ago had by 1990 become, to the subscribers who voted with their feet, irrelevant to the problems of the new decade. Initial enthusiasm for revelations began to give way to a sense of exhaustion and indifference as the grim reality of shortages took its toll on morale, though the circulation of the more radical and non-party papers increased.

The new-found press freedoms were constantly under pressure. The dangers were brought home to the editor of *Argumenty i fakty*, Vladislav Starkov, who printed a survey of readers' letters (40/1989: 1) which showed that the radical deputies in the new parliament were the most popular, with Sakharov in the lead, followed by Gavriil Popov, Boris Eltsin and Yuri Afanasev, and which painted Gorbachev in a less than flattering light. Starkov and a number of others, including Ivan

Laptev, editor of *Izvestiya*, and Yuri Afanasev himself, were carpeted by Gorbachev at a meeting on 13 October 1989 and by Medvedev on 16 October. *XX Century and Peace* also came under severe official pressure in late 1989 and its continued publication remained in doubt.

The new Law on Press Freedom of 12 June 1990 (*Iz.*, 20 June 1990) was designed to regulate the conduct of the media under conditions of *glasnost* and to consolidate the abolition of formal censorship and party control. The law on the media would act, as it were, as the constitution of *glasnost*, codifying freedoms that until then had been granted as concessions rather than rights. The law abolished censorship (except for security matters) and allowed any citizen or group to start a newspaper. It also contained a 'freedom of information' clause obliging government departments to answer questions put by newspapers. Journalists could exercise a 'conscience clause' not to write what their editors told them to, and gave editors, who could be either nominated by newspaper proprietors or elected by journalists, a degree of independence. Views over the press law differed. On the one hand, it was seen as advancing press freedom, with rights and limitations clearly delineated. On the other hand, there was concern that some of the clauses were unduly restrictive. Clauses allowing proprietors editorial control meant that the views of the CPSU, which owned the vast majority of papers, still carried undue weight.

The new Press law was nevertheless much more liberal than its draft versions. The simple registration procedures allowed what had been the unofficial Press to flourish, though inhibited by shortage of paper and access to printing presses. Freedom of the Press began to replace the Leninist view that the Press was the collective organiser and agitator of society. *Ogonëk* led the way in July 1990 in slipping off the tutelage of the CPSU. A management 'buy-out' created a registered self-financing independent journal. Local soviets also moved to establish their own papers. The Moscow city council planned at least four, including a national daily, *The Independent*. It also supported the creation of a *Time* equivalent, called *Stolitsa* (*The Capital*).

Jamming of the BBC and other Western stations was stopped soon after Gorbachev's accession. However, it was not until December 1988 that jamming of Russian language broadcasts by the overtly political Western stations, Radio Liberty and Deutsche Welle, came to an end. These stations had always played a vital part in keeping the Soviet population informed on world and domestic events, and had fostered public awareness of critical issues during *perestroika*. With the lifting of jamming and more liberal attitudes, these and other Russian language stations entered into a close relationship with the independent movement in the USSR.

Glasnost is a two-way process: not only does it allow the population at large greater access to information; it also forces the leadership to learn what the population is thinking and what everyone knows. Even before *glasnost* newspapers like *Komsomolskaya pravda* had pioneered the use of opinion polls, but now the government fully legitimated the scientific measurement of public opinion as part of its new responsiveness. The growing trust in the people was revealed in the emphasis on opinion polls and surveys on a range of contentious issues. The real nature of Soviet political culture could be examined and the proposition that the system created the people it deserved, thus inhibiting Gorbachev's reforms, could at last be tested.

Tatyana Zaslavskaya, who had spent much of her professional life at the Institute of Economics in Novosibirsk – a haven, as we have noted, for the more independent-minded economists and social scientists under Brezhnev – was the first head of the All-Union Centre for the Study of Public Opinion of Socio-Economic Problems, founded in 1988. It provided a scientific polling service led by a team, including Boris Grushin, Ludmila Khakhulina, Yuri Levada, Nikolai Popov and Valerii Rutgaizer. In a survey in autumn 1989 a profound pessimism was revealed about *perestroika*, with only one person in eight believing that it would improve life in the next few years and seven out of ten thinking that there would be little change for the better (*Ogonëk* 44/1989: 5). One surprising finding was that 45 per cent supported the development of the much-maligned co-operative movement, while only 30 per cent felt it should be banned. The divisiveness of the national question was starkly revealed, with 63 per cent of people from the RSFSR believing that a united country was essential, whereas only 10 per cent of those polled in Armenia and the Baltic states agreed and 30 per cent in the Ukraine. For 47 per cent of respondents in the Baltic self-determination was the key issue, not excluding secession from the union, while such feelings were shared by 21 per cent in the Ukraine and 17 per cent in Armenia (*Ogonëk* 43/1989: 4–5).

It should be stressed that even before the lifting of the restrictions on official information much was already known, often in distorted or exaggerated form but recognisable as a truth at variance with official views. *Glasnost* basically meant an increase in the amount of information made openly available to the public. The problem, of course, was what the newly informed citizenry would do with the information. This is where *glasnost* as information turns into *glasnost* as discussion and participation.

Discussion

Glasnost allowed controversies to be aired publicly. The demise of the notion of a single truth, termed by Solzhenitsyn the universal lie, permitted the reconstitution of a public sphere of debate and contestation. There were limits to the scope of discussion, and leadership policies themselves remained relatively immune to criticism. The experience of the 'hundred flowers' campaign in China in 1957 demonstrated that exhortations by Communist leaderships to 'let a hundred flowers bloom, let a hundred ideas contend' could, and usually do, end in tragedy; yet *glasnost* may well prove to be the exception.

The social sciences were rejuvenated and were now permitted to study contentious issues and to publish conclusions which were occasionally at variance with the official line. For years the social sciences had acted as a mouthpiece of official views, handing down 'authoritarian judgements' and 'indisputable truths' subject only to commentary. The stifling of the social and natural sciences came about because of the imposition of a set of normative principles which established *a priori* results, leaving scholars the task only of commenting on these 'eternal verities'. The empirical method of inductive analysis was rejected as a bourgeois sham. In the sciences the baleful effect of censorship was particularly serious and acted as a brake on scientific and technical progress. Developments in the West were not always reported, with controversial articles cut out of journals.

In a key speech to the Academy of Sciences on 17 April 1987 Aleksandr Yakovlev (1990: 214–35) condemned the loss of the 'ability for critical self-analysis' of social science, especially in the 1970s, and argued that the Soviet Union entered the 1980s 'with theoretical thinking largely dating from the 1930s'. He urged a non-dogmatic approach to Marxism–Leninism to allow the development of all branches of the social sciences, from law to sociology. The speech revealed both the limits and the achievements of *glasnost*.

The gulf between official statements and popular knowledge was nowhere so large as in the official treatment of Soviet history, and in particular Stalinism (Davies, 1989a). This was conceded by the decision in 1988 to pulp school textbooks on the history of the period and to commission a more truthful version for school use. The school history examinations of that year were cancelled since the history of the Soviet Union had become so distorted as to become meaningless. Gorbachev's own process of enlightenment about Soviet history can be used to measure the new honesty.

There has always been a tension in Soviet educational theory and practice. On the one hand, there is the legacy of the Enlightenment belief in the ability of education to create independent people free of prejudice, critical and self-affirming. On the other hand, Soviet education has been focused on vocational training and not on universal humanistic enlightenment. Under *perestroika* the new challenges of economic modernisation required a technically and vocationally directed education, but it was increasingly understood that a degree of critical free-thinking was also an essential element in the modernisation process. *Glasnost* allowed a rebirth of Russian and Soviet culture.

Participation

A greater trust in the population was to be reciprocated by a greater involvement on their part in solving the problems of society. An informed public is essential for participation in a democratic society. *Glasnost* was to be used as a form of public control over governmental bodies to expose bureaucratic mismanagement and corruption (Gorbachev, 1987a: 75–6). Hence an element of instrumentality remained as *glasnost* was proclaimed a new weapon in the armoury of socialism rather than simply a desirable end in itself.

Glasnost was a refutation of Andropov's belief that official corruption and social indiscipline could be dealt with by administrative methods by the regime itself. Instead, Gorbachev realised that such problems could be tackled only by enlisting the support of the public, and ultimately of an independent reformed judiciary. The supervisory role for public participation marked a return to the early days of Soviet power. *Glasnost* was envisaged as a form of *kontrol'*, in the sense not of control but of supervision, over the workings of the state apparatus somewhat akin to the role envisaged by Lenin for the organs of workers' control in the factories in 1918. Gorbachev described *glasnost* as an 'effective form of public control over the activities of all governmental bodies, without exception, and a powerful lever in correcting shortcomings' (1987a: 79).

Above all, *glasnost* was an invitation for a historic *rapprochement* between the regime and the cultural and technical intelligentsia and an invitation for them to participate in the reform process. Concessions to the creative intelligentsia allowed them to emerge, in the first years at least, as one of the key sectors supporting Gorbachev's reforms. He went out of his way to appeal for the support of the progressive cultural élite in the struggle against the administrative apparatus. On the eve of the writers' congress at a closed session on 19 June 1986 Gorbachev argued that 'society is ripe for a change. If we step away, the society will not agree to a return. The process must be made irreversible. If not us, then who? If not now, when?' and 'if we don't involve the people, nothing will come of it. All our plans depend on influencing the people' (*Time*, 5 January 1987: 54). Gorbachev liberated the intellectuals from the shackles imposed in the early years of Soviet power when they were intended to become, to use Gramsci's terminology, an 'organic' expression of the interests of the working class. *Glasnost* allowed intellectuals to return to a more 'traditional' free-floating and critical role in society. Gorbachev's reforms and *glasnost* have been undermining the roots of 'ideocratic' (Carl Linden) power, a system based on the dominance of an idea and programme.

The ideological downgrading of the role of the working class has been accompanied by the practical elevation of the intelligentsia. The Russian term 'intelligentsia' is broader than the English 'intellectual' and is not restricted to those with higher education. It is associated with notions of independent thinking and moral integrity, a definition far from the Soviet view of the intelligentsia as the massive third stratum of Soviet society complementing the two great classes of workers and peasants. Gorbachev's elevation of the intelligentsia was a sign of the transition from conformity to greater tolerance of diversity. The monolithic views ascribed to the working class by Leninist ideology have given way to the fractiousness of the traditional intelligentsia. However, Gorbachev shared the nineteenth-century view, passionately believed by the Russian Populists, of the intelligentsia as a group with a privileged understanding of how to make the world a better place, and that it is a dereliction of their duty not to participate in the struggle for progress. Thus the fateful conjunction was continued whereby the struggle for enlightenment, which necessarily involves an element of the 'ivory tower', becomes confused with the struggle for change. And therefore the baleful legacy of Marx's eleventh thesis on Feuerbach, which states that 'The philosophers have only interpreted the world. The point, however, is to change it', was perpetuated.

Stalin destroyed the flower of the old intelligentsia, including many in the Communist party itself, and in its place created a vast new office-holding and 'working' intelligentsia. The anti-intellectualism of Bolshevik workerism was one of the most pronounced features of early Soviet rule, and was present in Khrushchev's populism and Brezhnev's corporatism. Under Brezhnev the intelligentsia consolidated its position as specialist knowledge came to be valued, but the intellectual stagnation of his rule could find no role for genuinely critical or creative thinkers. They existed both within and outside the system, but became, in the words of the historian Natan Eidelman, rather like their predecessors under Nicholas I: 'superfluous people', with no outlet for their abilities in society (*ST*, 8 January 1989).

In marked contrast to his predecessors, Gorbachev respected and hoped to involve the intelligentsia in the process of change. Despite the official emphasis on his working background, Gorbachev is an *intelligent* himself both in terms of his educational background and in his intellectually questing personality. Gorbachev held repeated meetings with intellectuals, both Soviet and foreign, to argue his case for *perestroika* and to enlist opinion on his side. At a special meeting of the Politburo on 6 January 1989, for example, Gorbachev summoned a range of intellectuals and spoke of their special responsibility for keeping *perestroika* on an even keel. The meeting included such figures as Andrei Sakharov, Sergei Zalygin, the liberal editor of *Novyi mir*, and the conservative writer Yuri Bondarev. Reform, Gorbachev insisted, was to be a steady process avoiding, on the one hand, radical demands for political pluralism, a multi-party system and private ownership, and, on the other hand, conservative criticisms that *perestroika* was leading the country into chaos and which urged a return of a 'firm hand' to government (*P*, 8 January 1989). The cultural and technical intelligentsia, like other groups, began to split into various tendencies as *perestroika* matured.

Glasnost was an attempt to co-opt the cultural intelligentsia to support *perestroika*. Nevertheless, it was more than this, and it would be an exaggeration to argue that 'A cultural thaw should not be taken for more than it is: an endeavour on the part of the ruling élite to ingratiate itself with the social group that guarantees the symbolic reproduction of the system' (Tismaneanu, 1987b: 224). The intelligentsia was not something standing outside *perestroika* but could in many ways take equal credit with the party for generating the ideas that fuelled the official reform process. *Glasnost* is a basic demand of any serious intellectual, while *perestroika* as a whole was conceived by the intellectuals both in the party leadership and in academic think-tanks and, indeed, was part of the minimum programme of most dissidents.

The new openness after 1985 had, understandably, its most immediate impact in the cultural sphere. Cultural reform preceded economic reform as Gorbachev tried to mobilise the intelligentsia to support his changes against the entrenched bureaucracy. Under Khrushchev the thaw encouraged the cultural community to discuss matters of concern to themselves and society at large, while under Brezhnev free artistic expression was stifled. Only with the accession of Gorbachev did it appear that the hour of the intelligentsia had arrived.

Like the reforms as a whole, cultural life passed through three stages in the first five years of the reform process. The first up to 1986 witnessed the replacement of the old Brezhnevite leadership of the various cultural associations. The Minister of Culture from 1974, Peter Demichev, was at last retired in 1986. The second phase in 1987–8 saw the excited publication or release of materials that had gathered dust on shelves or in drawers, and was dominated by the old names of Khrushchev's thaw. The third stage from late 1988 saw a greater maturity as intellectuals began, tentatively, to believe that *glasnost* was more than a passing fad to be suffocated like so many such campaigns in the past. Within living memory the 'thaw' under Khrushchev had turned into the frost of the Brezhnev years. New writers and artists emerged who were not quite so mesmerised by the past but took as their subject material the life of the country under *perestroika*. The cultural intelligentsia, like the rest of society, began to divide into the broad camps of 'reformists' (the Gorbachevites), 'radicals' and 'conservatives'.

The 8th Congress of the Union of Writers (24–8 June 1986) proclaimed that it met in the 'spirit of the 22nd congress' of the party, which in 1961 had seen radical destalinisation and *perestroika*. The 75-year-old Georgii Markov became honorary president (a post vacant since the death of Konstantin Fedin), and he was replaced as First Secretary by Vladimir Karpov, then editor of *Novyi mir*. Under the editorship of Aleksandr Tvardovskii during Khrushchev's rule and up to 1969 the journal had been the flagship of the thaw. The link with the past was highlighted by the constant references to Tvardovskii during the congress, a physical link with the thaw-like policies that were now being put forward. The composition of the governing board was changed with the addition of 'reformists' such as Evgenii Evtushenko, Andrei Voznesenskii, Sergei Zalygin and Chingiz Aitmatov. However, the pressure for reform forced the addition also of 'radicals' such as Bulat Okudzhava, Bella Akhmadulina and Yuri Chernichenko.

Previously taboo topics could now be discussed, and previously banned authors were published, including Vladimir Nabokov, Andrei Platonov, Boris Pasternak's *Doctor Zhivago* and many more. George Orwell's *1984* was published in *Novyi mir* in the early months of 1989. Most significant in this respect was the publication of some of the religious, philosophical and historical writings of S.M. Solovëv. A new work by Chingiz Aitmatov, *Plakha (The Executioner's Block)*, stressed the need for an individual to achieve moral truth despite the obstacles that life places in the way. The country was also opened up to foreign artistic influences. An exhibition of Francis Bacon's paintings at the New Tretyakov Gallery in Moscow from September to November 1988 attracted large, if critically divided, audiences.

By November 1987 a special commission had restored some 6,000 books, previously held in 'special access' shelves, to public use. These included works by Lev Kamenev, Nikolai Bukharin, Leon Trotsky, Peter Kropotkin, Boris Savinkov, Paul Milyukov and the text of the abdication of Tsar Nicholas II (*Iz.*, 3 April 1988). Problems remained with access to 'sensitive' archival material, with much still restricted. Historians by 1989, however, gave mixed reports, with some being granted almost unlimited access to materials while others were able to view but not cite materials. Millions of sheets of valuable archival material are crumbling in appalling storage facilities, as in the depository on Pirogovskaya Street in Moscow. The director of the Chief Archive Administration, F. Vaganov, showed little interest in improving the situation (*P*, 1 June 1988: 4).

The changed atmosphere was particularly apparent at the 5th Congress of Film-makers, held in Moscow on 13–15 May 1986. Two-thirds of the old board were dismissed, including the First Secretary Lev Kulidzhanov who was replaced by Elem Klimov. This was a veritable 'earthquake' as Klimov put it, at about point 7 on the Richter scale. A 'disputes commission' was established which allowed the screening of previously banned works. The 'supervisory' functions of Goskino (State Film Administration) were fundamentally decreased allowing much greater autonomy for film studios. This culminated in the studios being placed on full *khozraschët* from 1 January 1989 whereby profitability became a major criterion. To many this meant that the tyranny of the bureaucrat had been replaced by the tyranny of the ruble, exposing production decisions to the mercies of the market-place.

Destalinisation was advanced by a number of films and documentaries. The film *Repentance* (1984) by the Georgian director Tengiz Abuladze boldly tackled the problem of Stalinism in a 'mythical realist' way. The liberalising head of the Central Committee propaganda department Aleksandr Yakovlev reported favourably to Gorbachev on the film, and after some resistance from Ligachev, who had overall responsibility for ideology, it was put on open release from 1 December 1986. The documentaries *Risk–2* and *More Light* examined the early years of Soviet power and the origins of Stalinism in a far more critical and truthful manner than in the past. The Latvian documentary film *Is It Easy To Be Young?* (1987) by Juris Podnieks shattered the complacent illusions about Soviet youth, a process continued by Vasilii Pichul's film *Little Vera* (1988) which revealed the harsh reality of working-class life in a provincial town. Aleksandr Proshkin's film *Cold Summer of '53* (1988) depicted the terror that a gang of released prisoners wreak on a Siberian village until it is saved by some political prisoners.

On television, also, *glasnost* revolutionised the content and presentation of programmes (Mickiewicz, 1988). The most exciting development was the emergence of bold new interview and documentary programmes like *Viewpoint* (*Vzglyad*) and *Twelfth Floor*, and the monthly *Before and After Midnight*, one of the most radical programmes, presented by Vladimir Molchanov. The Leningrad programme *Six Hundred Seconds*, presented by Aleksandr Nevzorov, focused on the exposure of corruption and incompetence wherever it might be found. The programme's sharply anti-Communist tone heralded the sort of investigative reporting that might become common once the compromises of *glasnost*, which Nevzorov openly proclaimed as fraudulent, were overcome. Television news became much sharper and tried to put into effect the principle of *operativnost'* (timeliness) in order to provide up-to-date and relevant information. In 1989 the Sunday edition of the nightly news programme *Vremya*, watched by an estimated 180 million people, was replaced by a news review programme called *Seven Days*, which aimed at lively and informative reporting.

Gorbachev's period in power has been marked by a new openness in the theatre. Moscow and provincial stages echoed to a chorus of plays that explored aspects of history, some of the more sordid undersides of Brezhnevite social stagnation and the poverty of a *perestroika*-obsessed USSR. Shatrov's plays raised hitherto suppressed themes and explored aspects of Soviet history peopled by characters who had become non-persons under Stalin. Lenin was seen in discussion with Trotsky and Bukharin who were no longer dressed in the livery of the devil (see pages 92ff).

The intelligentsia emerged as a powerful force in Soviet society, but in some of the republics, especially in the Baltic and Transcaucasia, their participation took a less than welcome form for the regime as they acted as the focus for nationalist sentiments. The Communist Party in these areas, when compared with the energy of the new groups, appeared a tired and declining force sustained in power not by conviction but by inertia. The popular fronts have been led by the cream of the native intelligentsia, lawyers, academics and artists. The 'superfluous people' now found a role for themselves, or had one thrust upon them, to speak as the conscience of their nations and of society as a whole. This has taken not only nationalist forms, but has also shown itself in concern for the environment and social questions.

Limits to glasnost

The first phase of *glasnost* devoted itself to the hesitant but increasingly bold exposure of past wrongs, present dangers, the years of lies and evil on a stupendous scale. After a few years, however, it became clear that a society could not live on a diet of exposure alone, and the artificiality of a process which could expose certain aspects of the past (above all the crimes of Stalin), but was not able openly to examine their source (Marx, Lenin, the October Revolution) or their present manifestation (the monopoly of power by a single party) was highly unsatisfactory and contributed to the crisis of *perestroika*.

Even though the language of reform accepted real internal problems in the system there were limits to permitted criticism. The existence of unelected, non-institutionalised and uncontrolled privileged hierarchies was only gradually examined. The gulf between permitted criticism and social and political realities was still not fully bridged. The distortions engendered by the seventy-year monopoly of power by a *dirigiste* party-state were only gradually exposed. The limits were marked in the first days after the Chernobyl explosion, and only after eighteen days did *glasnost* become evident (Lapidus, 1987). The full scale of the catastrophe at Chernobyl was hidden for several years. *Glasnost* was one of the casualties of intensified ethnic conflict in the Caucasus, and in particular the April 1989 massacre in Tbilisi. The editor of the journal *Glasnost*, Sergei Grigoryants, was subjected to harassment and the journal until 1990 remained 'informal', in other words not legally registered and thus subject to all manner of harassment. Moreover, *glasnost* did not shed much light on decision-making in the Kremlin.

Topics which for long remained 'blank pages' included much to do with Lenin, for example his justification of terror and the anti-religious campaigns of the early Bolshevik years. It was easy enough to condemn Stalin, but it was much harder for Soviet Communists to admit that Lenin also did much to damage the development of the socialist idea in the twentieth century. Tsipko (1988–9) and Selyunin (1988) prepared the ground for a critique of Lenin, and Eltsin conceded that it might be time for this to begin. He argued 'we have for much too long idealised and deified Lenin. Although he also made mistakes and changed decisions according to the situation. It is impossible to live by quotations alone' (*LF on EE*, 2/1989: 27). The Nazi–Soviet Pact of 23 August 1939 and the Warsaw Pact invasion of Czechoslovakia in 1968 were until 1989 treated tendentiously. Doubts were cast on the very existence of the 'secret protocol' of 1939 giving Stalin a free hand in Eastern Poland, the Baltic republics, Bessarabia and North Bukovina. Among the doubters was Valentin Falin, formerly ambassador to West Germany and head of the Novosti Press Agency, and at the time head of the CC's International Department. He reflected the common view that *glasnost* dwelt too much on the dark side of Soviet history and urged a balanced approach: 'If out of inertia we start painting Stalin as all black and call everything associated with him harmful or even criminal, I don't think that we will be doing service to the objective truth. . .' (*MN*, 36/ 1988: 8–9). By late 1989, however, the tide of *glasnost* appeared irreversible under the pressure of public demands for full truth.

The ultimate test of *glasnost* was the publication of Solzhenitsyn's *Gulag Archipelago*, which places the origins of Stalin's terror system firmly under Lenin's rule. The October 1988 issue of *Novyi mir* was due to announce the publication of several of Solzhenitsyn's works, including *Cancer Ward*, *The First Circle* and *Gulag Archipelago*, but on V. Medvedev's insistence the cover was withdrawn and the announcement cancelled. An assault upon Lenin would undermine the foundations of the legitimacy on which Gorbachev hoped to build a reformist consensus for *perestroika*. The debate revealed the growing cleavages in the cultural community. The conservative writer, Yuri Bondarev, who was also deputy chair of the Writers' Union of the Russian Federation, argued in late 1988 that the measures taken against Solzhenitsyn, including the 1974 decree stripping him of his citizenship and expelling him from the country, were correct, while a growing chorus of voices insisted that, irrespective of his political views, his works should be published. By late 1988 *glasnost* had reached a plateau. On the one hand, Medvedev prohibited the publication of *Gulag Archipelago*. On the other hand, *Novyi mir* published V. Korolenko's civil war letters to his student friend A. V. Lunacharskii, the commissar for culture, complaining about Bolshevik deception and terror of the intelligentsia and population in the Ukraine (*NM*, 10/1988: 198–218).

Battle was joined for the future of *glasnost*, symbolised by the struggle for the repeal of the 29 December 1988 regulations barring co-operatives from engaging in publishing. The struggle for *glasnost* was also one for the transformation of democratisation into democracy. The transition was boosted by the elections and the deliberations of the 1st Congress of People's Deputies and the first session of the new Supreme Soviet. Henceforth it would take more than a telephone call from a party official to stop a work being published. The Union of Soviet Writers, which had expelled Solzhenitsyn from its ranks in 1970, readmitted him in 1989 and demanded that Soviet citizenship be restored to him. At its meeting of 24 February 1989 the board voted for the publication of his *Gulag Archipelago*, and extracts were published in *Novyi mir* from August 1989.

Perestroika was characterised by Tsipko as a revolution of realism rather than Utopianism, liberating people from myths rather than enslaving them in new dogmas. He added, though, that the denunciation of Stalinism and the 'breach in ideological conservatism' had not opened the door to free philosophy, and that the de-ideologisation of thought was not yet complete (Tsipko, (November 1988): 45–55). While the victory of half-truth over the unmitigated lie was to be welcomed (*pace* Popkova, 1987: 240), the unstable compromise of *glasnost* could not last forever. A constant guerrilla war with the authorities sought to extend the bounds of the permissible. A situation of half *glasnost* could not last forever: either full freedom, exposure and recantation; or the consolidation of *glasnost* at an officially tolerated level falling somewhat short of complete freedom of the Press and information. In the first five years of *glasnost*, it should be stressed, the outer limits were constantly being pushed back, though not without the occasional setback. More and more sacred cows were sacrificed on the altar of *glasnost*.

The divisions between the three major factions of the intelligentsia were revealed vividly in the discussions at the 19th party conference. Bondarev argued that 'Some newspapers seem to understand *perestroika* to mean the destabilisation of Soviet society as we know it, the complete overhaul of beliefs and moral standards' (*XIX konf.*, vol. 1: 223–8). Vladimir Karpov, who could by now be classed as a conservative, made the somewhat surprising statement (from the man who headed the Writers Union) that 'Some people view *glasnost* as *carte blanche* to write whatever they please' (*Ibid.*: 140–5). Gorbachev himself took the middle 'reformist' line against the conservatives by arguing that 'If we give up the further development of *glasnost*, criticism, self-criticism and democracy, it will be the end of *perestroika*'; but at the same time he warned against the Press being taken over by the radicals by insisting 'we cannot permit the Press to be turned into the domain of any particular group', though he refused to identify himself with the conservative view of a 'liberal terror' being waged in the Press.

This line was partially endorsed by V. Afanasev, then editor of *Pravda*, who for example in November 1988 alleged that certain papers were abusing *glasnost* by using sensational stories on drugs and prostitution to boost circulation rather than to inform readers (*Ind.*, 3 November 1988). The conservative assault against liberal 'licence' culminated in a letter published in *Pravda* by six prominent figures condemning Vitaly Korotich, editor of *Ogonëk*. He later argued that 'Every social experiment of the century has been carried out on us. Now is the time to say that some were wrong' (*Ind.*, 9 February 1989). The group included the 'village' writers Vasily Belov, Valentin Rasputin and Viktor Astaf'ev as well as the film director Sergei Bondarchuk. They accused *Ogonëk* of 'distorting history, debasing cultural values and diminishing the social achievements of the people' (*P*, 18 January 1989: 6).

The assault revealed yet more cleavages among the intelligentsia, this time within the 'conservative' camp. The group of Russian nationalist conservatives had little in common with the *apparat* conservatives of the party and state, yet both shared a growing concern that *glasnost* exposed Soviet society to the corruption of the West and undermined traditional Russian values and culture. Rejoining the West politically was one thing, they argued, but opening up a relatively sheltered society to the alleged crassness and decadent commercialism of the West, especially America, was another. Various shades of populists and conservatives took it upon themselves to defend a people who supposedly had not been able to develop resistance to the virus of commercialism and for whom allegedly all things Western, by definition, were superior to the domestic version.

The divisions in the intelligentsia were at their most ugly in the plenary meeting of the RSFSR Writers' Union in mid-November 1989. The Leningrad Writers' Union was accused of being a 'Zionist organisation' even though at most a quarter of its 400 members were Jewish and all were writing in Russian. Jews were accused of having brought Russia to its knees (*Ind.*, 26 January 1990). Once again the age-old conflict between liberals and conservatives, Westernisers and Russophiles (and, in an extreme variant, Slavophiles) was being played out. The monthly journals could be divided between the two camps, with *Novyi mir*, *Znamya* (Banner) and *Oktyabr* on the liberal wing, ranged against *Nash sovremennik* (Our Contemporary) and *Molodaya gvardiya* (Young Guard), with support from the conservative papers *Literaturnaya rossiya* (Literary Russia), *Sovetskaya rossiya* (Soviet Russia) and the defence ministry paper *Krasnaya zvezda* (Red Star). In late 1989 the liberals established a new journal *Aprel* to put forward their view. It should be stressed that the gap between liberal reformists and moderate Russophiles was not so great, since both sought to achieve a type of democratic pluralist society. The difference was that the moderate Russophiles, represented for example by the journal *Vybor* (Choice), edited by Gleb Anishchenko and Victor Aksyuchits, argued for democracy with a Russian face.

The major achievement of *glasnost* was the reconstitution of the intelligentsia as a free-thinking and relatively independent group to act as a counterweight to the bureaucracy and the administrative system. As Korotich argued, 'If we are to escape the ruins of the planned society, we have to give society back to the intellectuals. You have to rebuild the brains of the country' (*Ind.*, 9 February 1989). However, the triumph of the intelligentsia was accompanied by the destruction of their special role as the conscience of the nation. *Perestroika* was accompanied by the transformation of the sociocultural structure of society. A 'normal' class pattern began to emerge, accompanied by the decline of the intelligentsia as a special group. Marketising economic reforms weaken the specific political role of the intelligentsia as society becomes less ideologically charged. A classic 'modern' Western pattern of class relationships is being shelled out through the decay of Communist power. The prominent role of the intelligentsia during *perestroika* was only a transitional one. Just as socialist revolution is the last political act of the peasantry as a class, so Communist reformism is the last class act of the intelligentsia.

At first the official view of *glasnost* was an instrumental one. It was regarded as a weapon of change rather than a policy that in itself could take any path it wished. It was designed to strengthen reformist socialism. Criticism was to be 'constructive' and imbued with the 'party spirit' (*partiinost*). As time passed, however, despite the inadequacies of the laws governing press freedom up to 1990, free speech was seized from below and thus the official bounds of *glasnost* were breached.

Glasnost acted as a slow letting off of steam, the gradual drip by drip revelations of the enormity of past crimes and present difficulties. It thus helped avoid the outburst of mass anger that the sudden complete truth provoked in East Germany and elsewhere after the revolutions of 1989. Tension over the scope and nature of *glasnost* was provoked in part by the fact that it promised more than *perestroika* could deliver. *Glasnost* created opportunities for movement towards democracy and suggested openings that the reformist definition of *perestroika* seemed to foreclose. The basic issue for the radicals was the transformation of *glasnost* into free speech. This was only gradually achieved through new press laws and laws guaranteeing civil rights.

Whatever the fate of Gorbachev and his reformist associates, the truth about the past and the present revealed by *glasnost* cannot be withdrawn. They have sunk so deeply into the national consciousness that no mere political counter-reform could root them out. In this respect the threshold of irreversibility has been crossed. Gorbachev's own speeches have highlighted the profound shortcomings of the system, and the official and unofficial Press have amplified and consolidated the details. *Glasnost* ultimately was the greatest guarantor of the irreversibility of Gorbachev's reforms.

Debrezhnevisation and the concept of stagnation

While destalinisation represents a direct assault on some of the most iniquitous features of the Soviet past and their legacy on the present, the process of debrezhnevisation has in many respects been no less challenging. On one level debrezhnevisation entailed the continuation of Andropov's anti-corruption campaign and the bringing to book of some of the more notorious criminals of that era. On a deeper level it represented the rejection or modification of a whole system of rule predicated on the neo-Stalinist compromise. The post-Stalinist era has ended and a new phase has begun. No longer will initiative be systematically undermined, culture stifled and social movements suppressed with the old vigour. The concept of stagnation tries to come to terms with the factors that gave rise to the sociopolitical stalemate of the post-Stalin era.

The Brezhnev era denied the conflicts that are the source of political change. The leadership gave up attempts at grandiose social engineering and propounded stability rather than change. It sought to manage society according to the ideas of 'developed socialism' and controlled modernisation within the terms of the 'scientific—technological revolution'. The neo-Stalinism of the Brezhnev years highlighted the difficulties of successful development into a thoroughly modern society, not only because the standard of 'modernity' constantly changes to encompass new social and technological developments, but also because of a reluctance to relinquish the controls that are the essential element of a political system based on the idea of a 'leading role' for the party. Neo-Stalinism represents an attempt to repress the spontaneity of social processes that is a mark of modernity.

Debrezhnevisation has involved the sloughing off of the Brezhnev generation of leaders. One of the first to go was Viktor Grishin, who in December 1985 lost his post, which he had held for eighteen years, as head of the Moscow party organisation. As a complacent member of the old guard and a paramount machine politician he had done little to avert the decay of the country's economic and moral infrastructure, and himself appeared tainted by the prevalent corruption. Moreover, it appears that he had opposed Andropov's candidacy for the leadership and had vied for the leadership against Gorbachev.

In December 1985, Grishin's successor as leader of the Moscow party organisation, Boris Eltsin — only months after his appointment as a CC secretary in July — delivered a harshly critical speech in Tashkent, the capital of Uzbekistan (*P*, 15 December 1985: 2). This was only the beginning of the unravelling of the greatest scandal of the Brezhnev era. During the twenty-four years of Sharif Rashidov's tenure as party leader in Uzbekistan the republic was the scene of several major scandals. Above all the huge cotton fraud between 1976 and 1983 cheated Moscow of some 3 billion rubles by claiming higher yields than those achieved. Uzbekistan had become the centre of what came to be called the 'mafia' of organised crime based on protection rackets, extortion, nepotism and corruption. Debrezhnevisation entailed a sustained assault on so-called economic crime which had moved beyond individual petty malfeasance into the wholesale corruption of Soviet economic mechanisms. The 19th party conference in 1988 was agitated by the allegations in *Ogonëk* that several delegates from Uzbekistan were involved in massive local corruption and that party membership was being used to protect them from investigation, with the connivance of senior party officials in Moscow (Hazan, 1990: 276—8).

Debrezhnevisation has entailed the exposure of the venality of Brezhnev's own coterie of leaders and families. The notable case was of Yuri Churbanov, Brezhnev's son-in-law, who had married his daughter Galina in 1971 and who used his new connections to become First Deputy Minister of the Interior between 1980 and 1984. He was sentenced to twelve years in a harsh regime labour camp in December 1988 for accepting bribes of some 650,000 rubles, much of it during trips to Uzbekistan. Churbanov's trial revealed the sordid underside of Brezhnevite stability, and he was accompanied in the dock by eight senior police officials from Uzbekistan, six of whom were also jailed. The former leader of the MVD, Nikolai Shchelokov, had apparently committed suicide in December 1984 as the investigators closed in on his own misdeeds, and now his deputy was also found guilty. Sharif Rashidov was fortunate enough to die in office in 1983 but the period leading up to the Churbanov trial was accompanied by a spate of suicides by officials in the republic. The bizarre case of the *raion* party leader, Akhmadzham Adylov, came to light revealing how he held court in an underground labyrinth in which he imprisoned and tortured those who offended him. Local party leaders had turned into feudal barons. The state prosecutor at the trial, Aleksandr Sboyev, summed up by stating that the trial had revealed how during the 'era of stagnation a web of corruption had spread across the land. . .eating into the souls of the people and undermining their faith in social justice'.

The leading investigators in unravelling the threads of scandal at the heart of the Soviet political system, Telman Gdlyan and Nikolai Ivanov, themselves became the target of conservative criticism. They were accused of having used 'Stalinist' methods to obtain evidence with the illegal detention of witnesses and harsh questioning methods. The investigators allegedly tried to use the Churbanov trial not to establish the guilt of a particular individual but to put the whole Brezhnev 'mafia' on trial in a manner reminiscent of the 'show trials' of the 1930s (*P*, 1 January 1989; *MN*, 2/1989). Gdlyan responded by alleging that the trial had been rigged to cover up the true extent of the corruption, discredit the investigators and divert attention away from those responsible, especially those at the centre. The Churbanov case in effect put the Brezhnev era on trial and revealed how easily the privileges and lack of accountability of a regime of mediocrities could turn into corruption (*P*, 30 August 1988). The assault on corruption and economic crime was simultaneously an assault not only on individual bureaucrats but also on the bureaucratic system that gave rise to it. The system had deposed Khrushchev, Soltan Darasov argued, in favour of its obedient tool Brezhnev (*Ob.*, 7 February 1988).

Gdlyan and Ivanov were elected by acclaim to the Congress of People's Deputies in spring 1989, demonstrating both the popularity of the anti-corruption campaign and the low esteem in which the old generation of officials were held. The Congress gave them a platform to press their accusations that their investigations had been obstructed at every turn by high officials in the Kremlin. Ivanov pointed the finger at Ligachev himself once again during his election, accusing him of being an accomplice in the Uzbek cotton scandal. The prosecutor-general,

Aleksandr Sukharev, reported to the CC plenum of 20 September 1989 that the charges of bribery against Ligachev were groundless. A special commission of the Congress again dismissed the charges against Ligachev and the 'Moscow bribe-takers', and instead found Gdlyan and Ivanov guilty of professional malpractice (*P*, 24 December 1989). The two were relieved from their posts, and in February 1990 expelled from the party. The affair dragged on, and a Supreme Soviet committee, co-chaired by Roy Medvedev, once again looked into the whole affair; in April 1990 they concluded that there were grounds to institute criminal proceedings against Gdlyan and Ivanov, and rejected the accusation against Ligachev. On 18 April, however, the Supreme Soviet turned down a request from the procurator-general to remove parliamentary immunity from them, and thus no criminal proceedings were instituted against them at that time. It was clear that the whole case was political, though cloaked in judicial rhetoric. Gdlyan at the mass demonstration on 4 February 1990 called for the resignation of the entire Politburo, including Gorbachev, on the grounds that they defended corruption.

Following his dismissal as Moscow party leader in November 1987 Eltsin bitterly noted that 'I underestimated the influence of the organised mafia in Moscow in all spheres' (*LF on EE*, 2/1989: 28). The concept of 'mafia' entered the language, encouraged by Eltsin's use of the term, to denote the privileges and conservatism of the authorities. Like the Italian mafia, this corrupt body had a thousand tentacles controlling all aspects of life. The authorities tried to restrict the term to the criminal gangs, but popular usage decreed otherwise. Gdlyan and Ivanov insisted that the two were in fact part of a single conspiracy. Their cause was boosted by the revelations of the scale of official corruption in East Germany following Honecker's disgrace in November 1989. This seemed to demonstrate that the Soviet and other Communist ruling classes had become one of the most venal, incompetent and useless ruling classes in history. The early idealism and self-sacrifice appeared to have degenerated into a self-serving and increasingly isolated ruling group. The political élite status that they so assiduously defended in the guise of the 'leading role' of the party became converted into a whole set of social privileges that they were naturally reluctant to lose. The leading role of the party began to degenerate into the dominant role of a social élite.

Debrezhnevisation played an important political function, giving Gorbachev's rule a clear identity and a scapegoat for the misfortunes of the country. Yet it was much more than simply a political manoeuvre on Gorbachev's part. The burden of guilt of a leadership that had destroyed a generation after 1964 began to be examined, and reasons explaining why the system could evolve in such a way were sought.

Debrezhnevisation encompassed the whole Brezhnev generation who had advanced on the graves of their predecessors in the Stalinist 1930s. In particular, Andropov's compromised past increasingly became the object of much speculation. In an interview in *Ogonëk* Vladimir Semichastny, Andropov's immediate predecessor as head of the KGB from 1961 to 1967, charged Andropov with participating in Stalin's purges and ignoring corruption under Brezhnev (24/1989: 24–6). It must be presumed that as head of the KGB he knew of the pervasive corruption in Central Asia and elsewhere, but kept quiet until it suited his purposes to lift the cover on the corruption in Brezhnev's immediate entourage.

Debrezhnevisation was accompanied by the removal of his name, together with that of Chernenko, from public places, enterprises and institutions. Gradually the assault against corruption was transformed into an attack on privileges. The Politburo in December 1988 decreed the closure of some thousand *Beriozka* shops stocking foreign goods for Soviet citizens with special coupons. The shops taking foreign currency remained untouched and closed to Soviet citizens. The number of official cars was cut by 40 per cent in February 1988. As *Argumenty i fakty* noted, an average provincial Soviet town had more official cars than the entire United Kingdom (240). The system of awarding state honours and medals also came in for criticism, with Brezhnev's own four gold stars as Hero of the Soviet Union for his modest war record particularly mocked (*P*, 3 April 1988). Roy Medvedev wrote that Brezhnev suffered a stroke in January 1976 and was pronounced 'clinically dead'. He recovered sufficiently to soldier on as head of state and party for another six years even though he 'stopped taking in what was going on around him' and 'found it more and more difficult to carry out the simplest of functions' (*MN*, 8 September 1988).

Debrezhnevisation, among other things, undermined the legitimacy of rulers in Eastern Europe who, to one degree or another, owed their longevity in power to Brezhnev. One after another they fell victim to popular revolts against Brezhnevism, which now meant that the regimes themselves were challenged, and in most cases destroyed.

The roots of Brezhnevism and stagnation began to be sought in earlier phases. The immediate perspective was an increasingly critical approach to the Khrushchev period. The brutal suppression of the Hungarian revolution in 1956 was condemned by its new definition as a 'popular uprising'. Khrushchev's suppression of the striking workers in Novocherkassk in June 1962, at the height of the so-called thaw, also received its share of critical attention (*Komsomolets*, 22 June 1988).

The definition of stagnation as developed in the early years of *perestroika* focused on the failings of the late 1970s and early 1980s. Burlatsky, however, extended the concept to cover the whole period. He argued that Brezhnev came to power in 1964 with almost no programme of his own other than staying in power, and disagreed with the idea of 'two Brezhnevs', the earlier one the proponent of moderate reform, the later one simply maintaining the *status quo* (in *Brezhnev* 1989: 34–46). The Brezhnev period is indeed of a piece with initiatives coming throughout, from the 1965 economic reform and the détente of the 1970s to the Food Programme of 1982. The problem, overall, was the diffused style of decision-making and ultimately the lack of final responsibility for ensuring the implementation of policies. For Burlatsky, the key lesson of the Brezhnev era is that statist socialism of the Stalinist or neo-Stalinist sort simply does not work: 'The state, far from promoting progress, was becoming more and more of a drag on society – economically, culturally and morally' (*G*, 17 December 1988). In short, the Brezhnev period demonstrated that there was no way of returning to Stalinism and that the administrative-command form of socialism was incompatible with technological, social and cultural progress.

All new Soviet leaders including, as the historian Vasilii Klyuchevsky noted, the Tsars in their day, have tended to denigrate their predecessors and hold them responsible for the shortcomings of the system. However, in the case of Brezhnev criticisms of his style of rule were rapidly transformed into a critique of the whole 'era of stagnation'. The sociopolitical and philosophical aspects of a concept of stagnation in the development of socialism began to be developed. The basic feature of this critique was an understanding that the stability of the Brezhnev years was vitiated by a number of factors that challenged both the practice of 'developed socialism' and the theoretical basis of a society allegedly marked by the absence of contradictions or of antagonistic groups or classes regulated by an omniscient and beneficent bureaucracy led by the Communist Party. The fundamental question is whether the Brezhnevite stagnation was a personal, conjunctural or systemic phenomenon. Did it reflect the failings of Brezhnev personally, a random conjunction of unfortunate circumstances, or the culmination of innate tendencies intrinsic to the system?

The central paradox is that Marxist socialism is a theory imbued with notions of progress and development which tends towards historicism, whose laws Marxism–Leninism seeks to explain and thus to control. However, the experience of the Brezhnev years insistently raised the question of whether Marxism can account for stagnation (Gellner, 1988: 93, 170–1). As Soviet society lost its dynamism, so Soviet social sciences began to stress stability over change, stasis over dynamism. The vision of the Soviet social system increasingly became one of a mechanism to be maintained rather than of a society to be transformed.

Already under Brezhnev the more dynamic concept of a 'political system' began to replace the rather static traditional notion of 'sociopolitical organisation' (cf. Hill, 1980). The elements making up the system, the party, Komsomol, trade unions and economic management as a whole, were to stand in a dynamic relationship with each other, implying a growing scope for autonomous action for each part. However, the radical implications of the idea were only fulfilled by Gorbachev. Under Brezhnev the language of 'developed socialism' considered the system in terms of a self-regulating mechanism in a vocabulary that was increasingly reminiscent of American functionalism. The focus was on how a political system achieves and maintains stability. The obvious criticism of this approach was that it lacked a mechanism, like totalitarian theory, to explain political change. The vision of developed socialism as a self-reproducing and self-maintaining system obviously suggested self-serving motives in that the necessity for change was denied and those trying to achieve change were discouraged.

There is a larger question of deciding whether the nineteenth-century view of societies as prone to indefinite change and progress is more accurate than the view which sees such periods of change as pathological symptoms of a breakdown in a primordial harmony and balance, the traditional Chinese or conservative view reflected in a perverse way by Stalinist romantic myths of harmony once class enemies had been destroyed. Brezhnevite conservatism and ideas of 'developed socialism' acted as the ideology of stagnation, albeit unwittingly. The problem for Marxist theorists was that once the sources of capitalist instability were removed – namely the class struggle, economic crises and exploitation – then it appeared that all that remained for the socialist system to do after the initial transition period was to sustain itself and run society according to its ideas of rationality. Hence it could be argued that there are entropic tendencies built into the theory of Soviet socialism itself. The tranquillity of the Brezhnev period suggested that the secret had at last been found on how to realise the functionalist dream of a stable self-perpetuating system.

The resonances between the stagnation of the Brezhnev years and the operation of an Asiatic Mode of Production (AMP) are quite striking. Gouldner pointed out that the notion of an AMP, raised by Marx but then left undeveloped, challenges the core Marxist notions of a unilinear process of change and the ideas underlying that change (Gouldner, 1980: 324–54). Soviet anthropological debates, as in other disciplines in the traditionally highly politicised world of Soviet social sciences, have often acted as a surrogate for debates of contemporary problems of society; one of the most interesting debates was over the AMP. Gellner succinctly captures the features of the AMP that challenge Marxism:

It is stagnant and self-perpetuating, thus offering no hope to the humanity caught up in its toils, unless it be accidental liberation from outside which, however, must then be contingent upon the existence of some other and less stagnant society, and on the conquest of the 'Oriental' society by it. It also offers the spectacle of a self-serving political order built upon violence, and serving the members of the state machine itself and no one else – in other words, a machine of oppression set up not in defence of [a] pre-existing class system, but by autonomous violence and coercion, and serving a class brought into being merely by its control of the means of coercion, rather than of production. (Gellner, 1988: 94)

The 'machine of oppression', of course, will be all the stronger when combined with control over the means of production as well as being in command of the state mechanism. The Gorbachev reforms to a degree confounded the view that fundamental change could only come from outside, and the dynamic concept of *perestroika* tried to develop an anti-stagnation ideology and practice based on the rejection of an administrative style of governance.

The basic question in examining Brezhnevite stagnation, which can be taken as only the sharpest manifestation of tendencies present at other stages of Soviet history as well, is whether the source of stagnation lay in the economic system or in the non-economic layers of social life. The immediate response may well be that in the Soviet context no such distinction can be drawn and that the 'administrative command system' was indivisible. There is certainly a dialectical relationship between economic and political stagnation.

The structure of the 'braking mechanism' was examined in a collection of articles of leading Soviet political scientists (*Mekhanism tormozheniya*, 1988). The source was seen to lie in Stalin's personal power and the birth of an administrative-command system dominated by a bureaucracy which survived into the 1980s. The clear conclusion was that stagnation was a far more complex problem than had been realised in 1985, and therefore would be a far more arduous task to overcome.

The economic and ideological aspects of societies marked by stagnation were provided by the Estonian philosopher Eero Loone (1988). The fundamental problem is how to define the concept of stagnation. Does it mean only a temporary phase of social paralysis, or is it a manifestation of a social system which has exhausted its potential and has thus become a historical dead end? If the latter, then Gorbachev's *perestroika* is much ado about nothing. The major question that arises is whether the 'stagnation' affected only the body politic, so that the economic sphere was able to achieve considerable, if distorted and expensive, economic development. In this case, the Brezhnev period simply saw the stagnation of the base come into line with the stagnation of the superstructure. This is not a wholly satisfactory formulation and comes close to the reductionism of Herbert Marcuse's *One Dimensional Man*, which makes social stagnation an outcome of the endless economic growth of liberal societies (Gellner, 1988: 171).

The whole concept of stagnation is thus problematical, especially in view of the dynamic social changes of the period. Some other organising principle must be applied to help understand the 'negative phenomena' of the Brezhnev years. The concept of stagnation is beset by problems such as when did it begin, have the factors which gave rise to it been overcome, what sort of stagnation are we talking about, what were its causes, and can it be ended within the framework of reform Communism? Has the idea of stagnation been set up as a straw man to provide an easy target against which the new leaders can display their dynamism? Is it a diversion to avoid making debrezhnevisation a dangerous partner of destalinisation and deleninisation, beset by the same questions over the nature of a social system that could allow itself to wallow in at least a decade of 'stagnation' while the 'propaganda of success' proclaimed it to be in the best possible condition and the vast majority of the political establishment gave standing ovations to themselves? Having been caught once by Stalin, how could the party allow itself to acquiesce in the personal vanity and dangerous illusions of a mediocrity like Brezhnev? These are the questions raised by the notion of debrezhnevisation but evaded by the idea of a narrowly defined period of stagnation.

Destalinisation and the new history

Glasnost was accompanied by a renewed challenge not only to Stalin's legacy but to the roots of Stalinism itself. Khrushchev's Secret Speech at the 20th party congress in February 1956 denounced Stalin the man but failed to develop a critique of the Stalinist system as a whole. The second destalinising congress, the 22nd in 1961, allowed more details of Stalin's crimes to emerge and launched a more vitriolic campaign against the man, but the structural and ideological sources of Stalinism remained unexplored. During the long years of Brezhnevite stagnation the topic was suppressed, although conservative attempts to rehabilitate Stalin failed.

The leadership changes of the early 1980s were remarkable for the almost complete absence, at least explicitly, of the issue of destalinisation. With the leadership question settled, *glasnost* allowed the causes and consequences of Stalin's rule to be explored. The issue, as under

Khrushchev, remained vulnerable to shifts in the leadership and at first was relatively restrained, but gradually discussion freed itself of leadership struggles and became an attempt to understand a complex phenomenon. The evaluation of Stalin challenges the Soviet regime to examine not only its own past but also the very nature of the type of socialism that it espouses.

In the political sphere the death of Stalin saw the re-establishment of the party as an effective organisation and the stabilisation of the bureaucratic apparatus, but despite over three decades of allegiance to the idea of 'reviving Soviet democracy' little substantive had been achieved. Above all, the actual question of 'Stalinism' was suppressed under Brezhnev. The mass coercion of the peasantry, the scale of the purges and size of the labour camp population, the miscalculations during the War, the deportation of peoples at the end of the War and many other of Stalin's 'excesses' remained shrouded in mystery. The reformist leadership gradually realised that as long as the history of the Soviet Union remained distorted even the positive achievements of the country were undermined. Khrushchev dealt with some of the symptoms, but the disease remained lodged in the Soviet body politic.

The first steps were taken by the cultural intelligentsia, many of whom had participated in the first wave of destalinisation under Khrushchev. At the Writers' Union Congress of the Russian republic in December 1985 Evgenii Evtushenko returned to the themes that had made him famous under Khrushchev: the problem of Stalin's crimes. The debate was taken up in literary journals, and once again the 'blank pages' in Soviet history were discussed. The film *Repentance* by Tengiz Abuladze exposed the guilt, compromises, suffering and silences of the Stalinist and post-Stalinist decades. Anatolii Rybakov's *Children of the Arbat* gave a vivid insight into the workings of Stalin's mind and revealed something of the reality of the purges of the party and industrial élites in the early 1930s. Aleksandr Bek's *Novoe Naznachenie* (New Posting) examined the bureaucracy and the cult of personality, including a study of the personalities of Stalin and Beria, when a high-ranking bureaucrat is forced to examine his past with the accession of Khrushchev.

The battle over the past has been as vigorous in the natural sciences as it has been in the humanities and social sciences. *Glasnost* allowed the publication of several novels describing the havoc wreaked by Stalinism in the sciences. Among them, Vladimir Dudintsev's *Belye Odezhdy* (Robed in White) analysed the impact on Soviet biology of the 1948 session of the All-Union Lenin Academy of Agriculture. A wave of persecution was unleashed against all those who refused to accept Trofim Lysenko's absurd views on accelerated genetic change of species. Daniil Granin's *Zubr* (Zebra) caused an uproar when first published in

Novyi mir in 1987. It was concerned with the rehabilitation of the Soviet scientist Timofeev-Resovskii, who left the USSR for Berlin in 1925 and worked there for twenty years, including under the Nazis. When the Soviet army reached Berlin in 1945 he was arrested and on his eventual return to the USSR faced persecution. In addition to his alleged collaboration with the Germans his work on genetics ran counter to Lysenko's.

Glasnost struck the greatest blow against Stalinism by eroding the culture of fear. The corrosive impact of fear on individuals and society in Stalin's last days in 1953 was explored by Boris Empolskii in his novel *Moscow Street*. The destruction of mutual trust is explored in Yurii Trifonov's *Disappearance (Ischeznovenie)*. The psychology that led to the trials and confessions of the Old Bolsheviks and which primed the fear was examined by Evgenii Ambartsumov. He recounts how the Menshevik emigré N. Valentinov (Volskii) met his old friend G. Pyatakov in Paris in 1928, soon after the capitulation of the Left oppositionists, and took him to task for his lack of moral courage. In reply Pyatakov referred to the true Bolshevik's lack of any restraints, moral, political or even physical: 'The true Bolshevik dissolves his personality in the party collectivity' and thereby removes 'any personal opinions or convictions.' This standard Bolshevik view is clearly reminiscent of Trotsky's opinion in 1925 that 'the party is always right.' What was once praised is now condemned by the author: 'That is how murderous and suicidal the moral nihilism that was once passed off as revolutionary spirit was!' (*MN*, 19 June 1988: 10).

In the theatre Mikhail Shatrov's plays *Dictatorship of Conscience* and *Onward, Onward, Onward* sought to draw a line between Lenin and Stalin and to insist that there were alternatives to Stalin. In particular, in the latter play he argued that under Stalin a bureaucratic degeneration of the Revolution took place. The latter-day bureaucracy did all in its power to prevent the performance of the play until Gorbachev himself insisted that for the the country and *perestroika* there was no alternative but 'onward, onward, onward'!

Academician D. S. Likhachev, a medieval scholar active in the popular movement to preserve Russian cultural artifacts, called memory 'the conscience of the nation'. The new destalinisation has been accompanied by an attempt to undo the falsification of Soviet history and to shed light on the blank pages (Davies, 1989a). Attempts were made in 1988 to establish a professional association of historians in order to further the moral recovery of the profession.

The first honest official Soviet biography of Stalin, the two-volume *Triumph and Tragedy* by Dmitrii Volkogonov, director of the Institute of Military History of the USSR, assailed Stalin's reputation as a military commander and gave fresh details of the terror. Roy Medvedev's *Let History Judge*, which first appeared in the West in 1976, was substantially reworked and now began to question the Leninist legacy. The book was published in the Soviet Union in 1989. These books and others re-examined the number of Stalin's victims in the three main categories: those executed for political crimes, mainly in 1937–8; those who died in the labour camps or during mass deportations; and the peasants who died during collectivisation and the famine of the early 1930s. A fourth category may be those who died unnecessarily as a result of Stalin's policies during the Second World War, especially in its early days.

The scale of the Soviet 'holocaust' was at last admitted. More than 10 million peasants were repressed during the collectivisation drive from 1929 to 1933 according to Vladimir Tikhonov, member of the Academy of Agricultural Sciences (*G*, 5 April 1988). Tikhonov, who later came to chair the All-Union Society of Co-operators, argued that collectivisation had ruined a flourishing agricultural system and that dekulakisation had destroyed the peasantry as a class and transformed farmers into workers without rights (*LG*, 5 August 1988). V. P. Danilov, one of the leading experts on the peasantry during the NEP, whose work was suppressed under Brezhnev, qualified this rather rosy view by pointing out that an exploiting kulak stratum was beginning to emerge in the midst of an increasingly differentiated peasantry in the 1920s (*Istoriya SSSR*, 3, May–June 1989: 3–62; see Davies, 1989b: 1–2). Nikolai Shmelëv (1987), an economist at the Institute of the USA and Canada, also drew on 'the destruction of the peasantry as a class' to illustrate that the Stalinist economic system produced for the sake of production, flouting all economic laws. He numbered the victims of dekulakisation at about 5 million, with some 17 million passing through the camps between 1937 and 1953. The famine of 1932–3 in the Ukraine, the Don region and the North Caucasus, in which some 5 million died (Conquest, 1986), is seen to have been largely 'artificial'. Even as hunger took hold troops were still seizing food and preventing starving peasants from leaving the area. Food was available elsewhere in the country but Stalin refused assistance, and indeed until late 1932 continued grain exports. The sheer scale of the 'murder-famine', as it is now called, or indeed Stalinist genocide against the Ukrainian people, has led to comparisons with the Jewish holocaust whose number of victims it exceeded. Conquest estimates a total death toll from Soviet agricultural policies in the 1930s at 14–15 million.

Gorbachev only gradually came to terms with the scale of the Stalinist horror. His speech to celebrate the seventieth anniversary of the Revolution in November 1987 steered a path between criticism and praise of the past. The role of leaders such as Bukharin, Trotsky and other of Lenin's colleagues was mentioned not altogether unfavourably for the first time in decades. Although he criticised Bukharin's policies Gorbachev called for more study. The speech was clearly a compromise and disappointed many who hoped for a more radical re-evaluation of the past, and of Stalin in particular. His assessment of collectivisation was that Stalin's farm policy had brought distortions and 'crimes' but had been necessary. In his book *Perestroika* Gorbachev again argued that industrialisation and collectivisation were necessary for the progress of the country. However, 'The methods and forms of accomplishing these reforms did not always accord with socialist principles' (1987a: 41). In his speech Gorbachev admitted that Stalin's victims ran into the thousands, but press comment in the following years further demonstrated how ridiculous an understatement this was.

On 4 February 1989 *Argumenty i fakty* suggested that 40 million people were arrested, executed or repressed under Stalin. Other papers reported the discovery of mass graves at Bykova, near Kiev in which, according to Memorial, the group organised to commemorate Stalin's victims, up to 240,000 bodies of those executed in the 1930s could be found (*LG*, 27 April 1989). The mass grave outside Minsk at Kuropaty is believed to contain some 50,000 victims of the purges (Ales Adamovich in *Ogonëk*, 25 September 1988). A mass grave near Donetsk in the Ukraine has also been found (*P*, 4 July 1989), and some 80,000 are believed buried in a mass grave near Chelyabinsk (*Ind.*, 6 September 1989). In Moscow itself the Kalitnikovskii cemetery has been revealed as a burial ground for those executed in the prisons, especially the notorious Butyrka, in the 1930s. Professor Yuri Polyakov, chair of the demographic history section of the Academy of Sciences, asserted at a news conference in October 1987 that Stalin's terror claimed over a million lives by the end of the 1930s and dismissed estimates of up to 19 million, the figure defended by Conquest (1971, 1986), as 'fantastical' (*G*, 10 October 1987). Roy Medvedev went further and suggested that up to 38 million people suffered at Stalin's hands, a fifth of the population, and claimed the lives of at least 12 million (*MN*, 23 November 1988). The KGB itself admitted in February 1990 that 786,098 people were shot between 1930 and 1953 out of a total of 3,778,234 who had been sentenced for counter-revolutionary activities in these years. These figures exclude the millions who died or were imprisoned as a result of collectivisation and famine (*Ind.*, 14 February 1990). Figures originally collected for Khrushchev showed a labour camp population rising from 179,000 in 1930 to 510,307 in 1934, 1,296,494 in 1936, 1,881,570 in 1938 falling slightly during the War and then peaking at 2,561,351 in 1950 (G, 10 March 1990). The KGB admitted indirectly that between the 1930s and the 1950s 3.5 million people had been 'exterminated' (*Ind.*, 27 March 1990). The debate over the number of 'excess deaths', as extrapolated from the census figures for 1937 and 1939, will continue until there is free access to NKVD and other archives, and the materials for the suppressed 1937 census made available (see Yu. Polyyakov, *A.iF*, 26/1990: 8).

As *glasnost* shed more light on the past it became clear that the accomplishments diminished steadily, while the crimes rose to become a veritable mountain of evil. Among the issues examined in greater depth than before was Stalin's role as a war leader. Details were revealed of the scale of the military purge just prior to the War. According to Nikolai Pavlenko, a military historian, between May 1937 and September 1938 a total of 36,761 Soviet officers and men were 'repressed' (*Ogonëk*, 25/1989: 6). Stalin's refusal to acknowledge the various warnings of German intentions on the eve of the War has also been revealed in numerous articles (e.g. *P*, 8 May 1989). The warning from Richard Sorge, a Soviet spy in Tokyo, that the date of the attack would be 22 June 1941 is well known. A more surprising revelation was that the German ambassador in Moscow, Count Friedrich von Schulenberg, an old-fashioned Bismarckian German nationalist, hoped to avert war with the Soviet Union, which he believed was not in Germany's interests, by warning Stalin (*P*, 22 June 1989). Once war had broken out and the Germans were approaching Moscow in October 1941, Stalin allegedly offered Hitler a deal (*ST*, 28 May 1989).

The purges were not restricted to the Soviet Union proper. Up to 100,000 people may have died in purges in Mongolia, a tenth of the population (*G*, 23 March 1990). After forty years of denials the Soviets at last admitted the existence of the 'secret protocol' of the Nazi–Soviet Pact of 23 August 1939 which gave *carte blanche* as far as the Germans were concerned to a series of Soviet 'war' crimes in eastern Poland and later in the Baltic republics. The notorious case of the disappearance in April 1940 of some 10,000 Polish officers and the murder of 4,500 more at Katyn in Belorussia was examined from 1987 by a joint Soviet–Polish commission. Its conclusions were to a degree pre-empted by the Soviet Press, which admitted what any honest person had always known, that the NKVD in 1940 and not the Germans in 1943 were the murderers (*MN*, 2 August 1989; 25 March 1990). This was officially admitted by a Tass statement on 13 April 1990, the fiftieth anniversary of the killings and of the mass deportation of some 1.5 million Poles to Siberia, half of whom perished there. The fig-leaf of rationality behind the Pact, that it won time for the Soviet Union to prepare its defences, has also been exposed as having been squandered and that Stalin was thoroughly duped by Hitler (Ernst Genri, *Moskovskaya pravda*, 18 May

1988). After the War mass killings took place throughout the Soviet-occupied zone of Germany.

The deportations from and executions in the Baltic republics after their recapture by the Soviet army in 1944 constitute a chapter of their own in the tale of Stalinist horrors. On 25 March 1949, for example, 43,000 Latvians were packed into cattle trucks at Riga's main station and shipped to Siberia.

Like debrezhnevisation, destalinisation has been accompanied by the attempt to remove physical traces of the cult of Stalin and his henchmen. Perhaps the most popular change was the removal of Andrei A. Zhdanov's name from Leningrad University, renamed after the War to celebrate Zhdanov's alleged heroic exploits in defending the city. The *Zhdanovshchina* of 1945–8 saw the persecution of writers such as Anna Akhmatova and Mikhail Zoshchenko and in the sciences saw the condemnation of 'professorial objectivism'. The Soviet Cultural Fund, headed by Likhachev, established a Council for Toponomy which sought to restore historical names to Soviet towns and places (*LG*, 20 July 1988). Immediate candidates were the return of the name Tver to Kalinin, Nizhnii Novgorod to Gorky, Samara to Kuibyshev, Mariupol to Zhdanov and ultimately no doubt St Petersburg to Leningrad.

Other aspects of the new wave of destalinisation saw the condemnation of the cult of the child informer Pavlik Morozov, who during collectivisation in 1932 denounced his parents as enemies of the state and was then murdered by enraged peasants. The mythical exploits of Alexei Stakhanov, who allegedly shifted 102 tons of coal, some 15 times the norm, in a single shift in August 1935 was exposed as having been a joint effort and staged from beginning to end. The search for the truth behind the disappearance in 1945 of Raoul Wallenberg, the Swedish diplomat who saved thousands of Jews in Hungary, continues.

The process of rehabilitation was resumed after the break of the Brezhnev years. The October 1987 plenum of the Central Committee established a Politburo commission chaired by Mikhail Solomentsev and made up of Viktor Chebrikov and Aleksandr Yakovlev to examine materials on the repressions of the 1930s and 1940s. The aim, according to Solomentsev, was to 'restore complete historical truth and justice' and to 'cleanse society from the grave mistakes and crimes of the past' (*P*, 19 August 1988). He condemned the end to destalinisation under Brezhnev. By August 1988, 636 people had been legally rehabilitated, covering not only victims but also family members who had often suffered as well. The commission also began to tread on the dangerous ground of establishing who was responsible for carrying out the repressions. As Solomentsev put it, 'The personal guilt of Stalin and the people closest to him before the party and the people for the mass repressions and lawlessness is dreadful. But the guilt of "the leaders" does not relieve the voluntary executors of responsibility, those directly involved in the infringement of socialist law, those who supported and blindly fulfilled inhumane instructions, committed outrages. It seems that the responsibility of people close to Stalin will become absolutely clear in the course of the commission's further work' (*P*, 19 August 1988). Yakovlev, now chair of the commission, revealed at the 28th congress that nearly a million people had been rehabilitated (*P*, 4 July 1990).

On 4 February 1988 Bukharin was posthumously cleared of criminal charges and in July, in the centenary year of his birth and fifty years after his execution in 1938, Bukharin was at last rehabilitated politically. This represented the political rehabilitation of the NEP itself, with which he had been so closely identified, and a rejection of Stalin's ultra-Left foreign policies from 1929 (Timmermann, 1989a). A. I. Rykov and M. Tomsky, who were purged with Bukharin for 'right deviationism' in the late 1920s, were also politically rehabilitated at this time. The Stalin leadership was found to have committed not only crimes, which however dreadful at least preserved the party's reputation for infallibility, but also policy mistakes, which was much more corrosive of party authority. Bukharin's rehabilitation raised questions about the other show trials of Soviet history. If Bukharin's trial in 1938 was rigged, what about the trial of the Mensheviks in 1931, or of the Socialist Revolutionaries in 1922 under Lenin? A Central Committee resolution published on 6 January 1989, which talked of hundreds of thousands of victims, proposed the blanket rehabilitation of all people convicted by the 'troikas', 'special boards' and the like with the exception of genuine traitors during the War (*P*, 6 January 1989). July 1988 also saw the political rehabilitation of two other of Lenin's colleagues, Lev Kamenev and Grigory Zinoviev, following their earlier judicial rehabilitation.

The victory of half-truth over the out-and-out lie typical of early *glasnost* was most apparent in the debate over the rehabilitation of Stalin's arch-enemy, Trotsky. One of the key elements of any genuine destalinisation would be the judicial, if not political, rehabilitation of Trotsky. Otto Latsis, deputy editor of *Kommunist*, insisted in an interview that while the criminal charges against Trotsky were unjust, his political rehabilitation, which would take the form of a return to membership of the party, was out of the question. Trotsky had been expelled from the party for 'anti-party activities' in 1927, before Stalin's consolidation of power (*Ind.*, 28 June 1988). However, Yuri Afanasev, director of the Institute of State Archivists, insisted that the process of rehabilitation should be taken to its logical conclusion (*G*, 18 June 1988). Trotsky's leading role in early Soviet history has already begun to be examined more truthfully (Volkogonov in *P*, 9 September 1988).

There is now a more honest evaluation of his views, and in 1989 a number of his works were published in the Soviet Union.

The scope of rehabilitations reflected the degree to which the party is willing to examine its history, but until the process is conducted independently of the party there will inevitably be doubts about the depth of the break with the past. The emergence of an active legislature in 1989 at last established a relatively independent forum in which to proceed, not only with destalinisation but also with debrezhnevisation. The Supreme Soviet forthrightly condemned Stalin's deportations of peoples as illegal, criminal and barbaric, and the body vowed that 'the violation of human rights and norms of humanity at a state level will never reoccur in this country' (*P*, 24 November 1989). The clamour for the rehabilitation of those persecuted in labour camps, psychiatric institutions and elsewhere in the years after Stalin's death, however, met with little official response.

Destalinisation from below was promoted by the establishment in 1988 of the Memorial group, whose honorary president was Andrei Sakharov and whose leaders include some of the most distinguished Soviet intellectuals such as the historians Yuri Afanasev and Roy Medvedev, the actor Mikhail Ulyanov, the writer and singer Bulat Okudzhava, Evtushenko and Boris Eltsin. By 1989 the group had branches in some hundred Soviet cities. Its aims included the setting up of local monuments and a memorial to Stalin's victims in Moscow, the upkeep of the graves of victims, an archive, a museum and a library of material to allow an examination of the precise scale of the Stalinist slaughter. In late November 1988 Memorial organised a 'week of conscience' in Moscow to bring home the full scale of Stalin's terror. This included the inauguration of a 'wall of conscience' where families of victims could pin up photos to help trace their fate. Memorial became one of the most important of the independent organisations and had an uneasy relationship with the authorities. The unhelpfulness of local officials and the KGB was criticised (*P*, 4 July 1989), and the problem remained of access to the files of the secret police. Official obstructionism forced the founding congress of Memorial to be postponed from late 1988 to January 1989. The authorities tried to limit Memorial to a single statue in Moscow, decided in July 1988, and hindered the other aims of the organisation. The conservatives in the party tried to neutralise grass-roots destalinisation by adopting Memorial's idea of establishing local destalinising committees, but made up of soviet deputies and organisations. The 'suffocating' process, whereby officialdom tries to dominate social life, has still not yet run its course.

As in the first wave under Khrushchev, Gorbachev's destalinisation was not confined to the Soviet Union but affected all socialist countries and the world. In China lip service was paid to destalinisation, yet the formulation which insists that Mao's 'merits were primary and his errors secondary' is one which is also applied to Stalin. The Soviets at least still have Lenin to revere in the place of Stalin, but without Mao the Chinese would be left as 'ideological orphans'. The revolutions of 1989 in Eastern Europe represented the final assault against the legacy of Stalinism in their countries. However, destalinisation is by no means something confined to socialist countries. For them the problem is clear, but for the rest of the world the nature of this twentieth-century madness has still not been adequately understood. In particular, Germany, which suffered its own descent into the abyss under the Nazis, has tried to understand the roots of the totalitarian phenomenon in its own history and culture. The *Historikerstreit* (historian's controversy) has linked the Soviet and German experience as part of a general European holocaust. The political implications of such a view have aroused enormous controversy in the Federal Republic since it relativises the Jewish holocaust; yet some of the views of Ernst Nolte, Andreas Hillgruber and Ernst Topitsch do shed light on the common origins and assumptions of the two major Molochs of the twentieth century, which together claimed between 70 and 100 million lives. The Soviet crimes against humanity, whose scale has been indicated above, were not unique. Destalinisation in the USSR has to be linked to an attempt to understand the monstrous nature of the early twentieth century.

Soviet historians have engaged in their own *historikerstreit* over Stalinism, and thus over *perestroika*. The central question is whether Stalinism was a natural evolution of the system bequeathed by Lenin or whether 'in the guise of socialism, [it] constituted a gross distortion of Leninist ideas about society' (O. Volubuev and S. Kuleshov, *SI*, 23 June 1988: 2–3). Conservative and radical views of Stalinism were vigorously debated at the time of the 19th party conference in 1988. Yuri Afanasev argued that a specific form of ownership based on function, tantamount to a kind of private property, had emerged in the USSR. He condemned the failure to deal with Trotsky in an objective manner, and decried the continued assumption that Lenin provided an answer to every question (*Literaturnaya rossiya*, 24, 17 June 1988). Pobisk Kuznetsov revealed the limits of destalinisation when he tried to refute Afanasev's arguments by emphasising that:

As the trailblazers of socialism, equipped with Lenin's guidelines for building socialism, we were unable and did not know how to be completely consistent, and external circumstances denied us that opportunity. That is why, the further we went, the more we deviated from Lenin's concept of socialism and thus produced a deformed socialist society. It is that deformed society and not the path that we travelled after October that we are rebuilding. We have not turned away from the path begun by the October revolution, as. . .Afanas'ev thinks; otherwise there would be no socialism in the world. (*P*, 15 June 1988: 3)

Kuznetsov further derided the idea of a 'Bukharinist alternative' in the 1920s to Stalin's path of development. In response Afanasev condemned evaluations that balanced the pros and cons of the Stalin period as an attempt 'to sacrifice Stalin to save Stalinism. That would mean missing the central point of the problem, evading the question of how far Stalin was the creator and at the same time the product of a system which was consolidated during his period in power.' This important debate finally examined the cardinal issues involved in destalinisation, namely, 'whether the society created in our country is or was truly socialist' and Lenin's role in developing a concept of socialism. For Afanasev, referring to his earlier article:

a) 'Despite tremendous sacrifices, we did not get socialism in the form in which Lenin and the Leninist cohort envisaged it in the 1920s', hence the need for *revolutionary*, that is, profound, structural *perestroika*; and b) The counter-revolutionary path of Stalin and his enormous apparatus was not historically inevitable and therefore justified, hence the opportunity in the course of *perestroika* to build on the unrealised, truncated, alternative economic, political, legal and sociopsychological potential of our country.

For Afanasev the alternative now was a democratic socialism that thoroughly repudiated the idea that socialism was being built *despite Stalin* and his deviations 'along an invariably glorious path'. The society inherited by Gorbachev in 1985 was not, according to Afanasev, a socialist society, even a 'deformed' one; hence a revolution rather than a reform was required to allow the Soviet people to start 'learning democracy' (*P*, 26 July 1988: 3).

The first steps have been taken to turn the searchlight of *glasnost* on to Lenin's rule. Contrary to the official view which argues that the murder of Tsar Nicholas II and his family in 1918 in Ekaterinburg was a panic local response in a time of civil war, it was now alleged that the shootings were sanctioned by the leadership in Moscow (Geli Ryabov, *MN*, 12 April 1989). In other words, terror and the shooting of children were inherited by Stalin rather than initiated by him. The full charge of Lenin's complicity in establishing the terror system inherited by Stalin is made in Solzhenitsyn's *Gulag Archipelago*, parts of which, as we have seen, were published in 1989 despite Medvedev's ban in November of the previous year. Vasilii Selyunin (1988) drew on quotations from Lenin to illustrate his ranting and personalised form of abusive attack. Selyunin directly stated that the system of forced labour and concentration camps was set up by Lenin during war Communism. A series of articles by A. S. Tsipko (1988−9) drew the theoretical threads between Lenin, Stalin and the Bolshevik revolutionary movement as a whole. He criticised the traditional class approach of Marxists, the belief that they have been vouchsafed a truth hidden from others, and scorned the attempt to build a democratic system on a non-market foundation, claiming that such a project was impossible and could in extreme circumstances 'become the basis for justifying any form of violence'. On the eve of Lenin's birthday on 18 April 1989 the actor Mark Zakharov suggested on the lively current affairs programme *Viewpoint* (*Vzglyad*) that Lenin's embalmed body should be removed from the mausoleum on Red Square and given a decent burial as desired by Lenin's wife, a view he repeated in a speech to the Congress in June 1989. The issue is an extremely sensitive one. As Sergei Sedov, the embalmer responsible for Lenin's body, argued, 'People who want to bury Lenin today really want to bury Leninism' (*P*, 27 October 1989).

While Stalin is dispensable to the legitimacy of Soviet power, Lenin is not. Gorbachev's appeals to return to an unsullied Leninism have been both an attempt to retain a version of revolutionary socialism and a way of maintaining the foundations on which to sustain Communist Party rule. The alternative to Leninist socialism, quite simply, is a return to multi-party democracy; hence the particularly sensitive nature of discussion of Soviet history under Lenin. The fundamental problem in coming to terms with the trauma of Stalinism is that the regime that gave birth to it is still in power. It is still difficult for Germany to come to terms with its Nazi past, but immeasurably more so for the Soviet Union. The Soviet past is still the Soviet present, whereas a clear line divides Nazi Germany from the liberal democratic present. Destalinisation can only be a partial process until it moves beyond re-evaluation and quantification of past crimes to the sincere repentance of the society involved. The recovery of memory is one thing, but a psychological vacuum remains until some sort of recovery of faith can help the society come to terms with what memory discovers.

Conservatives fear that destalinisation will inexorably lead to deleninisation. Such a consummation is, of course, devoutly wished by many. Destalinisation means a crisis of faith but at the same time provides a cause, if not an ideology, for the radical reformers. Destalinisation emerged as one of the central 'organising principles' of the reform process, a position it shares with nationalism and possibly religion. However, as *glasnost* revealed the scale and origins of Stalin's crimes the country's belief in its own past was perhaps fatally eroded. Destalinisation under Gorbachev was transformed into a slow-motion Nuremburg trial with potentially devastating consequences for the polity.

There are sociological limits to destalinisation, since a whole generation is implicated in the crimes and the ideology which condoned them. In a different way, this applies with even greater force to debrezhnevisation since those responsible for the policies which led to stagnation still hold important posts. Andrei Gromyko's *Memoirs* provide a fascinating portrait of the Stalinist ability to dissimulate and avoid facing up to the reality of the purges, the boundless cynicism of the Nazi–Soviet Pact which sought to share in a division of the spoils at the feast of dictators, and the narrow dogmatism which prompted the invasion of Czechoslovakia in 1968. Gromyko has disappeared from the scene, but still many lesser figures of that ilk remain. The Soviet leadership to a greater or lesser extent is still a beneficiary of Stalin's crimes. In China, the reformers tended to be the victims of Mao and thus could dissociate themselves from him. The equivalent category in the Soviet Union are all dead.

There are also historical limits to destalinisation. How far back is one to go without threatening the very legitimacy of the system? Khrushchev began his critique of Stalin from 1934. Others examined the faults in the NEP compromise of the 1920s. The critique could be extended to the nature of Lenin's rule. Even this is conditional and the first attempts have now been made to criticise the October Revolution itself. One does not have to stop there, and the limitations of the whole revolutionary movement of the nineteenth century can be taken into account in the evaluation of Stalinism, the approach taken by Nikolai Berdaev, with an awareness that there are Stalinist tendencies in the labour movements of all countries. Moreover, Stalinism is still sustained by powerful forces in Soviet society, as illustrated by Tofik Shakhverdiev's film *Is Stalin with Us?* (1989) (see also *Ogonëk*, 41/1989: 4). There remained a yearning for the 'strong hand' and the alleged 'order' of Stalin's years, and a rejection of *glasnost*'s 'blackening' (*ochernitelstvo*) of Soviet history, a term used by Ligachev to condemn the 'excesses' of *glasnost*.

Perestroika represented a dialectic between Gorbachev and Stalin. Both pushed through radical changes and there are some similarities in method. Both relied on the bureaucratic apparatus, however much they purged it, to promote revolutionary changes in society, and both also relied on popular enthusiasm harnessed 'for the good of the cause' and 'more socialism'. The fundamental difference, of course, is that whereas the enthusiasm was ultimately betrayed and used to disastrous purpose by Stalin, under Gorbachev it was intended precisely to overcome the legacy of Stalinism and to develop a humane type of socialism.

Towards a new concept of socialism

Zdeněk Mlynář, Gorbachev's room-mate at Moscow University in the early 1950s and a long-time friend, noted in 1985 that 'The choice of

Gorbachev was a novel event, offering a new chance for socialism' (cited by Hofheinz, 1987b: 164). Gorbachev tried to revive Communist ideology as a dynamic way of thinking about the human predicament and the development of human societies. Soviet ideology was rescued from the wooden formulae of the Brezhnev years when it was used to buttress the existing power system and the privileges of the *nomenklatura* class. The Leninist power system is a type of concretised ideology, and thus a change in institutions is usually reflected in a shift in ideology, and vice versa. Communist ideology, however, was always more than the forked tongue justifying the mailed fist. This view reduces ideology to propaganda, a way of justifying the policies of the power system. Ideology and authority have been in a far more complex relationship, but in its neo-Stalinist guise Soviet ideology was reduced to an ideology of political leadership to achieve economic modernisation and social welfare. It took no great intelligence in the 1980s to see that capitalism could provide both more effectively and at less cost. A new rationale for the system had to be found.

The problem for all Communist reformers is to find a satisfactory and convincing theoretical basis for change. The old model of socialism, for all its faults, was located in strong theoretical tradition, whereas reform socialism has constantly to create a philosophical space for itself between statist socialism and liberal democracy.

Chinese reforms even more than the Soviet ones lacked a theoretical foundation, and to fill the vacuum elements of Maoist ideology have been retained, buttressed by a belief that a rise in living standards will itself provide a new source of legitimacy for the regime (Cheng, 1989: 43). Neo-Maoism in this context thus paralleled the neo-Stalinism of the Brezhnev years, and the political stagnation thus engendered led to the events of 1989. Gorbachev has taken the contrary tack in the belief that political reforms should create the conditions for economic revitalisation.

Silviu Brucan argued that Gorbachev's greatest weakness was a lack of 'theoretical direction' (*Ind.*, 28 November 1988). While he was willing to respond in a pragmatic way to challenges, as in the moves to allow the long-term leasing of land to peasants, there appeared to be no overall theoretically defined substance to the reform process. On the world stage Gorbachev was able to change the post-war order. In domestic politics he came to power convinced that what the Brezhnev era complacently called 'real socialism' was a cruelly narrow and ineffective view of socialism. The reformed system was to be socialist but not Stalinist or neo-Stalinist. As the scale of the task revealed itself the piecemeal reforms turned into a general assault on the past and tried to create a new and more open-ended model for the future. *Perestroika* became a comprehensive attempt to reform the old model of socialism but it offered only an untried political and economic system to put in its place.

It is an exaggeration to talk of a single coherent ideology of reform, or indeed of a thought-out reform programme, which Gorbachev proceeded to implement. The concept of reform, given the name *perestroika*, became an ideology in the absence of a coherent reform programme. Hence the dynamic tension within *perestroika*: it was both a series of improvisations, often based on old theoretical formulations, *and* contained new ideas on democracy and society. As noted, it was both system-maintaining and system-transformative. Reform by definition is a transitional phase, a developing process which feeds on itself as it advances. The ideas which contribute towards an ideology of change are not always compatible but together contribute to achieve that 'restructuring of the mind' which is considered essential for reform (Lyubomirova *et al.*, 1989). Gorbachev's rhetoric lacks Khrushchev's bombast and is marked by an ideological modesty. His language is still heavily ideological but lacks grand formulations.

The deaths of Brezhnev and Suslov prompted a debate assessing how far the Soviet Union had gone down the path to a developed socialist society. At the June 1983 'ideology' plenum of the Central Committee Andropov urged flexibility in interpreting Marxism–Leninism and repeated earlier statements that the USSR was only in the early stages of socialist development, whereas Chernenko took a more dogmatic line in handling the sacred texts but argued that the country was well advanced in the transition to a mature socialist system (Andropov, 1983: 340–59; *P*, 16 June 1983). The implications of the contrasting views have been much debated. The key question was over the possibility of antagonistic contradictions under socialism and the nature of crises in socialist systems (Dahm, 1986). If Andropov was correct and the USSR was only at an early stage, then it suggested a need to develop heavy industry and to retain discipline to establish the foundations of socialism, whereas if a mature socialist society was already emerging then more attention could be paid to consumer goods and greater trust placed in a mature people. Democratic rather than disciplinarian measures would be appropriate. In his first years Gorbachev tended towards Andropov's views on economic development – hence the emphasis on investment in modernising industry and the cutback on the importation of consumer goods – but his political conclusions were diametrically oppposed. Gorbachev has not cited Andropov as the godfather of his reforms. His book *Perestroika* and his speech for the seventieth anniversary of the Revolution in 1987 made only formal acknowledgement of him. The reason is clear. Andropov's type of reforms were not to Gorbachev's taste and offered a very different idea of what had to be changed and how. Authoritarian *perestroika* was to give way to democratic *perestroika*.

Gorbachev did however take up Andropov's argument that ideology must be flexible to deal with changing reality. In his speech to party workers in Khabarovsk on 31 July 1986 Gorbachev condemned the 'dogma' of 'our home-grown scholastics' who turned socialist ideology into 'eternal truths' and impeded change (*Christian Science Monitor*, 4 August 1986:11). This part of the speech was broadcast in full that day, but cut from the newspaper reports on 2 August 1986. Gorbachev insisted that the very essence of Lenninism is 'an organic blend of theory and practice, an approach to theory as a tool of practice and to practice as a mechanism verifying the vaibility of theory' (*SN*, 1987: 402). Changes in ideology made possible changes in policy and institutions.

The party programme adopted at the 27th congress in 1986 was an updated version of the third party programme, initially introduced in 1961, rather than a new fourth programme. The programme was not the radical or innovatory document that some had expected. The intention, clearly, was to avoid giving the impression that the USSR had entered a qualitatively new phase in its development. In sharp contrast to the ebullience of Khrushchev's perspectives of 1961, the new programme was severely realistic, voicing general principles rather than specific goals (*Programme*, 1986; Gill, 1987; White and Pravda (eds.), 1988). The programme was neither a blueprint for the future nor a consistent programme for current reform. It accepted that the 'building of Communism' was not a smooth process but one subject to the vagaries of history. The concept of the 'state of the whole people' of the 1961 programme was further developed. The document offered few theoretical innovations or a new concept for the period, though it toyed with the notion of a subperiod of 'realistic socialism'. The draft programme (*P*, 29 October 1985) had talked of the current phase as one of 'integral socialism', presumably meaning that developments were now to be harmoniously combined to greater effect. The concept was omitted from the final version in favour of a modified notion of 'developed socialism', though Gorbachev warned against an overoptimistic interpretation of the concept (*P*, 7 March 1986). 'Developed socialism' no longer provided an adequate concept to understand Soviet reality and was replaced by the notion of an 'era of reform'. The 28th congress formed a commission to draft a new party programme (*P*, 14 July 1990).

The ideas fuelling the reform process have been eclectic. The reformers under Dubček in Czechoslovakia in 1968 began to develop a theory of reciprocal socialism in which party power was no longer imposed upon a passive society, but held its leading role through conviction and ability rather than traditional Communist power methods. The new openness of the system and the critique of Stalinist rule were, tragically, cut short and thus only the outlines of a new model of socialism were achieved.

The Czechoslovak experience contributed to the development of Eurocommunism, one of the major strands of reform Communist intellectual endeavour which sought to modify the dogmatism that sustained Brezhnevite orthodoxy. Some of the ideas which contributed to the Eurocommunist challenge of the 1970s reached back at least to the 1950s. In those years Palmiro Togliatti, the leader of the Italian Communist Party (PCI), cogently argued for polycentrism, the notion that there are many roads to socialism. The primacy of the Soviet model of socialist development was thus downgraded. Differing national roads to socialism had already been espoused by Communist leaders such as Wladislaw Gomulka in Poland in the immediate post-war years. By the 1970s Eurocommunism was exploring various aspects of Antonio Gramsci's thought, above all the notion of hegemony. The socialist revolution, Gramsci suggested, did not necessarily have to take place by a violent rupture with the past, as in the October Revolution of 1917. It could occur through a gradual 'war of position' in which the socialist forces could achieve influence and ultimately power through advances in the sphere of culture and society. There was no need for a violent assault on state power (Gramsci, 1971). The whole notion of the Leninist state was discredited and certain Eurocommunist parties, like the Spanish (PCE) under Santiago Carillo, went so far as to renounce Leninism altogether (Carillo, 1977).

The PCI rejected the Soviet model and in 1982 asserted that the evolutionary reserves of the Bolshevik Revolution had exhausted themselves. In place of the old idea of 'general laws', which Moscow claimed uniquely able to interpret, the PCI claimed many different paths to socialism; and in place of a 'world Communist movement' based on 'proletarian internationalism' it proclaimed a 'new internationalism' which encompassed various workers', social democratic and indeed ecological and feminist movements. The new internationalism allowed each party full independence, equality and mutual non-interference. The PCI's party congress of April 1986 continued its self-styled 'secularisation' or de-ideologisation, indeed 'Westernisation' in its attempts to become a 'modern reform party' (Timmermann, 1987: 4–7, 53–4). The transformation of the PCI under Achille Occhetto to some sort of liberal democratic party with a changed name which sought membership of the Socialist International demonstrated the historic reconciliation between revolutionary and evolutionary socialism. Eurocommunism challenged the division of the European Left brought about by the Bolshevik Revolution, and as the Berlin wall was dismantled in Germany, so in Italy the transformation of the PCI signalled the tearing down of a political Berlin wall. Eurocommunism, like *perestroika*, turned out to be only a transitional stage between revolutionary Communism and social democracy.

Gorbachev can be seen as a Eurocommunist. While by no means disclaiming Leninism as such, the import of his policies has been to modify Leninist practices. Soviet academics in the early 1980s were willing to accept that the Soviet model of socialism was not a universal precept (Butenko, 1982), a view Gorbachev accepted. The international Communist movement as such is dead (see Chapter 8) and the special links between the CPSU and other Communist parties have given way to a far more pluralistic interaction with various political forces in an interdependent world. Allowance for the national autonomy of Communist parties is clearly in the Eurocommunist tradition, and so is Gorbachev's tolerance for civil society, for the party to lead through hegemony rather than dictatorship, and his modifications to the theory of the socialist state; all mark him out as developing Eurocommunist ideas. Moreover, his emphasis on a common European culture exposed him to the charge of Eurocentrism, a complaint often levelled against the original Eurocommunists.

The ultimate trajectory of Eurocommunism was its transformation into a more radical version of social democracy, and Gorbachev's reforms followed much the same curve as the Soviet reformist leadership returned to the social democratic roots of Bolshevism and rethought its attitude to social democracy. Indeed, in some respects *perestroika* returned to the Menshevik argument that socialism is not an alternative to capitalist economic development but the end stage of it. This was implicitly a rejection of revolutionary Marxism in favour of the evolutionary perspectives of the Second International. Much of the ideological restructuring of the Gorbachev years tended towards the adoption of social democratic principles of political and social management. The Second and Third Internationals are indeed in practice coming together, and the historic division of socialism into a revolutionary socialist tendency led by the Bolsheviks and a democratic socialist branch represented by a number of West European social democratic and Eurocommunist parties is being overcome. The rejoining of these two tendencies at the same time lays the foundation for the physical reunification of Europe.

The '21 Conditions' adopted at the 2nd Comintern Congress in 1920 committed Communists to the struggle against social democracy, which Lenin considered had in 1914 betrayed socialism and in general had helped reconcile the working class to capitalism. However, the 1986 party programme no longer talked of 'right wing socialists' as 'the most important ideological and political prop of the bourgeoisie in the workers' movement', as asserted in the 1961 programme. Social democrats were now classified as part of the 'international Communist and workers' movement', though no ideological compromise was intended since both the revised programme and the party rules stressed the need for a determined struggle against 'revisionism and reformism'. However, the new social movements of the West now joined the long-established triad of existing socialist states, the international Communist and workers' movement, and the Third World national liberation movements as bulwarks of peace and anti-imperialism (*P*, 8 February 1986).

The corollary of the above is the rediscovery of the February 1917 'bourgeois democratic revolution', as it used to be dismissively termed in Soviet writing. The political practice of the February revolution included broad coalition politics, a popular front of all of 'democracy', as it was then called, based on a range of democratic popular institutions such as trade unions, soviets and dumas. Only the Bolsheviks stood apart, and in October 1917 they put an end to this profound democratic experiment. The February revolution has been rehabilitated to a degree by the publication of Vasilii Grossman's *Forever Flowing* in the July 1989 issue of *Oktyabr'*, in which Lenin is not only accused of bearing responsibility for the suffering of the country but also charged with terminating the democratic experiment: 'In February 1917 the road to freedom opened for Russia. And Russia chose Lenin.' Part of the reason for the descent into Stalinism of Bolshevik socialism is that in Russia the socialist revolution came before the democratic revolution had matured, and indeed, in its Leninist guise the socialist revolution deliberately set out to destroy the achievements of the February revolution. Now they are being restored.

One of the major sources of ideas for the reformers came from the experience of the NEP years in the 1920s. In particular, discussion focused on the ideas of Nikolai Bukharin. *Pravda* on 9 October 1988 linked Gorbachev's reform programme with Bukharin's fight against bureaucracy and his policies of balanced economic development. Bukharin's support for co-operatives, the market, his relative tolerance and his ability to look beyond the narrow interests of the working class to the good of all society were all cited as contributing to Gorbachev's *perestroika*.

At the same time Trotsky's theory of distortions has been brought out of the closet, although without attribution. Trotsky always denied that the 1917 socialist revolution had been transformed into some other system. For him the ascendancy of the bureaucracy and of Stalin personally only represented a degeneration on the basis of a fundamentally socialist foundation, the state ownership of the means of production. For Trotsky the bureaucracy was not a new class but only a stratum. The language of the modern reformers constantly returns to Trotskyist themes, but of course not by name. The idea that the basically correct Soviet system had somehow been distorted and all that was required was a stripping away of the accretions of the past has been a powerful one. Gorbachev and Khrushchev, like Trotsky, exhorted a return to an unsullied Leninism.

The rehabilitation of the NEP and the Bukharinist alternative to Stalinism has allowed the old unilinear version of Soviet history, as an ever-upward path, to be replaced by a dualistic version. Soviet reformers are drawing a sharp distinction between two models of Soviet power (Burlatsky, 1988b). The first is the war Communist model of 'administrative-command socialism', introduced between 1918 and 1921 and then once again taken up by Stalin in 1928 and which survived, with modifications, up to the time that Gorbachev's reforms began to transform the Soviet political system. The war Communism of the civil war period was characterised by the consolidation of authoritarian and administrative forms of economic and political management. All economic and political life underwent a massive centralisation, suffocating democratic initiatives and elements of the market in the economy. Hence the term war Communism is used to describe an overcentralised economic system in which resources are concentrated on narrow ends and in which political life is dominated by a bureaucratic apparatus.

Faced with economic breakdown and growing political fragmentation, Lenin in the months between February and May 1921 launched the NEP (see page 32f). What had begun as a retreat came to be seen as a viable path for the achievement of socialism, and was defended as such by leading Communists like Bukharin. However, the liberalisation of economic policy was not accompanied by the democratisation of political life. Indeed, the transition to the NEP saw for the first time the use of the term *perestroika*, but on this occasion it signified the intensification of war Communist political practices (Sakwa, 1989c). The tension generated by this discrepancy allowed Stalin to consolidate his power and in the late 1920s to bring the NEP experiment to an end. The 'revolution from above' once again brought war Communism back to economic life.

The first phase of Gorbachev's *perestroika*, the process of economic and allied reforms, can be seen as a historic shift from the old war Communist model of Soviet politics to a revival of aspects of the NEP. With greater or lesser intensity it was the war Communist model that dominated until the onset of the second phase of Gorbachev's reforms. The economist Nikolai Shmelëv argued in a famous article that it was now time to rapidly eliminate the war Communist legacy of running the economy through exclusively administrative methods. The NEP represented the transition from 'administrative socialism' to 'economic-accountability (*khozraschët*) socialism', releasing people's creative energies (Shmelëv, 1987).

The rather stark assertion of two sharply distinguished models does some damage to historical truth (cf. Cohen, 1985: 58) and blurs the elements of continuity and similarity between the two, though it serves the politically expedient end of endowing Gorbachev's reforms with an aura of historical and Leninist legitimacy. Lenin's own views of the NEP have been much debated: he insisted it was a system that would last 'for a long time and seriously' but, he added, 'not forever'. What would replace it? Lenin's fundamental belief was the bigger the better: a single state bank controlling investment capital and all aspects of monetary policy; even under the NEP he insisted on a state monopoly of foreign trade, which is only now being modified; large industrial enterprises were to swallow up smaller plants; and all of this was to be accompanied by rigid centralisation. Even before the onset of the civil war and war Communism in mid-1918 Lenin was advocating a type of state socialism which was only gradually modified after 1921.

In basic terms Leninism can be reduced to six major aspects: a theory of the organisation of the party and its leading role in society; a theory of imperialism and international revolution; the practice of class revolution; the building of the first socialist state based on the dictatorship of the proletariat; the practice of developmental socialism (in which socialism takes on the tasks of capitalism to industrialise and achieve modernity); and a theory of participatory democracy outlined in *State and Revolution* which can be called commune democracy. All of these to a greater or lesser extent were now reinterpreted and will be discussed in the appropriate places. With such a multi-planed *œuvre* it is not too difficult to find a Lenin of one's choice.

Neo-NEPism entails a still predominantly centralised system but with far more scope for the market and private initiative. It does not involve democratisation, despite a tendency to portray the NEP as a golden age of Soviet tolerance. Gorbachev's reforms, which combine economic and political reforms, are more than a neo-NEP but represent a radically new model of Soviet power. At root they reflect the crisis in developmental Leninism. The Bolsheviks came to power in a country which had neither the economic resources nor the social development expected by Marx to lie at the base of attempts to achieve socialism. The Bolshevik regime, of necessity, was forced to develop the economic base to match the political system. Rather than socialism being the fruit of capitalist development, it had to undertake the tasks fulfilled by capitalism but by novel means. Leninism thus had to find a way of optimising economic development and became, among other things, a theory of development. Developmental Leninism proved in the long run to be a relatively inefficient way of achieving economic modernisation, let alone political modernity.

The invocation of Lenin's authority was intended to endow reforms with a patina of ideological probity. Gorbachev created a mythological Lenin to suit his purposes, a Lenin of the last years before his death on 21 January 1924 as he fought to defend the NEP and assaulted the bureaucracy. The Lenin of the early NEP is portrayed as the forerunner of Gorbachev. The heart of Gorbachev's early ontology of reform was the concept of 'deformations and deviations'. This is clearly flawed since it could be argued that Leninism was part of the problem in the first place rather than a solution. This contradiction was avoided if not resolved by attempts to reinterpret Lenin, to mould him into a shape to suit the needs of the new generation of reform Communists. The fact that this has little in common with the historical Lenin does not seem to bother them unduly. The reinterpreters of Lenin are correct in arguing that under Lenin Bolshevism was still a diverse movement, bigger than Leninism itself and far broader than the Stalinism which followed. Gorbachev's reforms were initially an attempt to return to Bolshevism, reinterpreting Lenin in a way that vindicated the critiques of Leninism by such groups as the Democratic Centralists and the Worker Oppositionists. Under *perestroika* the debates of earlier periods of Soviet power over such issues as one-person management, egalitarianism, federalism and the meaning of social justice have been replayed. These debates were suppressed but never resolved. Now at last *glasnost* allowed the propositions of socialism to be tested against an actual rather than an idealised reality. By invoking the past to justify present changes Gorbachev revealed the ideological dependency typical of Communist leaders and inhibited the spontaneous generation of a rational ideology of reform independent of the writ of the past.

It is important to stress the Leninist roots of *perestroika*. While it may be irrelevant to ask whether Gorbachev is a Leninist, such a question can reveal something about the nature of the reforms. Gorbachev modified some of the key features of Leninism, yet at the same time extended others. As an attempt to translate theory into practice, Leninism is a dynamic and flexible corpus of thought. Up to early 1990 Gorbachev remained broadly within the Leninist tradition. He modified, however, the stark Leninist view of class struggle, of revolution and of the inevitability of conflict between systems caused, allegedly, by imperialism. At the same time Gorbachev defended the central Leninist proposition on the party's leading role, though he modified the ideological justification for it. He stressed the developmental aspects of Leninism over its revolutionary aspect, especially in the Third World (see Chapter 8).

While revolutionary Leninism may have suffered an eclipse, another element in Lenin's thought has been rehabilitated that had long been ignored, if not suppressed, namely his vision in 1917 in *State and Revolution* of a participatory form of democracy based on soviets. Commune democracy derives from a long tradition of Western political philosophy reaching from Marx to Rousseau and the Greek *polis*. It is the alternative to representative liberal democracy with its division of powers and emphasis on political rights based on a theory of competitive individualism. Lenin's espousal of commune democracy was a practical attempt to justify the destruction of the embryonic liberal democratic achievements of the February revolution and to develop a framework for the conduct of post-revolutionary politics. The soviets were to become the central institutional structure of mass participation and state power. The 'bourgeois' state was to be destroyed, and in its place a new socialist state was to be built: the state as such was to remain in the form of the dictatorship of the proletariat, though it was to contain the potential for its own withering away. In short, Gorbachev tried to revive the participatory element of Leninism, though he modified commune democracy to the degree that he imported some of the proceduralism and formalism of liberal democracy (Sakwa, 1989b).

During *perestroika* the relevance of ideas about commune democracy and the state have been defended (Lebedinskaya, 1988). E. Kuzmin argued that the divergence from Lenin's principles was caused by 'objective factors', above all socioeconomic backwardness, but that it was now possible to develop socialist popular self-management and socialist democracy (*P*, 24 August 1987). As in Lenin's time, there was little sense of a programme for the abolition of the state but there was a manifesto for the advancement of an inclusive participatory democracy. This was the justification for one-party democracy. While the means may have been democratisation, the end was not democracy in the liberal democratic sense. At stake was the revival and reinterpretation of the Marxist view of how to build an alternative to the liberal democratic state.

Soviet thinking on the relationship between class and state has always been marked by a tension between, on the one hand, a belief in the emancipatory potential of the proletariat and, on the other, the realistic appreciation that the much more immediately effective transformative agent was the state, especially in its modern form aided by sophisticated organisation, communication and technology. All the great socialist revolutions of our age have simultaneously, and perhaps primarily, been state-building endeavours. For ideological and historical reasons revolutions have led to the massive consolidation of state power. Marxism's reliance on the state as the agent of social transformation was reinforced by Lenin's strengthening of the socialist state to defend the Revolution in a hostile international environment. The novelty of Gorbachev's early reforms as far as socialism is concerned was the declining emphasis on the state; instead much greater faith was placed in society's ability to manage its own affairs.

The rethinking of the state has been accompanied by a re-evaluation of the role of class. In 1936 the notion of the dictatorship of the proletariat gave way to the idea of a multi-class socialist state, with the two great classes of the proletariat and the peasantry and a stratum not based on property, the intelligentsia. In practice Stalin insisted that the class struggle intensified as a system approached socialism, and thus justified his purges. Khrushchev in the 1961 party programme suggested that the absence of antagonistic classes rendered the notion of class struggle in Soviet society redundant. For his pains Mao Zedong labelled Khrushchev and his colleagues revisionists, asserting that all societies are class societies and that the class struggle would be waged in perpetuity. Gorbachev has taken up some of the ideas whose development had been stifled after 1968. A conference of sociologists in Minsk in that year asserted that Lenin's definition of class was no longer applicable to modern Soviet society. The old 'one class, one party' syllogism should, some of the bolder speakers argued, be replaced by a view of the party not simply as the vanguard of the working class but as a tool for the reconciliation of conflicts between diverse social groups. No longer was Soviet society viewed as homogeneous, as asserted by traditional Communist ideologues like V. Afanasev, but instead stratified and marked by class conflicts (Daniel Bell, *Dissent*, Fall 1988: 410). A.P. Butenko (1982, 1984) indeed argued that under socialism various contradictions, such as between productive forces and relations of production, and between production and consumption, were antagonistic and thus he denied the basic model of social harmony and non-antagonistic contradictions proposed by the concept of developed socialism. Gorbachev, freely borrowing from Zaslavskaya's Novosibirsk report, once again took up Marx's theory of contradictions, the main ones being, as Butenko pointed out, between the forces of production and the relations of production, and the class relations associated with this, and applied it to the Soviet Union with the bureaucracy instead of the capitalist class acting as the main antithesis of social control over the means of production.

Gorbachev's programme is an attempt to bring socialist Utopianism into line with changing reality. One of the main features of classical Bernsteinian revisionism is the rejection of the primacy of class politics. Marx identified Rousseau's general will with the interests of a single group in society, the working class. Gorbachev modified this in favour of a broader humanitarianism. The rhetoric of working-class power has been reduced and the role of class and class struggle in the development of socialist society has been played down. There is a fundamental reappraisal of the idea of an innate or pre-existing sense of class consciousness in the proletariat 'in itself' which could be awakened for the class to become one 'for itself' (Marx) or inspired by a revolutionary organisation from outside (Lenin). In this Gorbachev has taken the first steps on the theoretical path adopted by the Frankfurt School in questioning the proletariat's liberating role (cf. Kolakowski, 1978: 342). The new humanitarianism propounded by *perestroika* rejected class struggle as the primary motor of history, and thus allowed a moderation of the authoritarianism of seventy years of statist socialism in the USSR.

Gorbachev's appeals have been to the population as a whole rather than to any particular group, and policies have no longer been couched in class terms but have appealed to universal values. This allowed a greater role for the intelligentsia. Humanitarianism emphasises the common problems of all of humanity rather than the sectional concerns of any one group, or indeed nation (see *Winning the Human Race*, 1988). The denigration of class as the main criterion of policy formulation, however much this had been the case in practice in the past, exposed Gorbachev to the charge of élitism. His humanitarianism has been far from populism, and the interests of humanity are defined from the perspective of the 'authoritative part of society' (Gorbachev, 1987a: 153). This was accompanied by a condemnation of American mass society from a neo-Nietzschean perspective (Gorbachev, 1987a: 208).

Some of Gorbachev's statements are reminiscent of the arguments of the Praxis group of revisionist Marxists in Yugoslavia from 1964. Their revisionism asserted that Marxism provides the intellectual basis for reforms to existing socialist regimes, a belief that these systems are reformable while remaining Communist. Their emphasis on alienation, reification and bureaucracy all challenged basic Leninist notions of the leading role of the party and Soviet conceptions of state-centred socialism. They insisted that Marx's analysis of humanity's relationship with nature, as subject and object, precluded deterministic interpretations. Hence they emphasised that people were not 'determined' by nature or history, but that 'people make their own history', and that 'history did not make people'. They thus generated a new notion of freedom leading to criticism of Soviet state socialism. Gorbachev's emphasis on a humanistic form of socialism, and above all his stress on the 'human factor', may well have been taken from the pages of *Praxis* with its return to an allegedly more humanitarian young Marx in preference to the economistic and deterministic mature Marx. The humanisation of socialism indeed is the project of the Budapest school in later years (see D. Brown, 1988). As Communist ideology loses some of its Utopianism, or other-worldly aspirations, the way is opened to the rehumanisation of the socialist project. However, revisionism as defined here may well be doomed to fail since it is too close to the critical categories of Marxism that engendered the problems in the first place.

Perestroika has been seen as the transition from totalitarianism, which strives to control all aspects of social existence, to authoritarianism, a form of government which is relatively independent of democratic control but concedes areas of autonomy in social and economic life (see page 88). Gorbachev's reforms are a denial of the totalitarian aspirations which, however weakened, still lay at the heart of the system up to 1985, but the changes do not simply represent a transition to authoritarianism. The emphasis on self-management and the democratisation of society, however ambivalent, go much further (see Davis, 1990).

The continuing elements of authoritarianism can be much better understood as a form of democratic *dirigisme*. Party *dirigisme* was justified by the historicism of the old model of Soviet socialism, the belief that history is moving towards some defined stage guided by the party. This gave rise to the concept of 'building socialism', a necessarily mechanistic view of social development. The term has disappeared from Gorbachev's vocabulary and in its place a far more complex view of socialism as a set of organic human relations has gained prominence. The understanding of the individual and his or her needs has in this light been reinterpreted. For over seventy years the USSR has been looking for the 'new socialist person', and instead created *homo Sovieticus*, characterised by Aleksandr Zinoviev (1984) as egotistical, intrusive and concerned with the short-term maximisation of pleasure. The decline in historicism allowed a greater appreciation of the different paths that can be pursued by a socialist government. Not only has the variety of paths been accepted, but confidence in the end has also been lost, and in this there is a modification of the old Utopian belief in some beatific end state of Communism. *Perestroika* represented the end of teleology and a disjuncture in that the present is recognised to be the 'end', so to speak; thus the means to achieve a satisfactory 'non end' in the present becomes more important than the 'end' itself. Kant's categorical imperative has thus triumphed.

Closely associated with a re-evaluation of the role of class is a new approach to the role of property in social relations. For traditional Marxists, the private ownership of productive property was regarded as the major source of economic and political inequality. However, the hopes of the early Bolsheviks that the abolition of private ownership of the means of production would somehow lead to political equality were not realised. It became increasingly clear that the political system itself could give rise to inequality. For this reason the new analyses of Stalinism have examined the social forces that supported Stalin: forces that did not own property and hence were not classes in the classical sense, but which nevertheless constituted powerful social blocs.

The re-evaluation of the role of property opened the door to an increased emphasis on co-operatives and leasing, and ultimately private ownership. At the root of the old socialist vision was a view of private property as the root of all evil. In October 1988 the new head of the ideology commission, Vadim Medvedev, suggested that 'the relationship of property should be reorganised. We must overcome the separation which has grown up between the individual and state ownership' (*P*, 5 October 1988). This allowed a reappraisal of the role of the market under socialism. Medvedev went so far as to claim that 'The market – if speculative distortions are eliminated – is one of the greatest achievements of human civilisation' (*K*, 17/1988: 17).

One of the major ideological revisions of the Gorbachev years was the denunciation of egalitarianism as a primitive socialist ideal. In June 1931 Stalin had declared that 'equality-mongering' (*uravnilovka*) was anti-socialist, but under Khrushchev and Brezhnev it had returned in wage policy. The deleterious consequences on labour productivity has been much analysed since 1985, focusing on the lack of incentives for productivity. The neo-Stalinist commitment to egalitarianism led to passivity, inertia, the unchallenged rule of the huge socialist monopolies and a mentality of 'poverty in equality'. In a broader sense there has been some discussion which sees egalitarianism as the enemy of freedom. While egalitarianism might have lost some of its prestige, the development of a notion of social justice at the heart of the reform process acts to counter the growth of inequality (see Chapter 7).

Soviet ideology has been modified by several perspectives that, while by no means original in themselves, have together reshaped the Soviet way of viewing the world. Notable among these is the increased emphasis on environmentalism. In the past the proud boast of the Bolsheviks was that they could remould the world in the service of the proletariat. As Stalin put it, 'There are no fortresses that the Bolsheviks cannot storm.' The result of the exaggerated anthropocentrism was seen in the theories of Lysenko, which held that species could rapidly evolve to suit human needs. Nature was seen as a raw material to be moulded, and indeed despoiled, for the alleged good of humanity. While the constitution and media stressed the need for conservation, ecological concerns certainly lost out to the industrial lobby arguing for the most rapid economic development. Now the policy has shifted from declarations to a more profound respect for the environment. The new approach to nature at the same time means a new respect for the quality of human relationship, the moral ecology of politics (cf. Moiseev, 1989a).

The shift was preceded by popular anxiety over the wasteful and destructive patterns of economic development pursued by the Soviet regime. These concerns were vividly revealed in the decision to cancel the planned diversion of part of the flow of the Siberian rivers from North to South in August 1986 under the pressure of 'public opinion' (*P*, 17 August 1986). The plan would have been the largest civil engineering project on earth and entailed an extravagant diversion of scarce resources from more productive investment. For the first time in some fifty years the Gorbachevite reformers accepted that there must be limits to the frantic drive for the industrialisation of the country. In 1987 the ban on tree-felling and the phasing out of the two cellulose plants polluting Lake Baikal, the largest volume of fresh water in the world, were achieved after a twenty-five-year campaign by conservationists led by the writer Valentin Rasputin. It represented one of the more remarkable concessions to ecological security made by the government. No longer was nature to be indiscriminately plundered in the pursuit of economic growth. The Chernobyl disaster of 26 April 1986 meanwhile had further heightened ecological concern and led to a more cautious programme of building nuclear power stations.

Both the content and form of Soviet ideology began to change. The elements contributing to the new ideology could be almost indefinitely extended, including a new understanding of socialist efficiency and the realisation that Soviet isolationism was economically and politically detrimental, thus giving greater prominence to notions of globalism and interdependence (see Chapter 8). Gorbachev's speech to the United Nations on 7 December 1988 appeared to relegate the Russian Revolution to the past by stressing the new problems facing the world that transcended national boundaries.

Much of the above can be summarised as the social democratisation of Communist ideology. The basic problem for the reformist leadership was how to combine political democracy with an efficient economic system while preserving what were considered some of the social benefits of traditional state socialism. The 'Swedish model', in particular, exerted a growing fascination for Eastern Europe and the Soviet Union (Aslund, 1989: 184; Timmermann, 1989b). The key point was the realisation that Lenin's 'temporary' restrictions on democracy had been unduly prolonged, and now the experience of the Western socialist parties' use of the 'democratic institutions of capitalism' and of the market should be applied to the USSR (Lipitskii, 1989). Thus the market and commodity production are seen to be something common to both socialism and capitalism rather than being the exclusive attribute of the latter. They are, in short, neutral and independent of the political system (Timmermann, 1989b: 180). However, as noted above, there remained a firm rejection of convergence.

The ideological restructuring described above adds up to what is in effect a hybrid form of democracy suitable for late Communism. The sheer scale of the Soviet Union means that it will have to develop unique solutions to achieving a democratic polity. At the basis of the new model of socialism was a belief that economic revival requires a greater scope for individual freedoms and a new structure for political life. The authorities lacked the legitimacy or strength to impose painful economic solutions and hence sought to co-opt broader sections of society, but expanded power-sharing was more than a manoeuvre to blunt popular anger.

The new democracy was an attempt to achieve a synthesis of Soviet traditions and Western practices, the dominant role for the Communist Party together with elements of representative democracy. No doubt part of the reason for Gorbachev's reluctance to embrace full-blooded pluralism was the understandable fear that thereby the party might degenerate into a faction-ridden alliance of interests and groups. As we shall see, this indeed did take place. Instead of using class consciousness as the 'big idea' to promote cohesion in the party, Gorbachev turned to a broader conception of humanitarian and global values combined with responsive political leadership and effective participation. The new democracy represented the rediscovery of politics as a form of contestation, separation of powers and individual conscience.

Soviet ideology developed in response to attempts to change the outer world by a group who felt they had grasped, through Marxism, the secret of the march of history. Marxism had little to say about the inner life of the movement devoted to achieving the changes sanctioned by history. This is what *perestroika* entailed. Soviet leaders had an ideology of revolution and social transformation, but they lacked an ideology of reform. The old revolutionaries before 1917 in Russia could draw on a tradition some hundred years old on which to base their challenge to the old system, and they called on the rhetoric of ancient struggles of the poor and oppressed to sustain their challenge. The problem for modern reformers was that much of this rhetoric was closed to them, and they had to make do with apparently much more modest justifications for their attempt to change.

The debate over the speed and course of reform between, on the one hand, radical reformers and on the other, 'conservatives' like Ligachev and Chebrikov is reminiscent of the Left-Right debates of the 1920s. The struggle was between those in favour of, at the minimum, certain features of the NEP, and those who restricted themselves to modifications of the war Communist model. The latter blunted the radical thrust of Gorbachev's strategy, but were hesitant to brand the ideological *perestroika* 'revisionism', the worst charge in the Communist lexicon of abuse. The open use of the term would have exposed them to the charge that they were reviving Stalinist or Brezhnevite witch-hunts against ideological deviancy and debate. Perhaps rather than seeing Gorbachev's reforms as 'revisionist' one could argue that they were a long-delayed corrective to the ultra-leftism practised by successive Soviet leaders. One of the factors making *perestroika* such a tortuous process was the 'conservative role of dogmatic ideas on the nature of socialism which are deeply embedded in various groups of the population' (Nekipelov, 1989: 15). In particular, the conservatives objected to the challenge to Leninism and to the myth of 'building socialism'.

Gorbachev's speech on the seventieth anniversary of the Revolution on 2 November 1987 to a degree legitimated the concerns of the conservatives (*P*, 3 November 1987). His attempt to steer a middle course between the 'avant-gardism' of radicals like Eltsin and the 'conservatism' of Ligachev was clearly a compromise and was probably an inherently unworkable option. Either the reform process had to advance rapidly or it was doomed to languish and ultimately be stymied by the resistance of the bureaucracy. Gorbachev's 'turmoil' speech of 7 May 1988 sowed further confusion in the ranks of the radicals by talking of a panic taking the form of people asking: 'Isn't *perestroika* coming to mean the wrecking and rejection of the values of socialism?' (*SN*, 1988: 167). The fate of the 11 million strong band of professional ideologists and propagandists is clearly bound up with the fate of the ideology itself.

Such fears were given concrete form in the Nina Andreeva affair. Andreeva, a chemistry teacher in Leningrad, gave voice, with Ligachev's covert assistance, to a type of anti-cosmopolitan (i.e. anti-Semitic) Russian national Communism. The sacking of Boris Eltsin in November 1987 was interpreted by the conservatives as a sign that their star was in the ascendant. In her letter titled 'I Cannot Give up my Principles' she voiced the fears of the neo-Stalinists and conservatives about the destabilising effects of *glasnost* and *perestroika*, urged a 'balanced' assessment of Stalinism, voiced shock over the view that the class struggle was an obsolete concept and condemned classless 'humanism' and 'left-liberal intellectual socialism' (*Sovetskaya rossiya*, 13 March 1988). After a tense period of several weeks, in which the progressive forces went strangely quiet as a number of regional party leaders took this as the signal for an onslaught against radical *perestroika*, a vigorous, though confused, riposte was given in *Pravda* (5 April 1988).

Despite the radicalism of the 19th party conference resolutions, the following period was marked by a conservative counter-attack. Ligachev's speech in Gorky on 5 August 1988 has been noted (see page 52), and he was joined in the attack by Chebrikov (*P*, 2 September 1988). They were confronted by Yakovlev and Shevardnadze, and to a lesser extent Medvedev, who emerged as leaders concerned with elaborating the theoretical basis for a revised form of socialism. From this time a new sense of theoretical confidence allowed departures from a style of argumentation which relied on a precedent or statement from the life or works of Lenin. During a tour of Latvia and Lithuania in August 1988 Yakovlev noted that the Soviet people were 'learning the basics of Marxism all over again'. The primacy of the class struggle was rejected together with the belief that humanity could arrive at a conflict-free state. There were 'eternal' questions facing society and humanity which must be resolved time and time again. The difference between the socialist market and the capitalist one was seen to lie 'not by the movement of commodities, capital or even the workforce, but by the social processes which accompany it'. The alienating effect of old-style nationalisation was rejected and property, while on the whole remaining in the hands of the socialist state, was to become the property of a group of specific producers. This was to be achieved through long-term leasing of land, the creation of labour brigades in factories with the right to organise their time, and the extension of the co-operative movement to cover not only small-scale production but also larger enterprises. In the political sphere Yakovlev lauded the new 'pluralism of views and emerging polyphony' in Soviet society, and noted that this would inevitably be reflected in terms of nationality (*P*, 11 August 1988).

In autumn 1988 Gorbachev, though still not aligning himself with the radicals, dealt the conservatives some decisive blows (see page 16). In October the new head of the ideology commission swiftly raised the tempo of ideological restructuring now that Ligachev's restraining influence had been marginalised. In his first major speech Medvedev outlined a 'new conception of socialism' that was reminiscent of some of Bukharin's ideas (*P*, 5 October 1988: 4). Brezhnev's view that the Soviet Union had become a 'society of developed socialism' was rejected as a premature one which had ignored the real problems. The country had much to learn from the West, not simply in the realm of technology but also about the social and economic structures that sustained it. Medvedev's programme of political and economic change endorsed private enterprise and the role of the market as an 'indispensable means of economic co-ordination between production and consumption'. Co-operatives were to be developed and the NEPist idea of leasing industrial enterprises was brought out of the closet. Already the leasing of farms was being hesitantly introduced into agriculture, reflecting the changed appreciation of the role of property and state ownership and the relationship between the plan and market.

However, as during the first NEP, political reform was restrained. Medvedev conceded that the idea of 'socialist pluralism', espoused by Gorbachev over the summer of 1988, permitted the development of the host of social organisations, but it did not permit 'the artificial creation of other parties to oppose the Communist party's policies'. Medvedev expounded the idea that Soviet policy had moved beyond narrow 'class-based approaches', latterly espoused by Ligachev in Gorky in domestic and foreign policy. As usual, Medvedev was careful to stress that the ideological innovations were firmly in the Leninist tradition. All that they represented, he insisted, was a return to first principles freed of the distortions of Stalin and Brezhnev.

The ideological counter-offensive remained poised to attack and the debate continues. In February 1989 Chebrikov condemned the harm that 'certain so-called informal organisations' were doing (*P*, 11 February 1989). In the wake of election defeats in March 1989 the conservatives launched a bitter attack at the CC plenum of 25 April 1989. Many urged restrictions on unofficial organisations and the Press. Rahman Vezirov, at the time head of the Azerbaidzhani party organisation, argued that the mass media were biased towards 'people with certain views and intentions. . . They are trying to remove our ideological immunity, and inoculate our people with ideological Aids.' A barely concealed hostility to Gorbachev and the party's central bodies emerged in the speech of Ratmir Bobovnikov, the First Secretary of the Vladimir regional party organisation, in his argument that 'We must stop denigrating party workers. . . It's becoming impossible to find people willing to take lower-level local party jobs', and his warning from Lenin that 'One should think twice when your class enemy praises you.' Yuri Solovëv, the Leningrad party leader who had suffered a crushing defeat in the polls, blamed everyone except himself for his defeat. Gennadi Kolbin, at the time party leader of the Kazakhstan republican party organisation, bluntly warned Gorbachev that the lack of economic improvements would threaten the leader's own position. The confusion sown by the ideological restructuring was poignantly expressed by Ivan Polozkov, at the time leader of the Krasnodar *oblast* organisation: 'What is socialism today? What is the role of the working class? What are the political and philosophical principles of our society's renewal?' (*P*, 27 April 1989; see also Gleisner, 1989: 19–24).

Ligachev kept up his rearguard action against the 'new model of socialism'. He urged the party to resist forces that were trying to undermine socialism and that had a distinctly unsocialist view of *perestroika*, and wanted to create private property, encourage the market and establish a multi-party system (*P*, 9 September 1989). In an extensive interview Ligachev put forward a coherent conservative view of *perestroika*, arguing that socialism still had 'colossal resources'. He insisted that it was impossible to 'modernise socialism. . .using capitalist economic methods', and argued that the country did not need private property. For him the failings were purely technical and human, whereas the Soviet system was basically healthy. The key thing, he argued, was for the party to retain the unity of its ranks. There was no third way, either socialism or capitalism (*A.iF.*, 42/1989: 1–3). These views were reflected in the election of Polozkov as leader of the new Communist Party of Russia in June 1990 and in the debates at the 28th party congress.

In order to secure his flank against the charge of revisionism Gorbachev was careful to stress the socialist and Leninist pedigree of his ideas. He insisted that his changes, as he said in his Khabarovsk speech of 31 July 1986, should not be seen as a 'shaking of the foundations, a repudiation of our principles'. On the contrary, they were within the framework of socialism and were 'designed to fully develop the potential and superiority of the socialist system' (*Christian Science Monitor*, 4 August 1986: 11). However, the more radical of the reformers moved beyond these formulations and began thinking in post-Marxist terms. The cumulative impact of the revelations of *glasnost* and growing disillusionment provoked Len Karpinsky to lament that 'it is now hard to defend Marxism in public' (*MN*, 43/1989: 8).

Gorbachev took up the assertions that there was an ideological vacuum at the heart of *perestroika* in an important article called 'The socialist idea and revolutionary *perestroika*' (*P*, 26 November 1989). His arguments can be reduced to four. The first was his insistence that Marxism was not a blueprint to be implemented, but an idea to be developed: 'Some people try to reproach us that we have no clear-cut detailed plan to realise the concept of *perestroika*', Gorbachev admitted, but he insisted that it would have been a mistake 'to impose ready-made schemes upon society', which he argued had been the characteristic feature of Stalinism. The second point was the need to guarantee the socialist character of *perestroika* as the continuation of the ideals of the October Revolution. He insisted that the Revolution was not an error since there was no realistic alternative, and rejected the view that a bourgeois democratic republic had been an option in 1917. Instead the choice, he argued, was between the Bolshevik Revolution or 'an anarchic mutiny, a bloody dictatorship of the military and the establishment of a reactionary anti-popular regime'. The key point here was to discredit the idea of a democratic non-Marxist alternative to the October Revolution in 1917, and thus to rebuff the views of an increasing number of radical reformers that the Bolshevik Revolution had been a gigantic mistake which needed to be corrected immediately by shedding socialist dogmatism. Once again, Gorbachev insisted that it was Stalin who had deformed the Revolution rather than there being any intrinsic fault in the initial project. He went on to defend socialism as an idea, and asserted that Marxism could in no way be responsible for the 'deformations of socialism'.

The third argument held that while the party was to shed its day-to-day administrative and managerial functions, it was to become 'the centre for the elaboration of political and ideological platforms recommended to society and the state in the shape of its elective bodies'. The fourth argument concerned the balance to be drawn between pluralism and centrifugal tendencies in society. He insisted that 'A new quality of social being and a new aspect of socialism are crystallising in the competition of various economic and social forms, institutions and ideological trends.' The party would promote the development of pluralism, Gorbachev promised, but he warned that 'the party may not concede the initiative to either populist demagoguery, nationalist or chauvinist currents or to the spontaneity of group interests.' The country's ethnic diversity forced the retention of a strong hand in the form of the party, which would prepare the way for democracy. Moreover, there was a need for a consistent reforming force to push through the economic reforms, whose scale Gorbachev likened to a time of war, against the conservatism and bureaucratic inertia of the system.

There remained an ambiguity in Gorbachev's argument in that he had earlier noted that socialism was the 'natural product of the progress of civilisation and of the historical creative endeavour of the people': in other words, he espoused the earlier view of socialism as the successor to capitalism, and at the same time insisted it was the only alternative. Moreover, he failed to answer his own rhetorical question 'What meaning should be put into the notion of a new quality of society and new aspect of socialism?' The only clear answer, as we shall see in Chapter 4, was for the continuation of a leading role for the Communist Party, 'for the time being' at least.

The rejection of the old monolithic concept of state socialism meant, as Kryuchkov argued, that 'there is no universal model of socialism' and that 'attempts to unify and standardise social development in different countries are doomed to failure' (*P*, 5 November 1989). An ideology of reform was thus generated which went by the name of *perestroika*. *Perestroika* was in a sense the last Soviet mass campaign whose very success would make future national struggles on this scale, other than in times of national emergency, redundant, and indeed impossible. Struggles against leftists, rightists, kulaks, bureaucrats, alcohol and speculators should become a thing of the past.

This is not to suggest that there is an 'end to ideology' in the Soviet Union. Since the 1950s social scientists like Daniel Bell have predicted that the imperatives of industrialisation and modernisation would inevitably lead to a diminution in the role of ideology. Policy would become more instrumental as society became more complex and moved into the 'post-industrial' era. In the 1960s and 1970s the so-called behavioural revolution in Soviet studies, which focused on the actual behaviour of individuals and institutions rather than on programmatic statements or on the formal structures of power, gave a further boost to the end of ideology thesis. In East and West the prediction proved premature, if not wrong. Ideology in the Soviet Union, however modified, still plays a crucial role. Under Gorbachev there was still an attempt to limit the reforms to what was ideologically acceptable, even though the boundaries of the acceptable were pushed back dramatically.

We need to be clear about what we mean by talking of the 'end of ideology' or the de-ideologisation of Soviet politics under Gorbachev. It could mean that Marxism–Leninism no longer prescribes itself as the universal answer to all questions. There is a declining role for the ideology to act as a state religion demanding universal obeisance. There is a decline in Utopianism and the teleological elements of building socialism towards some end state. The belief that Marxism–Leninism is a rational way of developing society has declined. The primacy of class has been replaced by a broader humanistic vision. Despite all this, the argument that Gorbachev is a technocrat is not convincing. He believes in a major role for ideology in the transition to socialism, his key slogan is more socialism rather than less, and his revival of effective politics refutes the technocratic option of reform. But Gorbachev is a pragmatist marked by flexibility and a strong learning ability. Rather than talking of 'de-ideologisation' it might be better to think in terms of the secularisation of the ideology.

The whole notion of *perestroika* was clearly a highly artificial construct. *Perestroika* as an idea was used to control and direct the pace of change. In other words, *perestroika* acted simultaneously both as a motor and a brake, hence placing almost unbearable strains on it. Gorbachev's personal ability to learn from his mistakes was itself a powerful element in the process of ideological restructuring. In many ways thinking about ideas had been divorced from the business of staying in power. *Perestroika* was not a blueprint to be implemented but more a series of improvisations.

Marxism always proclaimed itself a rational-secularist way of thinking, but under Bolshevism it was marked by a pseudo-rationalism that destroyed creative thinking. Now Gorbachev returned to the older tradition. His achievement was not to proclaim any grand new theory but to modify and try to breathe new life into the old one. There was however a growing epistemological break in Soviet ideology in which the transition from a class-based to a humanitarian approach reversed Marx's own transition from a concern with alienation to an obsession with production. Gorbachev constantly called for more socialism. But what sort of socialism? It is unlikely that Gorbachev himself knew his final goal, the shape of the new society to be born out of *perestroika*, other than that it would look very different from the present version. The debate over ideology was a debate over socialism. The ideological upheaval in the Soviet Union had profound implications for socialists throughout the world. Gorbachev was no Martin Luther, nor indeed a Lenin, and was not prepared to countenance a schism in the true church in the cause of his convictions; he was rather a leader of a Counter-Reformation who tried to revive a stagnating revolutionary tradition (Michnik, 1988). Ideological *perestroika* after 1985 gradually generated an ideology of reform without which the institutional reforms would have been no more than castles in the air. The next step, though, was to provide an institutional framework to sustain and develop the new ideology.

4

DEMOCRACY, POLITICS AND THE PARTY

The Bolshevik Revolution was overinstitutionalised, in the sense that there were several potentially competing centres of power after 1917 including the trade unions, the secret police and the economic bureaucracy. Above all there was an unclear division of functions between the Communist Party and the soviets. Gorbachev sought to remake the state in order to overcome the constitutional confusion generated by parallelism, but there was little chance of success as long as political and state bodies competed for sovereignty. The problem facing the reformist leadership was to find a new basis for the political authority of the regime and to achieve some sort of democratic legitimacy drawing on the elements of consensus in Soviet society. A new way of conducting politics had to be found, but it remained unclear what form this might take. As S. K. Grossu, then leader of the Moldavian party organisation, put it in June 1988: 'The question of power, that is the central question of *perestroika*' (*XIX konf.*, vol. 2: 40). This can be seen both in terms of 'who rules' and also in the way that rule is conducted. The state began to be reorganised as part of the intended shift of power from political to state bodies and the principle of rule of law was established.

The socialist legal state and democracy

One of the central aspects of Communist reformism is the attempt to establish a legal and constitutional structure for politics. Indeed, reforms throughout history have been identified with a more prominent role for law. One of the watchwords of the reforms of Alexander II in the 1860s was *zakonnost*, or legality, which transformed the legal culture of late tsarism. During *perestroika* legal reform has taken the form of an attempt to establish a 'state governed by law' (*pravovoe gosudarstvo*). This entailed an effort to transform Soviet political culture by modifying socialism's traditional emphasis on collective rather than individual rights. Moreover, full Communism implied the end of the state, whereas a 'socialist legal state' suggests a retreat from the radical Utopianism of the Communist project.

In certain respects a socialist legal state is a contradiction in terms in that it places limits on the state's ability to transform society. It represents a major theoretical departure from the view of law propounded by early Soviet leaders. The last decades of tsarism had seen the transition of Russian legal philosophy from autocratic liberalism into a more democratic liberalism, which in turn became a democratic liberal socialism (Walicki, 1987). After 1917 this tradition was abruptly reversed and the legal system was constructed according to the principles of Marxist–Leninist ideas of class struggle and the necessity of a strong state to defeat enemies and build socialism. Theory, in other words, came before law, whereas in the West the political system and laws regulating the power system evolved simultaneously. This has added a distinctive colour to the Soviet view of law and human rights. As P. I. Stuchka put it in the early years of Soviet power, 'Communism means not the victory of socialist law, but the victory of socialism over law.' The Soviet legal scholar A. G. Goikhbarg argued in 1924 that 'Every conscious proletarian knows. . .that religion is the opium of the people. But rarely does anyone. . .realise that law is an even more poisonous and addictive opium for the same people' (cited Szawlowski, 1988: 379). The 'legal state' was considered to be not only bourgeois, but an absurdity as far as Lenin was concerned. In the 1920s E. B. Pashukanis proposed what was in effect a nihilistic theory of law which argued that under socialism society would be harmonious and self-regulating and therefore would not need to order social relations through the 'bourgeois' mechanism of law.

This approach was gradually modified but in essence remained in force until 1985. The director of the Institute of State and Law, N. Kudryavtsev, claimed that 'legal nihilism, the notion that we can do without laws, not only exists: these views are still rather widespread, especially among personnel at the lower levels of the state apparatus' (*Iz.*, 2 July 1987: 5; cf. Nersesyanits, 1989: 9). Indeed, the whole notion of a legal state was regarded as 'bourgeois liberal' until recently (Gryazin, 1988: 266). Gorbachev's own legal training as a 'jurist' led him to realise that 'democracy cannot exist and develop without the rule of law' (1987a: 105). The basic idea of the socialist legal state is to strengthen democracy through law and to avoid arbitrariness. Under Gorbachev a veritable revolution in legal culture was launched. The

19th party conference in 1988 set out a programme which tried to separate the legal system from the power system. The conference sought to clarify laws and thus reduce the scope for their arbitrary interpretation by the bureaucracy. The resolution 'On Legal Reform' called for 'the legal protection of the individual and secure guarantees of the Soviet people's political, economic and social rights and freedoms' (*XIX konf.*, vol. 2: 173). The individual, rather than the collective or the abstract interest of the class, state or Communism, as interpreted by the party, was thus made the fundamental unit of society.

A crucial aspect of this was that the party and its officials were no longer to stand above the law. No appeal to a higher law of class interests could take precedence over due process. Analysis moved from 'socialist legality' to a socialist legal state. The socialist legality espoused in the Khrushchev to Brezhnev years was an attempt to prevent the return of arbitrary terror, yet despite much legislative achievement (Butler, 1987) it remained limited in that the leadership was not willing to deprive itself of certain prerogatives in the pursuit of its own ends, such as the suppression of dissent. The USSR continued as pre-constitutional in the sense that the party remained the ultimate judge of what was legal and tolerated in the name of the defence of higher interests of the socialist state and the working class. It was against this double standard, which allowed the authorities to flout their own laws and constitution, that much dissident activity was directed. The reaffirmation of the leading role of the party by the 19th party conference, however, inhibited the creation of a socialist legal state. While the prerogatives associated with the 'leading role' may have been tempered, they were not abolished; hence the pressure for the repeal of Article 6 of the 1977 constitution guaranteeing the party's dominance.

The concept of a 'state governed by law' is derived from the German *Rechtsstaat*, and in Anglo-Saxon countries is simply denoted by the emphasis on the rule of law. The new concept of a socialist legal state incorporated the liberal democratic idea of checks and balances and the division of power, the heart of the Madisonian approach to government, into the practice of Soviet democracy. The traditional functions of Soviet constitutions were declaratory rather than explanatory. The functions of state and mass bodies were not defined and hence not limited, allowing the enormous concentration of power in executive bodies and the party. Now the task was to define the powers and functions of the four key structures of the Soviet polity: the Communist Party, the state represented by the soviets, the government bureaucracy headed by the Council of Ministers, and the judiciary. It should be stressed, however, that a legal state, as the Bismarckian Reich amply demonstrated, is not necessarily a democratic state; but it is a necessary condition for the development of one.

Substance was given to the idea of a *Rechtsstaat* by the constitutional amendments passed by the Supreme Soviet on 1 December 1988 after a short but vigorous debate. Fifty-five of the 174 articles of the 1977 'Brezhnev' constitution were changed. The amendments were passed by 1,344 votes to 5, with 27 abstentions. A new supreme organ of Soviet power, a Congress of People's Deputies of 2,250 members, was created (for details, see pages 142ff). Of these 1,500 were elected in national elections in March 1989, while the remaining 750 were nominated by a variety of 'social organisations', including the Communist Party, although this was dropped for future elections. The Congress elects a Supreme Soviet and a Committee of Constitutional Review with the crucial task of deciding whether acts are constitutional or not. Only the Congress can dismiss the President, modify the country's frontiers or repeal laws of the Supreme Soviet. It appoints the Procurator-General of the USSR and the supreme command of the armed services as well as electing the Supreme Court.

The amendments restricted the powers of the state but did not introduce a pluralistic constitution. They entailed a new approach to the state's responsibilities to citizens, though they did not discard the traditional emphasis of the citizen's responsibilities to the state. The amendments gave legislative force to the division of functions between legislative and executive bodies. Members of the executive, including ministers, were prohibited from being deputies to soviets. This, of course, diminished the effect of parliamentary accountability, but was designed to enhance the independence of deputies. It drew on American rather than British constitutional practice. All state bodies, including the Council of Ministers, were to be strictly accountable to the Supreme Soviet. Local soviets also were to share in the greater accountability of local executive bodies. The legislature and the government emerged as separate centres of power, and government appointees no longer needed approval only from the party, but the ratification of parliament as well. The amendments at last tried to give institutional force to the democratising reforms and to establish a state governed by law.

The appointment of the former head of the KGB, Chebrikov, to head the legal policy commission of the Central Committee did not bode well for the rapid implementation of the promise of the 1988 party conference to turn the USSR into a socialist legal state. While accepting much of the democratising agenda of legal reform, he retained the traditional stress on defending the interests of socialism, the state and society as a whole from 'anti-Soviet elements and extremists' (Chebrikov,

1989). Legal reform was always seen as an essential facet of *perestroika* and *glasnost*. At the conference Gorbachev insisted that 'Expansion of democracy and *glasnost* must go hand in hand with the strengthening of legality and with the instilling of unconditional respect for the rule of law.' Between September 1988 and September 1989 Chebrikov was in charge of the legal commission but Anatolii Lukyanov, Gorbachev's classmate at Moscow University, a reformist lawyer elected Vice-President of the Supreme Soviet in May 1989 and Chair in March 1990, was in charge of the detailed drafting of legislation to create a law-governed state. The first Congress in June 1989 established a large commission to draft a new constitution to replace the 1977 one. Its membership included Eltsin, Sakharov and seventeen First Secretaries of regional party organisations, and over half of overall membership was made up of senior officials. The new constitution would give expression to the idea of a law-governed state and the new respect for individual liberties.

The attempt to put the Soviet state on a new legal footing meant drafting a vast corpus of new laws. The legislative achievement of the first convocations of the Congress and the Supreme Soviet was quite awesome, with some fifty bills, some of them critical, facing the Supreme Soviet in the autumn of 1989 alone. They included new laws on press freedom, religious belief and much more. Economic reform meant that laws had to be devised hurriedly to regulate the new economic relations. The greater autonomy for enterprises, co-operatives and farms, and the joint ventures with foreign companies, all required a legal framework.

The development of a socialist legal state was intended to overcome the element of corruption that was built into the operation of the old system. Corruption is more than bribe-taking, nepotism and excessive privileges; it is rather the legal and political irresponsibility of those in power. In the Soviet context it came to represent a political challenge to the regime itself. The KGB played a key role in Andropov's and Gorbachev's anti-corruption campaigns to preserve Soviet government from degeneration. Gorbachev apparently believed that under Andropov the KGB was sufficiently reformed to enable it to play a key role in civilian politics. It was no longer the monstrous man-eating machine of the Stalin years, yet its very presence as an honoured guest at the table of power appeared anomalous. Chebrikov's replacement as head of the KGB in September 1988 was the career officer, General Vladimir Kryuchkov. He joined the Politburo as a full member in September 1989 and thus the KGB retained its seat, held since 1973. The KGB largely remained immune to criticism, and sought to remodel its image to avoid undue investigation into its past and present activities. The KGB, indeed, now appeared to favour an end to the 'cult of secrecy' in order to allow the USSR to become an 'information' society (V. Rubanov, *K*, September 1988). A special parliamentary committee was established to monitor the KGB (and the military). However, popular apprehension about the agency's extraordinary power behind Gorbachev's throne was not allayed. This was reflected in Aleksandr Kabakov's dystopia 'The man who wouldn't return' (*Iskusstvo kino*, June 1989) set in the Moscow of 1993 torn by civil war.

At the same time, a critical feature of the battle against corruption was the struggle to cleanse the militia itself from its association with organised crime forged under Brezhnev. The power of the interior ministry (MVD) was demonstrated when the minister Yuri Vlasov created, without advance notice, a special 'anti-riot' force in the summer of 1988 which was used against political demonstrations. His move to become premier of the Russian federation in October 1988 left the police without representation in the Politburo. *Perestroika* represented a reappraisal but not the abolition of the old war Communist iron triangle of Bolshevik power in which party rule was buttressed by the uniformed services and the bureaucracy.

An independent judiciary was regarded by the reformers as an essential condition for the success of *perestroika*. Under Khrushchev the law in particular had been abused by his excesses. His retrospective introduction of the death penalty for economic crimes in 1961 undermined attempts to restore legality in the post-Stalin world and demonstrated the vulnerability of formal legality in an authoritarian system. The major thrust of legal reform is changes in the judicial system, revision of the criminal code, formulation of the rights of defendants and their lawyers, the principles of Habeas Corpus (inviolability of the individual), and with it the presumption of innocence, and the introduction of twelve-person juries. A key element would be the introduction of adversarial proceedings in trials to undermine the powers of the Procuracy. Other planned reforms include making interference in the judicial process a crime, independence for judges and greater autonomy for lawyers, and a decrease in the number of capital offences.

In the spirit of the 19th conference steps were taken to put into effect a socialist legal state, something which proved a laborious and complex process (Baglai, 1989). The constitutional amendments of 1988 enhanced the independence of the judiciary. Judges were to be elected by the higher soviets, and their term of office was extended from five to ten years. Courts were to abide strictly by the constitution. The major change, however, was the revision of the criminal code of the RSFSR, the one on which all the other republics have traditionally modelled their criminal codes. In keeping with the new 'socialist humanism', the draft criminal code reduced prison sentences, restricted the death penalty and abolished internal exile (*Iz.*, 17 December 1988). The rights and freedoms of individuals were consolidated by the removal of the two 'anti-dissident' articles of the 1961 penal code: Article 70, covering 'anti-Soviet agitation and propaganda'; and Article 190−1, covering the 'spreading of anti-Soviet slander'. However, the new penal code retained an article against 'socially dangerous acts, damaging to the economic and political system of the Soviet Union', which placed a sword of Damocles above the heads of independent activists. The vagueness of the political provisions led to bitter disappointment on the part of the radicals, who urged Gorbachev in an open letter to come to grips with the conservatives and destroy the 'dictatorship of mediocrity' (*MN*, 52/ 1988).

The draft was placed before the Supreme Soviet in 1989 and led to much debate as the radicals tried to free the judicial system from the arbitrariness of the party and state apparatus. The final draft still failed to give legal recourse against decisions of the Communist bureaucracy.

The Soviet legal profession itself gradually fought and achieved greater autonomy. In December 1988 plans were announced to establish an Association of Defence Lawyers on the basis that 'A professional, strong, courageous and independent bar is undoubtedly one of society's aspirations and a necessary attribute of a state governed by law' (*P*, 19 December 1988). The legal profession was now to ensure that justice remained the prerogative of the legal system rather than 'outside agencies', the security police and the party. 'Telephone law' was abolished. The Vyshinskii approach to justice which argued that since all those involved in a trial, the judge, investigator and prosecutor, were all seeking to establish the truth, there was no need for defence lawyers was finally discarded (Z. Medvedev, 1986a: 41).

Human rights, of course, will figure largely in the codification of rights. Soviet legal reforms have been marked by a continuing ambivalence over the attitude to the Enlightenment belief that individual human rights are absolutely sacred and not dependent on any concept of duties. Communist law has always stressed that every right implies a duty (Anishchenko, 1987). Chebrikov did oversee the release of a large number of political prisoners and the relaxation after the Andropov purge of the human rights movement (see Chapter 5). At the 28th Congress in July 1990 the party committed itself to 'the earliest formulation of legal acts guaranteeing the rights and freedoms of citizens'. Political rights, personal property and privacy were all to be guaranteed, and the courts were to be given greater powers to protect civil rights (*P*, 15 July 1990).

The development of the 'socialist legal state' provided a framework for the relegitimising of the political state after the strictures of Marx and Lenin, and indeed Khrushchev's attempts to achieve its 'withering away'. One of the more problematical features of the Soviet polity for its first seventy years was the contrast between what could be called the strong state and the perennial constitutional chaos at the heart of the system. The totalitarian syndrome is marked by what Bialer (1980) called the shapelessness of government. The relationship between the elements of the state was governed by convention rather than by law. This in itself is not altogether deleterious, and the British governmental system provides an example of a system that has been able to evolve over a thousand years without a written constitution. But the British system operates within the context of a range of formal and informal constraints established by such landmarks as Magna Charta and Habeas Corpus. The Soviet system, however, was designed precisely to sweep away restraints on state power. The result was arbitrariness and massive coercion that peaked under Stalin but which characterised the system throughout its first seven decades.

The aim now is to rationalise and professionalise the system of state administration while at the same time bringing a more professional civil service under the purview of democratic control. The state is to be reordered, but it is to be limited as well. There is to be a division of powers with parliamentary control of the executive and an independent judiciary. The creation of a socialist legal state entails the retreat of state power and the development of a new relationship with a revived civil society whose rights and freedoms are guaranteed by law. The question remains for Gorbachev whether a system that managed for so long to insulate itself from the pressure of change from below is also impervious to change from above.

Electoral reform

The introduction of electivity into party, economic and social life was designed to act as the main weapon for democratisation. The absence of competitive parties allowed patronage networks to emerge under Brezhnev which provided an informal framework for policy coalitions and political ties. The existence of a fully-fledged party system, of course, does not eliminate patronage, but it is forced to operate in the context of competing and open politics. In the one-party state leaders at all levels maintained their administrations by semi-covert means, in particular by ensuring personnel placements to their advantage and building alliances with major interests. Competitive elections made transparent what had previously been fixed informally through patronage or officially through the *nomenklatura* system.

Electoral reform had long been on the agenda of socialist countries, and by 1985 had gone the furthest in Poland and Hungary. The results of experiments in these countries were studied by Soviet experts (Hahn, 1987), and some of the lessons were incorporated in the limited trials with multiple candidates in the June 1987 local elections, when competitive elections were held in some 5 per cent of constituencies (White, 1988b). By 1989 an electoral revolution led to the first non-Communist government since 1948 emerging in Poland. The power of the ballot box was something which Gorbachev himself had perhaps underestimated in his drive for electoral reform – or indeed hoped to use to dislodge the conservatives and break the resistance of the bureaucracy.

The new election law of December 1988 was designed to revive the role of central and local government (*P*, 4 December 1988). Elections for the 2.3 million soviet deputies in the country were gradually to become multi-candidate contests designed to judge the abilities and competence of the candidates. The choice initially was not between policies but personalities; however, this rapidly fell away as candidates put forward a range of platforms. In contrast to the old one-candidate elections, the new electoral law guaranteed 'the right to free and thorough discussion of the political, personal and professional qualities of candidates and the right to campaign for or against them'. Party officials who failed to be elected were urged to draw 'the necessary conclusions'.

The new Congress of People's Deputies was made up of three chambers of 750 members each, but, as noted, competitive general elections were to take place for only two of them. The third chamber consisted of representatives of social organisations with guaranteed seats, a system rather like that of the 'estates' in pre-revolutionary France. The Communist Party had 100 reserved seats, the trade unions and the co-operative movement also 100 seats each. There were 75 seats each for the Komsomol organisation, the women's councils, the creative unions, the scientific unions, and lesser numbers for other specified groups. In this way nominated party figures were able to enter parliament without facing popular elections, a strategem defended on the grounds that it was a way of overcoming manipulation by the conservatives. In December 1989 the system of nominations to the council of representatives was abolished.

The first test of the new law was provided in the elections of March 1989. Two-thirds of the Congress's 2,250 deputies were to be elected by secret ballot in constituency elections. Members of public organisations, including religious activists, were granted the right to be nominated as long as their platform did not 'contradict the constitution or the laws of the Soviet Union'. The nomination procedure was cumbersome. Candidates could not simply be nominated to be placed on a ballot paper but had to pass a two-stage process. In the first, their names had to be proposed by a factory, office, registered association or at a local meeting of not less than 500 people and accepted by at least half those present. The fact that most informal political associations had not been registered automatically excluded them from nominating candidates. The second stage consisted of vetting at a 'pre-election meeting' where the candidate again had to receive the support of over half those present. At both stages registration committees vetted the nominated candidates.

The 100 seats reserved for the Communist Party were filled by exactly 100 candidates at the 10 January 1989 Central Committee plenum, a group who went on to be accepted with no discussion by the CC on 15 March. Most of these were high-ranking national party leaders, but excluded Boris Eltsin. The social parliament element was defended as providing direct access to parliament for organised groups, but it clearly violated the principle of one person, one vote. It was at the January plenum that Gorbachev denounced the 'group egoism, ambition and political careerism' typical of multi-party systems. No group was allowed in any official way to challenge the Communist Party or to publicise their views in the media. The same meeting, which lasted a mere four hours, also adopted the party's election 'manifesto' (*P*, 8 January 1989). Since it was the only one allowed there was a certain falseness about the whole procedure and it cast doubts on its declared aim of achieving 'the renovation of the socialist idea itself'.

Not surprisingly, the radicals found fault with the electoral system. The absence of formal criteria by which candidates were allowed to stand gave the party bureaucracy in the localities great scope for manipulation, as in the elections to the June 1988 party conference, and made it difficult for radicals to enter parliament. The obstacles faced by Sakharov once the nomination process got under way in December 1988 vividly illustrated the point. The *apparatchiks* in the Academy of Sciences ensured that he was not selected as one of their candidates even though sixty scientific organisations had nominated him. After a long struggle against the leadership of the Academy, led by a grass-roots 'electoral club', the membership on 21 March forced the nomination of Sakharov, Shmelëv, the space scientist Roald Sagdeev and other liberals for its twenty reserved seats in a second election on 20 April. Elsewhere stormy nomination meetings took place like those for Korotich, who acted as a focus of criticism that dared not be directed against Gorbachev himself, and other reformers such as the economists Gavriil Popov, Shmelëv and Aganbegyan, Sagdeev and Zaslavskaya, all of whom were rejected by nomination meetings in the constituencies. Some of the rejected liberals, like those in the Academy, gained seats through the 750 reserved seats for social organisations. Eltsin himself was nominated as the candidate for the national territorial seat for the whole city of Moscow.

Despite the complicated electoral system the elections did provide some surprises. By the closing date of first-round nominations on 24 January 1989 7,351 candidates had been found for the 1,500 ordinary constituencies. In the second stage, lasting until 22 February, special 'registration' meetings decided whose names would finally appear on the ballot papers. A total of 2,901 candidates finally stood in the election of 26 March, nearly two per seat for the 1,500 contested seats, half of which were ordinary constituencies and half 'national territorial' seats. Of these 85 per cent were members of the Communist Party, a higher proportion even than in the old uncontested elections; a quarter were classed as workers, 1 in 10 were collective farmers, and 1 in 6 were women. In 385 constituencies, especially in the Ukraine and Central Asia, the second stage was manipulated by 'the bureaucracy' so that only one name, usually a local party official, was carried forward whose only hurdle was to gain 50 per cent of the vote. In the quarter of the seats where only one candidate ran, the choice facing the voter was either to cross out the name or to place the ballot paper untouched into the box. In 953 seats there were two candidates, while in the remaining 162 constituencies there was a choice of three or more candidates up to the record of twelve in the Gagarin district of Moscow. These were particularly common in the Baltic, where to prevent manipulation the second stage tended to be skipped altogether.

Election platforms devoted little attention to foreign policy but concentrated on welfare issues such as low pensions, environmental problems, economic reform and shortages. The more radical campaigners in addition condemned privileges, the bureaucracy and the legacy of 'administrative command socialism'. The campaign revealed a deepening polarisation of Soviet politics, but by the same token revealed a thirst for genuine politics that effectively politicised a large proportion of society. The essential issue was over the pace, and thereby the nature, of *perestroika*, and ways of dealing with the economic crisis. The inculcation of a 'culture of democracy', however rough at the edges, was the great achievement of the election campaign.

Eltsin's programme represented a radical populist assault against 'the bureaucracy', party privileges and corruption. He also urged the reform of the electoral system to allow free, equal and direct elections, and urged guarantees against the return of authoritarian power and personality cults. His criticisms cut to the heart of *perestroika*, and indeed on 19 February he remarked 'There has not been any thought-out concept of *perestroika*, with phased development. The result is nil' (*Ob.*, 5 March 1989). The diffuseness of his programme was reflected in his disparate sources of support, ranging from radical democrats to the nationalist Pamyat group. He was above all a Moscow phenomenon, but no doubt his views found much support throughout the country. The attempts of the conservatives to discredit him only served to increase his popularity as a symbol and a cause, reflected in ever-larger demonstrations in his support. A special commission of the party to investigate his alleged 'deviations from the party line' during the campaign, above all his call for party privileges to be abolished, the establishment of parliamentary scrutiny over the party, and his insistence at his nomination meeting on 21 February that 'The idea of a multi-party system ought to be discussed and studied', came to naught. Eltsin's populist campaign evoked comparisons in the West between him and Mussolini, and indeed the 'Eltsin phenomenon' was seen as neo-Fascist in its manipulation of crowd moods and anxieties and condemnations of abstract villains like 'the bureaucracy' and 'the mafia' (*Ob.*, 26 March 1989).

Voter turnout on 26 March 1989 varied from traditionally high rates of over 95 per cent in Azerbaidzhan, Georgia, Kirghizia, Turkmenia and Uzbekistan to 87 per cent in Estonia and the RSFSR, and down to 82.5 per cent in Lithuania. The lowest rate of 72 per cent was in Armenia, still recovering from the earthquake of December 1988. The regional variations can be explained by the share of urban population, the proportion involved in agriculture and the number of candidates per seat (Berezkin *et al.*, 1989). Eltsin soundly defeated his opponent, Evgenii Brakov, director of the ZiL car plant. He was swept to the Congress on a turnout of 83.5 per cent with a vote of 5.3 million, 79 per cent of a constituency of 6.7 million, the single largest popular vote of any member of the assembly. Eltsin's victory represented a sharp rebuff to those who had supported his fall in November 1987 and marked a political comeback unprecedented in the USSR's history. A general law of the election appeared to be that the more radical the candidate and the further from officialdom, the more likely they were to be elected.

In the Baltic republics the Communist parties were routed by the local popular fronts, which had put up a strong field of candidates with a clear programme. The party leader of Lithuania, Algirdas Brazauskas, survived only because his Sajudis opponent withdrew from the contest, while the 'opposition' won outright in 34 of the 39 out of the republic's 42 seats which it contested. Candidates of the Latvian Popular Front took 24 of the 29 first-round seats. Jan Vagris, the leader of the Latvian party, was opposed by Juris Dobelis, a leader of the National Independent Movement. In Estonia the party and the nationalist movement had achieved a working relationship. The Estonian party leader Vaino Valjas was permitted an unopposed run, while the Prime Minister Indrek Toome and the President Arnold Ruttel gained, like the party leader, 90 per cent of the vote. Fifteen of the 23 candidates supported by the local Popular Front won, while four candidates from the rival Russian Interfront were elected.

In the Congress as a whole 87 per cent were Communists, a higher proportion than in the old Supreme Soviet where they made up 73 per cent. The new intake, however, were more professional and included fewer workers and *apparatchiks*.

In the 64 constituencies where out of several candidates none had achieved 50 per cent, run-off elections between the two most successful candidates were held on 9 April. It was at this stage that Roy Medvedev and Yuri Chernichenko, a radical journalist working for *Ogonëk* magazine, were elected. In the 198 constituencies where only one or two candidates stood but still failed to be elected, new elections with new candidates were held on 14 May. Among those elected at this stage were Evtushenko and Korotich in Kharkov and, by a huge majority in Leningrad, Nikolai Ivanov, the leading prosecutor against Brezhnevite corruption and the scourge of Ligachev.

Despite the lack of choice, some thiry-four party leaders who stood unopposed were defeated in the election, including a full sweep of six of the Leningrad party and soviet leaders, and the party and soviet leaders in Kiev. Twenty per cent of the party officials standing in the elections lost. The major anomaly of the half-reformed electoral system and the existence of the dual party and state hierarchies was that the losers in elections did not need to resign their party posts; yet in 1989 their positions became untenable once they had been defeated in the popular vote. A post-mortem on the elections took place at the 25 April 1989 plenum of the Central Committee, in which Gorbachev claimed that the election results were a victory for *perestroika* and a defeat for conservatism. His sanguine approach appears justified, given the high proportion of Communists elected. People did not vote against Communists as such, only against bureaucrats and conservatives. As noted, at this plenum the conservatives blamed everyone except themselves for the defeats (page 121). Yuri Solovëv, the leader of the Leningrad regional party organisation for four years, blamed his defeat on the shortcomings of *perestroika*, and Bobovnikov, head of the Vladimir party organisation, blamed his defeat on shortages of soap, the Press for discrediting the party, and even the Politburo (*P*, 27 April 1989).

No action was taken against the losers at the plenum, but in the months to come most were replaced. On 6 July 1989 a meeting of the leadership of the Leningrad regional party organisation, under Gorbachev's watchful eye, relieved Solovëv of his job and replaced him by Boris Gidaspov, one of the few Leningrad leaders to have won a convincing victory in the elections. In November of that year Anatolii Gerasimov, head of the Leningrad city party organisation who had also been defeated in the elections, was removed from his post and the city and regional organisations were united under the leadership of Gidaspov (*P*, 22 November 1989). His support for a type of conservative populism at a rally on 22 March 1989 was marked by his denunciation of 'unlimited democracy' (*G*, 29 November 1989). It appeared that once again the Zhdanov–Romanov tradition of hardline Leningrad politics would be continued as Gidaspov denounced the marketising reforms espoused by Abalkin: 'Today we have a great deal of democracy and *glasnost*, but no order or organisation. . . Socialist ideals are deliberately confused and the people duped by sweet fairy tales about "people's capitalism", unlimited democracy and non-party *glasnost*' (*Sov. Rossiya*, 22 November 1989). Rather than engaging in radical democracy, the Leningrad bureaucracy sought to save itself by stressing a type of technocratic socialism whose standard-bearer was Ryzhkov.

On 21 November Lev Zaikov, who had taken over from Eltsin in November 1987, was himself removed from his post at the head of the Moscow party organisation and replaced by Yurii Prokofiev who, while defeated in the March elections, pledged himself to play 'an active part in the further democratisation of our society' (*P*, 22 November 1989). He appeared to favour different platforms in the party but drew the line at organised factions, and warned that the party had very little time in which to reform itself. The removal of the long-time leaders of the Ukrainian and Moldavian republican party organisations, Shcherbitskii and Grossu, respectively, clearly signalled that in advance of the local elections the reformist leadership in Moscow was trying to prevent a recurrence of the defeats.

The election marked an irreversible step in the evolution of *perestroika* as politics entered the streets and popular consciousness. The various popular fronts and other radical groups, including an increasing number of voters' clubs and associations, represented a growing challenge to the party's comfortable hegemony. The machine politics of bureaucratic socialism, and its attendant empty shelves, mismanagement and corruption, suffered a stinging defeat. Gorbachev made the best of Eltsin's victory and of the elections in general. Indeed, the popular enthusiasm and involvement in the first semi-free elections in some seventy years testified to the passions that had been kept muzzled for so long. The new politically aware electorate handed Gorbachev yet another cudgel with which to beat the conservatives in the Central Committee and the laggards of *perestroika* everywhere. He argued that the election had been a referendum in favour of *perestroika* which had now become 'a truly national movement' no longer restricted to 'enthusiasts and trailblazers'. He dismissed the arguments of the defeated and noted that 'Some have gone so far as to say that both democracy and *glasnost* are very nearly a disaster. . .and that *perestroika* has gone too far' (*P*, 26 April 1989). Some of the shine, however, was taken off Gorbachev's charisma by the fact that he and 99 other leading party figures had used the party's guaranteed 100 seats to avoid facing elections themselves.

The elections of spring 1989 had important international ramifications. The Soviet leadership appeared willing to tolerate defeat and diversity, and thus encouraged East European countries to be bolder in dismantling Soviet-type socialism. The elections in Poland in June 1989 saw the opposition gain sweeping victories in the 35 per cent of the seats in the lower house of the Sejm allotted to them and 99 out of 100 seats in the newly created Senate, the odd seat having been won by a candidate whose name began with a 'z' and thus escaped the cross that eliminated all the others. Despite declining support the party in Hungary agreed to hold multi-party elections in Spring 1990, and in preparation turned itself into a socialist party. Though poorly reported in China, the Soviet elections raised ever more strongly the question of Chinese political democratisation, an issue which the students took to the streets in the following months.

The second convocation of the Congress in December 1989 abolished the quota system which had guaranteed seats for the party and other social organisations (*P*, 23 December 1989). In future elections Gorbachev would have to put himself to the test of a popular vote. The electoral process was simplified by dropping the system of pre-election registration meetings, which had proved an effective barrier to the radicals earlier in the year, in favour of the direct nomination of candidates from constituencies without any preliminary stage.

Some of the lessons of the spring 1989 elections were taken to heart and led to modifications in the electoral procedure in the fifteen republics for local and republican soviets. Each republic adopted its own rules amidst much controversy in the summer and early autumn of 1989. The Supreme Soviets of the Baltic and the RSFSR led the way in abolishing the reserved seats for 'social organisations', but in Belorussia and Kazakhstan they were kept. The republic and local elections were held, with the exception of Georgia, between December 1989 and March 1990. The percentage of single-candidate elections fell in comparison with the spring 1989 elections and once again *apparat* candidates were defeated by the democratic movement. Voter turnout declined, in Moscow falling from 83.5 per cent in spring 1989 to 70 per cent, signalling perhaps a growing disillusion with the existing system. The proportion of party members and candidates fell sharply to 49.1 per cent in the RSFSR as a whole, but the proportion remained high in the autonomous Russian republics at 88 per cent (*Sovetskaya rossiya*, 28 March 1990). A far greater proportion of 'radicals' were elected than the third in the earlier election despite countless cases of ballot rigging by the authorities and smear campaigns against independent candidates. Above all, a whole new generation of radicals entered active politics and decisively altered the conduct of Soviet politics.

The democratic forces in the RSFSR coalesced to form the Democratic Russia bloc, an umbrella organisation ranging from reform Communists to democratic Russian nationalists. It was the equivalent of the various 'civic forums' in Eastern Europe. Out of the 1,026 seats in the Russian parliament, Democratic Russia won 370, including 59 out of the 66 seats allocated to Moscow. In the elections to the presidency of the Russian republic in May 1990 the bloc was strong enough to defeat Polozkov's candidature and to elect Eltsin. Eltsin then set about creating a sovereign, democratic Russia. In Moscow, Democratic Russia won 292 out of 465 seats to the city council, and the alliance between reform Communists and non-Communist democrats was symbolised by the election of Gavriil Popov as mayor of the city and Sergei Stankevich as his deputy. In Leningrad, 355 out of 400 seats were gained by the Election-90 coalition, who elected Anatolii Sobchak as mayor. Eltsin, Popov and Sobchak announced their resignation from the Communist party at the 28th party congress, and proceeded to develop the institutions of democratic government and a market economy freed from the tutelage of the Communist bureaucracy. Elsewhere, independent democratic workers' candidates won in industrial towns like Kemerovo and Novokuznetsk in Siberia, and the Democratic Labour Movement and its allies took nearly all the seats in the Vorkuta city soviet (see Chapter 6).

The 1990 republic and local elections marked a decisive step towards the pluralisation of Soviet politics and the revival of independent soviets. Radical democrats won resounding victories in the big cities, but in smaller towns in the provinces the party bureaucracy clung on to its power. The limitations of both the 1989 and 1990 elections reflected the hybrid and compromised nature of the new democracy. At root, there was the natural fear of the Communist Party that free elections would sweep them from power, as indeed was the case in Poland in 1989, and in the GDR, Hungary, Slovenia, Croatia and Czechoslovakia in 1990. A whole new stratum of politicised society began to edge its way towards power. The emergence of informal structures such as voters' clubs and electoral coalitions clearly marked the first stage in the evolution of the Soviet polity into a genuine multi-party system. The peaceful electoral revolution was perhaps the greatest achievement of *perestroika* up to 1990, yet its greatest challenge lay ahead, the contested multi-party elections for the Congress of People's Deputies designated for 1994 in which the Communist Party would have to fight on equal terms with other parties.

Democratisation of the state

Russian and Soviet experience of representative democracy has not been a happy one. During the revolution of 1905 Nicholas II was forced to concede an elected Duma, or parliament, but was able to restrict and manipulate the suffrage to the extent that it lost much of its effectiveness and popular legitimacy. The government was not directly accountable to it, and thus Western practices of responsible government were stifled. In its few months the Provisional Government failed to establish an effective system of local or central government, and in any case the system of 'dual power' meant that the soviets, councils first elected in 1905, remained unintegrated in the new system of democracy. After October 1917 all administrative power was effectively transferred to the soviets, but political power remained the prerogative of the Bolshevik Party. The Constituent Assembly elected in November 1917 gave the Bolsheviks only 25 per cent of the seats, and at its first meeting in January 1918 was dissolved. Local soviets, the congresses of soviets, and, from 1936, the Supreme Soviet all remained in the shadow of the party.

Gorbachev insisted that the new democracy would focus on 'freedom, democracy and humanism' in the framework of individual rights in a 'representative parliamentary democracy' based on the rule of law. In developing such a model the USSR would draw on the experience of West European social democracy (*P*, 26 November 1989). The new democracy at first tried to forge a link between economic democracy, in the sense of a degree of worker self-management and shop-floor democracy, and the traditional socialist aspiration of achieving a high degree of political participation. Under Gorbachev a distinctive hybrid form of democracy emerged made up of three distinctive elements. The first was an emphasis on some form of economic democracy, which will be examined below. The second was the attempt to breathe life into participatory political democracy or commune democracy. Marx had called for the conversion of representative institutions from the 'talking shop' politics of parliamentarianism to 'working bodies' (Marx, 1968).

The soviets for Lenin represented the mechanism whereby this could be achieved (Lenin, 1977: 46). However, the soviets failed to play this role in the first seventy years of Soviet power, not only because of adverse economic and international circumstances, but also because of flaws in the very theory of unified executive and legislative power. The lack of checks and balances and the absence of the separation of powers allowed the enormous accumulation of power in the hands of executive bodies.

The third strand of the new democracy was an attempt to overcome the deficiencies in the practice of direct democracy while not embracing full-blooded liberal democracy. The commitment to elements of commune democracy is now accompanied by the proceduralism of liberal democracy, the separation of powers and accountability. In his speech to the Supreme Soviet on 29 November 1988 Gorbachev argued that 'The question of power is the most important question in any society', and the session went on to adopt the constitutional amendments that began to regulate the relations between governmental, state and party bodies (*P*, 30 November 1988). The acceptance of checks and balances in the Soviet system broke with the tradition of Marxist commune democracy which stipulated the fusion of executive and legislative powers. However, the problem remained of how a system of checks and democratic proceduralism could be established against the power of the Communist Party. The leading role of the party excluded an unconditional acceptance of the 'dictatorship of parliament'.

After several false starts since the death of Stalin, Gorbachev like his predecessors insisted on 'the need to restore completely the role of the soviets as bodies of political power and as the foundation of socialist democracy' (1987a: 112). The cardinal task of political reform, he insisted, was to breathe new life into the soviets (*SN*, 1988: 440). Thus the slogan of 1917, 'All power to the soviets', has been resurrected, with many of the same ambiguities. The revival of the soviets inevitably entailed the danger of the emergence of a type of dual power between the party and the soviets, a problem Gorbachev hoped to avoid at the 19th party conference by making the local party and soviet leaders one and the same person. The idea was condemned by a number of speakers, including Abalkin and Eltsin. Clearly the measure, which ran counter to the leadership's stated intention of separating the functions of party and state, was a political compromise but was justified as a practical necessity to avoid conflicts and to enable the party to retain a degree of control over the soviets. While this might help reduce personal clashes, the institutional tensions between the two organisations were not resolved. How is it possible to separate the party and the state in a one-party state?

The constitutional amendments of 1988 began to put an end to the rule by party committees by empowering a reorganised two-tier legis- lature. The Congress of People's Deputies meets on average twice a year for about two weeks each time. At its first session it elected from its members a 542-member Supreme Soviet, an executive President, and his Vice-President. In yet another blow to Brezhnev's policy of 'stability of cadres', the amendments stipulated the obligatory turnover of up to a fifth of Supreme Soviet deputies every year to provide fresh energy between elections. The system is rather like the US Senate where a third of its members come up for election every two years. The President and all deputies are elected for a maximum of two five-year terms, and can theoretically be recalled at any time. The danger, however, is that expertise gained in a term of office may be lost just as it comes to fruition.

The Supreme Soviet is a full-time parliament on the Western model, holding two three- or four-month sittings a year. Half of its members were picked on a regional basis, with for example each of the fifteen union republics having an entitlement of eleven seats each, to make up the Soviet of Nationalities. The other 271-member house, the Soviet of the Union, is chosen taking into account the distribution of the population. The responsibilities of the Supreme Soviet included appoint- ing the Prime Minister and approving his or her ministers. The Supreme Soviet became a parliament with full-time paid MPs who, for the first time since the 1920s, freely used their right to vote against government programmes.

Deputies now became parliamentarians, but the mandate (*nakaz*) mechanism still means that they are delegates rather than representatives as in liberal democratic systems. The *nakaz* feedback mechanism has been strengthened through more meetings with electors, more detailed practical reports and with major programmes submitted for discussion by the population. This is intended to overcome what had been a lamentably low level of public awareness of matters discussed by soviets, especially the lower-level ones (*P*, 24 August 1987).

The Congress of People's Deputies met for the first time for fifteen days from 25 May to 9 June 1989 with its main task the election of the Supreme Soviet. Despite the radicals' insistence that membership should be more than a pre-ordained choice of the Politburo to be rubber- stamped by the assembly, the Supreme Soviet on 27 May was in fact elected from pre-arranged lists for every region, which in most cases numbered exactly the same as the number of places. Thus there was great scope for bureaucratic manipulation. Moreover, the system of negative voting meant that instead of voting *for* someone, deputies voted *against* by crossing out names on the ballot paper. Hence there was a structural bias in favour of the obscure since those who were well known were more likely to be crossed off, leading to the emergence of what has been called a 'parliament of mediocrities'. As the most famous politician after Gorbachev, Eltsin failed to win one of the eleven places out of twelve candidates for the Russian republic in the Soviet of Nationalities, but later took the place of a deputy who made way for him by resigning. Many other radicals failed to be elected because the Moscow deputies submitted fify-five names for twenty-nine places in the Soviet of the Union.

The radicals were severely disappointed by the composition of the new Supreme Soviet, and many echoed Yuri Afanasev's sentiment on 27 May that a 'Stalinist–Brezhnevite' body had been chosen (*P*, 28 May 1990). Those who shared his view about the 'aggressive and obedient majority' in the Congress went on to found what was in effect a separate faction, the 'interregional group' of radical democrats. This group could count on a maximum of a fifth, some 450 deputies, out of the 2,250 at the Congress. The division had a class aspect, since the majority of the radicals were intellectuals, whereas the 'obedient majority' tended to be workers by origin though often bureaucrats by profession. These could barely restrain their animosity against the 'Moscow intellectuals'. The division contained within itself the embryo of a multi-party system.

Gorbachev was elected the Supreme Soviet's first executive President on the first day with a minimum of debate and no alternative candidate, though eighty-seven voted against him, thus perpetuating the lack of choice that he had so much criticised in the country at large. As President, the constitution granted him the exclusive right to nominate a candidate for the post of First Deputy Chair of the Supreme Soviet, in effect Vice-President. He proposed his close ally, Anatolii Lukyanov, who was duly elected, but only after severe questioning by other deputies. On 8 June Ryzhkov was confirmed in his post of Prime Minister.

The status of the Congress remained unclear. Nominally the supreme authority, it appeared to duplicate the Supreme Soviet. The Congress granted itself the power to review and amend all laws passed by the Supreme Soviet and thus acted as a second chamber. The functions of the four-fifths of the deputies not in the Supreme Soviet at any one time was also unclear. It was conceded that any deputy, not only those in the Supreme Soviet, could be a member of standing committees, allowing a broader range of specialist input. Half the places on the committees would be reserved for them, and indeed the work of the 23 parliamentary standing committees was assisted by 250 members of the Congress who were not members of the Supreme Soviet. Congress delegates argued that not only those elected to the Supreme Soviet but all 2,250 deputies should become professional politicians and give up their jobs. On 26 May the Congress decided that 'as a rule' Supreme Soviet deputies, in keeping with the professional nature of the new body, would have to give up their former jobs. This formulation allowed party officials, with Gorbachev at their head, to keep their second jobs while simultaneously acting as deputies. Once again, the party's leading role allowed it to flout the rules it imposed on others.

The debates of the Congress, which were televised live, enthralled the nation. The populace did not remain passive, however, and Eltsin's initial failure to be elected to the Supreme Soviet was protested by a mass demonstration on 28 May at the Luzhniki stadium. Voters, moreover, inundated deputies with requests and instructions. The heated debates between what rapidly emerged as a division between liberals and conservatives could be witnessed as part of the new *otkrytnost*, openness in the sense of laying bare. Most remarkable of all was the sight of Sakharov, who only three years earlier had languished in exile in Gorky, at the podium of the nation's supreme assembly. Under the cover of parliamentary immunity the deputies enjoyed to the full their new rights to freedom of speech and day by day pushed back the frontiers of *glasnost*. On 2 June Yuri Karyakin urged that Lenin should be removed from the Mausoleum and given a decent burial next to his mother. He and other speakers called for Soviet citizenship to be returned to Solzhenitsyn (*P*, 5 June 1989). The massacre in Tbilisi on 9 April, in which twenty-one had died, was a constant theme of the Congress. The Minister of the Interior was held accountable for forcefully breaking up demonstrations, and the KGB itself was labelled by Yuri Vlasov an 'underground empire' which should be severely cut back and moved out of the Lubyanka (*P*, 2 June 1989). A personal attack on Ligachev on 1 June by Chernichenko asked why a man who had failed in ideology and who was ignorant about agriculture should be placed in charge of such a critical area (*P*, 3 June 1989). Eltsin on 31 May once again proposed a radical programme of reform, including a new law to define the powers of the party, limits to the powers of the head of state and all privileges of the *nomenklatura* to be abolished. He also held Gorbachev personally responsible for many of the failures of the first four years of *perestroika* (*P*, 2 June 1989).

The new Congress was a far cry from the old ceremonial rubber stamp legislature typical of Communist systems and on several occasions showed a new self-confidence in calling the government to account. The Congress marked a turning-point in Soviet politics and established a counterweight to the party apparatus and the governmental bureaucracy. The Soviet Union could never be ruled as before. The debates at the Congress, with their fearless denunciations of corruption, the bureaucracy, shortages and much more besides encouraged the public to become politically active. In particular, the debates acted as the catalyst for miners' strikes over grievances that had long been suppressed.

However, the hopes of some that the Congress would act as a type of constituent assembly and place the Soviet Union on a new road were disappointed. The reform programme of the radicals, which included such elements as full-scale marketisation of the economy, changes in the electoral law, the repeal of restrictive decrees on demonstrations, decentralisation of powers to the republics, and a calling to account of those responsible for the foreign policy errors of earlier governments, failed to be adopted. Many of the aspirations of deputies from the Baltic and elsewhere were not realised. Above all, no clear decisions were taken on the separation of the functions of the party and state. This prompted Sakharov on the last day of the Congress to announce his 'Decree on Power' which warned of the excessive power in the hands of the President and called for the annulment of Article 6 of the Constitution, the absolute subordination of the Supreme Soviet to the Congress, the transfer of the power of appointments from the party to the Congress, the transition to a professional army, and the creation of a 'federal ethnic constitutional structure' to create a 'union of equal republics joined by a federal treaty' (*XX Century and Peace*, 8/1989: 9– 12). In short, he called for the genuine implementation of the slogans of 'all power to the soviets' and the creation of a law-governed state. While this might not feed the people, only this, Sakharov insisted, could 'create political guarantees for the solution of these problems' (*P*, 5 June 1989).

The new Supreme Soviet has a supervisory capacity, especially in overseeing the budget, checking the ministries and their agencies, and reviewing legislation. Fears voiced in the debates on the amendments on excessive centralisation were tempered by attempts to establish some control over power. The Supreme Soviet was given the right to repeal decrees of its own Presidium and instructions of the President, and to recall any elected or appointed official if they failed in their duties; it was also made mandatory for the government to report back to the assembly at least once a year. In an attempt to avoid another Afghanistan, or indeed Czechoslovakia, the Supreme Soviet reserved to itself the exclusive right to authorise the use of Soviet troops beyond the country's frontiers. The system of standing committees was much strengthened. They can summon and interrogate ministers and officials, and took up this new power with undisguised relish.

The first Congress elected Gennadi Kolbin, leader of the Kazakhstan party organisation, as head of the People's Control Committee, a combined government and volunteer body of inspectors designed to ferret out corruption and maladministration and to improve efficiency.

The role of the Committee of Constitutional Review was defined at the second meeting of the Congress in December 1989 as an independent body which decided on the constitutionality of laws. It was made up of a chair, a deputy and twenty-five legal and political specialists, of whom one at least would be drawn from each republic (*P*, 26 December 1989). Contrary to the hopes of the radicals, it was not constituted with the authority of a supreme court, and thus weakened the power of the judiciary in the new quadripartite relationship between it, the party, the legislature and the government.

The USSR relived the period that the United States passed through from the Declaration of Independence in 1776 to the adoption of the American Constitution in 1787. The basis of a federal democratic republic and the role of the President was as much contested then as it is now (cf. Sundquist, 1986: 19). The new Soviet parliament borrowed much from the procedures of the US Congress. The political scientist, deputy mayor of Moscow and interregional deputy Sergei Stankevich, indeed, studied the American constitutional system and sought to introduce some of its methods. However, the legacy of the old model of commune democracy, with its emphasis on fusing executive and legislative functions, remained, as in the proud assertion that the Congress and the Supreme Soviet 'not only issue laws, but also directly take an active part in administration' (Solodukhin, 1989: 21).

The spring session of the new Supreme Soviet ended on 4 August 1989 after a five-week session in which it passed much vital legislation. The autumn session began on 25 September 1989 and faced a mountain of legislation. Despite the criticisms of the radicals the Supreme Soviet in a remarkably short time became a genuine national parliament, acting as the first port of call for all the major issues facing the country. It developed the procedures of liberal democratic parliaments, with the first and second reading of bills, amendments, early day motions and so on. Moreover, it increasingly asserted its prerogatives against the government and, indeed, the party. The mere fact that a parliament existed began to marginalise the party, its Central Committee, and even more so its apparatus. It seemed to prove that a culture of democracy can emerge with quite astonishing rapidity, though this still failed to quell the doubts of those who thought the country could be ruled only by authoritarian methods. However, the emerging situation of dual power was vividly manifested in summer 1989. The legislature was on holiday, and the party apparatus ruled supreme, issuing an ill-considered denunciation of democratisation in the Baltic on 26 August (see page 236).

The reform of local government was envisaged as the third stage in the reform of government, following the changes in central authority and in the principles of federalism. At the January 1987 Central Committee plenum Gorbachev argued that elected bodies should have greater authority over executive ones (1987e: 321–5). In order to make soviets more accountable to the electorate and to prevent the traditional dominance of the legislative side by the executive, most full-time soviet officials were prohibited from standing in elections to soviet executive committees. Moreover, the powers of the deputies have been increased to remedy their traditional weakness relative to the powers of the bureaucrats. The soviets were to be in a position, according to Gorbachev, to decide on all local affairs and become fully-fledged bodies of people's self-government (*SN*, 30 November 1988). The budgetary rights of local soviets have been increased, as well as their control over local economic life. However, one of the dangers is to avoid the problems of China and Yugoslavia where decentralisation was unaccompanied by democratisation. In those countries there was a tendency for central control over enterprises simply to be transferred to local authorities, which then in their own way could impede the autonomy of enterprises and the development of market relations.

The key process was the transfer of legislative power from the Communist Party to the local soviets, a transition hastened by the victory of the democrats in the spring 1990 elections and the abolition of the political privileges enshrined in Article 6 of the constitution. The fragility of the powers of the soviets, however, was demonstrated by the presidential decree in April 1990 depriving the Moscow Soviet of the right to license gatherings within two miles of the Kremlin, and the transfer of the two Moscow papers, *Moskovskaya pravda* and *Vechernyaya Moskva*, to the sole authority of the Moscow party organisation. Thus the democrats in the Moscow Soviet lost any direct way to put over their views. Once again the inherent instability of parallel and competing centres of power in the Soviet polity was revealed.

The reforms tried to develop an effective government responsible to parliament and thus to the people. This entailed the creation of ministries which were no longer extensions of party organs, which at its crudest meant that ministries were not much more than the executive agents of departments of the Central Committee. The number of ministries was reduced in Gorbachev's early years by the creation of the so-called 'superministries'. In October 1985 a Bureau for Machine Building was created to co-ordinate the eleven civilian ministries in the field (*P*, 18 October 1985). In November agriculture followed with the formation of the State Agro-industrial Committee (Gosagrom) (*P*, 23 November 1985). The amalgamated ministries shed up to a third of their staff. Between 1986 and 1990 the number of ministries fell from 55 to 37, and the number of state committees from 23 to 19.

The Council of Ministers was drastically reduced in size, derived in part by the merging of ministries into larger bodies. The Council of Ministers is appointed by and formally responsible to the Supreme Soviet. It tried to become the effective government of the USSR, performing executive and administrative tasks, though it was later overshadowed by the Presidential Council. It remains, however, the primary organ of the state bureaucracy and as such has come in for special criticism. At the same time its role as a policy-making body was limited both by the existence of the party's Politburo and by the reactivated Supreme Soviet, its Presidium, Chair and committees.

The embryonic separation of powers was seen in the prohibition against being simultaneously a minister and a deputy. However, while the government as a whole became responsible to parliament, if ministers do not sit in parliament they cannot be questioned in the chamber, though of course they can be called before a standing committee. This separation is reminiscent of the American system, where parties also were condemned by the founding fathers, rather than the European party-based governments accountable to and sitting in parliament.

Prospective ministers have to demonstrate their competence and be recommended for confirmation by the relevant standing committees of parliament. In June 1989 confirmation hearings began for the new government presented by Ryzhkov made up of 57 ranking ministers and 13 deputy premiers. The number had fallen sharply from the old 115-member Council of Ministers, with the greatest fall in the number of economic portfolios, down from 52 to 32. Only ten of the ministers in office in 1984 survived. Abalkin was confirmed as a deputy premier in charge of a new state committee for economic reform. The first non-Communist minister was Nikolai Vorontsov, in charge of the state committee for nature conservation. One of the notable casualties of the new democratic procedures was Vladimir Kamentsev, chair of the Foreign Economic Commission and a deputy Prime Minister, who was accused of nepotism and bureaucratism. Other victims included the incumbent culture minister, Vasilii Zakharov, and Vladimir Gribov, nominated to head a more powerful central bank, Gosbank, and Polad Polad-Zade, recommended to chair the ministry of land reclamation, the body that had laid waste vast tracts of Central Asia and Russia. Their candidatures were withdrawn by Ryzhkov and alternatives proposed. Those who were confirmed often had a stormy ride, as the defence minister, Dmitrii Yazov, discovered.

The constitutional changes of 1988 elevated the status of the government in relation to the party. This was reflected in the new prominence given to the role of the Prime Minister, and Ryzhkov's own personal profile was raised sharply and in effect he became second only to Gorbachev himself. This recreated something like the situation obtaining at the close of Stalin's era, when Georgii Malenkov felt confident that the prime ministership was enough to ensure his succession to Stalin, only to be outwitted by the party's First Secretary, Khrushchev, who went on to establish a thirty-five-year dominance of the party.

As long as a 'leading role' continued to be reserved for the party the revival of the soviets as effective decision-making centres remained in doubt. The constitutional amendments of 1988 provided no clear delineation of the functions of party and soviet bodies despite the constant calls for this to be achieved (e.g. Gorbachev, *SN*, 24 February 1988: 69). In rather traditional language the party was urged to promote the development of the soviets, but not to substitute for them (the process known as *podmena*) or to interfere in their work (*PZ*, 4 February 1988: 19).

Gorbachev argued that the values of the October Revolution, of freedom and democracy, were to be revived to overcome the 'authoritarian methods of power established in the early 1930s' which had limited effective participation in public affairs and led to the domination of representative bodies by the apparatus (*P*, 30 November 1988). While he admitted that the reform of the political system was an extremely complex task, the roots of the distortions were still not fully examined. The monopoly of Communist Party power was broken, and in its place an unstable new type not even of dual power but of 'quadruple power' emerged in which the soviets, the government, the presidency and the Communist Party vied for influence and power.

Participation and workplace democracy

Socialist self-administration (*samoupravlenie*) and the disappearance of the state as a distinct entity were very much played down by Brezhnev. The administrative grip over participation was strengthened. Chernenko's time in power had been, in words at least, a quasi-populist one in which calls were made for greater participation in administration and for a revival of local soviets (*P*, 11 April 1983). During *perestroika* the reformists sought to put into effect traditional Soviet rhetoric on self-management, realising that it would be impossible to achieve a structural transformation of society without challenging the bureaucratic administrative-command system by enlisting the support of forces from below. The strategic policy of the 27th congress was the development of 'people's socialist self-management in an increasingly comprehensive way' (*Materialy XXVII s"ezda KPSS*: 54), though the theme was not highlighted by the revised party programme of 1986. As *perestroika* deepened, the attempt to expand 'popular self-management' became one of the cardinal principles of the new democracy and was lauded as one of the features that distinguished it from liberal democracy. The socialist political system indeed began to be defined as a system of popular self-management (*K*, 8/1986: 17).

Gorbachev's calls for popular initiative can be seen as an attempt to fulfil Article 9 of the 1977 constitution which called for the 'ever broader participation of citizens in managing the affairs of society and the state'. This itself harked back to Khrushchev's idea of a 'state of all the people' in 1961, and indeed to Lenin's *State and Revolution* of 1917. Participatory democracy was used to counter the social forces which benefited from the administrative-command system bequeathed by Stalin and Brezhnev. The democratisation of social life was designed to encourage the 'human factor' in the arts, the sciences and the economy, and as such democratisation has become 'the soul of *perestroika*' (*PZ*, 4/ 1988: 16). For Gorbachev, democratisation and *glasnost* were not just instruments to stimulate the economy but the essence of socialism and a guarantee of the irreversibility of *perestroika* (1987a: 63). By overcoming civic passivity, mass participation was intended to establish a bulwark against a return to the past or the revenge of the bureaucracy.

Gorbachev tried to strip participation of much of its old formalism and to imbue it with a new effectiveness. However, he was not concerned with 'smashing the state' but rather with its regulation, making him a reformer rather than a revolutionary. While the reformers were in favour of greater popular participation, this was seen as complementary to state procedures rather than a substitute for them.

The system of nationwide discussions preceding the adoption of important documents lost some its earlier formalism and allowed some genuine popular participation in the drafting of legislation. Gorbachev revealed that over 6 million suggestions were received during the discussion preceding the adoption of the revised party programme in 1986 (*P*, 26 February 1989). The law on nationwide discussions of 30 June 1987 established a legal framework for them, but fell short of prescribing mandatory referenda (*P*, 1 July 1987). The five-week discussion preceding the adoption of the constitutional amendments of November 1988 evoked some 300,000 contributions leading to changes in half of the draft articles.

The proclamation of the soviets as bodies of people's self-government has been discussed above, but it should be noted that their procedures have been modified to make participation more effective. In addition to the strengthening of the *nakaz* system, 'socialist self-government' has been expanded by allowing recesses in soviets to allow more discussions and more reports to keep the public better informed. Consultative councils under popular governmental bodies have been proposed not only to oversee but also to initiate legislation.

The reforms saw the emergence of a public opinion no longer cowed by fear and as a force in its own right. This is particularly in evidence with ecological issues. The creation of the public opinion centre headed by Tatyana Zaslavskaya has been noted (p.70). Its purpose was to discover public views on social and economic issues (*P*, 18 March 1988: 2). Zaslavskaya drew the link between participation and the need for full information, not only for the leadership but for the public as well: 'People will trust and support you only if you trust them' (*P*, 6 February 1987). The new centre made greater use of public opinion surveys through such measures as telephone sampling. The feedback mechanism of letters to the media was further encouraged, though with the rider that all letters were to be signed to prevent anonymous denunciations.

One of the major elements of any attempt to achieve greater participation in political life must be to expand its accessibility to women, so often screened out by a multitude of factors built into existing structures. In his opening address to the 19th party conference in June 1988 Gorbachev noted that 'women are not duly represented in governing bodies' (*P*, 29 June 1988). Zoya Pukhova, chair of the Soviet Women's Committee, agreed. She argued that the 'new thinking' should be applied to change old-fashioned attitudes. She pointed out the gap between the official policy of equality for women and the reality in which women lost out to men in career opportunities. They received little help in looking after children and the home. The grandiose promises of each five-year plan regarding women had not been translated into effective policies (*XIX konf.*, vol. 2: 78–82).

After 1918 the independent women's movement in the Soviet Union had gradually been incorporated into Bolshevik-dominated structures, and under Stalin the relatively autonomous Bolshevik *zhenotdely* (women's departments) were abolished. Women remained without effective representation until *perestroika*. The women's councils (*zhensovety*) and the Women's Committee created by Khrushchev were largely ceremonial. From 1985 the women's councils were transformed into a mass organisation. Within months of Gorbachev's speech on the subject some 240,000 had been established, reviving an approach popular in the early years of Soviet power. However, apart from the general aim of involving women in political and economic life it was not clear what their precise functions were to be. They duplicated other political organisations like the trade unions, and indeed the newly created 'councils of labour collectives' (see page 157). The *zhensovety* are organised in the traditional hierarchical structure of democratic centralism, with horizontal links as usual rather weak, undermining contacts between them. The network of women's councils was subordinated to the Soviet Women's Committee in a structure passing from the enterprise up through the town, region and union republic women's councils. The Soviet Women's Committee dominates the life of the councils in a traditionally bureaucratic manner with little voice for rank-and-file members (*MN*, 29/1989: 12). The challenge remains to transform the organisation from a quango (quasi non-governmental organisation) into an effective campaigning organisation.

The major assemblies of the restructured democracy are still overwhelmingly dominated by men. Only two women achieved top rank. Aleksandra Biryukova was a Central Committee secretary and then from 1988 a candidate member of the Politburo. In July 1990 Galina Semenova joined the reorganised Politburo and became a Central Committee secretary (*P*, 15 July 1990). The proportion of women elected to the Congress halved, falling from 33 to 17 per cent (*P*, 5 April 1989). The Supreme Soviet's 'commission for women's issues, protection of the family, maternity and childhood' reflected the traditional limitations of such bodies in lacking a concept of paternity or parenthood. Economic reform poses a major challenge to the role of women in work and society, and in particular their right to work in a situation where unemployment is expected to rise. Social difficulties for women abound, including the lack of child care facilities and the problem of contraception in a country where the number of abortions equals the number of births. The dilemma of combining primary responsibility for home-making with professional or political duties (the double shift) did not decrease under *perestroika*. If anything, problems of gender typing have become worse as beauty contests have emerged and official propaganda has stressed the nurturing role of women and the value of the strong family. Gorbachev himself wrote of the need to 'make it possible for women to return to their purely womenly mission' (1987a: 117). The larger issues of the meaning of women's equality under reform Communism, and the nature of social justice where the privileges of the élite are being challenged but those of men over women are little discussed, remain to be resolved. This is a challenge being taken up by the independent women's movement (see page 209).

Effective participation is based on tolerance for differing viewpoints. Gorbachev insists that 'We must treat diversity as normal, as the natural state of the world, not with clenched teeth as in the past' (*Iz.*, 28 October 1986: 3). This was not accompanied by a revival of Khrushchev's populism but tried to outflank the bureaucracy by achieving a level of popular democracy. The powers and privileges of top officials and the corruption of individuals have been condemned, but the assault against the bureaucracy has taken place in the framework of the socialist legal state rather than in the dissolution of the state into full-scale self-managing bodies which was Khrushchev's ultimate purpose. Self-management under Gorbachev was the partner of a democratised state, rather than its alternative.

This entailed a realisation that Lenin's vision in *State and Revolution* was flawed. Lenin's insistence that under socialism people would participate 'not only in voting and elections, *but also in the everyday administration of the state*' is accepted, but the further argument that 'Under socialism *all* will govern in turn and soon will become accustomed to no one governing' (Lenin, 1977: 116) has been modified. The latter proposition, which even Lenin did not think was an immediate prospect, in effect meant the abolition of politics in favour of expanded administration which failed to provide channels for effective mass participation in policy-making. In its place a massive bureaucracy emerged whose roots are only now being analysed. Kudryavtsev pointed out that in all the years of Soviet power no serious study had been made of the bureaucracy (1989: 5). Soviet sociologists are now making up for lost time (e.g. Shubkin, 1988, and Makarenko, forthcoming).

While Gorbachev condemned the particularly virulent form that Soviet bureaucracy has taken, he was not opposed to bureaucracy as such. He was well aware that modern administrative theory has not yet been able to find a way of dispensing with the services of a bureaucracy and that traditional Marxist views on the subject were Utopian. Gorbachev hoped to shed some of the millions of Soviet bureaucrats and to establish democratic oversight over the workings of the apparatus as a whole. A strengthened system of appeals against the actions of officials has been introduced through an expanded system of citizen's complaints (*P*, 21 October 1987: 3). A law of 30 June 1987 gave citizens for the first time the right of legal appeal against the violation of their rights by public officials. The new law provided a mechanism for the implementation of the vague rights contained in Article 58 of the 1977 constitution which asserted that officials could be sued, but failed to say how. The measure revealed Gorbachev's determination to establish a legal framework to encourage greater popular participation without fear of recrimination.

Russian political culture has often been argued to be subject-participant, a relatively passive approach to political processes (see page 368). The experience of *perestroika* demonstrated that given the right opportunities political culture can change very fast. Fears of popular passivity gave way to concern that there might simply be too much involvement in ways that threatened the integrity of the system and could lead on to anarchy. Gorbachev urged the development of an active citizenry, but he qualified this by insisting that they should be 'politically aware'. What this means in practice is that participation should be channelled in system-supportive ways. There are two ways the leadership can achieve this. The first is by creating a set of institutions that can integrate popular activity in forms that do not threaten the system. The second is by appeals to political maturity and indirect censorship. Gorbachev increasingly tended towards the first option, though did not eschew the second. The institutional changes from above combined with popular pressure from below began to establish a momentum for change that became well-nigh unstoppable.

The emergence of a vigorous public opinion meant that *perestroika* was no longer, if it ever was, the preserve of the intelligentsia. The involvement of large numbers from all social groups in the elections democratised *perestroika*, as it were, and these people then went on to show their feelings in demonstrations and rallies that came to make up a whole new type of political activity under *perestroika*. Every citizen faced by a choice at the ballot box develops a degree of independence of mind that is difficult to erase. The masses, as it were, once again become active participants on the stage of Soviet politics, rather than auxiliaries in the crowd scenes.

This is particularly in evidence in the workplace. The attempt under *perestroika* to breathe new life into economic democracy is seen as fulfilling the promise of socialism (Litvin, 1987). Gorbachev's reforms have been marked by a strong, indeed dialectical, awareness that productive forces can be creatively developed only if the relations of production do not act as a fetter. In this he returned to Marx and rejected the division between the economic and the political, and for a time dismissed Lenin's view that 'Industry is indispensable: democracy is a category proper only to the political sphere' (cited D'Agostino, 1988: 17). Reform of the economy from above was accompanied by attempts to involve workers from below. The strategy tried to defuse the sort of working-class pressure that gave rise to Solidarity in Poland. A democratic system of workers' self-management was designed to balance the introduction of economic accountability (*khozraschët*) envisaged by the Law on State Enterprises which was adopted on 30 June 1987 and which came into force on 1 January 1988. The law gave workers the right to elect the managing director as well as a council of workers' collectives. The reform of industry was to be accompanied by its democratisation, a dual programme that found one undermining the other.

There were four main aspects to the democratisation of industry. The first was the attempt to make the concept of the 'labour collective' a living force in the life of the enterprise. This was to be achieved by the creation of enterprise, shop and brigade councils (soviets) of self-management, whose formation had already been suggested by the 1977 constitution and developed by the 1983 Law on Labour Collectives. The 'councils of labour collectives' are somewhat reminiscent of the factory committees of 1917–18, which were later incorporated into the trade unions, and may possibly in time share some characteristics with the workers' council established during the Hungarian revolution of 1956. The early history of the councils showed that a disproportionate share of places was taken up by administrative personnel, whereas the latter were not meant to make up more than a quarter of the total (*PZ*, 4/1988: 17). Their purpose was to exert a degree of democratic control over production decisions and the life of the enterprise.

The second strand in the democratisation of work was the introduction of the 'electoral principle' into the workplace. The original view that managers were to be elected by general meetings or conferences of labour collectives was modified by Ryzhkov at the second Congress (*P*, 14 December 1989). Even in the first variant the choice was not left entirely to the work collective since the party conducted a guiding role in 'personnel policy', though this was to have been achieved through 'exclusively democratic methods' (*PZ*, 4/1988: 18). Article 6 of the Law on State Enterprises affirmed the guiding role of the party in self-management (*P*, 1 July 1987), though the *nomenklatura* system was weakened. Elected managers are more able to resist party demands, but not those of the workers.

The third element was the revival of the trade unions themselves. Experience of Solidarity in Poland revealed what could happen if the gulf between workers and their alleged representatives became too large. The strike wave culminated in the miners' strikes of July 1989 (see pages 210ff), which showed what could happen if the gulf between a bureaucratised union hierarchy and a dissatisfied labour force became too large at a time of falling living standards and political turmoil. During *perestroika* the unions were urged to become the genuine representatives of the working class. However, the relationship between the councils of worker collectives and the trade unions is not always clear. In principle, the trade unions have been exhorted to defend the rights of workers, whereas the role of the councils is to provide a mechanism for worker participation in management, which on occasions may still require vigorous union intervention to defend workers' interests. The unions clearly refused to remain the Cinderella of Soviet politics. However, as during war Communism, when hopes of the unions actually taking over the management of industry were dashed, they are still bypassed by a range of bodies.

A meeting of the All-Union Central Council of Trade Unions (AUCCTU) in September 1989, in the wake of the miners' strikes, vowed to redirect itself 'towards defending the legitimate rights and interests of working people'. The leader of the 140 million-strong national union organisation, Stepan A. Shalaev, admitted that the strikes had revealed a 'crisis of confidence in sociopolitical structures, including trade unions'. He urged that mechanisms similar to collective bargaining should be found to identify and settle conflicts at an early stage, and though strikes were instrumental in advancing the workers' cause they were to be avoided. The development of effective social policies, the employment of young people in cost-accounting plants, and combating latent unemployment and indeed unemployment in certain regions were seen as the main tasks of the union movement. He also urged a struggle against greedy co-operatives and the creation of a trade union council for the Russian federation (*P*, 7 September 1989). The resurgent union leadership immediately set about braking the economic reforms by urging a freeze on basic food prices until 1991. The new leader of the AUCCTU, Gennadi Yanaev, elected in April 1990, fought hard to ensure that the burden of radical economic restructuring would not fall too hard on workers. The contradiction between a revived worker democracy and marketising economic reform emerged in all its harshness, underlining the fact that earlier opportunities for bitter 'medicine' had been missed. A more assertive union movement made industrial rationalisation that much more difficult.

The fourth aspect of democratisation of work was a new approach to industrial relations. A draft bill in April 1989 to regulate labour conflicts was superseded by a more detailed one in August which for the first time made strikes legal, but introduced several restrictive clauses (*Trud*, 16 August 1989). Strikes were prohibited in strategic sectors like railways, civil aviation and other public transport, the defence and energy industries, and in government administration, the police and com-munications. Strikes could be mounted only after an elaborate procedure, including a three-day 'cooling-off period', then a five-day period in which a 'conciliation commission' from both sides should look into the dispute. If still no resolution could be found an arbitration tribunal made up of local judges and parliamentary deputies could be called on, who were to give a verdict within a week. If all that failed then the strike weapon could be used as an 'extreme measure' but only after five days' notice had been given, and a majority of the workforce had voted for action in a secret or open ballot. Picketing was illegal and strikers would lose their pay. To balance these restrictions, managers held responsible for causing the strike could be sacked, and not only official unions or councils of workers' collectives but also other bodies empowered by the workers, like the shop-floor committees which emerged during the miners' strike, could represent the workers.

Soviet ideas on worker self-management were still a long way from those introduced in Yugoslavia under Tito. Yugoslav reforms were accompanied by a theoretical reappraisal of the role of ownership under socialism, which led to the introduction of the notion of 'social ownership' encouraging worker management through councils. In Yugoslavia, however, the bureaucracy remained, albeit at a lower level, leading to the loss of national economies of scale and to nationalism. The democratisation of industry in the Soviet Union during *perestroika* tried to avoid pitting one sectional or national interest against another and was based on the ideal of collective social harmony in the workplace (Bova, 1987), although there was a growing awareness that a degree of contestation is not necessarily a bad thing.

There is a contradiction between the attempt to improve efficiency and the attempt to augment democracy in the workplace, a contradiction faced by Lenin in his usual resolute style. The two principles can come into conflict in the election of factory and farm managers, posts requiring skills, a variety of expertise and experience. The Press was full of stories of the election of popular but weak directors. In the West the training of managers and the recruitment of personnel has developed into a whole 'head-hunting' industry, and yet the Soviets at first opted for democratisation instead of professionalisation. The two are not necessarily opposed and resources have now been allocated for the training of middle managers, but there is the risk that in elections popularity may not coincide with managerial ability and that hard decisions, like redundancies, will be postponed. It is for this reason that by the fifth year of *perestroika* the balance shifted away from worker self-management towards a more professional managerial ethos.

Leadership and policy-making

In his book *On Socialist Democracy* Roy Medvedev in 1975 predicted the emergence of a reformist leader of the type of Gorbachev, and the book outlined a political programme which in essentials forecast the strategy of *perestroika*. Change from above sponsored by a reformist leader reinforced the role of leadership in the Soviet system focused on Gorbachev himself. Reformists have rallied to his banner. Korotich argued that 'There is no alternative. If Gorbachev goes, the system goes with him. Gorbachev is the only way to make us part of humanity again' (*Ind.*, 9 February 1989).

Gorbachev represents the third generation of Soviet leaders. The first were the Old Bolsheviks, Lenin's colleagues who made the revolution and who were destroyed by Stalin. The second generation was the Stalinist one, which included Khrushchev, Brezhnev and their successors. Gorbachev's generation has experienced years of reform and counter-reform since 1953, and for them the Revolution is already a fading historical memory.

When he came to power, Gorbachev's personal legitimacy was immediately high, and to a degree in his first years he was able, by putting forward a vision of reform, to restore a greater sense of legitimacy to the system as a whole. By 1989, however, the Gorbachev honeymoon period was definitely over. *Perestroika* had provided few material benefits, and the image of the reforming tsar gave way to comparison with failed modernisers like the Shah of Iran.

For Burlatsky the Brezhnev era demonstrated the urgency of reforming the system of leadership selection in the Soviet Union. This was to be buttressed by Khrushchev's idea of the rotation of leaders implemented by a democratic electoral procedure. Above all, he argued that the mandate of the Politburo was insufficient and that the necessary authority for effective leadership could be legitimated only through direct popular elections (*LG*, 15 June 1988). Some of this was achieved and the role of leadership under Gorbachev changed in many ways. The role of leader was formalised and leadership was placed in a constitutional framework. The tendency for the principle of collective leadership to be transformed into exaggerated individual leadership was given the force of law while at the same time constrained by law.

The expansion of presidential powers took place in two stages. The 1988 constitutional changes tried, Gorbachev argued, to give the President enough power to organise the work of the Supreme Soviet and its Presidium while avoiding the excessive concentration of power in one person. The principle of collective leadership, he insisted, was being retained (*P*, 30 November 1989). The President had wide powers to nominate the Prime Minister, to manage the country's foreign policy, be the commander-in-chief of the armed forces and sign all laws into effect. To help him do this a presidential staff began to emerge. The Soviet parliament was now headed by an executive President who acted as the major initiator of policy. According to the 1988 amendments, the Congress could recall the President by secret ballot, thus establishing a degree of restraint on the emergence of elective dictatorship. The indirect method of electing the President, however, reflected the compromises and contradictions in the democratisation process. The

Congress became the electoral college for the presidency, rather like the old electoral college in the United States. The executive President thereby was deprived of a popular mandate and his authority was weakened. The next president would be elected by popular vote in five years.

Despite the constant invocation that it was the party which launched *perestroika* and was responsible for its implementation, it would be more accurate to say that it was one person, Gorbachev, who launched the policy against the protests of the party apparatus and the howls of the conservatives. The President of the USSR, like the French and American Presidents, took to addressing the nation directly on matters of concern. Gorbachev defended his accumulation of power, which by 1989 included being General Secretary of the Communist Party and chair of the Russian Bureau, President of the Supreme Soviet, leader of the legislature as head of the largest (and only) party, and chair of the Defence Council, as a matter of practical politics. There was some justification for this, since clearly only a firm hand could ensure the success of reforming legislation against the conservatism of the Central Committee and even of the Congress.

While the reformists pinned their hopes on a powerful leader forcing reforms from above, the creation of a powerful presidency was greeted with misgivings by some of the more radical figures. In the elections for the presidency in May 1989 no alternative candidate was put forward by the 'democratic minority', which later constituted itself as the 'interregional group', let alone by the conservatives. Sakharov and nine other deputies abstained from the vote because of the absence of a serious alternative candidate. In introducing his Decree on Power on 9 June 1989 Sakharov warned that 'The concentration of such power in the hands of one person is extremely dangerous, even if this man is the initiator of *perestroika*.' He identified a growing loss of confidence in the nation's leadership, leading to drift and disillusionment. In his proposed Decree he foresaw direct nationwide elections for the posts of President and Vice-President (*XX Century and Peace*, 8/1989: 9–10). Elsewhere he warned that the plan for political reform was a 'time bomb' giving the Kremlin a dangerous monopoly of power: 'A head of state with such powers in a country that does not have a multiparty system is just insanity. . .Today it is Gorbachev, but tomorrow it could be someone else. There are no guarantees that some Stalinist will not succeed him' (*Ind.*, 3 November 1988). Gorbachev had avoided, at least for a time, the fate of Pozsgay in Hungary, whose courage had done so much to stimulate radical reform only to then find himself discarded by the ensuing democratic revolution. The liberal authoritarianism represented by Gorbachev's accumulation of power created the framework for a revived *dirigiste* style of leadership, now no longer focused on the party but on the presidency. Thus party-guided *perestroika* gave way to presidential *perestroika*.

Disappointment at the failure of the Congress to institutionalise the democratic revolution and the mounting economic, social and national crises led certain observers to argue in favour of the 'firm hand' with dictatorial powers to push through the reforms against the opposition of the conservatives and the bureaucracy (Klyamkin and Migranyan, *LG*, 16 August 1989). Migranyan (1989) urged reformists to take 'more serious and radical steps to stop the fall in their authority and seize the initiative'. In a crisis there were fears that Gorbachev might have to displace democracy and act like Cromwell as Lord Protector for the duration. Gorbachev appears to have taken heed of such advice, and the resolution adopted by the February 1990 Central Committee plenum spoke of the need to give the President 'the necessary powers. . .to maintain stable development, to speed up *perestroika*, to guarantee its irreversibility, to ensure the normal and effective functioning of all state and public institutions in the process of democratisation. . .' (*P*, 13 February 1990). Contrary to expectations, no mention was made of direct national elections for the strengthened presidency.

The second stage of Gorbachev's presidential coup was resisted by the radicals, but on 13 March 1990 the powers of the presidency were strengthened by the emergency third convocation of the Congress of People's Deputies. Gorbachev, who had previously been only President of the Supreme Soviet, on 14 March was elected President of the USSR with powers and status akin to those of a French or American President. The new presidency had wide executive powers including the power to declare martial law, to impose direct presidential rule within the country and to declare war against other countries. The President had the right to appoint the Prime Minister and individual ministers and to rule by decree (*P*, 16 March 1990). However, presidential powers were rather less than Gorbachev's original proposals. The declaration of a state of emergency required the sanction of the Supreme Soviet in the republic concerned, or the USSR Supreme Soviet. The President could not appeal to the Congress if the Supreme Soviet overrode his or her veto. And, thirdly, the members of the Committee of Constitutional Review would be appointed not by the President but by the Chair of the Supreme Soviet. Despite these concessions Gorbachev was elected the nation's first President by a surprisingly low margin, 1,329 out of 2,245 (59.2 per cent), with 495 votes cast against, reflecting considerable unease at the emergence of a 'new tsar'.

A Presidential Council of seventeen was established, composed, in the first instance, of the Chair of the Supreme Soviet (Lukyanov was elected to this post), the Prime Minister (Ryzhkov), the Minister of Foreign Affairs (Shevardnadze), the Minister of Defence (Dmitrii Yazov), the Minister of the Interior (Vadim Bakatin), the head of the KGB (Kryuchkov) and the head of the State Planning Commission (Yuri Maslyukov). These were appointed *ex officio*, and the others were appointed at the President's discretion. These were Yakovlev, a minister without portfolio, Evgenii Primakov, the Chair of the Council of the Union of the Supreme Soviet, Grigorii Revenkov, a member of the USSR Supreme Soviet, the Russian patriotic writer (and only non-Communist on the Council) Valentin Rasputin, the Kirghiz writer Chingiz Aitmatov, the self-declared social democrat economist Stanislav Shatalin, the director of a successful Latvian agricultural enterprise Albert Kauls, a leader of the United Front of Workers Venyamin Yarin, a leading physicist Yuri Osipian and Valerii Boldin, the head of the Central Committee's General Department. A Council of the Federation was also established with representatives of the fifteen republics, which often met in joint session with the Presidential Council. At the same time, Gorbachev's 'kitchen cabinet' took on a more prominent role. The academic Georgii Shakhnazarov, who favoured a multi-party system and an American-style presidency, had been advising Gorbachev for some years. The philosopher Ivan Frolov remained close to decision-making even though he was now editor of *Pravda*. Anatolii Chernyaev was formerly one of five CC international department chiefs and now advised Gorbachev on foreign policy. The fourth adviser, the radical economic reformer and expert on prices and finance, Nikolai Petrakov, became in effect the presidential spokesperson on economic affairs. In addition, the President now had an official spokesperson, Arkadii Maslennikov, who took over some of the functions of the Foreign Ministry spokesperson, Gennadi Gerasimov.

Thus the Politburo and Central Committee were effectively marginalised; indeed, the Politburo met infrequently in the following months, and when it did meet it concentrated on internal Communist Party matters, a trend confirmed by the 28th congress. The problem remained, however, of the relationship between the remaining 'efficient' (to use Walter Bagehot's term) parts of the power system, the President, the Supreme Soviet and the Council of Ministers. Lukyanov argued that one of the major tasks of the presidency was to co-ordinate the work of the three (*P*, 2 April 1990), but this was unlikely to satisfy Ryzhkov who saw his power of ministerial appointment eroded.

The gap in executive leadership in the country had thus been filled, but the creation of an executive presidency without the check of a parliamentary opposition or constitutionally defined powers illustrated the pitfalls of one-party democracy. The trenchant criticisms of the new structures of strong executive power, somewhat reminiscent of the presidential structures established by De Gaulle for the Fifth Republic in France in 1958, spilled over into personal criticisms of Gorbachev's leadership style. However, accusations that Gorbachev had become, in institutional if not personal terms, a dictator, were probably exaggerated. While impatient, headstrong, and on occasion intolerant, Gorbachev did not appear to be made of the stuff out of which dictators are forged. His willingness to acknowledge mistakes and the rejection of any cult of infallibility acted as a degree of insurance against dictatorship. It would appear almost too Machiavellian to suggest that Gorbachev deliberately undermined the authority of the Communist Party in order to put himself forward as President. Nevertheless, fears that the new institutions of leadership could provide the basis for a less scrupulous successor to establish dictatorial control were well founded.

Forty years of Yugoslav reform Communism seem to have led in at least one constituent republic, Serbia under Slobodan Milosevic, to the prospect that the dictatorship of the proletariat would give way to the rule of a dictator or a benevolent autocrat who could impose a solution. Such a ruler would not necessarily act as a counter-reformer but as an enlightened despot who could force through reforms against entrenched opposition and bureaucratic inertia. Indeed, the proponents of the 'new authoritarianism', such as the social scientist Liu Donghua and Zhao Ziyang's adviser Bao Tong, saw the road to democracy and modernisation as passing through the authoritarianism which seems to have been effective in Taiwan, Singapore and South Korea (*Ind.*, 29 March 1989). However, the proponents of the 'new democracy', like Su Shaozhi, identify the authoritarian principle as having caused the problems in the first place, and in its new guise was not likely to work more effectively than in the past.

The relationship of leadership to the political system has changed. The consolidation of Gorbachev's position as President, albeit elected by the Congress rather than directly by the nation, made him independent from the Politburo, whereas the General Secretary had traditionally, in theory at least, been no more than first among equals. It should be stressed that the political system up to 1989 placed limits on leadership, and Gorbachev was forced to use the threat of resignation more than once to have his way. The Khrushchev reforms did not extend to constitutional reform, and the 'administrative-command' system was able to eject him with little effort. Now a parliament emerged as a counterweight to plots in the Politburo directed against the General Secretary. Public opinion itself would have made a conservative coup against Gorbachev a dangerous affair and one which could not have been restricted to the magic circle of the leadership alone. Decisions in the Politburo apparently were now taken by votes rather than the old method of consensus, and the old facade of unity began to crumble. The transformation of the Politburo at the 28th party congress in 1990 (see p. 174) and the reorganisation of the Central Committee in any case signalled the end of the old style of closed politics and brought divisions into the open.

The popular legitimacy for leadership changed. The hero-worshipping charismatic leadership of the past, however uncharismatic the individual leader, now gave way to a more critical attitude. The cult of Lenin remained but it lost some of its awesome magical properties as the Communist agitprop apparatus was deflated. Charisma will now really have to be achieved by the personality of the incumbent as leadership becomes based on legal rationality.

The political culture of the polity also changed. As the old authoritarianism declined it became easier to establish whether the alleged ingrained respect for the 'strong tsar' of Russian political culture was in fact a credible interpretation of popular attitudes. Was the strong leadership from Peter the Great to Stalin a need generated by the nature of the system or by the nature of the people? The populace was now urbanised and educated and this clearly affected the quality of leadership and its relationship to society.

During *perestroika* there was an assault on the *dirigisme* associated with the administrative-command form of socialism. *Dirigisme* was originally associated with the French state's attempt to direct the economy, but it now tends to be used in an expanded sense of state and individual leadership over society as a whole. Soviet *dirigisme* emerged out of what Trotsky called substitutionalism, where the leader dominates the party machinery, the party machinery the party as a whole, and the party the working class and society. In the early Soviet model of socialism economic *dirigisme* was transferred wholesale into the realm of politics as state management came to be seen in terms of an expanded form of administration. The leadership of the party became personified in the form of Stalin, and thus the cult of personality only represented a focusing of an intrinsic *dirigisme* on to a single person. Stalinism represented a shift from the leadership of the party to the leadership of the leader. Even with the stress on collective leadership after his death, the defence of the party's leading role was inevitably associated with 'command and administer' methods. The emphasis on *dirigisme* in the form of the party's leading role was indeed the defining characteristic of the unreformed USSR.

With the onset of democratisation the party's leading role was redefined and there was an expanded role for self-management. The redefinition of *dirigisme* at the centre was to be reflected in more open and democratic leadership in the localities. Officials were exhorted to be more considerate and to govern by conviction rather than by bureaucratic orders. Officials were to learn the 'art of political leadership' in order to inculcate a 'culture of democracy' into society as a whole. A whole new type of 'civic responsibility' (*grazhdanstvennost*') was urged (Moiseev, 1988). The new definition of leadership moderated the party's *dirigisme* over social and economic processes by separating 'ruling' from 'governing'.

Another aspect of leadership in transition was a style of policy-making which tried to combine strong leadership with democratic procedures. A new policy process was required to overcome the system's entropic tendencies by ensuring not only that decisions were taken but that they were implemented. The politics of *perestroika* heightened the role of leadership. The reform process was always in danger of being hijacked either by the radicals, who urged the removal of restraints on *perestroika*, or by the conservatives, who wished to control the pace of change. The dialectic of reform added a new dynamic to the already powerful tendency in the USSR towards strong leadership, in this case to prevent *perestroika* falling prey to either the radicals or the conservatives.

The limits to the 'institutional pluralism' achieved under Brezhnev can now be seen against the backdrop of a more assertive leadership. The autonomy of institutions and the bureaucracy were sharply reined in by the revival of a strong political centre. At the same time, however, the limitations on leadership were starkly revealed by the struggle to achieve radical reform. The ambiguities resulting from the attempt to combine a more dynamic leadership with democracy provided one of the more unsettling of the paradoxes of *perestroika*. It is clear that *dirigisme* was still very much part of the Soviet system. The party's leading role in the first five years was only being redefined, not abolished, and Gorbachev's personal leadership role surpassed that of any leader since Stalin. The need to push through reforms heightened the role of leadership, but at the same time it ran counter to the spirit of the reforms.

A degree of authoritarianism remained in the very process of democratisation. Gorbachev as leader used the traditional methods of manipulation in order to get his policies through. This was most vividly in evidence at the 19th party conference when the democratising resolutions were adopted without specifically having been debated. The dramatic personnel changes which consolidated the first stage of the presidential revolution were ratified by the CC on 30 September and the Supreme Soviet on 1 October 1988, both meetings lasting about an hour, with unanimous votes and no debates. The tension between a programme of Communist reformism and democratic leadership increasingly came to the fore. Korotich argued 'I too could criticise Gorbachev, but I won't, because to undermine him would be fatal. It would help his enemies' (*Ob.*, 12 February 1989). While the temporising of the reformists was understandable in refusing to give cause for complaint to the conservatives, it made the advance of democracy all the harder. As radicals like Sakharov argued, what sort of democracy can be born by undemocratic means?

The general problem facing any Communist leader who engages in reform is that the power of the government as such tends to decline as the reform process develops, power here being defined as the government's ability to mobilise resources with popular and institutional backing. One by one the levers of power were broken. Assaults on regional bureaucracies, for example, encouraged them to develop countermeasures to defend their position. In response, Gorbachev's leadership strategy was a cautious one, a gradual consolidation of the position of the reformers, interspersed with the sudden counterthrust.

In a period of democratising reform the relationship between leadership and politics changed. Leadership and policy-making in the Soviet Union can be seen as having been involved in a process of broadening over the years. This reflected an expanding role for politics, defined briefly as debate over policies. Under Stalin policy-making was largely restricted to the leadership and politics took the form of struggles between small groups at the apex of the political system. We know, for example, that in the immediate post-war years there was a broad division between the 'party revivalists', led by Zhdanov, and those who stressed the role of the state, led by Malenkov. Under Khrushchev and Brezhnev the scope of effective politics was broadened to include the social, political and professional élite, marked in particular by a greater role for specialists in policy-making. The third stage under Gorbachev saw the repoliticisation of society, not in the old sense of the administrative regulation of every significant life-choice, but allowing society a degree of effective choice and methods of articulating preferences. Society itself has been encouraged to involve itself in the management of common affairs through elections and participation. The monopoly of the bureaucracy over politics was broken. Experience from Eastern Europe suggested that the fourth stage in the broadening scope for politics would take the form of the recreation of multi-party politics. This opens the door to the revival of the socialist critique of liberal democracy, and thus the cycle would perhaps begin anew. Gorbachev long resisted crossing the Rubicon in the belief that an effective form of one-party democracy could be created at the third stage.

As the financial, economic, nationalist and political crises deepened in

1989 Gorbachev's popularity and authority continued to decline. This was not so much due to dashed expectations of consumer plenty and liberty, since few Soviet people believed that these could be achieved by *perestroika*, but by the absence of hope that *perestroika* could find even partial solutions to any of the problems facing the country. However, no effective alternative Communist leader emerged. The March 1989 elections brought to the fore Eltsin as a charismatic and popular figure, and his election as president of the Russian republic in May 1990 undermined Gorbachev's position as leader.

Divisions over the strategy for *perestroika* were reflected in what appeared at times as confusion in the policy-making process itself. Strong reformist leadership in a fluid political structure meant that decisions appeared to be made on an *ad hoc* basis with no effective means of ensuring their implementation. The attempt to achieve compromises between conservatives and radicals often led to unworkable policies. The institutional and political stalemate was thus reflected in chaotic policy-making.

This was partially a reflection of the limitations on leadership in the Soviet Union. The Anglo-American assessment at the beginning of Bush's presidency that Gorbachev could be overthrown by his domestic opponents if he stumbled, and that his position depended on the speed with which he could find effective economic policies, was essentially correct. The position of a non-dictatorial leader is dependent on success in policy, and no amount of consolidation can compensate for failure. Despite Gorbachev's great concentration of power he still had to lead as a member of a collective, and thus in practice had less effective power than a leader of, say, a British party returned to power with a large majority. The principle of collective leadership changed as the executive presidency began to carve out a degree of autonomy, but was constrained by an active legislature wary of the excessive concentration of power. The Politburo gave up its traditional prerogatives only when faced with a catastrophic political breakdown in 1990. Gorbachev made himself independent of the party apparatus to a degree unequalled since Stalin.

The *nomenklatura* class as a whole placed limits on the effective scope of leadership power. At the same time, the traditional interplay between the power and authority of the individual leader did not diminish during *perestroika*. The actual structure of policy-making had still not been formalised, leading to the weakness of executive power noted by Ryzhkov and others. Policy implementation had not improved much from Brezhnev's day, despite the vigorous new leadership, as the party and state machine was reorganised. There simply seemed no effective way in which Gorbachev could impose his writ on, say, the Baltic or the

Caucasus. This took place against the background of a growing distrust of authority spawned by the revelations about the monstrous doings of Stalin and the corruption of the period of stagnation. The traditional sources of authority, the party and the Communist project, weakened, and the hesitancy in embracing democratic legitimation led to a dangerous vacuum into which all sorts of populists, authoritarians, anti-Semites, chauvinist nationalists and others stepped.

The party and politics

Perestroika of the economy and democratisation of society were not intended to undermine the Communist Party's leading role but rather to enhance it. Gorbachev frequently argued that 'the *perestroika* drive started on the Communist Party's initiative, and the party *leads* it' (1987a: 55). In other words, the fact that the party had begun the reform process allegedly gave it the right to continue ruling. The party, though, had to reform itself. Gorbachev argued that 'It is the party that bears responsibility for the development of the process of democratisation. But if it is to be capable of expressing the requirements of the new stage it must itself undergo change.' He insisted that 'The party cannot lag behind the processes that are taking place in society' (*P*, 15 July 1987). However, by early 1990 it had become clear that the party *had* lagged behind developments in society, and it was forced to change its role and organisation.

In contrast to the 1961 party programme, which focused on the state and society, the revised 1986 programme adopted by the 27th congress emphasised the party, insisting that the Party's 'leading role in the life of society inevitably grows' (*Programme*, 1986: 82). More responsibility was placed on Communists and party bodies; hence their effectiveness was to be improved. The definition of democratic centralism was expanded to stress the role of 'business-like' discussions within the party and the development of 'Leninist norms' of party life by the encouragement of criticism and self-criticism. None of this was particularly new, but the difference was that the Gorbachev leadership actually tried to revive and democratise inner-party life. This was reflected in modifications to the party rules, though on the whole there were few major changes. A fifth point was added to the definition of democratic centralism insisting on a 'collective spirit in the work of all organisations and leading Party bodies and the personal responsibility of every Communist for the fulfilment of his duties and party assignments' (*Rules*, 1986: 12). No specific measures were adopted to ensure 'the principle of the systematic renewal of the composition of Party bodies (*ibid.*: 13). The comment that 'Any manifestation of factionalism or group activity is incompatible with Marxist–Leninist Party principles' (p. 5) was balanced by the injunction that 'Those who suppress criticism or victimise anyone for criticism shall be penalised strictly' (p. 7).

Gorbachev's intention was not to create a new party but to reform the old. In Hungary the radical Communist reformists sought to transform their party (HSWP) into a leftist party on Western social democratic lines, to be called the Hungarian Socialist Party, and the PCI took the same step in December 1989. For Gorbachev the aim was to democratise the party so that its leading role could be achieved in a political, rather than administrative way. New vigour was given to the old attempt to separate the functions of the Communist Party and the state. Chernenko's speech to his nominating plenum of 13 February 1983 urged a clear demarcation of the functions of the party and the state, insisting that the party was to be an instrument of 'political leadership' rather than the day-to-day manager of social and economic affairs (*P*, 14 February 1983).

The democratisation of the party was to take several forms. One of them was the attempt to revive an interactive form of politics within the party itself, and thus to ensure the involvement of all Communists on a democratic basis in party life. This involved the rejuvenation of primary party organisations. Discussions were to lose their 'formal' nature to allow genuine debate. *Glasnost* was to operate as much inside the party as in society. The democratisation of the party necessarily alters radically what it means to be a Communist (*P*, 2 May 1988).

Another aspect was the improved selection of recruits and the purging of undesirable elements. The 1986 rules allowed non-members to participate in discussions about the qualifications of candidates. The minimum entry age to the party was raised (with the exception of Komsomol members) to 25 (*Rules*, 1986: 8). The party's elective bodies were to develop a new relationship with the membership and to stop 'over-organising' meetings (*P*, 21 November 1987). The report-back link between executive bodies and the membership was to be strengthened, establishing a degree of democratic control from below. This was to be balanced by the injunction for more reports from lower to higher bodies to avoid the gulf between the two. The candidate stage for party membership was dropped in 1990, and at the same time resignation from the party became much easier (*P*, 28 June 1990).

The major thrust of inner-party democratisation comes from the development of the 'electoral principle'. This began with the election of offices within party committees and was later extended to the election of committees themselves with fixed terms for party officials. The new emphasis on openness in party operations urged by the new rules included the open election of certain posts in lower-party bodies. The *nomenklatura* system of appointments was undermined by the introduction of an increasingly effective 'electoral principle' and was in danger of simply withering away. It still operated, however, in the guise of the party's 'personnel policy'. Party recommendations (the *nomenklatura* system) and democracy were not considered incompatible (*P*, 16 November 1987: 2).

A leader's authority is achieved through success in policy. For Gorbachev this was slow in coming, but one of the major factors which helped tide him over the lean years of *perestroika* was the new approach to politics itself. Already at the 27th party congress his speech on behalf of the CC was called the 'political report', restoring the word 'political' that had been current in Lenin's day and that had last been used at the 16th congress in 1930 (Rigby in Miller *et al.* (eds.), 1987: 14). The political dimension was restored to discussion in the party suggesting that there were choices to be made, replacing the choicelessness typical of the Stalin to Brezhnev years.

The reforms signalled not the dissolution of democratic centralism but its adaptation to new social and political challenges, illustrating Gramsci's contention that 'democratic centralism provides an elastic formula, which lends itself to many embodiments; it lives to the extent to which it is continually interpreted and adapted to necessity' (Waller, 1981: preface). At its March 1989 congress the PCI went much further in its burial of what were considered to be the coercive mechanisms of democratic centralism, but hesitated to legitimate the formal right of individual Communists to dissent from collective party decisions. In the USSR the ban on 'horizontalism', in which lower-level bodies relate directly to each other thus avoiding the higher instance, was modified to allow platforms but much to the disappointment of the radicals, factions with their own organisations were banned by the statutes discussed by the 28th party congress (*P*, 28 June 1990). Fear of horizontalism had for years led to an excess of 'verticalism', but by 1990 a number of groupings had emerged in the party that rendered void the old ban on factions.

The attempt to lessen the party's direct role in running social affairs was implemented in a highly ambivalent manner. It is difficult to see how the election of party First Secretaries as simultaneously the chairpersons of the local soviet executive committees could advance the cause of separating the functions of party and state, a point forcibly driven home to Gorbachev at the 19th party conference and later. The attempt to expand the bifunctionalism of party leaders would only perpetuate the traditional confusion. As a result it encountered much opposition and was only patchily implemented. The limits to the democratisation of the party were revealed in the choosing of candidates to the 19th party conference and the 28th congress. The old methods were very much in evidence, and once again instead of elections by the mass of the membership there was a tendency towards the usual 'selection' by the local party committee.

The party's *apparat* has also been reorganised and personnel reshuffled in order to facilitate the separation of the party and state. In a series of dramatic changes designed to accelerate economic reform the top bodies of the party were restructured at the emergency plenum of the Central Committee on 30 September 1988. The Central Committee apparatus underwent the most significant change since its consolidation in the early 1920s. The Secretariat, as such, was abolished and replaced by six new commissions (party development and personnel policy; ideology; social and economic policy; agrarian policy; international policy; and legal policy) to manage the twenty departments of the old Secretariat, half of which were responsible for managing the economy. The number of departments was soon reduced to nine. The commissions replaced the old system of some twelve powerful secretaries in charge of the departments staffed by *apparatchiki*, the full-time party bureaucrats, in which there was little scope for outside supervision or participation.

Aleksandr Yakovlev was transferred from the CC department responsible for the mass media, where he had vigorously urged *glasnost* upon the Press, to take charge of the new international policy commission. Chebrikov, who had headed the KGB since 1982, was made responsible for the new legal commission whose major task would be to oversee the legal reforms necessary to curb the powers of his old agency. Nikolai Slyunkov headed the commission on economic and social affairs. The commission's brief was to decentralise the economy by reducing the powers of the ministries and transfer them to factory managers. A framework was to be established where the initiative of managers to innovate and introduce new technology could be rewarded. Georgii Razumovskii was placed in charge of the crucial commission for party development and personnel policy. In other words, the critical decisions on the hiring and firing of personnel would pass through his hands. Vadim Medvedev was placed in charge of the ideology commission which combined the work of the three old departments responsible for propaganda, culture and education. Finally, Ligachev was placed in charge of the difficult position of overseeing the modernisation of Soviet agriculture through the new agriculture commission. The appointment of a man with a known and often expressed distrust of market mechanisms to oversee their introduction into agriculture through long-term leasing and other methods was surprising, and its immediate effect was to undermine the already delicate tissue of peasant confidence in the reform process. The suppression of the kulaks in the late 1920s after a decade of exhortation to 'enrich themselves' is still a vivid memory scorched on to the collective psychology of the Soviet peasantry.

The new commissions were headed by Politburo members and made up of members of the Central Committee supported by a much reduced bureaucracy. They functioned rather like Senate or parliamentary committees in the West, and thus duplicated the work of the Supreme Soviet's standing commissions. Gorbachev created what he hoped would be an effective tool to drive through the reforms. The net effect was to remove the party apparatus from detailed economic decision-making, leaving the two commissions for agriculture and socioeconomic policy to set general policy. The commission heads took over much of the detailed work of the Politburo, and meeting together could well have made up a separate inner body analogous to the six-member Standing Committee of the Chinese 23-person Politburo. Previously the division of functions within the top party bodies was somewhat ambiguous. The Politburo had been responsible for formulating policy, while the task of the Secretariat had been to secure its implementation. The responsibilities of the twelve secretaries overlapped and covered a range of the old departments. The assignment of specific responsibilities to individual Politburo members now rendered it more like a traditional cabinet system with personal responsibility for policies.

The leadership of all the fifteen republics was converted to the new model. As part of the October 1988 reshuffle, Vitalii Vorotnikov was made President (chair of the Supreme Soviet) of the RSFSR, by far the largest republic. He had been Prime Minister of the republic for five years, a post now taken by the head of the interior ministry since 1986, Alexander Vlasov. Each republic, as the union as a whole, was to have an executive President. As a concession to Russian nationalism and as part of the conversion to a more federal type of party, the party in the Russian federation was given its own sixteen-person bureau, presided over by Gorbachev himself and reliant on the existing staff of the Central Committee. The leaders of the Moscow and Leningrad party organisations, Yuri Prokofiev and Boris Gidaspov, respectively, were given seats on the Russian Bureau.

Following the spring 1990 elections Gorbachev's programme of bifunctionalism was implemented by the election of Communist leaders to chair local and republican soviets. In Uzbekistan, for example, the republic's party leader was elected President of the republic in March. In Russia, however, a new Communist Party of the RSFSR, with 58 per cent of total CPSU membership, was founded in June 1990 headed by Ivan Polozkov.

At the Central Committee plenum of 5–7 February 1990 Gorbachev proposed a radical restructuring of party organisation. The party was to become more 'federal' in form (*P*, 13 February 1990), the Central Committee was to be reduced in size and the Politburo rechristened a Presidium (*P*, 28 March 1990). No agreement could be found on how to extend electivity, and the 16 March CC plenum decided to let each of the party's 164 regional organisations decide on how to elect delegates to the July party congress (*P*, 17 March 1990). All bar 29 decided on direct constituency elections, but this did little to diminish the influence of the conservatives. Despite the fact that surveys showed that the views of the Democratic Platform (see p. 181) were supported by some 30 to 40 per cent of party members (*Demokraticheskaya platforma*, 2 (April 1990): 1–2), they gained no more than 100 out of the 4,700 seats at the congress.

At the 28th congress from 2 to 13 July 1990 some of the more radical proposals for party reorganisation were rejected. Yet the new rules did make some significant organisational changes. Politburo membership now became formalised with the *ex officio* addition of the General Secretary, the new deputy General Secretary and the first secretaries from the 15 republics. The old pattern of overlapping membership was eliminated, and none of the other seven members of the enlarged 24-member Politburo were ministers or members of the Presidential Council (see Appendix 2). Yakovlev, Shevardnadze, Ligachev, Medvedev and other key figures of the first five years of *perestroika* were no longer members. The centre of decision-making clearly shifted to the Presidential Council, which Medvedev joined on 17 July, and the Politburo was marginalised and to concern itself with purely party affairs. The Central Committee Secretariat was substantially renewed (see Appendix 3). As Ligachev informed the congress, the Secretariat after its reorganisation in September 1988 had more or less ceased functioning (*P*, 5 July 1990:2). The status of candidate (non-voting) member of both the Politburo and Central Committee was abolished. The Politburo was to meet once a month, while day-to-day business was to be handled by the revived Secretariat, meeting once a week.

The Central Committee itself was substantially renewed, with a lower holdover rate (those who had been part of the previous composition) even than the 23 per cent who survived in 1939. Some 35 full members and 21 candidate members elected at the last congress in 1986, slightly over 10 per cent, survived in 1990 to make up the new 412-member Central Committee (*P*, 15 July 1990). The conservative mood of the conference was reflected in Yakovlev's failure to be elected. To secure himself against the type of vote that unseated Khrushchev in 1964, for the first time the General Secretary was elected by the full congress and not by the Central Committee. In a contested vote on 10 July, Gorbachev defeated his opponent, Teimuraz Avalyani, a local party leader from Kiselevsk, by 3,411 votes to 501. The new post of deputy General Secretary was created to manage the day-to-day business of the party. Contrary to expectations, Gorbachev remained General Secretary (as well as President). Ligachev also failed to be elected to the new Central Committee, and his defeat by a substantial margin, 776 votes to 3,109, in the contest for the post of deputy by Gorbachev's candidate, Vladimir Ivashko, former president of the Ukraine, signalled Ligachev's political demise. (For further analysis of the congress, see pp. 386–8.) The congress, however, failed to resolve the debate over the party's role in society and the democratisation process in the country.

The onset of an era of reform once again forcibly raised the question of the party's leading role. The principles enunciated at the party conference in June 1988 were designed to remould the party's conception of its leading role in society. The internal life of the party was to be changed as well as its relationship with mass organisations, above all the soviets. The party was to withdraw from the minute supervision of all aspects of policy, especially in the economy, and to concern itself with general policy guidelines through political leadership rather than detailed commands.

Modification of the party's definition of its leading role takes place in the context of an evolving concept of a political system. At the 25th congress of the CPSU in 1976 Brezhnev outlined four tasks of the Soviet political system: the perfection of the socialist state system; the consolidation of socialist democracy; the development of the legal basis of the state and social life; and the rejuvenation of public organisations (*XXV sëzed KPSS*: 106). As noted (page 88), the idea of a dynamic 'political system' replaced the more static notion of 'sociopolitical organisation'. It allowed scope for such bodies as the party, governmental bodies, Komsomol and trade unions to interact dynamically as relatively independent bodies. The degree of independence and manner of interaction, however, was still not clear.

At the 27th congress Gorbachev argued that accelerated economic development could not be achieved through economic reform alone but also required changes in social relations and the development of socialist democracy and self-management. The bloated party and state bureaucracy, overcentralisation, one-person commandism and initiative-free careerism all hampered effective economic reform. Political and economic reform were placed in a fateful dependency on each other. Economic reform is hard enough, as the experience of *perestroika* and the last thirty years amply demonstrate, but political reform directly challenged the existing distribution of power, privileges and ideology. There is the further question of just what political system suits the requirements of a reformed economic system. Does it automatically follow that a marketised economy requires a pluralistic political system?

The question became ever more pressing: how compatible was the modernisation of Soviet society with the continued retention of a party which claimed the leading role in all significant political processes? In keeping with the two sides of *perestroika*, the system-supportive and the system-transformative, at first there was no intention of undermining the one-party system, only of modifying its practice. Democratisation was not an open-ended process but was to be 'guided into the necessary channels' by the party (*PZ*, 4/1987: 17). Democratisation was not to deny but to strengthen the leading role of the party. But this was now to be exercised in a new way, giving up the old practices of 'banning, rejecting, abolishing' (Gorbachev, *P*, 15 July 1987). It was to be achieved through ideological guidance. Gorbachev accepted that democratisation of society entailed changes to the party's 'role as the political vanguard of society' (*P*, 21 November 1987), but the shape of these changes was not clear. The traditional confusion between providing ideological guidance and acting as a legislative and executive agency in place of soviet and governmental bodies was to be eliminated.

With the exception of the overthrow of Bela Kun's Communist rule in Hungary in 1919, and again in Hungary in 1956, no Communist Party in power had been overthrown by domestic political forces. The only alternative to party power in Leninist thinking until recently was counter-revolution. Georges Sorel, writing of the dictatorship of the proletariat at the turn of the century, opined that 'the greatest miracle that could ever be recorded in history would be the voluntary abdication of dictatorial powers' (cited by Michael Lewin, 1989: 167). And yet this was something, *mirabile dictu*, that the Polish and Hungarian parties in 1989 contemplated with something approaching equanimity, and a *fait accompli* that was forced on the East German, Bulgarian and Czechoslovak, not to mention Romanian, parties. The process was not easy however, and as a Polish official noted, 'All the textbooks tell how difficult it is to seize power. But no one has described how difficult it is to relinquish power' (quoted by Timothy Garton Ash, *Ind.*, 12 May 1989). By August 1989 the first non-Communist Prime Minister since 1948, Tadeusz Mazowiecki, was in power in Poland, at the head of a coalition led by Solidarity, and within six months he was joined by a number of others in Eastern Europe.

Party rule from Poland to Azerbaidzhan was visibly crumbling. Communist parties seemed to melt like icicles in the sun. The East European revolutions demonstrated that Communist power is all of a piece: remove one element and the whole structure comes tumbling down. What appeared monolithic had by the erosion of time become hollowed out. The structures of Communist power appeared brittle like ice: impervious to frontal blows, but susceptible to the warming rays of mass demonstrations, national aspirations, popular movements and the activism of reborn civil societies. Election results in Hungary demonstrated that however hard the Communist Party tried to change its image, the legacy of forty years was not easily forgotten or forgiven. There appeared to come a point when the traditional party was perceived to be simply irrelevant to the country's needs. The argument of the Czechoslovak refomers that power was not something gained by the party for all time but had to be won in daily life and successful policies may have been convincing in the 1960s but was barely viable in the 1990s. The former Communist parties in Eastern Europe lost their subventions from public funds, and found themselves in a critical financial position. The 'leading role' of the party, as enshrined in the national constitutions, was removed and new rules were adopted for the registration and financing of political parties.

A similar process was at work in the USSR itself. The speed with which the party's authority and internal coherence dissolved during 1989 is quite astonishing. By July Gorbachev admitted that the party's prestige had fallen sharply (*P*, 21 July 1989). The party apparatus lost many of its traditional levers of power by the abolition of posts and departments, and it became clear that it was unable to transform itself into even the new type of body envisaged by Gorbachev, let alone the radical campaigning party desired by the radicals. The struggle focused not only on defining, and thereby limiting, the powers of the party, but on whether Article 6 of the 1977 constitution, which stipulates the party's leading role, should be dropped.

Events in Eastern Europe and the deadlock in Moscow encouraged the 140,000-strong Lithuanian Communist Party (LCP) at its 20th congress on 19 December 1989 to declare itself independent. Its leader, Algirdas Brazauskas, had long argued that republican parties should be autonomous. The LCP thus returned to its social democratic roots of the early part of the century. The fear that the LCP would suffer in the general defeat of party officialdom expected in the local elections precipitated the split with Moscow. They wished to be seen at the head of the two forces waxing strongly in Lithuania, nationalism and radical political and economic reform. However, V. Medvedev warned in Lithuania that the triumph of centrifugal forces in either the country or a republic would spell the end of *perestroika*. Already in spring 1989 the 33-strong Estonian delegation to the first Congress, many of whom were Communists, supported moves to delete Article 6 from the constitution.

The various popular fronts in support of *perestroika* in the Baltic republics became mass movements that marginalised the established party. To the extent that conflicts no longer always and necessarily had to focus on the party, this could be considered a positive development. The conflict over Nagorno-Karabakh, for instance, was increasingly fought out between soviet bodies rather than party organisations. However, to the extent that this made the party irrelevant it could not be welcomed by the leadership.

The leading role of the party was still defended in theory, but in practice the emergence of independent social, political and national movements eroded the notion of much of its content. The back of the CPSU was broken in the Caucasus over Nagorno-Karabakh, and in the Baltic because of the almost universal alienation of the population over 1940 and post–1944 Stalinist and neo-Stalinist policies. An opinion poll carried out in June 1989 revealed declining confidence in the party and its ability to perform an effective leadership role. Thirty-nine per cent of those polled believed that the prestige of the primary party organisations had fallen sharply, a view shared by a quarter of Communists themselves. Several polls discovered that Marxist–Leninist rhetoric was rejected by 40 per cent of young people (14–18 years), and disillusionment with socialism was widespread among the new generation. *Pravda* argued that the problem was not so much the party's leading role, but the way that it was implemented. The paper admitted the unpopularity of party functionaries and argued that the only way to overcome this was to replace the practice of appointments through the *nomenklatura* system by democratic elections, and that the *nomenklatura* system should be dismantled in its entirety (*SN*, 18 October 1989: 358).

The leading role of the party was achieved by a network of some 440,000 primary party organisations based in workplaces. In Eastern Europe democratisation meant that cells began to be withdrawn from workplaces. Should the party leave the factories and let the managers get on with managing? This must, sooner or later, be a consequence of the marketisation of the economy in the USSR and elsewhere. The question of the party's assets was also raised. Where did the money come from to build their lavish headquarters up and down the land, to create and maintain elaborate rest homes, restaurants and much more? Party funds alone would not have been sufficient.

The Communist Party became increasingly ideologically and politically confused. If membership were to be separated from privileges and jobs, then membership would no doubt plummet, a trend already marked in Eastern Europe. There has traditionally been a tension between the CPSU being a 'mass' and 'cadre' party, a tension between both 'leading' society and 'representing' society. Leading society necessarily implies recruiting the 'brightest and the best', whereas representing society means recruitment should reflect the composition of society as a whole. Recruitment policy became confused, reflecting doubts over the party's role. The growth of party membership declined and a growing number left the party (*P*, 4 March 1989; *Iz. TsK KPSS*, 1 and 3/1989). The annual growth rate between 1981 and 1986 was 1.7 per cent, whereas in the three years following the 27th congress in 1986 the growth rate fell to 0.8 per cent (*Iz. TsK*, 2/1989: 138). According to Razumovskii at the 28th congress, 136,600 left the party in the whole of 1989, whereas 82,000 left in the first quarter of 1990 alone (*P*, 5 July 1990: 4). The full and candidate membership of 19.4 million in late 1986 will in all likelihood be the high watermark of CPSU membership. Between 1985 and 1 January 1989, 863,400 left to give an official membership of 19.3 million on 1 October 1989 (*Dialog*, 1/1990). By 1 January 1990 Gorbachev reported a membership down to 18.8 million (*P*, 12 March 1990). *Pravda* indeed coined a new term for those leaving the party, 'refuseniks' (*otkazniki*). In the Baltic and the Caucasus the party had already been eclipsed by the genuinely popular people's fronts, and in the rest of the country informal organisations rapidly gained support. The more *glasnost* revealed about the party's far from glorious past, and the more *perestroika* was compromised, the greater was the disillusionment.

Alienation from the party in society was matched by disorientation within. Eltsin sharply indicated the absence of democracy in the party by arguing that 'practically everything has been decided and is decided by the apparat' (*LF on EE*, 2/1989: 24). He cited the example of the theses prepared for the 19th party conference in whose drafting the majority of the Central Committee played no part even though they were issued in their name. The 19th party conference revealed internal party divisions to the public for the first time, identifying the personality clashes and policy differences. Abalkin argued that the original concept of *perestroika* was not working and that the whole approach to economic reform had to be rethought. He also insisted that there must necessarily be limits to the degree of democratisation possible within the framework of the one-party system (*XIX konf.*, vol. 1: 114–19). Yurii Bondarev was openly critical of *perestroika*'s gamble on the future 'without knowing if there is a landing strip at the other end' (*P*, 1 July 1988).

In October 1988 Vadim Medvedev argued that provided the Communist Party accepted the rights of individuals and groups to express their views and to advance their interests, there was no point in organising separate parties (*P*, 5 October 1988). The party should not be reduced to a co-ordinating body but should retain its central role guiding society and public life. This contention, however, rapidly became untenable, and throughout 1989 the debate over the party's leading role and the limits to pluralism raged, deepening the sense of a profound political crisis. In February 1989 Chebrikov denounced 'certain so-called informal groups' who, while ostensibly supporting *perestroika*, 'are in fact damaging it'. In traditional language he condemned 'anti-socialist elements' who might challenge the Communist Party's monopoly of power (*P*, 11 February 1989). For the conservatives, the restructuring of the party's role began to look suspiciously like its deconstruction. At a meeting on 10 March 1989 Lev Zaikov made the rather surprising claim that 'One of the most important achievements of the current changes is the restoration and strengthening of the party's prestige', and he condemned the idea of a multi-party system on the grounds that parties cannot be 'made to order' but are a product of 'the historical development of specific social groups having particular political interests'. He concluded that 'a multi-party system is not a guarantee of democracy in society' (*P*, 11 March 1989: 2).

The debate over the role of unofficial groups allowed liberal positions to be advanced with increasing confidence. A. K. Masyagin, a consultant to the Central Committee's party development and personnel commission, noted that the country's political landscape had been modified by the emergence of such groups as the popular fronts in the Baltic and argued that 'the day may come when party organisations have to put into practice ideas like co-operation, partnership and even formal agreements with these groups. And the sooner they come to terms with the new reality on the basis of democracy, pluralism of opinions, *glasnost* and lack of prejudice, then the sooner they will gain the credit of trust from the people' (*P*, 13 February 1989).

Eltsin's comments on the possibility of a multi-party system during the spring 1989 election campaign led to a storm of protest, and the 16 March 1989 CC plenum set up a commission to examine whether he was in breach of party discipline. Yet a few months later the work of this commission appeared to have fizzled out as no longer relevant. By February 1990 Eltsin had moved to a position sharply critical of Gorbachev personally, and insisted that the party had to end its political monopoly, 'the worst scourge of the Stalinist system' (*Ind.*, 6 February 1990).

The political pluralisation of the Soviet Union necessarily raised the question of whether the leadership of the CPSU could remain united. As *perestroika* deepened, pressure mounted against the veto on horizontalism. The party, created and moulded in different circumstances, had to respond by more than an internal restructuring – rather by a fundamental regrouping. The conservative, reformist and radical wings found themselves the kernels of new political organisations. Polish, East German and Hungarian experience illustrated how the pressure of reform may become so intense that to all intents and purposes the party disintegrates. Some of the more radical in the party began to call for the 'ban on factions', imposed in March 1921 as a temporary measure, to be lifted. This would allow the opposing tendencies in the party to become open (Kurashvili, *XX Century and Peace*, 5/1989). From at least the 19th party conference divisions within the party, above all between conservatives and radicals, were brought to the surface. The much-vaunted unity of the party began to fracture over the fate of *perestroika*. The personal conflict between Eltsin and Ligachev represented a profound conflict over policies. In effect, the 'ban on factions' began to lose any practical meaning.

Competitive but single-party elections raised fundamental questions about the party's right to a leading role in society. The democratisation of the party, while necessary, was not a sufficient response to the growing challenge of multi-partyism. The real test for the new democracy was whether the party could be transformed into a real campaigning *political* organisation. A multitude of political organisations in society challenged the party's monopoly of power, and the party itself began to fragment along political lines. These can be seen on a spectrum ranging from the radicals, such as the Moscow Party Club of Radicals, who strove for a thoroughly democratic *perestroika*; the liberals, who focused on marketising economic reforms within a more democratic framework; several varieties of populists whose concerns ranged from attacks on privileges to the proletarian populists who insisted on revived class politics; the conservatives, who accepted change but not too much; and the reactionaries who bade their time in offices and thought of the glorious days of 'building socialism'.

The interregional group of deputies was established on 29 July 1989 by some 400 radical Congress deputies to provide a forum for alternative policies. The mere existence of the organisation, most of which were Communists, meant that the party's vaunted unity had come to an end, though they were still bound by the rules of party discipline and democratic centralism. The next step urged by the group was for a formal end to the constitutionally guaranteed leading role of the party, which would usher in a multi-party system.

In January 1990 radicals from 102 cities met to establish a pressure group called the Democratic Platform, and one of its leaders, Vladimir Shostakovskii, rector of the party academy in Moscow, called for the establishment of 'factions' in the party (*Ind.*, 29 January 1990). The Democratic Platform coalesced out of a number of political clubs and brought together Communists disappointed by the failure to implement the radical proposals adopted by the 19th party conference in June 1988. In their programme the Democratic Platform called for a two-stage transformation of the Communist Party: in the first, the party was to become a democratic organisation in which different opinions could be formalised into fractions; and in the second stage it would become a normal parliamentary party functioning in a multi-party system (*P*, 3 March 1990). By April 1990 the CC estimated that the Platform had the support of some 30 per cent of Communists (*G*, 20 April 1990). As the Platform prepared for its conference in June, talk of an open split with the Gorbachevite party gained currency. The Central Committee apparatus responded by an open letter entitled 'For Consolidation on a Principled Foundation' denouncing the Democratic Platform and urging the expulsion of its leaders and a purge of radicals (*P*, 11 April 1990). According to Gavriil Popov this signalled 'the declaration of civil war in the party' and hastened preparations for a split even before the July party congress.

The conservatives also began to coalesce into groups. On 16 February 1990 they banded together in a parliamentary group called Union (*Soyuz*), with some 100 Supreme Soviet deputies. The formation of the group reflected the fears of Russians living outside the RSFSR about the break-up of the union (*Ind.*, 17 February 1990). Their political programme favoured a moderate form of *perestroika*, with restrictions on private ownership and limited marketisation.

In the party the Marxist Platform, compiled by social scientists and party officials in Moscow, urged the transformation of the Soviet Union into a post-Leninist type of democratic socialism based on revived and decentralised soviets with a socially owned but self-managed economic system. They sought to retain developed social guarantees, and denounced the social democratic path taken by radical *perestroika*, warning of its rightward evolution towards liberalism (*G*, 20 April 1990). Conservative Russian Communists gathered in a two-day conference in Leningrad in April 1990 to further the cause of the creation of a separate Russian Communist Party, an aim achieved in June 1990. In this way the evolution of the country towards a multi-party system was accompanied by the disintegration of the Communist Party itself.

The party's leading role was the cardinal question of *perestroika* and was not lightly renounced. The whole concept of *perestroika* was meaningless without a guiding hand. The Brezhnev doctrine, which asserted that the revolutionary advances in a country are irreversible and should be defended either on their own or by the efforts of fraternal socialist states, was irreversibly abandoned in 1989 in the USSR's relations with Eastern Europe. The fundamental question facing the reformers, however, was the degree to which it was applicable to Soviet domestic politics itself. Could the Communist Party really contemplate giving up power, and if so, was it not the duty of conservatives (or loyal Communists) to prevent this occurring? The decentralisation of the economy, they insisted, was not to be accompanied by the fracturing of the political monopoly of the Communist Party (*P*, 26 March 1990).

The idea of a multi-party system was supported by reformist leaders like Eltsin, and the public opinion centre headed by Zaslavskaya admitted on 17 March 1989 that almost half of Moscow's population was in favour. The 1989 elections clearly demonstrated that the party as such was no longer attractive, and that its reformist wing alone could achieve victory in the test of public voting. The Vorkuta miners in summer 1989 demanded the abolition of Article 6 of the constitution, and in November they resumed their strike as an overtly political act demanding its abolition. Ligachev, however, insisted that while free dialogue of differing views was acceptable, it had to remain within the one-party system (*G*, 4 March 1989). Sakharov on numerous occasions argued in favour of genuine 'political and trade union pluralism'. A multi-party system was increasingly seen as unavoidable and the only way out of the political and economic crisis. The leading reformers like Yakovlev and, to a lesser extent, Medvedev came to admit that the constitutionally guaranteed leading role of the party was ultimately incompatible with the type of society that they hoped to build. The question was not 'if' but 'when' the party would drop its claim to a monopoly on formal political life.

In the middle of the miners' strike on 18 July 1989 Ryzhkov warned that the party was losing its power and authority and was in danger of becoming irrelevant. The party could no longer rule in the old way, but had not found a means of ruling in a new way, he argued. The several branches of government had to be harmonised or the forthcoming local elections would result in 'soviets without Communists'. He failed to mention that this was the imputed slogan of the Kronstadt insurgents in March 1921. He called for a dramatic reorganisation of the Secretariat and the Politburo, and for Gorbachev to be relieved of some of his duties to allow him to concentrate on restructuring the party (*P*, 21 July 1989). In other words, he admitted that there was not only a political crisis, but also a crisis in effective government.

While Gorbachev was willing to renounce *dictatorial* powers, up to 1990 he was not prepared to give up a monopoly of power for the party. In countless speeches he insisted that continued party rule was the guarantee for the success of modernising Soviet society through *perestroika*. This was understandable since, as a man shaped by the party, he felt that he had no one else but the party and its officials to rely on. By retaining the leadership of the party together with the executive presidency Gorbachev tried to avoid becoming a general without an army. The 'socialist pluralism of opinions' and the growing autonomy of groups, mass organisations and national republics was not to flourish into full independence.

Gorbachev in 1989 was at a loss to comprehend the forces he had released by permitting relatively free elections. At the 6 January 1989 meeting of the Politburo and intellectuals Gorbachev insisted that *perestroika* would not be allowed to grow out of socialism. *Glasnost* should not be used as a cover for attacks on the Communist Party, 'which has worked out and proposed *perestroika*' (*P*, 8 January 1989). At the Central Committee plenum of 10 January 1989 he condemned pluralism, but conceded that the party's leading role was not a God-given right; rather its vanguard position in society had to be earned through policies that appealed to the Soviet people. He insisted that 'trust in party policies and support for them in society are increasing in the course of *perestroika*', but 'the credit of trust is not granted forever' (*P*, 11 January 1989). Gorbachev on several occasions dismissed the idea of a multi-party system as 'rubbish'. In a broadcast on 21 January he insisted that the Communist Party had to remain the 'integrating force' in Soviet society, and condemned those arguing for a multi-party system as 'demagogues and irresponsible elements' (*G*, 17 February 1989).

At the Central Committee meeting of 19–20 September 1989, which was televised for the first time, Gorbachev brought forward the date of the next full party congress by some six months to October 1990 (later advanced to July). Only the congress could re-elect a Central Committee and thus remove a stronghold of the conservatives. The congress was intended to put an end to the disarray in the party's ranks and to create a renovated and democratic party freed of the dogma of the past, as Gorbachev put it at the plenum (*P*, 20 September 1989).

The rout of old-style parties in Eastern Europe added urgency to the democratisation of the Soviet party. Gorbachev's tone had changed by November, and his arguments were now couched in terms of expediency rather than dogma. Whereas he appeared sanguine about the loss of the constitutionally guaranteed leading roles elsewhere, he argued that it would be 'advisable' for it to continue in the Soviet Union (*P*, 26 November 1989, and see pages 122–4). While no longer quite so assured about the party's automatic right to rule, he insisted that a one-party system would have to continue in the USSR for some time. The basis for party dominance was expanded and demystified and came to include four elements: the party as the defender of socialism; the party as the only integrating force in a vast multinational country; the party launched *perestroika* and is responsible for developing effective policies for its implementation; and the party can become an effective democratic force in society by democratising itself. The article represented a shift away from the old definition of the leading role which saw the party as a vast placement bureau, appointing cadres to staff the universal bureaucracy. But above all it signified an epistemological shift in the rationale of a leading role for the party. Until then it had been legitimated in charismatic terms, the party's collective charisma leading the society to socialism. Now it was based on legal–rational grounds, with legally defined functions and based on rational and pragmatic reasons. In the past there could be no argument against the metaphysical definition of the party's role; now it could be contested on the same terms in which it was presented, as 'advisable', or indeed inadvisable, 'for the time being'. Kryuchkov had earlier stressed the pragmatic argument that the party's role could not be decreased since it was the only force that could counteract the centrifugal trends in Soviet society (*P*, 5 November 1989), and the interregional group welcomed Gorbachev's article as a step in the evolution of a more radical *perestroika* (Sergei Stankevich, *Ind.*, 4 December 1989).

A ratchet effect operated as each new step of boldness by the independent movement, the national republics and the East European revolutions pushed the USSR inexorably towards the pluralisation of its political system. The legitimacy of one-party rule was rapidly eroded. The issue of the party's monopoly could not be deferred to the congress. At the CC meeting of 9 December 1989 Gorbachev warned that undue delay in making the necessary changes would lead to the sort of 'excesses' already witnessed in Eastern Europe, and he called for an expanded plenum early in the new year to discuss the question (*P*, 10 December 1989). The interregional group pressed their demands for the abolition of Article 6, and called for a general strike on 11 December to put pressure on the leadership, though in the event it was called off. For the radical democrats the abolition of Article 6 meant the end of 'totalitarianism in the party' (Stankevich, *Ind.*, 4 December 1989). The motion to discuss the abolition of Article 6 at the second Congress meeting on 12 December 1989 gathered a surprisingly high 839 votes, two-fifths of the total of 2,033 deputies attending. Gorbachev's view that discussion of the issue was premature gained 1,138 votes, and 56 abstained.

On 9 January 1990 the Lithuanian Supreme Soviet voted to delete parts of Article 6 from its republican constitution and drafted laws that would allow the registration of the many groups that already existed, thus ushering in the era of competing parties. In his visit to Lithuania on 13 January 1990 to try to heal the rift Gorbachev for the first time appeared to concede the imminent possibility of a multi-party system. He remarked that 'I see no tragedy in a multi-party system if. . .it arises as a result of a normal historical process and answers the needs of society', but he added that it was 'no panacea' for the Soviet Union's ills (*P*, 14 January 1990).

Grass-roots revolts led to the dismissal of a number of leading conservative party leaders in early 1990. Among them was Vladimir Kalashnikov from Volgograd, and the party leaders in Chernigov and the oil town of Tyumen. On 4 February, on the eve of the crucial plenum, some 150,000 people demonstrated outside the Kremlin in favour of the abolition of Article 6. Eltsin told the crowd that 'the present Central Committee is incapable of bringing democratic change', and insisted that the years of *perestroika* had only brought 'half-measures and compromises' (*Ind.*, 5 February 1990). They warned Gorbachev that this was his last chance. One of the speakers remarked that the sheer weight of numbers would make it feasible to storm the neighbouring KGB headquarters in the loathed Lubyanka (*Ind.*, 7 February 1990). The fact that there was no violence demonstrated the maturity of the crowd: but the large numbers attested to popular anger as well. Even as the plenum met, Leonid Bobikin, regional party leader in Sverdlovsk, the scene of the 'vodka riots' in December 1989 protesting the absence of food and drink, was voted out. Meeting with Ukrainian miners Gorbachev outlined his thinking that the party had no claim to a monopoly and was prepared for political dialogue with those who were 'acting to assist *perestroika* and renew our life' (*P*, 5 February 1990).

Faced with what appeared to be a terminal crisis within the party, and the danger of an East European type of popular revolution from outside, Gorbachev faced the expanded CC plenum of 5–7 February 1990, attended by some 200 miners' representatives. Introducing the party's platform 'For a Humane, Democratic Socialism' for the 28th congress, Gorbachev admitted that the mass of political clubs and independent groupings in society had created a *de facto* pluralism (*P*, 6 February 1990). The platform argued that 'The development of society does not preclude the possibility of forming parties', and insisted that 'The Soviet Communist Party does not claim a monopoly and is prepared for a political dialogue and co-operation with everyone who favours the renewal of socialist society.' The old 'barrack-room, hierarchical' view of democratic centralism was to be modified and groups could draw up their own platforms, but were forbidden to create 'factions' with their own rules and organisations (*P*, 13 February 1990). Gorbachev insisted that the party had to earn its 'leading role' through the ballot box in competition with other parties, though the actual timing of the formal introduction of a multi-party system was left unclear. The convocation of the 28th party congress was brought forward to July 1990, when the democratisation of the party and society would be discussed. Gorbachev insisted that the party would fight to retain its dominant role, 'But it will do this strictly within the framework of the democratic process, giving up any legal or political advantages.' The party had to shed the 'ideological dogmatism ingrained in past decades' and 'We must abandon everything which led to the isolation of socialism from the mainstream of world civilisation' (*P*, 6 February 1990).

Gorbachev was assailed by the conservatives and the plenum gave a foretaste of the party congress in July. Anatolii Kornienko, First Secretary of the Kiev party organisation, demanded an explanation for the absence of all reference to ideology in the draft platform. Valentin Mesyats, leader of the Moscow regional party, called for a sharper definition of the party's platform; otherwise it would become irrelevant. Ligachev's speech calling for discipline and order was cheered to the echo as he outlined the conservatives' credo against private property and 'against turning the party into an amorphous organisation, a political club'. His views were echoed by Vladimir Brovikov, the Soviet ambassador to Poland, who argued that *perestroika* had brought the country 'into crisis, anarchy and economic decay'. He blamed Gorbachev for an obsession with 'total democratisation of society without discipline or order'. Gidaspov, the conservative technocrat from Leningrad, insisted that 'only the Communist Party can be the guarantee of socialist development'. He had only recently announced that he would not run in the local elections, knowing full well that he would be soundly defeated. He added, correctly, that 'for all practical purposes executive power in the country is now in disarray.'

The radicals also found the draft platform not wholly to their liking. Eltsin once again accused Gorbachev of making excessive concessions to the conservatives and warned that the party was 'on the edge of crisis'. His ten-point programme called for the full recognition of private property, the decisive shift from the planned to the market economy, the voluntary union of nations and republican parties, and equal rights for all political parties. His call for the renunciation of the principle of democratic centralism to allow genuine pluralism in the party was supported by Yuri Prokofiev, leader of the Moscow party organisation, who urged greater independence for primary party organisations and a more effective voice for rank-and-file Communists in party life. Evgenii Velikhov, an adviser on scientific matters, suggested that the party should split into two (*P*, 7 and 9 February 1990, *SN*, 7 February 1990). In the vote on the third day, in which the observers took part, only Eltsin voted against the programme on the grounds that it did not go far enough. The conservatives fell into line, well aware that Gorbachev was their only effective shield against a mass uprising, though the summer party congress would in all likelihood see the end of party careers for most of them. There was no doubt that V. Medvedev was correct when he noted that the party's voluntary renunciation of a monopoly of power averted the immediate danger of mass unrest that might have turned into civil war (*Ind.*, 9 February 1990).

The third (extraordinary) convocation of the Congress on 13 March 1990 amended Article 6 to remove the Communist Party's political monopoly, but on the very same day the powers of the presidency were strengthened. At the same time Article 7 of the constitution, which stipulated which social organisations could take part in effective political life (above all the trade unions and Komsomol), was also amended to remove the restrictions on other political parties, social organisations or mass movements as long as they remained within 'the framework of the constitution and Soviet laws' and did not advocate the use of force to change the constitutional system or the state.l Gorbachev's acceptance speech focused on the need to establish a new structure of parliamentary and local government to avoid a power vacuum as the Communist Party withdrew from its 'direct interference' in political and economic life (*P*, 16 March 1990). Ryzhkov returned to his theme of the crisis of executive power and stressed the need to 'redistribute power'. In an interview he argued 'The party is relaxing its grip on power while executive power is still weak and has yet to adapt to the new system' (*P*, 14 March 1990).

Pressure for democracy, however, began to take to the streets creating an unpredictable and tense situation. The gulf between rank-and-file Communists and the bureaucratised leadership appeared ever wider. The question became still more acute about exactly how the party's renunciation of full authority in government would be translated into allowing other organisations a share in running the country. New laws had to be adopted for the registration of parties. Support gathered for the establishment of 'round-table' negotiations, a process that had been so effective in dislodging Communist power in Eastern Europe, to be held in the USSR with all political groups to avoid mass disorder. The interregional group had put forward the idea in late 1989, and in January 1990 the new leader of the Moldavian party, Pëtr Luchinsksii, added his voice to the proposal (*Ind.*, 22 January 1990), which was supported by the second massive national pro-democracy demonstration on 25 February 1990, the anniversary of the February revolution of 1917. Like the February revolution, stalled reforms from above gave way to mass peaceful revolution from below.

Thus began the fourth phase in the development of the reforms since

1985. This phase could not but be a transitional period as the attempt to achieve some sort of viable late Communist alternative to capitalist modernity gradually gave way to the post-Communism already embraced in Eastern Europe. The transition from party to presidential *perestroika* in itself solved none of the Soviet Union's pressing problems. It provided no democratic consensus for the drastic economic measures, like the price reform, return of the land to peasants or privatisation, that were required. Neither did it offer a solution to national tensions. This could only come in the fifth phase of reform, a government with a popular mandate operating on a parliamentary majority. The fourth phase was a hybrid, neither Communist nor capitalist, but worst of all, not an effective system in any respect. Estimates suggested that in a free competitive ballot the Communist Party would gain some 20 per cent of the vote, patriotic parties some 30 per cent, and some sort of social democratic force 50 per cent (Andrei Piontowski, *Ind.*, 5 February 1990). However, the fourth phase did offer the possibility of a solution to the crisis of political and executive power in the Soviet Union, and thus prepared the way for the solution of the other problems.

The issue of the party's leading role affected not only the conduct but also the nature of Soviet politics and the type of society that it should be. In his article 'Why is it so difficult to tell the truth?' the sociologist Igor Klyamkin (1989) argued that the party's leading role was based on a 'dual monopoly: on decision-making and lack of accountability to anyone', a monopoly achieved in the 1920s through the suppression of democracy and the obsession with party unity. A claim to a monopoly on political life not only poisoned the conduct of politics as a whole in the country, but also inhibited the democratisation of the party itself. The attempt to justify the party's continued leading role on the fact that it initiated *perestroika* was seen increasingly as the tautology it had always been: it was the party that had led the country into crisis, so it could hardly base its claim to continuing rule on its attempt to overcome the problems of its own making.

The debate over the leading role of the party was a debate over the development of *perestroika* and differing concepts of social justice. In addition, ideological debates were accompanied by sociological factors. The vast mass of medium- and low-level Communist bureaucrats, the *nomenklatura*, who for some seventy years maintained their grip on political and social life in their bailiwicks, had a vested interest in the party's leading role. The challenge was to close the gap between the *pays légal*, the official sphere staffed by a multitude of petty officials, and the *pays réel*, the actual life of society and the aspirations to fulfilment and autonomy of the Soviet people. A weakening of the party's political role without the corrective of popular competitive democracy may see the

the emergence of a tendency, already witnessed in Poland, for the existing political élite to be transformed into a new bourgeoisie as part of the transition to a post-Communist system. The United Front of Workers (OFT) indeed made this point. The political revolution against the power of the *nomenklatura* may find that the latter take their revenge by returning to haunt society in the form of a social consolidation of their privileges. The political revolution of democracy would thus become a social revolution of property. The post-Communist 'new class' may be little less insalubrious than their predecessors. The push for multi-partyism can in a broader sense be interpreted as an attempt by a 'rising bourgeoisie' to consolidate their social privileges in a more effective type of class power, secure in their property and political rights (see page 308). While there are elements of truth in this view, it falls into the classical Marxist trap of reducing the political institutions and freedoms of modern society to a specific form of ownership and production.

Even before *perestroika* the party's leading role was in a state of slow dissolution. The relative destalinisation of the political system and the de-ideologisation of certain realms of private endeavour were slow to develop, yet the party's role in regulating social life was gradually modified. Certain areas slipped into a twilight zone of depoliticised personal concerns, ranging from the arts to petty economic activity. Gorbachev's accession accelerated the process, and it looked all the more dramatic for the speed with which it was forced to go to make up for the lost years of the stagnation period.

The question has been revived as to whether pluralism was ever part of Lenin's conception of socialism. In the first months of Soviet power a limited role was allowed to the Left Socialist Revolutionaries in coalition with the Bolsheviks, and there was some scope for the anarchists and Mensheviks. By the summer of 1918 the evolution of Soviet institutions allowed no serious role for other parties. In late 1922 and early 1923 Lenin returned to the idea of allowing the political representation of different interests, but only under the aegis of the Communist Party. Classic Leninism was indeed based on the vision of 'one class, one party, one truth'. However, while effective political pluralism rapidly expired, Lenin's rule was marked by constant debates that validate contemporary arguments in favour of the 'pluralism of opinions'.

As long as the leading role of the party was defended, the democratisation associated with *perestroika* was not much more than a liberalisation of the system. Any party-led democratisation process finds itself at the mercy of those who are supposed to implement it. The attempt in Hungary from 1968 to 1973 ran into the sands of conservative and bureaucratic resistance. The basic problem was to find a way of reconciling the maintenance of the vanguard role of the party, the essence of Leninism, and democratic reform. The balance was a fine one and even such a skilled leader as Gorbachev found it hard to maintain. The fundamental paradox of trying to encourage popular support and participation while preserving the party's monopoly of power was unresolved. In Hungary and the USSR, one-party pluralism acted as a transitional phase towards a genuinely democratic regime. As Gorbachev pointed out, the basic issue is one of power, but the growing crisis of legitimacy translated into a crisis of power. The redefinition of the party's functions ultimately had to include sharing power with others.

The leading role of the party traditionally meant much more than acting as a hegemonic force in a coalition; rather it expressed the priest-like functions of the source of authority, wisdom and guidance. Communist rule has always been based primarily on its claims to a privileged relationship with the working class and the belief in its special mission in history. Now the party relaxed the old insistence on *partiinost* in culture and social life, but tried to find new ways to defend its relevance. There has been a slow shift in the basis of legitimacy from the party as the representative of a class to the representative of a modern nation. This shift was consolidated by Gorbachev, but there remained the problem that a party authority based on national legitimation was open to conflicting interpretations of national interests, whereas authority based on class is more easily manipulated to achieve a definition set by the party itself. It was both ruler and high priest, whereas in the nation there can no longer be such a close relationship between power and ideology.

Even with the abolition of the privileges guaranteed by Article 6 the party tried to dominate the pluralised political system. In Sverdlovsk on 26 April 1990 Gorbachev conceded that the Communist Party had been the core of the administrative-command system and its 'political mechanism', yet he insisted that it should regain its Leninist role as the political vanguard (*P*, 27 April 1990). However, powerful new parties were not willing for long to see their rights eclipsed by some remnant of an old ideology or to fall into the trap of taking responsibility for economic transition and austerity without genuine power. The times when a government was the obedient tool of the Politburo, but in which the latter bore no responsibility for the consequences of its decisions, has passed. Now the government indeed bore responsibility but once again fell under the shadow of the institutions of the strengthened presidency. The Communist Party lost its monopoly on power and had to fight for the implementation of its policies (cf. *P*, 16 March 1989: 6). By spring 1990, however, it became increasingly difficult to talk of the CPSU as a functioning political party at all as its factions lined up for the decisive confrontation at the party congress.

A revised role for the party requires its wholesale removal from the factories and into the localities where it will have to campaign like any other party. The Communist Party began with a head start because of the divided nature of the opposition. In contrast to Poland, there was no overwhelming support for an alternative in Russia. Chinese and Hungarian experience showed that it was very hard to dislodge party officials from economic decision-making and management. Traditions of parallel government die hard. The secession of the party from direct influence in government and economic affairs was only partial. Ultimate control until free elections remained in the hands of the party, but the divestiture of some of its functions meant that it no longer bore direct responsibility for all shortfalls and problems. However, years of economic mismanagement, only exacerbated by the compromises of *perestroika*, discredited the party. It was no longer seen as an effective tool of either political or economic management.

While the party did not willingly give up power, developments in Eastern Europe and in Soviet society rendered the defence of a monopoly on political life increasingly dysfunctional. Gorbachev had destroyed Marxism–Leninism as an official ideology providing a 'scientific approach to the management of society', while at the same time he tried to maintain the leading role of the party without such a theoretical base. The party's monopoly on truth was renounced while there was an attempt to retain its effective monopoly on political life. Party rule was therefore increasingly suspended in the air and was threatened with collapse into a welter of jostling groups, nascent parties and indeed civil war. One-party Communist rule without a satisfactory rationale for it was simply not sustainable without coercion.

The new democratic revolution

From 1987 democratisation became the cardinal value of Gorbachev's reforms. The nature of this democratisation, however, remained ambiguous. Democracy was to be grafted on to an existing system rather than acting as its successor. As the party's platform for the 28th congress put it, 'In Lenin's words, we should combine the advantages of the Soviet system with the advantages of parliamentarianism' (*P*, 13 February 1990). Every achievement was qualified, and it took a continued struggle before the two main demands of the Czechoslovak revolution of November 1989, an 'end to the Communist monopoly' and 'free elections', were achieved. The USSR's seventy-year history of Communist power entailed a much more complex democratisation process than elsewhere. Since 1917 the party had become thoroughly entwined with the state, and its ideology was the corner-stone of the very existence of the polity. It appeared that the over-hasty attempt to separate the ideology and the party's organisation from the state might lead to the collapse of the state in its entirety and the emergence, possibly after a 'time of troubles', of some new form of dictatorship.

The decay of Communism in the USSR was accompanied by a second democratic revolution, the rebirth of a specific hybrid form of democracy under *perestroika*. The onset of late Communism, and indeed post-Communism, can be seen in certain respects as a replay of the democratic revolutions of earlier centuries on both sides of the Atlantic. Much of the language and debates of the contemporary period is couched in terms which echo the debates of the earlier period, such as the balance to be drawn between community and individualism, social responsibility for public welfare and private rights, the balance of powers between executive and legislative, and the dangers of 'faction', as Madison put it. The new Soviet democracy realised that there can be no definitive answers to such questions, and accepted that each society and each age must strike a balance in keeping with its traditions and resources.

While by 1990 the reforms had restored a sense of democratic proceduralism to government, what was achieved was clearly not liberal democracy. Liberal democracy operates in markedly different ways from Sicily to San Francisco and would, no doubt, take a markedly different form again when introduced into the Soviet Union. Gorbachev's fundamental belief was that the reforms could generate genuinely democratic practices that related to Soviet and local conditions and experiences. The constitutional reforms under Gorbachev were designed to institutionalise the reform process instituted from above, but their major drawback was that they failed to provide an effective mechanism to institutionalise political activity from below. The law-governed state was still undermined by the elements of arbitrariness that could be limited only by the advance of democratic controls.

The question facing Communist leaders was whether reform would turn out to be a democratic revolution against socialism, or could result in a form of democratic socialism. The answer would appear to depend on the flexibility and adaptability of the leaderships themselves. The rebirth of democracy did not take the form of simply adopting the whole paraphernalia of liberal democratic societies. It may come to that, and the East European countries set off in that direction, but the democratisation process of *perestroika* can be characterised as a 'new democracy', to distinguish it both from the old Soviet notion of democracy and from Western democratic practice.

There was growing pressure from below for a new political order. There was a growing realisation of the need for independent political institutions of a reborn civil society on which an effective state could be built. The ground swell of an independent society began to be felt in the USSR as much as it had been earlier in Poland and Hungary. Pressure from below combined with divisions at the top provided the conditions for the end of one-party rule in the Soviet Union. The development of institutional mechanisms to structure the rebirth of autonomous social groupings was the major challenge facing *perestroika*. Under Lenin a gulf in all but name was drawn between democracy and socialism: it was Gorbachev's aim to bring the two together (*P*, 15 July, 1990).

In July 1989 Ryzhkov stated that the spring elections had created 'a real and mighty power in the land'. The spring 1990 elections to the republican and local soviets established a dense network of reformed soviets endowed with a democratic legitimation achieved at the ballot box that rivalled the local party organisations. The emergence of dual power, between revived central and local legislatures and the party's Central Committee and local apparatus, had to be resolved one way or another. The stalemate otherwise would repeat the 'dual powerlessness' that Trotsky noted in 1917. A structural instability emerged in the Soviet system of government that undermined legislative processes and prevented a firm new principle of democratic legitimation emerging. Under Brezhnev the rule of the apparatus was not democratic but it at least provided clear lines of command. Now there was no knowing where effective power lay. The emergence of the strong presidency only confused matters further.

This dangerous situation was conditioned by theoretical hesitancies. Democratic *perestroika* was premised on achieving a law-based state regulated by the principles of parliamentary democracy, while at the same time governed by the Communist Party which at every turn must flout the basic rules of parliamentary democracy. The longer this impasse continued, the worse its effects. Soviet thinking was still torn, on the one hand, between the principles of community, represented by the totalising role of the Communist Party and, on the other hand, allowing full play to the divisive group interests of civil society and the multi-party system (cf. page 36). The whole political culture of Bolshevism began to change. The authority of the party used to be derived from its claim of a direct relationship with society in the context of a modernising and revolutionary ideology. This predominantly political domination now began to give way to an attempt to find some sort of plebiscitary legitimation. At the same time, bureaucratic dominance found itself vulnerable to the democratic challenge.

Under Gorbachev the way was opened for practical analyses of how to organise the state's business in order to increase democracy and effective participation, and to limit governmental and administrative arbitrariness. In this respect Gorbachev returned to the ideas of the Democratic Centralist group of the civil war period. They too developed a programme for reform based on a constitutional definition of Soviet governance, an effective role for local government through the soviets, an effective central legislative body, and in general an emphasis on due procedures and legality in which the Communist Party played its part but did not stifle the rest (Sakwa, 1988a: 186−8 and *passim*).

The political project of *perestroika* was quite the opposite of that outlined in the *Communist Manifesto* − which was to make public power lose its political character. On the contrary, *perestroika* sought to imbue public power with a renewed political content. By politicising government, the reformers hoped thereby to make it more accountable. The state was no longer seen as the barrier to human emancipation and democracy, the view of the classical socialists and Lenin − the latter argued in *State and Revolution* that 'So long as the state exists there is no freedom. When there will be freedom, there will be no state' − and instead the remade Soviet state was seen, in a Hegelian way, as the vehicle for humanitarianism and democracy.

The new democracy gave rise to a new type of politics. Dubček in his Bologna University speech of 13 November 1988 insisted that politics was an end in itself: 'In 1968, we learned that the key to overcoming the crisis, to make socialism richer in every sense, was not to be found in the sphere of economics alone. The key was, and remains, in politics' (*Ind.*, 14 November 1988). The question still remains: what is the 'new Soviet democracy' to be like? The development of a self-managing society of commune democracy was constrained by the party's claim to a leading, though modified, role. The adoption of the proceduralism and formalism of liberal democracy was later accompanied by a stress on professionalism and the legitimation of group interest politics. Gorbachev's calls for 'the combination of democratic centralism and self-management' (1987a: 34) were soon found to be irreconcilable.

The pluralism associated with the 'new democracy' is to a degree inspired by classical liberal rhetoric, but in a structural sense has been a response to the stresses envisaged and provoked by the introduction of market forces. The traditional political structures, as in Poland and Hungary, were unable to respond adequately to the bankruptcies, unemployment, inflation and closures required by thoroughgoing economic reform, and indeed feared that popular resentments would find an easy target in a retained monolithic political structure. Political pluralism thus served the functions of diffusing popular resentment and allowing a pluralistic debate between revived trade unions, parties, ecological and consumer groups, to name but a few, to find solutions.

A key paradox of Gorbachev's strategy, as it must be for any Communist reformer, is that while seeking to restrict some of the party's power, it is the party which is ultimately the major instrument to ensure the implementation of reform policies. Without the party's leadership the reforms could take unexpected and, from the leadership's point of view, undesirable directions. Too much civic freedom, too active independent associations and too much private enterprise could all conspire to transform reforms designed to modernise the existing socialist system into something altogether different. The aim was to generate a momentum of change, but at the same time to retain control over that momentum. The fundamental paradox of *perestroika* is that for society to become what the reform Communists wanted it to be – full of initiative, economically active and secure in its rights – the party itself had to renounce its political monopoly, and in so doing lost control of *perestroika*. Gorbachev looked for a new form of democracy, beyond parties and relying on groups under the aegis of a single party. But politics is about organisations and meaningful opposition, which can be provided only by organised parties proposing alternatives and alternation. Can politics take place under conditions of choicelessness?

The creation of the Congress and the new Supreme Soviet marked the transition from the liberalisation of the existing system, where rights could be granted or withdrawn by the authorities as an act of generosity or spite, to its democratisation, where popular rights can be demanded and defended from the authorities. The elections of spring 1989 and the first meetings of the Congress, while in many ways a breakthrough, left the radicals profoundly disappointed. The elections were conducted in much the same way as in the past through controlled nominations. The committee chairs were selected not by open contests but once again by nominations, largely from the old guard. The Congress was hailed as a 'school for democracy' for the country as a whole. The new parliament's ability to mature was hampered by the political immaturity which is implicit in a one-party system. Recourse to non-democratic means is forced to ensure certain policies, even if they are designed to accelerate democratisation.

The old confusion about limiting governmental power by abolishing the state now gave way to an institutional attempt to control government. The practice of Soviet parliamentarianism was still ambiguous, and revealed the limits to the de-ideologisation of Soviet political life. Parliamentarianism without politics, in the sense of competing parties, is liable to degeneration. Mechanisms to provide for the 'circulation of élites' in these circumstances have a somewhat artificial air about them, and are likely to degenerate in the long run to the stifling monopoly of the ruling group or faction, as took place in Mexico under the tutelage of the Party of the Institutionalised Revolution (PRI). The revival of Communist representative institutions borrowed much from the proceduralism of Western liberal democracy while insisting that its essence – competing parties on the floor of the house – was not appropriate. This helps explain why some of the problems of the American system, principally the weakness of government as such and its physical isolation from accountability on the floor of the chamber, have now been replicated in the Soviet system. Parliamentarianism without parties (bar one) represented a hybrid form of democracy. It increasingly became clear that one-party democracy was incompatible with the type of democratic hopes put forward not only by the independent movement but by sections of the reformist leadership itself. There was, however, no unanimity on how to move into the next phase. Hence the growing pressure for the recall of the Constituent Assembly after an interval of some seventy years to take up the problem of state-building in a democratic Russia.

The reform of the Soviet political system increasingly became not just a political question, but a technical one as well. The aim was to design an effective democratic system. Political scientists played a growing role in the debates over the structure of the new institutions of power and Soviet democracy. It was among the social scientists that the seeds of *perestroika* were sown during the Brezhnev years, with the most notable figures being Georgii Shakhnazarov, now president of the Soviet political science association, and Fedor Burlatsky; they have now been joined by a younger generation including Igor Klyamkin and Andranik Migranyan. They are today faced with the awesome task of remaking the Soviet state to sustain a viable democracy. For them, an ordered governmental system is the guarantee of freedoms, a principle reminiscent of the early liberals who saw the regulated state as the only mechanism to restrain the passions of the state of nature and the egotism of civil society.

The alternative to one-party democracy was the pattern emerging in Eastern Europe. The Communist parties there were forced to transform themselves into democratic parliamentary parties whose mandate from Lenin to rule had been withdrawn, and instead they returned to the political market-place of civil society to fight for support and votes like any other party.

The danger of the semi-reformed system of one-party democracy was that it might simply denote the transition from traditional Soviet *dirigisme* towards a new form of societal corporatism. Already under Brezhnev elements of state corporatism had emerged, a system in which large institutions like the trade unions and the ministries themselves managed to gain a degree of institutional independence by exploiting the absence of dynamic leadership at the top, though they were still unable to appoint their own leaders. Now under Gorbachev these bodies, including the party itself, may achieve the ability to run their own affairs but, in the absence of an effective integrating mechanism and fully democratic politics, they could carve out areas of autonomy and monopoly.

The major problem in trying to remake the institutions of Soviet democracy, according to both the theorists of the new authoritarianism and the populists, is the absence of a proper state. Eltsin, for example, argued that '. . .our political structure is not ready [for democratisation]. There is no legal state. . .we only do things as if there was one' (*LF on EE*, 2/1989: 25). Migranyan (1989a) also argued that there cannot be a proper state without a developed civil society, and in the interim a strong authority is the only force that could establish the conditions for its development. As noted, *perestroika* entails a revolution against the classical Marxist view of the state and returns to the Hegelian roots of Marxism in seeing the state as the only universal force capable of integrating the passions of civil society. Marx had assumed that the last universal class in history, the proletariat, would perform this function. Lenin then tried to implement this by the simple expedient of striving to destroy civil society in its entirety and thus to eliminate conflict and egotism. For Hegel, however, the universalising functions of the state were to operate in tandem with a vigorous civil society, with all its attendant particularism, and did not entail its destruction. Gorbachev has returned to Hegel's insight, and the project for the post-*perestroika* period is to institutionalise an effective state with a vigorous civil society. The one cannot survive without the other: to paraphrase Gorbachev's nationality policy, a strong state and a strong civil society.

The Communist Party tried to straddle both, yet it could not be enmeshed in the state and at the same time pretend to be just another element of civil society. The longer the choice was delayed the more profound became the political crisis. In Hungary, Poland and elsewhere the Communist parties were forced to choose and have returned to civil society, the sphere where political parties properly belong. There they had to fight on equal terms with other elements of civil society and give up their Leninist pretensions of being a crucial element of the state.

The new democracy could not for long remain a guided process. The March 1989 elections saw for the first time how politics could begin to escape the control of the bureaucracy. The local elections of 1990 further unleashed forces that they were unable to control. One of the main aims of democratisation was to separate normative politics from administration, to allow the emergence of impartial and effective governance. However, *perestroika* was predicated on a single party's claim to a monopoly on government, however diluted this monopoly may have become, and thus it was not possible to separate the party from the state. By 1990 it had become clear that effective and democratic governance could be achieved only beyond the framework of *perestroika*.

5

THE INDEPENDENT MOVEMENT AND CIVIL RIGHTS

The Soviet authorities since at least the death of Stalin have been faced with the growing autonomy of society from party-state structures. This has taken a variety of forms, but the common dimension is a striving for independence by groups and individuals. The challenge facing the reform Communists was to find a way of institutionalising the growing pluralisation of society, and at the same time to ensure the civil rights of citizens.

The independent movement

The basic dynamism of the independent movement derives from the revolt of the individual against all-encompassing notions of class, an approach which Gorbachev himself to a degree shares. For Lenin, politics emerged from the conflict of classes, and under socialism politics was destined gradually to give way to the 'administration of things' as classes disappeared. For Gorbachev, the end of the centrality of class conflict meant the revival of politics against the stifling monopoly of the administrative-command system. The rule of the state over society increasingly became monopolistic rather than monolithic. Under *perestroika*, however, there remained a totalising impulse which tried to restrain the autonomy of society.

The reforms since 1985 can be seen as part of a broadening struggle of the independent movement against the bureaucratic administrative system. From the totalitarian perspective the emergence of an independent movement entails the overcoming of the atomisation of society. This can be seen in terms of the apotheosis of civil society, a sphere independent of and legally guaranteed by the state. A civil society is one where rights are effectively secured and in which interest groups can

200

assert themselves. It is a pluralistic approach to politics. Civil society represents the nascent entrepreneurial class, the independent groupings, freedom of expression, religious freedom and a thousand other forces that were harassed and suffocated after October 1917. Despite persecution, elements of civil society and a sense of what constitutes 'normal life' and decent human relations survived to take revenge on Stalinism and all its works. Civil society has been gathering strength in the Soviet Union in a myriad of covert ways, increasingly overtly under Gorbachev, and this gathering force of individual and group initiative constantly burst the bounds that mere 'democratisation' placed on it.

Despite the attempt to revive effective participatory mechanisms after Stalin, Brezhnev's rule saw the progressive disengagement of the population from enthusiastic involvement in the procedures of Soviet democracy. Participation became instrumental, to achieve limited aims in housing or for career advancement. Disengagement became most pronounced among a whole generation of the best and the brightest intellectuals of all professions, especially among the young (J. Millar (ed.), 1987). *Perestroika* saw the re-engagement of the population in Soviet political life, often in ways that the leadership would have preferred not to have seen.

The emergence of a second economy to make up for the inadequacies of the administrative-command economic system was accompanied by the development of a semi-underground 'second polity' made up of various elements including nationalist groups, religious movements and associations with overtly political demands. This second polity in places merged in its analysis, aspirations and composition with the official system, the within-system reformers identified by Shtromas and others. With the onset of Gorbachev's *perestroika* this second polity emerged as a force in support of reform. Gorbachev was not so much stimulating change as taking advantage of forces that were clamouring for something new.

The alternative to disengagement was the attempt to achieve within-system reform. Gorbachev is often given credit for ideas that originated elsewhere. In particular, the similarity between some of the unofficial demands for democratisation and his reforms are striking. These demands, when voiced earlier, led to the imprisonment or exile of their champions, like Lev Timofeev and Sakharov. Under Gorbachev the line between official and unofficial thought was blurred as a continuum from reformists to radical independents was created. This was seen clearly in the establishment of a ginger group in October 1988 called 'The Moscow Tribune' pressing for radical political and economic change. It included about a hundred intellectuals, including Sakharov and Yuri Afanasev and some of Gorbachev's academic advisers such as Sagdeev and Zaslavskaya on the 'liberal' wing of the reform process. They demanded the release of all political prisoners, the rescinding of the public order regulations of 28 July 1988, and thorough constitutional and economic reform. They were motivated by concern that the reforms had little to show for themselves after three years, and by fears of a counter-attack by the more conservative reformers (*Ind.*, 14 October 1988). The real lines of fracture can perhaps be seen, on the one hand, between the conservatives and conservative populists in the leadership allied with various national Bolsheviks in the independent movement and, on the other hand, between radical reformers like the Democratic Platform within the system and democratic groups in society. The latter were united in a basic desire to see society purged of bureaucratic socialism and its attendant inhumanities. A new reformist social democratic bloc of the centre was in the making which came to fruition following the 28th party congress.

Gorbachev came to power after a period of severe repression against the so-called dissident movement and, indeed, against all forms of independence. The collapse of *détente* and the onset of the 'second cold war' from 1979 to 1985 conspired to destroy dissent, and in mid–1979 the Soviet regime decided to wipe it out once and for all (Reddaway, 1983). Gorbachev radically modified policy towards dissent, and the rapid pace of reform increasingly made the term anachronistic. Dissent had always been an ambiguous term and operated at several levels ranging from resistance within the system to the brave actions of a small group of overt dissidents. *Glasnost* brought hitherto heterodox views and critical opinions into the mainstream of Soviet political life, and the repression of earlier years gave way to a more tolerant atmosphere. Attention now focused on the restoration of normal political life.

There is considerable debate in the Soviet Union about what to call the emerging civil society. Earlier notions of 'resistance' to the system have now given way to a far more active approach to politics and are therefore no longer adequate. The notion of an 'opposition' applies mainly to those directly engaged in political struggle, and thus excludes the great mass of cultural and other types of activity. While the term 'independent movement' has its drawbacks (independent from whom?; can such a disparate range of groups and tendencies be called a movement?), it does at least have the benefit of conciseness and universality, and we shall use the term for convenience.

The problem for reform Communists was to establish structures that could institutionalise the growing independent movement in time before the whole polity was overwhelmed, a problem particularly acute in the field of nationality politics. Under *perestroika* the party did not unequivocally renounce its claims to a monopoly of political power so that while a return to the old system was virtually impossible, the conditions for the emergence of a new balance of stability of the Western type, with changes of government and of ruling party, were still not achievable. The rules of the old political game were swept away, but no one was quite sure what the new ones were. The Gorbachevite leadership's expectations that the intelligentsia, workers and various groups could be incorporated into an expanding notion of democratic *perestroika* were swiftly dashed. National movements and social groupings resisted co-optation into a reform process whose limits and scope were defined by the existing Communist leadership. Instead, they fought for greater autonomy in a more pluralistic society. Thus dissent metamorphosised into the independent movement.

The concept of 'independence' in the Soviet political context reaches back to the first years of the Revolution, when the Menshevik trade unionists made it their key slogan (Sakwa, 1988a: 71–5). The fundamental principle of the new movements, however sympathetic to the aims of *perestroika* or to Gorbachev personally, was that informal associations, and indeed official social organisations, should retain a degree of independence from official ideology and organisation, and above all should retain their independence from the Communist Party and the KGB.

The rebirth of politics witnessed the growth of a multitude of groups and civic organisations, known as informal associations (*neformaly*), which forced the pace of the pluralisation of Soviet politics. The campaign preceding the 19th party conference in 1988, and even more the elections of March 1989 and early 1990, allowed these groups to mobilise to unseat complacent bureaucrats and to gain places in representative bodies. This political activity began to coalesce into distinctive political programmes in preparation for the emergence of a multi-party system.

The informal groups developed into a dense network of alternative, though shifting, political structures. Officially some 30,000 *neformaly* had emerged by late 1987 (*P*, 27 December 1987) and by early 1989 there were at least 60,000 (*P*, 10 February 1989). Many of them were concerned with sport and other leisure activities, but a large number were involved in political life. At least 500 parties of one sort or another existed by 1990. A second polity had therefore emerged to challenge the official political system.

Gorbachev sought to incorporate the flourishing informal groups and independent activity, and even the miners' strikes of summer 1989, into *perestroika* as pressure groups to accelerate economic and social reform. He remained ambivalent, however, about their role in the reformed political system, and this very ambivalence increasingly became the source of growing tension at the heart of political reform. Few members of the informal organisations were elected to the Congress of People's Deputies in the spring 1989 elections, and thus they remained largely outside the semi-reformed political system. Many more, however, entered the local and republic soviets in early 1990.

The independent movement consists of a range of groups and ideas that operate beyond the bounds of *perestroika*, defined here as an officially inspired programme for the renewal of Soviet socialism. Strands of the independent movement coincided with the official goals of *perestroika*, as in the various popular fronts in defence of *perestroika*, but ultimately they had an agenda of their own. However, in so far as *perestroika* was an expanding concept some of the trends *within* official *perestroika* – the radicals, reformists and conservatives – increasingly allied with movements in society and thus blurred the line between the independent movement and the official political system. Growing aspirations for independence within the system and the emergence of formal competitive politics, just as with dissent, began to render the term 'independent movement' anachronistic. With the rise of such movements as the interregional group of Congress deputies and the Democratic Platform the contrast between intra- and extra-systemic independence was blurred. The greatest achievement of the independent movement would be its own disappearance into the mainstream of an expanded democratic political sphere.

Informal organisations focus on politics, culture, nature, religion, sport and so on. We will focus on some of the main political tendencies, noting that space does not permit a full analysis of these, let alone discussion of activity in the provinces and republics. It was to be expected that in the first enthusiastic phase of their activity, and in the absence of formal rules governing group processes, the majority of the groups would tend to represent ideas rather than interests as such. With the passage of time it became clear that the Western pattern of interest group formation began to be reproduced, with a broad division into economic groups, which 'protect and promote the specific economic interests of their members', and ideological groups, which 'promote or defend legislative or administrative change for ideological reasons rather than to forward their members' particular financial interests' (Marsh, 1983: 3).

Soviet informal associations run in a spectrum from anarchist and socialist to democratic, national democratic and chauvinist-nationalist, but no single classificatory system can do them justice. Informal sociopolitical associations emerged in the spring of 1986, though some have their roots in pre-networks of earlier years. A law on associations came into effect at that time which established a procedure for their registration under the sponsorship of an official organisation, but most groups simply ignored the bureaucratic procedure involved and hence remained 'informal'. One of the earliest groups in 1987 was the Club of Social Initiatives (CSI), involving among others Gleb Pavlovskii and Boris Kagarlitsky. CSI acted as an umbrella organisation, including Club Perestroika, a social democratic grouping advancing a distinctive programme of its own. In August 1987 the CSI reached agreement with the Moscow party committee, then chaired by Eltsin, to hold the first conference of 'informals', attended by some 300 groups from 12 cities. The major achievement of the conference was to set up a broad informational network and it was the starting-point for the Memorial organisation, one of the most effective organisations in the USSR. The conference represented the birth of a conscious alternative political movement. The CSI itself continued as a co-ordinating centre for a network of small socialist clubs.

Club Perestroika in Moscow grew out of a series of meetings in spring 1987, and in January 1988 split into two wings. Perestroika–88 took a more libertarian view and turned into a pluralistic discussion club before its disintegration, while Democratic Perestroika sought to find practical ways of achieving reform. Democratic Perestroika adopted its separate statutes in January 1988. In May 1989 it convened a conference with forty-six delegates from clubs in the capital and some five other towns and advanced the idea of establishing a social democratic association that could ultimately grow into a party. The platform argued that *perestroika* had to become a genuine mass movement since the leadership had lost its direction, and insisted that 'our main task is to move from a post-totalitarian society to a normal, civilised, democratic society' (G, 5 July 1989).

Disappointment at the absence of concrete measures for the democratisation of political life in the official theses for the party conference in May 1988 stimulated some socialist-minded independent groups to draft a 'Public Mandate to the Party Conference' at two one-day conferences on 5 and 12 June, proposing the radical democratisation of the Soviet system; the removal of all governmental functions from the CPSU; the transfer of all power to freely elected soviets released from the tutelage of the party; the abolition of the *nomenklatura* mechanism of appointing office-holders; the right for independent groups to nominate candidates and propose alternative policies in elections; open access to the media for independent groups and the right to establish independent publications; the extension of the rights of national minorities including the abolition of point 5 in internal passports stating nationality; and greater democracy in the management of enterprises, with power vested in democratically elected councils of labour collectives (*LF on EE*, 1/

1989: 18–20). The Mandate has been quoted at some length since it provided one of the most developed leftist perspectives for the radicalisation and democratisation of *perestroika*. It had little to say, however, on the crucial question of the type of economic reform that they would support, thus allowing ample scope for continuing debate about the relative roles of plan and market and compensation for social dislocation caused by economic reform.

A conference of socialist-minded independent groups in Moscow on 5–12 June 1988 led to the creation of the Moscow Popular Front (MPF) as an umbrella organisation for existing groups, which then set up affiliated branches. The idea of setting up popular fronts then spread throughout the country. The Popular Front was an extension of the existing Federation of Socialist Clubs (FSOK) but appealed to a broader audience including Communist reformists and the democratic movement on the lines of the Estonian Popular Front. The MPF rejected the argument of the Democratic Union that agitation should focus on the creation of a multi-party system and instead tried to work within the framework of *perestroika* (*LF on EE*, 1/1989: 22; Mike Urban in *Détente*, 14/1989: 3–8). The affairs of the Front were managed by an organising committee. Debates in the Popular Front focused on whether it should become a broad federation of separate groups with their own views or a homogeneous single organisation with a single platform, or indeed whether it should style itself socialist or simply democratic. By late July 1988 twenty-two groups were functioning within the Front, which sought to establish some sort of legal relationship with the authorities (Kagarlitsky, in *LF on EE*, 1/1989: 6).

The MPF held its founding congress in May 1989 with representatives from some forty political and ecological clubs from the capital. The Front called for direct elections for local soviet leaders and for the national President, the review of Article 6 of the 1977 constitution and the legalisation of other parties, and insisted that economic reform should not be at the expense of working people. Its basic programme was for a form of democratic socialism, yet a sizeable minority argued that the whole concept of socialism had become so discredited that their name should simply be the 'Democratic Party' rather than a reconstituted socialist party (*G*, 5 July 1989). The semi-official stance of the Moscow Popular Front led to the withdrawal of the CSI, Memorial, Democratic Perestroika and others. The major criticism that has been directed against 'socialist renewalists' is that they have no concept of independence. Hence they are seen to be compromised by an unduly close relationship with the authorities. At worst, their complaisance turns into indiscretions which compromise other activists in the independent movement.

The welter of radical groups includes *Obshchina* (Commune), an anarchist—syndicalist populist group which rejects the socialist label in favour of calling itself a historical—political association. *Obshchina* is always a prominent feature at demonstrations, with their red flag with a clenched fist in black in the centre, and with their paper by the same name on sale, having reached a circulation of some 10,000. The group was involved in the demonstration of 28 May 1988 of about 600 people, with other groups such as 'Civic Dignity' (*Grazhdanskoe Dostoinstvo*), a constitutional democratic (Cadet) association, and the 'Union of Worker Communists'. These groups come under the umbrella of the 'Federation of Socialist Clubs' (FSOK), which issues a journal called *Levyi povorot* (Left Turn). In addition to the groups mentioned above FSOK includes groups like *Svoboda* (Freedom), 'Forest People', 'Alliance Che Guevara', 'Alejandro Diaz International Brigades' and many more. More structured organisations include 'Activists for a Democratic Perestroika' and the group led by a council including Boris Kagarlitsky, 'Socialist Initiatives' (SI), not to be confused with the now defunct 'Club for Social Initiatives'.

The variety of non-socialist political groups is far too complex to analyse in full here but a brief suggestion of the major lines is in order. There is an emphasis on achieving accurate non-official information. In this respect the journal edited by Sergei Grigoryants, *Glasnost*, must take pride of place. It has provided a forum for some of the more interesting independent analyses of *perestroika*. Closer to the official definition of *perestroika* was the journal *Referendum*, edited by Lev Timofeev. The attempt to provide accurate information was the aim of *Ekspress-khronika*, started in summer 1987 and edited by Aleksandr Podryabinek. Several cities saw the establishment of information networks, the most effective being the Moscow Bureau for Information Exchange (M-BIO), led by Vyacheslav Igrunov. In early 1990 Aleksandr Suetnov established a Centre for the Study of Social Movements. By early 1990 there were some 500 independent newspapers and journals in Russia alone, and some 700 more in the other republics.

The Democratic Union (DS) was established in February 1988 and its founding congress was held on 7—9 May 1988 amid police disruption. The party was initiated by the Western-orientated liberal grouping called Democracy and Humanism. From the first it took an overtly non-socialist stance. The congress condemned the system of rule instituted by the October Revolution and Leninism, both of which in its view led to totalitarianism, and called for genuine political pluralism encompassing a multi-party system and parliamentarianism; free trade unions; complete economic freedom for all citizens; the division of powers between the executive, legislative and judiciary; full civil liberties; a free press; and real rights of nations to self-determination up to secession (*LF on EE*, 1/1989: 25).

The Democratic Union, with branches by February 1990 in over 80 cities and a membership of over 5,000, was the first national independent oppositional party since the 1920s. However, the party failed in its first three congresses to establish a genuine national organisation with defined structures and thus fell prey to factionalism, in which in a perverse way it took pride. It brought together activists from the old 'dissident' movement of the 1970s, including the underground free trade union SMOT, and the new movements of *perestroika*. The DS stressed the politics of the street and one of its leaders, Valeriya Novodvorskaya, at a demonstration in Pushkin Square on 25 June 1988 held up a banner that said 'The one-party system spells doom for *perestroika*.' Such direct challenges to the political authority of the Communist Party, driving a wedge between the party and reform, led to more repressive measures against demonstrations. The Democratic Union, though not banned like the Karabakh Committee, operated at the very limits of official tolerance. The party was split over whether to contest the 1990 local elections, with the Moscow and Leningrad branches calling on voters to boycott them, while the Kiev group participated. The party called for Western-type liberalism without an understanding of Western liberal democratic processes.

Some of the patriotic and nationalist groupings will be examined in Chapter 6. Two overtly political organisations will be mentioned here. The first is the Russian Popular Front (RPF) founded by Igor Shamshev in October 1989 at a congress in Yaroslavl. It combines Russian nationalist concerns with demands for a multi-party system. Like most national movements, the RPF condemned the destruction of monuments of Russian culture by Soviet power, stressed ecological concerns and sought to recover the true history of Russia from seventy years of distortion. The RPF is not a party as such but plans to co-ordinate various patriotic and democratic movements and individuals. It organised the alternative demonstration on 7 November 1989 which called for the abolition of Article 6 and the resignation of Gorbachev. Unlike the DS, the RPF aims to fight elections, and with the help of Memorial, one of its constituent organisations, has had representatives in almost every town. One of its candidates in the local elections of 1990 was Viktor Aksyuchits in Moscow, perhaps one of the most outstanding of a new generation of political leaders beginning to emerge outside the Communist system.

The Christian Democratic Union of Russia was established in August 1989 by Aleksandr Ogorodnikov, and by February 1989 had held two congresses where it adopted its programme and statutes. However, the party failed to establish a national organisation because of ambivalence over the status of the Ukraine and over the type of federation envisaged with such areas as the Baltic. Despite having received the endorsement, and financial assistance, of the Christian Democratic International meeting in Guatemala in November 1989, the party is still restricted to a tiny membership dominated by Ogorodnikov personally.

Most informal groupings do not fall easily into a Left-Right categorisation. The emerging feminist movement, for example, reflects the divisions of society. The limitations of the women's councils (see pages 153–4) led to the creation of a number of independent women's associations such as the Association of Women Engineers, the Movement for Biologically Pure Food, and the Union of Mothers of Student Conscripts (*MN*, 29/1989: 12). An independent publication started by Olga Lipovskaya in Leningrad called *Zhenskoe chtenie* (Women's Readings) sought to make Western feminist literature available to a broader Soviet audience.

Ecological concern gave rise to one of the largest mass movements, with a wide range of groups promoting, defending or protesting a number of issues. Among the most important were the Social-Ecological Union, a Green Party in the Baltic, the Third Way (*Tretii Put'*) in Kuibyshev, and hundreds more. They all challenge the destructive pattern of Soviet industrialisation and promote an awareness of the importance of the spiritual values of a civilisation. In particular, spurred on by the Chernobyl disaster of 26 April 1986, a number of groups protested against the construction and exploitation of nuclear power. About 10 per cent of Soviet power needs are met by nuclear power, and this was planned to increase sharply. Ecologists warned against the dangers of nuclear technology, recommended renewable sources of energy and urged the better use of existing resources and energy conservation. Public opinion did have some successes, including halting construction of nuclear power stations in Minsk, Odessa and Krasnodar, and the decision to decommission the Erevan power plant after the Armenian earthquake of December 1988. Large parts of the Ukraine, one-third of Belorussia and two regions of Russia remain contaminated years after Chernobyl, accompanied by the birth of deformed children and a high incidence of leukaemic and other radiation-induced illnesses. Struggles to save the Volga from pollution and hydroelectric schemes achieved some success.

The destructive pattern of Communist economic development forged a link between environmentalism and nationalism. The ecological movement as a whole became a major force for the democratisation of Soviet society, and at the same time focused on the dangers of the exploitation of high-risk technologies by undemocratic regimes. As if to prove the point, the government in April 1989 imposed a ban on the reporting of nuclear accidents, reminiscent of the secrecy surrounding the explosion at the Kyshtym nuclear waste dump in the Urals in the 1950s and the fire at Beloyarsk nuclear power station near Sverdlovsk in 1978.

Gorbachev showed an awareness of environmental issues, and they figured largely in the confirmation proceeding of the Supreme Soviet from May 1989. Ryzhkov was accused of 'ecological illiteracy' by Academician Aleksei Yablokov for his support of the further development of the chemical industry of Western Siberia, an area already suffering from catastrophic pollution. A State Committee for Environmental Protection was established in March 1988, and in July 1989 Nikolai Vorontsov took over its leadership from Fedor Morgun as the first non-Communist minister since 1918. A new ecological code was devised establishing rules for the conservation and rational use of natural resources. The new minister found in the independent ecological movement a valuable ally to combat the obstructionism of the economic bureaucracy.

The status of the *neformaly* was unclear. They were tolerated, occasionally harassed, and neither wholeheartedly welcomed nor prohibited. There have been conflicting views in the leadership over how to proceed, with frequent rumours of government plans to step up coercive measures against them. Gorbachev at the 19th party conference gave a cautious welcome to the burgeoning independent groups 'reflecting all the diversity of social interests', though he interpreted them as a way of articulating interests *within* the one-party system (*XIX konf.*, vol. 1: 74–5). In one way or another the authorities tried to place organisational and ideological restrictions on the independent social movements, though such limits in places looked porous. The government hoped to weld the groups into obeisant 'popular front' organisations in support of *perestroika*, as a form of reactive democracy to take the place of a more proactive form of democratic participation. The attempt to achieve a subaltern democracy in liege to the party in fact failed, and the various popular fronts and groups were the advance guard of the post-Communist order. As the conservatives quite rightly recognised, whatever the protestations of support for *perestroika* of the various popular fronts and informal organisations, their striving for independence inevitably challenged the party's leading role. The long awaited Law on Social Organisations of June 1990 granted them full legal rights as long as they were registered and met a minimum number of requirements (*P*, 4 June 1990), and thus the *neformaly* movement as such came to an end.

The new tolerance for active citizenship was ambivalent when it came to workers' strikes, whose number increased rapidly as *perestroika* advanced. The response to worker militancy depends on contrasting interpretations of the nature of the working class created by fifty years of industrialisation and on its role in Soviet politics. Is there something in the caricature of the Soviet working class as a lumpenproletariat drunk most of the time and expecting to be paid for doing nothing, or is the image of the heroic clean-shaven conscious working class building socialism so beloved of Communist propaganda more accurate? The truth as usual does not lie in the middle but somewhere else entirely. The working class in the Soviet Union is as divided as any group in society, and no monolithic consciousness, or lack of it, can be attributed. As Zaslavskaya has long argued, 'The driving force of behaviour is personal and group interest' (1989c: 59).

One of the fundamental paradoxes of Soviet power is that the working class that it created remains in an ambiguous relationship with the power system that gave it birth. An autonomous 'class consciousness' has emerged which has certain expectations of the power system, as in social and employment policies, but which also evinces certain critical tendencies and, as *perestroika* develops, an increasingly independent stance. The blue-collar working class, for example, is not as integrated into the power structure as the Communist leadership might have hoped and expected. As *perestroika* began to bite, working-class resistance increased against attempts to solve the economic crisis at the expense of living standards and social welfare. The growing autonomy of Soviet working-class independent organisations ultimately poses the greatest challenge to Communist reformism.

The rising number of strikes during *perestroika* were provoked by many issues, but central to them has been an attempt to harness improvements in the internal ecology of working conditions in enterprises to the enhancement of the larger environment by combating pollution. A two-day strike in 1989 in the granite quarry in the city of Priozersk near Lake Ladoga, for example, demanded better working conditions and improved environmental protection. Pollution from the giant steelworks and power stations in Kemerovo in Siberia has reached such a state that it has been dubbed the 'Siberian Chernobyl', with smoke from its plants reaching Lake Baikal 750 miles to the east and drivers forced to use headlights in the middle of the day (D. Wilson, G, 20 July 1989).

The most serious labour stoppage since the 1920s was the miners' strike which began on 10 July 1989 in the town of Mezhdurechensk in the Kuznetsk coal-mining region (Kuzbass) of Kemerovo province, and which spread in a matter of days to all the major coal-mining areas including the Pechora coalfield near Vorkuta in the Komi Autonomous Republic and the largest, the Donetsk Basin (Donbass) region of the

Ukraine. At its peak some half a million miners were on strike, with a further 160,000 other workers in ten towns involved in stoppages in support of the miners' demands. The miners organised strike groups and in the ten towns these were supplemented by area strike committees. Unlike the emergence of Solidarity in 1980, these did not rapidly coalesce into a single umbrella organisation covering different regions and industries. Also, unlike Solidarity, no attempt was made to distinguish between trade union and political demands. However, like the Polish strikers the Soviet workers showed a high degree of discipline and organisation, maintaining order by patrols in conjunction with the police and blocking entrance to alcohol shops. As in Poland, other workers showed a keen sense of solidarity with the striking miners. These strikes prepared the way for an independent trade union movement.

Demands focused on pay and conditions, in particular food and soap supplies, safety and pensions, but also centred on reorganising managerial, union and financial structures, and on more local autonomy, self-management, pollution control and a national debate on the new Soviet constitution. The Pechora miners put forward some of the more radical demands, including the insistence that all power should indeed be handed to the soviets; that the guaranteed seats of deputies from 'mass organisations' to the Congress should be cancelled; that Article 6 of the constitution guaranteeing the party's leading role should be abrogated; and that the national President and the chairs of local soviets and city and regional departments of the MVD should be elected by secret and direct ballots. Coming from Vorkuta, the site of several of Stalin's liquidation camps, the radicalism of the miners at Pechora is perhaps not surprising.

Miners won the right to sell coal produced over and above the amount contracted to the state. The government in the form of the coal minister, Mikhail Shchadov, conceded most of the strikers' demands, and an emergency programme worth £10 billion of purchases of scarce consumer goods from abroad was announced. The strikes revealed a high level of distrust of the government, and promises were accepted only after they had been written down and publicly displayed or announced at the highest levels, notably by the head of a government commission on the strikes headed by Nikolai Slyunkov. Local party leaders in particular were excoriated by the strikers. Following the actions the strike committees were turned into permanent 'workers' committees' to make sure that the concessions were implemented.

Gorbachev's reaction to the strikes was very different from Khrushchev's in 1962, when a strike by workers in Novocherkassk near Rostov was suppressed with great brutality by the army leading to over twenty deaths. The 1989 strikes showed just how far *glasnost* had gone, and official coverage on the whole was informative, although frequently condemned by the miners for its distortions. Gorbachev recognised that the miners' demands were on the whole compatible with his own programme, and was thus with good conscience able to make concessions. However, addressing the Central Committee on 17 July, amidst bitter clashes between conservatives and reformists, Gorbachev warned that 'A real threat is emerging of the weakening of the Communist Party's leading role in *perestroika* and, consequently, in society.' Two days later in a speech to the Supreme Soviet he argued that people 'hostile to the socialist system' were 'trying to manipulate the strike', and he singled out the Democratic Union for particular criticism. On television on 23 July he interpreted the strikes as a statement of support for *perestroika*, but warned of the grave dangers they presented for reform, and the next day he described the strikes to the Supreme Soviet as 'the gravest test since *perestroika* was launched four years ago'. Unlike the nationalist unrest, workers' strikes challenged the very legitimacy of a system established on the claim that it represented the working class. Independent forces were emerging that were propelling *perestroika* in new directions and at the same time probably guaranteeing its existence: any attempt by the conservatives to put the clock back would be challenged by a newly revitalised working-class movement.

Shaken by the force of the strikes, Gorbachev denounced extremists of both Left and Right. He argued that '*Perestroika* continues to experience strong resistance from dogmatic, conservative forces, many of whom view the democratic steps as a deviation from socialist principles.' As for the other wing, 'Of late there has been a notable increase of social groups under the influence of left wing radical ideas. They are for more resolute actions, for speeding up reforms. Among them populist ideas are widespread, as well as leftist demagogic calls for social justice within a total levelling of society' (*G*, 20 July 1989). In October 1989 the Supreme Soviet banned all strikes for fifteen months. This did not prevent the Vorkuta miners laying down their shovels in autumn 1989 to declare an overtly political, indeed revolutionary strike, demanding the abolition of Article 6, direct elections for the presidency and a prohibition against the head of the party simultaneously being President of the country.

Despite the anti-strike legislation the number rose, leading to raw material and fuel shortages. A total of 7 million working days were lost in 1989. Of the average 30,000 workers on strike every day in 1989, half were in Transcaucasia (*SN*, 1990: 67). In the first quarter of 1990 an average of 100,000 were on strike every day, compared to 100,000 at the height of the miners' strike the previous year (*P*, 29 April 1990).

Attempts to create independent trade unions in the late 1970s and early 1980s had been met with fierce repression. In the wake of the miners' strikes an independent trade union was established in the Kemerovo region of the Kuzbass in September 1989. It joined the existing association of socialist trade unions, *Sotsprof*. Speaking in *Moscow News*, one of its leaders, Lev Volovik, argued that 'The AUCCTU is an organ of state power...So we had to take things into our own hands.' In late 1989 the Vorkuta miners left the official trade union movement. 'Workers' unions' and 'workers' clubs' began to mushroom with little distinction between trade union and political activity. They became one of the major elements in the local popular fronts and the kernel of an independent trade union organisation. Representatives of some 150 unofficial workers' organisations gathered for their first congress in the Siberian city of Novokuznetsk on 30 April 1990, and in June 1990 an independent miners' trade union was established at a conference in Donetsk. Active citizenship was indeed developing a dense network of an independent polity that soon came to rival the official one.

Aspirations for a degree of independence were not restricted to the multitude of unofficial groups but penetrated official mass organisations. The case of Komsomol (VLKSM, or All-Union Leninist League of Communist Youth) helps illustrate the distinction between autonomy and independence. Independence is the aspiration of various groups to enjoy areas of action in which they are responsible only to themselves and to interact with other groups on a contractual, equal and constitutional basis. In other words, they form the basis for civil society. Autonomy, on the other hand, is somewhat akin to state corporatism, where an organisation retains a certain degree of organisational autonomy but all key decisions on personnel and policy remain the responsibility of the state. Movements emerged in Komsomol which urged the transformation of autonomy into independence. In its early years this organisation was noted for its radicalism and striving for independence as a partner with the party in the building of a socialist society. While officially remaining independent, from 1920 its scope for autonomy was severely limited. It became a classic 'transmission belt' of party policies to young people. Komsomol did not so much represent youth as organise them. By the Brezhnev era membership was seen as a duty or as a springboard for a career in Soviet politics or administration. Reform was much overdue.

One of the first major acts of Communist reform processes was to reform the youth organisation. During the Prague Spring the Czechoslovak youth organisation was in effect disbanded and a radical independent organisation took its place. In the Soviet Union Komsomol was one of the slowest organisations to respond to the challenge of democratisation. Eltsin criticised its bureaucratisation: 'The Komsomol organisation has become much too bureaucratic and is too enveloped in the hands of the party organisation. It needs to be much more independent and needs to have a greater overall strategy for dealing with the specific problems facing the youth of the country today' (*LF on EE*, 2/1989: 24). Yet once changes began it became clear that the independent movement is far broader than the old circle of dissidents and encompasses groups within official organisations like Komsomol.

A rank-and-file movement emerged demanding independence from the Communist Party. Two years of growing activity by the *Politklubi* (Political Clubs), like one called 'Torch' involving Komsomol activists, culminated in the formation of the Democratic Faction and the 'Surgut Initiative', a splinter group akin to the Democratic Platform in the Communist Party. At a national delegate conference on 15–16 October 1988 an eight-point reform programme drafted by the Faction was adopted demanding freedom for groups and factions in Komsomol to organise and publicise their views and greater accountability of the leadership to the membership. This could be achieved, they argued, by abolishing the post of First Secretary of the organisation and instead making the head of the parliamentary group in the Congress of Deputies the leader of Komsomol. Accountability could further be ensured by replacing its present territorial structure by one based on interest groups (*G*, 21 October 1988). The aspiration for Komsomol autonomy was reminiscent of the demands put forward by V. Dunaevskii and other Komsomol leaders during the civil war. Ironically, it was Bukharin who led the struggle to destroy Komsomol aspirations for relative independence within a broad Communist movement (Sakwa, 1988a: 207–12). As in 1920, the 1988 programme demonstrated that one of the major guarantees for independence within official structures was the abolition of democratic centralism.

Komsomol, like the Communist Party, began to disintegrate. From 42 million in 1985, membership fell to some 30 million by early 1990. In early 1989 the Lithuanian branch seceded from the parent organisation. At the 'Forum of Young People of the Soviet Union' in November 1989, addressed by Gorbachev amidst much rousing rhetoric, a minority called for the complete political pluralisation of the country and the abolition of Article 6 (*Ind.*, 22 November 1989). The Komsomol congress in April 1990 condemned the CC letter of that month calling for the expulsion of radicals as a 'grave political mistake'. Komsomol, like the party, was increasingly marginalised by the emergence of independent groups.

The Soviet army itself was not immune from the strivings for an independent civil society (Galleoti, *Détente*, 17/1990). Morale in the army fell sharply as pay and conditions deteriorated. Defeat in Afghanistan and the use of the army for civilian policing purposes, as in Armenia and Tbilisi, and indeed in the 'invasion' of Azerbaidzhan in January 1990, led to disillusionment. In October 1989 an officers' trade union called Shield (*Shchit*) was formed in the army, aiming to defend the rights of military personnel. The union urged the professionalisation of the army and the end of dual military and political command, and aimed to ensure that the army would not be used against its own people.

Groups act in a variety of ways but ultimately involve a relatively small number of people. Far more dramatic was the emergence in 1988 of mass political actions, dismissively labelled 'rally democracy' by the authorities, the most notable being the sustained popular mobilisation of the Armenian population demanding the return of Nagorno-Karabakh. Although the Crimean Tatars had demonstrated since the 1960s, this now became a common occurrence. Attempts by local party officials to gerrymander elections to the party conference in June 1988 and to the Congress of People's Deputies in spring 1989 led to demonstrations in Omsk, Kuibyshev, Astrakhan, Sakhalin and elsewhere. In Sverdlovsk mass demonstrations supported Eltsin's nomination.

The constraints on independence were not only ideological; they also took more direct forms, including police action against 'rally democracy'. There is every justification for the KGB and others to be concerned about the dangers of political instability unleashed by the relaxation of political controls. The CIA counted some 600 popular disturbances in 1987–8, about half of them over ethnic issues. In 1988 alone there were national demonstrations in nine of the fifteen republics (R. Gates in *ST*, 30 October 1988). The basic question remained whether the KGB would tolerate moves towards free speech and freedom of association.

In response to the demonstration of Crimean Tatars in Red Square in the summer of 1987 the Moscow city soviet announced a set of 'Temporary Regulations' on 11 August banning demonstrations in the city. The then chair of the Moscow soviet, Saikov, did not hide his loathing of public gatherings and was firmly convinced that politics should remain the preserve of the constituted authorities. The Temporary Regulations were adopted by towns throughout the country, and in some places, such as Minsk, were openly declared to be permanent. In September 1988 the government promulgated a nationwide ban, adopted on 28 July, on 'anti-Soviet' demonstrations, carrying the penalty of severe fines and labour camp for organisers. The decree, signed by Gromyko without any public consultation, authorised troops to enter houses and workplaces. Informal organisations lost the right to register and hold meetings and instead had to seek special permission from the local soviet to hold demonstrations or marches. Hence precisely in areas where the local authorities were the least reconstructed and thus needed the pressure of demonstrations, meetings were the most difficult to hold. Hundreds were detained as a result of this new public order legislation.

Months of increasing intolerance for 'rally democracy' spilled over into the violence of the night of 8−9 April 1989 in Tbilisi. Demonstrations had continued for a week demanding Georgia's secession from the USSR, provoked by Abkhazia's attempts to secede from Georgia, and on that night around 10,000 people had gathered peacefully outside the government offices. The attack at 4 a.m. was unprovoked, and in a frenzy troops killed twenty-one demonstrators with sharpened shovels, gas and truncheons. The repercussions of that night of violence were to stretch long into the future and engendered fears that political controversy in the Soviet Union could escalate into civil war. Deputies at the 1st Congress of People's Deputies in May−June demanded an independent inquiry into the events, including an investigation of the actions of the military and interior ministry troops under the command of General Igor Rodionov. The commission, which included Sakharov, Likhachev and Sagdeev, surprisingly came to no clear conclusion about who was responsible for giving the order to use force, but *Ogonёk* pointed the finger at Ligachev. The latter, in his speech to the CC plenum on 6 February 1990, insisted that the decision had been taken by the full Politburo meeting of 7 April 1989, a version disputed by Shevardnadze who insisted that no full Politburo meeting had taken place that day.

A new law published on 10 April 1989 made 'crimes against the state', namely 'appeals to overthrow the Soviet state and social system or change it in a manner contradicting the constitution', punishable by up to three years' imprisonment. Meetings organised by the Democratic Union, such as one on 23 April 1989, were broken up with some violence and forty-seven arrests, including one of the group's leaders, Evgeniya Debryanskaya. The onset of the new age of Soviet parliamentarianism, however, meant that the handling of internal dissent entered a period of tolerance. Trials and sentences for political crimes were virtually abandoned. While public meetings still have to be sanctioned by the local authorities, if permission has not been sought or granted meetings go ahead anyway with the authorities tending to turn a blind eye. In the wake of the Tbilisi massacre rallies by independent political groups and activists were more often than not granted official permission, or at least tolerated without police interference. As Gorbachev put it, 'People are beginning to act like citizens again.' This was confirmed by the demonstrations of 4 and 25 February 1990. The new politics revised the approach to citizenship and began to acknowledge that participation can take a multitude of forms.

Many of the informal groups established during *perestroika* and the conflicts between them are similar to the groupings of 1917 and earlier. However, seventy years of Soviet power have made some of them rather wiser, and no equivalent to the Bolshevik Party has emerged. Most groups protest their loyalty to the democratic process, and thus the emergence of a vigorous independent movement is one of the guarantees of the consolidation of a pluralistic and democratic Russia.

Human and civil rights

The new approach to dissent after 1985 meant undoing the repressive legacy of the past. Anatolii Shcharanskii was released in exchange for three Soviet spies in early 1986. In mid-year Irina Ratushinskaya, one of the most courageous poets of our day, was released from labour camp after a long campaign. However, in December 1986 news arrived of the death of a brain haemorrhage of the dissident Anatolii Marchenko. Against all the provisions of the RSFSR criminal code his wife had not been allowed to visit him in Chistopol' prison for two and a half years. Above all, in December 1986 Andrei Sakharov was not only released but rehabilitated. Gorbachev clearly wanted to indicate his role in this by phoning Sakharov personally in Gorky. Over 600 political prisoners were released in 1987–8, including a large group in early 1987. Their release, however, was conditional on signing a pledge not to engage in political activity. By late 1988 Soviet officials estimated the number of political prisoners at between 11 and 52, while Amnesty International claimed 140, and in late 1989, 81.

The connection between religion and dissent has long been recognised, and under *perestroika* it has became one of the most important elements in the independent movement. Relations between the Russian Orthodox Church and the state have undergone a dramatic transformation since 1985 and allowed the promise of the separation of Church and state finally to be achieved. The 1918 constitution separated the Church and state in Soviet Russia, yet the state was never prepared to allow the Church to manage its own affairs. Under Lenin the Church was divided and assaulted. The Orthodox Church focused on survival and accommodation with the secular authorities, symbolised by the accords accepted by Metropolitan (later Patriarch) Sergei following the death (or murder) of Patriarch Tikhon in gaol in 1925. Sergianism came to symbolise religious compromises with the authorities.

Collectivisation was accompanied by an assault on the Church which saw many closed or demolished, notable among them being the Church of Christ the Saviour opposite Red Square in Moscow, whose site was to have been a grandiose palace of soviets but in the event became an open-air swimming pool. The 1929 Law on Religious Association limited religious worship to churches and forbade Sunday schools, charitable work or any other aspect of normal pastoral life. By 1939 only about 4,000 of the 50,000 churches in existence in 1917 were still in use, and only 7 of the 163 bishops and some 500 of the 51,000 priests remained. The concordat between the Church and the state in 1943 represented only a brief respite as Stalin sought to broaden support for the war effort. Stalin allowed the Church to re-establish an ecclesiastical administration and to re-open some churches and some seminaries to train priests. Khrushchev relaunched the anti-religious crusade and by 1986 only 6,794 of the 15,000 churches open in 1953 had survived. The Church was placed under an even more invidious form of supervision. The Council for Religious Affairs (CRA), a secular body, closely monitored the behaviour of all priests and bishops and supervised their selection and placement. The remarkable aspect of these years is that despite the persecution, some 40 to 50 million people remained Orthodox believers to see in the new relations permitted by *perestroika*.

The movement to revive the religious life of the Orthodox Church contributed its share of victims to the administrative-command system. In 1974 Aleksandr Ogorodnikov established a Christian seminar, and soon after he was arrested and sent to a labour camp, only being released as part of the amnesty in February 1987. Father Dmitrii Dudko established a 'religious–philosophical' seminar with no political aims but excluded party members. It became woven into the tapestry of Russophilism. Father Gleb Yakunin's fight for human rights among believers from 1965 and against the compromises of the Church hierarchy led to his imprisonment in 1979. He also was released in 1987. In 1971 the journal *Veche* was founded by Vladimir Osipov, devoted to revive Russian national culture, to restore a sense of pride in Russia, to contribute to the solution of the social problems of alcoholism, corruption and the breakdown of the family, and to help maintain the purity of the language. Osipov realised that some new moral order had to be created to fill the gap caused by the crisis of faith generated by destalinisation. The Russian Patriotic Union founded by Osipov was severely harassed by the authorities. The group reflects the growing interest in the return of a monarchical system to Russia as a symbolic point of authority.

Under Gorbachev an extraordinary *rapprochement* between the Church and the state took place. The Council on Religious Affairs rescinded the 1961 edicts passed as part of Khrushchev's campaign restricting the life of the Church, and the 1929 laws were no longer enforced. By April 1989, 1,610 new Orthodox congregations had been registered and about 937 churches returned to their congregations. There was a veritable resurrection of organised religion, with nearly 1,000 churches opening in 1989, and about 300 mosques. Three monasteries were returned to the Orthodox Church, including the Danilov in Moscow which became the administrative centre of the Church, and permission was granted to rebuild the Church of Christ the Saviour. Charitable work was permitted, bans on ringing bells were lifted and religious instruction allowed. The majority of the 400 recognised religious prisoners of early 1988 were released, including Deacon Vladimir Rusak who had been sentenced to twelve years under Gorbachev for writing a history of the Church since the Revolution. Only some thirty recognised religious prisoners remained in January 1989, though the numbers sentenced under non-political articles is not known. Religious literature could now be published or imported much more freely. The celebration of the millenium of Christianity in the Russian lands was marked by the return of the Kiev Monastery of the Caves (Pecherskii), which had been closed as a religious community in 1961, to the Orthodox Church. It marked the site of the first baptism of the Russian peoples under Prince Vladimir in 988.

Gorbachev's opening to the Church was made possible by the ideological shift from the emphasis on class to human or universal values, and more specifically by the depoliticisation of social relations. Another factor was the growing realisation of the leadership that the Church could play a part in combating the moral decay of the Soviet people and imbuing a sense of social cohesion. While the Orthodox hierarchy long supported Soviet foreign policy, and in particular the peace campaign, the voice of the Church on certain social issues was now welcomed. A letter from the aged Archbishop Mikhail of Vologda condemning pop music and television was published in the party press, the first time a Church letter on a social theme had appeared there since the War (*P*, 21 December 1987). The Church worked closely with the All-Russia Cultural Foundation, headed by Likhachev, to raise money for a 'Russian People's House' in the capital. In effect the Orthodox hierarchy entered into a new patriotic concordat with the authorities which allows it to act as the champion of Russian national values, a role which carries dangers of exclusivity with regard to other faiths and peoples. Moreover, too close a relationship with the state entails the danger of moral compromises unless the government unequivocally accepts religion as a human right rather than as a useful element in policy.

Despite significant improvements relations between Church and state under *perestroika* were still strained. In February 1989 Konstantin Kharchev, the head of the CRA, introduced a draft law on freedom of conscience and belief. The judicial status of the Church, especially over ownership of property, began to be regularised, parents were allowed to bring up their children in a religious way, and religious conscience was accepted as grounds for avoiding conscription, though some equivalent service was required. The draft marked a great improvement over earlier laws, yet failed to guarantee believers the same rights as atheists. The law itself was open to restrictive interpretations, and retained the mechanisms of control over the Church through central and local secular regulatory bodies, the KGB, and financial controls which included very high taxation (*P*, 6 June 1990).

Even this was not achieved without a battle against the ideological hardliners. Kharchev, a victim of this struggle who lost his post as chair of the Council of Religious Affairs in summer 1989, gave a vivid insight into the struggles in an interview later in the year. The law on religion and freedom of conscience was constantly postponed as debates raged over how liberal it should be, with the KGB more tolerant since Chebrikov's departure yet keeping a strict eye on developments. Kharchev's radicalism extended to suggesting that the Council itself should be disbanded in favour of some parliamentary regulatory body, and he offended the Orthodox hierarchy by suggesting that the pre-revolutionary Synod should be revived to elect the Patriarch, and thus give him some independence *vis-à-vis* the authorities (*Ogonëk*, 44/ 1989: 9–12). His successor, Yuri Khristoradnov, is a far more cautious man.

A meeting of religious dissidents in March 1989, which included Ogorodnikov, editor of the independent *Bulletin of the Christian Community* and founder of the Christian Democratic Union, condemned the proposals. The demands of religious activists focus on three issues: the legal status of the Church should be changed so that it can own property (at present it merely leases churches and land from the state); religious people should have equal rights to combat anti-religious propaganda, including access to the Press and television; and the rights of religious communities to run Sunday schools and clubs, and to do charitable work, should be legally guaranteed. One of the major problems hindering the religious revival of the Church is the lack of democracy within it and the complaisant attitude of the Orthodox leadership, including Patriarch Pimen (who died in April 1990) and his successor, Patriarch Aleksei, to the Soviet authorities, the legacy of Sergianism. Independent Orthodox activists, however, are not united, with Yakunin fighting for reform from within the Church, though highly critical of the hierarchy, while Ogorodnikov takes a more militant line.

One of the more difficult Stalinist legacies in religious life was the fate of the Ukrainian Catholic Church, known as the Uniates, who were accused of collaboration with the Nazis and forcibly merged with the Orthodox Church in 1946. The Uniates of Western Ukraine practise Orthodox rites but since 1596 have owed their allegiance to the Roman Pope. The Uniates for long remained the largest denomination still banned and repression against its some 4 to 5 million followers continued up to 1989, with fines, detentions and imprisonment, and services forced to take place in the forests. The authorities apparently feared the Uniate Church as a focus for Ukrainian nationalism, and the Orthodox hierarchy wished to retain it as part of its congregation. The relegalisation of the Uniates was opposed by several powerful forces, and Kharchev's support for their legalisation was one of the reasons for his dismissal. Party conservatives feared the alliance between religious and nationalist movements, while the Orthodox hierarchy was apprehensive of a loss of property and prestige. Gorbachev himself appeared to favour legalisation since it would help achieve foreign policy goals, notably the restoration of relations with the Vatican, in principle achieved during his visit in November 1989, and the possibility of a visit by the Pope to Moscow.

The Union of Evangelical Christians and Baptists was the fastest growing denomination in the post-war period because of its more flexible organisation compared with the Orthodox Church. During *perestroika* the five million strong Protestant churches grew rapidly and developed more foreign contacts.

The Lithuanian Catholic Church has acted as the focus of independence. Vilnius cathedral, which had been used as an art gallery, was returned to the Church in 1988, and in early 1989 its leader, Bishop Julijonas Steponavicius, returned to the cathedral to resume his duties after a break of twenty-eight years in internal exile. In Latvia the Lutheran Church plays a less central role as the focus of nationalism.

In Armenia Christian nationalism and faith are closely entwined. The Church here suffered dreadfully, with only 52 of the 1,500 parishes surviving, and not a single one in the disputed Nagorno-Karabakh autonomous region.

Despite certain periods when the Soviet state managed to work reasonably well with sections of Islam, the profound theism of Islam inevitably jarred with the atheist state. Muslims in Central Asia, Azerbaidzhan, on the Volga and even in Moscow have been remarkably adept at retaining the essentials of their faith, especially in matters concerning the family and community such as circumcision, marriage and burial, without coming into direct conflict with the authorities. The hegemony of Islam over some 60 million Muslims, one-fifth of the total Soviet population of 287 million, in Central Asia and in Azerbaidzhan can be likened to that of the Catholic Church in Poland, and in similar ways managed to insulate a people from the extraordinary onslaught of Communist ideology. Of the 25,000 mosques in Russia before the Revolution, only about 400 were operating in 1989. A report in 1986 noted that there were 3,761 atheistic 'political information groups' in Azerbaidzhan (pop. 6.8 million), 6,911 propaganda collectives and 32,250 instructors trained in anti-religious agitprop (*Ob.*, 12 October 1986). In the late 1970s a more militant form of fundamentalism began to make itself felt, fanned by the Shiah Islamic revolution in Iran, though the fact that the majority of Soviet Muslims are Sunni (except Azerbaidzhan, where the Shiahs dominate) has to a degree limited the impact of Muslim fundamentalism. By their nature little is known about the Sufi Brotherhoods, which derive from the groups who fought Russian colonisation in the nineteenth century and who remain loyal to what they consider a pure form of Islam. They remain beyond the pale of officially regulated Islamic communities, which the government oversees through four 'spiritual directorates', but their influence, and those of various Muslim Brotherhoods, is increasing. Muslim forms of the independent movement do not take only a religious form. In 1988 several oppositional groups became active in Central Asia. In Uzbekistan 'Islam and Democracy' emerged in Tashkent, and *Birlik* (Unity) became the nucleus of a popular front organisation.

Perestroika brought an end to the worst aspects of official suffocation of Jewish culture and religion. In February 1988 an academy was established to train rabbis. A fortnightly newspaper began publication in April 1989 with the title *Herald of Soviet Jewish Culture*. In 1989 the Solomon Mikhoels Cultural Centre opened in Moscow, named after the great actor murdered on Stalin's orders in 1948. The centre provided Hebrew lessons and a forum for Jewish art, music and history, and in general a base for the restoration of the national culture of the USSR's 2 million Jews. At the opening ceremony in February 1989 the president of the World Jewish Congress, Edgar Bronfman, argued that however many emigrated there would always be a Jewish community in the USSR: 'If we do not want to lose them as Jews, we must teach them to be Jews.' The centre, however, was rapidly eclipsed by other Jewish organisations. In December 1989 a National Council for Soviet Jewry was established, the first such national organisation permitted since the Bolshevik Revolution. In addition, a Jewish Information Centre opened in Moscow. The revival of Jewish political, cultural and religious life, under the aegis of the confederation of Jewish organisations and communities of the USSR (VAAD), was balanced by Jews finding themselves the scapegoat for the shortcomings of *perestroika* among certain groups like Pamyat.

The release of most political prisoners was accompanied by an increase in Jewish emigration, sharply curtailed after 1980, and the solution of a number of vexed 'refusenik' questions. Iosif Begun, for example, was granted permission to leave in 1988, seventeen years after he first applied to leave for Israel. At the European Security Conference in Vienna in January 1989 the Soviet Union promised to resolve all outstanding refusenik cases within six months, though by the end of the allotted period many cases still remained. The major cause for refusal is alleged knowledge of state secrets, or the refusal of relatives to sign waivers that the applicant has no outstanding financial commitments.

The emigration question clearly affects Soviet relations with the West, in particular the United States and West Germany, and in general reflects the rights granted to society as a whole. The Helsinki Final Act of 1975 does not provide for a general right of emigration or free movement, but stipulates only the *freer* movement of peoples in a 'positive and humanitarian spirit'. Only 460 Soviet Germans emigrated in 1985 and some 1,000 Jews in 1986. Emigration policy was reviewed with an eye to clearing the backlog of refusenik cases (*P*, 19 January 1987), and emigration rapidly increased. In 1987 8,155 Jews left, the great majority of whom were refuseniks, 22,000 in 1988 and 60,000 in 1989, exceeding the record of 50,000 who left in 1979. As numbers rose, the proportion opting to go to Israel declined from 31 per cent in January to 10 per cent in December 1988, and in response the United States began to impose entry restrictions on Soviet Jews. The rate of Jewish emigration increased sharply in 1990, spurred on by fears of pogroms. The source of such rumours was unclear, but clearly played a part in the twilight world of Moscow politics as the old system was destroyed and the new democratic one struggled for life. In particular, Russian nationalist groups pointed out that every time such rumours swept the city it was their meetings that were cancelled and their activities restricted. As the United States began to close its doors to mass Jewish migration the proportion going to Israel rose to over 40 per cent.

Restrictions on emigration continued though they were gradually eased and codified. The major problem increasingly became the prohibitively high cost of a passport and the shortage of plane tickets. An increasing number of Germans, Jews and Armenians, distraught following the earthquake and violence with neighbouring Azerbaidzhan, emigrated. In 1988, 52,000 Germans left, compared with a total of 74,000 between 1964 and 1984, but in 1989 an astonishing 100,000 left, out of a total of some 2 million. In 1989 Soviet citizens were able to apply for five-year passports and far more Soviet citizens travelled abroad on personal business; a growing number also left to take up permanent residence abroad (*P*, 25 March 1989). The major problem was that while the UN Charter on Civil and Political Rights held that departure was a *right*, Soviet procedures transformed it into a *privilege*. A new and more liberal emigration law is planned. The solution to problems of emigration and freedom to travel is a way of giving content to the Soviet idea of a 'Common European Home' and signalling compliance with the Helsinki Final Act and the Vienna concluding document.

The new approach to politics is sustained by a re-evaluation of human rights. This entails a less reserved acceptance of the 1948 Universal Declaration of Human Rights. Article 17, for example, defends the 'right to own property', which is being developed in the form of co-operatives, leasing and landholding. However, Soviet theory still stresses social as well as political rights. The Soviet process of 'learning democracy' does not mean that the Soviet Union is willing to 'take lessons from the West' (*P*, 23 February 1989: 4). Soviet acceptance of the Helsinki process since 1975, and Gorbachev's wholehearted espousal of the 'third basket' agenda of human rights, eroded the previous omnipotence of the state in Soviet thinking. Deputy foreign minister Anatolii Adamishin argued that 'The Soviet leadership is offering the world a conception of a new political mentality based on the unquestionable priority of general human interests', and insisted that this was in no way 'a deviation from genuine Marxism', by discovering a Lenin who 'stressed that human life and the possibilities for its all-round development were most precious' (*G*, 13 December 1988). Acceptance of a 'higher law' of universal human rights set clear limits to the prerogatives of the state in both domestic and foreign policy. The state-building drive set in motion by Lenin began to falter under Khrushchev and is now being reversed.

Changes in Soviet policy and practices led to the 35-nation Helsinki review conference in Vienna in January 1989 to agree to a human rights conference in Moscow in late 1991. Agreement was conditional on the release of all political prisoners, the solution of family reunification cases, the removal of articles in Soviet penal codes making political or religious beliefs and expressions an offence, and the guarantee of free access for journalists and observers. For the Soviet leadership the conference in Moscow signalled the return of the Soviet Union to the family of nations as a respected and equal member, and as a jewel in the crown of its domestic democratisation drive. Yuri Reshetov, responsible for humanitarian affairs at the Soviet foreign ministry, insisted that 'humanitarian problems are as important as political and economic exchanges' (*G*, 5 January 1989). It was far more than a propaganda exercise, and played a role in consolidating the human rights advances in the country. The fact that attendance by the major Western powers was conditional on human rights improvements gave leverage to organisations like '1991 Watch', established to monitor the Soviet Union's treatment of its citizens in the run-up to the 1991 conference. No such conditions had been attached to the original Helsinki meeting in 1975 and its follow-up conferences, allowing Brezhnev to flout its human rights provisions. Questions on emigration rights, discrimination, freedom of cultural and religious expression, prisoners of conscience and other issues meant that the Moscow conference remained in doubt until the last moment.

The reformist leadership tried to put an end to psychiatric abuse. In one of the most notorious cases the Donetsk miner Aleksei Nikitin was committed to a psychiatric hospital when he tried to set up an independent union in the 1970s and again following Solidarity in 1981. The psychiatrist Anatolii Koryagin declared him sane, and for his pains was sent to a labour camp and only released in 1987. In March 1988 a decree transferred 'special' psychiatric hospitals from the Interior Ministry to the Ministry of Health, though this did not occur immediately. Families of inmates can now appeal against the diagnosis. A group of US psychiatrists was allowed 'on site' inspection of Soviet psychiatric hospitals in January 1989. Re-entry to the World Psychiatric Association, from which the Soviet Association of Psychiatrists withdrew on the eve of its expulsion in 1983, could only come after the mechanisms that had made possible such abuses were completely eliminated, and past abuses and present practices investigated. The verdict remains mixed (see *NYR*, 8, 22 December 1988; 16 February 1989) and the USSR has been granted only provisional membership.

A key body in the USSR's attempt to improve its human rights record is the Commission for Humanitarian Affairs and International Co-operation, chaired by Fedor Burlatsky, established in early 1988. Burlatsky called for the release of all Soviet political prisoners and insisted that psychiatric abuse was part of the larger question of 'giving legal protection to the rights of individuals, and to unofficial civic groups' (*G*, 18 January 1989). Part of the problem is the definition of a political prisoner. For the West they are usually defined as people imprisoned for their beliefs, religion or ethnic origin who have not advocated the use of violence. The great majority of remaining Soviet political prisoners are people who are not readily identifiable as such since they have not been imprisoned under the two former articles of the RSFSR criminal code dealing with anti-Soviet activities or the two articles dealing with religion, namely Article 142, 'violation of the law separating Church and state, or school and state', and Article 227 dealing with forbidden religious services. Sergei Grigoryants, for example, was imprisoned on the fabricated charge but non-political crime of speculating in antique art, and others were trapped by the anti-parasite laws or on trumped-up charges of 'hooliganism'. Hence Gorbachev's pledge to West German Chancellor Kohl in October 1988 to release all political prisoners by the end of the year was difficult to verify.

The basic task for the Commission and the independent movement as a whole is to ensure that the achievements of *perestroika* are given constitutional form and legal guarantees. It is one thing when existing laws are interpreted in a benevolent manner by bureaucrats, but another when these same bureaucrats can be held accountable to parliament and the law. Progress has primarily been achieved as a result of political decisions and only slowly been reflected in institutional changes. As noted above, the creation of a 'socialist legal state' is an attempt not only to change the application of the law but also to modify the laws themselves to eliminate the arbitrariness that has characterised the Soviet approach to human rights for so long. Fears are particularly acute that if Gorbachev were to fall the instinctive authoritarianism of the Communist administrative-command system might well reassert itself. Moreover, traditional Soviet attempts to insulate their human rights record from outside interference are now much more subtle and take the form of the concept of 'freedom of choice', buttressing an absolute concept of national sovereignty under whose banner the state retains the right to treat its citizens as it sees fit. The Soviet Union, however, has modified the view that the rights of nations take precedence over human rights since the Helsinki process made human rights an international matter. On the other hand, Gorbachev's argument that there is a moral equivalence between Soviet human rights behaviour and that of the West, while valid to a degree, is weakened by the confusion in Soviet thinking between human and social rights. *Glasnost* has revealed the traditional Soviet argument that the poverty, unemployment and homelessness of the West are denials of human rights impossible under socialism for the demagogy that it always was.

While much has been achieved, there are still vexed issues that require solution. Among them are the system of internal passports and the *propiska* system of residence registration, which restricts internal migration and acts as a system of police monitoring. Article 198 of the old RSFSR criminal code dealt with 'malicious violation of passport rules'. Large, though decreasing, areas of the country are still closed to foreigners and Soviet citizens alike. Soviet passport holders abroad are no longer required to endure the cumbersome invitation procedure to return on visits, but still have to obtain a stamp from the embassy abroad. Soviet citizens wishing to travel to the West are hindered by the non-convertibility of the ruble. A free press as such is only just emerging, elections are hedged in by numerous qualifications, and political groups are still subject to harassment. As noted in Chapter 4, while the new penal code marks a significant consolidation of rights, a clause against 'socially dangerous acts' remains. Only when such issues have been dealt with, and the list gets shorter all the time, can the Soviet Union be regarded as a 'normal' state. If the term had not already been abused by the Czechoslovak hardliners after 1968, the term 'normalisation' would indeed be appropriate to describe the political and human rights' advances under *perestroika*. It should also be stressed that regional variations abound, with 'normalisation' by 1990 having gone much further in the Baltic and much more slowly in the Ukraine.

The emergence of a strong domestic independent movement and a new approach to human rights have had profound implications on Soviet international relations. *Perestroika* allowed the reunification of domestic and external currents of independence, and in particular some of those exiled by Brezhnev have been allowed to return on visits. Shevardnadze opened the door to reconciliation with the 20 million Soviet citizens living abroad (*MN*, 4 January 1989). As the USSR for the first time took the lead in stressing human rights, the oppressive regimes of Eastern Europe were delegitimised even further and were challenged to reform. Their failure to do so led to their fall. Moreover, while the issues of human rights and disarmament are independent, clearly the elimination of human rights' abuses created a better atmosphere for diplomacy.

Under Gorbachev the radical expansion of permitted political activity has led to a remarkable reversal which has left the conservatives as the minority. They are the ones now who have to get used to being the outsiders. The *apparat* almost daily finds new ways of impeding change. The film about life in the first Soviet labour camp in the Solovki islands was withdrawn from Moscow cinemas after only a week, despite – or indeed because of – enormous queues. The 'week of conscience' in 1988 to commemorate Stalin's victims had to surmount a range of obstacles, and when it met it could do so only in an outlying factory club. The obstacles facing Memorial have been noted above (page 98), and the list could be continued indefinitely. The attitude of the conservatives was summed up by *Pravda*:

> The slogans of democratisation, *glasnost* and increased human rights and freedoms are being increasingly manipulated by various groups of people who while passing themselves off as advocates of *perestroika* are in fact its vicious opponents. These people would like to turn democracy into licence, *glasnost* into

insults, and to turn rights and freedoms into a one-way stream drifting towards law-lessness and permissiveness, without any obligations to society and the law. It is the self-appointed leaders, extremists and nationalists who hide their true faces behind a mask of commitment to *perestroika*, who have on their conscience the events in Armenia and Azerbaidzhan and the disturbances in Tbilisi. (*P*, 10 April 1989)

Such intemperate language remained common during *perestroika* and showed the prevalence of old thinking. Action like the Chinese government's suppression of the Tienanmen democracy movement in June 1989 could never be entirely ruled out until a stable democratic system had been consolidated.

The advances in individual and social rights are being gained through struggle. While *perestroika* might have begun as a 'revolution from above', the challenge of the independent movement inexorably trans-formed it into a struggle for reform and civil rights from below. The enormous development of groups means that democracy is no longer an abstract slogan but is beginning to exert pressure of its own in pursuing its own varied, and often contradictory, demands. While democratisa-tion was offered from above, it is being won from below. However, both are in danger of being lost unless some effective means is found of regulating relations between groups and of mediating political conflict. In their early stages neither the Congress nor the Supreme Soviet was capable of this, and the growing mutual intolerance between groups soured the political atmosphere and heightened the danger of some sort of official backlash and civil war.

The application of the idea of civil society to the consolidation of the independent movement entails a specific approach to the pace and scale of reform. Many of the activists in the independent movement are well aware of the need for a 'responsible' approach. For example, Viktor Aksyuchits put forward the classic liberal view that 'the striving to achieve complete freedom immediately is the fastest way to even greater servitude.' He insisted that 'Only the gradual forming of civil society, the broadening of rights and freedoms of people and society, will allow the new forces to consolidate themselves' (*RM*, 17 February 1989: 3).

Gorbachev's reforms allow an unprecedented degree of interest aggregation and articulation. Yet the major problem is that the institutional reforms were only slowly able to transform the social relationships between bureaucratic agencies and social groups or, put more broadly, between state and society into a stable pattern of democratic bargaining. The rather limited espousal of 'socialist plural-ism of opinions' meant that attention was not focused with sufficient urgency on the problem of providing institutional and legal regulation of interest group activity. The danger then emerged, as the conservatives hastened to point out, of 'anarchy', which meant no more than the emergence of powerful groups, particularly in the sphere of nationality politics, in the absence of a settled framework of interest adjudication. The hesitations of reform Communism in institutionalising the pluralisation of Soviet politics only strengthened the hand of those who sought to exploit the already weak legitimacy in Communist ideology for interest group activity.

The emergence of a broad range of *neformaly* began of itself to change the nature of Soviet democracy. An active and organised citizenry provides the kernel for the rebirth of a pluralistic democracy based on a revived civil society. However, restraints on this evolution remain, as discussed above, focusing on the continued role of the Communist Party and its evolving thinking on the relationship of socialism and democracy. The leading role above all meant a claim to a privileged relationship to ideology, if not quite the ideological or political monopoly of old, and this of itself meant that while the 'socialist pluralism of opinions' might be tolerated, the institutionalisation of these opinions into contesting parties was inhibited by the continued emphasis on the 'socialist choice' of October 1917 and the 'Communist perspectives' of Soviet society (*P*, 15 July 1990). Official Soviet thinking only gradually lost the commune democratic emphasis on the internalisation of political conflict. The prejudice against contestatory politics, however, did not mean that there was no role for an expanding public sphere of contending groups and ideas, only that it was to be limited by what Jowitt (1975) termed 'inclusion', the broadening coalition of groups under the hegemony of party rule.

The exalted status of certain sections of society institutionalised by the leading role of the party was challenged by the independent movement. While the Gorbachevite reformers conceded the principle of universal citizenship by their remodelling of the political institutions of the nation to allow effective popular participation and contested elections, in so far as the leading role of the party was defended the quality of citizenship remained unequal. The independent movement ultimately successfully challenged the party to grant universal and *equal* citizenship for all individuals and groups in society – in short, to allow genuine pluralism and the institutionalisation of diverse groupings within the political system.

6

NATIONALISM AND THE STATE

The Soviet Union is unique and in many ways is not a nation at all but an empire, a unique assembly of countries at different levels of cultural and economic development, a heterogeneous collection of peoples who happen to share a continent and to be contiguous. However, during *perestroika* it became clear that they all shared a desire to regain their personalities and to achieve a degree of genuine control over their cultures and destinies. What was the nature of the nationalism sweeping the Soviet Union under *perestroika*, and how was the concept of 'nation' to be applied? How did nationalist assertion relate to the development of the democratic revolution in the country as a whole? The problem for the Soviet leadership was to find a way of combining the democratic aspirations of nationalities with the continued unity of the state, and in this it was found wanting.

Nations and nationalism

Soviet federalism was always of a distinctive sort. The USSR came together in December 1922 as a federation of republics with all the trappings of statehood rather than as autonomous units of a unitary state. In other words, the aspiration to statehood of the peoples who made up the original federation was accepted and given a political framework. The fact that the statehood aspect of ethno-federalism was undermined does not alter the basic principle that the Soviet Union was always in principle more than a single state but rather a federation of nations. To this degree the idea of the Soviet Union as an empire is misleading. A return to the first principles of the USSR as a federation of states would entail the economic and political autonomy of each of the fifteen republics, including control over the uniformed services, and

231

provision for the other 85-odd ethno-linguistic groups. The status of the 'minorities' within each republic, which in Kazakhstan and Kirghizia make up the majority, would also have to be safeguarded. Some 25 million Russians and about 35 million other nationalities live outside their own borders, suggesting that any harshly territorial resolution of nationality problems are either ruled out or would lead to great dislocation.

The year 1988 was one of nationalist assertion, inaugurating a period that became the sternest test of the democratic aspirations of *perestroika*. From the Baltic to the Caucasus Communist Party rule and the old model of federalism were challenged by massive nationally based movements. The Soviet authorities gradually lost their grip on political authority. Since Khrushchev's time several communities learned the practice of popular self-defence, notably the Crimean Tatars, Jews and others with specific grievances. Now the other communities of the USSR, including the Russians themselves, learnt how to promote their perceived interests. The resurgent nationalism of some of the Soviet Union's 100-odd peoples challenged the very existence of the multinational state.

Soviet federal policies nurtured the languages and cultures of even quite small peoples in nationality units ranging from the fifteen union republics, twenty autonomous republics, eight autonomous regions (*oblasti*) and ten autonomous districts (*okruga*), with their own indigenous political, social and cultural élites, languages, schools and universities. The internal passport system distinguishes between Soviet citizenship and nationality, the latter being the notorious fifth point in the internal passports. Nationalism was sustained, and indeed generated, by the ethno-federal framework. Cultural policies promoted the development of Sovietised national cultures within the structure of national social development. Modernisation broadened the social and political élites and provided the basis for literate and nationally conscious populations.

The nationality crisis under Gorbachev demonstrated that the old methods of managing nationality questions had clearly outlived their efficacy. *Perestroika* was not in itself at first the cause of the problems but provided the opportunity for their long-delayed solution. For many years prior to Gorbachev's accession there had been a perceptible strengthening of national self-consciousness among Russian and non-Russian nationalities alike. Already under Brezhnev some of the issues faced later were strongly in evidence, such as the absence of a coherent demographic or labour policy, and confusion over investment priorities, and the consolidation of local political and social élites. Problems in the republics which had been forcibly incorporated into the USSR had been smouldering for years, and in other parts ancient national and local conflicts long predating Soviet power had never been satisfactorily resolved. With Gorbachev's thaw the nationalisms that had been kept in a state of suspended animation for some fifty years stepped out of the Soviet ice age to breathe and fight again.

The break-up of the old centralised command economy opened the door to the growth of localism and nationalism. It should be noted that many of these movements were not simply 'nationalistic', but part of a broader struggle for 'national justice' and an element in what could be called 'national democratic' movements. To paraphrase Stalin, the struggles were national in form but democratic in content. As the problems of *perestroika* multiplied, the fires of nationalism were stoked. By early 1990 some thiry-five borders within the USSR were disputed between different national groups. We will briefly examine each area before analysing the new federalism.

The Baltic republics

The Baltic republics had gained their independence in the wake of the collapse of the tsarist empire at the close of the First World War, an independence recognised by the Soviet Union in treaties of 1920 with the three republics. The circumstances surrounding the incorporation of the Baltic republics (and Moldavia) into the USSR stoked the fires of nationalism. The official view was that they had joined the union voluntarily in 1940, but the popular movements insisted that they were forcibly annexed by the terms of the 'secret protocols', an annexe to the Soviet–Nazi Pact of 23 August 1939, and a friendship treaty of 28 September. Occupied by the Germans from 1941, they were reconquered by the Soviet army in 1944. Stalinist deportations following the reincorporation of the Baltic republics in 1944 added further bitterness to the relationship with Moscow. Their incorporation into the Soviet Union was never recognised by the Western powers, and indeed Sweden was the only Western country to do so. Sporadic guerrilla warfare continued up to 1952, accompanied by the execution and deportation to Siberia of some 700,000 Balts, of whom 300,000 were Lithuanians. Following Stalin's death repression was eased, but the native cultures were undermined by restrictive policies and by extensive industrialisation that in Latvia and Estonia drew in large numbers of immigrants.

Only after enormous popular pressure did the Soviet government even acknowledge the existence of the protocols. A parliamentary commission established in June 1989 headed by Yakovlev finally accepted that the documents did indeed exist, and that they were illegal and invalid, but refused to accept that the Baltic became part of the USSR only through the use of force legitimated by the protocol. Instead, Yakovlev argued, it was the historical link between the Baltic and Russia and fears of Nazi expansionism which were the crucial factors in the incorporation of the states into the USSR (*P*, 18 August 1989). Yakovlev failed to mention, however, the various treaties signed between 1926 and 1933 between Moscow and the then independent states guaranteeing mutual sovereignty. Logically, these should come back into force if later agreements are nullified, and it was with this argument that the Baltic republics pursued their struggle for independence.

In the Baltic republics a novel form of social organisation emerged. These were the various popular fronts whose initial aim was to unite Communists and non-Communists, indigenous peoples and immigrants alike, on a platform of radical democratic *perestroika*. By 1990 these mass movements had become political parties in all but name and came to challenge not only the Soviet Communist Party but the very cohesion of the USSR itself.

In each republic the path to independence took a different route. The national democratic movement in Estonia was fanned by its cultural and linguistic affinities with neighbouring Finland. By 1989 only 62 per cent of its population of 1.6 million were Estonians, while 28 per cent were Russians. The Estonian Popular Front in Support of Perestroika was the first to be established in April 1988 as a broad democratic movement with the support of the local party and Soviet authorities. Its key demands were for Estonian to become the sole state language in the republic, the transition to full cost accounting, the extension of republican sovereignty, the solution of ecological problems and the dismissal of the First Secretary of the Estonian Communist Party. These demands were later broadened to include economic autonomy and the restriction of immigration of outsiders (i.e. Russians). As in Armenia, the local party and cultural organisations aligned themselves with the Popular Front in order not to be completely marginalised, but throughout the Baltic the major problem from the first was the diffidence shown by the Russian-speaking minority in joining the organisation. The founding congress of the Estonian Popular Front met in early October 1988. It described itself as neither a party nor an opposition, though it fought the elections of spring 1989 and firmly supported the plans of the Estonian Communist Party to achieve economic autonomy for the republic.

The Popular Front, however, was increasingly marginalised by the 499-member Congress of Estonia, sponsored by the Citizens' Committees led by Trivimi Velliste. It was elected in early 1990 in a vote in which some 600,000 native Estonians took part. The Congress, which claimed to act as the supreme authority of the Estonian nation on the grounds that it drew its legitimacy from pre-war independence, in turn elected a 78-member Committee of Estonia. These organisations adopted an almost Gramscian strategy war of position as one by one the institutions of statehood fell under their control. In the local election of 18 March 1990, 78 of the 105 seats in the parliament were taken by the Popular Front, Free Estonia and other independence groups, leaving only 27 seats for the pro-Moscow International Movement. A parallel polity began to emerge which put into sharp relief the alleged illegality of the official Soviet bodies.

Rather than declaring independence as in Lithuania, on 30 March 1990 the Estonian parliament passed a decree no longer recognising the force of the Soviet constitution in the republic on the grounds that since 1940 Estonia had been an occupied country and thus *de jure* independent. Soviet laws were simply suspended. A transitional period was announced leading to full independence from Moscow. On 25 March, the Estonian Communist Party, at its 20th congress, declared itself independent from Moscow and adopted its own platform and statutes, but provided for a six-month transition period until the 28th party congress in July.

Latvia finds itself in potentially the most difficult position since barely a majority, some 51 per cent of its population of 2.8 million, are native Latvians, while 33 per cent are Russians. Moreover, Riga is the centre for the USSR's Baltic military region. The Latvian population feels itself the most threatened by cultural and ecological annihilation, while the incomers are strong enough to organise resistance to nationalist measures. In 1987 an independent Latvian Ecology Club (VAK) was established, the forerunner of the Popular Front of 1988, 80 per cent of whose members were Latvians. Delegates representing 300,000 members at the Front's 2nd congress in October 1989 shifted from a position of 'sovereignty within the USSR' to demands for outright independence for a democratic parliamentary republic, though they accepted a transitional period in which a multi-party system and a market economy would be established. This brought them closer to the Latvian National Citizens' Committees (LNNK), which demanded immediate independence. Relations between the local Communist Party and the movement were less close here than in the other two republics. In the elections to the local soviets in December 1989 supporters of independence won three-quarters of the 14,000 seats, while in the elections to the 201-member Supreme Soviet on 18 March 1990 the Latvian Popular Front achieved a small majority with 131 seats, just short of the two-thirds majority of 134 needed to make constitutional changes on its own.

Latvia was the first republic to change its constitution to allow a multi-party system in late 1989. On 15 February the Latvian parliament called for 'the restoration of the state independence of Latvia' and denounced the July 1940 vote of the republic's parliament, after rigged elections, to join the USSR. In Latvia, as in Estonia, a Citizens' Movement registered some 730,000 who could prove they were native Latvians. Elections to a Citizens' Congress were held in April 1990 for a Congress of Latvia to meet in May. Also, as in Estonia, a division took place between the LPF, which espoused the parliamentary road to independence, and the Citizens' Movement, which argued that since the existing parliament was constituted within the framework of an illegal occupation, genuinely national agencies should be used rather than tainted Soviet ones.

In the event, on 4 May 1990 the Latvian Supreme Soviet adopted a declaration of independence similar in form to that adopted in Estonia on 30 March. The declaration restored the authority of Latvia's 1922 constitution, the basis of its inter-war sovereignty, but allowed a transitional period of unspecified duration to allow negotiations with Moscow over the details of the transition from *de jure* to *de facto* full statehood. Thus the 1940 annexation was rendered null and void. The social and political rights of all citizens of the republic were to be protected, and the President of the republic, Anatolii Gorbunis, and the Prime Minister, Ivars Godmanis, trod a cautious path to avoid the confrontation provoked in neighbouring Lithuania.

Lithuania is the largest of the three republics with a population of 3.6 million, 80 per cent of whom are native Lithuanians, 8.6 per cent Russians and 8 per cent Polish. The popular front organisation was established in 1988 and achieved some early successes, including the resignation of the old guard Communist leadership of the republic, including the First Secretary, Ringuadas Songaila, who had sent riot troops on 28 September 1987 against a peaceful demonstration in the main square of Vilnius. He was replaced by the reforming Algirdas Brazauskas on 20 October 1988, on the eve of the founding congress of the Lithuanian Movement for Perestroika (Sajudis) on 22–23 October. As in the other republics, the congress called for radical reform and democratisation, with a strong emphasis on national and human rights. It goes without saying that the 'leading role' of the party was nowhere mentioned and indeed the door was opened to a multi-party system. Gorbachev conveyed a message to the congress which he hailed as 'a positive force which can serve *perestroika* and strengthen the Soviet Union'.

However, attacks in the central media against the 'provocative' materials printed by Sajudis and by some 40 other publications, including the alleged 'ultra *perestroika*' tone of some Komsomol publications (*P*, 22 February 1989) suggested that *glasnost* had reached the limits of toleration in the Baltic. A vitriolic campaign against the Baltic republics was launched by Ligachev in August 1989. A strong attack on Sajudis (*P*, 23 August 1989) and its leader Vytautas Landsbergis, was followed on 26 August by a broadcast in which the Central Committee castigated the republics for adopting 'openly extremist and separatist positions'. They were held responsible for whipping up 'nationalist hysteria' and of trying to separate the republics from the rest of the country. Party committees and officials who had played up to nationalist feelings were condemned. In the elections of 24 February 1990, the first free multi-party elections in over half a century, Sajudis and its allies gained the necessary two-thirds majority in the Lithuanian Supreme Soviet to make constitutional changes.

The Baltic populations complained about the bureaucratic mismanagement of their economic development. Unwanted factories had been built in unsuitable places, polluting the environment and drawing in labour from other republics, thus threatening the entire native cultural community. In Estonia protest was aroused by plans to expand oil-shale and opencast mining of phosphorite; in Latvia by plans to build a hydroelectric dam and by the pollution of the Gulf of Riga; and in Lithuania by the construction of a third nuclear RBMK (the Chernobyl design) power station at Ignalina. The solution to environmental and economic issues for the local leaders was the wholesale transfer of economic management from the incompetent Moscow bureaucrats to republican economic self-management. The independent movements in all three Baltic republics called for radical reform and defence of the national languages and culture. These demands were supported by massive and heart-moving displays of national feelings. In all three republics, and some others, the national flags banned by Stalin were restored.

The movements helped accelerate the transition to full republican economic autonomy. A law passed by the USSR Supreme Soviet on 27 November 1989 gave the Baltic republics a large degree of economic independence. Nearly three-quarters of Baltic industries from 1 January 1990 passed into local control, leaving heavy industry, fuel and raw materials the responsibility of all-union ministries. Most local tax revenue and foreign currency would also remain in the republics, and they controlled land and resources. The Baltic gradually became a free enterprise zone in which each republic gained a degree of economic autonomy, including independent trading with the rest of the world and the right to issue their own currencies. The Baltic republics moved towards the creation of a local Common Market by 1993, with the aim of integrating their economies and with the co-ordination of their external economic activities. The Baltic Common Market was to be governed by a Baltic Council modelled on the European Commission.

Nationalists in the Baltic saw independence as the only way of avoiding civil war; yet their struggle for independence made that war more likely and weakened Gorbachev's position. The debates surrounding the constitutional amendments of 1988 revealed widespread suspicion of Moscow's intentions. Political change fused with ethnic passions in a potentially lethal combination. The Baltic states and Georgia feared that their already narrow room for manoeuvre would be further circumscribed by clauses which contradicted promises for increased regional autonomy. In particular, they objected to the complicated electoral procedure and draft clauses that gave the Congress an automatic right to declare republican laws 'unconstitutional'. The Estonian parliament, even though elected in the old way, on 16 November rejected the amendments in their entirety and declared its sovereignty in local matters by granting itself the right of veto over central government decisions and laws. Another resolution stated that all land, air and mineral resources in Estonia were the republic's exclusive property, while the 1977 constitution stated that they belonged to 'the Soviet people'. Both measures were declared unconstitutional by a commission of the Supreme Soviet in Moscow on 19 November, as was Estonia's recognition of the right to own private property. This was forbidden by the 1977 constitution, which recognised only 'personal' property. The Supreme Soviets in Lithuania and Latvia stopped short of Estonia's drastic measures, but supported the demand for changes to the constitutional amendments. Concessions were made by increasing the number of representatives from the fifteen republics to the parliament and, in December 1989, in giving each republic representation on the Committee of Constitutional Review which decides whether laws passed in the centre and the republics conform with the constitution.

In January 1989 Lithuanian was declared the state language of the republic, to the protests of non-Lithuanians in the republic. Similar problems were faced in other republics, including Tadzhikistan and Moldavia, where the issue was sharpened by the attempt to return to the Latin alphabet. Changes to local language laws were designed to make the native language the state language within each republic.

In the run-up to the elections of 1990, each republic adopted its own electoral laws. Changes were made to citizenship laws as part of the process which limited the electoral rights of recent migrants. A law adopted by the Estonian parliament on 8 August 1989, after years of deliberate Russification, qualified only those who had lived in a constituency for two years or five years elsewhere in the republic. This was in marked contrast to the extreme liberalism of the election law in general which allowed opposition groups to stand. The two other Baltic republics and Azerbaidzhan adopted similar laws. The Estonian law went the furthest; it was declared unconstitutional by the Presidium of the Supreme Soviet on 16 August 1989 and gave the republic until 1 October to modify the law in line with the constitution, which was done.

These laws provoked the anger of the non-titular populations. In the Baltic republics (and Moldavia) movements were founded on behalf of the Russian working class, predominantly in the big plants directed from Moscow. The Latvian Interfront, in the most Russianised of the three republics, was one of the earliest and strongest. Together with restrictive electoral laws, the most contentious issue was language, since if the native language became the official one the rest would be left in a difficult position (*P*, 1 March 1989). In response to the new laws, in the summer of 1989 tens of thousands of the Russian-speaking minority in Latvia, who totalled some 600,000, used strikes for openly political purposes, closing dozens of the largest factories and disrupting the railways for ten days. Many of the Russian-speakers, of course, identified with the aspirations of the local populations, but found that opportunities for compromise became narrower. The immigrants feared that the language and citizenship laws would make them second-class citizens, presaging cultural and job discrimination. The Russian 87 per cent of Daugavpils, the Eastern Latvian port city, threatened secession from any self-proclaimed Republic of Latvia. The Unity (*Edinstvo*) organisation in Lithuania and the International Movement (*Interdvizhenie*) in Estonia warned that they too would take action if the republics restricted immigrant rights. A widespread suspicion in the Baltic held that conservatives in Moscow were orchestrating the backlash to discredit the radical reforms.

The popular fronts contained many Communists, yet they could not but act as opposition parties in all but name. As long as the local parties conceded the demands of the fronts for human and national rights, political and economic reform, and environmental security, then the basic contradiction between the movements and the party could be glossed over. The signal fact, however, was that the Communist parties in the three republics lost control to popular forces. The Baltic governments' reform programmes went much further than the official aims of *perestroika*. Some of these demands gradually filtered into the party's reformist wing and became official currency of democratic *perestroika*. All three local Communist parties found themselves losing membership. However, the attempt to make the Soviet Union a loose federation in which only defence and foreign policy remained the responsibility of the centre went too far even for the most radical of the Soviet leaders. What would happen when the Moscow authorities decided that enough had been conceded and that it was time to draw the line? In Eastern Europe in 1989 it was discovered that Moscow in effect had no 'bottom line'; but Lithuania found that within the USSR there were limits to the independence that Moscow was willing to concede.

Matters came to a head when the Lithuanian Communist Party decided at its 20th congress on 19 December 1989 by 855 votes to 160 that a formal split from Moscow was the only way to preserve its credibility in the local elections. Sajudis had already penetrated the party itself, with six out of the fourteen members of the Lithuanian Politburo also members of Sajudis. The transformation of the local Communist Party into a social democratic one gave it a great degree of popular legitimacy. Gorbachev's refusal to consider the use of force against Lithuania in his address to the CC plenum called to discuss the emergency on 25 December meant that some sort of political solution had to be found (*P*, December 1989). Gorbachev's three-day visit to Lithuania in January 1990 convinced him that for the national Communist Party to remain a genuine force in politics it too would have to transform itself (*P*, 14 and 15 January 1990). At the February plenum of the CC the first steps were taken on this road, but they were accompanied by an appeal to the Lithuanian Communists not to split from the national party. At a time when the Lithuanian parliament denounced the republic's accession to the Soviet Union in 1940, the first step towards secession, the room for manoeuvre by either side narrowed. The choice facing the Lithuanian Communists was either subordination to Moscow and defeat in local elections, or a continued fight for their independence.

The election of Landsbergis rather than Brazauskas as President of the republic on 15 January 1990 set the scene for the crisis over Lithuanian independence that would either destroy the unity of the Soviet Union or undermine the aspirations of democratic *perestroika*. Gorbachev's hope that political and economic autonomy could restrain nationalist pressure, and that indeed the Baltic could become a showpiece for radical *perestroika*, stumbled on what he perceived to be the ultra-nationalism of the region. It became clear that the East European option of full independence was not open to Soviet republics. But, as in Eastern Europe, the populations did not wait for official permission before they began their revolutions. Gorbachev's concession in Lithuania promising a law establishing a mechanism for a republic to secede appeared irrelevant to peoples who were achieving independence by their own efforts. The European Community option for a looser and more democratic type of federalism appeared to put the cart before the horse:

first independence, the nationalists argued, and then some sort of renegotiated treaty for economic and political co-operation. The attempt to reform the Soviet economy while simultaneously renegotiating the principles of federalism made both more difficult. The disintegration of the economy was increasingly accompanied by the dismemberment of the country.

The Lithuanian parliament's vote on 11 March 1990 for the restoration of pre-war independence confirmed the split between the radical 'Kaunas faction', who led Sajudis, and the Vilnius independent Communist faction led by Brazauskas. Even though Brazauskas joined the government of Kazimiera Prunskiene as a deputy prime minister, the division remained which hampered the creation of a united team to negotiate with Moscow. In a flood of legislation that ran contrary to Soviet legislation the Lithuanians proceeded to establish the institutions of an independent state. The country was renamed simply the Lithuanian Republic, dropping the intervening 'Soviet Socialist'; new identity cards were introduced; laws were passed setting up its own border forces and security forces; and the spring conscription to the Soviet army was halted. Sajudis called for all Lithuanians serving in the Soviet army to desert.

The newly inaugurated executive President soon showed his 'iron teeth'. Gorbachev's first *ukaz*, a term used by the tsars to describe edicts of the first importance, called for the confiscation of private arms, followed by a series of intimidatory gestures including military sabre-rattling, the capture of deserters and the occupation of printing works belonging to the Communist Party. Gorbachev's initial insistence that he would restrict himself to political measures gave way to a range of economic sanctions, including cutting energy and food supplies.

Gorbachev's options were dangerously limited by the Lithuanian declaration of independence. If he acceded to the republic's demands, then no doubt Estonia, Latvia, Georgia, Azerbaidzhan and Moldavia would soon follow, and his own position would be jeopardised by a conservative backlash allied with the military and the KGB. However, if Lithuanian aspirations were crushed with excessive force, then five years of adroit diplomacy on the world stage would be undermined. Understanding Gorbachev's dilemma, the West at first remained largely passive in the face of Soviet actions against Lithuania. The West imposed trade curbs, but did not endorse the reconstitution of Lithuanian independence. Gorbachev insisted that talks with Lithuania could only proceed if the 11 March declaration, which he declared on 13 March to be 'illegal and invalid', was rescinded. He refused to negotiate as this would betoken an act of recognition. The challenge was ultimately reminiscent of that of Czechoslovakia in 1968. The Soviet invasion of that year did not derail the process of *détente*. Lithuanian expectations of Western support were no doubt exaggerated. From the Lithuanian viewpoint, however, there was a clear logic in making a dash for freedom at a time when the Soviet Union was at its weakest. The Lithuanians had hoped to use existing Soviet institutions to find a path to independence, but found that they lacked the physical means to sustain their bid for freedom from Moscow.

Moldavia

Moldavia, formerly Bessarabia, was annexed from Romania in 1940 as part of the division of spoils permitted by the secret protocol of 1939. In Moldavia the local language, a dialect of Romanian, was forced to adopt the Cyrillic alphabet. As elsewhere, the reimposition of Soviet control in 1944 was accompanied by the mass deportation of peasants and others. By 1985 there were few books in the native language or provisions for its teaching. The language issue became the focus of discontent for the majority of Moldavia's 5 million people, and at the same time the bone of contention with the non-Moldavian 35 per cent, mainly Russians and Ukrainians, who had immigrated since the War.

The cultural movement began in May 1988 when the local Union of Writers formed a group on national and environmental conditions. The obstructiveness and savagery of the local party, headed by Semën Grossu, one of the two remaining Brezhnev appointees at the head of a republican party organisation, transformed the essentially moderate movement for the re-Latinisation of the alphabet into a powerful nationalist movement which organised a series of mass demonstrations. A green movement emerged protesting against the environmental degradation of the republic caused by chemicals, and others condemned the Stalinism of the local leadership. These coalesced by January 1989 into the Moldavian Popular Front (*Al Moldovei*, MPF), which then held its inaugural conference in May. Its demands included the replacement of the Brezhnev generation of leaders, the Moldavianisation of education, though respecting Ukrainian and Gagauze minorities, an end to migration from Russia and other republics, full sovereignty, the reinstatement of the old red, yellow and blue flag, and the establishment of a Moldavian Orthodox Church (G, 31 August 1989). Naturally, closer links with Romania were desired, but this was not a pressing demand until the overthrow of Ceausescu across the border.

Laws that made Moldavian the official state language and restored the Latin alphabet were passed on 31 August 1989. As in the Baltic, non-Moldavians established a movement called Unity (*Edinstvo*) which organised political strikes involving some 100,000 people in summer 1989, even though the law made provisions for the use of Russian in 'inter-ethnic communication'. Under pressure, the law was later moderated to recognise both Russian and Moldavian. Moldavia itself has a minority people, the Gagauze, some 160,000 strong who live in the south of the republic. They are a Christian Turkic group who demanded autonomy in order to preserve their language and culture which they felt was in danger of dying out. Their language was also protected in the modified language laws of the republic.

In response to the violence accompanying and following the 7 November 1989 celebrations of the Revolution, Grossu was finally replaced as leader of the republican party by Pëtr Luchinskii on 16 November. The MPF insisted on full recognition for itself, and opposed plans to establish a separate autonomous republic for the Gagauze. The non-Moldavian minority continued its agitation against the nationalists by organising a referendum in Tiraspol, 87 per cent of whose population are non-Moldavians, which voted in favour of creating an autonomous republic for the area.

Transcaucasia

Some fifty different groups live in the Caucasus, divided by language, ethnicity and religion. The first major nationalist conflict erupted over Nagorno-Karabakh, an autonomous region within the Azerbaidzhan Soviet republic. On 5 July 1921 Nagorno-Karabakh, 90 per cent of whose population at the time were Christian and Armenian, was transferred from the direct control of Soviet forces to the jurisdiction of Turkic and Shiah Azerbaidzhan by the Bureau of the Caucasian Party Committee under pressure from Stalin. On 16 July the CC of the Armenian party rejected the decision but was unable to reverse it. From this act of Stalinist high-handedness, accompanied by centuries-old rivalries, sprang the demonstrations that began on 20 February 1988 for its transfer to Armenia. During the last 60 years the number of Armenians in Nagorno-Karabakh has fallen from 142,000 to 136,000, from 94 to 76 per cent of the population of 160,000 in 1979.

Democratisation within the framework of *perestroika* emboldened the Karabakh regional soviet on 20 February 1988 to petition for its transfer to Armenia. By Soviet law this should have been dealt with by the USSR Supreme Soviet within a month. Instead, it delayed a decision for five months, thus allowing events to escalate out of control. The Armenian leadership of the region interpreted Article 70 of the 1977 constitution, which declared the right of nations to self-determination, as permitting a region to choose which republic will govern it. Article 78, on the other hand, stated that the territory of a union republic could not be altered without its consent. In this case the transfer of Karabakh to Armenia, the clear expressed wish of the majority of its population, would not have altered the boundaries of Azerbaidzhan. However, the restrictive interpretation of this clause and fears by Moscow that territorial shifts could set a dangerous precedent led to catastrophe.

The slaughter of thirty Armenians at Sumgait on 27 February 1988 was probably instigated by the Azerbaidzhan 'mafia' with the connivance of the party leadership. Many questions remain unresolved, including why troops stationed in the suburbs did not intervene earlier. Instead of answering the Karabakh soviet's request, the Soviet government sought to placate the population by promising economic and social improvements in Karabakh. While welcome, this concession, typical of much of Gorbachev's handling of nationality issues, was too little too late. The population took to the streets in the region and in Armenia proper in ever larger numbers. The use of force on 5 July 1988 at Zvartnotz airport in Erevan, in which one Armenian youth died, provided a foretaste of the violence by troops in Tbilisi in April 1989. A whole nation learnt how to organise and act collectively and legally. In June 1988 the Karabakh regional authorities decided unilaterally to withdraw from Azerbaidzhani control.

Popular demands for transfer were supported by the Armenian and Karabakh Communist Party organisations. Even so, party authority was undermined by the Karabakh Committee made up of academics, writers, journalists and local officials acting in a personal capacity. The Karabakh Committee established local committees throughout the republic and in effect acted as a shadow government with immeasurably more authority than the official Communist Party. The Armenian Church headed by Catholicos Vazgen began to play a role analogous to that of the Catholic Church in Poland during the first Solidarity period, and similarly urged non-violence. The 'leading role' of the party and Soviet power in general effectively collapsed, first in Armenia and then in Azerbaidzhan.

The USSR Supreme Soviet meeting of 18 July 1988 was marked by intolerance and inaccurate speeches, including that by Gorbachev himself. The request of the Nagorno-Karabakh soviet was rejected (*P*, 20 July 1988). Instead, on 12 January 1989 local government in Nagorno-Karabakh was dissolved and the area was transferred to the direct control of Moscow under a commission headed by Arkadii Volskii. Seventy-eight people had been killed in 1988, and at least 150, despite direct rule, in 1989 as the area degenerated into civil war and a blockade of Armenia by Azerbaidzhan. The solution that Gorbachev refused to countenance was to turn Nagorno-Karabakh into an autonomous republic, with its own Supreme Soviet and government.

The analogy with Ulster gave way to comparisons with the Lebanon. Despite this, the Supreme Soviet in November 1989 decreed the end of direct rule in the area and the return of administration to Azerbaidzhan. In response, the Armenian parliament voted to unite with Nagorno-Karabakh. The continued stalemate was thick with portents of catastrophe for the region and the nation. The Karabakh Committee acted as a steering committee democratically controlled by mass meetings. In July 1988 one of its leaders, Paruir Airikyan, like many others under Brezhnev, was stripped of his Soviet citizenship and expelled from the country. Following the Armenian earthquake the majority of committee members were arrested. By September 1989 hundreds of thousands of Azeris demonstrated and struck in Baku demanding the return of Karabakh to Azerbaidzhani control.

A powerful Azerbaidzhani Popular Front (APF) in effect replaced the legally constituted authorities, and by late 1989 party authority under the leadership of Abdul Rakhman Vezirov had, as a member of the APF put it, vanished 'like a bubble of soap'. Less than half of the republic's party membership of 384,000 in 1987 remained by 1990. Support for the APF was fed not only by the conflict with Armenia, but also by five other factors. The first was Azerbaidzhani nationalism, fuelled by bitterness at separation from the Azeris in neighbouring Iran, from whom they were divided by a treaty of 1828. This led to the breaking down of the border between Azerbaidzhan's Nakhichevan autonomous republic and Iran on 31 December 1989. The second was religion, Islamic fundamentalism being fanned by the Iranian Shiah revolution. The third element focused on economic grievances, in particular Moscow's exploitation of Caspian oil reserves with little benefit going to Azerbaidzhan. Over 90 per cent of the republic's industry was controlled by Moscow. The fourth factor, as in other republics, was the ecological catastrophe facing the region. Above all, however, political factors focused on Azeri resentment at Moscow's subordination of the republic and on hopes for an independent, democratic and pluralistic republic. The elections to the Congress in spring 1989 had been blatantly rigged. It would appear that in Azerbaidzhan at this time a liberal agenda of democratic rights and separation of powers took precedence over Muslim fundamentalism.

Fears of civil war in the region between Armenians and Azerbaidzhanis came to tragic fruition following a blockade of Armenia and pogroms against the 200,000 strong Armenian population in Baku in January 1990. These pogroms may well have been officially organised, and on the eve of the Soviet army invasion Vezirov was unceremoniously replaced. The APF in effect took power, leading to the invasion of Soviet forces on 19 January in which at least 200 died. What was officially called an 'anti-Soviet insurrection' was crushed and the APF harassed but not banned.

As we saw when discussing the Baltic, the ethnic and civil unrest began to affect the armed services. Following Lithuania's declaration of independence Lithuanian conscripts deserted, and everywhere conscripts demanded the right to serve only on the territory of their republics. The old Soviet army practice of bullying new recruits, *dedovshchina*, took on an ugly ethnic dimension as conscripts far from home were beaten up. The number of people trying to avoid military service rose sharply, and there were mass protests against the call-up of reservists to be sent to the Caucasus. After the hopeless war in Afghanistan, there was little enthusiasm to be caught up in yet another insoluble conflict. Moreover, changing demographic patterns meant that one in three conscripts were now Muslims.

Georgia had known a period of independence from 1918 to 25 February 1921, when a passing army overthrew the Social Democratic government and incorporated the nation into the union despite a treaty of 1918 which recognised the republic's independence from Soviet Russia. Some 65 per cent of its 5.5 million people are ethnic Georgians, yet fears remained of its 'Russification'. In Georgia environmental movements and nationalists united in many organisations, including a Popular Front, the Ilya Chavchavadze Society, the National Independence Party and the National Democratic Party to name but a few, to fight the plan for a new Transcaucasian railway which threatened ancient monuments, the unspoilt habitat from which Tbilisi drew its water, and forests. Demographic issues also played their part, directed against the fast growing Azeri population. The Georgian nationalist movement was fragmented and lacked the cohesion and discipline found in the Baltic. In a series of large demonstrations it called for outright independence in a capitalist and multi-party state. On 20 March 1990 the Georgian Supreme Soviet abolished the Communist Party's guaranteed monopoly on power, and postponed the local elections until the autumn to allow preparations to be made for genuine multi-party elections. Thus Georgia, like the Baltic, set out on the path of independence.

However, the independence that it sought for itself Georgia was unwilling to grant to its own minority peoples, in particular the autonomous republic of Abkhazia on the Black Sea, which it had gained in 1921. With the onset of *perestroika* the long suppressed movement for the secession of Abkhazia, which contained 10 per cent of the republic's population, from Georgia swelled into a mass movement leading to ethnic clashes in July 1989 in which twenty-one people were killed. Tensions also ran high between Georgians and the South Ossetian autonomous region: Georgians argued that they were second-class citizens in their own land, while the latter demanded to join Russia. The Adzhars and Meskheti Turks in Georgia also sought greater autonomy.

The cloud of military intervention that had long hung over the nationalist movements finally burst with disastrous consequences with the army attack on demonstrators in Tbilisi on 9 April 1989, in which twenty-one were killed (see page 216). The Georgian nationalist demonstrations had been provoked by the Abkhazian demands for secession. The demonstrators demanded the area's complete integration into an independent Georgia. While Khrushchev in 1962 had been able to suppress information about the Novocherkassk massacre, these events, the largest known official killing since then, could not be hidden in an age of *glasnost*. The military option in dealing with nationalism was seen to be counter-productive. The attempt to discredit Gorbachev by the old leadership of the republic and, more than likely, conservative forces in Moscow backfired sharply against their cause. Following the deaths of 9 April a new party leader, Givi Gumbaridze, replaced Dzhumbar Patiashvili, who accepted responsibility for the clashes. In his address to the Georgians following the incident Gorbachev made plain his view that 'The restructuring of inter-ethnic relations is not the replanning of borders or the breakdown of the national-state structure of the country' (*Ind.*, 13 April 1989).

The massacre thoroughly discredited the existing authorities and boosted the movement for independence. A 'parallel parliament', like the Estonian and Latvian ones, was created, the 45-member National Forum, to challenge the existing Supreme Soviet. The collapse of Communist Party authority strengthened the National Democratic Party and the National Independence Party.

Central Asia

The first riots of *perestroika* took place in Alma Ata in December 1986, protesting against the appointment of the Russian, Kolbin, as party leader in Kazakhstan. Tension had apparently been provoked by corrupt local élites who tried to muddy the already murky waters. In Kazakhstan only 36 per cent of its 16.5 million population were Kazakhs, while 41 per cent were Russians. Central Asia is at the blunt end of ecological concerns, especially over the Kara-Kum canal depriving the Aral Sea of water. Economic mismanagement here has taken place on a grandiose scale in the obsessive pursuit of cotton monoculture. The region has become the Soviet Union's own Third World. For example, 90 per cent of the cotton and 70 per cent of the raw silk produced in Turkmenistan is processed outside the republic, thus depriving it of employment, manufacturing skills and value added. Republican *khozraschët* and economic autonomy would allow Turkmenistan to process the raw materials and thus allow it to move away from its dependence on primary products.

Stalin's legacy of deportations in particular affects Central Asia, where the deported peoples were dumped: Balkars, Chechens, Crimean Tatars, Greeks, Ingush, Kalmyks, Karachai, Koreans, Kurds, Meskhetian Turks and Volga Germans. Nationality grievances moved beyond vertical divisions between the centre and the localities, and took on an ugly lateral dimension in the form of intercommunal rivalry and massacres. In June 1989 Uzbek gangs in the Fergana valley hunted down and slaughtered some 100 Meskhetian Turks who had been deported by Stalin from Georgia, wounded 1,500 and drove a further 16,000 out of Uzbekistan. The Crimean Tatars make up 4 per cent of Uzbekistan's population of 19.9 million, 65.9 per cent of whom are Uzbeks and 11 per cent Russian. In February 1990 anti-Soviet riots broke out in Dushanbe, the capital of Tadzhikistan, in which at least twenty-two died. Tadzhiks account for 60 per cent of the 5.1 million population, about a quarter of a million of whom were unemployed. Inadequate housing, poor living conditions and unemployment, especially among the young of the fast growing population, were the factors which fuelled these riots, just as fear of unemployment played a part in the strikes in the Baltic by immigrants.

These incidents revealed the high degree of political instability in Central Asia as Soviet power began to fragment. This was confirmed by the breakdown of political authority in Dushanbe. Soviet power was restored only by the use of troops, but not before the headquarters of the Communist Party had been burnt down. Not to be left out, riots broke out in Frunze, the capital of Kirghizia's 4.3 million people as Uzbek fought Kirghiz in Osh in June 1990. In these areas national independence as such was not the central issue, but rather political democracy and economic autonomy.

Belorussia and the Ukraine

Eighty per cent of Belorussia's population of 10.2 million are ethnic Belorussians. Nationalist and democratic movements were stymied by the conservatism of the local party leadership, and a local popular front only emerged late and then had to use facilities provided by the Sajudis movement in neighbouring Lithuania. The local intelligentsia and activists succeeded in establishing a Belorussian Popular Front (BPF) in Support of Perestroika only in June 1989. In contrast to the close relationship between the party and the fronts in the Baltic, the Belorussian party organisation, headed by Efrem Sokolov, maintained a resolute hostility even though some 14 per cent of the 361 delegates to the founding congress in Vilnius were Communists. The Front's main goal was declared to be a sovereign Belorussia 'based on the principles of democracy, humanism and social justice', and vowed to achieve 'the establishment of people's power and the rebirth of the Belorussian nation' (G, 26 June 1989).

In the elections to the Belorussian Supreme Soviet in spring 1990 the opposition fought only 149 of the 310 seats, winning 59 of them. Fifty of the seats were reserved for social organisations. The leader of the BFP, Zenon Pozniak, was among the victors. In the local elections the opposition took control of Minsk city soviet.

The Western swathe of Belorussia is made up of territory taken from Poland during the War. The Poles living there, together with those in southern Lithuania, called for their own autonomous republic within a reorganised federation of Soviet republics.

The language issue is a vital one in Belorussia and the Ukraine as much as it is in the Baltic and elsewhere. In 1958 Khrushchev no longer made it compulsory to teach a child its native language, while Russian remained compulsory throughout the union. The number of Ukrainian and Belorussian speakers declined precipitously. An education in the dominant language of the state, Russian, was considered advantageous. In urban areas of Belorussia few local language schools could be found, while in Kiev in 1987 a mere 12 per cent of schools taught in Ukrainian. Popular campaigns to make study of the local language, literature and history compulsory, led by the Ukrainian Writers' Union, failed to gain the support of the local party.

With a population of 52 million, of whom 72 per cent are Ukrainian and 20 per cent Russian, the Ukrainian republic is second in population only to Russia itself and is a major industrial and agrarian region. The Soviet Union could survive without Lithuania or Georgia, but without the Ukraine it could not. Vladimir Shcherbitskii was the last Politburo survivor of the Brezhnev years, having joined in 1971 and become head of the republican party organisation in May 1972 with the brief to destroy the nationalist legacy of his predecessor, Pëtr Shelest. It is still not clear why his foot-dragging approach to *perestroika* was tolerated for so long before his replacement by Ivashko in autumn 1989. Shcherbitskii ruled the republic for seventeen years with an oppressive grip, and in the 1989 elections to the Congress tried, though in the event unsuccessfully, to guarantee the election of conservative party leaders by ensuring that one-third of them ran unopposed. His attempts to avoid a similar fate by tailoring the electoral law for the local elections of 1990 failed and the opposition in November 1989 forced the abolition of the system of reserved seats for social organisations.

The national movement was from the first led by the Ukrainian Writers' Union, and its newspaper provided a forum for discussion of collectivisation and the famine of 1932–3, the purges, ecological problems and Chernobyl, and language and cultural issues. Memorial focused attention on the Bykov mass grave near Kiev, which as noted may hold between 150,000 to 240,000 victims of the purges of 1937–8. The city of Lvov, taken from Poland in 1940, exhibited the most radical and strong movements.

The founding congress of the Ukrainian Popular Front (*Narodnyi Rukh*), which was formed in November 1988, took place on 8–10 September 1989 in Kiev with 1,120 delegates representing some 300,000 members from language groups, the Uniates, the intelligentsia and, in particular, members of the Ukrainian Writers' Union who had long agitated for the democratisation of the republic, miners and other workers who sought more trade union independence, Memorial, environmental groups in the republic which had witnessed the world's worst nuclear disaster at Chernobyl, managers who wanted more decentralisation, outright nationalists who sought to restore the independent Ukraine that existed in 1917–18, and many other strands of Ukrainian nationalism and democracy. One-fifth of the delegates were Communists. Adam Michnik represented Solidarity from neighbouring Poland and announced with some prescience, 'We are witnesses of a new chapter in history between post-Communist nations. We now have the chance of ending Stalinism and totalitarianism in Eastern Europe' (*Ind.*, 9 September 1989). He went on to give advice on how the workers, above all miners, could make common cause with the intelligentsia. *Rukh* demanded full financial self-accounting for the Ukraine, the adoption of Ukrainian as the republic's official state language and as the only language in education, the right to own and inherit land, and environmental conservation.

Rukh was boosted by the agitation over the selection of candidates to the 19th party conference and the chicanery of the local party machine in the spring 1989 elections. With a membership which by then had reached half a million, it fought the local elections of 4 March 1990 as part of a Democratic Bloc with groups like Green World and the Ukrainian Language Society. The Bloc fielded candidates in less than half of the 450 constituencies, giving the Communist Party a clear advantage. Nevertheless, *Rukh* gained control of the Lvov and Kiev city soviets, and indeed all the deputies from Western Ukraine to the Supreme Soviet were non-Communists. *Rukh* had agreed with the democratic workers' movement not to field candidates in Eastern Ukraine, where there is a predominantly Russian-speaking working class. The opposition won control of Kharkov and Donetsk city soviets. In sum, *Rukh* won 85 of the 450 seats, and the workers' opposition 25, and together they constituted themselves as the Democratic Bloc in the Ukrainian parliament. Following the election the leader of *Rukh*, Ivan Drach, and its secretary, Mykhaylo Horyn, declared their intention to transform the movement into a fully-fledged opposition party campaigning for political pluralism, democratisation and independence from the Soviet Union (G, 7 March 1990).

Russia

The Russian Soviet Federated Socialist Republic (RSFSR) is itself a microcosm of the multinational USSR, and 147.4 million (120 million of whom are ethnic Russians) of the country's total population of 286.7 million live there. The native peoples of Russia are facing the same pressures that indigenous peoples are facing throughout the world as industrialism encroaches on their habitats. There are plans to restore some of the national districts, especially in the far north, which existed in the 1920s and 1930s in areas which do not have autonomous regions. Long before *perestroika* certain homeless nationalities were agitating for redress of their grievances, above all, return to a native homeland. In 1957 Khrushchev had restored autonomous republics to all the deported nationalities with the exception of the Crimean Tatars and the Volga Germans. The Crimean Tatars demonstrated in Red Square in summer 1987; in June 1988 they were denied their request for the return of an autonomous homeland but were allowed to resettle in the Crimea on an individual basis.

A German autonomous republic had existed on the lower Volga between 1924 and September 1941, when Stalin accused them of 'harbouring spies and saboteurs' and deported some 600,000 Germans, who had settled there under Catherine the Great, to Central Asia and Siberia where some 2 million now live with few German language facilities. The Germans had been rehabilitated in 1964, and in 1972 they were permitted on an individual basis to resettle on the Volga. In March 1989 an All-Union Society of Germans (*Wiedergeburt*, or Rebirth) was established to agitate for the restoration of a German autonomous republic on their former territory between Volgograd and Saratov. It seemed in late 1989 that their hopes would be fulfilled, but Gorbachev's antipathy to changing borders has already been noted, especially since the local population protested. Gorbachev hoped that economic and cultural improvements would be sufficient: such an approach may have worked twenty years ago but has little chance of satisfying national aspirations today. The only option for the Germans seemed to be emigration , which the Federal Republic of Germany assisted.

The census of January 1989 showed that the Russian share of the total population of the USSR had fallen to 50.8 per cent from 52.4 per cent in 1979. This confirmed the continuing fall in the average annual rate of increase of Russians. The Russian national question is the most complex of them all. Russian nationalism is by nature divided into innumerable currents. A widespread perception among Russians is that they have had to bear a disproportionate part of the burden of empire without a corresponding share in its benefits. Standards of living in the RSFSR are lower than in many other republics, the countryside has been ravaged by collectivisation, pollution, and incompetent economic and social policies, and Russian culture and religion have been oppressed. While other ethnic groups have a buffer between their nationalism and the Soviet state, one aspect of which is that they can at least hold the Russian 'elder brothers' responsible for their sufferings, Russian nationalism lacks any mediating dimension and is confronted directly with understanding how and why the structures of the Soviet state, which they have staffed in such numbers, could have wreaked such a mortal toll on them.

The Russian population lacked an encompassing national dimension in the struggle for change under *perestroika*. However, what united Russians, Ukrainians, Balts and the other peoples was a common struggle against Stalinism and the 'administrative-command system'. It should be stressed that Stalinism was not a Russian colonial endeavour pillaging the non-Russian republics for the benefit of a Russian imperial class, but the universal suppression of the rights of all Soviet peoples, however much Russification may have been used to bolster imperial authority in the non-Russian republics. The principle of *divide et impera* came as naturally to Stalin as it did to Caesar and Robert Clive.

Since the 1930s the Communist leadership has been willing to use Russian nationalism to buttress the authority of Marxism–Leninism, and as democratic *perestroika* faltered an alliance began to be forged between the Communist Party *apparat* and Russian populist and conservative nationalism to retain the unity of the Soviet state against the smaller nationalities and radical democratic movements. Something of the sort took place with the rise of Slobodan Milosevic in Serbia. While the Soviet state is federal, Gorbachev insisted that the Communist Party should remain unitary. But as the nationalist movements came to the fore local parties increasingly identified with them and the party began to fracture into its constituent elements. Over half of all Communists in the country, 10.6 million, were in the Russian part of the country, so the establishment of a Russian party organisation would eclipse all the others. The fear of boosting centrifugal forces and the stress on the unitary nature of the party led to a reluctance to create a separate republican party; instead a Russian Bureau of the CPSU Central Committee, abolished in 1965, was created (see p. 173). This was not enough for Russian Communists, and as noted in June 1990 a separate Communist Party of the RSFSR was created.

One of the key aspects of the *perestroika* of nationality relations was to give a new identity to the Russian republic, and its governmental institutions were reorganised and strengthened. In contrast to the other fourteen republics, many functions for Russia were carried out by all-union bodies which, according to Yuri Manaenkov, a secretary of the CPSU Central Committee and a member of the Russian Bureau, 'had a highly negative effect on the interests of both the republic and the entire union' (*P*, 9 November 1989). A series of new republican ministries was created. A Russian academy of sciences was planned, as well as Russian trade union and Komsomol bodies. Under Eltsin's presidency the Russian parliament gave shape to Russia's rebirth by such acts as a declaration of state sovereignty (*Sov. Rossiya*, 14 June 1990) and a decree on power (*A.i F.*, 25/1990), which separated governmental office from party-political interference. Under the new prime minister, Ivan Silaev, the Russian government was thoroughly reorganised.

Yanov warns that liberal Russian nationalism may develop into a 'Fascist nationalism', fuelled by the tradition of Slavophilism and the 'Russian idea' (Yanov, 1987). While Brezhnev's institutional anti-Semitism, such as restrictions on entering Moscow State University, all but disappeared, and emigration policy was relaxed, a tide of anti-Semitism emerged. The Pamyat (Memory) organisation originated under Brezhnev as a cultural group concerned with the preservation of monuments and the environment, but as *perestroika* deepened it became a more overtly political body combining apparently contradictory fears about the 'cultural genocide' being practised against the Russians, popular Stalinism, anti-imperialism, anti-Semitism, anti-Westernism and anti-Freemasonry in a virulent and heady brew of chauvinism and xenophobia. They identified the hand of Jewish speculators behind the new co-operatives. Pamyat groups were organised in several Russian cities and held black-shirted rallies. There was a widespread suspicion that behind Pamyat lay the divisive hand of the KGB. The Fascist overtones of the movement, whose size and support are not clear, were a sharp reminder that *glasnost* could bring to the surface all sorts of forces that had lain dormant in the Soviet body politic. In all republics, as if in reaction to the forced harmony of earlier years and the chaos and failures of *perestroika*, anxieties took the form of racism against the other and discrimination against outsiders. Russian democratic nationalists in particular felt that the influence of Pamyat, a small group with ties to the conservative *apparat* as well as the KGB, was exaggerated as a very effective stick with which to beat them. The historical role of the Russians meant that legitimate Russian nationalism was often seen as threatening. For some unknown reason the authorities long failed to use existing laws against those inciting racial hatred, and only in February 1990 for the first time started proceedings against two members of Pamyat under Article 74 of the RSFSR Criminal Code (*LG*, 21 February 1990).

Much discussion about reform is permeated by the 'Russian question', the eternal problem of changing and modernising a society that seems impervious to change for a long period, then like the Russian spring embarks upon a period of frenetic activity, only to fall dormant again. Aspects of the 'Russian question' include the nature and diversity of the people, the size of the polity, the type of governmental institutions that could represent its peoples, the mystical belief in Russian exceptionalism, and the burden of history in a country in which attempts to reform since Peter the Great have tended to go disastrously wrong.

National Bolshevism which favoured the retention of the multinational state and felt that Communist power was one way in which this could be achieved, re-emerged with considerable force. While this conservative and nationalist approach might have been a healthy development in a pluralistic society, under *perestroika* it was tainted by two aspects. The first was its neo-Stalinism and glorification of past discipline. The second was the anti-Semitic tone of some of the writing. Neither should be exaggerated, and to a degree can be understood (though by no means justified) by the sense of devastation of Russian national culture over the last seventy years reinforced by an apprehension of being beleaguered by the strident nationalism in the non-Russian republics.

Fears that *perestroika* would open the door to degenerate aspects of Western culture were taken up by Aleksandr Prokhanov in his idealisation of the veterans of the Afghan war, the *Afghantsy*, as a force to cleanse Soviet society (*LG*, 16 May 1988). Prokhanov was a leading exponent of national Bolshevism, but he was neither neo-Stalinist nor anti-Semitic (*Détente*, 9–10/1988: 24–9). Russophile writers like Valentin Rasputin and Fedor Abramov sought to find the roots of Russian culture in the villages, and criticised the policy of rapid industrialisation and urbanisation that has destroyed the Russian countryside. Russian nationalists like Igor Shafarevich have identified a pervasive Russophobia in the attempts to calumny any display of Russian self-identity or self-examination as a harbinger of Russian imperialism and pogroms (cf. Shafarevich, 1989). One liberal strand inspired by Solzhenitsyn would look upon the dissolution of the USSR with equanimity since it would allow Russians to concentrate on finding their own special spiritual path. Not for them the view that however bad the USSR might have been, at least it was theirs. Several monarchist organisations emerged, such as the Russian Orthodox Constitutional Monarchist Party that held a founding congress in May 1990, and the old white, blue and red Russian flag became increasingly popular.

Hundreds, if not thousands, of local popular fronts were established, but no single overarching Russian nationalist movement emerged, though the Russian Popular Front began to play this role. The embryonic multi-party system in the country was reflected in the many divisions in Russian society. Echoes of the Russian nationalist backlash in the Baltic and Moldavia were heard in the founding congress of the United Front of Russian Workers (OFT), established in Sverdlovsk in September 1989. This was a conservative working-class organisation, sponsored by Ligachev, with links to the Russian minorities in the Baltic states. It denounced liberal economic reforms, condemned the 'bour-geois democracy' of the liberals in parliament in favour of workers' democracy, and opposed the nationalism of the non-Russian republics. The group feared that *perestroika* was leading to chaos, a theme expounded by Ligachev, and warned that economic decentralisation could lead to the breakup of the union and condemned the uncontrolled development of market relations (*Sovetskaya rossiya*, 13 September 1989).

More radical democratic organisations also emerged. In October 1989 representatives from 35 popular fronts from the RSFSR held an inaugural congress which demanded straightforward constituency elections for local and national assemblies, the transformation of *glasnost* into full freedom of speech, and an end to the leading role of the party by deleting Article 6 of the constitution. As noted, a Bloc of Democratic Russia uniting some fifty organisations was created later in the year to fight the local and republic elections of 4 March 1990. In other words, patriotic Russian nationalism and radical reform Communists joined forces to achieve the democratisation of the country. The Bloc achieved impressive results, taking a majority in the Moscow and Leningrad city soviets. Following the elections the contours of a post-Communist Russia began to emerge. A notable event was the foundation of the Russian Christian Democratic Movement (RCDM) on 24 March 1990, one of whose leaders was Viktor Aksyuchits, who had won a seat to the RSFSR parliament. His co-founders were Father Vyacheslav Polosin,

Gleb Anishchenko and Father Gleb Yakunin. The RCDM tried to bring together democratic elements from the Russian Popular front and the Russian Orthodox Church, and was the kernel of a future Christian democratic party. Based on Christian principles of charity and solidarity, the RCDM called for a multi-party democratic Russia and favoured the re-establishment of the old Russian parliament, the Duma, a free market economy and equal rights for all citizens irrespective of their nationality, and guaranteed the right for each nation to leave the union or to decide on what basis to become a member.

Gorbachev was both ambivalent to and understanding of Russian aspirations. The rapid rise of Aleksandr Yakovlev could be taken as a sign of ambivalence, since he had been 'exiled' by Brezhnev to Canada in 1973 for his forthright condemnation of extreme Russian nationalism (*LG*, 15 November 1972). He was one of Gorbachev's closest allies on the Politburo. However, Gorbachev showed great understanding, and indeed sympathy, with Russophile ideas. His rejection of the Siberian rivers diversion scheme won him much support from Russians. In his Krasnodar speech in September 1986 he quoted Dostoevskii's views on the openness of the 'Russian heart', though he hastily added that this now applied to the whole Soviet people (*Moskovskaya pravda*, 19 September 1986). Furthermore, his support for Likhachev's Fund for Soviet Culture actively supported by his wife Raisa, demonstrates a respect for the Russian past. Likhachev's book (1981) on what it means to be a Russian reflected certain Russophile ideas, and they emerged as one of the key elements of the independent movement which flourished under Gorbachev (Hammer, 1987; Szporluk, 1989). Gorbachev's Presidential Council included the Russophile, Rasputin.

From the above analysis it is clear that every nationalism in the USSR is the product of a different history and culture, and thus each needs to be understood in context. It is equally clear that nationality relations are focused not only on the vertical relationship with Moscow, but also on horizontal relationships with other nationalities. Nationality unrest was fuelled by some seven factors, not all of which applied to all peoples: the principles of federalism; the experience of non-Soviet statehood and the way republics were incorporated into the USSR (Baltic, Moldavia, Western Ukraine, possibly Georgia); deportations; pattern of development which led to population shifts undermining the indigenous groups (Latvia, Kazakhstan); wasteful industrialisation leading to environmental degradation (everywhere); corruption and the struggle against it (above all Central Asia); and the failure of *perestroika* itself to deliver tangible economic benefits and guaranteed political rights. The social processes that gave rise to the informal groups acted with redoubled pressure when combined with national issues, no less in Russia as in other republics. It was quite clear that the official definition of Soviet federalism could not satisfy the aspirations of unofficial nationalism.

The new federalism

Gorbachev insisted in his speech to the Supreme Soviet on 29 November 1988 that it was not *perestroika* that was to blame for nationalist unrest, but rather '*perestroika* has exploded the illusory peace and harmony which reigned during the years of stagnation' (*P*, 30 November 1988). This was indeed the case, but the process of reform itself exacerbated existing tensions. Political conflicts over democratisation, pluralism and economic reform fused with long-standing nationality disputes, giving a harder to edge to already difficult issues. Gorbachev assumed that nationalist aspirations were compatible with his definition of *perestroika*, but it became increasingly clear that *perestroika* was only the gateway through which the nationalist movements tried to bolt from the Soviet stable.

The rise of separatist nationalism can be seen to be a consequence of the inadequacies of the unreformed Soviet state. While Marxist theory on nationalism promised a functionalist Utopia where co-operation based on class internationalism would replace competition, seventy years of Soviet power failed to develop effective neo-functional strategies to bring together the peoples of the USSR. The notion of 'a new community of Soviet people' proved hopelessly inadequate, while the hypercentralised state was unable to provide viable structures for the harmonious development of the country's many peoples. The key problem for *perestroika* was to establish new and clear principles of federalism. The 1977 constitution talked of a 'voluntary' association of equals, but at the same time proclaimed contradictory principles of federalism with scarcely a hint of embarassment. Article 72, for example, granted the fifteen union republics 'the right freely to secede', while Article 73 tied them irrevocably to the USSR. The 1977 constitution's provisions regarding the federal system had to be revised to take into account the aspirations for political and economic autonomy of the republics. A new basis to the Soviet federative system had to be devised, but a degree of complacency prevailed in the early years.

One of Gorbachev's gravest mistakes was to underestimate the force of nationalism, and in this area the skills revealed in foreign policy were notably absent. In his 29 November 1988 speech he argued that the first stage of reform was to deal with restructuring central and local soviets and electoral reform. Only the second stage of the 'political transformation' would deal with 'harmonising relations between the Union of Soviet Socialist Republics and its constituent republics': 'Questions of the status of union republics, the extension of their rights and capacities in political, economic and cultural life, the consolidation of our federal Soviet socialist state will be discussed at that stage. The same applies to autonomous formations – republics, regions and districts' (*P*, 30 November 1988). However, the nationality issue rapidly developed into a series of major crises. Delays in calling a long-promised Central Committee plenum to deal with the issue only made matters worse. The fact that the attempt to resolve the question was initially confined to the party and not to an emergency constitutional conference or the Congress of People's Deputies also demonstrated the attempt to deal with the issue in traditional ways.

Gorbachev never really understood the force of the non-Russian national democratic movements. Sakharov criticised in particular Gorbachev's handling of the Nagorno-Karabakh issue. Sakharov supported Armenian claims over the area, and condemned the arrest of the Karabakh Committee, calling them the new prisoners of conscience. Gorbachev's haranguing of speakers during the Supreme Soviet debate on Nagorno–Karabakh was tactless and brutal, and he further alienated many Armenians by his clumsiness during his visit to the earthquake zone in December 1988. On his visit to Kiev in 1988 he talked of Russia rather than the Ukraine twice. The question arises whether Gorbachev had a nationality policy at all. In this area he appeared to be more at a loss than in other policy areas, perhaps because he too here fell prey to the 'propaganda of success' that he condemned so vigorously elsewhere. Gorbachev appeared to share the feelings of Woodrow Wilson's interlocutor at the Versailles peace conference in 1919 who asked, 'Is every language to have a nation for itself?' The basic Gorbachevite strategy was to promote autonomy without independence, to draw the teeth of the independence movements and to forestall demands for secession.

The declining economic effectiveness and weakening popular legitimacy of Communist regimes led several in Eastern Europe to play the 'national card' in order to bolster their authority. This option was simply not available to the Soviet leadership, unless it took the divisive form of expounding national Bolshevism, a Sovietised form of Russian nationalism, which would mean the end of the Soviet Union as we know it. While nationalism in Eastern Europe, with the exception of the GDR, Yugoslavia and minority groups, was broadly integrative of the polity, in the Soviet Union under *perestroika* it has been profoundly disintegrative. The problem for the Soviet leadership was how to reconcile the expansion of legitimate national aspirations while preventing this becoming out and out secessionism.

The 1986 party programme asserted, rather prematurely, that 'the nationalities question inherited from the past has been successfully solved in the Soviet Union.' The programme predicted the long-term drawing together (*sblizhenie*) of the Soviet peoples, but stated rather more forcefully than usual the view that there would remain certain national characteristics marked by 'complete unity' (*polnoe edinstvo*) rather than the fusing (*sliyanie*) of peoples. The programme dropped the implication of Russian leadership over other nationalities in the new community of 'the Soviet people' (*Programme*: 47–8).

The challenge facing the Gorbachevites was to find adequate neo-functionalist strategies, in terms of institutions and policies, to implement the functionalist perspectives of Soviet nationality policy, the achievement of a higher type of unity for a large number of disparate peoples. The key issue was the relationship of nationalism to the state. The Soviet Union, strictly speaking, was not a nation but a federation of states in the form of fifteen autonomous republics. The Soviet multinational state is a distinctive entity and cannot easily be compared with the older empires like the Habsburg or Ottoman ones. The dynamics of its creation and perpetuation was based not only on conquest, dynastic accumulation and economic aggrandisement, but also on a distinctive ideology of Marxist internationalism. The dominant role of the Russian core was based not on an appeal to Russian nationalism as such but on the sheer preponderance of one people, half of the total population, and its historical role. As noted, Russians did not benefit materially from their sub-imperial role, and indeed found themselves somewhere in the middle of a league table of prosperity among the fifteen republics. While the Russian language became the *lingua franca* of the union, and a distinctly Sovietised version of Russian culture was propounded, national languages and cultures were sustained, however tenuously, by ethno-federal policies. While Russification policies were pursued in language and culture, the glue that held the Soviet state together was not so much Russian nationalism as a supranational ideology consolidated in the form of a unitary Communist Party. The dissolution of Marxist–Leninist ideology was accompanied by the disintegration of the multinational state.

Three layers of the Soviet 'empire' can be identified. The first is the internal empire within the borders of the USSR itself. The second was made up of the six East European 'buffer states', donated as a legacy of Yalta, and the third the far-flung countries like Cuba and Vietnam. The collapse of the second empire magnified the unrest in the first.

Nationalists drew the parallel that if Poland could gain genuine independence from Moscow, then why not Lithuania or any other republic? At the same time, the new Soviet approach to the Third World in effect represented a retreat from the burden of empire (see Chapter 8). Developments in all three rings of empire affected each other. The disintegration of the first empire was hastened by the burden imposed by the cold war and the diversion of resources to the military. As with earlier empires, the factor of imperial overstretch identified by Paul Kennedy (1988) led to domestic disintegration. Gorbachev faced the dilemma confronting De Gaulle in 1958: France could not retain its North African empire, but the 'conservatives' at home and in the colony would not accept independence for Algeria. At the same time, faced by the secessionist demands of the republics, Gorbachev could say in the manner of Churchill that he was not elected President to preside over the dissolution of the Soviet Union.

Elite integration through party and other mechanisms of political, educational and professional advancement was traditionally the major way in which national élites were co-opted into the Soviet multinational system. Such a strategy could be really effective only at a time of economic development; at a time of recession national stability was threatened as different ethnic groups compete for scarce investment, jobs and prestige. The vertical distinction between sections of the élite, many of whom had earlier been imprisoned for nationalist activity, and society was dramatically bridged by the emergence of 'popular fronts'. The 'people' and 'élite' joined forces to press for greater national autonomy, forcing the central government to find a new type of nationality politics that went beyond the cultivation of pliant local élites to encompass the mass of the people.

The republics had many of the trappings of a traditional nation-state, though until Gorbachev the institutions served largely to formalise Moscow's control. Two major changes took place during *perestroika*. The first was that the dormant national state institutions awoke and sprang into life. If the federal structure previously was a façade, it is now filled with content. The second change was that the unitary role of the party began to be modified. Under Brezhnev the national party leaderships, especially in Central Asia, began to reflect in a form of degenerate nationalism the social demands of the locality rather than the centre. This process was initially sharply truncated under Gorbachev as part of the struggle against corruption. However, the new party leaderships, especially in the Baltic and Transcaucasia, began to identify with the aspirations of the local indigenous population, if only to avoid being bypassed altogether, in a form of democratic nationalism. Indeed, local parties began to fall under the control of popular fronts.

Official response to the tide of nationalist unrest became increasingly harsh. Gorbachev's televised presidential address to the nation on 1 July 1989 clearly showed his alarm in his insistence that 'the fate of *perestroika* and the unity of our state is at stake. Irresponsible slogans, political provocations, setting one nation against another, could lead to disaster for us all.' The very future of the Soviet state hung in the balance. He vowed that separatism would not be tolerated and suggested four ways of resolving the issue. All citizens were to be assured the exercise of their rights guaranteed in the constitution; the right for ethnic groups to develop their own language and culture was affirmed; there should be radical economic and political reform in the republics, though avoiding 'economic autarchy and cultural isolation'; and finally, Communists and members of the local intelligentsia should use their influence to calm the situation. On 26 August 1989 the Central Committee issued a sharp condemnation of the unrest and warned the Baltic states that they were heading for 'the abyss'. Ligachev went on television on 2 September calling for measures to stop the 'erosion of socialism', though he insisted that he had in mind political rather than repressive measures, above all the tightening of party discipline. Gorbachev argued in a televised address on 9 September that excessive nationalism threatened the cohesion of the Soviet Union and the entire strategy of *perestroika*

Gorbachev believed that democratic legitimation and nationalist aspirations were compatible. There came a time, however, when the argument that democracy was incompatible with the continuation of the union seemed to prevail. In the absence of an effective 'leading role' for the party and a declining sense of Soviet nationhood, what indeed could keep the union together? Gorbachev's answer was that it was precisely democracy and economic reform that could forge a new basis for unity. While each republic is linked by a multitude of economic and social ties with the others, many of which were deliberately designed to make them interdependent, the political and moral elements in national movements were consistently underestimated by Moscow.

Rather than a bold and voluntary reconstitution of the union through some form of constituent assembly, the new federalism emerged in a piecemeal and not altogether convincing way. Sakharov described the Soviet Union as 'the last colonial empire in the world', an empire that had accumulated contiguous territories since Ivan the Terrible in the sixteenth century, and argued that the 'empire-like' structure built by Stalin on oppression should be dismantled in favour of a voluntary confederation. There had to be a return to first principles to allow 'maximum independence' for the 100-odd ethnic groups (*Ogonëk*, 31/ 1989: 18–22). A voluntary economic confederation may well make each unit more efficient. Gorbachev and his allies were looking for a formula that could secure the interests of the centre, the titular nationality in each republic, the smaller peoples with or without their own autonomous regions, and the minorities and non-titular nationalities in all the republics. The American republic passed from confederalism to federalism between 1776 and 1787, whereas the evolution of the Soviet Union may well be in the opposite direction, from federalism to a democratic confederalism.

The basic slogan of the long-postponed September 1989 Central Committee plenum on the national question was 'a strong centre and strong republics' (*P*, 20 September 1989). This still begged the question of the nature of the relationship between the two and failed to provide an effective solution to the problem of an equitable relationship between Moscow and the republics. The theses on the nationality question adopted by the plenum went part of the way to satisfying local demands for economic decentralisation and the preservation of 'national uniqueness'. This was to be achieved, however, in the context of the 'revolutionary renewal of Soviet society' and the retention by the centre of responsibility for defence, foreign policy and overall economic policy. The rights of republican parliaments remained relatively limited and could be overruled by the centre. While Stalin's negative influence on nationality policy was condemned, the document conceded that some sort of *modus vivendi* had to be found with his legacy, such as the use of Russian for intercommunal discourse. Russian was now to be made the state language throughout the Soviet Union. Discrimination against minorities in the various republics was condemned, a riposte amongst other things to the Estonian law of August 1989 which placed limits on the voting rights of recent immigrants into the republic. The theses insisted that all Soviet citizens were to have the same rights throughout the Soviet Union, and indeed the vow to strengthen the rights of minorities provided a formula laden with potential conflict. The rights of not only the fifteen union republics but also the thirty-eight autonomous republics, regions and districts were to be strengthened, and possibly some others created. The nationalities deported by Stalin were to be rehabilitated and compensated.

No clear principles were enunciated over the relative validity of all-union and republic laws, and indeed of what precisely republic 'sovereignty' was to mean in practice, but union republics were permitted to question all-union laws before a constitutional court. Thus Estonia's law of November 1988 declaring that all-union laws were not valid unless ratified by its Supreme Soviet was dismissed. No mention was made of the existing Article 72 of the constitution giving the republics the right to secede from the union. No concessions were made to Baltic hopes of a transformation of the federal principles of the December 1922 treaty that created the USSR into a federal system of equal republics, thereby loosening their ties with the centre. Moreover, the hopes of the Lithuanian Communist Party to set itself up as an independent party was given short shrift, and the theses insisted that 'The division of the CPSU into nationalities is unacceptable in principle.' The sanctions that could be employed by the centre to enforce its will and the provisions of the new nationality policy were left vague. The distinction made between the rise in national consciousness, which was seen as positive, and nationalism, which was being abused by 'irresponsible charlatans and nationalist-careerists' was a subjective one and promised yet more conflicts.

A law on 'Economic Relations between the USSR and Union and Autonomous Republics' in April 1990 proposed far greater powers for the republics in taxation, finances, investment policy and economic management. Republics would be able to trade directly with other countries, and even override decisions of the central authorities if they ran counter to the republic's interests (*P*, 17 April 1990).

In an apparent concession to separatist feelings, in his presidential acceptance speech on 15 March 1990 Gorbachev urged the rapid drafting of a new union treaty which would guarantee the republics real sovereignty within a renewed Soviet federation (*P*, 16 March 1990). The creation of the Council of the Federation gave all fifteen republics a direct voice in policy-making. In keeping with his promise on his visit to Lithuania in January 1990 a Law on Secession was passed in April 1990 that made secession possible only after two-thirds of a republic's electorate had voted in favour in a referendum. This was to be followed by a five-year transition period during which the other republics could voice objections, and a second conclusive referendum could be held at the request of just one-tenth of the voters. Finally, the measure had to be confirmed by the whole Soviet parliament (*P*, 8 April 1990). As a number of deputies pointed out, the law was designed to prevent secession rather than to make it possible. The Baltic republics in any case denied that the law could apply to them since their whole strategy was to argue that they had never been incorporated into the Soviet Union legally in the first place.

The Moscow authorities insisted that local Communists use their influence to calm nationalist passions, yet many found themselves in an ambiguous position. A large number of Communists joined the popular fronts but at the same time owed ultimate allegiance to the all-union party. Local Communist Party leaderships were in an even more difficult position, finding themselves on the one hand in the vice of pressure from Moscow to restrain the independent movements, while on the other the

Congress elections of 1989 and the local elections of 1990 clearly taught these leaders that they had to take into account the influence of the powerful 'informal' movements like the popular fronts and the growing independence parties. The Lithuanian party took the lead in resolving the crisis of loyalty between Moscow and the locality, and plumped for the latter.

One of the greatest challenges facing the reformers was how to integrate the many nationally-inspired emerging civil societies into an all-union reformed political society. This problem would have been difficult enough to resolve in a single homogeneous republic, but was almost impossible in a multinational state. The divisions and egotism of civil society, condemned by Hegel and Marx, in the late Soviet context took on an avowedly nationalist colouring. The Soviet state as the representative of the universal or general interest to a large extent lost its legitimacy as a result of Stalin's crimes and Brezhnev's chauvinistic policies, and it now lost credibility because of the half-heartedness of the *perestroika* of national relations. The sheer size of the Soviet Union and the disparate and intermingled nature of its population led many to suggest that democracy simply would not be viable in such a large country. The integrity of the nation, it was argued, could be maintained only by a strong hand at the centre, a principle to which Gorbachev adheres. The example of India, with a population over treble that of the Soviet Union, suggests that sheer size and heterogeneity are not in themselves obstacles to multi-party democracy. In certain respects the very diversity of the Soviet Union helped retain a degree of cohesion since the many nationalist movements that have emerged during *perestroika* lacked a unified or co-ordinated organisation, whereas in the more homogeneous countries of Eastern Europe relatively unified nationalist sentiments fused with the political opposition. In the Soviet Union nationalist movements were fractured by linguistic, cultural, religious and economic factors which to a degree counteracted each other. The long-delayed development of stable and equal relations between the USSR and the countries of Eastern Europe indicated a possible form of relations between the peoples of the USSR.

The dialectic between nationalism and civil society is a complex one and operates at several levels. Nationalist demands encouraged the development of independent groups which lie at the basis of civil society, yet the nationalism of these groups often took authoritarian forms that undermined the democratising impulse of a political project which aimed to encourage the development of civil society. Marx and Hegel had considered civil society the site of conflicts and divisions in society, and nationalist civil societies seemed to confirm the view of socialists who argued that principles of unity and harmony, traditionally associated with the internationalism of the workers' movement, should take precedence over group and national egoisms. Nationalist unrest challenged the very basis of the new politics emerging in the Soviet Union. The alternative to command socialism appeared to be not democratic socialism wedded to the democratic proceduralism of liberal democracy but chauvinistic nationalism.

The unfreezing of nationality politics within the Soviet Union and of politics in Eastern Europe opened the door to revanchist claims to territory. The dead hand of the administrative-command system had at least kept the border issue closed. Some Romanians claim Bessarabia, now Moldavia, and north Bukovina, which was incorporated into the Ukraine. There remains the eternal question of the status of Lvov, a Polish city surrounded by a Ukrainian hinterland. Grodno and other towns in western Belorussia and south-east Lithuania are as Polish as Poznan. Such fears fuelled support for the maintenance of a strong Soviet state as a policeman of the Eastern Eurasian land mass. All of this however, should not be exaggerated, and the territorial conflicts of the inter-war years will not simply be resurrected. Polish revanchism, for example, on what is now Soviet territory is kept in check by the fact that the USSR is the guarantor of Poland's Western border with Germany along the Oder-Neisse line. The new democratic governments of Poland and Czechoslovakia, moreover, declared the inviolability of existing frontiers. The whole structure of international relations in Europe has changed from the naked power struggle politics of the inter-war years to new forms of political, economic and security co-operation.

Most nationalist movements passed through a stage of 'cultural democracy' to an understanding of 'national democracy' which came into conflict with Gorbachev's understanding of the new democracy of reform Communism. It was not at all clear whether the independence movements were more keen to throw off Moscow's power or to reject the Communism, however reformed, that Moscow's rule represented. Secessionist nationalism could be seen as a particularly sharp manifestation of the localism that accompanied the decay of the old hyper-centralised model of socialism. Omsk and Tomsk required economic autonomy and local decision-making on cultural and social questions as much as Tbilisi and Vilnius, yet lacked the focus of nationalism to put over their case to Moscow. The republics and the localities alike insisted that the problems that could not be solved at the national level could well be resolved through flexible local management. However, as *perestroika* staggered from crisis to crisis the national groups became convinced that the Soviet Union was ultimately so irremediably authoritarian and irreformable that the only way for them to achieve democracy was through national independence. The strategy for a quick dash for freedom while the empire was distracted by *perestroika*, before the lid comes crashing down again, is one they learnt from the Finns and the Poles, who gained independence when the Russian state in effect collapsed during the Revolution of 1917.

The problems facing Gorbachev were those of any great empire facing the prospect of decolonisation, and the model for future relations remains unclear. As Communist leaders in the Baltic argued, Gorbachev had to make the union something that none of the republics would want to leave. The radicals in the Baltic soon moved beyond the struggle for a type of internal Finlandisation, which would have given them the right to establish their own domestic economic and political policies but limited their foreign policy options. Georgian radicals from the first sought Austrianisation, effective independence limited only by guarantees of neutrality.

The fundamental question facing the Soviet republics, as for the peoples of Western Europe, is whether the nation-state is indeed the terminal point of history. Is there an alternative form in which peoples can express political and cultural aspirations? The question facing the peoples of the Soviet Union as elsewhere is the degree to which a nation can remain without a sovereign state. The peoples of the USSR are locked into a supranational state where decisions are taken far from their own republics or regions. The Soviet leadership had to find effective democratic mechanisms to satisfy the conflicting demands of local autonomy and national leadership and to bind together the disparate peoples of the union. They struggled to judge the degree to which national autonomy was compatible with the unity of the state and the interests, as they saw it, of the party. As time passed the problem became one of finding new intrastructural sources of loyalty beyond party unity and taking into account the declining effectiveness of ideological cohesion, the lack of economic rationality in the old Soviet model of socialism and the discrediting of the concept of class internationalism as the basis for empire. The struggles in the Baltic and elsewhere brought home the lesson that working-class solidarity had not replaced nationalism as a focus of loyalty. This of itself, as the partisans of the world society school of international relations would argue, does not render the search for a new basis of internationalism redundant. A new model of Soviet federalism that accepted a rich tapestry of ethnic diversity based on equality between peoples was one step taken by the Gorbachevite leadership. Another was the understanding that the logic of economic rationality could serve as the basis for a new type of federalism. The problem was that they could not find a way of putting these principles into effect within the framework of *perestroika*.

A new basis of legitimacy for a multinational empire had to be found if anything like the Soviet Union was to continue. In many respects the Soviet Union was an anachronistic political unit. Given the experience of the dissolution of the Austro-Hungarian and British empires, the survival into the twenty-first century of a large multinational state, though based on different principles from the former empires, would be a historical oddity. The Ottomanisation of the USSR might be achieved through democratisation, though the experience of Yugoslavia, the only other federal Communist state, is not encouraging. Moreover, the ideology of socialist modernisation was also discredited. The belief that only a state encompassing differing levels would allow the developed parts to assist the modernisation of the relatively less-developed regions was undermined by the bureaucratic mismanagement of the economy and resources. Advances were made, but the question increasingly arose whether these gains could have been achieved at less cost by some other means.

The problem for the Gorbachev leadership was to avoid what they perceived as the Balkanisation of the Soviet federal state into competing and discriminatory statelets. The search for a new form of integration that provides mutually beneficial economic relations while allowing sufficient local sovereignty to satisfy nationalist aspirations is one that is not unique to the USSR but faces such regional groupings as the European Community. In the light of the development of the Single European Market in Western Europe, the transformation of the USSR into a Eurasian Economic Community leading to a United States of Eurasia might not be wholly unrealistic. Alternatively, the institutionalisation of the Common European Home in a set of economic, political and security organisations leading to a United States of Europe stretching from the Atlantic to the Pacific would inhibit yet more civil wars between the peoples of Europe and Asia. The integration of the Soviet Union into a larger European Community, of course, would create huge difficulties but would present the most exciting challenge of the twenty-first century. The achievement of some sort of 'post-imperial' solution for a 'socialist commonwealth' of the USSR or, indeed, a simple post-Communist Eurasian community of peoples, became the greatest challenge facing the country.

7

PERESTROIKA OF THE
ECONOMY

Economic reform lay at the heart of *perestroika*, yet the compromises and setbacks in this field jeopardised the attempt to democratise Soviet society. This chapter will begin by summarising how the reformers have tried to deal with some of the main economic problems. It will then briefly examine some of the critical issues surrounding labour and social policy before, in the final section, analysing the travails of economic *perestroika* and the political and theoretical issues associated with the 'new economic model of socialism' that is being born with so much pain.

Restructuring the economy

The major flaws of the Soviet economy as bequeathed to Gorbachev in 1985 can be summarised as follows. There was a wasteful use of resources, with Soviet products using 2 to 2.5 times as much energy and raw materials as comparable Western goods. There was an inflexibility in the hierarchical multilevel institutional structure which stifled enterprise initiative. The vertical channels of command were clogged with detailed instructions. There were major shortcomings in the planning mechanism itself. There was a resistance to technological innovation because of a lack of incentives at enterprise level and the barriers to communication with and travel to the West. There was a poor division of labour, especially on the international level, and too many costly products using large resources. Investment performance was poor, with too many schemes started and an extraordinarily long gap before coming on stream, and resources were not used effectively to boost the productivity of existing plant. There were few incentives for enterprises to produce cost-effective goods of quality and variety to satisfy consumer demand. Plan fulfilment still functioned basically on gross output indicators, despite many attempts to find better ways to stimulate enterprise performance. High reserves of labour were 'hoarded' for a rainy day, leading to very low productivity. The old methods had achieved impressive growth rates in earlier years, but these declined to close to zero in 1981–5, and in 1989 any growth was more than accounted for by inflation. In Soviet parlance, the Soviet economy had developed in an 'extensive' way, by increasing the inputs of labour and capital. The challenge of *perestroika* was to move to 'intensive' growth, the more effective use of inputs.

Gorbachev had read the Novosibirsk report of April 1983 which contained one of the most trenchant critiques of the Stalinist command economy heard in official circles since 1934. The basic charge was that the structures of economic management had remained largely the same as those created in the 1930s, while the nature of the economic system had changed out of all recognition. The vast ministerial apparatus acted as a brake for the further development of the economy and held back popular initiative (Zaslavskaya, 1984). Despite attempts at reform in the post-Stalin period, notably the Kosygin/Liberman reforms of 1965, the economy entered a period of 'stagnation'. Early pronouncements referred only to the decade after 1975, though later the term was stretched to cover the whole of Brezhnev's rule, and in some instances the entire post-Stalin period. In strictly economic terms the real downturn in economic performance came after 1975, and in agriculture from 1979.

Gorbachev's economic policies began with the promise of a revival of some of the practices of the NEP, but soon such comparisons could be made only on a very general level since the detailed requirements and problems of the state-run Soviet economy in the 1980s differed so drastically from those of the 1920s. The first variant of economic reform under *perestroika* had the traditional hallmarks of Stalin, Khrushchev and Brezhnev. The slogans of 'invigoration' and 'acceleration' (*uskorenie*) set very ambitious tasks for the economy, with output to be doubled by the year 2000 and production and productivity to rise substantially. Every family was to have its flat and there were to be major increases in the number of sanatoria and other public facilities (Ryzhkov, 1986). These ambitious, if traditional, targets were predicated on a leap in productivity which there was little reason to expect. Only in 1987 did economic reform become a programme of structural change of the whole organisation of the economy, but the actual implementation of reform was marked by hesitations and confusion (Aslund, 1989).

In many respects the economic reform began with a false start. Even before coming to power Gorbachev's speech for the 113th anniversary of Lenin's birth in April 1983 emphasised heavy industry, especially the machine-building sector. He called for the technological modernisation of industry, thus shifting away from building new plant to the modernisation through reinvestment of existing ones (*P*, 23 April 1983). His was a classic exposition of the Andropov programme of economic reform, and it began to be implemented once he was in power. At the 27th party congress Ryzhkov promised that the productivity of Soviet workers by the year 2000 would outstrip the world level. He promised huge investments in the twelfth five-year plan (1986–91), with an 80 per cent increase in the engineering sector and a third of all state investment going into agriculture. In the face of a decline in foreign exchange earnings caused by falling world prices for oil, gas and coal the USSR cut the import of consumer goods by some R8 billion, thus forcing sacrifices on an already starved consumer market. The first effects of *perestroika* for the Soviet consumer were less choice and fewer goods. Gorbachev learnt the hard way that economic reform cannot take place in an environment of forced growth but needs to develop at its own pace. The strikes in the 'summer of discontent' in 1989 vividly demonstrated the failures of economic *perestroika*. *Perestroika* had come a long way since 1985, but still found itself only at the beginning of a structural transformation of the economy.

Statistics

Any attempt to reform the Soviet economy requires accurate statistics. The scale of the accumulated problems and the progress of *perestroika* need to be measured. In the late 1920s Stalin brought the Central Statistical Board (TsSU) to heel, and since that time accurate data about social and economic processes were simply not available to Soviet policy-makers. The article by the journalist V. Selyunin and the economist G. Khanin (1987a) launched a bold attack on Soviet statistics, claiming systematic distortion and falsification at enterprise and ministerial level and by statisticians. The major charge was that official statistics had grossly overstated the growth of national income since the late 1920s by not taking inflation sufficiently into account. They argued that the official index of growth between 1928 and 1985 had been exaggerated by a factor of 13. In other words, rather than net material product – NMP is the Soviet version of GNP which excludes services, though since services are so underdeveloped NMP differs little from GNP – increasing 86-fold between 1928 and 1985, it only rose by some 6–7 times. National income data in recent decades, they suggested, had been inflated by giving undue weight to oil exports and the rapid growth of alcohol sales, and inadequate attention to depreciation on machinery. Their estimates are probably too low, but not by much, and Western research suggests that a more accurate figure would be a 10-fold increase in GNP terms and 11-fold in Soviet terms, excluding the service sector. These figures give an annual growth rate of 3.1 per cent, which is comparable to that achieved by the EC in the 1960s and 1970s (M. Kaser, *THES*, 30 October 1987: 15). The corollary of such estimates is that instead of the Soviet economy being something over half the size of the American one, it is in fact somewhere between a quarter and a third.

In mid–1987 the lack of credible material on which to base reform led to a reorganisation which converted TsSU into a more prestigious State Committee for Statistics (Goskomstat). It was to become an authoritative body for the gathering and publication of statistics. The committee had a lot of ground to make up, especially since it had to relearn basic methodology and to retrain a generation of statisticians more used to obfuscation than revelation. More information became available on labour and demography, including factors like age, sex, infant mortality, life expectancy, employment and so on, though new statistical series on agriculture and investment offered little new by 1989. Attempts have been made to produce internationally acceptable statistics on overall GNP growth. Statistics remain politically charged and here, as elsewhere, the struggle continues.

Finances and price reform

One of Gorbachev's first acts on coming to power, spurred on by Ligachev, was to launch a vigorous anti-alcohol campaign (*P*, 5 April and 17 May 1985). The campaign, quite astonishing in its scope, had its roots in the 1920s, with even some similar slogans revived. Production was cut back sharply, vineyards destroyed, prices steeply increased, beer halls closed, and the number of retail outlets and the hours they served drastically reduced. The loss of some R10 billion a year in tax revenue to local and central authorities placed a heavy burden on an already overextended budget. The government hoped to recoup the losses through savings in other spheres, since it was estimated that for every ruble in alcohol revenue, 1.4 rubles were lost in economic output or increased social expenditures. The campaign was applied unevenly, and especially vigorously by Boris Eltsin in Moscow, which with 4 per cent of the population accounted for 20 per cent of the revenue drop. Some even called for the restoration of the 'dry law' of 1914. But the chances of a successful prohibition are about the same as in the United States in the 1920s. The campaign, conducted in an administrative-command way, was reminiscent of Stalinist crusades, permeated by an authoritarianism and irresponsibility as of old, but in the conditions of the 1980s it was wholly inappropriate and aroused enormous popular resentment against Gorbachev personally. The campaign was a clear failure at all levels: the losses to the state budget; alienation of the drinking population and the viniculturalists; and the encouragement of a huge growth in the production of *samogon*, bootleg liquor, leading to sugar shortages. By 1988 it was admitted that the anti-alcohol campaign was a disastrous and expensive failure, and in early 1990 it was abandoned.

Attempts to improve the quality of goods added an extra element of state interventionism and disrupted work patterns. In 1987 the State Quality Control Board (Gospriëmka) rejected goods worth R6 billion as substandard, though they entered national production and output statistics as if they had entered the market.

From about 1978 the Soviet Union began to run a budget deficit which by 1985 had reached R37 billion. This was increased by the loss of revenues associated with the anti-alcohol campaign, heavy defence spending and the falling price of oil, together with events like Chernobyl and the Armenian earthquake. From the late 1970s enterprises had become less profitable and thus furnished less revenue to the state budget. The budget deficit was long hidden by supplying state enterprises with credits and then ascribing these credits as actual revenue. In fact, as Finance Minister Boris Gostev informed the Supreme Soviet on 27 October 1988, some 24,000 out of 46,000 state enterprises (52 per cent) were loss-making. The early miscalculations of *perestroika* severely underestimated the budget deficit and instead of cutting state expenditure, increased it by taking on extra social and investment commitments while maintaining the military budget. Gostev announced a budget deficit of R35 billion in October 1988, and then in March 1989 the need to borrow R63.8 billion, making a total deficit of some R100 billion, 11 per cent of GNP (*Iz.*, 30 March 1989). Yurii Maslyukov, chair of the State Planning Committee (Gosplan), revealed to the Supreme Soviet on 5 August 1989 that the budget deficit for 1989 was projected to rise to R120 billion, or 13.8 per cent of GNP on a total budget of R494 billion. Thus under Gorbachev the deficit in the Soviet state budget rose from about 3 per cent of national income in 1985 to some 14 per cent in 1989. In comparison, strong growth meant that the US federal deficit fell back from 6.2 per cent in 1983 to 3.1 per cent in 1989 of a GNP of $5,200 billion, and the federal debt had stabilised at some 42 per cent of GNP. Maslyukov also revealed that the Soviet national debt was R312 billion and growing faster than that of the United States. The absence of a convertible ruble means that the Soviet deficit has little significance for the world economy, but until the books are balanced ruble convertibility cannot be contemplated.

The cutback in alcohol sales and the scarcity of consumer goods led to a gap in the domestic market which was not compensated by removing potential purchasing power. The great mass of money in circulation was not backed up by goods and paid services (*P*, 15 January 1989), leading to powerful inflationary pressures which according to official figures reached 8 per cent in 1990 (*Ind.*, 18 April 1990). Moreover, the way that the budget deficit was financed was inflationary, including loose controls over money supply and the printing of money to cover the deficit. Wages in the three years to 1989 rose by some 8 per cent per annum, and in 1989 rose twice as fast as prices. In an attempt to stop the wage–price spiral, wage limits were imposed for fifteen months by the government in September 1989, limiting increases to 3 per cent, though enterprises producing consumer goods were exempt because of the government's commitment to overcoming the acute goods famine. At a time when inflation was running at over 5 per cent, this meant an actual fall in spending power for most workers.

The enormous subsidies holding down prices make statistics on inflation almost meaningless. The pricing system had taken shape in the late 1920s and now reflected neither the costs of production nor the demand for products. Prices were set centrally by officials in Moscow who were unable, and often unwilling, to reflect costs and consumer preferences. The much-vaunted price stability in the Soviet Union has gradually been transformed from an object of pride to an embarrassment, beginning with the economists and then increasingly in public perceptions also. Rents had not risen since 1928, gas and electricity rates were the same as those of 1946, bread cost as much as it did in 1954, and meat and milk prices had last risen in 1962. Compared with income these prices were by no means low, and indeed justified low average wages, but they failed to reflect the high cost of production, the difference being made up by subsidies which for food drained the budget of some R60 billion a year by 1988, and which reached R100 billion in 1990 on a total retail turnover of R500 billion (*SN*, 1990: 114). By 1990 food subsidies absorbed 15 per cent of the Soviet budget.

A price reform was accepted by most reform economists as an essential precondition for the success of *perestroika*. The aim would be to tie salaries to achieved results, and to remove some of the subsidies on food, transport, gas, electricity, water, local phone calls and housing. Price reform would, moreover, allow full play to the crucial 'value added' factor, one of the key motors of economic dynamism. Improved wages paid for by increased productivity were in principle to offset price increases in a more marketised economy. Price reform, in effect a euphemism for price increases, is both the most explosive and the most necessary element in the reform programme. The major problem is how to achieve a price reform while fulfilling official promises that living standards will be safeguarded. Price rises have led to the fall of more than one Polish leader, and bedevilled the march towards the socialist market in Yugoslavia and China. Gorbachev's hesitancy on this issue may in addition owe something to his memories of the bread riots under Khrushchev that culminated in the shootings in Novocherkassk in 1962. Price reform on its own would tend to provoke inflation and thus had to be tied to changes in property rights. The reduction of subsidies on food and services and the concomitant price rises would add an enormous inflationary impetus to an already overheated economy, though it would help bring back a correspondence between money supply and goods and services.

Thus political fears and the dangers of inflation led to the postponement of the price reform until a balance had been achieved between supply and demand of consumer goods. Matters in fact worsened, with wages tending to rise faster than both output and productivity and increases in money supply threatening to get out of control. The budget was put under further pressure in 1989 by the emergency purchase of R10 billion worth of consumer goods to defuse the critical political situation and to absorb some of the surplus spending power. Virtually all growth in the Soviet economy in 1990 was projected to be devoted to providing consumer goods. The increases in investment in consumer goods announced in 1989 heralded the long-awaited decisive shift from sector A (producer goods) to sector B (consumer goods), one aim of the Kosygin reforms of 1965. For far too long consumer goods had to make do with the 'residuary' after defence and heavy industry had taken their share. Some of the foreign currency to finance this shift was to come from cutting capital goods imports, which in itself threatened the long-term productivity of the economy. The attempt to 'saturate the market', as advocated by Shmelëv, was designed to absorb some of the purchasing power, depress inflationary pressures and remove some of the political dangers to *perestroika*, yet in strictly economic terms it was a diversion from the main tasks. There is a tendency for reform Communists to deal with the economic consequences of reform by applying political measures, which in turn undermine the logic of the economic reforms.

Various ideas were proposed to reduce the budget deficit, including sharp cuts in defence spending and prestige projects. On the income side, new ideas were proposed like issuing loan certificates for specific projects, interest-free bonds, and for money to be made by the 'privatisation' through long-term leasing, and possibly even the sale, of housing and land. Shmelëv warned of a financial crisis leading to a political crisis like that of France in 1789, and argued that more radical measures had to be taken to bring down inflation and cut the deficit. His 'alternative economic programme' proposed cuts in food subsidies, an end to grain imports (on which some $5 billion a year were spent), the dismantling of the collective farm system allowing peasants to buy their land outright, the payment of peasants in hard currency for output above the plan, the closure of unprofitable factories and the release of gold reserves to import Western consumer goods.

The large savings of the population demonstrated the surplus purchasing power, too much money chasing too few goods. As the shops became emptier savings increased dramatically by R17.7 billion alone in the first half of 1989 on top of the R280 billion, or R1,000 for every Soviet man, woman and child, already held. This was more than five times the personal bank deposits in the United States. These vast liquid reserves raised the average prospect of a currency reform, intended to eliminate the 'hot money' reserves of the second economy but which would no doubt depreciate the value of people's hard-earned savings, as happened in December 1947 when Stalin exchanged all personal savings above R3,000 on a ten to one basis. Fears of a currency reform led in late 1989 to a flight from money to jewellery and other valuables. There was a real danger of hyperinflation, already suffered by Poland in 1989. Inflationary pressures were also fuelled by poor controls over investment, especially in the construction industry, with the value of unfinished projects rising dramatically and thus not returning goods to the economy to absorb purchasing power. The huge money overhang made possible the inflated earnings of the emerging merchant class, which fuelled popular resentment against the reforms in their entirety.

In 1988 Gootov outlined ambitious plans for the future, including the creation of a stock market where shares in state-owned companies could be traded, but all these plans only added gall to current shortages. In October 1988 the Politburo committed itself to the international convertibility of the ruble by the year 2000, and the government announced a range of measures towards the goal including a 50 per cent devaluation of the currency for foreign trade purposes in December 1988. In 1991 a new exchange mechanism for the ruble was to come into operation. One of the major immediate problems, however, was the artificially high level of the ruble, trading officially at R1.10 to the pound (60 kopeks to the dollar) in December 1988; yet its real level was more accurately reflected in the black market rate of R10–15 to the pound. This was tackled by a 10-fold devaluation of the ruble in November 1989 for tourist transactions. Lack of confidence in

Moscow's policies encouraged the Baltic republics to introduce their own currencies.

A reform of the taxation system tried to restore the Soviet economy to normality. Up to 1989 the maximum tax rate for earnings over R100 was a 13 per cent flat rate. A progressive income tax was introduced from 1 January 1990, with tax cuts for lower incomes and a maximum of 50 per cent for high earners of R1,501 or more a month.

The 1990 budget announced by the new Finance Minister Valentin Pavlov to the Supreme Soviet on 25 September 1989 estimated expenditure at R488 billion and income at R428 billion, giving a deficit of R60 billion, half the 1989 level of 120 billion. Investment in heavy industry was to fall for the first time since the 1920s, with the money diverted to projects which would give a more rapid return and to technology. The defence budget was severely cut (see pages 334–6) and defence conversion accelerated to provide the consumer market with goods. Only by cutting the budget deficit could inflation be restrained and confidence restored in the ruble. Pavlov announced that the national debt had risen from R300 billion to R400 billion and the foreign debt to R58 billion, some £30 billion of which was hard currency debt (*P*, 26 September 1989).

Gorbachev informed the 19th party conference that the failure to make progress in the area of price reform hampered the development of the reform process as a whole: 'Without price reform we cannot and shall not be able to create satisfactory economic relations in the economy.' It is in this area that the greatest contradiction of *perestroika* emerged. By 1989 the majority of enterprises were operating on *khozraschët* (see below), yet the old price system remained in confusion. Pricing policy remained arbitrary, with prices often unrelated to the cost of producing an item or the demand for it. Soviet theory had earlier considered that laws of supply and demand did not operate on Soviet territory, but what made matters worse for radical reformists was that the acceptance that economic laws did in fact cross over from the capitalist world was not accompanied by the necessary actions. The price system was based on scarcity and, while abundance is a long way off, the existing price mechanism only exacerbated the shortages. Price rises reject any attempt at egalitarianism or state-directed rationing, and instead allow the market to determine patterns of distribution.

Abalkin, chair of the State Commission for Economic Reform established in 1989, stressed the importance of financial stabilisation in a more marketised economy. He accepted the diversity of models of socialism, including the social democratic model, but stressed that reforms would not simply negate Soviet experience but would build on them to renovate the socialist idea (*P*, 11 November 1989). On 13

November 1989 he outlined a series of stages of development of Soviet economic reform. The first would last until late 1990 and would include a standardised law on taxation, price reform, wide-scale leasing which would gradually be converted into co-operatives, shareholding societies or other forms, financial stabilisation and the elimination of loss-making enterprises. As the miners' strike in summer 1989 made clear, decentralisation without price reform was meaningless. In the second stage, from 1991 to 1992, loss-making farms would be wound up, credit facilities extended under the state bank (Gosbank), market forms of transactions developed widely and a stock exchange created. In the third stage, from 1993 to 1995, the transition would be largely complete and this would prove a testing period for the new system, with financial normalisation, a healthy consumer sector and the growth of foreign trade. The last stage, from 1996 into the new century, would see the new system of social and economic relations settle down (*SN*, 6501/1989: 387). Such plans, and this was just one of many that came and went, were a far cry from the 'dash for the market' masterminded by the Polish Finance Minister Leszek Balcerowicz, which from 1 January 1990 saw the rapid destalinisation of the Polish economy, albeit at the price of an increase in unemployment, a fall in output and sharp price rises. Opinion polls nevertheless revealed popular support for the harsh measures, which if they succeed in stabilising the economy would represent a veritable 'second miracle on the Vistula'.

The critical delay in the early years of *perestroika* and the development of democratisation made the hard choices all the more difficult. The emergence of mass independent organisations ready to defend living standards made the struggle against inflation and the budget deficit that much worse in the absence of a popularly elected government. Possibly it could not be solved at all within the framework of democratic *perestroika*, giving support to those who advocated a form of authoritarian government which could impose the necessary sacrifices on society.

Industrial reconstruction

Soon after coming to power Andropov stressed the need for greater autonomy for production units, enterprises and farms (*P*, 23 November 1982). The attempt to free production from the stranglehold of the bureaucracy, the planners, ministries and party officials, has been the core of the economic strategy of *perestroika*. The successful manager of the Ivanovo Machine-Tool Building Association, V. P. Kabaidze, astonished delegates and delighted viewers when he declared at the 19th party conference that he had no need for the ministry of machine building, under which his plant came: 'What can the minister give us? Nothing at all'; instead the ministry inundated him with superfluous instructions that only slowed things down (*P*, 1 July 1988). As a practical manager Kabaidze insisted that running a business should be left to the managers, but could enough entrepreneurial managers be found? Kabaidze's plea to reduce the huge and unnecessary state managerial structure can be taken as the *leitmotif* of industrial reconstruction under *perestroika*.

At the root of the Gorbachevite destalinisation of the economy is the reform not only of management but also of managerial relations in general. Joseph Berliner (1957) had long ago demonstrated that the Stalinist command economy could not be understood through a simple totalitarian model where commands from above led to the corresponding actions in the factory. Instead, managerial behaviour included a variety of informal responses not intended by the authorities in order to circumvent shortages and contradictory demands from planning and ministerial agencies. The classic example of this was the hoarding of labour and other reserves in order to provide a cushion to insulate themselves from sudden demands or shortages. Resistance to innovation and other problems of managerial behaviour were identified at least forty years ago, but have still not found a solution within the framework of central planning with its mandatory output targets and centralised distribution of resources. *Perestroika* modified the framework of central planning, like so many earlier economic reforms, and it is not this which makes it interesting. Its chief interest is that *perestroika* had the potential for reducing almost to zero the central planning mechanism and with it the central economic bureaucracy. Its failure to do so constitutes the cardinal failure of the *perestroika* phase of Gorbachevite reformism.

The major mechanism whereby enterprise autonomy, and with it responsiveness to the real costs of production, could be achieved in the socialist economy is *khozraschët*. This is usually translated as 'economic accounting', 'cost accounting' or 'profit and loss accounting', but no English phrase can cover its various connotations which include an enterprise covering its expenses from sales and thus introducing some form of profit motive. *Khozraschët* was one of the main slogans of the early NEP, and since the 1960s has hesitantly been introduced into Soviet industry. A constant debate in socialist economics is over the level at which *khozraschët* should be applied: the individual enterprise, a production grouping of factories (trust), or a particular ministry or republic. Clearly, the combination of a planned economy with an awareness of costs and profits is inherently unstable because of the lack of a mechanism to judge acceptable cost.

The June 1987 CC plenum endorsed the major items of a radical reform proposed by academic economists and some of Gorbachev's political associates. The 'Basic Provisions for the Fundamental Restructuring of Economic Management' marked the first steps towards a radical overhauling of the Soviet economy that would take decades to implement. The basic idea was a decentralisation of the operation of state industry with greater autonomy for individual units. The principles were incorporated into the Law on State Enterprises, which from 1 January 1988 moved 60 per cent of state enterprises on to a system of self-management, with the rest going over on 1 January 1989. Enterprises were allowed to engage in 'wholesale trade' with each other and set their own prices. Managers were no longer allocated machinery and raw materials by the planners in Moscow but had to negotiate in a semblance of a market, and obligatory targets were no longer imposed from above. In theory, self-financing enterprises failing to reach a certain minimum standard of profitability would face bankruptcy and closure. At least 13 per cent of the 46,000 enterprises were estimated to be effectively bankrupt. Unprofitable departments and enterprises were able to shed workers and reduce wages.

Amendments to the Law on State Enterprises in 1989 and 1990 further weakened an enterprise's dependence on central planning and even allowed them to break away from their parent ministry. Strict limits were placed on the amount that the ministry could demand from enterprises, in particular through state orders (*goszakaz*), as controls were further loosened. Enterprises were allowed to deal with foreign firms, including capitalist ones (*P*, 11 August 1989). As part of the transition to *khozraschët* a new breed of managers began to emerge. Some have been sent to business schools in the West, and others trained at a new Institute of Management in Moscow.

There was to be a new role for planning, with a shift from directive planning to overall strategic guidance of the economy. In February 1988 the head of Gosplan, Nikolai Talyzin, was moved to chair the Bureau for Social Development and replaced by Yurii Maslyukov. The change revealed concern about the failure of the economy to respond to what was hoped to be the new stimuli. It also reflected perhaps the reluctance of Gosplan to give up its detailed oversight over the economy. Central planning began to retreat, but only reluctantly. Gostev informed the Supreme Soviet on 27 October 1988 that in 1988 the state, through the system of state orders, would buy 86 per cent of production, but in 1989 planned to take only 25 per cent, the rest being disposed of on the open market if a purchaser could be found. This did not take place and in early 1990 state orders still took 90 per cent of enterprise output. The system of state orders was simply another way of setting plan targets and limited enterprise autonomy by not allowing managers to choose what to make. Moreover, instead of enterprises being allowed to keep their profits, up to 80 per cent was taken by the relevant ministry. As in earlier reforms, the transition to *khozraschët* and freer wholesale trade was marked by the understandable attempt by the bureaucracy to retain its prerogatives. The ministerial bureaucracy itself was buffeted by contradictory demands and its resistance to losing instruments of control cannot be ascribed purely to malevolence.

Moves towards the liberalisation of individual economic activity were preceded by harsh laws against so-called 'unearned income' (*P*, 28 May 1986), which struck against unofficial private initiative. As with many measures of *perestroika*, it was a case of one step forward and two steps sideways, with an own goal thrown in for good measure. The 'Law on Individual Labour Activity' of 19 November 1986 came into effect on 1 May 1987 (*P*, 19 November 1986). Certain kinds of one-person business were permitted which legalised, and thus made liable to taxation, the existing network of private enterprises operated in tandem with, or on the side of, official occupations. Individuals were allowed to open businesses ranging from restaurants to small consumer goods factories and to provide repair services, private lessons and a number of other services in competition with the often low-quality state-run businesses. This return to private enterprise was strictly limited, permitting only groups of family members living under the same roof to work in one business. The work was to be carried out only in a person's spare time from a state job. The rules were later relaxed.

As the social problems of *perestroika* accumulated, the earlier emphasis on reinvestment in industrial capacity shifted, as noted, to an almost desperate effort to ease the plight of consumers. Investment shifted to the consumer sector, which was planned to grow 2.3 times faster than heavy industry in 1989. The 1989 draft plan approved by the Supreme Soviet on 28 October 1988 was for the first time orientated towards meeting consumer needs. Moreover, new laws on consumer protection have been drafted.

The decentralisation of the economy through 'republic *khozraschët*' has been one of the main demands of nationalist movements (see page 236). Estonia led the way in this respect, with the Politburo in May 1988 agreeing to transfer key economic sectors, though excluding engineering and instrument-making, thus giving the republic much greater autonomy in managing its economy. Some of the problems which could not be solved at national level may find solutions in the republics.

The reform of economic management appeared to advance at a crawl, apparently for much the same reasons as the failure of earlier economic reforms, namely contradictions within the reform programme itself, leadership conflicts and bureaucratic resistance. Obstructionism was not necessarily due to the hostility of individual bureaucrats, though there was no shortage of this, but the very structure of the reforms set enterprises against ministries, forcibly raising the question of whether the ministries were required at all. However much they were reorganised, with reductions in departments and staff, the direct relationship between enterprises and ministries had probably outlived its day. Instead, if the ministries were to be kept at all, radical reformers advocated that they should restrict themselves to the management of whole industries through the sponsorship of research, investment and social programmes. They were to lose responsibility for marketing and supplying materials and equipment to enterprises and instead concentrate on supplying producers with market information and specialised research and development. The director of Uralmash, the giant Urals engineering plant, Igor Stroganov, argued that his plant could do without ministries, but in a survey 59 per cent of directors feared that the abolition of the tutelage of ministries would cast them out into stormy waters for which they were unprepared (*MN*, 2/1989: 12).

The decentralisation of the economy was promoted by the 'Law on Leasing' introduced in the Supreme Soviet on 23 November 1989. The law greatly expanded the legal rights of leaseholders, and correspondingly weakened the veto powers of the bureaucracy over their activities. Leasing was to be encouraged in all spheres but was expected to yield rapid results in agriculture. Workers were allowed to buy out an enterprise that they had leased from the state with the guarantee that there would be no 'expropriation' in the future, but whether farmers could buy land was unclear. The law marked a big step towards the creation of the 'commodity market economy' that had for so long been promised, but continued uncertainties over taxation held back their development.

The first three years of radical economic reform from 1987 to 1990 seemed to show that from being one of the most overmanaged economies the Soviet Union was moving to become one of the most mismanaged. This was reflected in a zero growth rate, shops lacking 243 out of 276 basic consumer items, static farm output and inflation. The 1.7 per cent rise in industrial output in 1989 was the worst result since 1945, and was more than eaten up by inflation. Despite all this Ryzhkov's proposed five-year plan for 1991–5, announced to the Congress on 13 December 1989, was marked by compromises. Price reform was once again delayed to 1991–2 after 'broad public discussion', and 'rigid directive measures' would remain in force until then. As noted, in the interests of discipline enterprise managers would be appointed rather than elected. Ryzhkov ruled out the introduction of private property, denationalisation and monetary reform. Instead, a range of financial measures would be directed against the second economy, reckoned to equal about 20 per cent of the country's total GNP of R866 billion. Some of the 13,000 loss-making farms were to be offered for sale to their employees, or leased to others (*P*, 14 December 1989).

Ryzkov's plan of June 1990 for the transition to a 'regulated market' appeared finally to have broken the deadlock over radical reform. The 57 industrial ministries and commissions were to be converted into trade associations, Gosplan was to become an economics ministry, and in the two years from 1 January 1991, 60 per cent of state enterprises were to be denationalised and broken up, leaving only the 'commanding heights' in the hands of the state. Yet the degree to which the market would be regulated remained ambiguous, and the attempt to launch the whole reform with steep prices (subsequently reversed) jeopardised the whole plan. Thus central planning was to be retained for the foreseeable future. On offer was a hybrid economy limping between the market and the plan.

Reintegration into the world economy

In 1922 a state monopoly was imposed on foreign trade and all external economic contacts, setting the Soviet Union on the path of economic autarky and limited integration into the world economy. Under *perestroika* foreign trade and economic co-operation with non-socialist countries were seen as one of the main ways to achieve the Soviet Union's reintegration into the world economy and economic modernisation. In his speech of 7 December 1988 at the United Nations, Gorbachev unequivocally announced the Soviet Union's desire to rejoin the world. With the official end of the cold war in 1989, this in practice meant associating with the international organisations and agreements, for so long condemned by the USSR, that regulate the world economy. At the Malta summit in December 1989 Bush invited the USSR to become an observer at the General Agreement on Tariffs and Trade (GATT), a 97-nation agreement which seeks to extend the frontiers of free trade and to undermine protectionism. The USSR sought also to join the World Bank and the International Monetary Fund.

The Soviet Union had much ground to make up. Its trade represented only 4 per cent of the world total, and 60 per cent of that was made up by the export of raw materials. The Soviet Union's trade pattern has become increasingly diversified, though 60 per cent was still with Eastern Europe. The Council for Mutual Economic Assistance (CMEA, or Comecon) was established in 1949 as a response to the Marshall Plan for the reconstruction of Western Europe, which the countries of Eastern Europe were forbidden to join by Stalin, and later tried to match the European Community. At first the CMEA was used as an instrument for the bilateral exploitation of member countries by the Soviet Union. In May 1958 a plan was adopted to revive CMEA by the specialisation of member countries. The plan would have consolidated the position of the more developed countries to the detriment of the less developed ones, such as Romania, which would have been locked into the role of primary agricultural producers. In the ensuing struggle the plan was modified. With the added membership of Cuba and Vietnam the CMEA took on additional liabilities. In 1986 the Soviet Union provided $23 billion in aid to the developing world, with the bulk going to just those two countries; thus the USSR is now unwilling to take on further clients.

On 13 December 1989 Ryzhkov proposed transforming the CMEA into a trading system based on a convertible currency reflecting world prices, a type of Eastern common market (*P*, 14 December 1989). However, with the onset of post-Communism in Eastern Europe the CMEA, as an effective economic co-ordinating organisation, appeared to fall still more into disarray. The East European dash for the market from 1990 saw their central planning mechanisms dismantled, and their growing links with the EC increasingly made the CMEA irrelevant to their needs. At the CMEA meeting in Sofia on 9–10 January 1990 Poland, Czechoslovakia and Hungary threatened to withdraw from the organisation unless it was fundamentally restructured, while East Germany's incorporation into West Germany meant the loss of a crucial member of the group. Thus the Soviet plans for reform of the CMEA were too little and too late: soon after the loss of its political authority in Eastern Europe, its economic position was also eroded.

Foreign trade amounts to less than 10 per cent of Soviet GNP and the Soviet presence in the world market is negligible. In 1987 trade with Britain accounted for only 1.6 per cent of Soviet foreign trade and only 0.7 per cent of British trade. The Soviet Union now ran a net trade deficit with the West, and it was feared this would increase as the EC consolidated the single market towards 1992. In 1989 the USSR ran an overall trade deficit of R3.3 billion, the first in fourteen years, reflecting falling prices for oil, falling Soviet exports of coal and oil and increased imports of food and consumer goods. In 1988 the CMEA and the EC recognised each other for the first time, making possible the proliferation of diplomatic and economic contacts. However, while the EC was able to negotiate on behalf of all its members, no such right was conceded to the CMEA and instead agreements with individual CMEA countries were made. An extensive trade and co-operation treaty with the EC and the USSR was signed in November 1989, which included the transfer of high technology to the USSR. But providing an economic basis for the 'common European home' was beset by problems of incompatibility and the different requirements of the two halves of Europe.

Soviet foreign currency indebtedness was a growing problem, though it was not quite such a burden as in Hungary, Yugoslavia and Poland. Increased purchases of foodstuffs, machinery and consumer goods led to a massive (by Soviet standards) debt of $6.3 billion by 1975, rising to $25.5 billion in 1984 and $28 billion in 1989. On 9 June 1989 Ryzhkov told the Congress that the country was running a hard currency debt of R34 billion, financed largely by the sale of gold. With the fall in the price of oil in the mid–1980s the foreign exchange position of the Soviet Union took a turn for the worse. New lines of credit were granted by West European banks in late 1988 totalling some $7 billion. By early 1990 the USSR found itself in difficulties in servicing the hard currency debt.

With past experience in mind, attempts have been made to restrict borrowing. Western support for a Marshall Plan for Eastern Europe and the Soviet Union could be considered only after the revolutions of 1989, but Soviet membership of the EC investment bank, created to channel resources for post-Communist reconstruction, remained in doubt. In any case, the USSR was too developed and too large an economy to be considered in the same light as the war-ravaged economies of the 1940s. Similarly, the Soviet leadership accepted that there should be strict monitoring of how the funds would be spent. Reform economists divided over the advisability of taking extra foreign credits to finance *perestroika*. The West's grudging offer of loans was seen as forcing the Soviet Union to utilise its own resources more effectively, and to avoid the wastage of the 1970s where Western credits helped defer the structural reforms required by Communist economies. Talk of a 'Marshall Plan for *perestroika*' was seen to be an unrealistic programme, though it may become politically necessary.

Gorbachev energetically sought to have the trade sanctions imposed by the West in response to the Soviet invasion of Afghanistan lifted. In particular, the Paris-based seventeen-nation Co-ordinating Committee on Multilateral Export Controls (Cocom) imposed harsher controls on the export of strategic and high-technology goods to the Eastern bloc. These were eased only from early 1990. At the same time, granting the USSR most favoured nation status by the United States would act as the seal of approval on Soviet reintegration into the world economy.

The reformist leadership in Moscow came to see joint ventures, rather than the earlier enthusiasm for the international division of labour, as a way of bringing the Soviet Union up to world technological and quality levels. A new state foreign economic commission was created in August 1986 which deprived the ministry of foreign trade of its old monopoly. In January 1988 the two bodies were amalgamated to create a new ministry of foreign economic relations. It retained wide-ranging rights to regulate foreign trade (*P*, 17 January 1988). The bureaucracy was cut back, with the commission reducing the number of its foreign trade branches from forty-five to twenty-five, but still remained considerable. The radical reform of foreign trade granted ministries, departments, union republics, enterprises and organisations the right to conduct foreign trade, giving them direct access to foreign markets. The problem remained of finding sufficient high-quality goods to export (*P*, 22 January 1989). From 1 April 1989 all registered state, co-operative and other organisations gained the right to export and import goods and services. Despite all this, in 1988 70 per cent of Soviet exports were still made up of fuel and energy. There is no clear reason why registration has to take place at all other than providing revenue through the registration fee. In short, after three years of reorganisation 'administrative methods of management remain, and genuine cost accounting is absent in foreign trade' (Bondarev, 1989: 16).

Commercial partnerships with the West are expected to increase. In the first version, all joint ventures had to be based in the Soviet Union and structured with a 51 per cent Soviet share and 49 per cent foreign participation. These laws were relaxed in October 1988 to allow a foreign partner to hold a majority shareholding in a firm, and even to appoint Western managers. From 1 July 1990 foreign interests could acquire 100 per cent control of Soviet enterprises. The company rather than the state could determine the level of salaries and terms of employment and dismissal. In other words, Soviet employment laws would not apply to them. By 1989 structures were in place for expanded foreign investment and trade, and yet Soviet officials complained about the relatively few joint ventures that had been established and the slow pace of investment. By 1 January 1989 a total of 191 joint enterprises had been registered, 164 of which were with capitalist countries (*P*, 22 January 1989). Western reluctance in large part stemmed from fears about the stability and durability of the reforms, but also arose through specific economic concerns about the continuing unresponsiveness of Soviet economic mechanisms and the difficulties associated with repatriating profits because of the non-convertibility of the ruble, the postponement of the price reform and the high official exchange rate. The penetration of the Soviet market by joint ventures remained very difficult and revealed a yawning culture gap. A test case of the new approach was the joint venture between Macdonalds of Canada and the

Moscow Public Food Service Production Association, which opened its first outlet in February 1990.

Ryzhkov supported the creation of 'special economic zones' to attract foreign investment and technology to the Soviet Union, on the model of the Chinese zones. Already joint ventures in the Soviet Far East were exempt from taxation for three years as opposed to the two elsewhere. In return for investment, foreign companies would gain cheap labour, land and plant. Soviet special zones were developed in the Far East around Nakhodka, and around Leningrad.

Agriculture

Improving the consumer economy became Gorbachev's greatest challenge. The decline in real living standards struck at the heart of *perestroika*'s promise of achieving comparability with the West. The official admission in 1989 that 1,000 of the 1,200 items on a model shopping list were in chronically short supply only brought home the fact that the agricultural sector had not recovered from the ravages of collectivisation. The first years of *perestroika* were marked by a sharp deterioration in the supply of agricultural produce to the shops. In eight of the fifteen republics meat was being rationed (*P*, 2 September 1988), other basic foodstuffs were being rationed throughout the USSR, there was the endemic shortage of sugar, used to make home-brewed alcohol, soap and other goods, and even in the Ukraine by early 1989 rationing had been introduced for potatoes. The economic journal *EKO* calculated that Soviet farming and labour productivity were only 10 per cent of American rates (*ST*, 22 January 1989) despite the fact that some 35 per cent of the Soviet population were employed in agriculture. The United Kingdom, with 3 per cent of its population working on the land, produces as much wheat as Kazakhstan, some ten times the size of Britain. From a peak harvest in 1978, when 237 million tonnes of grain were reaped, the following years were marked by a sharp deterioration, with only 179 million tonnes being gathered in 1987 and 195 in 1988, 17 per cent below target. The pre-war grain harvest of 1913 in Russia, with slightly different borders, was 86 million tonnes, yet seventy years later the harvest had not much more than doubled (Z. Medvedev, 1986a: 33). The very structure of the Communist organisation of agriculture bred inefficiency and waste.

The catastrophic supply situation placed a heavy burden on the Soviet balance of payments, with the USSR importing a quarter of its butter and cooking oil, a third of its sugar and two-fifths of its potatoes and onions, not to mention the 35 million tonnes of grain that had to be imported in 1989. Reductions in some of the R5 billion spent annually on purchasing grain and other foodstuffs from abroad began to be diverted to domestic farmers and to satisfying the home market with imported goods, thus soaking up some of the cash reserves in the economy.

Gorbachev, as the party official responsible for agriculture, had ramme of 1982, and it was e was a continuation of the nto agriculture since 1971, crease in output of only 25 g the population increase. ent in grandiose irrigation ore effective use of existing bution, and greater incent- *restroika* the level of capital splaced from its formerly rastructure – roads, storage hing food queues led to a ulture.

 ary responsible for agricul- ll for radical solutions to showed that fairly rapid productivity and marketing rimary producer. Yet once rs like Ligachev prevented decommunalisation. While rovide all the answers the evelopment of an efficient sector (cf. Shanin, *Iz.* 26 measures was attempted.

 sation was endorsed by the nt, the 'collective contract achev's agricultural reform. to achieve certain results llowed to keep part of the o teams, links and families, rn to family farming as in to work clash with fears of growing inequality and 41). The take-up of the was relatively slow because ucratic hurdles that had to ngs of the family members increased there was a common complaint that there was little to spend the money on. The system of payment by 'final result' was often introduced as an alternative to the family contract system, though it does not seem to have been particularly successful.

The size of the private plot was increased and more were made available. Peasants were permitted to sell the food grown on their plots, collective or state farms directly in cities, at metro stations and elsewhere, bypassing the state distribution system. After sixty years of suppressing such private trade, by its restoration the authorities admitted the inadequacy of state distribution.

The problem remained of excessive centralised direction and mis-planning. This was if anything exacerbated by the attempt in November 1985 to reduce duplication and to raise the status of agricultural administration by merging five all-union agricultural supply ministries and a state committee to create a new 'superministry', the State Agro-Industrial Committee (Agroprom), headed at first by Vsevolod Murakhovskii. In the localities all branches of the food industry were concentrated in Raion Agro-Industrial Complexes (RAPO), founded in 1982 to co-ordinate the food programme, which created a powerful new layer of bureaucracy. The rhetoric in favour of devolving initiative to farms themselves appeared to run into bureaucratic obstacles. 'Instead of destroying the bureaucracy', *Pravda* admitted, 'we on the contrary strengthened it.' Gosagroprom had a staff of 4,500 in Moscow, 200,000 specialists and an army of nearly 2 million officials covering the country in a dense layer (*P*, 6 March 1989). The plenum of 15–16 March 1989 decided to abolish Agroprom: having created a monster, they sought to take credit for its destruction. In its place a commission under the Council of Ministers was to act mainly as a purchasing and support agency, and much more responsibility was to be devolved to individual farms, regions and republics.

Among the new ideas was leasing. At first leases were for relatively short periods and only in mid–1988 were fifty-year leases introduced for families or other groups. The aim was to restore the bond between the land-worker and the earth, in short to recreate the peasantry, though fifty years was far too short a period to restore the land to health. In the event the take-up by farmers of long-term leasing was very slow. This reluctance is not surprising. There is a small pool of dedicated skilled small farmers; fears of yet another shift in state policy which would open the rural entrepreneurs to the charge of 'kulak' once again as in 1929; the perception that a lease is not ownership, thus discouraging a long-term commitment to a plot of land; confusion over rights of inheritance; the conversion of the most active elements in the country-side from agriculturalists to tractor drivers or mechanics, whose skills are industrial and not suited to the long-term nourishment of the earth but rather to its rapid exploitation; the structure of rural employment, which has placed women in the hardest and least skilled of agricultural professions; the drift to the towns of the young and more dynamic elements given the lack of social facilities and housing in the villages; the lack of roads and infrastructural development; the burden of bureaucracy that acts as a deadweight on initiative and local responsibility; and the hostility of local farm management to individual or family farming. Leasing within the structure of collective ownership did not appear to offer much of a solution, and even in 1989 peasants could still be described as 'serfs' of the collective and state farm managers (*Ogonëk*, 42/1989: 1–2).

In certain areas, like Estonia, the Law on Individual Labour Activity was applied to agriculture allowing leases to be converted into private landholding 'in perpetuity'. With a pool of skilled farmers with memories reaching back to before their incorporation into the Soviet Union in 1940 agriculture quickly recovered. Many of the details of the scheme in the rest of the country remained open to restrictive interpretation since key questions like the right to own and sell tractors, farm buildings and other inputs, access to the open market and rates of taxation remained vague. This was addressed by the 'Law on Land' (*P*, 7 March 1990), introduced together with a new 'Law on Property' to the Supreme Soviet in February 1990. The law allowed tractors and other machinery to be privately owned, thus making it possible for peasants to farm their own land, but the power of the collective farms remained intact. The key point was that the law abolished the state monopoly on land effected by the Decree on Land imposed the day after the victory of the Bolshevik Revolution in October 1917. Farmers now had the right to own land, on which they paid an annual tax, and to pass it on to their children, but were not allowed to sell it or give it away, or to employ others to work on it. The law, as usual, was a compromise, as in its refusal to endorse explicitly the notion of private property.

The majority of state and collective farms were technically bankrupt and survived only through state subsidies. By 1991 loss-making farms were to be closed. The idea that bankrupt collective farms could be turned over to leaseholders was firmly quashed by Ligachev: 'It was not for this that we established Soviet power', he asserted (*ST*, 5 March 1989). Ligachev's solution to the agricultural question was the merging of stronger farms with weaker ones, thus undermining the more successful and creating even greater problems of size. Moreover, Ligachev held back the democratisation of management on the farms themselves through the election of farm chairs with a choice of candidates.

A top-level meeting on 12 October 1988, from which Ligachev was notably absent, heard Gorbachev urge the 'privatisation' of agriculture. However, the CC plenum devoted to agriculture on 15–16 March 1989 retained the collective farm structure, though it allowed the expansion of contract working and leasing. State orders were gradually to be replaced by market relations in which producers and the state would agree to a contract 'on an equal basis'. Gorbachev's analysis of the problems facing agriculture was devastating, including a condemnation of the famine resulting from Stalin's collectivisation and an admission that millions, rather than the 'few thousands' he had mentioned in November 1987, had suffered from forcible and accelerated collectivisation (*P*, 16 March 1989). Nevertheless, the principle of collective farming was to be retained though in conjunction with long-term leasing. Farms and other units were still bound to deliver set amounts to the state before being able to dispose of the surplus on the market. As Ligachev stressed at the plenum, agriculture was to continue to develop 'along socialist lines'. The proposals were clearly a compromise and were dead even before they were published in the Press.

From August 1989 the state offered to pay farmers hard currency for above-plan output of quality wheat and other key crops. Collective and state farms were to receive a set sum in convertible currency for average output above base years, which for hard wheat was 1981–5. In 1988–9 the government imported 36 million tonnes of grain costing the exchequer R5 billion. The extra offered to Soviet farmers was two-thirds of world market prices; thus if the scheme is effective there should be significant hard currency savings.

While problems with production are bad, those with distribution are catastrophic. Gorbachev himself estimated that half of the fruit and vegetables earmarked to supply Moscow rots before it reaches the shops, and in the country as a whole the figure was 40 per cent (*P*, 30 July 1988). Shmelëv estimated the wastage at some 60–70 per cent, and argued that a quarter of all the grain produced by the country went to waste (*ST*, 20 November 1988). V. Tikhonov estimated that of the 90 million tonnes of potatoes harvested annually, only 24 million actually reach the consumer (*Ind.*, 25 April 1990). Anyone who has waded through the rotting slime of one of the huge vegetable depots in Moscow is surprised that a single cabbage makes it to the shops. Some of these depots have now been transferred to co-operatives. Much of the extra spending on agriculture was to go into infrastructural projects like storage, roads and distribution, together with improvements to social conditions in the countryside, an aspect that had been neglected under Brezhnev.

The failure of agriculturalists to free themselves from the clutches of the bureaucracy revealed the gulf between Gorbachev's rhetoric on breaking down the Stalinist structures in agriculture and the rather diffident policies actually proposed. The fate of agriculture vividly illustrates the organisational and ideological resistance to change in the Soviet Union. At the 19th party conference Gorbachev talked of restoring sovereignty to the peasant, making him or her the 'real master of the land'. How the sense of ownership could be achieved while maintaining common ownership was something that was not explained. The failure of agriculture is increasingly taken as symbolic of a larger failure. As Eltsin argued at the 19th party conference, seventy years of socialism had failed in its basic task, of feeding and clothing the population (*XIX konf*, vol. 2: 59).

Science and technology

Soviet hopes of 'catching up and overtaking the West' in both economic output and technological level from the 1930s fell prey to the inherent difficulties of providing incentives to managers for technological innovation. Faced with taut plans managers saw little reason to disrupt existing processes to gain the unsure benefits of innovation. There was no in-built mechanism for technological modernisation within the enterprise, and the system relied on specific orders from above to innovate, or the pressure of foreign competition, as in the defence industries, to maintain world levels. It has often been pointed out that if Soviet performance is compared to its own past, then the achievements would be a source of justifiable pride. However, Soviet performance cannot be judged in isolation, and the rapid pace of economic and technological change in the West in most sectors outstripped that of the USSR. Contrary to expectations, socialism did not of itself release a vast source of creative energy. The technological and managerial revolution in the West exposed the shortcomings of the Soviet economy until by 1985 the need for change became overwhelming.

Managers, workers and administrators are all far better qualified than in the past. The Soviet Union now boasts some 22 million university graduates compared with only 1 million in 1941. The number of scientists has more than doubled from 665,000 in 1965 to 1.5 million in 1987, but with a preponderance of older people, and with too many relatively low-grade engineers and too few in the developing biological and chemical sciences (J. Cooper, *THES*, 6 November 1987: 16). Despite a vast scientific establishment Soviet scientists published little of world class and won few Nobel prizes. Soviet science was harnessed to the task of production rather than abstract research, and as in other areas was suffocated by bureaucracy in a highly centralised framework. Some of these problems are now being tackled.

The education system, despite a reform in 1984 and the presence of an élite section which is the equal of any in the world, found itself unable to cope with the demands for a flexible and technologically aware society. Too much time was spent on rote learning or on manual tasks such as lifting potatoes in the autumn. Many schools, especially in the countryside, lacked basic facilities. Educational reform under Gorbachev has continued the stress of the 1984 reform on vocational training (Connor, 1986: 36–9).

Gorbachev admitted the technological backwardness of the Soviet Union and, echoing earlier Stalinist calls, urged not only that world levels be reached but that they should be surpassed. A range of reforms have been undertaken to improve the quality of scientific work, including the closure of certain institutes which had produced little, better monitoring of individual performance and the introduction of *khozraschët* to allow market winds to blow away some of the dust of the past. Decentralisation and individual responsibility have become the key policies in a new environment which has moderated its obsession with 'state secrets' and allowed a much greater flow of information. Indeed, the CC in June 1988 committed itself to make the country an 'information society'. *Glasnost* itself provides an atmosphere much more conducive to the enquiring mind. Information technology and computerisation can now develop.

Co-operatives

During the civil war Lenin had taken a dim view of the role of the co-operatives and had preferred to rely on state organisations for retail and distribution. However, with the onset of the NEP in 1923 he returned to the question in *On Co-operation* and argued that they could play a critical role in educating society, above all the peasants, towards a more socialistic form of economic activity. He argued that 'the system of civilised co-operators is the system of socialism.' By 'civilised co-operators' he presumably meant a non-capitalist form of co-operation. The deterioration in state provision of goods and services in the early years of *perestroika* led to more attention being paid to them. Co-operatives emerged as a middle path between state socialism and free market individual capitalism. They appeared to offer a way of rapidly improving certain quality of life industries without placing an additional burden on the state exchequer. Moreover, they appeared to be a way of reconciling the encouragement of private enterprise with the prejudices of orthodox Marxism–Leninism. However, the notion of 'civilised' co-operation, if not always explicitly, placed powerful restrictions on the development of the co-operative sector.

The Law on Co-operatives of 26 May 1988 (*Kooperatsiya i arenda*, vol. 1, 1989: 173–231) gave them equal rights with the state sector of the economy and released them from the clutches of the state planning system. They were allowed to trade abroad without the intermediary of state bodies, though this was hampered in practice by the authorities. Introducing the law to the Supreme Soviet on 24 May 1988, Ryzhkov argued that co-operatives would help absorb some of those made redundant by state enterprises, and would act as flexible small to medium-sized production units geared to the market. He condemned those who saw the co-operative sector as a departure from socialism. 'This was the result of distorted notions of socialism', he insisted (*G*, 25 May 1988). He envisaged a growing industrial role for the movement. The law removed limits on the profits and incomes of members, a break with practice since 1929.

Adoption of the new co-operative law was complicated by the new tax laws that came into effect from 1 April 1988, allowing local authorities to take up to 90 per cent of co-operative profits. The tax rates set by the local authorities were often punitive, though allegedly designed to allow a flexible response to local needs (*Iz.*, 23 February 1989: 2). The controversy illustrated the contradictory development of *perestroika*: on the one hand, for the first time local soviets were allowed to keep local tax revenues and not simply pass them on to central government, a reform that gave them an independent budget for the first time; on the other hand, the clause allowed conservatives in local soviets to stifle the development of the co-operatives. In the event, the Supreme Soviet challenged the finance ministry, a further sign of growing legislative independence of the administrative system, and modified the tax law, though it remained a source of controversy in the following years.

The incident revealed the confusion in the government and party over the role of the co-operatives. This was further demonstrated by the administrative decree, adopted without any discussion, of the Council of Ministers of 29 December 1988 which severely limited the range of co-operative activity (*Kooperatsiya*, vol. 1: 270–3). Film and video production, medicine, jewellery manufacture and much more were banned, but above all publishing was proscribed as a legitimate co-operative activity. This unleashed a vigorous debate in which both sides appealed to the law, a sign that law was beginning to be perceived as more independent of the administrative system.

The co-operative movement expanded at great speed, and in two years had grown from under 1,000 to some 133,000 by June 1989, employing nearly 3 million people with a turnover of some R13 billion (*Commersant*, No. 0, August 1989: 4). Co-operatives tended to concentrate on consumer goods and service industries like restaurants, repairs, beauty salons and clothing, rather than moving into manufacturing. This was understandable, given the environment in which manufacturing industry had to operate. A particularly fast-growing sector was the medical co-ops in which doctors and nurses joined to provide services directly to the customer, though they were not permitted to do surgery or abortions and some other activities. Their success revealed the depth of patient alienation from the state health sector and the poor remuneration of its staff. Consumer co-operatives, which had long operated in the countryside, were revived in Leningrad (*SN* 1990: 130) and other towns.

The growing differential between the earnings of successful co-operative members and the typical state employee fuelled a powerful current of hostility. The fires of envy were stoked all the more by the poor quality and inflated prices of many co-operative goods. Residual prejudice against private enterprise at a time of shortages also played its part, with the development of co-operatives being seen as the restoration of capitalism through the back door. Their unpopularity stemmed from the difficult circumstances in which they were forced to operate, with rising inflation and unemployment and an almost anarchic economic environment giving great scope for making large profits out of sharp practices, like buying goods at state prices and retailing them with enormous 'value added'. The flaunting of new-found wealth enraged the population. Within the nexus of state economic relations a new economic system and social class was being shelled out, coexisting uneasily with the state sector and state employees. *Perestroika* appeared like a period of reconstruction after a fifty-year war against private initiative, and as in any post-war period shortages provide rich pickings for 'spivs' (*zhuliki*). Even worse, *perestroika* revealed a widespread lawlessness in which organised crime seemed to operate with impunity. The Interior Minister, Vadim Bakatin, revealed that Soviet crime increased by 31.8 per cent in 1989, and by 17 per cent in the first three months of 1990 alone (*P*, 17 April 1990). The co-operatives were at the mercy of the Soviet mafia, with the conviction that the authorities did not do enough to protect them (*P*, 23 March 1989). The relatively affluent, defenceless and unpopular co-operatives offered easy pickings for various protection rackets, in particular around the Riga station in Moscow. *Perestroika* brought to the surface the widespread and pernicious level of lawlessness that was endemic to Soviet society.

By 1989 the unpopularity of the co-operatives had become general and drew all sorts of administrative measures against them. One of the demands of the Donetsk miners in July 1989 had been the 'prohibition of co-operatives and disbandment of existing medical and food co-operatives' (point 22). This call was taken up by the AUCCTU in September 1989 when it passed a resolution condemning the 'deformations' in the co-operative movement and urged the disbandment of 'greedy' co-operatives that failed to charge state prices for their goods, including those providing catering services (*P*, 7 September 1989). Such expressions of popular distaste boded ill for the further development of the co-operative movement. The problems facing the co-operatives revealed the difficulties in the creation of a 'socialist market' in commodities and services. Plans to limit profits and prices by administrative means demonstrated a lack of faith in the free market. By 1990 the 'third path' of co-operative consumer socialism could be judged a failure in the existing conditions, and the hopes of radical economic reformers now focused on the rapid transition to a full-blooded private property market.

Labour and social policy

Economic Stalinism represented an unbalanced pattern of development which lavished resources on heavy industry while consumer goods, service industries and welfare in general were funded on what Gorbachev (1987a: 99) and others called 'the residual principle', what was left over after satisfying the needs of production. It became clear that Malenkov's and Khrushchev's partial redressment of the balance was not enough, and that Brezhnev's commitment to expanding the social sector grossly underestimated the scale of the changes necessary.

One of the greatest challenges facing the Gorbachevite reformers was to provide the economic and social environment which could achieve a transformation in the relationship between labour and work. According to Hough, the Kirilenko group in the 1970s was working towards economic reform and was prepared to accept such items as wider pay differentials among workers, but the regime settled for social stability and egalitarianism at the cost of economic stagnation. The pillars of the old neo-Stalinist social compact included full employment, a rough equality (excluding the élite) and the promise of rising standards of living. These were eroded by the marketising reforms, and indeed Gorbachev argued that 'socialism has nothing to do with equalising' (1987a: 100). Stalinism imbued the Soviet worker with a profound conviction of equality, even though Gorbachev like Stalin before him realised that 'equality-mongering' (*uravnilovka*) is an obstacle to economic productivity. The removal of subsidies on all but medicine, education and some other items was to be balanced by increases in wages. In the early period of *perestroika* many wages actually fell because of the new quality control measures, but by 1989 average monthly pay rose by 9 per cent to reach 240 rubles – rising much faster than productivity and thus fuelling inflationary pressures. Wage policy lost the emphasis on narrowing differentials that had occurred under Brezhnev.

Compensatory mechanisms were introduced which, while protecting living standards, tended to aggravate the original problem. Wages were raised, only exacerbating the tendency for output and supplies to fall behind income growth, leading to even longer queues and inflation. By 1989 this changed to attempts to restrain wage growth; yet cash reserves and savings grew even faster than before, rising to 120 billion and 340 billion rubles respectively by June 1990, since there was little to spend the money on, thus adding further to the inflationary pressures. In 1989 alone wages rose five times faster than output.

Policy in the Gorbachev years focused on a variously defined notion of 'social justice'. For Gorbachev this meant adequate remuneration for a job well done, restoring the basic principle of socialism: 'From each according to his ability, to each according to his work' (1987a: 31). A new ethic of labour was to emerge, making the people 'the true master of production, rather than the master in name only' (1987a: 83). The new approach was directed against the alienation and corruption of the Brezhnev years, and also against those securing an 'unearned income' by speculation and so on. An unpublished section of Zaslavskaya's Novosibirsk report stressed the disastrous decline in the work ethic among Soviet workers, and noted how this would hamper any attempt at economic reform (Bialer, 1986: 134). This was amply borne out by the experience of *perestroika*. A common complaint is that the Soviet worker has forgotten how to work well and up to a high professional level. The old economic mechanism encouraged workers to prefer a quieter life even if it meant lower wages since there were few incentives to work harder. Zaslavskaya frequently stressed the social repercussions of an economy which encourages cheating and makes people dishonest (1989c).

Perestroika involved a transformation of employment patterns. According to the State Labour Committee, manufacturing and heavy industry were to shed some 16 million workers, a fifth of them by 1991. In addition, millions would have to be lost from the 14 million, some 12 per cent of the country's total workforce, staffing the administrative empire, quite apart from the 11 million more in administrative jobs in the enterprises and farms. All of this threatened the traditional social compact where workers were guaranteed a job for life, however badly paid, and in which the quality of work played little part. A whole new social ethos had to be achieved, and in many ways this was the greatest challenge of *perestroika*.

At the 27th party congress in 1986 Gorbachev had scoffed at fears of a labour shortage, and indeed marketisation of the economy raised the spectre of unemployment – not least among the bureaucracy. The onset of cost accounting meant that factories cut back sharply on their surplus labour. By late 1989 some 3 million people out of a total workforce of 164 million had lost their jobs because of *perestroika*, a figure that could reach 16 million by the year 2000. The number in the early 1990s would be swelled by at least half a million servicemen released from the armed forces. Unemployment was particularly high in Central Asia, where according to some estimates up to a quarter of the labour force are unemployed, and an even larger proportion underemployed, many of whom took part in the ethnic disturbances. An association of the unemployed claimed that 23 million, or 14 per cent of the workforce, were unemployed (*P*, 30 October 1989). In January 1990 Goskomstat revealed that if women, invalids and people temporarily between jobs were added to the 3 million out of work already admitted, the total unemployment figure was 13 million (*Ind.*, 26 January 1990).

Unemployment challenged the basic socialist promise of a job for everyone, enshrined in Article 40 of the 1977 constitution, and prevented the emergence of any consensus on the definition of social justice under *perestroika*. Enterprises were no longer responsible for finding jobs for those made redundant. New schemes were launched for retraining and redeployment. In 1988 a nationwide system of job centres was created, together with a system of unemployment benefits to be paid for a maximum of three months. The intention of the reformers, of course, was not to provoke unemployment but to stimulate the redeployment of labour from declining manufacturing industries to areas of shortages, like some of the more remote regions, new industries, the co-operatives and so on. The Law on Employment was expected to sanction unemployment, though at the same time creating a legal framework for job mobility.

In his first period in office Gorbachev failed to understand that consumption gains could not be postponed indefinitely. The emphasis on high reinvestment in heavy industry suggested that once again improvements in the standard of living would be delayed, thus undermining incentives to improve labour productivity and alienating the population from *perestroika*. The standard of living of the average East European is only one-third that of Western Europe. According to

Brucan, 'That ratio can't continue to get lower without the risk of socialism becoming meaningless' (*G*, 12 November 1988). The new economic model began to address such issues. However, from the first days of *perestroika* there was a glaring contradiction between the ambitious social goals of the reformers, such as ensuring housing for all by the year 2000, and its investment priorities in modernising Soviet industry. The medium-term goals in social policy seemed far beyond the capacity of the system given the actual rates of economic growth (Connor, 1986: 31). The outlook for consumers of goods and social services under *perestroika* was bleak.

Resources can be devoted in three basic ways: to defence, investment or consumption. Gorbachev increased investment in plant and techno-logical renovation, energy and agriculture, and until 1988 maintained defence spending. The source of funding for social spending and consumption in that year, however, began to be diverted from defence spending. Funding for 'non-productive' sectors like health, education, housing and culture were no longer to be granted on the residual principle but came to be seen as crucial to the development of the Soviet economy as a whole, above all to boost productivity and for the maintenance of social peace. Exhortations for more sacrifices lost their power, and with democratisation the population began to demand satisfaction today. Temporary relief for consumer goods shortages came from an emergency programme of foreign spending. The democrat-isation of Soviet politics was thus reflected in a new attention to the social needs of the population rather than prestige projects like space and defence.

The large underclass of the Soviet poor was at last recognised. About half the Soviet population lives in households with an income of R100 or less. Ryzhkov's economic report to Congress on 7 June 1989 revealed that some 40 million Soviet citizens lived below the poverty line of R75 a month. These included pensioners, peasants on poor-quality land and unskilled workers. While prices were subsidised they could survive, but subsidies are a regressive form of support in which the better-off gain the most, being more likely to consume heavily subsidised items like meat. To compensate, despite the inflationary dangers, social spending was sharply increased. Pensions were increased from 1 January 1990 at a cost of R6 billion a year, with an average rise of 15 per cent, though for those whose pensions were already lower than average, such as collective farm workers, the average increase was 43 per cent. The basic minimum pension rose from R46 to R70 a month. This of course placed yet another burden on a budget already running a huge deficit.

As noted, at the centre of *perestroika*'s social policy was an expanded concept of social justice. Conservatives used it to defend the level of achieved equality, job security and so on, that were considered the gains of the Revolution. In the hands of conservative populists, like Gidaspov, social justice was used as a weapon with which to beat the co-operatives and the marketising reforms as a whole. For Zaslavskaya the term signified a meritocratic 'equality of opportunity', allowing a differentiation of achieved result. All, however, were agreed that social justice must establish a link between the quality of work and the rewards.

Radicals like Eltsin made the term social justice their own, and used it to challenge technocratic *perestroika* and the privileges of the élite. Eltsin's critical approach to Soviet society began to spill over into public in late 1987. Gorbachev urged him to postpone his criticism of the slow pace of *perestroika* until after the celebrations of the seventieth anniversary of the Revolution. Yet at the Central Committee plenum of 21 October 1987 Eltsin pointed out the injustice of workers spending hours in queues for near-meatless sausages while the tables of the élite groaned with caviar and sturgeon. He asked to be spared Raisa Gorbachev's 'petty interference and her daily telephone calls and scoldings'. Despite all the resolutions the bureaucracy remained bloated: 'Comrades, it must be clearly understood that, as long as we do not break up the army of bureaucrats and red-tape merchants. . .there will be no path for *perestroika* and all our resolutions and directives will be buried by a flood of instructions and circulars' (*LF on EE*, 1/1989: 22–3). As usual, Eltsin's speech spared no feelings, but it lacked any clear political concept or theoretically worked-out position. It reflected a radical leftist populism, attacking party privileges in favour of a programme of social justice. In contrast to the Thatcherite economic reformers, who accepted the need for greater social inequality and differentiation to improve labour productivity, Eltsin argued for greater social equality. His own authoritarian approach to personnel management while in power in Moscow endowed his programme and personality with a Peronist stamp. Eltsin, however, is not simply a populist or a crude egalitarian, as in his argument that 'if someone receives a suitable compensation for work done, bureaucrats have immediately retorted "you are growing rich!" ' (*LF on EE*, 2/1989: 30). His criticism of élite life-styles, and of Gorbachev's personal enjoyment of luxuries, was described in bitter detail in his autobiography (1990).

The role of the party in securing social justice (full employment, welfare, health) traditionally legitimated its leading role. Under *perestroika* Soviet ideas about the state in this field had a double, and incompatible, edge. With the onset of marketisation a prop to Communist party-state power was removed. Yet at the same time there was a new emphasis on the state (or the community) as the guarantor of equal opportunities and as the provider of universal welfare. The

Communist Party entered the era of multi-party politics as the defender of a social democratic agenda of health, education and other welfare rights (*P*, 15 July 1990).

A new economic model of socialism

The crisis of centrally planned economies indicated that something was wrong with the traditional model (Bleaney, 1988; Winiecki, 1988). The state socialist pattern of development achieved impressive results in the first 'extensive' phase of industrialisation, the generous input of labour and material resources, but was unable to respond to the challenge of 'intensive' development, utilising existing resources to maximum advantage. The difficulties in achieving advanced modernisation may well be found in the unbalanced pattern of primary modernisation: the inflexibility of planning; the bureaucratisation of agriculture; a structurally unsound service and distribution sector; outmoded technologies in industry, and so on. The Stalinist developmental model was ultimately incapable of sustaining the transformation of society into economic modernity.

The economy that Gorbachev inherited in 1985 was in all essentials basically the one constructed by Stalin from 1928. However, the problems began to mount to reach a 'pre-crisis' by 1985. Destalinisation is not something applicable to the political sphere alone. Reform of the economy entails a profound destalinisation of economic thinking and practices. Economic destalinisation entails increased personal economic autonomy, increased consumption and the dismantling of centralised economic command mechanisms. The reformation of the old war Communist approach to economic policy represents far more than a break with a particular Soviet leader of the past. It represents a profound challenge to traditional socialist notions of how an economy should be organised. The belief, for example, that the socialist state should have a monopoly on foreign trade was not Lenin's alone. It was Trotsky who in 1922 achieved the imposition of the monopoly against the advice of the commissar of finance, G. Yu. Sokolnikov.

The new thinking in Soviet economic policy has had a more difficult passage than that in foreign policy. The reason is simple: the heart of socialism is a critique of capitalist economic rationality and an attempt to achieve an alternative. The problems of a Marxist form of development have been much debated over *perestroika*. Selyunin (1988) sought to demonstrate that war Communism, the economic system developed during the civil war of 1918–20, was not simply a response to war and economic dislocation but an attempt to implement essential Marxist ideas on economic organisation entertained by the Bolsheviks and Lenin even before the Revolution. In their view the destruction of free trade and the market economy in favour of state control over the means of production was an essential feature of socialism. The elimination of financial incentives thus required some form of economic coercion. The ideological legacy of old socialist ideas on how to run an economy still bears its bitter fruit, and was reflected in the hesitations and equivocations of Gorbachev's economic reform. As Gavriil Popov, the editor of *Voprosy ekonomiki*, delicately put it: 'We still live according to the ideas of [Marx's] *Capital*, a book of brilliant analysis but one that reflects the situation in the last century' (*Iz.*, 11 June 1989: 3).

In contrast to his sure touch in foreign policy, Gorbachev made serious misjudgements in economic reform. Given the enormity of the problems this is hardly surprising. The *uskorenie* phase of economic reform was predicated on the assumption that there was still some mileage in the old system, and that planning and economic organisation only needed to be radically improved rather than transformed. Yet the mistakes were not Gorbachev's alone, and as we saw earlier when discussing leadership, there was no clear policy-making consensus. A combination of bureaucratic inertia, stymied leadership, ideological hesitancy and, perhaps most importantly of all, leadership divisions led to political compromises. Aslund (1989, ch. 2) analyses the various trends in the leadership, ranging from the radical reform position espoused by Gorbachev, Shevardnadze, Yakovlev and Medvedev; Ryzhkov's cautious reformism which sought to retain a key role for central planning, a position supported by Slyunkov and Maslyukov; Zaikov's technocratic rationalisation; to Ligachev's stress on socialist morality and opposition to private property in the means of production. No credible economic policy around which a consensus could be built emerged either within the political leadership or, it should be stressed, in society as a whole.

The pace of *perestroika* was much slower than expected, and indeed the only fruits seemed to be a price spiral, a growing budget deficit, inflation and falling living standards. The social sphere did benefit, however, from increased spending on health and education, with large wage rises for teachers and medical staff, and an increase in pensions. The government was careful to ensure that the price rises ensuing from the attempt to reduce food subsidies did not reduce living standards, above all for those on fixed incomes like pensioners, though this simply meant shifting the budget deficit from subsidies to compensatory payments.

The government miscalculated in believing that in conditions of democratisation the Soviet population would be willing to tolerate yet more short-term sacrifices on the premiss that the future would be better. The leadership failed to recognise the need for immediate improvements in quality of life indicators, in the supply of food, consumer goods and services. Otherwise, the tasks of *perestroika* would be greeted with scepticism. Instead of importing high-quality goods so that immediate improvements could be seen, there was an attack on the 'import scourge'. With little to spend money on, savings expanded, fuelling inflation and eroding incentives. Moreover, there was a contradiction in the simultaneous emphasis on high growth and high quality, aims which in the short term were not complementary (Hewett, 1988). Investment strategy was unbalanced, with a programme of heavy industrial reconstruction taking precedence over the immediate satisfaction of consumer demands. *Perestroika* was predicated on creating an environment where initiative and harder work were rewarded, yet from an individual's point of view there was little incentive to modify traditional economic behaviour.

The manner in which the reforms were implemented in itself created problems and economic disruption. This was seen vividly in the case of quality control, in which an extra-economic agency, Gospriëmka, tried to impose quality rather than trusting in the market to eliminate low-quality goods. Since 1918 Soviet governments have been unable to use financial means effectively to control economic behaviour. The attempt to reform Stalinist industrial management while postponing the reform of prices and the state monopoly over goods exacerbated the sort of disequilibria that the reforms were trying to overcome. The 1988 plan, for instance, retarded reform implementation by failing to incorporate the necessary changes in planning methods.

The absence of a developed alternative model of economic relations was reflected in the piecemeal way in which economic reforms were implemented. The various policies making up the economic reform were not complementary. They lacked a mechanism to introduce cumulative gains and inherent dynamism to the economy. When the Bolsheviks came to power in 1917 they knew the broad outlines of the economy they desired and precisely what needed to be destroyed, but modern reformers had no clear idea of what they would like to take the place of the existing economy and hence they were not sure what to destroy of the old.

The haphazard introduction of economic reform inevitably led to havoc and infringed basic economic laws. Moreover, the lack of a cumulative element in the reform process meant that it was characterised by constant superhuman efforts, like the old economy with its storming, rather than by a self-sustaining dynamic. At the 19th party conference, a mere twelve months after the adoption of the Law on State Enterprises, Leonid Abalkin was once again calling for 'a totally different economic system, precisely the one we agreed upon a year ago'. He pointed out the lack of economic logic or consistency in the economic reforms to date. He provocatively declared that the emperor of economic reform had no clothes: despite all the talk there had not yet been a radical transformation of the economy. Moreover, he implied that the leadership was somewhat deficient in its understanding of the basic rules of political economy. He cited the twelfth five-year plan which ran counter to economic logic by striving simultaneously to achieve higher growth rates and higher quality (*XIX konf.*, vol. 1: 114–19). The strategy was Gorbachev's, and Abalkin came perilously close to taking *glasnost* beyond what was deemed proper, reflected in Gorbachev's waspish response to the speech. Abalkin derided the decree-mania of the Soviet leadership and their belief that the introduction of a resolution on its own solves a problem. Reformers, as much as the early revolutionaries or the stagnationists, are prone to the illusion that policy-making is as good as policy implementation. Abalkin, in short, was urging the leadership to pay more attention to the *economics* of economic reform. At the conference Gorbachev rebuked Abalkin for being an 'economic determinist' and thus implied that the latter lacked a full understanding of the social and political context of the reforms. Nevertheless, it appears that Gorbachev, as usual, was willing to learn from the views of others and from experience. The lack of success of the reforms reflected not only the shortcomings of the government bureaucracy but signified a deeper failure in the conceptualisation of the reforms themselves.

A new generation of Soviet reform economists emerged and academic economists under Gorbachev played a prominent role, although their views have been balanced by party and ministerial officials. It was the academics who had moulded the June 1987 package of economic reforms. Their implementation, however, lay with the bureaucracy, and thus their fate remained uncertain. The creation of the Central Committee's economic and social policy commission in September 1988, headed by Slyunkov, was an attempt to give overall guidance to the process of reform. This function was eroded by the emergence of an effective legislature, and in June 1989 Abalkin was appointed a Deputy Prime Minister and chair of the new State Commission for Economic Reform.

Reform economists, from Aganbegyan to Abalkin, Shmelëv and Popov, provided cogent criticisms of the old economic mechanism and the inadequacies of the transitional period. As *perestroika* entered its dog days from late 1988 there was a perception that the old economic mechanism had been destroyed, but a new one not yet built. Academician Viktor Belkin noted that 'the economy is increasingly cannibalistic, feeding on itself', and Vladimir Tikhonov warned of impending famine (*G*, 10 July 1989). The economic indices for the first quarter of 1990 were disastrous, revealing falling output, a trade deficit, rising inflation and worsening consumer shortages (*P*, 29 April 1990). The transition from the 'command economy' to the 'regulated market economy', as the new model came to be called, proved to be more difficult than expected, not least because no one knew what a 'socialist market' should look like. Popkova indeed ridiculed the attempt to create 'market socialism', arguing that it was absurd to put the two words together (1987: 240). The economic system entered a state of endemic civil war in which no one any longer knew the rules: market forces were not allowed free play while central administrative mechanisms began to be dismantled. The national market itself began to break down as towns and regions sought to protect their supplies. The economy became 'primitivised' as it turned towards barter and other non-monetary relations (*P*, 30 April 1990). By any reckoning this was a recipe for chaos. It appeared that there had to be a clear choice: either a plunge into the market or a return to the protective fold of the command economy. The delay in making this choice led to the economic chaos and shortages that provoked the social and political crisis of 1989–90.

Gorbachev in effect admitted as much, and in his presidential acceptance speech of 15 March 1990 he promised the radicalisation of economic reform and warned of harsh measures to come on taxation, spending and prices. He urged the rapid 'demonopolisation' of the economy to create a 'full-blooded domestic market' with a stock market, full-scale commodity exchange, central bank control of the money supply and realistic interest rates (*P*, 16 March 1990). The new concept of economic reform moved towards the Scandinavian model of a 'regulated market economy'. The Polish model of a dash for the market became increasingly attractive to Soviet reformers, but appeared to be ruled out by Gorbachev for fear of strikes and mass protest. Part of the problem was the lack of domestic capital to fund the privatisation of the economy. The transfer of enterprises to workers was also ruled out since, as noted in Chapter 4, the emphasis on workers' self-management, the heart of the first stage of Gorbachev's reforms, had by 1990 given way to an emphasis on professional management. Moreover, social and political inequalities in Soviet society meant that the costs of radical economic restructuring would be unfairly distributed. No natural consensus could be formed to back drastic measures.

Abalkin and Pavel Bunich, the deputy chair of the Supreme Soviet's economic reform commission, favoured a much faster pace of reform than that espoused by Ryzhkov. All options entailed political costs which the Presidential Council appeared unwilling to accept (Petrakov, in *Rabochaya tribuna*, 24 April 1990). Ryzhkov's confused attempt to impose price rises from July 1990 as part of the turn to the 'regulated market' were characterised by Bunich as 'all shock and no therapy'. Only a government with the popular legitimacy like that enjoyed by Mazowiecki's in Poland could hope to impose shock therapy and expect to survive. Gorbachev himself lacked the authority to drive through harsh measures, having refused to go to the country for a mandate for the presidency. Once again, radical and speedy measures were tempered, and the Soviet economy lurched with both the brake and accelerator pedals pushed firmly down. The failure to take a decision as to whether to maintain the system or to transform it meant that the economy was in danger of spinning out of control.

The ministerial bureaucracy found itself in the unenviable position of being denounced while at the same time given responsibility for implementing the reforms. The levers of control for a state committee are fairly limited. For example, Gosplan and Gossnab (the state supply agency) primarily operate through state orders or control figures in order to balance the economy; yet their use leads to the charge that they are abusing their prerogatives in order to defend their privileges. By imposing massive state orders on enterprises the ministries tried to retain their monopoly on output and hence impede a factory's ability to dispose of goods in the market-place. But as far as the ministry is concerned, it needs a particular plant's output in order to achieve targets further downstream. The problems were exacerbated by the attempt to operate a reformed economy while maintaining the old economic institutions, and so once again we return to the question of the nature of reform.

Earlier attempts at economic reform in the USSR and elsewhere gave mediocre results primarily because they tried to insert market mechanisms into the command economy. The economic debates of the 1980s returned to some of the themes of the 1960s, but with the difference now that the problems appeared to be that much more intractable and were enriched, if not embittered, by the experience and sense of failure and wasted time of the era of stagnation.

The debate over the new economic model began in a surrogate and veiled manner: in terms of the reform experience of Hungary, China and Yugoslavia. With the development of *glasnost* such subterfuges were soon dropped. But the Chinese reforms did exercise an attraction for some leading Soviet officials, and Fedor Burlatsky (*LG*, 16 June 1986) gave a positive and honest evaluation of them. While the Chinese leadership under Deng Xiaoping since 1978 had called for economic decentralisation and market mechanisms, and had condemned the harm caused by taut planning, the stresses also began to mount. Gorbachev declared that the Chinese approach to solving the problems of mature socialist economies was not applicable to the Soviet Union. The Hong Kong paper *Far Eastern Economic Review* (14 August 1986) reported that in mid-1985 at a closed meeting of Warsaw Pact party secretaries discussing economic problems, Gorbachev sharply condemned the plans of some of the participants to apply the experience of the Chinese reforms and Yugoslav market socialism. 'We shouldn't be thinking about lifebelts, but of the ship itself. And this ship is called Socialism', he declared.

During *perestroika* the Soviet Union tried to find its own solutions to its own distinctive problems. The debates at the Congress demonstrated that the reformist leadership had no coherent plan for solving the country's economic crisis. While the elements of a possible strategy were aired, no section of the leadership was able to devise a strategy to implement the desired reforms. Oleg Bogomolov insisted that a new economic model for socialism had to be found. Among its priorities was agricultural reform and the satisfaction of the home market. The suspicion arose, not least among the conservatives, that the new economic model of socialism was nothing less than capitalism. The Poles from 1989 abandoned all attempts to hide marketising economic reform under a fig-leaf of socialist rhetoric, and boldly dashed for the market. In the Soviet Union the attempt to find a new economic model suitable for late Communism modified traditional economic policy while trying to retain socialist legitimacy.

The Soviet economy is highly politicised, with the regular and often misplaced intrusion of political bodies in economic affairs. Few if any modern economies exist without state intervention, yet in the Soviet case politicisation took an extreme form. The very paradigm of socialist economic development favoured state intervention operating in giant factories, and fetishised the industrial proletariat working within a centralised planning system. The Stalinist state found its natural counterpart in a centralised economy, inhibiting the development of a modern economy and a differentiated society. The Soviet command economy was quite an effective mechanism for modernising a relatively backward society and economy (though no doubt more effective mechanisms were available at far less cost), but whether it is capable of running a modern system was the fundamental question that faced reformers for at least thirty years. What had once been taken as the indisputable elements of a socialist economy, such as social ownership of the means of production, were now questioned (Nekipelov, 1989).

Reformers now accepted that modern economies require pluralism, decentralisation and autonomous units of varying size.

Shmelëv (1987) argued that the country had 'lost the habit of doing anything that is economically normal and healthy, and gained the habit of doing everything that is economically abnormal and unhealthy'. He argued that 'We have to introduce into all spheres of our social life the understanding that all that is economically inefficient is immoral, and all that is effective is moral' (G, 8 February 1988) – which is rather reminiscent of Deng's argument, that so outraged the leftists in China, that it does not matter what colour a cat is as long as it catches mice. The problem here was the inability to create an industrial culture based on innovation, quality, care and finish. The case of the exploding Soviet colour television sets, which cause over half the household fires in Moscow, is well known. Quantity, bulk, 'storming' work, rushed plans, these are the typical features of the old system (with the exception of certain military enterprises), that left the Soviet Union far behind Japan and increasingly even the newly industrialised countries (NICs).

The emerging new economic model moderated the traditional Soviet obsession with large-scale industrialism. Stalinist industrialisation subordinated environmental and social concerns to the simple achievement of 'gross output', a basic quantitative indicator that acted as the engine of distorted Soviet economic development. The new economic model of socialism borrowed some of the ideas of Tolstoy, above all his emphasis on the transformation of people's relationship with the natural world. Boris Mazurin's article on a Tolstoyan 'Life and Work' commune outside Moscow, and repression against it from 1928 (NM, 9/1988: 184–226), lamented the brutal suppression of yet another of the rich tapestry of experiments in the 1920s by Stalin's centralised model of the socialist economy. The alienation that this engendered was now explored (Belov, 1988), and the emphasis has fallen on a new symbiosis of industry and the environment. However, the Soviet attempt to embrace consumerism has come just at the time when the Green movement has challenged the dangers that the expansion of consumer needs poses to the very texture of the earth itself.

The development of a large co-operative sector appeared as the harbinger of a form of consumer socialism, rejecting the production-orientated nature of the old model. An economic reform of this sort would be slanted to the market, depriving central managers of their authority and devolving it to plant managers and technical specialists. Over the years various Communist regimes have introduced elements of market socialism in order to achieve greater efficiency for the command economy. The question now is whether the market can be introduced for its own sake.

This is associated with the problem of equality. Is there a primeval striving for equality in Russia that acts as the major barrier to economic liberalism, an equality that transcends liberalism's equality of opportunity and is rather a precise equality of no one having more than anyone else? The old communal structure of landholding clearly encouraged this primitive equality, and Lenin and Stalin both inveighed against *uravnilovka*, or equality-mongering. Under Gorbachev successful co-operatives drew the hostility of those tied to a state salary. Is this resentment against marketising reform part of a traditional culture of envy? Is the cultural climate of Russia simply inhospitable to capitalism and all of its works? Public opinion surveys suggest not, especially among younger and better-educated people (*Iz.*, 1 September 1989).

The attempt to stimulate initiative implied a re-evaluation of the individual and a reappraisal of the emphasis on communal and collective ties. Seventy years of state-dominated economic development undermined individual initiative in the economy. The destruction of the independent peasant sector and the flourishing co-operative movement at the end of the 1920s, together with the imposition of a harsh centralised command economy, left little scope for dynamism from below. The 1980s in the West, if only imperfectly and inconsistently, advanced under the slogan of the enterprise culture. Gorbachev hoped to weld elements of a culture of enterprise to a developed system of social provision. The major challenge is whether this is possible, or indeed desirable. It is open to attack from both those who emphasise the relaxation of state control over the economy, and those who insist that the state alone can ensure not only a fully developed welfare state but also a full-employment economy. The modern social democratic ideal of a mixed economy became increasingly attractive to Soviet reformers.

One of the methods to achieve greater individual responsibility for economic performance was a new approach to property and ownership. The traditional Soviet, and indeed socialist, view of property is changing, though not without the resistance of Ligachev and others. While the Left Bolsheviks of the early Soviet years sought to destroy individual attachment to an enterprise stimulated by a sense of ownership, *perestroika* seeks to re-create a sense of personal involvement in economic performance using, if necessary, private ownership. In his speech on the seventy-second anniversary of the Revolution the head of the KGB Kryuchkov reiterated that *perestroika* was a 'revolution within the revolution', and pointed out that the key issue in the economic reform was the problem of property: 'The essence of this problem is the need to return the means of production to the actual ownership and disposal of the people and to release their creative initiative', and he urged 'a variety of forms of socialist property' (*P*, 5

November 1989). A revised 'Law on Property' giving equal rights to three forms of property – state, co-operative and individual – was passed by the Supreme Soviet on 6 March 1990. The law talked of citizens', rather than private, property, and the terminology revealed once again the hesitancies of the leadership and represented only a partial legalisation of private property. The law allowed people to own and inherit flats, and allowed private businesses, though the hire of non-family labour, the 'exploitation of man by man', remained forbidden.

A reform of property rights entails a revolution in social relations. Ownership began to shift from the state, at the disposition of a narrow political class, to broader private or co-operative ownership. Opposition can therefore be interpreted either as an ideological commitment to socialist common ownership and against 'the restoration of capitalism', or as the defence of the class interests of the 'privilgentsia'. The emergence of a middle class based on private or co-operative property is obviously incompatible with the power of the 'new class' of the Communist bureaucracy. Friedrich von Hayek's argument that capitalism is a necessary condition for an open society, on the grounds that a diffusion of ownership allows alternative power bases in society, has been taken up by the reformers (Hanson, 1989: 6). Soviet debate over the respective roles of the plan and market is therefore a debate over power and democracy. Nove (1983) argued that the abolition of the market implies a strong authority to regulate the economy which is incompatible with decentralisation and local democracy. In other words, espousal of the market, as Hayek and von Mises argued, is as much a political as an economic programme. The political economy of Gorbachevite socialism clearly understood the link between economic decentralisation and the attempt to democratise Soviet society. The end of economic monopoly entails a modification of political monopoly.

An alternative view would argue that rather than the second Russian revolution allowing a rising bourgeoisie to displace the old ruling class, in fact the old class in this revolution is transforming its previous exclusive rights to the fruits of state ownership into ownership for itself (see page 189). In other words, the 'new class' is turning into a new bourgeoisie. In Poland new laws on private enterprise in 1988 saw the sale of public property to middle-level managers, many of whom were Communists, the heartland of the *nomenklatura* class. The transformation in ownership enabled a transition from a ruling class into the new owning class. Such a process in the Soviet Union might well facilitate the decline of the party by giving its members a new role, but it could equally be seen as the plunder of national resources.

The new approach to ownership allowed the development of a degree of economic pluralism. The three main sectors of the national economy

– private, state and co-operative – became subject to the same laws and competed on an equal basis. The privileged monopoly position of the state sector was weakened. The issue, of course, is as much a theoretical as a political one since economic pluralism entails a shift from the old collectivist ethos to one in which a nascent entrepreneurial class can gain a foothold.

Communist reformism is based on the belief that plan and market are compatible, and that such a hybrid economy can provide an effective base for political democratisation. Certain economists are not sure. Shmelëv emerged as one of the most cogent partisans of Thatcherism as the solution of the USSR's economic woes. Market forces were to be used as a battering ram against the administrative-command system. He urged a vigorous programme of privatisation in which unemployment should be allowed to find its own level. He dismissed concern about social inequality and income distribution as marginal to the main task of achieving an effective economic system.

The central issue appeared to be over the nature of a socialist commodity market. Elements of the market had always existed in the Soviet economy, and conservatives argued that all that was required was a relaxation of controls to allow more scope for individual, co-operative and joint ventures. Radical reformers could no longer see any distinction between a capitalist and a socialist market, though operating in different sociopolitical contexts. In other words, for them market relations are not necessarily related to capitalism (Vodolazov, in *Inogo ne dano*: 441–67). The black market in any case always existed under socialism, performing certain functions that the official economy failed to achieve. The whole notion of a 'socialist market' could be seen as an ideological camouflage for traditional Soviet distaste for the market. The more radical Soviet economists put it simply: a good market, whatever it is called, is one which saturates the economy with goods, and a bad one leaves the shelves bare.

There was a nascent market economy pressing at the gates of the state-regulated economy, creating a situation analogous to that of the 1920s. Ultimately, a decision had to be taken since the balance between the official and the second economy was inherently unstable and depressed the dynamism of both. The attempt to bolt the elements of capitalism on to an essentially socialist system created a very peculiar animal indeed, and encouraged rapid profit maximisation rather than long-term investment. The Law on Unearned Income of 1986 and the anti-corruption campaign depressed the spirit of enterprise. Corruption reached disastrous and debilitating proportions, but in a sense corruption was a morbid symptom of stifled entrepreneurial energy. The 'black economy' was estimated to have an annual turnover of some R80 billion in 1988. Some of what was called 'corruption' represented attempts by citizens to achieve a degree of economic independence by giving private lessons and other activities that gave 'unearned income'. Much of this was the only genuine earned income, since the money received at the official job was often paid for putting in an appearance only. The struggle against corruption became a weapon forged by Andropov to crush individual enterprise. Only in June 1990 was the green light given for the development of the market, albeit 'regulated'.

Up to 1990 the embryonic market economy was stifled and overregulated in order to prevent it overwhelming the state economy. Despite official strictures against 'over-organisation' in the political sphere, in economics the administrative system lost few of its powers. Gorbachev warned industrial managers in a speech on 15 February 1989 that a culture of spivs (*zhulikov*) was emerging that needed to be combated. But what is a spiv other than a person who fills the gaps in the official economy? When is an entrepreneur showing initiative a spiv? The ideological self-definition of the culture and regime will shape the course of economic development, which in turn will provide a new identity for the country.

From the above it is clear that *perestroika* was an evolving concept of economic reform. It was to be an extended process applying the scientific-technological revolution to the Soviet economy. The system of management was to be overhauled allowing greater initiative to enterprises and individuals, though the degree of worker participation in management was not clear. A new type of social justice was to emerge, though this was to mean social fairness and the elimination of some privileges rather than an attempt to achieve equality. It was based on *glasnost*, open discussion and accurate statistics. It sought to reintegrate the Soviet Union into the international division of labour and the world economy. Above all, economic *perestroika* tried to realise the alleged potential of socialism through the use of the 'human factor'. Gorbachev called all this 'in essence, revolutionary'.

Gorbachev's own position on the details of economic reform also changed. He began by stressing that the first task was to strengthen the centralised management system and to improve the quality of the middle-level ministerial bureaucracy, then to increase enterprise powers. The attempt to combine strong ministries with strong enterprises soon foundered since strong ministries jealously defended their powers over enterprises. At the same time, the emphasis on improved personnel retained elements of the old 'cadres decide everything' approach which eschewed structural changes. From 1987 the emphasis shifted to allowing more autonomy for enterprises. The destalinisation of the economy ultimately entailed a relaxation of the party's commitment to an exaggerated notion of economic *dirigisme*. The reforms at first, however, did not involve the abandonment of central control and throwing the economy to the wolves of the market. Instead there was a partial demonopolisation together with greater powers for republican and regional authorities. The ultimate shape of the reformed Soviet economy was not clear as the 'commodity-producing market economy' struggled with the command system.

In many respects the Soviet domestic economy is a nineteenth-century system facing twenty-first-century challenges by returning to nineteenth-century values. Discussion of the politics of economic reform is clearly coloured by one's view of Soviet politics. Simply to list the various sources of opposition or support presupposes a degree of pluralistic interplay. However, the fact that analysis focused on the leader's ability to push through reforms highlighted the highly concentrated nature of Soviet politics. The major question remained: even if the reform programme as outlined by *perestroika* was implemented in its entirety, if the bureaucracy leapt to fulfil the new tasks, would the aims of the reformers have been achieved? Would a dynamic and self-sustaining new model of the socialist economy have emerged? Experience suggests that this was unlikely to have been the case.

The major constituency for marketising economic reform to date has been found among the liberal intelligentsia and a relatively small section of the political leadership. The enthusiasm for liberal economic reform among peasants and workers has been tempered by an awareness of the penalties, such as higher prices, reduced economic security and harder work. According to Zaslavskaya the postponement of the price reform was due to adverse public opinion, it being supported by only 16 per cent in one poll. Similarly, 58 per cent in another poll considered unemployment intolerable (G, 18 March 1989). There was clearly a constituency to be found by a populist leader who could campaign on the basis of 'social justice' while making inflationary promises and gathering a Peronist coalition.

There are powerful pressures restraining the attempt to restore elements of economic rationality, as defined by radical reformers, to the Soviet economy (cf. Gerner and Hedlund, 1989). The radical measures of *perestroika*, such as the liberalisation of co-operative policy and the expansion of joint ventures with foreign business, in their early stages were so hemmed in by restrictions imposed by the ideological cautions of the conservatives that they were unable to bear healthy fruit. It made rational economic sense for a co-operative to try to maximise its short-term profits in an unstable political and financial environment. The radical economic reform programme called for the abolition of the centrally planned economy, the abolition of price controls and food subsidies, the convertibility of the ruble, the radical weakening of the ministerial system and so on. The government temporised, and by 1989 began to reap the harvest of disaffection not because of its boldness but because of its timidity. Much of the economic reform legislation on its first appearance was such a compromise that it pleased neither the conservatives nor the radicals. More importantly, it was not effective, and it appeared that there was no middle path for reform.

Given the right economic policies the USSR is placed to become perhaps the most dynamic economy of the twenty-first century. Already on the eve of the First World War Russia was the fifth largest economy and in per capita GNP terms equal to Japan, whereas now while it might be the third largest economy in the world its per capita GNP is half that of Japan. Soviet reserves of natural resources are second to none in a whole range of items. The USSR has a large educational and scientific base and in several sectors, like metallurgy and long-distance energy transmission, leads the world, while its defence sector on the whole has kept up with global developments. There is a natural resilience to the Soviet economy that even the dislocation of *perestroika* may not completely undermine. If agriculture and the allied food industries and distribution could be made effective, there are enormous reserves available for an economic surge comparable to post-war Germany and Japan. The German 'economic miracle' (*Wirtschaftswunder*) engineered by Konrad Adenauer and his 'social market economy' were based on an undervalued currency, low incomes depressing internal demand, the removal of past liquid savings, low spending on defence, and paternalistic though not excessively interventionist government in a relatively free market economy, with the labour movement to a degree incorporated into a capitalist hegemony. By 1990 it became clear that this formula could not be applied to unlock the potential of the economy in a country with superpower aspirations and ensnared in the ideological contradictions of *perestroika*.

All previous attempts at Communist economic reform have failed, as discussed in Chapter 2, and *perestroika* followed much the same path. It is difficult to establish a typology of the failure of Communist reforms since each country's road to failure is paved with its own particular good intentions. In the USSR the political reforms were inalienably tied to the economic reform, since it was difficult to envisage a thriving democracy based on economic ruin. A deteriorating economy generated forces and conflicts that sought to find expression. It became clear that the economy could not be decentralised and the 'leading role' of the plan weakened, while trying to retain the vanguard role of the party in the political sphere. In addition, as the Poles and others discovered, even in conditions of post-Communism it is not easy to dismantle a command economy. *Perestroika* was based on the belief that there was a middle way between capitalism and Communism. This middle road, however, could not be found.

8

THE NEW REALISM IN FOREIGN POLICY

On coming to power Gorbachev was faced with a dire legacy. After six years of war in Afghanistan Soviet forces were no nearer victory. In Eastern Europe political stagnation and economic crisis threatened a new wave of unrest. Relations with the West were at their worst in thirty years. *Détente* had been broken on a number of policy issues, including wars in Africa, human rights, the deployment of Soviet SS-20 missiles, the invasion of Afghanistan and the imposition of martial law in Poland. Brezhnev's foreign policy had culminated in the nightmare of encirclement by hostile powers. The USSR had painted itself into a corner with poor relations with all of its neighbours; even its allies were sullen and rebellious. The situation was only exacerbated by Andropov and Chernenko as Soviet foreign policy continued to be gripped by a lack of direction. Soviet prestige in the world was eroding and under a series of ailing leaders appeared rudderless and dangerous. The Soviet Union was in the grip of the paradox of external expansion and internal decline (Bialer, 1986).

Gorbachev was forced to retrieve the situation. The necessity for change was apparent to all but the staunchest conservatives. His accession radically changed the international atmosphere and established a new context for East–West relations. The succession crisis was over and the scene was set for a period of new realism in Soviet foreign policy. His rule was immediately marked by a new vigour in the international sphere.

The Soviet Union under Gorbachev launched one of the most sustained and far-reaching reforms in the principles and conduct of its foreign policy in its entire history. *Perestroika* of the domestic economy and polity was accompanied by a radical reappraisal of its foreign policy. A foreign policy NEP was inaugurated as part of the USSR's domestic *perestroika*. The linkage between domestic and foreign policy is an axiom of the Marxist–Leninist approach to international relations, and from the very beginning Gorbachev insisted that restructuring of the country's foreign relations was an integral part of domestic *perestroika*: 'The organic ties between each state's foreign and domestic policies become particularly close and practically meaningful at crucial moments. A change in domestic policy inevitably leads to changes in the attitude to international issues' (1987a: 132). The extent and nature of these changes in Soviet international politics will be the subject of this chapter.

The new political thinking

The change in tone and substance of Soviet foreign policy since Gorbachev's accession is now subsumed under the general rubric of the 'new political thinking' (*novoe politicheskoe myshlenie*, or NPT). The degree to which the NPT was really new, or just a tidying up of the old, needs to be assessed. It appeared at first that Soviet foreign policies since 1985 could be considered part of a 'new realism', following on from the disastrous period of the second cold war, entanglement in a hopeless war in Afghanistan and an accelerated arms race. The new Soviet foreign policy was indeed an attempt to recover credibility and effectiveness after the difficulties of the past, but it soon became clear that it was far more than this. As the domestic reforms deepened, so the dynamic between internal reform and foreign policy strengthened the innovative features of Soviet foreign policy.

Many tributaries contributed to the development of the NPT. Above all, there were the intellectuals within the Soviet academic establishment who, even during the 'era of stagnation' under Brezhnev, had been putting forward alternative ideas. Jerry Hough, for example, identified many of these in the field of Soviet relations with the Third World (Hough, 1986), and Neil Malcolm in the study of Soviet–American relations (Malcolm, 1984). The NPT gave a boost to the scope and originality of the *mezhdunarodniki*, specialists concerned with various aspects of the study of international relations. In particular, the journals *Voprosy filosofii* (Questions of Philosophy), *Voprosy ekonomiki*, and the Institute of Social Sciences of the Central Committee, headed by Fedor Burlatsky, played a key role in developing the new thinking (Hamman, 1989). In foreign policy, as in other spheres, under the glacial torpor of the Brezhnev years new currents of thinking were maturing that under Gorbachev burst out in full flood.

The new thinking transformed the way that international relations (IR) is studied in the USSR. The subject, while only relatively recently recognised as a separate discipline, gained in size and importance. In the past the many works on aspects of the field had been provided by historians, lawyers and others applying the skills of their own profession rather than the specialised approaches of IR specialists. From about 1970 IR became an established subject, but only in the late 1980s were undergraduate courses organised (Light, 1987b). The emphasis, in this field as in the other social sciences, had traditionally been the study of 'questions whose answers are known beforehand', restricting itself to commentaries on established truths. Now Soviet scholars became more adventurous in examining contentious issues and scrutinising formerly closed areas. This established a dynamic for the deepening of the new thinking as ideas were fed into the study and conduct of foreign policy.

Several commentators have noted, not without a degree of irony, the similarity between the NPT and certain concepts popularised by US academics and politicians in the 1970s (see, for example, Falk, 1971; Keohane and Nye, 1977). The ideas included notions such as common security, the predominance of global issues over the old US–Soviet rivalry, the need for co-operative solutions through agreements guaranteed by international agencies, and the call for arms control and political accommodation in US–Soviet relations. The old adversarial style of superpower relationships was to give way to an understanding of the need to take into account the fears of the rival (Hoffman, 1988: 24). Of particular importance was the concept of interdependence (*vzaimozavisimost'*) which US scholars in the early 1970s applied to the global economy and, more boldly, to international politics itself. These ideas were taken up by some of Carter's advisers and by Carter personally. However, the Soviet Union under Brezhnev proved unreceptive and Gorbachev in his early years found himself ranged against Reagan, a man to whom these notions were anathema. Interdependence, of course, clearly runs the risk of opening the way for a degree of superpower condominium over the affairs of the world, or, in an alternative scenario, of a condominium of developed countries over the less-developed ones. Gorbachev warned against this danger.

Gorbachev added little that was original to the new thinking. Margot Light points out that the new Soviet ideas are similar to older concepts in Western social science, such as dependency theory, interdependence and transnationalism, and ideas of post-industrial society (Light, 1987a: 216). In the sphere of relations between Communist parties there are many points of similarity between the new thinking and the views put forward by Togliatti and his successors in the PCI, often against considerable Soviet hostility. At Enrico Berlinguer's funeral in June 1984 Gorbachev is reported to have said that 'Berlinguer's criticisms [of the USSR] were not without value' (Timmermann, 1987: 62–3).

Gorbachev's political report to the 27th party congress first introduced the new ideas in a systematic way. The speech dispensed with the
old formal order of dealing with countries and instead focused on key
issues in foreign policy, above all dealing with relations with capitalist
countries (*P*, 26 February 1986). Much of his speech, like the new
edition of the party programme, used standard Soviet language in
dealing with the alleged exploitation and militarism of capitalism,
though having restated the official formula of peaceful coexistence he
saw in scientific and technological advances and intensifying inter-
imperialist rivalries new challenges for the world as a whole. Multinational corporations were singled out for special attention with their
vast resources accounting for over a third of capitalist production and
more than half of its foreign trade. While not denying crisis tendencies,
Gorbachev's report was remarkable for emphasising the development
rather than the decline of capitalism. The dominance of capitalism in the
Third World was conceded with almost no reference to anything that
the USSR could do about it. The speech was notable for its awareness of
ecological issues and the depletion of natural resources, which could be
solved only by international co-operation.

In sharp contrast to Brezhnev's formulation of *détente* as meaning
only the abstention from the use or threat of force in relations between
states, and as having nothing to do with the class struggle within states
expressed through civil wars, guerilla warfare or *coups d'état* which
marked the world revolutionary process, Gorbachev stressed interdependence. This implied a shift in the definition of peaceful coexistence
from competition to co-operation in an ever more integrated global
society. Collaboration was to take the place of the competition
structured into the very notion of peaceful coexistence (cf. Mitrany,
1946). The Brezhnevian 'fight for peace', in which every blow against
imperialism signified the consolidation of peace, gave way to an
exhortation to respect fundamental human values in managing the earth
and its resources. Ideological struggle between capitalism and socialism
was played down in favour of globalism and interdependence. The
speech represented a sharp break with the adversarial and confronta-
tional approach of previous Soviet leaders in favour of co-operation,
global interdependence and disarmament. No longer could the Soviet
Union restrict itself to a primarily military response to outside threats.
Gorbachev clearly warned that the militarisation of the Soviet foreign
policy agenda should be reversed in favour of domestic economic reform
and the search for points of agreement rather than differences with the
West.

While on the whole fairly traditional in its perspectives, the 1986
party programme made an interesting shift of emphasis in seeing

disarmament and arms control as the major guarantees against war, whereas the 1961 version placed the emphasis on strengthening the socialist bloc (Gill, 1987: 53). The change reflected the recognition that capitalism, though still considered doomed in the long run, was not in imminent danger of collapsing; hence a long-term pattern of war-reducing measures was necessary. Gorbachev's foreign policy represented an important stage beyond traditional views of peaceful coexistence, which implied an adversarial relationship, towards a more co-operative approach in which all states have 'perfectly legitimate interests'.

The concept of interdependence gave rise to the idea of a 'comprehensive system of international security' (CSIS), first mooted at the 27th congress and then on several later occasions including speeches to the United Nations (e.g. *P*, 17 September 1987). The idea was quite dramatic in its scope. In the military sphere it included the renunciation of war against each other or third parties by the nuclear powers, the destruction of nuclear and chemical weapons, preventing the arms race reaching into space, and reducing conventional forces to a level of 'reasonable sufficiency'. The concept of interdependence allowed a new approach to the question of security which was no longer simply defined as a military problem but cast in terms of economic, ecological and political concerns and based on humanitarian considerations. The political aspects included non-interference in 'the right of each people to choose the ways and forms of its development', just solutions to regional conflicts and international crises assisted by international mediation, and a whole raft of confidence-building measures. In the economic sphere Gorbachev's proposals ranged from the renunciation of economic sanctions unless ratified by the world community, the settlement of the debt issue, a 'new international economic order' (NIEO) ensuring economic security for all nations, reduction of the debt burden, the diversion of resources from military expenditure to assist developing countries, and the global attempt to solve pressing problems.

On human rights Gorbachev urged an increased exchange of information in the arts, sciences, education and medicine, and greater contact between peoples. There should be greater international co-operation to defend personal, political and social rights 'while respecting the law of each country'. All nations have a right to exist; hence there was a need for non-intervention in other peoples' affairs. Such a formulation revealed the tension in the new thinking between a radical reintegration of the Soviet polity into world society and the traditional emphasis on Soviet exceptionalism as a state bounded by no rules other than those defined by the needs of building socialism. The CSIS was basically an appeal to implement the principles declared in the UN Charter adopted at the founding congress in San Francisco in 1945.

Soviet ideas were still vague on many issues, as for example the idea of the NIEO and the transfer of resources to less-developed countries (LDCs). There was, moreover, much that was obviously self-serving in Gorbachev's definition of CSIS, especially in the military and human rights fields; yet taken together the ideas represented the launching of a visionary agenda whose implications were only gradually realised.

However much Gorbachev referred to Lenin in advancing his version of the interdependence of the world, it was a radical repudiation of Lenin's views of a harsh division into two contending systems, even though Lenin accepted a degree of interaction between the two in his notion of peaceful coexistence. The view that 'Mankind has lost its immortality' (Gorbachev, 1987a: 138) and the unprecedented diversity and interconnectedness of life, according to Gorbachev, required new thinking: 'Our world is united not only by internationalisation of economic life and powerful information and communication media but also faces the common danger of nuclear death, ecological catastrophe and global explosion of the poverty–wealth contradictions of its different regions' (Moscow forum, *SN*, 1987: 59; see also 2 November 1987 speech, *SN*, 1987: 401 and *P*, 3 November 1987). The question mark over human survival encouraged the search for the CSIS. Instead of focusing on the differences between the two systems, capitalism and socialism, the new thinking emphasised what the world has in common.

One of the major themes in Soviet post-war thinking in international relations was the concept of the 'correlation of forces'. There was a deeply held belief that the correlation of forces was ineluctably tilting in the Soviet Union's favour because of the expansion of the bloc of socialist countries, the independence and nationalist movements in the Third World and the end of colonial hegemony by leading West European powers, together with the stiff resistance to US neo-colonialism and imperialism, and the growing economic and military strength of the USSR relative to the rest of the world. It was this tenet that lay at the basis of the concept of peaceful coexistence and *détente*. This optimistic prognosis of a changing correlation of forces in favour of socialism was played down if not altogether abandoned. For Brezhnev *détente* was only possible, as he put it in June 1975, 'because a new correlation of forces in the world arena has been established', and *Pravda* earlier had insisted that 'peaceful coexistence does not mean the end of the class struggle between the two social systems' (*P*, 22 August 1973).

The new thinking modified the belief in the inevitability of a long-term struggle between the two systems: if victory was not inevitable, then perhaps the struggle itself might not be worth waging. The renunciation of historicism meant that international relations were no longer seen in terms of a zero-sum game where a gain for the USSR was seen as a defeat for the USA, and vice versa. Wars of national liberation and other struggles were now seen in a new light. The new view of security as a political rather than a largely military issue led to a series of radical reappraisals of the nature of war and peace as a whole. Above all, the Leninist tenet that there could be no peace until socialism was established on a global scale was rejected. The new thinking reversed this formulation and argued that peace was the basic condition for the construction of socialism. Hence the so-called world revolutionary process was marginalised in Soviet thinking and the emphasis shifted to achieving the highest possible level of international support for the new approach in Soviet foreign policy.

At the root of the NPT was a changing evaluation of imperialism. In the seventieth anniversary speech of 2 November 1987 Gorbachev posed three crucial questions. The first asked whether imperialism was inherently aggressive or could it be dealt with and its more dangerous manifestations blocked (*SN*, 1987: 402). Gorbachev's answer was basically in the affirmative. In his earlier speech to the 27th party congress he insisted that 'the US ruling class is linked to the military–industrial complex' (*SN*, 1986: 89), but it could and must be contained. The final resolution of the congress argued that 'In modern day conditions, imperialism is a growing threat to the very existence of mankind. Militarism is its most monstrous offspring, seeking to subordinate the whole political machinery of bourgeois society to its influence and interests, and to exercise control of spiritual life and culture' (*SN*, 1986:123). But as a result of the concept of interdependence there is a 'struggle of opposites' to reach peaceful conclusions to diverse issues: even the thick skulls of Western imperialists understood the fragility of the world today. Could capitalism adapt itself to a nuclear-free world, to an equitable economic order and to intellectual openness between systems? Gorbachev's answer was equivocal, but suggested that inter-system rivalries had moderated and the trends that led inevitably to war had weakened. Indeed, the lesson of the war against Fascism showed that alliances are possible between socialist and capitalist states, especially in the face of nuclear catastrophe.

The second question was associated with the first: can capitalism free itself from militarism and function without it in the economic sphere? The 'economic miracles' of Japan, West Germany and Italy suggested that this was indeed the case. Capitalist development can take place in the absence of major arms spending. For the United States the 'permanent war economy' initially stimulated the economy but then burdened it with debt and public squalor. In other words, militarism aggravates domestic problems so if only capitalists opened their eyes they would understand that it would be even in their interests to demilitarise.

The third question asked whether the capitalist system could do without neo-colonialism, 'currently one of the factors essential to its survival'. Here the answer was more negative, and Gorbachev made the almost unprecedented concession that 'The calls for severing the historically shaped world economic ties are dangerous and offer no solution.' Despite this, neo-colonialism and the increasing burden of Third World debt had to be moderated in some way. Gorbachev was by temperament an optimist and could not leave the question there. He put forward the solution (to which we will return) in the form of 'disarmament for development' (*SN*, 1987: 403).

The new thinking was based on a changed evaluation of the role of class in international relations. The most radical change was to redefine and temper the concept of the international class struggle which had served to fuel the Soviet confrontation with the West. As Gorbachev pointed out in Krasnoyarsk in September 1988, stripped of the ideological animus there was no fundamental territorial, economic or social conflict with the West. The Helsinki conference in 1975, for example, ratified the post-war boundaries of Europe. There were some things more important than the class struggle: the survival of humanity. Gorbachev was well aware of the debates about declassing and the alleged 'disappearance of the working class' (*SN*, 1987: 403). However, he insisted that the working class had the potential to play a decisive role in curbing militarism. The fundamental point is that international relations are no longer (if they ever were) seen as the playing out of the class struggle in the international arena. In this case Gorbachev once again created a Lenin to suit his purposes. He claimed that this principle was derived from Lenin who allegedly could see further than the class-imposed limits of the proletariat: 'More than once he [Lenin] spoke about the priority of interests common to all humanity over class interests' (1987a: 145). This is the opposite of our usual understanding of Lenin's thought, and nowhere was the dramatic deleninisation of Soviet foreign policy more visible than in the changing emphasis from class to humanitarianism. Be that as it may, this reading was reflected in the revised party programme of March 1986 which no longer defined peaceful coexistence as a 'specific form of class struggle'. Humanitarianism in domestic affairs suggested that the interests of one class cannot be placed above those of society as a whole, and in foreign affairs that the interests of one nation cannot be placed above humanity as a whole. Hence it implied a multilateralism in all aspects, from nuclear disarmament to ecological issues to regional conflicts.

The new political thinking modified the Soviet view of international relations. At a conference at the Ministry of Foreign Affairs on 25 July 1988 Yakovlev insisted that in the context of a nuclear world peaceful coexistence could no longer be seen as a specific form of class struggle: 'The struggle between two opposing systems is no longer a determining tendency of the present-day era' (Hazan, 1990: 424–8). With the declining role of the international class struggle the emphasis shifted from what divided the world to focus on the world's common problems. The role of the USSR in the world began to be rethought. The new approach to class in international relations provided the focus for criticisms of the new thinking. The traditionalists managed to retain much of their commitment to proletarian internationalism, the dominance of class over nation, in the programme adopted in 1986, which sat uneasily with the new wind in other sections stressing the independence of Communist parties and the need for 'comradely' relations between them. Gorbachev stressed the theme of 'unity in diversity' in his speech to the 27th party congress. However, Ligachev constantly stressed that Soviet diplomacy should continue to base itself on the 'class character of international relations'. On 4 August 1988 he asserted that class remained firmly at the basis of a socialist foreign policy (Ligachev, 1989: 290–1).

With his effective demotion and replacement by Vadim Medvedev in September 1988, the 'humanistic' understanding of international relations was even more vigorously espoused. In his inaugural speech Medvedev rebutted Ligachev's assertions about the irremediably class-based nature of foreign policy. The paths of socialism and capitalism would not converge, but in a strange formulation he argued that their paths would 'inevitably cross each other' since both systems operated 'within the same human civilisation'. Medvedev used the traditional Leninist concept of peaceful coexistence, but stripped of its subsequent 'deformations' which insisted that struggle, albeit peaceful, between socialist and capitalist nations only reflected fundamental class conflicts. Peaceful coexistence, Medvedev now argued, was a developing process whose future could not be predicted (*P*, 5 October 1988).

The new understanding of class was related to the loss of the old optimism on the decline of capitalism. Soon after the War Evgenii Varga, director of the Institute of World Economy and World Politics in Moscow, was disgraced for suggesting that the War had infused the capitalist economies with renewed vitality. Gorbachev's new thinking finally accepts that capitalism will, in the short run at least, retain its viability. This does not mean, however, that the old homilies about the 'further exacerbation of the general crisis of capitalism' have disappeared from public declarations (e.g. *SN*, 1986: 123).

The new thinking was above all conditioned by a re-evaluation of the nuclear threat. This focused on four issues: (a) Military and technical means cannot be relied upon to safeguard peace. This means that security 'is increasingly seen as a political problem, and it can only be resolved by political means' (*SN*, 1986: 88); (b) New weapons themselves change the rules of the game since the decision-making time in the event of perceived attack is now reduced to a few minutes at most; (c) The US military–industrial complex is still seen as the main motor of the arms race, but it can be offset by the arguments adduced above, and by popular pressure which will be discussed below; (d) The modern world is seen as an interrelated system and 'has become too small and fragile for wars' (*SN*, 1987: 57). There is no alternative to co-operation and interaction between countries. Furthermore, the USSR proclaimed itself to be 'unequivocally defensive' and at the 27th congress renounced the first use of nuclear weapons. As an act of good faith the leadership announced a moratorium on nuclear testing and allowed great scope for extended verification. All of this was predicated, as Gorbachev vividly put it, on the premiss that 'there would be no second Noah's ark for a nuclear deluge' (1987a: 12).

The idea of 'reasonable sufficiency' signalled a shift in military doctrine, reflecting a new understanding of the dynamics of inter-national relations in the nuclear age. It provided the theoretical basis for Gorbachev's disarmament policies. Valentin Zhurkin, the first head of the Institute for European Affairs, argued that at current arms levels no attack could be made with impunity since the side attacked would need to use only a small percentage of its strategic arsenal in response. The conclusion was that both sides could reduce their nuclear (and indeed conventional) arsenals at once without prejudicing their security (*G*, 18 November 1987). Soviet policy-makers now agreed that the level of military confrontation had to be reduced and that security could not be achieved by military means alone.

This opened the door to an even more profound development, namely what Henry Kissinger called the 'delegitimisation of nuclear weapons'. Reagan's 'Star Wars' project in a convoluted way shared this vision, and at its most idealistic strove to make nuclear weapons obsolete. The convergence in thinking provided the background to the astonishing boldness of the discussion between Reagan and Gorbachev in October 1986 in Reykjavik for the abolition of all nuclear weapons in ten years. Nuclear disarmament was not Gorbachev's policy alone, though it was given eloquent voice by him. At the 27th congress he stated that 'the CPSU has put forward a coherent programme for the total abolition of weapons of mass destruction before the end of this century' and went on to say, 'Our ideal is a world without weapons and violence' (*SN*, 1986: 88). Later he argued that the fundamental principle of the new thinking is that: 'Nuclear weapons cannot be a means of achieving political, economic, ideological or any other goals' (1987a: 140). Gorbachev admitted that the idea was truly revolutionary because it meant discarding traditional notions of war and peace: 'Clausewitz's dictum that war is the continuation of policy only by different means, which was classical in his time, has grown hopelessly out of date' (1987a: 141).

The new view of the world and the belief that 'security has become indivisible' (1987a: 142) entailed a fundamental rejection of the concept of deterrence. This was argued on the usual grounds of the possibility of technical mistakes, that it encouraged a constant proliferation of weapons systems and so on, but the NPT advanced a new argument to be used against those accustomed to the balance of terror of the last forty years. Deterrence, the Soviets now argued, was a policy based on intimidation and imparted a poisonous dynamic to international relations and politics (*SN*, 1987: 59).

Closely associated with the concepts of reasonable sufficiency and CSIS was the notion of 'disarmament for development', outlined by Gorbachev in his seventieth anniversary of the USSR speech (*P*, 3 November 1987). It was a classical exposition of the 'guns or butter' argument, focusing on the belief that the reduction of the military burden was an essential condition for economic reconstruction. It was justified on several grounds, including the argument that imperialism had changed sufficiently to allow the USSR to dismantle some of its weapons systems. The example of certain countries seemed to be overwhelming: Japan, Germany and Italy experienced economic miracles when freed from the burden of military expenditure. China showed how another socialist country could undergo relative disarmament in order to concentrate on economic reform. At first the Soviets were equivocal about the application of 'disarmament for development' to the USSR itself, and there seemed to be a view that there was no absolute choice between guns and butter; they tried to achieve both, albeit neither of consistently high quality. The US experience could be used to demonstrate that guns put butter in the mouths of many people. Disarmament for development became an important factor in world politics and was taken up by the Delhi Declaration on Principles for a Nuclear-Weapon-Free World of November 1986 (*SN*, 1987: 144–5).

By late 1988 Soviet policy lost its equivocations, and began a programme of arms reductions unprecedented in its history. At this point it became clear that NPT was essentially derived from domestic factors to allow the reform of the Soviet economy and polity.

The new view of the world had many implications. Among them was a rejection of the traditional link in Soviet thinking between war and revolution. No longer was it acceptable to argue that wars give a great boost to the revolutionary process, as at the end of both world wars. The Soviet Union abandoned the belief that a Third World War would lead to new positive social upheavals (Gorbachev, 1987a: 147).

Another consequence of the new thinking was the shift in ideology away from the Leninist understanding of the concept of international-ism, away from the dream of world revolution. The concept was still occasionally plied on ceremonial occasions, but it was in effect mothballed. In Soviet–East European relations there was a change from 'proletarian internationalism', under whose banner the Warsaw Pact invaded Czechoslovakia in 1968 and under whose slogan the country was 'normalised', to 'unity in diversity'. This implied a more dynamic and interactive relationship between the USSR and its allies. The 'Brezhnev doctrine' of limited sovereignty (see page 35) was dropped and the Soviet Union renounced its claim to infallibility in dealings with other countries. This was manifested in the Soviet–Yugoslav Declara-tion at the end of Gorbachev's visit in March 1988: almost every Yugoslav demand of the last forty years for the independence of Communist countries was conceded without a struggle (*SN*, 1988: 108–9). Gorbachev announced that 'The time of the Communist International, the information bureau, even the time of binding international conferences is over' (*SN*, 1987: 404). In this context his rider that 'the world Communist movement lives on' appeared more as a pious sentiment than a practical reality. For him, 'All parties are completely and irreversibly independent' within the framework of the world socialist system (*SN*, 1987: 404).

Relations between the superpowers in the context of the new political thinking has been a matter of some debate. The issue focuses on whether a bipolar or multipolar dynamic to international relations had become dominant. The leading exponent of the view that Soviet foreign policy has moved away from its dogged obsession since 1945 with its relations with the United States, managed for so long by Andrei Gromyko, is Jerry Hough (Hough, 1985). At the 27th party congress Gorbachev argued that 'in world politics one cannot confine oneself to relations with any single, even a very important, country', (*SN*, 1986: 88) and he told his foreign ministry officials that the world should no longer be seen through the prism of US–Soviet relations (*G*, 25 November 1987). The shift was precipitated above all by the perception of America's growing weakness. In relative terms, the post-war period has been the story of US decline, which is now accelerating, from its position of absolute dominance. In addition, two other centres of 'imperialism' have emerged, Japan and the European Community, which while weak militarily challenged US economic and technological superiority. The

USSR itself had matured and become not just a regional but a global power which could afford to take a broader view of the world.

It should be stressed, however, that the bipolar view cannot be wholly discarded since the centrality of arms control issues renders the Soviet–US relationship central not only to themselves but to the rest of the world as well. The very structure of international relations in the late twentieth century ensures the survival of a degree of bipolarity. In contrast to Hough, the veteran Soviet social scientist and political commentator Fedor Burlatsky argued that the Soviet–US relationship is too important to be relegated even for a short time (Simes, 1987: 486).

Multipolar themes in Soviet foreign policy have been reflected in the concept extolled by Gorbachev of 'Europe, our common home'. The relative decline of the United States was accompanied by the long-awaited and not yet fully realised rise of a new Europe. The Soviet attitude to the EC changed dramatically, but perhaps of even greater significance was the concept of a European cultural dimension. Gorbachev's speeches are littered with references to Europe, 'the core of modern world civilisation', torn between two warring blocks. He was careful to avoid the suggestion that he was trying to split the two pillars of NATO, America and Europe. There was the obvious danger, apparent to the USSR as it was to the rest of Europe, that a reduced US military commitment to Western Europe might be replaced by a non-nuclear Europe dominated by the regional superpower, Germany, whether united or not. Another view saw the outcome as a Finlandised Europe in the shadow of the USSR. Yet there are major opportunities for a specifically European approach to world affairs, a Europe that stretches 'from the Atlantic to the Urals', 'a cultural–historical entity united by a common heritage' (1987a: 197). The European theme should be placed in context, however, since Gorbachev went to Vladivostok and talked of 'the Pacific, our common home'; to Murmansk, and looking to Scandinavia, proclaimed 'the sub-arctic, our common home'. All that remained was for him to go to Ulan-Bator and talk of 'Asia, our common home'! The Soviet Union's sheer size of necessity gave it a multipolar perspective. Nevertheless, it is clear that Gorbachev was the first thoroughly European leader that the Soviet Union has had – and that includes Lenin. In fact, he was so European that he shared the alarm of many on the Continent of the 'serious threat' hovering over European culture emanating 'from an onslaught of "mass culture" from across the Atlantic' (1987a: 208). In this there is that welcome edge of élitism which has characterised Gorbachev's thought. He concludes: 'No one can replace Europe with its vast possibilities and experience either in world politics or in world development. Europe can and must play a constructive, innovative and positive role' (1987a: 209).

His appeal was not to any Europe, but to the Europe of the Renaissance and the Enlightenment, the Europe of high culture.

Another feature of the NPT was a much greater willingness to compromise within the context of more flexible foreign policies. According to some reports Gorbachev was convinced that Soviet 'stubbornness' was one of the major symptoms of the period of stagnation. In domestic affairs stubbornness took the form of refusal to negotiate with society, resulting in economic and political stagnation. In foreign policy obduracy led to the erosion of the USSR as an alternative model of development and to the single-minded emphasis on the military element in international relations. The new self-critical spirit can be likened to America's doubts following its defeat in Vietnam. Soviet intransigence now gave way to bold proposals on arms control, human rights and regional issues, with foreign policy marked by much greater openness and honesty. As Gorbachev put it, there must be more light in international affairs, and he called for more democracy in international relations (1987a: 158). The new emphasis on international co-operation and the marked decline in Soviet arrogance was reflected in Gorbachev's speech to the United Nations of 7 December 1988.

This new honesty allowed the first steps to be taken towards discussion of some of the more contentious issues in the history of Soviet foreign policy. Above all this focused on the relationship between Stalin's terror and foreign policy, including the Nazi–Soviet Pact of 23 August 1939 and its secret protocol allowing the Soviet occupation of eastern Poland, the Baltic republics and Moldavia. Another issue was Soviet responsibility for the cold war. According to N. Popov, in *Literaturnaya gazeta* in August 1989, Soviet behaviour under Stalin was largely to blame for the cold war since the Soviet Union had created a 'culture of confrontation' with the West which allowed it to be blamed for the USSR's own shortcomings. The traditional Soviet view held that the cold war had been launched by Churchill in 1946, with American support, whereas Popov argued that it reflected 'a continuation of the opposition to the Stalinism of the 1930s' which was marked by bloody purges and campaigns beginning with the Shakhty affair of 1929. Overcoming the continued abhorrence of Stalinism, identified in the West with the politics and ideology of Communism, and to win trust was the major challenge facing Gorbachev: 'Shaking off Stalinism is a hard and painful process'. Other key issues, among many and discussed elsewhere, are the murder of Polish officers, the invasion of Czechoslovakia in 1968 and responsibility for the war in Afghanistan.

An interesting feature of the NPT was what was called the 'charm offensive', or put another way, the development of people's diplomacy. Gorbachev informed the 27th party congress that 'we have addressed our proposals not only through the traditional diplomatic channels but also directly to world public opinion, to the peoples' (*SN*, 1986: 88). This has echoes of Trotsky's calls during the negotiations at Brest-Litovsk in 1917 for the German working class to overthrow its militaristic leaders and his statement on taking office in November 1917: 'I shall issue a few revolutionary proclamations to the peoples of the world and then shut up shop.' The October Revolution, in certain interpretations, put an end to politics as administration replaced government, and in international relations too the great power tradition of diplomacy was to end.

Of course, Gorbachev did not reject traditional diplomacy, but he supplemented it by direct contacts with influential people, the moulders of public opinion. People's diplomacy allowed a much greater degree of human contact between East and West, with new agreements on pupil and student exchanges and an expansion of ordinary and political tourism. The reason for this was straightforward: the USSR concluded that 'the interests and aims of the military–industrial complex are not one and the same as the interests and aims of the American people' (*SN*, 1986: 88). In general, Gorbachev was keen to take advantage of the emergence of a range of new social movements in the West (*SN*, 1987: 403). Policy was 'to take into account the opinion of what may be called the most authoritative part of the public' (1987a: 153). This explains the variety of fora, gatherings and jamborees hosted by the Soviet Union, and Gorbachev's hectic round of encounters with the famous and the notorious.

As part of the same process the view of Western 'progressive forces' was revised, with the tacit admission that the old reliance on Western Communist parties had in fact weakened Soviet influence. Co-operation with these progressive forces was to be based on a 'new international-ism', an idea developed by the Romanians and the Italians to stress the independence of their parties. The gradual overcoming of the historical division between revolutionary Leninism and social democracy was already apparent at the 27th congress, where among the 153 delegations 33 were social revolutionary and national democratic parties, and 23 socialist and social democratic parties, 15 of whom were members of the Socialist International (Timmermann, 1987: 64).

The new political thinking itself became a factor in international relations. As Gorbachev put it on 2 November 1987, 'The new thinking with its regard for universal human values and emphasis on common sense and openness is forging ahead on the international scene, destroying the stereotypes of anti-Sovietism and dispelling distrust of our initiatives and actions' (*SN*, 1987: 402). Indeed, under Gorbachev Soviet foreign policy was imbued with a dynamism and boldness that was striking in comparison not only with the Soviet Union's own past but with the dearth of new ideas in international affairs as a whole and in Soviet economic thinking.

New thinking in practice

After 1945 the Soviet Union became first a regional power and then a global power, yet until 1985 Soviet foreign policy still bore the aggressively defensive stamp of the years of isolation of the inter-war period. It was Gorbachev's achievement to imbue Soviet foreign policy with a new confidence and sense of security that did not see every concession as a defeat and every negotiation as a test of survival. The Soviet Union now claimed to have taken up the mantle of responsible world leadership and appeared ready to accept the compromises that such a role requires. In nearly every sphere of Soviet foreign policy there was evidence of a new approach, of the new political thinking in action.

Perestroika saw a spate of innovative foreign policy initiatives, particularly in the sphere of arms control, in which Gorbachev more often than not was personally involved. He absorbed the reports of specialists but proved himself relatively independent of the foreign policy establishment and of interest group pressures. Policies were designed to exploit new opportunities for trade and to create the conditions conducive to the success of domestic modernisation. To this end Soviet foreign policy was restructured to place limits on East–West competition and to broaden the goals of policy. As in other policy areas, the momentum for change came from a combination of personnel changes, institutional reorganisation and policy initiatives.

The personnel changes were radical but took place over several years. The first major shift was the replacement of the veteran foreign minister, Andrei Gromyko, by Eduard Shevardnadze. In July 1985 Gromyko was promoted to the largely ceremonial presidency and thus his icy grip on Soviet foreign policy was prised lose. He had served twenty-eight years as Soviet foreign minister, a tenure comparable only to those of Talleyrand and Metternich in the nineteenth century. From 1946 to 1949 he was Soviet ambassador to the United Nations, where he used the Soviet veto with such liberality that he became known as 'Mr Nyet'. After serving four years as deputy foreign minister from 1953, he became foreign minister in 1957. He supported Soviet intervention in Czechoslovakia in 1968 and probably helped frame the Brezhnev doctrine. As Brezhnev's health deteriorated in the 1970s foreign policy formulation appears to have passed more into his hands, strengthened by his becoming a full member of the Politburo in 1973. While in favour of *détente*, his interpretation of the process was narrow. Against the advice of several leading academics, he supported the invasion of Afghanistan in December 1979 and thus bore a large degree of responsibility for the ensuing disaster. The guiding principle of his stewardship of Soviet foreign affairs was the relationship with the United States. All other countries were regarded as no more than bit players in this central drama.

Shevardnadze proved himself an able and personable diplomat and an effective agent of the new political thinking. His appointment reflected Gorbachev's intention to modernise and de-ideologise Soviet diplomacy. His relative inexperience in foreign affairs allowed Gorbachev to take a prominent role in foreign policy management. Even after Shevardnadze had grown in the job, foreign policy was very much managed as a team but dominated by Gorbachev personally. At the conference of the Ministry of Foreign Affairs (MFA) in July 1988 Shevardnadze, like Yakovlev, called for a radical rethinking of Soviet foreign policy, urged that policy be developed on the basis of common sense rather than dogma and insisted that in relations with other countries 'general human values' were 'more important than class interests' (*Mezhdunarodnaya zhizn'*, 9/1988).

The institutions managing foreign policy were restructured to help achieve the goals of the new thinking. Until September 1988 the Central Committee Secretariat had departments covering the main foreign policy fields: the International Department dealing with East–West relations, and a Department for Liaison with Communist and Workers' Parties of Socialist Countries. Together they constituted the nerve centre of decision-making. Gorbachev placed diplomats acquainted with the West in key positions at home. The head of the International Department between 1955 and 1986, exceeding Gromyko's tenure as foreign minister, was Boris Ponamarëv. He was replaced by Anatolii Dobrynin, the Soviet ambassador to Washington since shortly before the Cuban missile crisis who had remained to serve under six US presidents and five Soviet leaders. He was well acquainted with Western thinking and in a position to revitalise the department. Aleksandr Yakovlev, who spent ten years as ambassador to Canada and then headed IMEMO (the Institute of World Economy and International Relations), became a full member of the Politburo and head of the Secretariat's propaganda department, taking a major interest in international affairs. The department handling relations with the socialist world was headed by Vadim Medvedev.

In line with the 19th party conference call for the separation of party and state, in September 1988 the CC Secretariat was reorganised into six commissions (see page 172). Aleksandr Yakovlev's appointment as head of the new International Policy Commission was not a challenge to Shevardnadze's position as the manager of current Soviet foreign policy since his brief was to nurse relations with ruling and non-ruling Communist parties as well as to develop a long-range perspective for Soviet foreign policy. He took over the functions of Medvedev, who moved to head the new ideology commission, and of Dobrynin at the head of the old International Department, who was removed from the Secretariat. The removal of Gromyko from the presidency completed the process of distancing him from the management of foreign affairs. The dualism in Soviet foreign policy between traditional diplomatic methods and party relations, a legacy of Comintern and Cominform, was decisively shifted in favour of the former, with the new stress being placed on state-to-state relations. The domestic emphasis on raising the prestige of state bodies was thus reflected in foreign affairs.

The new sophistication of Soviet foreign policy and the stress on traditional diplomacy was borne out in the reorganisation of the MFA. Under Gromyko's stewardship the MFA had grown in stature and played a larger role in policy formulation, and the changes under Gorbachev only confirmed the process. The appointment of Gennadi Gerasimov as a spokesperson for the ministry reflected the desire for *glasnost*. The deputy foreign minister Yulii Vorontsov took on a Kissinger-like role with shuttle diplomacy in the Gulf and elsewhere.

Specialist bodies such as IMEMO and the USA and Canada Institute, long headed by Georgii Arbatov, were increasingly important sources of specialised information and advice to the leadership. The move away from the old obsession with US–Soviet relations was reflected in the creation of a new Institute of European Affairs under the USSR Academy of Sciences. The institute symbolised the decline of the old two-camp mentality by studying both Eastern and Western Europe. These institutes played a critical role in generating the ideas that fuelled the new thinking, and their lively debates reflected the greater autonomy of academic life from the needs of the power system.

While the voice of the academics, professional diplomats and civilian defence analysts has risen, the influence of the KGB and the military on formulating policy has waned. Following Marshal Ustinov's death in December 1984 his successor as Minister of Defence (nominated by Chernenko) Marshal Sergei Sokolov, a man in his seventies, obtained only consultative (non-voting) status on the Politburo. The flight of Matthias Rust to Red Square in summer 1987 permitted Gorbachev to change key figures in the military, including the replacement of Sokolov by General Dmitrii Yazov. The clear aim of Gorbachev's personnel changes was to reassert the fundamental principle of civilian rule over the military which had weakened under Brezhnev. Sokolov and Yazov were pointedly not given voting seats on the Politburo, which had become usual since 1973 when Grechko, and then from 1976 Ustinov, a man with a long career in defence industries and thus not a career soldier, had joined. The lower prestige of the military was reflected in the fact that while Yazov remained only a candidate member of the Politburo, Kryuchkov, head of the KGB, was made a full voting member, missing the candidate stage, in September 1989. Military power remained a high priority under Gorbachev, but he began the arduous task of reducing the burden.

The new thinking entailed a revolution in military doctrine. In a speech in Tula in 1977 Brezhnev had modified the Soviet view on the possibility of a limited nuclear war and moved towards the standard Western view that a nuclear engagement would lead to Mutually Assured Destruction (MAD). The military were not convinced, and it took the full power of Gorbachev's leadership to change military doctrine. The new doctrine was 'non-offensive defence' which moved away from the old Soviet forward, offensive strategy, forged in memories of the Second World War and NATO encirclement and Western nuclear superiority in the first post-war years. From the 1970s the modern exponent of forward defence, which envisaged a massive Soviet *blitzkrieg* before NATO could decide to use nuclear weapons, was the then Chief of General Staff Nikolai Ogarkov, whose retirement opened the way for a changed posture and thus to improved relations with China and the West. An important confidence-building measure was the new Soviet openness in military matters and the promise to reveal its true defence budget, a tacit admission that the published figure of R20.2 billion was meaningless (see below). The idea of 'necessary sufficiency' promised a reduction in forces to a level where they could implement a defensive strategy only.

Perestroika's emphasis on transferring resources from defence to the modernisation of the civilian economy was accompanied by the decline of military influence on policy formation and by increasingly sharp criticisms of the military. The final act of the personnel changes of September–October 1988 was the retirement of Ogarkov from his post as Commander-in-Chief of the Western Theatre of War, in command of all forces ranged against NATO on the European front. Ogarkov had been remarkably successful in seeing his views implemented. He had masterminded the deployment of SS–20 missiles from the late 1970s, a highly provocative act which triggered the counter-deployment by NATO of cruise and Pershing–2 missiles and fuelled the second cold war. Leading reformers under Gorbachev criticised the move as both unnecessary and inflammatory and Gromyko later admitted that

Brezhnev had not fully realised the implications of deploying the missiles. Ogarkov had been granted the great increases in military spending he had demanded to prepare for large-scale non-nuclear offensive war against NATO. His position clearly became uncomfortable with Gorbachev's insistence on the adoption of defensive war plans and his willingness to discuss deep cuts in conventional forces. The retirement of this hawkish military figure, who had presented the convoluted Soviet justifications for shooting down the Korean Airlines flight 007 in September 1983, removed yet another legacy of the Brezhnev–Andropov period of foreign and defence policy.

Gorbachev's overriding aim was to free both economic and foreign policy from the burdens imposed by the arms race. The nuclear threat meant, in the words of Georgii Shakhnazarov, a key adviser to Gorbachev, that 'the struggle for survival is more important than the struggle for class, national or any other interests' (*K*, 3/1989: 69). This understanding, together with the decline in the old optimism that history was working in the Soviet Union's favour, led to a shift away from the view that peace could be assured only by the advance of socialism and that, on the contrary, peace was a condition of socialist development. The new emphasis was on 'necessary military sufficiency' rather than an open-ended commitment to military expenditure. The new thinking, and in particular the idea of 'reasonable sufficiency', opened the door to fruitful talks since the Soviets now accepted the possibility of deep, and not necessarily symmetrical, cuts in weaponry and the need for extensive verification.

Gorbachev's speech at the United Nations on 7 December 1988 promised unilateral cuts in conventional forces of 500,000 men, some 10 per cent of the Soviet army, and the withdrawal of some 50,000 men and offensive weapons from Eastern Europe. As Khrushchev realised, strategic offensive weapons are relatively cost-efficient, accounting for only some 10 per cent of the Soviet military budget. The big economic benefits are achieved by cuts in conventional forces, not only in financial terms, which given an official budget deficit in 1988 of some R135 billion was not negligible, but by the release of labour power. The resentment aroused by Khrushchev's demobilisation of 1.2 million men in the late 1950s was one factor leading to his overthrow in 1964. Military misgivings at Gorbachev's cuts, which included the retirement of many career officers, may well have been reflected by the retirement of Marshal Sergei Akhromeev, Chief of the General Staff, on the day of Gorbachev's UN speech and his replacement by the 49-year-old Mikhail Moiseev, the representative of a new generation.

There was a continuing dialectic between economic reform and military commitments. The achievement of the Soviet Union's global status had come at huge financial and political costs. Shevardnadze talked in terms of what can be called *khozraschët* in the international sphere, to make foreign policy more cost-effective by avoiding wasteful expenditure on defence and excessive foreign commitments (*P*, 5 July 1990). Quality was to take the place of quantity both in terms of personnel and equipment. The military budget was cut and the process of defence conversion, whereby parts of the defence industry and some of its administrative capacity are redirected to supply the consumer market, was accelerated. Debate began about even more radical cuts in armed forces of up to 50 per cent and ending conscription by the creation of a professional army on British lines. The idea of the creation of a network of territorial militias reflected the traditional Marxist distaste for standing armies, buttressed by revulsion at Stalin's militarism and his legacy of 'barracks socialism'.

In 1989 full statistics on defence spending were for the first time provided to the Congress. Gorbachev revealed that the Soviet Union had allocated R77.3 billion for defence, some R32.6 billion of which was for weapons procurement (*Ind.*, 31 May 1989). In his report on 7 June 1989 Ryzhkov outlined plans to cut defence spending by half by 1995. Defence spending was announced to be running at 15 per cent of the budget, more than double the American rate. Controversy over Soviet defence spending as a proportion of GNP, however, continued, with the 1988 CIA estimate of 15–17 per cent now being dismissed by Soviet estimates as being too *low*. The figure depends on the size of Soviet GNP, which the economist Viktor Belkin claimed to be only 28 per cent of the United States level rather than the accepted 50 per cent. On the basis of this Bogomolov estimated defence spending to be some 20 to 25 per cent of GNP (*Ind.*, 25 April 1990). The defence budget in 1989, unchanged from 1988, was for R20.2 billion, but this, as Gostev admitted, only covered the upkeep of personnel. The true figure would have to include weapons research and procurement. The 1990 budget presented by the new finance minister Valentin Pavlov on 25 October 1989 implemented a cut in defence spending of 8.3 per cent, with spending down from R77.3 billion in 1989 to R70.9 billion in 1990. This was the first step to an overall cut in military expenditure of 14 per cent by 1991 announced at the 1st Congress. The costs of maintaining the army and the navy were planned to fall from R20.2 billion in 1989 to R19 billion in 1990, spending on military research and development in 1990 by R2.2 billion and spending on military construction by 15 per cent (*SN*, 1989: 331).

The size of the army was reduced by half a million to 4.5 million in 1989, in keeping with Gorbachev's promises at the United Nations. Shevardnadze revealed that the war in Afghanistan had cost the USSR

R60 billion, some R8 billion for every year of the war (*P*, 5 July 1990). The popular Press increasingly called for the conversion of the conscript army into a professional force about half its present size. The military became the butt of unprecedented criticism and from all accounts the morale of the officer corps sank. An article in March 1989 denounced its excessive secrecy, the overblown powers of the ministry of defence, which claimed that its interests were the same as those of 'the entire people', and the privileged resources of defence industry plants, and called for a professional army and the ending of conscription (Albert Plutnik, *Iz.*, 20 March 1989). The Supreme Soviet in summer 1989 exempted advanced students from conscription, which at a stroke deprived the army of 175,000 of its brightest recruits. Liberal officers even went to the extent of establishing an informal trade union, *Shchit* (see page 216).

The intervention of the army in Soviet domestic politics is possible but unlikely. Traditionally, the party kept tight control over the military and the system of political commissars remained in place. Gorbachev moreover assiduously appointed those whom he considered trustworthy, including Yazov himself and Moiseev as Chief of the General Staff. Gorbachev remained head of the Defence Council, the supreme military body. Rumours, however, suggested growing military dissatisfaction with Gorbachev's policies. On 25 February 1990, the day of the large demonstrations in Moscow and elsewhere, units were allegedly armed in Moscow's suburbs. The key point is that on a number of issues – the future of East Germany and the fate of the Warsaw Pact, the CFE talks in Vienna and the handling of the Baltic crisis – sections of the military were dissatisfied with what they considered was Gorbachev's capitulation to the West and to domestic democratic forces. Gorbachev could not ignore the discontent among his high command. Nevertheless, if there was to be a coup, it was less likely to come from the remnants of the Brezhnev-era generals than from conservative, patriotic and disaffected colonels.

Arms control initiatives, including a moratorium on nuclear testing from 1985, were matched by a series of concrete proposals which were no longer directed mainly at Western public opinion but rather to policy-makers. In the United States Reagan's fading presidency was prepared to enter into a series of arms reduction agreements. The meeting between Reagan and Gorbachev in Geneva in October 1985 was the first summit for nearly a decade. At the Reykjavik summit the complete elimination of nuclear weapons was discussed. An INF treaty actually eliminating categories of nuclear weapons was signed at the Washington summit in December 1987. The arms control process continued towards a START (Strategic Arms Reduction Talks) treaty at the Moscow summit of May 1988. The START negotiations face formidable obstacles because of the complexity of the issues involved and the balance to be drawn between nuclear and conventional forces. Negotiations over reductions in conventional forces continue towards a Conventional Forces in Europe (CFE) treaty.

A major concern of Soviet foreign policy was the relationship with the United States. The bipolar structure of international relations was legitimised at Yalta in 1945, but by the 1980s had been undermined. The emergence of regional powers such as China and Japan, the integration of Western Europe and the strivings for independence in Eastern Europe all challenged the post-war 'realist' order in which the ideological struggle between capitalism and socialism was focused on the rivalry between the two pre-eminent states of each camp, the United States and the USSR. Already in February 1985, in a speech during the Supreme Soviet election, Gorbachev called for a less obsessional relationship with the United States and a new approach to relations with Europe and Japan (Tatu, 1987: 108), policies that had begun under Andropov. The process was helped by the removal of Gromyko, the main proponent of the bipolar view. By the early 1990s the dissolution of the blocs could be contemplated as a result of the East European revolutions and the unification of Germany.

The *détente* of the 1970s focused on superpower relations, whereas the 'new realism' policies pursued by Gorbachev took a larger global view with greater sensitivity to the views of smaller states. The reasons for the failure of the original *détente* of the 1970s need not detain us, but it is worth noting that differing perceptions and different expectations of what each side would obtain from the process lay at the root of its failure. The new thinking suggested that the USSR had had exaggerated hopes of the economic and technological benefits that it could obtain from the process. Moreover, at the basis of *détente* was the idea of a controlled buildup in arms, whereas Gorbachev tried to establish a dynamic for 'build down'.

Improved relations with Western Europe were pursued within the framework of the 'common European home', an idea borrowed from Brezhnev but appropriately first raised by Gorbachev in Paris in 1985. De Gaulle's idea of a Europe 'from the Atlantic to the Urals' was given content by talk of common problems facing the environment, the development of integrated power and communications systems, greater freedom of information and improved economic links (Stent, 1989). At the 27th congress Gorbachev called for an 'end to the schism of Europe', and on 10 April 1987 in Czechoslovakia he stated:

> We are firmly opposed to the division of the continent into military blocs facing each other, against the accumulation of military arsenals in Europe, against

everything that is the source of the threat of war. In the spirit of the new thinking we advanced the idea of the 'common European home'...[with] the recognition of a certain integral whole, although the states in question belong to different social systems and are members of opposing military–political blocs ranged against each other. (*SN*, 1987: 129)

West European economic integration towards 1992 raised the prospect of yet another profound division on the Continent, this time imposed not by arms but by economics. To avoid this, in June 1988 Comecon signed a first agreement with the EC, and individual East European countries led by Hungary moved towards establishing associate status with the EC. The idea of the common European home opened the door to the overcoming of the blocs and the division of Europe. Above all, it made possible much greater East European initiative both domestically and in their relations with Western Europe.

Gorbachev was committed to the preservation of the post-war frontiers of Europe, but with far more open and friendly contacts between nations. It was in Europe that the 'de-ideologisation' of foreign policy moved the furthest. The Federal Republic of Germany consolidated its economic links with Eastern Europe and hoped to expand its derisory trade with the USSR, which in 1988 accounted for only 1.5 per cent of its exports and 1.8 per cent of its imports, mainly natural gas and oil. The Soviet lack of hard currency and absence of quality products to sell inhibited trade with the West. However, the FRG in the person of its foreign minister Hans-Dietrich Genscher was the most critical of NATO's plans for nuclear modernisation of short-range Lance missiles, which would fill the alleged gap created by the abolition of intermediate-range missiles, and was most receptive to the new ideas from Moscow.

The notion of a world Communist movement barely survives. The Yugoslav, Chinese and Italian parties have been particularly sensitive about any attempts by Moscow to reassert its 'leading role' in the international Communist movement. As noted, the Soviet Union now relies more on traditional forms of diplomacy and state-to-state relations and less on party-to-party diplomacy which, according to Gorbachev, 'sometimes sugar-coated the truth or, worse still, dealt in Aesopian fables' (1987a: 155). The new emphasis on state relations helped allay fears of revived 'hegemonism' and promoted more equal relations between sovereign Communist states. The new thinking conceded that the attempt to use ideology as a cohesive force in relations between Communist states was counter-productive. This proposition had been argued by the Chinese at least since their return to Communist international relations in 1980 (Timmermann, 1987: 59). Politics took the place of ideology in relations between Communist states.

The new thinking to all intents and purposes accepted that the world Communist movement was irremediably fractured by ideological and political differences to such a degree that the very term 'movement' was no longer applicable. Just as the Soviet Union itself defined socialism to suit its own state interests, so other countries, as soon as circumstances permitted, followed suit. Yugoslavia, China and most East European countries continued the Soviet tradition of conflating socialism with national interests. Gorbachev came to terms with this and accepted that 'unity in diversity', as he put it at the 27th party congress (*P*, 26 February 1986) – a term borrowed from Togliatti – was the best that could be salvaged from the debris of the world Communist movement (Timmermann, 1987). Soviet plans for a fourth world conference of the Communist movement, following on from those of 1957, 1960 and 1969, first mooted under Brezhnev in 1981, were not renewed by Gorbachev. Rather than building cohesion these conferences only highlighted the divisions in the so-called socialist camp. Brezhnev made up for their absence by meeting with socialist leaders while holidaying in the Crimea, and Gorbachev maintained links by a series of personal visits to almost all the socialist countries. Gorbachev's acceptance that there are many ways of building socialism (*P*, 3 November 1987) vindicated earlier arguments in favour of polycentrism by denying the possibility of a leading centre in the world Communist movement.

The problems associated with implementing such ideas were immediately apparent in Soviet relations with Eastern Europe. The legacy of nearly fifty years of Soviet domination and occasional resort to brute force engendered a tradition of bitterness and hostility. Both the legitimacy of the Soviet presence and the system that it to a greater or lesser degree imposed were fragile. Soviet political and economic stagnation spilled over to Eastern Europe in possibly an even more accentuated form than at home. Decommunisation in Eastern Europe could not but lead to desovietisation. Gorbachev was forced to redress past inequalities in the relationship and to find a new basis to relate to the individual needs of each country.

On a practical level a whole range of initiatives was launched ranging from the promotion of technological modernisation, improvements in product quality (especially for goods destined for the Soviet market), and encouragement of Soviet-style political reforms. A major question facing the NPT was whether the de-ideologisation of international relations, which it advocated in East–West relations and international affairs as a whole, applied to Soviet relations with Eastern Europe. Since the death of Stalin Soviet relations with the area were based on a complex mix of security and ideological considerations, the one being seen as buttressing the other. The NPT and such notions as a 'common

European home' decoupled security from ideology. During his visit to the Ukraine in February 1989 Gorbachev stated that Moscow was now 'not only in theory but also in practice rethinking its relations with socialist countries'. The new approach was based on 'unconditional independence, full equal rights, strict non-interference in others' internal affairs', and the righting of earlier wrongs (SN, 1989: 72). 'Freedom of choice' for socialist countries meant that the Soviet model of development and politics was no longer regarded as the only acceptable one for the region and instead, as Gorbachev informed Miklos Nemeth, 'each ruling Communist Party fulfils its tasks in accordance with its historical conditions and national values, and works out its policies independently' (SN, 1989: 73). Liberal Soviet academics went so far as to suggest that the export of the Stalinist 'command administrative' model itself provoked the cold war and promoted decades of instability and economic stagnation in the region (MN, 35/1988: 6–7).

The acceptance of diversity in the world Communist movement meant that Gorbachev did not force the pace of change on Eastern Europe. Whereas Khrushchev initially was keen to export destalinisation, Gorbachev was noticeably reluctant to export democratisation. As he put it in Czechoslovakia in April 1987, 'We are far from intending to call on anyone to imitate us' (SN, 1987: 127). This disappointed advocates of radical reform who hoped that he would throw the whole weight of his authority to impose change on stubborn neo-Stalinists, but Gorbachev added the rider that 'We do not hide our conviction that the process of reconstruction undertaken in the Soviet Union corresponds to the essence of socialism.' In Czechoslovakia the principle of non-interference meant that the USSR could not officially revise its view of 1968 until the Czechoslovak leadership itself did so. The diplomatic discretion of the Soviet leadership, however, did not prevent reformist sections of the revived Soviet media from going further and re-examining the events of 1968 or urging peace with Solidarity in Poland.

The new model of relations between socialist countries developed under the rubric of 'unity in diversity'. For many years 'proletarian internationalism' in Communist relations was the counterpart of democratic centralism in domestic affairs, and as the first disappeared so the second was weakened. However, there were obstacles in the evolution of Eastern Europe from a 'buffer zone' to Finlandisation. The concept of 'historic choice' was used in the middle period of *perestroika* to suggest that once embarked on the socialist path of development, a country cannot turn back, though the indigenous party can redefine socialism. At the Polish party congress in June 1986 Gorbachev declared, 'To threaten the socialist system, to try to undermine it from the outside and wrench a country away from the socialist community means to encroach not only on the will of the people, but also on the entire post-war arrangement, and, in the last analysis, on peace' (*SN*, 1986: 455). However, by 1989 the unlinking of security and ideology had advanced so far as to allow each nation to redefine its destiny to combine political freedom, economic efficiency, social justice and ecological security. The language of proletarian internationalism gave way to a new concept of socialist sovereignty which rejected the limits imposed by the Brezhnev doctrine. The new internationalism was no longer based on the priority of transnational class values but on equal relations between sovereign states.

In the wake of the Czechoslovak revolution of November 1989 the Soviet Union unequivocally denounced the leadership since 1968 and welcomed 'The first step. . .in dismantling the Stalinist system which has existed untouched for many years' (*P*, 27 November 1989). As the regime established by the Soviet tanks in 1968 crumbled, Supreme Soviet deputies began to insist on the truth being told about one of the last blank pages unexposed by *glasnost*. *Pravda* under its new editor, Frolov, indeed welcomed the popular revolution and suggested a new history of 1968 (*P*, 27 November 1989). The silence that continued to be maintained over the Soviet leadership's role in reimposing the Stalinist system was finally broken when in December 1989 the Warsaw Pact meeting, at which Gorbachev briefed his allies on the Malta summit, unequivocally denounced its suppression of the Prague Spring, and the Supreme Soviet in December 1989 followed suit.

Fear of the spillover effect from democratisation in Eastern Europe was one of the major factors that prompted the termination of reform in Czechoslovakia in 1968 and Poland in 1981. The spillover effect of Gorbachev's policies to Eastern Europe was an ironic reversal of earlier expectations. In turn, the demise of Communism in Eastern Europe then fed back into Soviet politics. Even if Gorbachev were to be removed there was little likelihood that the Soviet Union could reimpose its authority in its former 'buffer states'. The 1989 revolutions in Eastern Europe, and Gorbachev's benign acceptance of the changes, meant an irreversible shift that no combination of forces in the USSR could change. A coalition of the conservative old guard, the party apparatus, the KGB and the military could combine to try to halt the reforms in the USSR, but their levers of influence over Eastern Europe have been broken forever. Short of fighting a war on all fronts, there is little that they could do.

Perestroika led to changes in the CMEA (see page 282f.) focusing on the development of economic co-operation between member countries, improving its own organisation and working out strategic perspectives for long-term co-operation. From the outset Gorbachev made clear his belief that the deterioration in economic performance affected all members of Comecon to a greater or lesser degree, and that solutions therefore would have to be sought throughout the alliance. Economic reform in these countries was no longer restrained by Moscow but actively encouraged to provide a more dynamic economic base to the whole alliance. The USSR under Brezhnev had to fund not only its own neo-Stalinist deal but also those in Eastern Europe, partially financed by the acceptance of shoddy goods from the area. The change in domestic economic policies and the rejection of the old corporatism forced a re-evaluation of the old patterns of economic relations. The aim of economic integration in the form espoused by Khrushchev was shelved, but the development of economic integration to promote scientific and technological modernisation remained. Joint enterprises between Soviet and East European companies were launched to share technological expertise, marketing and resources, but the distinctive interests of each country were no longer sacrificed in pursuit of alleged common goals (Light, 1988: 306–7). However, barriers to intra-bloc trade were erected as countries tried to prevent the export of scarce goods. The debt burden of these countries and the widespread shortages led some commentators to talk of the 'Africanisation' of Eastern Europe.

Shevardnadze emerged as the great proponent of cost-effectiveness in Soviet interstate relations, and in particular with bloc partners. He warned that 'It is in no way necessary to proceed from the fact that relations with friends must be of a loss-producing nature' (cited by Svec, 1988: 991). The Soviet Union was no longer willing to bail out uncompetitive economies, allies or not. Yet another of the paradoxes of *perestroika* in this respect was that Soviet attempts to make its allies economically viable encouraged them on to paths away from Moscow, and indeed, away from Communist rule altogether.

As the East European countries achieved independence after their revolutions in 1989, the traditional pattern of economic relations with the Soviet Union changed dramatically. Poland led the way in late 1989 with its insistence that trade should be conducted on the basis of hard currency rather than the transferable ruble, a notional currency used to conduct trade. From 1991 Soviet–Hungarian trade was to be conducted purely in hard currency. Trade within the CMEA moved away from the old cumbersome government to government procedures to more flexible enterprise links and a greater responsiveness to the laws of supply and demand. In other words, an organic form of the international division of labour began to assert itself. The freedom for manoeuvre for Eastern Europe, however, was limited by its dependence on Soviet oil and gas. With fewer natural resources than the USSR, these countries were always part of a larger economic interdependency with Europe as a whole. These economic links were ruptured by Stalin, and only now were they gradually restored.

The Warsaw Treaty Organisation (WTO, or Warsaw Pact) was always more than a military alliance; it was also used as an instrument of political integration. Warsaw Pact summits provided opportunities for the co-ordination of policies. Gorbachev allowed the countries greater latitude in developing their own foreign policies and relations with the West. The sovereignty and political equality of member states was stressed and the Warsaw Pact no longer spoke with one voice.

Détente in Europe and the improvement in superpower relations allowed a degree of demilitarisation. Gorbachev's UN speech of 7 December 1988 announced the removal of six Soviet divisions numbering some 50,000 troops and 5,000 tanks from Eastern Europe. Two of the five Soviet divisions in Czechoslovakia, one division with some 15,000 of the 60,000 Soviet troops in Hungary, and three of the nineteen divisions in the GDR were to go. In addition, East Germany, Poland and Hungary sought to relieve the onerous burden of defence spending by announcing cuts in military expenditure and armed forces. The devaluation of the military element had proceeded so far that by early May 1989 Shevardnadze could state that he could imagine no occasion in which Soviet troops might intervene in a Warsaw Pact country (*Ob.*, 21 May 1989). Demilitarisation affected not only international relations but Communist politics as a whole. As 'barracks socialism' gave way to democratisation not only was the military influence on society reduced, but party influence in national armies also waned.

While Moscow maintained a benevolent neutrality during the Eastern European revolutions of 1989, insisting that the internal affairs of each country were its own business, it did insist that each country should respect its treaty obligations. Above all, this meant continued allegiance to the Warsaw Pact. This leaders like Mazowiecki were willing to do, especially when faced with the prospect of a united Germany. The Warsaw Pact thus became transformed from a military alliance, though its effectiveness in this respect had long been doubted, into a political–military alliance guaranteeing mutual security and the post-war borders. At the same time, post-Communist East European countries began to negotiate the removal of all Soviet troops from their territories. Czechoslovakia led the way, and all 72,000 Soviet troops were to leave by the end of 1991. In Hungary also troops began to leave in 1990. However, even if the two major alliance systems, NATO and the Warsaw Pact, were to be negotiated away, it appeared that something like the Warsaw Pact or a pan-European security system would have to be re-created, this time not directed against an ideological foe but for the mutual security of all European states, large and small.

An increasingly important aspect of post-cold war politics was the role played by the Conference on Security and Cooperation in Europe (CSCE). The Helsinki process imbued European international relations with a new dynamic, and elevated the status and effectiveness of the diplomacy of the smaller nations. It also provided a forum for the definition and monitoring of a developing standard of civilisation in international affairs. The Vienna agreements of January 1989 established a rolling series of conferences, including the one to be devoted to human rights in Moscow in 1991, to culminate in a full review conference in Helsinki in 1992. By request of the USSR the conference was brought forward to meet in Paris in October 1990. It was to act as the peace treaty that never took place at the end of the Second World War and to help manage the changes in Europe.

Sino-Soviet relations in the 1980s improved steadily as both countries launched ambitious reform programmes. In a speech in Tashkent on 24 March 1982 Brezhnev noted the 'enormous' potential for Sino-Soviet relations (*P*, 25 March 1982). The Chinese responded with the 'three obstacles': large Soviet forces on their 4,500-mile common border; Soviet forces in Afghanistan; and Vietnamese forces in Cambodia. Andropov and Chernenko both made conciliatory gestures, but it was only under Gorbachev that relations improved as one by one the 'three obstacles' were removed. The Soviet Union completed its withdrawal from Afghanistan by 15 February 1989, it announced the removal of some 200,000 troops from Mongolia and Central Asia, and Vietnam withdrew from Cambodia in 1989. Already in 1986 in Vladivostok Gorbachev had accepted the *thalweg* (main current) principle for the demarcation of the Sino-Soviet river border. The year 1988 saw not only the end of the cold war in the West but also the end of hostility in Sino-Soviet relations, which helped pave the way for Gorbachev's visit to China in May 1989. Against the background of the challenge to Deng Xiaoping's authority by the occupation of Tiananmen square, Gorbachev called for the total demilitarisation of a border where clashes in 1969 had nearly led to war. Despite the suppression of the democracy movement Sino-Soviet relations remained on a good neighbourly basis, demonstrating the decline in the divisive role of ideology.

The shift from party to state lines of diplomacy had earlier taken the ideological edge off differences and fostered the practical development of economic contacts. By 1989 the USSR had become China's fifth largest trading partner, rising from $363 million in 1983 to $2.6 billion in 1986 (Zagoria, 1989: 122), with a rapid growth in cross-border trade. The two countries found many points of mutual interest as part of their economic modernisation programmes, and their economies are more compatible, especially through the widespread use of barter, than with the NICs of the region. It was in the interests of neither side to return to the 1950s type of relationship. Sino-Soviet *rapprochement* reduced the scope of manoeuvre by their allies in East Asia, above all Vietnam and North Korea, which were no longer able to play one off against the other.

Improved relations with China were only one part of a broader interest in the Pacific region. Gorbachev made it clear in his 'Vladivostok initiative' of 28 July 1986 that the Soviet Union regarded itself as 'an Asian and Pacific country'. He insisted that 'the situation in the Far East, in Asia as a whole and in the ocean expanses washing it, where we are permanent inhabitants and seafarers of long standing, is to us a matter of national, state interest' (SN, 1986: 337–43). The speech vividly demonstrated the link between domestic restructuring and international relations. Reminiscent of Peter the Great's comment on Petrograd regarding the West, Gorbachev described Vladivostok as 'our wide open window on the East'. Gorbachev was well aware of the shift of economic and political power from the east to the west coast of the United States, and from the Atlantic to the Pacific Basin. The Pacific Rim is made up of thirty-four countries and twenty-three island states containing more than half the world's population. It possesses 21 per cent of the world's oil resources, 63 per cent of the wool, 67 per cent of its cotton, 87 per cent of its natural rubber and 94 per cent of its natural silk, while the growing number of NICs is transforming the area into a manufacturing centre to rival Europe and north-east America.

The Soviet strategy in the region was to restore political and economic relations with China, to establish a presence by consolidating ties with the newly independent countries of the south Pacific, to decrease military activity in the region, and to promote international trade to allow the transfer of the technology and economic power of the leading Asian capitalist countries to assist Soviet economic development. The USSR now paid court to ASEAN, once denounced as an 'imperialist' force, and is establishing a dialogue with its members. In short, the Soviet Union tried to increase its presence in the region, but by effective diplomacy rather than by threats and sanctions. Rather than retreating into a 'socialist isolationism', Gorbachev broadened the scope of Soviet global diplomacy.

Gorbachev called for a Helsinki-style conference on Pacific economic co-operation, perhaps in Hiroshima, the designation of the southern part of the Pacific as a nuclear-free zone and the establishment of nuclear-free zones in Korea and South-East Asia as well. By 1990 earlier Soviet offers to dismantle its naval base in Cam Rhan Bay in Vietnam in exchange for American withdrawal from the Clark air force base and the Subic Bay naval base in the Philippines were replaced by unilateral Soviet withdrawal.

The new Pacific policy was reflected in an upgrading of the study of the region. The Far East Science Centre in Vladivostok became a full Division of the USSR Academy of Sciences, and a new Soviet National Committee for Asian-Pacific Co-operation sought to promote regional co-operation. Economic ties were discreetly developed with Taiwan and South Korea, and vigorously pursued with Japan. The latter's involvement in the proposed Chinese-type special economic zones in the Maritime and Khabarovsk territories was considered crucial.

In the Pacific-Asia region the new Soviet approach, as elsewhere, faced a legacy of distrust and hostility. Bipolarity was never dominant in the Pacific, given the economic power of Japan and China's balancing role, yet both superpowers saw the area as yet another arena to fight out the cold war. Of all the developed countries Japan was the least impressed by the Gorbachev reform process and the new thinking. The stumbling-block of the four southern Kurile Islands (called the Northern Territories by Japan), occupied by the Soviet Union since the end of the Second World War, appears to be insurmountable. For the Japanese the issue is one of vital principle, whereas for the Soviet Union the transfer of territory would open the door to a whole range of irredentist demands. One side or the other would have to pay a high political price to gain the economic benefits of improved bilateral trade. Gorbachev's 'charm offensive' failed to find grace in Tokyo.

The problems of the Pacific are not restricted to the international sphere but encompass the legacy of Moscow's own relations with Siberia. Magadan, Kolyma and Sakhalin are still littered with the bones of Stalin's labour camp victims, and the secrecy and closed nature of the region is only slowly thawing. Vladivostok has been declared an open city. The area has its share of blank pages, such as the deportation of the Soviet Koreans to Central Asia, the expulsion of the Chinese minority and the fate of religious minorities. Soviet efforts are greatly hampered by the abysmal level of economic development achieved by its own Far Eastern territories. Gorbachev insisted that they achieve at least self-sufficiency in food. These regions do not stand as a shining example to the rest of the Pacific world. The impermeability of the region is one reason for Japan's disillusionment with trade with northern Asia.

One result of the NPT was to marginalise Third World revolutions. The new thinking stressed that revolutions are not essential for economic development but that, on the contrary, economic development is the basis for social revolution. In this way the Soviet Union's own experience was no longer projected on to the rest of the world. In sharp contrast to Khrushchev, Gorbachev was neither a populist at home nor a romantic revolutionary abroad. He understood that socialist expansionism brought not economic advantages but military and economic burdens and strained the credibility of the Soviet government both at home and abroad. It became clear to the Gorbachev leadership that Soviet activism in the Third World had damaged other foreign policy goals, above all relations with the United States. To balance this, Gorbachev's thought was imbued with anger at the sufferings of the Third World and he rejected the idea that national liberation movements were declining (*SN*, 1987: 403).

The 1986 party programme barely mentioned the Third World, and then only in the context of East–West relations. The Third World merited only two paragraphs, compared with thirty-eight at the 26th congress in 1981, in Gorbachev's political report to the 27th congress (Jukes, 1987: 190). In the past the Soviet Union refused responsibility for developing the Third World, arguing that developmental problems were the legacy of colonialism and should be remedied by the imperialist powers. The USSR under Gorbachev continued its financial commitments to Third World members of the CMEA (Cuba, Vietnam and Mongolia) and to a lesser extent with the states of a 'socialist orientation' like Angola, Mozambique, Ethiopia, South Yemen, Cambodia, Laos and Nicaragua. However, the USSR's trading links with non-CMEA states grew faster than with the CMEA states. Further, the Soviet Union actually encouraged its allies to diversify their links towards greater co-operation with capitalist states (Cassen (ed.), 1985: 245). Not only did the economic terms of trade move against the Third World, but also the political balance since the new diplomacy weakened the bargaining position of the South in playing East against West.

The reappraisal of relations with the Third World had begun under Brezhnev (Valkenier, 1983; Fukuyama, 1986; Hough, 1986). The basic point had been that in a world threatened by nuclear catastrophe and ecological disaster the survival of humanity must take precedence over revolutionary change in the Third World and elsewhere. Moreover, a strong sense of disillusion with the slow rate of economic and political progress of LDCs pursuing a socialist-orientated path was evident in Soviet thinking from at least the mid-1970s. This applied equally to the economic prospects of socialist-orientated states, where the emphasis was now on economic development, and the political reform of vanguard parties who were urged to seek broader bases of national legitimacy. In short, the new thinking urged LDCs to think less of revolution or socialism and more of development and some form of democracy.

In a sense this is a return to the old socioeconomic determinism of Marx, who highly valued the economic progress brought by capitalism, albeit imported in the holds of gunships, and a downgrading of theories of imperialism (i.e. Leninism) which suggested that countries were forced into making a leap into socialism however underdeveloped their social, economic or political infrastructure. Such views ultimately affect thinking on the Soviet Union's own leap on to the socialist path in 1917.

This is not to suggest that the new thinking abandoned the LDCs altogether to the tender mercies of capitalist development. Gorbachev's speeches have been imbued with a passionate advocacy for a solution to the problems of the Third World and debt entrapment. 'Disarmament for development' concerned not only the USSR itself but also the hope that resources wasted on arms could be better spent assisting LDC development, as put forward in the CSIS at the 27th congress. The USSR itself now accepted that it bore a responsibility, as a developed industrial nation, for the rest of the world. The first fruits of this reappraisal were already in evidence by 1986, when for the first time according to the OECD the USSR gave a greater proportion of its GNP in development aid than either Britain or the United States (*Ind.*, 3 September 1987).

There have been calls for greater study and understanding of the history and politics of Third World countries, rather than the projection of aspirations and prejudices. The playing of the 'great game' of superpower geostrategic and ideological rivalry in the Third World led to a simple division between 'ours' and 'theirs'. Now it is accepted that some of 'ours', the 'states of socialist orientation', suffered from the burden of administrative-command methods and the absence of democratisation. Now it has been suggested that a variety of developmental paths are acceptable (D. Volskii, *Iz.*, 22 December 1988).

Under Gorbachev the USSR decreased its sponsorship of Communist movements and governments throughout the world. The shift was in keeping with the CSIS which, Gorbachev stressed during his meeting with Castro in April 1989, meant that 'the security of each state can only be guaranteed in a trustworthy fashion within the system of overall international security.' East–West security was to take precedence over North–South issues. Understandably, the Third World was wary of CSIS since it focused attention on the Security Council at the UN, beyond their control. The new thinking in general can be seen to be exclusive since it strengthened existing élitist institutions at home and in international affairs. Soviet policy towards the Third World was increasingly marked by pragmatism rather than by messianism which, as Khrushchev discovered, is very expensive. Retreats from Afghanistan and elsewhere suggested that the Soviet age of expansionism was over. However much tempered by caution, opportunism and pragmatism, and whatever the motives fuelling it, Soviet foreign policy since 1944 had an expansionary dynamic at its core. The new thinking began to overcome this dynamic as co-operation replaced competition.

At the 27th congress Gorbachev called the Afghan war a 'bleeding wound' and indicated a readiness to withdraw 'as soon as a political settlement is reached'. Soviet military power was not able to break the power of the Mujahadeen, supplied by the United States, Pakistan, China and Iran. Afghanistan had become a diplomatic albatross, alienating the Muslims, the Third World and China, and obstructing the course of East–West relations. Moreover, the Soviet Union needed to husband resources for domestic reconstruction rather than military adventures. Despite attempts to start negotiations there were major offensives in early 1986. The withdrawal of 8,000 men that summer was clearly part of a routine turnover of personnel, and included a large proportion of construction battalions who had finished their tasks. However, Soviet determination to end its military involvement led to the rather undignified spectacle of Moscow's manipulation of leadership changes in Kabul. Babrak Karmal, who had been installed in Amin's place following the Soviet invasion in December 1979, was replaced by Najibullah, who was apparently more amenable to entering peace negotiations. At Geneva in 1988 UN-sponsored talks between Pakistan and Afghanistan, with Moscow and Washington acting as guarantors, led to accords signed on 14 April for a 'front-loaded' removal of Soviet forces whereby the bulk would leave fairly rapidly by 15 August and the rest by 15 February 1989.

The Soviets apparently conceded the possibility of a non-Communist regime in Afghanistan as long as it was neutral. By the beginning of the withdrawal of the 'limited contingent' of some 115,000 men in May 1988 Soviet forces had lost 13,310 men killed and 35,478 wounded. The retreat was, however, a military one, and the Soviet Union was careful to try to retain political and economic influence in the country. This was facilitated by the splits in the opposition. Nevertheless, the scale of the Soviet defeat should not be minimised. This was the first war that the Soviet Union had lost since the reverses of the early days of the Second World War. It was the first withdrawal from occupied territory since the Bolshevik Revolution, with the exception of the retreat from northern Iran in 1946 and Austria in 1955. It provided yet another blow to the Brezhnev doctrine of the irreversibility of Communist revolutions. Yet it was a mark of Gorbachev's skill that he managed the Soviet retreat from this shameful war with a degree of dignity.

Soviet withdrawal from Afghanistan was part of a larger tide of retreat. In Angola, Cambodia, Namibia, Nicaragua and elsewhere the goal of stability and peace took precedence over the establishment of yet another 'socialist' state. Indeed, Soviet overtures to South Africa and Israel suggested a change of priorities and a more realistic appreciation of the complexities of regional conflicts.

One of the key principles of the new thinking is interdependence, and a concrete manifestation of this was participation in intergovernmental organisations (IGOs) and non-governmental organisations (NGOs). Of all international organisations the UN is one of the most important and has been the main focus of the new Soviet diplomacy. The 'Mr Nyet' policies of yesteryear gave way to a far more positive approach which encouraged a remarkable revival in an organisation that in the early 1980s was plagued by financial crisis and bitter North–South and East–West hostilities. The removal of Gromyko alone was a major step in improving the climate. The USSR used its position as one of the five permanent members of the Security Council, together with Britain, France, the United States and China, to try to solve some of the major crises in the world, such as the Gulf War, Namibia, Spanish Sahara, the Middle East and Cambodia. The Soviet Union hoped to use the Council as a forum for the resolution of regional disputes, opening it to the charge from the ten non-permanent members and the floor of the General Assembly that a new five-power condominium over world affairs was emerging. Such feelings were encouraged by the Soviet idea, prompted by dissatisfaction over UN monitoring of Pakistan's adherence to the Geneva accords on Afghanistan, of establishing a standing UN army under the control of the permanent members of the Council. The Soviets also proposed the conversion of the Trusteeship Council, responsible now for only one trust territory, into a World Ecological Council. Moreover, in keeping with the new approach to the Third World the Soviet delegation increasingly bypassed UNCTAD, the body dealing with trade and development and dominated by the Third World, and in its place used the hitherto lowly UN Economic and Social Council. The more open Soviet approach was spiced with new ideas, but fundamental problems such as Third World debt remain unresolved.

A new realism for a new society

The new political thinking modified the old approach to international relations. It was motivated by an urgent sense of the dangers of the nuclear threat and the senselessness of an ever-escalating arms race. Soviet foreign policy now espoused the concept of 'reasonable sufficiency' which allowed a degree of 'disarmament for development'. Deterrence was rethought and to a degree nuclear weapons were delegitimised. The new thinking stressed the global interdependence of the human race of whatever political creed or class when faced by ecological catastrophe and economic deprivation. In the Soviet view, security became indivisible: neither East nor West can be secure at the other's expense. The new realism no longer believed in the inevitable tilting of the 'correlation of forces' in socialism's favour, and even imperialism was not now seen to be quite so red in tooth and claw. The Soviet view of the world changed. No longer was it considered simply the scene for class and inter-system rivalries but as the habitat of the human race which the Soviet Union could help protect. Parochial and regional perspectives were broadened to take in the global view.

The frozen patterns of the post-war world thawed. The legacy of Yalta began to be overcome and the division of Europe healed. Gorbachev's speech to the UN General Assembly of 7 December 1988 signalled his willingness to put an end to the cold war, and by 1990 a post post-war world emerged. Soviet domestic changes encouraged a new role in the world. If previously economic weakness was compensated by reliance on military power, now a more balanced view emerged to overcome the one-dimensionality of the Soviet Union as a super-power.

Kissinger argued for a 'new Yalta' in which the West would offer the Soviet Union new security guarantees in return for the pledge of political liberalisation in Eastern Europe. Such a new Yalta would once again have tried to settle the fate of Eastern Europe in Moscow and Washington and would thus have been reminiscent of the first Yalta. In the event it proved unnecessary as 'people power' swept the neo-Stalinists out of power in Eastern Europe.

On the eve of the Malta summit Gorbachev's speech in Rome on 30 November 1989 called for the second Helsinki conference to be brought forward from the scheduled date of 1992. The conference would provide the scaffolding with which to build the common European home as 'a commonwealth of sovereign democratic states, with a high level of interdependence and easily accessible borders' (*SN*, 1989: 413). The centrality of a cultural concept of the common home was made explicit in the link he drew between the revolutions in Eastern Europe and the humanistic, democratic and open traditions of Western civilisation. The new Europe would be based on the rule of law, the retention of the existing borders, and non-interference. German unification was thereby, for the time being at least, rejected.

The Malta summit of 2–3 December 1989 put a diplomatic end to the cold war. The problem now was how to manage the transition to the new pattern of international relations in the 1990s. The basis of the new order consisted of a twofold Soviet withdrawal, from Eastern Europe and from the global arms race, and in return Gorbachev sought assurances that the West would not destabilise the political situation which might threaten the integrity of the Soviet Union itself. The Malta summit was notable for Bush's engagement on precisely that issue, and a rejection of some of the advice of some of his advisers that Gorbachev's problems were not America's concern. Bush realised that Gorbachev's survival was in America's best interests. The summit was notable in yet another respect, in that it recognised that the cold war had begun in Europe and that it could only end in Europe with the European nations taking control over their own destiny. Nearly forty-five years after Yalta, the ghost of Stalin in European international relations had finally been put to rest.

Soviet political and economic weakness during *perestroika* was compensated by the quality of Gorbachev's leadership in international affairs. Malta was no Brest-Litovsk where concessions were forced on a desperate Soviet leadership, but a meeting of equals on the world stage. It should not be forgotten that as the two leaders met the Soviet Union still had nearly half a million troops in Eastern Europe, the vast majority of them in East Germany. Moreover, the Soviet Union remained a nuclear power with the capacity to reduce the world, and itself, to ashes.

The new order of international relations saw a unilateral Soviet retreat from its global aspirations, and it became more firmly than ever a European power. Soviet plans to create a new structure of European international relations were intended to avert the Balkanisation of the eastern part of the continent. The Balkanisation of the USSR itself, however, became a real prospect. There is little doubt that Soviet global power will decline in the 1990s leaving only one superpower, balanced by the emergence of a united Germany. Indeed, the process of managing superpower decline is the essence of the changing nature of European international relations.

The view that the cold war reflected tensions *within* the two major blocs (Kaldor, 1979; Chomsky, 1982) rested on the assumption, as far as the Soviet side was concerned, that international tension helped justify authoritarian domestic policies by appealing for unity and discipline in the face of the external danger. By drawing the tooth of the 'imperialist threat' Gorbachev thereby lost one of the props sustaining the old distribution of power. Whatever the outcome of *perestroika*, barring dramatic events, it will be very difficult to revive the image of the enemy. Indeed, liberal Soviet writers now admitted that the USSR contributed to the cold war not only by confronting the enemy without but also by persecuting the alleged enemy within.

It remains to be considered whether we can really talk of a new Soviet foreign policy. Has the undoubtedly innovative new political thinking been translated into a new structure of Soviet international relations? Or is Soviet foreign policy under Gorbachev simply an attempt to salvage a disastrous legacy and to prepare for a renewed offensive against the West once the economy has been reformed and society revitalised? In other words, can the new Soviet policy be classed as a *peredyshka*, a breathing space like Lenin's won by the treaty of Brest-Litovsk in March 1918 in preparation for a renewed offensive against capitalism once circumstances permit? The degree to which ideology modifies overt behaviour in foreign policy is always a matter of debate, and no less so when new thinking in international relations is grafted on to domestic ideological upheavals.

On the negative side of the scales it could be argued that up to 1990 much remained of the old thinking. Soviet foreign policy was still saturated with the manichaean view of the world, the competition between two contestatory social systems. As far as Brezhnev was concerned, *détente* was a phase of peaceful coexistence and considered a way of managing conflict. Peaceful coexistence is a theory of cold war between social systems. Under Gorbachev conflict between systems and states gave way to a new emphasis on collaboration, in keeping with the functionalist arguments of David Mitrany (1946). There is no doubt that the new thinking re-evaluated the cornerstone of the cold war, the ideological struggle between capitalism and socialism, whose physical manifestation was the conflict between the major representatives of the two systems, the United States and the USSR, but the notion was not altogether abandoned. Competition remained and so the concept of peaceful coexistence was still valid, albeit in a new form of co-operative peaceful coexistence. The grounds on which the conflict was fought were broadened both ideologically, on who really represents the best interests not only of the working class but of the human race as a whole, and spatially, with the new interest in the Pacific and Latin America.

While there was a partial 'end of ideology' in foreign policy and a scaling down of Soviet ambitions, the realist school of international relations would argue that the very structure of the nation-state as the basic building block of international relations means that an adversarial stance is inevitable. The failure of the Soviet strategies pursued during *détente* and the second cold war led to a necessary reappraisal and refinement of tactics but not to a change of strategy. The major concerns of foreign policy remain the same, but the way that they are pursued has been modernised. The *perestroika* in international relations was designed to make existing policies more effective to keep the USSR a credible world power. Under the guise of a new responsibility and willingness to share the burden of global management the Soviet Union was able to achieve more in five years than decades of bluster and threat by Brezhnev and his predecessors. In other words, there was no suggestion of a turn inwards on the Chinese model. In Russian history it has always been the modernisers rather than the conservatives who have pursued the most ambitious foreign policy.

This 'hawkish' view can be countered by a number of arguments. We have to define what are the 'existing policies'. The emergence of a more pluralistic political system in the USSR would suggest that the notion of an 'overall strategy', a deep structure which is unevenly articulated, is at best vague and at worst fundamentally misleading. It would be surprising if a group of leaders who were deeply divided on domestic policy should find unanimity in foreign policy. It became clear that there was no 'bottom line' in Soviet foreign policy as even basic policies were revised, such as the Soviet attempt to keep some sort of hegemony over Eastern Europe. Moreover, one of the axioms of international relations is that for any power 'the goals are less important than the means taken to achieve them, the intensity with which the objectives are sought, and above all the manner in which the policy is conducted' (Hoffman, 1988: 24). Although the concepts of the new thinking ran ahead of actual practices, there were many tangible changes. Military expansionism was renounced and co-operative solutions were advocated for common problems of humanity. The Soviet Union now participated actively in a number of world organisations as a responsible partner. Indeed, the USSR now acts as a 'moderate' or satiated power.

Above all, the gravity of Soviet domestic problems meant that even if the new thinking began as a strategem to gain time before advancing again, it was clear that by 1990 the USSR was absorbed in a series of domestic crises. This helped accelerate the implementation of the co-operative strategies advanced earlier, such as the demilitarisation of international relations. The disintegration of the old authoritarian polity in the face of the democratic challenge meant that the idea of a monolithic 'rational actor model' in Soviet foreign policy had to be abandoned. It was no longer convincing to talk in terms of a 'techno-bureaucratic' élite in the USSR whose goal was not the old Brezhnevite stability but its own internal cohesion and political viability (see, for example, Tismaneanu, 1987a: 78–84).

To many observers it seemed that international relations were returning to a nineteenth-century pattern of four or five great powers shadow-boxing and moving into uneasy alliances to promote national interests, stripped of the ideological animus which characterised the cold war. There is some truth to the view of an increasingly de-ideologised world, but it should be noted that ideology is still an important factor in international affairs. Even *realpolitik* is ideologically conditioned. However, the fundamental originality of the new thinking was the transformation of the relationship between Soviet ideology and foreign policy. Gorbachev insisted on the need to 'separate carefully ideological differences from interstate relations' (*P*, 31 July 1985), and that 'Ideological differences should not be transferred to the sphere of interstate relations' (1987a: 143). In certain respects there was an epistemological break under Gorbachev in Soviet foreign policy. Contrary to the fundamental Marxist–Leninist assumption that there cannot be harmony in industrial society or international relations, Gorbachev identified the source of disharmony not in class conflict alone but in a broader disequilibrium in human affairs. He overcame not only Lenin's legacy in foreign affairs, but also Marx's, expressed above all in the reunification of revolutionary socialism and social democracy.

The 'world society' school of international relations, in contrast to the realists, saw much greater scope for co-operation. Hedley Bull's discussion of international society and the problem of ethics argued that the ethical norms of domestic behaviour should be applied in the international arena (Bull, 1979). The USSR now joined the 'family of nations' and the interstate system of international society (Gladkov, 1989). This allowed the transformation of *détente* into *entente*, a broader and more co-operative relationship between capitalism and socialism. Countries like Japan still lacked the military strength to dance in a global 'concert of nations'. Modern capitalism was so thoroughly internationalised that nation-states themselves were perhaps less important as dancing partners than giant corporations and international organisations. The emergence of regional groupings like the EC further eroded the autonomy of nation-states. This put in doubt one of the major axioms of both Western and Soviet writings on international relations, the implicit acceptance of the rational actor model whose basic unit on the international stage is the nation-state. Above all, nuclear weapons precluded a return to nineteenth-century great power diplomacy. The new stress on interdependence, IGOs and NGOs in the new thinking implicitly accepted the tension between the nation-state and the problem-solving capacity of supranational organisations. However, neither the Soviet Union nor the West was able to resolve the contradiction between world society and the egoism of nation-states.

The new Soviet thinking was derived from both domestic factors and an intellectual revolution. Paul Kennedy argues that the United States, like the earlier empires, was unable to sustain its global interests without accumulating huge debts caused by military expenditure. The phenomenon of 'imperial overstretch' occurs when the diversion of resources into military spending caused by extended strategic commitments weakens a country's competitiveness leading to relative decline (Kennedy, 1988). The new thinking was a Soviet response to this problem, but it also came from an intellectual appreciation that international relations in the nuclear age must be more than an endless zero-sum game to be played with the West. At the same time, thinking about international relations and Soviet domestic problems combined in the understanding that economic strength was no less important than political power. This new realism underlay the attempt to 'normalise' and 'rationalise' the USSR's international position, and indeed, to make its foreign policy more cost-effective.

The new thinking did not enjoy an easy victory in the Soviet leadership, as Ligachev's criticisms made abundantly clear. The military establishment may resent its exclusion from the top echelons of policy-making and its relative downgrading. The middle ranks of the KGB may also find the confusion engendered by a more open politics threatening and insist on the reassertion of discipline. The list could go on, but the essential point is that the new thinking was not, and could not be, irreversible. This made the task of Western policy-makers more complex since a response to Gorbachev's initiatives in such areas as arms control might open the West to the threats of more militant successors. Sakharov argued that the West should support *perestroika* because, if it failed and Gorbachev fell, the Soviet Union could revert to expansionism. Hence Western leaders such as Thatcher, while diffident about cashing in the 'peace dividend' offered by the end of the cold war, did not seek to exploit the social and political difficulties to weaken the Soviet Union or to hasten the demise of the Warsaw Pact as a whole.

Just as many of Khrushchev's ideas in international relations were developed in the last years of Stalin, so many of Gorbachev's ideas emerged in the years prior to his accession both at home and abroad. Yet there is no doubt that taken as a whole the new political thinking stimulated an original Soviet foreign policy. In particular, the downgrading of the class element in international relations allowed the triumph of the concept of national sovereignty as the guiding principle in relations between socialist and other states. The end of Utopian aspirations allowed the state to be rehabilitated in both domestic politics and as the major actor in international politics. This made the respect of international law, so much emphasised by Soviet writers in relations with the world at large, also possible in socialist interstate relations. The interactive relationship between theory and practice in Gorbachev's foreign policy enriched both. Under Gorbachev Soviet foreign policy in both thinking and practice entered a qualitatively new phase and it would not be too much of an exaggeration to talk of a revolution in foreign policy. In its seven decades the Soviet Union passed through the stages of revolutionary enthusiasm and revolutionary defencism to pragmatic opportunism and its present maturity. In the life of a nation a few decades is not very long. Under Gorbachev the Soviet Union's foreign policy finally entered adulthood; but it may be as well to remember Wordsworth's dictum that 'the child is father of the man'.

9

THE SECOND RUSSIAN REVOLUTION

In this chapter we will sum up the experience of the first five years of *perestroika*. *Perestroika* proved that systemic change was possible in the Soviet context, but the nature and causes of the changes were less clear. Were we witnessing the evolution of totalitarianism into authoritarianism, or the transformation of an authoritarian system into a democratic one? The nature of the change can be examined by studying its causes. Was it provoked by the maturation of society and economic modernisation, by an ideological crisis of the system or, more specifically, by not the success but the perceived failure of the old pattern of development and its lack of viability in an increasingly interdependent world? Indeed, was *perestroika* above all a response to the stark challenge posed by the dynamic development of the West? We have argued that the official definition of *perestroika* tried both to preserve the system and to transform it, to stimulate change and to control it. The divisions within the reform Communist camp based on different evaluations of the scale and pace of change required were reflected in the compromises and hesitations of *perestroika* itself. *Perestroika* encountered opposition from all sides, and the attempt to reform the Soviet system while keeping many of its key features led to compromises that satisfied no one. The new model of socialism was a hybrid form of democracy that failed to gain popular support.

Problems of *perestroika*

The fundamental problem of *perestroika* was how to change a system designed to withstand change. The extraordinary resilience of the system planned by Lenin and built by Stalin, though perhaps not on precisely the same lines, was tested in war, famine, stagnation and several attempts at reform. Nearly everybody had learnt to live with the old system and got something out of it, not only the élite but the common people as well. Moreover, a large part of society was compromised in the crimes, excesses and follies of the past, from Stalin's torturers, Khrushchev's enthusiasts and Brezhnev's bureaucrats. Faced with entrenched structures, could a gradualist strategy be adopted of piecemeal reforms, or did the Soviet system stand or fall as one piece? Could some of its building blocks be changed without bringing down the whole edifice?

Russian and Soviet history has been marked by periodic bouts of reform. These have been of two sorts. The first was the imposed modernisation from above of the type of Peter the Great and Stalin, despots who sacrificed society in order to modernise it. The second type of reform was that launched by Alexander II and Gorbachev. These have been long-term programmes which sought to activate society and encourage the development of a vigorous civil society as the basis for a viable state and an effective economic system. The parallels with the great reforms of the mid-nineteenth century under Alexander II are striking. The earlier reforms included the abolition of serfdom, the creation of elected local government, the relaxation of censorship and the development of a modern legal system. The major parallel is the development in both periods of an active citizenry with regulated duties and protected rights. At the end of war Communism the sociologist Peter Sorokin characterised Soviet power as a 'new serfdom' of the Soviet citizenry in thrall to an ubiquitous political and economic bureaucracy. Just as the great reforms of Alexander II began with the abolition of serfdom in 1861, so Gorbachev began to overcome the 'new serfdom' imposed by the administrative-command model of socialism.

The fate of the earlier reforms and those of Gorbachev is also instructive. The historian Aleksandr Yanov has advanced a theory of Russian history based on the cycle of despotism, reform and stagnation. In the first phase a reforming but authoritarian leader imposes modernisation on society. This gives way to a phase of more rational reform in which the tyrant is denounced and his victims rehabilitated. This period then peters out amidst corruption and bureaucratic inertia, which gives rise to yet another push from above to overcome the stagnation, and thus the cycle is renewed (cited by G. Hosking, *Ind.*, 13 January 1989). The unhappy fate of Alexander's reform, undermined by his successor Alexander III under pressure from terrorists and revolutionaries, and then destroyed by the Bolsheviks, is also instructive. The key question was the compatibility of revived and independent political and economic forces with the remaining structures of the bureaucratic and authoritarian system.

Stephen Cohen (1985) saw post-Stalinist history as torn between reformist and conservative traditions. His conclusion was that the USSR's political culture was inhibitive of reform rather than stimulating it. A similar conclusion was reached by Gerner and Hedlund (1989) on the grounds that the rationality of the Soviet system ran counter to that of liberalising reforms. Gorbachev was therefore forced to undertake a reform contrary to the flow of Soviet politics and could not even build on the various strands of a reform tradition. His predecessors had been too effective in stifling the regenerative forces that arose within the system, from the Democratic Centralists to the dissidents. When examining the roots of Stalinism Soviet commentators wondered why it was so easy to create an administrative-command system but so hard to dismantle it (*P*, 30 September 1988).

Before Gorbachev there was a sustained and fairly high level of 'structural violence' in the political and economic mechanisms of the system. It was Gorbachev's achievement to reduce this to something approximating the level found in advanced capitalist countries. *Perestroika* can be likened to a society emerging from a long period of war. Oskar Lange observed that Communism is the war organisation of capitalism (cited by Gerner and Hedlund, 1989: 35), but under Gorbachev it tried to become a viable and effective alternative to capitalism. This meant undoing the legacy of war Communism in its various guises, and it is, in this sense, a post-war society. Much of the behavioural pattern of the Soviet population is reminiscent of a society scarred by the trauma of war, with universal shortages, rationing, the emergence of spivs, the urge to recount one's doings in the war, all combined with an almost palpable relief that the long emergency is over and that the burden of fear has lifted.

Perestroika was increasingly fractured. There were those like Roy Medvedev who believed in a scientific and gradual approach to reform. These were balanced by more enthusiastic reformers like Eltsin. Opposition to the Gorbachevite reforms can be identified on both ideological and social grounds. It is impossible, however, to gauge the precise level of dissatisfaction, although Gorbachev readily admitted its existence. In Khabarovsk on 31 July 1986 he angrily condemned lethargy, incompetence and corruption among party officials. He attacked 'our public officials [who] sometimes have the most serious failings', and called for vigorous 'self-cleansing' within the party (*P*, 2 August 1986). In his Krasnodar speech in September 1986 Gorbachev noted the opposition to *perestroika* on the part of workers and peasants, and exclaimed 'how strong conservatism is, how hard it is to dislodge' (1987e: 94).

Various groups can be identified that at one stage or another showed a degree of ambivalence towards radical reform. They can be placed into five main categories (the reservations of the military and the KGB are discussed elsewhere). The first are the ordinary citizens who felt the negative effects of Gorbachev's reforms on their everyday lives. The anti-alcohol campaign served to alienate many, and the anti-corruption campaign closed various channels by which the bureaucratic system could be circumvented. This might have been tolerable if the shops had become fuller and standards of living improved. In fact, life under *perestroika*, in material terms, became harder for the majority of Soviet people. No state-employed social group, even skilled workers, stood to gain much from *perestroika* in the short term. Economic reform involved harder work and higher prices. Kagarlitsky argued that the great majority of the population were simply unready to accept marketising reforms based on the assertion of technocratic criteria of economic efficiency and capitalist methods (*LF on EE*, 2/1989: 31). Gorbachev was to feel the anger that this provoked during his walkabout in Krasnoyarsk in September 1988. The equation between material dissatisfaction and gratitude for *glasnost* and the new politics was difficult to judge, but there is no doubt that the former took the edge off the latter. The demonstrations in favour of democracy on 4 and 25 February, and 15 July 1990 revealed that *perestroika* was falling behind popular aspirations. Hostility to Gorbachev himself was revealed at the 1 May 1990 celebrations, when he was jeered off the Mausoleum accompanied by placards bewailing 'Seventy-two years on the road to nowhere'. It became clear that he could not be both a transformer and a conserver, and he personally began to be seen as an obstacle to radical change. Not only the conservatives but the Communist reformists themselves were in danger of being swept away, like the governments of Eastern Europe, by popular democratic revolutions.

The second group were the so-called conservatives who objected to liberalising economic laws and other flirtations with the market on ideological grounds. The use of the term 'conservative' to describe the more moderate reformers is, of course, purely a matter of convention. Communist conservatism shares some of the concerns of classical Western conservatism, as in the stress on some sort of organic community, but in the Soviet context it led to policy prescriptions at variance with neo-conservatism in its continued loyalty to 'leftist' policies and a veneration for statist socialism. Chinese usage of the 'remnants of leftism', referring to those who still hold to Maoist extremism, is more accurate. Moreover, there were at least three types of 'conservatism': the 'old left' conservatives like Ligachev, Polozkov and their ilk, who argued that more could be salvaged from Soviet history and politics than the more radical reformers would concede; the 'conservative populists' like Gidaspov, who tried to forge an alliance with the traditionalist working class and nationalism; and the 'new Left' conservatives, many of whom came from the independent movement itself, like Kagarlitsky, who argued that Gorbachev had lost all sense of a socialist alternative and that *perestroika* was turning out to be not much more than capitalism with a socialist face. It should be stressed that the new Soviet Left are here labelled 'conservatives' only in the sense that they criticised excessive marketisation: they tended to favour a type of self-managed socialism.

Old Left conservatives like Ligachev were worried about the implications of an economic reform which increased the role of the market and raised the spectre of the erosion of what they considered basic socialist values, such as full employment, a commitment to equality and a centralised state structure. The capitalism that was chased out the front door in October 1917, they feared, might creep in through the back door of *perestroika*.

The spectre emerged of an unholy neo-Marxist alliance between the more conservative sections of the political élite, uneasy with the radical moves towards democratisation, and an alienated part of the working class opposed to the social disruption caused by marketisation. The military–industrial complex and the party *apparat* would join with Russian chauvinist nationalism and workerist populists. The emergence of the United Front of Workers of Russia (OFT) and the Joint Council of Russia in late 1989 (Tolz, 1989a), made up of party *apparatchiks*, traditionalist workers, some Russian national Stalinists, but most of all factory- and university-based intelligentsia, demonstrated that while the working class may have been displaced from its privileged ideological position, workerist ideas remained strong in popular consciousness. There was still a residual belief that the prejudices of working people were somehow superior to the affectations and artificiality of the civilisation of the intelligentsia. Marketising economic reform and liberal political reform were condemned as alien to Soviet traditions, and indeed as part of a Judaeo-Masonic conspiracy in which liberal reformists were allegedly implicated (Wishnevsky, 1989). In fact, as Gleisner points out, the OFT represents a return to some sort of Left Communism – indeed, a return of some of the thoughts of the Left Communists in 1918, and in particular a form of working-class rule operating through soviets and a socially-assured economy. The Marxist Platform shared some of these ideas.

Conservative populism became the greatest obstacle to *perestroika*, indeed to the return of the USSR to world civilisation, unabashedly defined as the norms of the world society rooted in the culture of Western Europe (Gong, 1984). The appeal to the working class was still strong in the rhetoric of the party, especially when repressive measures were being contemplated. These are justified by the formulation, still to be found in Gorbachev's speeches but above all used by the conservatives, that 'the working class demands' this or that, such as a crackdown on 'demagogues and those who permit political speculation on the process of democratisation and *glasnost*', and that 'The working class has not yet had its say. It is high time it did' (G, 27 July 1988). The conservative use of workerist symbols, of course, has no time for an independent working-class movement, one of the preconditions for making democratic *perestroika* irreversible.

Socialist conservatism was one of the major obstacles in the way of democratic *perestroika*. Gorbachev himself just a few years ago could have been labelled a conservative. There is no evidence to show that he came to power with a hidden agenda, but the major difference between him and his colleagues was his open mind, his learning ability and his boldness in drawing what he felt were the necessary conclusions. The conservative defence of the basic outlines of the old model of socialism was based on firm arguments. They did not oppose most of Gorbachev's reforms as such, but feared that the reform process would escape the control of the Communist Party and become self-sustaining with a social dynamic at variance with party policy and ultimately party rule itself. The ambivalence of the concept of Communist conservatism is further illustrated by the fact that some radical reformers like Eltsin once had reservations about capitalist methods of modernisation, such as wage inequalities and unemployment. Above all, the very structures of the Soviet system generated so-called conservative attitudes and patterns of behaviour. This was illustrated at the 19th party conference where many speakers, such as Grossu and Kalashnikov, mouthed reformist platitudes in a Stalinist language. In the manner of Soviet campaigns of old, *perestroika* became reified, and treated as if the abstract idea was a material force.

The gathering pace of political reform posed the threat that Communism would reform itself out of existence. The turmoil of *perestroika* seemed to confirm the conservative view that democratisation was opening the door to destabilisation. Economic dislocation, national and ethnic rivalries and disaffection gave rise to the 'anarchy scenario'. According to Soviet figures between January 1988 and November 1989 300 people were killed, more than 5,000 injured and 360,000 forced to flee their homes because of pogroms, riots, and intercommunal clashes (B. James, *International Herald Tribune*, 8 November 1989: 3). As in China, many of those concerned about *luan*, or chaos, were not secret Stalinists but were rather in favour of traditional order and a model of socialism they understood. Gidaspov stressed that 'We lack what was always the Bolsheviks' strong point – clear-cut programme targets and the ability to show clear prospects to the people' (*P*, 28 November 1989). The response by some liberals to the crumbling of order was to sponsor the 'new authoritarianism', while for the conservatives the old authoritarianism was sufficient.

Conservative counter-reform was not a programme for the restoration of neo-Stalinism as such, but was designed to curtail liberal democratisation. Counter-reform meant not opposition to reform itself but an alternative to democratic *perestroika* emphasising the maintenance of the social promise of bureaucratic socialism, full employment and the planned economy. Nevertheless, this did not add up to a set of convincing or coherent alternatives. However much the conservatives may have cavilled at the pace of Gorbachev's reforms they had little to put in its place.

While the so-called conservatives lacked a common alternative policy or the means to pursue it, what they did have was the ability to impede the adoption and implementation of radical policies. They all made fine speeches about the wonders of *perestroika* but for them, as Shmelëv pointed out, *perestroika* was just another campaign, another of the zigzags of Soviet politics like Stalin's espousal of democracy in the 1930s. The greatest strength of the conservatives was that inertia was on their side. Simply by carrying on in the old way they could sabotage democratic *perestroika*.

The personal element in the drive to reform is perhaps best illustrated by the fact that each major manifestation of conservative sentiment occurred when Gorbachev was absent. For example, on 13 March 1988 the critique of *perestroika* by Nina Andreeva was published when Gorbachev was abroad and Ligachev was in command. In the summer of 1989 when Gorbachev was on holiday a nasty campaign against Baltic nationalists and popular democrats revealed what would be in store if Gorbachev lost out in a power struggle. The conservative suggestion that Gorbachev had turned a pre-crisis into a full-blown crisis struck a powerful chord in the mind of a section of the establishment. Following Eltsin's dismissal *Pravda* mocked Gorbachev's speeches at the January and June 1987 CC plenums by arguing, in language reminiscent of Gorbachev's, that 'democracy means disorder and anarchy' (*P*, 16 November 1987).

The third group was the bureaucracy, which was ruthlessly purged and criticised. Clearly party and state bureaucrats did not take kindly to the torrent of abuse launched against them. In his extraordinarily vituperative speech to a closed meeting of some forty Soviet writers on 19 June 1986 Gorbachev singled out the state planning agency: 'For Gosplan there exist no authorities, no General Secretaries, no Central

Committees. They do what they want' (*Time*, 5 January 1987: 54). The assault against the bureaucratic élite was both political and social: political in that the prerogatives of the administrative class were undermined; and social in that their privileges were condemned.

The Soviet administrative system developed a distinctive type of bureaucratic culture which stood in an ambivalent relationship to the reforms as a whole (Hill, 1986). The assault against bureaucratism often took the form of an attack against bureaucracy as such. However, as noted, the reformers did not want to abolish the bureaucracy but to make it work better. One of the greatest challenges facing Gorbachev was to turn the bureaucracy into a civil service based on meritocratic recruitment and formal rules. However, while during *perestroika* the bureaucracy lost its old teleological aspirations, it remained a political bureaucracy. The ambivalent approach fuelled the Trotskyist view of *perestroika* which suggested that Gorbachev hoped to preserve, albeit in a new guise, the power and prestige of the bureaucracy. For them, the radicalisation of the reforms was achieved by the pressure on the bureaucracy by millions of Soviet workers, and only sustained pressure could ensure the defeat of the bureaucracy and a return to genuine workers' democracy (e.g. E. Mandel, 1989).

While the social bases of support for *perestroika* tended to be diffuse, Soviet political society generated specific groups who were threatened by the reforms. The language of the Gorbachevites increasingly identified an 'exploiter class' of functionaries in party, state and industry. To dislodge this 'new class' some of the more radical reformers talked of the necessity for a 'social revolution' of reform to expropriate the exploiters. The technocratic language of the first years of reform, which envisaged a smooth process of *uskorenie* to tap the reserves of socialism, gave way to what amounted at times to the language of class war. In effect, *perestroika* turned into a controlled coup against the bureaucracy and ultimately against the party apparatus itself. The conservatives could with some justification warn Gorbachev that thereby he assaulted the basis of his own power.

Eltsin was the leading exponent of the idea that political power had been transformed into excessive social privileges. After his demotion several speakers at the 19th party congress continued his condemnation of the privileges of the élite and the theme was strong at the 1st Congress of People's Deputies. The struggle was hampered by the intention to avoid the language of revived class struggle in keeping with the revised perceptions of class and practical considerations. While the existence of antagonistic social groups in Soviet society was at last recognised, the application of a revolutionary Marxist class analysis to the power structure of the Soviet Union was avoided. At the February 1988 plenum of the Central Committee Gorbachev insisted that the fight for *perestroika* 'does not acquire the form of class antagonism' (*SN*, 1988: 62). Nevertheless, a *Pravda* editorial soon after added that 'Although the struggle [for *perestroika*] does not take the form of class conflict it is still very bitter' (*P*, 5 April 1988). Rather than attacking the élite or the bureaucracy as a class, which would be the Maoist approach, the focus was on individual shortcomings.

The failings of *perestroika* itself were taken up by Sergei Andreev (1989). He warned that *perestroika* was being deliberately undermined by the 'new class' of industrial and party bureaucrats and that Gorbachev refused to face up to the full implications of this. Economic chaos actually served their interests by allowing them to retain control over economic management. In an unusually direct personal criticism of Gorbachev, Andreev argued that the reforms could well play into the hands of the 'new class' unless marketisation reduced the power of the ministries. The attempt to maintain the party's 'leading role' hampered an effective assault on the bureaucracy. Only an effective legislature could bring the party leader, who should not simultaneously be President, to account. The power of the 'new class' should be effectively balanced by popular democracy. Such a force began to emerge through contested elections, an active legislature and popular movements.

The fourth challenge to the 'new democracy' of *perestroika* was posed by a type of radical populism. The leading exponent of this was Boris Eltsin in his first incarnation under *perestroika*. At the October 1987 Central Committee plenum Gorbachev accused Eltsin of being 'politically illiterate', and though his phenomenal success in gaining 89 per cent of the popular vote in the March 1989 elections might suggest an astute political brain, there remained a suspicion until 1990 that Gorbachev's judgement contained more than a hint of truth. Eltsin, however, appeared able to present himself as a man of the people, expressing their aspirations and grievances in simple terms. This was revealed during his two years as leader of the Moscow party organisation, though he also showed himself to be a poor manager. Eltsin's short but effective speech to the 19th party conference – especially when contrasted with the aggression of Ligachev – won his place in people's hearts, confirmed by the March 1989 elections. But, to paraphrase Lord Blake, just because Eltsin is popular does not make him a populist. By the time that he was elected president of the RSFSR, Eltsin had matured. His masterly handling of competing views in the Russian parliament revealed him to be a skilled and tactful politician. Moreover, his commitment to democratisation and the power of the soviets, and to remedying Russia's many ills, could not be questioned. His economic policy focused on allowing individual and market initiative by dismantling the manifestly ineffective old bureaucratic system.

The fifth threat to Gorbachev's evolving vision of guided *perestroika* came from what can be loosely termed the democratic challenge, both from within the party itself, taking the form of an embryonic social democratic party based on the Democratic Platform, and from the various groups outside the official political process analysed in Chapter 5. In effect, by 1990 *perestroika* as a directed process of reform Communism was dead, and a struggle for democracy began. Society in the shape of the independent and national movements began to liberate itself from the legacy of Stalinist socialism and resisted attempts at inclusion in the expanding consensus of *perestroika*. Representatives of various popular and informal movements could see no reason to ally with a power system, however liberal and enlightened in comparison with its predecessors, which for over seventy years had tried to undermine civil society. Moreover, it could be argued that the socialist bureaucracy had fulfilled any historical role that it might have had in laying the basis for an industrialised modern society and could no longer offer anything more than a discreet withdrawal into history. 'No vengeance, just go', as placards in Prague put it in December 1989. Gorbachev's reforms from above gave way to the revolution of self-emancipation from below. Liberalisation of Soviet socialism no longer appeared enough. As far as the national question was concerned, the basic dilemma was how to combine liberalisation of the political system while retaining a multinational system in which several elements clearly preferred not to be members. There appeared simply to be no democratic way of reconciling such sharply opposed views.

By early 1990 Eltsin argued that the country faced bloody revolution unless the party accelerated the pace of reform to appease popular anger. For him, the revolutionary situation had arisen because of 'compromises and half-measures' (*P*, 8 July 1990). Semi-democratisation had created a situation where disorder threatened to overwhelm the country, and the semi-legal status of mass movements in society left the political system vulnerable.

Gorbachev's institutional bases of support changed over the years. In his rise to power he had allied himself with the KGB's anti-corruption drive. He had also been able to win the acquiescence of the military, who understood that only a modernised economy could sustain a military technology comparable to that in the West. These two sources of institutional support in the early years of *perestroika* were inevitably short-lived ones. Like Prince Hal, sooner or later Gorbachev would have to break with his Falstaffian friends as the reforms entered a new stage of maturity. Reliance on the intelligentsia broadened into an appeal to the population as a whole, an appeal which was weakened by the failure of the benefits of Communist reform to outweigh the costs. The processual nature of *perestroika* made it liable to periodic crises.

Gorbachev was unable to translate his enormous prestige in the international sphere into effective policies at home. The leadership of *perestroika* itself bore a severe burden of responsibility for hasty campaigns and the impetuous introduction of ill-considered legislation. The anti-alcohol campaign is a case in point, together with the creation of the Gosagroprom monster, restrictive decrees against the co-operatives and repressive public order laws. Brezhnev's stagnation and the whole history of the Soviet Union could not be called upon to exonerate the leadership's mistakes (cf. A. Gerasimov, *Iz.*, 23 April 1989). The economy was the Achilles' heel of *perestroika* and here achievements lagged far behind those in politics, though in both cases achievements lagged far behind aspirations.

By late 1988 it was clear that there was a crisis of confidence in reform Communism. Too many promises had been broken in the past, and there were too few concrete improvements in the present. Popular disaffection was fuelled by the awareness that the problems of the economy and declining living standards were real, whereas the improvements remained no more than the pious hopes of the Gorbachevite reformers. Talk of democracy and the promise of improved living standards as a result of *perestroika* inevitably raised political and economic expectations, though Gorbachev from the first tried to damp down the latter while raising the former. The raised expectations were translated into insistent popular demands for genuine political and economic choice.

The travails of *perestroika* from 1989 led to a rediscovered awareness of the Kremlinological analysis of Soviet politics, focusing on whether Gorbachev could survive as leader. Khrushchev's enforced departure in 1964 set a precedent which was much discussed in the Soviet Press. However, the Central Committee under *perestroika* was no longer the body it once was, and Gorbachev's position was more secure. The conservatism of the CC, up to its renewal at the 28th party congress in 1990, was balanced by the radicalism of sections of the Supreme Soviet and even more of the underemployed four-fifths of the Congress. The overthrow of Gorbachev could no longer, as in 1964, be decided by the party apparatus alone, but would have to reckon with parliament and the people. The refusal of the conservatives to take up the gauntlet of his threatened resignation on several occasions, notably in December 1989, suggests that at the time they saw no alternative to his leadership. The consolidation of the presidency in 1990 confirmed Gorbachev's independence from the old structures of collective leadership, though it did not render him immune from group pressures from the KGB, the military, increasingly militant official and unofficial trade unions and democratic organisations.

While *perestroika* was much larger than one man and could continue without him, it was equally true that without Gorbachev the reform process could have very quickly become lost in the wilderness for another forty years. Gorbachev as a born optimist was of the school of thought that the necessity of reform was so obvious that it could not fail. The necessity for some sort of reform, however, was on the agenda for at least forty years and yet remained unfulfilled. There is no room here for Carlylian hero worship, but for a strictly political appraisal of the traditionally leadership-dominated structure of Soviet politics. Without popular controls, as Sakharov frequently pointed out, there was a danger of the leader evolving towards a form of personalised authoritarianism. A hectoring and intolerant note on occasion crept into Gorbachev's speeches, reflecting some of the misconceived, personalised and authoritarian campaigns under *perestroika*.

One of the major questions facing *perestroika* was the 'reformability' of the Soviet people itself. The classic typology of political culture by Almond and Verba (1963) identified three types derived from the way that people relate to politics. The first is the parochial culture, focused on the locality and in which political life is felt mainly in the form of the soldier, police and the tax collector. The subject political culture includes a greater awareness of government but a passive approach to politics. In a participant culture people have an active interest in political activity and become involved in policy-making. After thirty years of Stalinism and twenty years of stagnation and artificial enthusiasm the Soviet people increasingly showed signs of what could be called a 'new parochialism', aware of political life but withdrawn into personal and local concerns, focused on the workplace, leisure and the home. By encouraging greater participation Gorbachev tried to overcome the growing parochialisation of Soviet politics. The ambition of Gorbachev's reforms was to transform the Soviet polity from a subject–participant political culture to a participant one within the framework of a revived socialism. The developing 'culture of democracy' was intended to encourage a participatory self-managing society to emerge. He tried to remake the political culture of both the élite and the masses, used to years of authoritarianism.

There remains a question of the relationship of political culture and reform Communism. Too often in the past the failings of the Soviet system were ascribed to the inadequacies of the people themselves. Allegedly, they were apathetic and receptive to authoritarianism because of centuries of subjection. This was a convenient way of diverting attention from the failings of Soviet socialism itself. Now the responsibility for shortcomings could not so easily be placed at the door of the old regime or on a people who had now been moulded by the Soviet system itself. Already, in a manner reminiscent of Brecht, the Soviet people have been blamed for the failings of *perestroika*. Ryzhkov justified the delay in the price reform on these grounds. Rather than accepting that *perestroika* was so defined that it could not unleash the creative energies and entrepreneurship of the people, the people were described as having failed the test of *perestroika*. The argument that 'Political culture here is as undeveloped as the food distribution system' is ascribed to the 'deeply ingrained conservatism and suspicion of ordinary Russian people', as Jonathan Steele put it. This affects both political life, where there is not 'a society of eager democrats just waiting to emerge' from the tutelage of the party, and economics, where there is a lack of an entrepreneurial spirit because of what Andrei Fëdorov, the head of the Moscow Association of Co-operatives, called the 'anti-market culture' of the last seventy years (G, 18 January 1989). There is an element of truth in such arguments; yet the apathy, caution, lack of an acquisitive mentality, wariness of change, fear of new thinking and so on are born of a rational response to the structures in which people live and work. The restrictions on the development of the co-operative movement have been described, and the limits to pluralism inhibited the development of an autonomous political life. The influence of concepts of political culture in reform processes must be treated with extreme caution.

The irreversibility of reforms can never be guaranteed, but with the passing of each day it became more difficult to uproot them. *Glasnost* made known things which could never be made unknown. A culture of democracy began to replace the climate of fear. The active participation of millions in open and contentious public life could never be erased. The elections of spring 1989 marked a watershed in this respect, and the local elections of 1990 confirmed the rebirth of an active citizenry. Hundreds of thousands took the opportunity of freer travel to see life in the West for themselves. Reform of the legal system began to establish the rule of law rather than bureaucratic whim, and the new religious and political freedoms were to be guaranteed by the new constitution. The consolidation of economic reform remained tenuous; but the co-operatives, the farmers leasing and owning the land, joint enterprises and increasingly autonomous state enterprises could not be removed without a repeat of the Stalinist civil war of the state against its own people. Republics like Estonia, Latvia and Lithuania would not give up their economic and political sovereignty without a struggle. Even the army could not be relied upon as the tool of the party bureaucracy since elements of democratic control had been introduced by the legislature. The danger remained, however, and Sakharov warned of the possibility of a military or right-wing coup (*Ogonëk*, 32/1989: 26–9).

At what point does a reform become irreversible? Is there a point of no return, a threshold of irreversibility? In the economic sphere there cannot be such a point. In Communist regimes politics is 'in command' and can almost at will reverse economic reforms despite the profound socioeconomic processes at work in society. The key element in irreversibility lies in changing the political sphere sufficiently. Every tilt towards the conservatives appeared to dash hopes for irreversibility, but every tilt to the radicals could indeed unleash irreversible but uncontrollable forces. In a sense the question of irreversibility is falsely posed since, as Hegel pointed out, history is both continuous and discontinuous, and there can never be a return to the *status quo ante*. The undoubted necessity of *perestroika* did not ensure its irreversibility. However, there is a political process of irreversibility that is built into any system of social evolution. There is very little chance that the monolithic Stalinist system could return, not all of Khrushchev's reforms were reversed, and it is unlikely that the comfortable *nomenklatura* rule of the Brezhnev years could be restored. Pre-reform conditions no longer exist and cannot be recreated but, as the Chinese repression of 4 June 1989 illustrated, the old politics can be reimposed.

Perestroika contained the potential for system transformation, the emergence of a polity beyond the one-party state, the command economy and the dominant ideology. Yet each step was accompanied by travail. To be effective there can be no such thing as the 'last reform' beyond which everything is fine and functioning splendidly. Reform cannot be artificially stopped at a certain stage – otherwise it will lack the momentum to remain at that stage. Irreversibility in the context of Gorbachev's reforms meant not a return to Stalinism or even Brezhnev, but the avoidance of political commandism and *dirigisme*. The major guarantee for the irreversibility of Gorbachev's reforms was the achievement of legal guarantees against arbitrary state power, the establishment of strong legislative bodies and the consolidation of independent democratic political organisations. Any coup would then have to be directed against not just one person but against parliament and the people as a whole.

Gorbachev's reforms appeared torn between two opposing tendencies: those that were system-supportive, preserving the main elements of the system as established in the course of seven decades; and those that were system-transformative, dismantling the administrative-command system and opening the door to the transformation of the system in its entirety. Z (1990) indeed charged that Gorbachev hoped through 'soft Communism' to salvage what could be saved from the existing system. Gorbachev shaped *perestroika* as a door leading from one system to another, but he hesitated to use it. While useful, a doorway is not a place one would choose to spend much time. To change the analogy, *perestroika* in a sense only identified the disease, and indeed exacerbated the symptoms, but the healing process could only begin once *perestroika* was transcended.

Compared with earlier reforms *perestroika* was remarkably successful. It might not have put meat in the shops or soap on the shelves by the end of its first five years, but it changed dramatically and in many ways irreversibly the moral and political climate of society. A democratic political culture began to emerge. Much was given by the authorities as part of a 'reform from above', which by 1990 had still not been fully transformed into a 'revolution from below'. There remained an ideological codicil to all the reforms which could at any time be invoked. The conduct of official politics was still stamped with the birthmarks of the Bolshevik Revolution. Gorbachev himself trod a cautious path between radicalism and conservatism, and sought to prevent democratisation escaping the control of the authorities. The conservatism in the party and managerial apparatus was deeply rooted and struck a responsive chord in broad layers of society schooled in the hypocrisy of neo-Stalinism. As Andreev pointed out, why should the managerial 'new class' promote reforms that would undermine their power? A class based on economic *dirigisme* and political commandism would have little *raison d'être* under conditions of marketisation and democratisation. Zaslavskaya indeed saw *perestroika* as a social revolution, 'a second revolution of a socialist type', to overcome the 'exploitation of the *nomenklatura* stratum over the rest of the population' (*Iz.*, 24 December 1988: 3). The 1989 East European revolutions gave vivid force to Djilas's prediction that 'when the new class leaves the historical scene – and this must happen – there will be less sorrow over its passing than there was for any class before it. Smothering everything except what suited its ego, it has condemned itself to failure and shameful ruin (Djilas, 1957: 69).

Gorbachev was willing to enlist the support of an independent society to counteract the apparatus, to use democracy as a battering ram against the administrative system, and it was this that made *perestroika* unique in the history of Soviet reformism. Perhaps the greatest success of *perestroika* was the awakening of a popular movement and genuine civic consciousness, the like of which had not been seen since 1917. Ultimately the only guarantee of the irreversibility of *perestroika* and its transformation into the true democratisation and pluralisation of society was for it to become the property not of a reforming élite but of the whole people. This could be achieved only by bursting the bounds of the 'socialist pluralism of opinions' and creating competing centres of power, a mass independent movement and a vigorous civil society institutionalised in the structures of a reformed political system.

Socialism and reform

Gorbachev's reforms were the culmination of a thirty-year cycle of reform and conservatism and represented the most thorough attempt to come to terms with Stalin's legacy. They were more than this, however, as they tested models of socialism inspired by Marx and developed by Lenin. They represented, as Gorbachev put it in his 7 December 1988 United Nations address, the end of the post-revolutionary era. The whole stage of development begun by October 1917 moved into a qualitatively new phase as the system born of the Revolution gave way to a post-Bolshevik type of socialism. The aim, however, was to achieve not the post-Communism of Eastern Europe but a type of late Communism that could equal the late capitalism of the West. But the popular unrest from 1989, together with the disintegration of the Soviet polity itself, led to a second Russian revolution that put an end to the compromises of *perestroika* and prepared the way for post-Communism in the USSR itself. The argument of George Kennan's Long Telegram of 22 February 1946 appeared to be vindicated, that the Soviet Union as an ideologically charged power contained the seeds for its own destruction.

Instead of inheriting a developed economy from capitalism, as envisaged by Marx, the Bolsheviks believed that there was an alternative path to reach the stage where Communism could be realised. Instead of being the successor to capitalism, Soviet socialism tried to become its alternative. Soviet-type systems were built on fairly simple premises. A dominant Communist Party would guide political and intellectual life. A strong state would eliminate private ownership of the means of production and rationally plan and achieve society's development by concentrating all resources in its hands. Given the failure of the Revolution to spread as expected to the advanced centres of capitalism, a degree of economic and political isolation was accepted as necessary for a time until the final achievement of Communism on a world scale. Human resources would be mobilised on a grand collective scale to achieve directed goals, and individual and group needs would be subordinated to the larger purpose. However, while both Marx and Auguste Comte argued that society was moving towards universality, the one that actually arrived in the Soviet Union was very different from the one envisaged by the great modernist thinkers of the earlier age.

As *perestroika* developed it appeared that the crisis of the old model of Communism inexorably deepened. Not only did *glasnost* shed light on the tragic shortcomings of the past, but the crisis also seemed to have spread from one country to another as both the old systems and the reforms themselves acted as a catalyst to exacerbate existing problems. The massacre in Tienanmen Square on 4 June 1989 was simply the most dramatic sign of a Communist world system in crisis and, for many, was a vivid demonstration that reform cannot be irreversible. The old Communist model of social development was now seen to have been a costly historical detour. Historicism thus returned through the back door with the end condition not Communism but an efficient utilisation of capital and individual freedom. The current period might well be described as the fourth phase of Kolakowski's great trilogy on Marxism, the Foundation, Golden Age and Breakdown. The current period can be labelled the Retreat.

The new conception of socialism under *perestroika* no longer saw itself as transcending capitalism but as learning from it, no longer its inheritor but its partner. The fundamental premiss of *perestroika* was that a reformed socialist system could provide political freedom, economic efficiency and the truth about its own past crimes and present inadequacies. Indeed, for Gorbachev and his allies not only can a socialist society be democratic, but only a socialist society can be genuinely democratic. *Perestroika* came to represent the search for a humane, democratic socialism as the Communist Party put it in its programme adapted at the 28th congress (*P*, 15 July 1990). But what if it did not exist?

On witnessing the defeat by Napoleon of Prussian forces at the battle of Jena in 1806 Hegel proclaimed the 'end of history', meaning the triumph of the political and philosophical principles on which the French Revolution was built – liberty, equality and fraternity, and the revolutionary view of the individual's political and economic role in society. The development of political philosophy could not be taken further and thus, in that sense, history ended (cf. Fukuyama, 1989). Marx, however, begged to differ, and argued that the ideals of the French Revolution, with which in principle he had no quarrel, could not be fulfilled in a class-divided capitalist society. Lenin then sought to implement the alternative view with the Revolution of October 1917. The East European revolutions and the second Russian revolution, however, appeared to demonstrate not only the failure of the Bolshevik path of development but of the Marxist critique of Hegel in its entirety. These revolutions returned not only to the principles of the February 1917 'bourgeois democratic' revolution but to the French Revolution itself. The Russian revolution of February 1917, the second revolution if the first had been in 1905, had only been the long-delayed triumph in Russia of the agenda set by the French Revolution over a hundred years earlier. Hence Gorbachev's expectation that *perestroika* could stabilise the Bolshevik Revolution, just as the 1688 Glorious Revolution in England or the July 1930 'bourgeois' Revolution in France had eliminated the excesses of their respective great revolutions, was disappointed. From this perspective the Bolshevik Revolution had only been a long and tragic hiatus before *perestroika* once again made possible a return to the challenge of the February revolution, and with it of liberal democracy and economic individualism.

Herein lay *perestroika*'s triumph and tragedy. The triumph was the realisation that a new model of human and economic relations was required; the tragedy lay in the attempt to work within the confines of the Marxist and Bolshevik project while at the same time trying to transform it. This is not to suggest that liberal democracy could be picked from the shelf of a Western superstore. Each 'post-historical society', as Fukuyama would put it, moulds the agenda of the French Revolution to suit its specific historical and cultural conditions: the Americans stress liberty; the Swedes equality; while the Russians may well place the emphasis on fraternity.

Perestroika was both a choice and a historical necessity. Yet economic failures and nationalist unrest led to a profound unease with the way that Gorbachev tried to achieve the reformation of the Soviet system. His approach comprised a type of reform Communism that can be termed 'Gorbachevism'. Above all, Gorbachevism was an attempt to create a distinctive humane and democratic model of socialism suited to Soviet conditions and moulded by the historical traditions of the Soviet Communist Party, but at the same time returning to some of the ideas of the February revolution. While borrowing much from the West, both in terms of ideas and technology, the new thinking in the broadest sense was an attempt to generate a convincing alternative to capitalism and liberal democracy, a new politics of feasible socialism.

The new model of socialism attempted to understand the power system that actually emerged after 1917. Marx's historicist view that the abolition of private property in the means of production would complete the process whereby class power passed from the aristocracy to the bourgeoisie and then to the working class, where it would remain 'at the end of history' since there was and could be no successor class, was shown to be seriously flawed. Power, considered as a set of relationships, was appropriated by what has variously been called a central political bureaucracy, a new class and much else besides. The key point was that at its most benign the type of socialism that emerged in the Soviet Union, leaving aside personalities, was an extraordinarily exaggerated form of the social democratic project for the rational management of society by a public sector bureaucracy. From town hall to the Kremlin this is a statist form of social management that tends to disenfranchise the population from effective participatory democracy and subjugates it to the despotism of the specialist and the bureaucracy. It is not surprising that much current Soviet criticism of the administrative-command system sounds rather like the new Right critique of the welfare state in the West.

The central shift was from an economistic socialism, where social ties are determined by the relationship between things, such as the ownership of the means of production, to a humanistic socialism where the emphasis is on the relationship between people. Both these aspects can be found in Marx and can conventionally, if inaccurately, be seen as a contrast between the humanistic young Marx, concerned with human alienation and ways of overcoming it, and the economistic old Marx, whose vision was allegedly narrowed by immersion in economics. Gorbachevism vigorously returned to the 'young Marx'.

Perestroika was an attempt to demonstrate that there are alternatives to a monolithic, centralised and stifling form of Communist rule. The debate about alternatives focuses on the viability of Bukharin's programme in the 1920s, and indeed whether Leninism under Lenin was an alternative to what came later, and whether the elements of continuity between Lenin and Stalin were purely contingent. The Bolshevik alternatives to Lenin himself have not as yet been aired to a large degree, presumably because most held views that Lenin himself labelled as ultra-leftist. This does not apply to the coalitionists, who in the first weeks after the Revolution argued for a broad-based government, or to the Democratic Centralists who already in late 1918 insisted that a new constitution had to be devised that could defend the soviets from the encroachments of the Bolshevik party machine.

The coda of the reforms is that Bolshevism is bigger than Leninism. The fact that so many of the current debates are almost precise replicas, indeed a continuation, of those in the early years of Soviet power is not accidental. For some sixty years the contentious issues in 'socialist construction', as it used to be called, were suppressed rather than resolved. Now Gorbachev allowed these questions to be examined, and some of the alternatives put forward by the Bolsheviks in contrast to Lenin's and Stalin's views are being explored. By 1990 this was not enough, and the ideas of the Menshevik and even non-socialist opponents of Leninism were now given a more sympathetic hearing.

The most profound aspect of destalinisation is the modification of the materialist foundations on which it was based. History itself seems to have revolted against Marxist materialism. As Arnold Toynbee insisted, spiritual values ultimately play the decisive role in the development and maintenance of civilisations. In particular, for Toynbee Christianity provided a bulwark against the assault on the values of his civilisation. For Gorbachev, too, the profound spiritual crisis of Soviet society by the early 1980s was one of the cardinal problems he faced on his accession. He tried to restore a sense of human values and freedom, albeit couched in socialist terminology. This entailed the repudiation of the traditional Left Bolshevik obsession with the economic essence of socialism, a view that the conservatives still retain. The editors of *Pravda*, in their response to Afanasev's assertion that 'I do not consider the society created in our country socialist, however "deformed" ', acidly commented: 'Has Yuri Afanasev really "forgotten" about such defined features of our social order as the socialist system of the economy, based on the social ownership of the means of production, the absence of exploiting classes and unemployment. . .' (*P*, 26 July 1988). For Gorbachev, however, the new Soviet notion of freedom was more than an abstract idealism; rather it was rooted in European cultural values, including the Marxist critique of liberal freedoms. It tried to combine positive and negative freedoms in an original synthesis.

Gorbachev appears to have accepted, consciously or not, Aleksandr Bogdanov's argument in his Utopian novel of 1908, *Red Star*, that even after socialism was established there would remain problems such as environmental imbalances, the dangers of atomic power and the relationship of science to society (Adams, 1989). Moreover, in his other writings Bogdanov developed a critique of Lenin's concept of power and the relationship of the party to society that retains its validity today (Sochor, 1988). Gorbachevism represents not only a historic reconciliation of revolutionary socialism with democratic socialism, but also a reconsideration of some of the debates that wracked the party even before the Revolution, and in particular the 'God building' controversy of Bolshevism's early years. The debate over the alternatives to Stalinism thus now shifted back to the rich debate over the alternatives to Lenin.

Gorbachevism restored a sense of motion and dynamism to the Soviet system and its ideology. In an important article in the early 1970s William Taubman took up Samuel Huntington's idea of the shift in emphasis in the study of social systems from the study of the given to emphasising the notion of development through various types of modernisation theory, a veritable 'change to change'. Taubman applied the notion of change to the study of Communist systems, though perhaps rather prematurely (Taubman, 1974). No longer was socialism defined as a state of being, the implication of Brezhnevian 'developed socialism', but as something to be changed and revived. The emphasis shifted from stasis and stability to dynamism and change. Soviet socialism has not lost its prescriptive element, the need to conform to a certain vision of what a socialist system should be, but under Gorbachev there was scope for experimentation.

At the base of Gorbachev's approach to politics is a profound reaffirmation of modernity. Contrary to Jean Baudrillard and other apostles of post-modernism, Soviet politics in the age of Gorbachev, perhaps reflecting its 'backwardness', gave solidity and meaning to processes that are melting away in Western philosophy. The very notion of 'reform', of 'change' and 'renovation', of 'progress', speak of modernity rather than post-modernity. The return to Enlightenment ideals, universal values and consensus, all suggested that *perestroika* represented the completion of the modernist project (cf. Habermas, 1985). Gorbachev's discourse was redolent of the nineteenth century but spoke of things of the twenty-first. The Soviet project at the end of the twentieth century was an attempt to restore 'real' politics and rejected the Baudrillard view that the real is no longer real in modern society. Instead Gorbachev posited a new vision of universality, of collective values and truth in a world that has meaning and can be interpreted using critical and common-sense faculties. Thus under Gorbachev the Soviet Union adopted the modern concept of political philosophy and the individual, the modernity proclaimed by the French Revolution.

Despite their early modernist flavour Gorbachev's reforms moderated what Karl Popper called 'historicism', the belief that history is a single unified process governed by intelligible laws of necessary development that inevitably lead towards a higher stage of human existence. The eighteenth-century writings of Voltaire and Condorcet were redolent of historicist assumptions that culminated in the nineteenth-century constructions of Hegel, Comte and Marx. From the Soviet historicist perspective phenomena could be understood only in terms of the place they occupied in the overall scheme of historical development. Soviet Marxism–Leninism remained a last redoubt of nineteenth-century universal progressivism based on an optimistic assumption of a rational and better world to come, while at the same time denying the rationality on which it was based. The irony of *perestroika* was that while Marxist historicism was abandoned a Hegelian historicism emerged to take its place.

A philosophy purged of Marxist historicism meant that the Soviet study of history lost some of its normative content. This necessarily elevated a Weberian approach to the study of the social sciences that stresses the distinctiveness of particular social formations whose features are the result of specific relationships rather than part of a pre-ordained march of history. Although the Communist Party continued to claim a leading intellectual role, it ceded its claim to absolute ideological sovereignty. This allowed a separation of knowledge and power, and encouraged the autonomy of a range of institutions to field their own ideas. As in the United States, a network of policy intellectuals emerged in or close to the corridors of power, above all in the institutes of the Academy of Sciences.

Gorbachevism entails a new understanding of democracy. V. Medvedev (1988) embraced the democratic forms of 'bourgeois democracy' that had long been decried by Soviet ideologists such as elections, civil liberties and representative assemblies, and thus separated democratic from class politics. It could be argued that the attempt to introduce democracy not only into political life but into the economy as well was based on a misreading of liberal democracy as full democracy. As Schumpeter (1943/1987) and others have pointed out, there are parts where liberal democracy does not reach, and factory management is one of them. From the Left Communists to the present there has been a search for a viable form of economic democracy (Kowalski, 1990, ch. 5). The partisans of New Left *perestroika*, represented by Kagarlitsky and others, revived the tradition of workers' democracy and self-management.

The rather confused reform of the government and the state left many in doubt as to whether a viable and democratic system could emerge. Gorbachev rejected elements of the tried and tested Leninist power structure; yet he refused, understandably, to adopt uncritically the Western model. The whole credo of Gorbachev's reforms was the belief that there was an alternative to capitalism and liberal democracy. Could he find, and indeed is there, a third path of late Communism? Max Weber was highly critical of the capitalist system, but could not conceive of a rational alternative. Gorbachevism, nevertheless, is dedicated to finding this alternative. Just as the co-operative movement was the 'third path' between statist socialism and capitalism, so Gorbachev sought to find a political third path, a type of co-operative or communitarian socialism. The basic problem is that no one knows what a democratic socialist state would look like. What sort of economic system would be able to combine economic viability with the social demands of the socialist programme? (See Brus and Laski, 1989.)

The new understanding that market relations in the economy and mixed forms of property are the basis for a new type of Soviet democracy is clearly analogous to the classic liberal belief that property and commodity exchange endow the individual with an independence that allows equal exchange in the political market-place. Soviet thinking thus returned to the cardinal principle of classic liberalism that capitalist production is the core of political emancipation. Late Communism thus looks suspiciously like early capitalism. It awaits only its own Marx to expose the alleged hypocrisy of an economically generated political system.

Gorbachev's programme was always one of radical Soviet socialist democracy rather than a liberal constitutional one. The notion of commune democracy re-emerged at least in the early period of *perestroika*, as a project capable of achieving the politics of feasible socialism. Gorbachevism modified Marx's and Lenin's theoretical anti-statism and emphasis on untrammelled popular power in a unified executive and legislative framework and, shorn of its excesses, a new form of commune democracy was in the making. The aim was to devolve more power to the soviets, more control over executive bodies, greater independence for judicial and constitutional bodies, a redefined role for the party, and scope for the pluralisation of Soviet politics and society. The new democratic revolution in the Soviet Union was based on a hybrid form of constitutional commune democracy.

The new democracy, however, was flawed by the imperfect relationship of the political system to civil society. There was a possibly fatal absence of a clear means of integrating political and civil society. Social movements and a pluralistic society, a civil society of sorts, either remained outside the main institutions of Soviet power and thus acted as a source of dissension, or were entrained into a system that still retained a totalising tendency towards what could be called overincorporation, not just part of a stable mechanism while retaining a separate corporate identity, but transformed into something like the 'transmission belts' of old.

One-party pluralism, however democratically practised, could not but add an element of authoritarianism to democratic *perestroika*. Reform Communists insisted that without the party *perestroika*, as currently understood, would not be *perestroika* at all but the swan-song of the old regime. The central paradox was that the only way for the aims of democratic *perestroika* to succeed was by putting an end to *perestroika* as a governed process and allowing the spontaneous resolution of conflicts without the guiding force of the party. The Democratic Union and other groups sought to transform party *perestroika* into people's *perestroika*. It was on the rock of party leadership that Gorbachev hoped to build the church of *perestroika*, but it was this rock that well-nigh broke the democratic potential of the reinvigorated society.

The Gorbachevite developmental and political model, despite its innovatory features in comparison with the old Soviet system, retained much from the past. By early 1990 the radical reform Communist Yuri Afanasev had become convinced that party *perestroika* could not lead to a genuine transformation. Soon after a vigorous speech on the first day of the 3rd Congress (12 March 1990) denouncing Lenin, whom he accused of having 'founded a system built on violence and mass terror', and condemning the whole history of Soviet Communism since 1917 as a disastrous mistake, he gave up his party card in April on the grounds that the party was beyond redemption (G, 20 April 1990). Thus the radicals increasingly became convinced that the transformatory side of *perestroika* would be defeated by its system-maintaining side, and so many left the party and urged a regrouping of political forces in the country.

The transformation of party *perestroika* into presidential *perestroika* in 1990 only served to underline *perestroika*'s tendency to rely on undemocratic methods to achieve democratisation, as in the reserved places for 100 Communist deputies to the Congress of People's Deputies. The problem is one which faces all developing countries, and one which Russia has faced in the past. Lenin's view of Peter the Great's modernisation drive as one which sought to 'drive out barbarism by barbaric means' aptly sums up the Bolshevik Revolution itself. The fundamental question was whether the Gorbachevite reformers had sufficiently distanced themselves from the old Leninist morality where the end justified the means, however barbaric. In other words, have the reformers been able to generate a new ethic to sustain the reforms? It is clear that democracy can be achieved only by democratic means and cannot be imposed by *diktat* from above. As John Stuart Mill always argued, to achieve democracy one needs to learn democracy.

While Communism promises the abolition of the state, all socialist revolutions to date have strengthened the powers of the state. The autonomy of the Bolshevik party from the working class was translated after 1917 into a remarkable autonomy of the state from society. One of the major achievements of *perestroika* is that it established a dynamic for this process to be reversed, for the state to retreat. In the jargon of *perestroika*, this was known as breaking down the administrative-command system. The basic process of *perestroika* was a twofold withdrawal: of the state's minute supervision of economic and social life; and the party's detailed guidance over politics and society.

Gorbachev argued that the USSR needed another revolution to break the drift from revolution to stagnation. The question remains of just how relevant the concept of revolution is in a post-revolutionary society. A revolution in the Marxist sense suggests the replacement of one class by another. In the Soviet context it is not clear which class was transforming itself from a 'class in itself' into a 'class for itself' and trying to assert its class power. The complex Soviet social structure and multifaceted process of reform cannot be reduced to a single class dimension.

The semantic and political distinction between concepts of 'socialism' and 'Communism' should be stressed. While socialism, as a practical programme for the improvement in people's daily lives, has shown itself capable of development and flexibility, Communism, as a project for the radical transformation of human nature and the state, lost its vision of the future. Communist reformism in practice meant the abandonment of Communism in favour of socialism; and late Communism in the Soviet Union represented an attempt to find an effective form of social democracy while retaining elements of Leninism. As long as one-party rule remained the Soviet Union could not be classified as a post-Communist system. *Perestroika* can be characterised as a programme to achieve a form of de-ideologised late Communism whose essence is rule by hegemony and consent, effective participation, welfarism and above all legal restraints on coercion and arbitrary power.

Although *perestroika* was accompanied by a significant broadening of political participation it remained a directed process, a 'revolution from above' guided by the reformist wing of the party. Roy Medvedev insisted that 'Even after the removal of its [the CPSU's] guaranteed monopoly under Article 6 of the constitution, it will remain the ruling party for a long time to come' (*G*, 20 April 1990). 'Revolution from above', however, gradually became 'reform from below' as popular pressure began to propose alternative programmes. The reforms launched by Gorbachev had the potential to achieve the transformation of the USSR, but they were not intended to turn the country into a post-Communist, post-Leninist, let alone post-socialist society. The retention of the party's leading role inhibited the development of procedural democracy. For Gorbachev the new model of socialism was far more than a Sovietised version of the Swedish welfare state. The aim of *perestroika* was not to abolish the Soviet system but to renew it, hence the 'revolution within a revolution' was indeed a reform.

The dilemma for Gorbachev was how to prevent the growing initiative of the people that he himself stimulated, ultimately challenging the party's monopoly on power. Gorbachev envisaged the party as a flexible and humane body encompassing all sections of society and not bound by any dogma. In this vision the focus was on attracting the right people into government and parliament. The new model of socialism associated with Gorbachevism was very much a long-term process of directed change. However, the very gradualism of *perestroika* entailed its own problems. *Perestroika* at various times appeared to be marking time following a sharp break from one plateau to the next – indeed, from one ontology of reform to another. But once on the latest plateau there appeared to be a loss of direction. An extended plateau followed the 19th party conference despite the personnel changes of autumn 1988 and the constitutional amendments. Even the elections of March 1989 were unable to reanimate enthusiasm for *perestroika* as such, and the personnel changes of September 1989, which just a few years earlier would have been greeted with astonishment, now appeared to be of little real significance.

This reflected more than continued dissatisfaction with the lack of food and goods in the shops; it represented a perception that unless an ideological breakthrough occurred *perestroika* had nowhere to go. Movement was vivid and rapid in Poland and Hungary, but the Soviet Union appeared trapped in contradictions and compromised with its ideological legacy. The 15–16 March 1989 CC plenum on agriculture, for example, still held out the prospect of socialism in the USSR, but a pale consumer socialism of food and shoes. For most of the population it was clear that food and shoes, on the whole, could be produced more effectively and at less cost by capitalism. Why try to find an improved socialist way of producing them when an alternative model was already available in the West?

In effect the new model of constitutional commune democracy was not capable of generating popular enthusiasm, perhaps because of a perception that the continued stress on exaggerated leadership would render it ineffective. Whereas the Czechoslovak reformers of 1968, and the revolutionaries of 1989, went to the very heart of the problems and tried to create a genuine democratic form of socialism, there remained a lack of focus to *perestroika*. Certain topics remained taboo, certain issues proscribed, certain powers inalienable, all of which endowed the process with an air of impermanence. Gorbachev was a master politician but even he could not have his cake and eat it: popular democracy but centralised party rule; *glasnost*, but not too much; the market, but combined with the planning system; national autonomy but not independence. Enthusiasm was certainly rekindled substantially in the Gorbachev years but not directly for *perestroika*, rather for what people could get out of it: national justice or autonomy, religious freedom, publication, or business opportunities. *Perestroika* allowed all these to happen but at the same time limited them. Hence official attempts to make *perestroika* a popular cause of democratised socialism failed dismally.

Soviet reforms, unlike those in Hungary and Czechoslovakia, were autonomous in the sense that no one was likely to invade the Soviet Union if it deviated too far from the received model of socialism. This in a sense made the reformist leadership its own policeman. The reforms were indeed self-limiting (cf. Staniszkis, 1984). The danger as perceived by the conservatives was that Communist reform would simply become a vehicle for the restoration of capitalism. The restoration of politics and the growing autonomy of administration meant the end of Communism as a distinctive practice of directed politics, as pa. aspiration to abolish politics altogether. The restor tended by definition towards post-Communism, and a whether an effective concept of late Communism could t seemed to run against the grain of history.

The spectre that haunted the Communist leaderships was meant the self-liquidation of the system. Reform, in other w   ume to mean not a better version of the existing model, but anot..er model altogether. This was decisively rejected by Gorbachev, notably in his Council of Europe speech in Strasbourg on 6 July 1989 where he condemned the view that 'what is meant by overcoming the division of Europe is actually "overcoming socialism" ' (*Ind.*, 7 July 1989). As years passed, with a deterioration in overall economic performance and declining standards of living, a crisis of legitimacy began to take shape, one which threatened the legitimacy of *perestroika* and ultimately Gorbachev's own position, but above all the legitimacy of the attempt to create a more democratic form of socialism. The old command form of socialism appeared to have failed to deliver the goods, and the question was raised ever more insistently whether the new form could, however much purged of 'distortions and deviations'. Once the attempt was abandoned in Eastern Europe, Gorbachev's Communist reformism became even more untenable.

The issue cuts to the very heart of the reform process. Is pluralism, and indeed, liberalism irremediably bourgeois and capitalist, and is any concept of 'liberal Communism' a contradiction in terms? If so, Gorbachev's liberalisation of the Soviet system had nowhere to go. In historical terms, it had no future, no niche in the pantheon of human society other than as a curious example of dead-end evolution dating back to the late twentieth century. Gorbachev tried to introduce elements of democracy and the market economy while maintaining the socialist nature of the system. Can the system reform and remain socialist, let alone Communist? If it remains Communist, can it reform? The fundamental belief at the root of Gorbachev's reformism is that Soviet socialism is not a 'dead-end' social formation but one capable of development. This is a belief that entails an act of faith. As we saw in our discussion of the concept of stagnation (page 82 ff), the nature of the crisis of the 1970s and 1980s is one which raises important questions about the whole pattern of Soviet development. *Glasnost* allows *perestroika* to interpret reform as a moment of truth: the lies and distortions of the past are exposed in order to develop a programme for the future. But the truth was more painful and deeper, and entailed the anguished examination of present ideas of socialism which may well also bear within them the seeds of a new stagnation.

..he question can be examined in two ways. The focus can be on either the political conditions for economic reform or the economic pre-conditions for political reform. With the first, the major question is whether even a reformed Communist system is compatible with a marketised economy. The major source of legitimacy for the system of 'guided democracy' was that it was able rationally to direct society to achieve certain socioeconomic goals. Once these goals are left more to the market, and the direct administration of the economy recedes, the rationale for the party's leading role is eroded. If the market is found essential in the economy for its superior allocative abilities, then the corollary might well be drawn that this applies equally to political life. Such a view is reinforced by the simultaneous retreat from the belief that the social interest can be known at all, and the realisation that such grandiose claims only buttressed the power of an increasingly grubby priestly 'new class'.

The political effect of marketising reforms is not clear. It could be argued that the guarantee of even relative success for some sort of market socialism is a plurality of political views and procedures. Could the market be introduced in the economy while restricting the pluralisation of political life by retaining the one-party system? The Gorbachevite model of socialism argued that one-party pluralism would be sufficient to express the various interests of society. Hungarian and Polish experience suggests that economic liberalism gives rise to demands for political liberalism, and that the longer this is resisted the smaller the long-term role for the party. As the Hungarian and Lithuanian Communist parties realised, better to lead from the front than to be forever chasing the popular movement. It was questions such as these that in 1990 shattered the unity of the CPSU. The social democratic Democratic Platform urged the rapid transition to a pluralistic political system and a market economy, whereas the Marxist Platform, while rejecting a guaranteed leading role for the party, remained loyal to some sort of self-managing constitutional commune democracy.

Brus (1973, 1983) has long argued that democracy is a prerequisite for a market economy to be able to function effectively. However, this statement should be modified, as Batt argues, by a more detailed analysis of the precise level of deconcentration and pluralisation of the political system that might be appropriate to allow the market to be able to work efficiently (Batt, 1988, part 1). This is clearly a crucial argument, since liberal democracy and statist socialism are not simply reverse sides of the coin but merge imperceptibly in a whole range of pinkish blues of social and Christian democracy where a social role for the state is defended. However, if this argument is taken further to suggest that a rebuilt and relegitimised leading role for the Communist Party – with adequate channels for participation of group influence which do not become excessive bulwarks for the defence of sectional interests – can be an effective partner for the marketising economy (as argued by Batt), then we arrive at precisely the central question on the viability of Gorbachev-type reforms. The non-democratic market variant will always be prey to the temptation of the state, especially in times of crisis, to encroach not only on the prerogatives of the market but also on the residual freedoms allowed to a more pluralistic society. It might in addition be a system forever in a state of tension, with not enough pluralism to allow the market to work and not enough rewards from the market to compensate for the absence of democracy. Either there is a social interest that can be interpreted by command mechanisms, in which case the leading role of the party is defensible and indeed rational, or the social interest is a variable determined by the balance of societal forces at any particular time, in which case party dominance is a distorting and irrational factor. All societies achieve integration in a variety of formal and informal ways, but experience tends to suggest that a single dominant party which hopes to avoid the pitfalls of corporatism is not an effective way of reconciling interests or acting as a viable long-term partner for a market economy.

The central question is whether the 'new democracy', which tried to combine a continued leading role for the Communist Party with democratic government and effective popular participation, was ever a viable programme. The restrictions placed on the development of pluralism in the first five years of *perestroika* echo some of the arguments of the early American democrats. James Madison, writing 'On Factions' in *The Federalist* no. 10, argued: 'There are again two methods of removing the causes of faction: the one, by destroying the liberty which is essential to its existence; the other, by giving to every citizen the same opinions, the same passions and the same interests.' Madison criticised both methods and proposed a third option, for the government to control the tides of factionalism which essentially must be allowed. Gorbachev moved the Soviet system from the first to the second and was not quite sure how to institutionalise the third. The problem, as always, focuses on the role of the Communist Party. What would the party do in conditions of liberty? Its whole purpose was to lead and guide, and it would find itself redundant if the polity no longer required such guidance. Gorbachev tried to break this vicious circle by reconciling party leadership with democracy. The ambiguities in the practice of the new democracy were the result. The new semi-democratic political institutions of *perestroika* were tested in the harsh fires of national and industrial unrest, and proved reasonably effective. Their very success made the vanguard role of the party not only redundant but counter-productive, acting as a force of disorganisation rather than stability.

The election of Ivan Polozkov as first secretary of the Communist Party of the RSFSR in June 1990, at a conference of delegates to the 28th party congress which then turned itself into the founding congress, appeared a decisive turning-point. The spectre was there for all to see of a party unable to reform itself. The election of an *apparat* politician of the worst kind, who had revealed his antipathy to market reforms by the suppression of the co-operative movement in Krasnodar *krai*, where he had previously been first secretary (*P*, 18 October 1989), boded ill for the fate of reforms, and presaged a period of tension between the Russian Communist Party and the Russian parliament, headed by Eltsin.

The 28th party congress saw the reorganisation of the Politburo, the adoption of new rules, the expansion of the Central Committee, and the adoption of an interim programme. 'Towards a Humane, Democratic Socialism', pending the adoption of a new programme (see p. 174). By making himself elected by the full congress, Gorbachev at a stroke freed himself from the traditional 'circular flow of power', in which the General Secretary had to be careful to pack the Central Committee with his supporters to avoid being voted out. The compromises incorporated into the congress's resolutions, and indeed the strong undercurrent of 'Old Left' conservatism in the debates, left the radicals disappointed. The congress equivocated over the withdrawal of party groups from the workplace, the security forces and the army and the transformation of the party into a territorially-based parliamentary party. The departification of the uniformed services and labour became one of the main demands of the democratic opposition in order to dismantle the strongholds of the bureaucratic administrative system. The RSFSR parliament had already declared party organisations in these bodies illegal. In comparison with Ligachev, Ivashko as deputy General Secretary might well have appeared a centrist, yet his record in the Ukraine and speeches in the Central Committee suggested that he was a loyal *apparatchik* (see *Iz. TsK KPSS*, 6/1990: 75). The failure of the party to change its name seemed to represent the larger failure of the party to change its nature.

The much heralded split in the party did not take place at the congress, yet Eltsin's walk-out from the hall, closely followed by the announcements by Gavriil Popov and Anatolii Sobchak that they, too, would leave the party, symbolised both the failure of the party radically to reform itself, and the fact that parallel structures of power to the old party-state were emerging. The leader of the Democratic Platform, Vladimir Shostakovskii, also left the party, and Vladimir Lysenko announced that the Platform would be constituting themselves as a separate organisation within the CPSU for the time being.

The features of the emergent post-Communist and post-*perestroika* order take some four forms, all predicated on a declining role for a single ideology claiming a monopoly on the truth. The first was the 're-formation' of the traditional Soviet class structure. The development of marketising economic reforms meant that a 'new bourgeoisie' based on property and wealth began to take on a stronger identity against the old hierarchy based on privilege and power. The class position of the intelligentsia and of the new economically independent entrepreneurial class begins to be consolidated in new forms of class power. The second feature is that the 'leading role of the party' is sufficiently undermined to allow an embryonic or a fully-fledged multi-party system to emerge. 'Normal' political life is resumed with a free press, independent trade unions and a mass of competing interest and pressure groups. Above all, there is an accelerated process of party formation. At the 28th congress the Democratic Platform announced that in the autumn of 1990 it would be setting up a new oppositional party. They would be joining what was already becoming a very crowded forum as *neformaly* groups and popular fronts began to transform themselves into parties.

The third process was the consolidation of the soviets as alternative power centres. The election in March 1990 of a radical democratic bloc headed by Ilya Zaslavskii in the October district of Moscow, for example, meant that the district became a haven for independent groups. There they could be registered and find accommodation. Even as the 28th party congress met, the newly-elected RSFSR Supreme Soviet gathered to debate the formation of a 'coalition' government under the prime minister, Silaev, and the contrast between the two gatherings could hardly have been greater. In Moscow and Leningrad, in the Russian republic, in the Ukraine, Armenia and in other republics the outlines of a post-Communist order became increasingly distinct. The fourth element was the crisis in executive authority that we have mentioned several times before. Ryzhkov's government and its laws began to take on that aura of futility and impermanence that marked the activities of the Provisional Government in 1917. Instead, it was the laws passed by the parliaments of the individual republics that increasingly gained solidity. Problems in the economy and society that the all-union government had signally failed to solve were now tackled by the republics themselves.

These processes increasingly marginalised the Communist Party, and indeed Gavriil Popov noted that earlier a party congress would have been a major event, now the significance of the 28th party congress 'should not be exaggerated' (*Iz.*, 29 June 1990). Eltsin drove home the point at the congress when he argued that the fate of *perestroika* and the country's development would be 'solved by the people beyond the walls of the building, by the soviets of people's deputies'. The congress could only deal with the 'fate of the party itself', and not even that but the fate of the party apparatus. The party had to be separated from state functions and to transform itself from an 'apparatus' party to a 'parliamentary' party joining with all democratic forces in a multi-party system. Otherwise the Soviet party would meet the same fate as the East European ones (*P*, 8 July 1990: 4). The top leaders had to report on their activities in the preceding five years. Yakovlev questioned the whole basis of Soviet development in suggesting that the 'radical modernisation of society' had been delayed 'by some fifty years' (*P*, 4 July 1990: 3). The commission drafting the new party programme was to report back by the middle of 1991, in advance of the next party congress whose meeting was set for some time in 1992. With the departure of Eltsin and others from the party, the stream of resignations was expected to become a flood. No one could predict the shape of the party at the next congress, but that it would be smaller was not in doubt.

The emergence of a type of dual power between the soviets and the Communist Party was only one element of a very complex political situation. The emergence of an executive presidency only complicated the transition of the Soviet Union from late to post-Communism. Above all, the very existence of the USSR in its old form, despite Gorbachev's attempt to negotiate a new union treaty, was put in question as one by one the republics followed the lead of the Baltic and the Russian republic and passed laws on their own state sovereignty. No one could predict the shape of the post-USSR policy, if it existed at all, other than that it would have to take the form of a voluntary union of free republics. If one of the legacies of the French revolution was the vindication of popular sovereignty in some form of liberal democracy, then the other was the triumph of nationalism. Europe in the nineteenth century was convulsed by the state-building endeavours, the attempt to achieve statehood for nationalities, of countries like Italy and Germany. Following the First World War and the dissolution of the Austro-Hungarian empire the nations of Eastern Europe achieved statehood, albeit with contentious frontiers and with large minorities. Now the territory of the Soviet Union underwent a similar process. Without Communist ideology was there any justification for the retention of the Soviet Union?

The second Russian democratic revolution meant that after some seventy years the civil war that had begun in 1917 finally came to an end. And it was the forces represented by the February 'bourgeois democratic' revolution that finally triumphed over the revolutionary socialism espoused by the October revolution. The disintegration of the party itself reflected this fundamental ideological and political cleavage. As long as the battle was against Stalinism and neo-Stalinism, the liberals and reform Communists could more or less work together. When the question arose of what to put in its place, then the ranks of the reformers divided, and the party itself split, between those who endorsed a radical, liberal, political and economic agenda, and the so-called conservatives who hoped to retain, in the words of the programme 'Towards a Humane, Democratic Socialism', the 'socialist choice' and 'communist perspectives' of the country (*P*, 15 July 1990). They avoided the question of who had actually made this 'choice', and the features of the 'communist perspective'. While late Communism, and indeed the notion of post-Communism, tend to focus on the negation of past mistakes, the problem now was one of affirmation: what was to take the place of past structures and ideas?

Gorbachev's aim was a dynamic and efficient economy accompanied by a reactivated society and revived political institutions. The aim was not democracy in the liberal democratic sense but some form of constitutional commune democracy. Commune democracy is a radical project for a participatory society based on socialist property. Gorbachev was thus quite sincere in his endless espousal of 'more democracy, more socialism'. The contradiction between the enormous sound and fury of *perestroika* and its limited achievements lay in the problem that no one, not least Gorbachev, knew what the constitutional commune democratic form of socialism would look like other than that it would be very different from the old model of state socialism. In his second speech at the 28th congress Gorbachev noted the 'explosion of freedom' in the country and the politicisation of society, and he poured withering scorn on the 'conservatives' in the party who could not adjust to the new realities. As for those who suggested that the Soviet Union should have taken more resolute steps during the East European revolutions of 1990 including possible intervention, Gorbachev was nearly speechless with anger: 'Well, do you want tanks again. Shall we once again teach them how to live?' He analysed the crisis in the party and defended its role in the vanguard of democratisaion. He correctly identified the key issue as 'what do we understand by socialism?' (*P*, 11 July 1990).

After five years of *perestroika* it became clear that Gorbachev was willing to sacrifice the essentials of the Marxist–Leninist ideology, and indeed the constitutionally guaranteed leading role of the party, to achieve his goal. The mere fact, however, that an alternative was being sought to the 'normality' associated with Western democracies meant that while Soviet politics had become secularised and relatively deideologised (that is, in comparison with its own past), it still retained elements of Utopianism, the search for the politics of feasible socialism.

Perestroika is in all likelihood the last great myth (in the Sorelian sense) of the Soviet Union. Gorbachev sought through the mythologisation of *perestroika* to capitalise on the Soviet system's enormous mythologising capacity to achieve change. But the very mythologising process was undermined by *glasnost's* profoundly subversive character once it had escaped from the instrumentality that the authorities had hoped to impose on it. The movement for social and political renewal outgrew the initiator of *perestroika*, and this was both the triumph of the Soviet peoples and a personal tragedy for Gorbachev. He unleashed forces that he could no longer control, and it appeared that his own capacity for development began to exhaust itself. By 1990 he was no longer leading from the front, a characteristic noted in the preface, but was overtaken by events and was always one step behind the popular movement.

The political crisis from 1988 was pregnant with resonances with the early years of the century. The blockage on institutionalising the democratic forces in society under the late Tsarism had led on to revolution. A crisis of power dragged on despite Gorbachev's assumption of the strengthened presidency. The attempt to 'consolidate' on a centrist position, the programme of the 28th party congress, was no longer viable because there was no longer a centre. The polarisation of politics, as in 1917, reflected the reality that there could be no third way between parliamentary power and the *dirigisme* of the party apparatus. By prolonging the crisis of dual power the country entered the antechamber of civil war. The urgent economic and national crises did not allow the country the luxury of a prolonged political crisis, and the tenacity of the party apparatus in clinging to power led precisely to the worst result. Not for Russia and the USSR what Lech Walesa called 'the gift of history' in Poland, the forced but ultimately voluntary withdrawal of the Polish Communist Party in July–August 1989.

An assessment of *perestroika* is open to an optimistic and a pessimistic reading, and the two are not entirely incompatible. The optimistic view would point to the undoubted gains of *glasnost*, the new honesty in history and the social sciences and the removal of the pervasive fear and threat of coercion. People were no longer comrades but once again became citizens as large sections of society were drawn into active politics. The international climate improved beyond measure and the East European countries freed themselves from the legacy of Stalinism. The list could be extended indefinitely, but the key point was the rapid construction of the scaffolding for the edifice of parliamentary politics in the individual republics and in the union as a whole in the Congress of

People's Deputies and the Supreme Soviet. Above all, in the heartlands of the republic all this had taken place without bloodshed.

The pessimist would have no problem conceding all of this and yet retain a sceptical view of the country's evolution. No amount of sociological determinism on the maturation of Soviet society could deny the fanatical grip on power of the party apparatus and of the bureaucratic system as a whole, its continued use of chicanery and demogogy to retain its privileged position justified by its defence of the so-called socialist choice of the country. Moreover, how could one speak of deideologisation when Gorbachev accused Eltsin in May 1990 of not having used the word socialism once in his programmatic speech as a candidate against Polozkov for the presidency of the RSFSR? Eltsin neatly responded by saying that there were many different sorts of socialism, including national socialism. The army itself increasingly reflected the disintegration of the polity. At the founding congress of the Communist Party of the RSFSR in June 1990 General Albert Makashov assaulted Gorbachev's record both at home and abroad. The KGB, as usual during *perestroika*, tried to ride with the hounds and run with the hare, but the case of Major-General Oleg Kalugin, the KGB head of counter-intelligence in the 1970s, who exposed the continuing arbitrariness of the organisation, indicated on which side the KGB would come down. Kalugin accused the KGB of being 'a state within a state' with its agents everywhere from the Russian Orthodox Church to many of the new parties. The country was a giant concentration camp, he argued, dominated by a 'party-police system' (*A. iF.*, 26/1990: 6–7). Kalugin himself was stripped of his rank and exposed to criminal prosecution. At the 28th congress Kryuchkov supported Ligachev's version of authoritarian *perestroika* and condemned Shevardnadze's alleged excessive demilitarisation of Soviet foreign policy: 'We have something to defend, and we need something to defend it with' (*P*, 5 July 1990: 3).

The whole notion of stagnation, as we have seen, might be something not only applicable to the Brezhnev years but might well be the underlying feature of the whole pattern of Soviet development. In that case, the Gorbachevite formulation of *perestroika* was doomed to failure. The economic problems could not be tackled until the political crisis was resolved, and were probably terminal under any conditions. The only hope was for the individual republics to distance themselves from the sinking ship of the Soviet state. And, to cap it all, the pessimist would argue that the political developments of the first five years of Gorbachev's reforms had given not democracy but freedom, not liberty but licence, and revealed the intrinsic inability of Russians, especially after seventy years of Soviet power, to channel political energies into system-integrative ways.

And indeed, the country needed more time for the independent movement to mature, for the new parties to consolidate themselves, to build structures and support, and for democratic and liberal consciousness themselves to ripen. It could be argued, and this was the implication of the arguments in favour of the strong hand of the 'new authoritarianism', that what the system needed was not democracy but liberalism in order to undermine the totalitarian structures in politics and society. Liberalism can long survive without democracy, as England demonstrated in the two hundred years up to the mid-nineteenth century. Liberalism entailed the separation of powers, an independent judiciary and private property. Liberal democracy only came later, and it could be argued that the two terms are contradictory: the totalitarian potential of democracy was demonstrated by Soviet history; and, indeed, a strong case can be made that the democratic agenda undermines liberalism, and *vice versa*. Fate was not to give Russia and the other republics the necessary years. The unreformability of the apparatus, the economic crisis and the national conflicts meant that immediate solutions had to be found. Russia and the other republics had to achieve in a few years what the Western democracies had taken centuries to build. The experience of post-war Germany and Japan, in their different ways, suggests that this is possible.

Between these two perspectives it can be seen that Russia and the USSR would require between two and two hundred years to emerge from the multiple crisis. Two years might see the emergence of effective parliamentary parties and the development of liberal and democratic institutions, a new federal structure for the republics and Russia itself, and a reasonably functioning economic system. However, two hundred years would be required for the restoration of the organic structures of the fibres of society, so rudely torn by the sad events of the twentieth century. The rural population and land workers, and the land itself, will take decades to return to a modicum of health. The economic structures of society cannot simply be reoriented to a market system: the technological, managerial and psychological infrastructures are lacking. Above all, the liberal mentality and the democratic proceduralism have to grow in organic inter-relationship with the structural adaptation of society itself to the 'standards of civilisation' operating elsewhere: toleration, the defence of the rights of minorities, formalism, patience and parliamentary proceduralism. All of this has began, but it will take decades, if not centuries, to overcome the legacy of Utopian socialism and the crisis of early twentieth century Russia.

Perestroika clearly showed much continuity with the Bolshevism of the past. The commitment to a renewed Marxian socialism, to October 1917 and Lenin's bequest, was more than rhetorical and placed the reforms in the tradition of the previous seventy years. From this perspective Gorbachevism represented no more than the honest, indeed idealistic, application of the stock of ideas that were the very currency of the Bolshevik socialist revolution. Thus *perestroika* was perhaps the last, and most appealing, of a long line of permutations of the Soviet system. Gorbachevism did not represent quite such a break with the past as the apostles of *perestroika* tried to make out.

However, the novel elements are striking as system-maintenance gave way to system-transformation. The psychology of Gorbachev's reform Communism was a future-oriented outward-looking form of politics. It allowed the country's reintegration into the world economy and society. Nevertheless, a post-Communist system cannot altogether shed the legacy of its Communist past. This might take the form of a strong commitment to the public provision of welfare, full employment and liberal social legislation. Some of the more negative features may also be present, with an authoritarian political ethos, envy of the more successful based on the psychology of 'equality in poverty', intolerance of minorities, and a strong military and security apparatus. The 'new bourgeoisie' may engage in a buccaneer form of capitalism, with an eye to the quick profit and a carpet-bagging attitude to what had formerly been state property.

A post-Communist system will not necessarily be a more democratic, open and just system. If the reforms do not produce tangible results fast enough, if no feasible reformed socialist system can be devised, if no stable constitutional structure can be created, then the chronic economic crisis and political instability might well promote a yearning for the 'new' or the old authoritarianism. Such a post-Communist outcome would be deideologisation compensated by coercion, a Francoisation of the Soviet political system, or indeed a march into Fascism through democratic elections as in Germany in 1933. The varieties of post-Communism range from a renewed Stalinism to a form of national Bolshevism purged of Marxism, military dictatorship, national fragmentation and civil war – and, the possibility must not be excluded – some form of liberal democracy. Russia has to learn over again that there are no short cuts to democracy other than democracy itself.

Perestroika and the world

The speed and scale of the East European revolutions of 1989 raised ever more insistently the question: could a Leninist type of socialism survive in the Soviet Union once it had been transcended in Eastern

Europe? Could a reform policy rooted in the traditions of 1968 and 'socialism with a human face', which in effect sought to institutionalise a type of one-party pluralism, be viable in conditions far removed from those pertaining a generation ago? The profound question facing the reformers was that not only did Marx never indicate what came after Communism: according to the scheme of historical materialism nothing *could* follow it. Classical Leninists always believed that, ruling out military reverses, Communist revolutions were irreversible. Now the revolutions in Eastern Europe made plain that Marxist–Leninist regimes were distinctive phases in historical development that would, sooner or later, be replaced by something else. Quite what, Soviet reformers did not know.

Perestroika yet more firmly entwined the destiny of the Soviet Union with that of the West and the world. The Soviet need to concentrate on domestic reform prompted a thorough evaluation of its foreign policy and indeed the very principles on which it had conducted its international relations since 1917. A system driven by ideological and programmatic aspirations voiced in global terms run by a small group who regarded themselves as the vanguard of a world revolutionary process, however tempered this aspiration may have been in practice, was transformed into a more genuinely national form of government which moderated some of its global and teleological aspirations. The de-ideologisation of Soviet foreign policy meant that the USSR was now committed to the stability of the international system rather than to its destruction.

The new basis for East–West relations was both cause and effect of *perestroika*. Looked at in the long view, beginning with Peter the Great's attempt at modernisation, *perestroika* was accompanied by a remarkably peaceful international climate. Indeed, the last 400 years of European politics have been conducted against the backdrop of war or the threat of war, the rise and decline of great powers, whereas at present the rise of a relatively united Europe and the relative decline of the United States and the USSR as superpowers may well not be accompanied by wars but by the boredom at the end of history, as Fukuyama (1989) playfully put it.

The new political thinking in international relations modified the Soviet Union's relationship with all other countries and processes. As far as global international relations were concerned, Gorbachev sought to find a way out of the 'exterminism' of the post–1945 period in which, according to E. P. Thompson, the arms race and the associated conflicts between states had acquired a momentum of their own beyond the control of individual governments (Thompson, 1982). Rather than taking the extreme 'green' position of those like Rudolf Bahro, who advocated the radical repudiation of industrial civilisation and the modern society that spawned nuclear weapons in favour of an ecologically sound spiritual transformation (Bahro, 1974), Gorbachev hoped to transform the existing structures of society to negate the exterminism implicit in the nuclear arms race. He thus confirmed the earlier Soviet modification of Lenin's thesis that true peace could only be achieved through socialism, since imperialist capitalism was prone to war. Khrushchev's view that nuclear war was not inevitable was taken further to eliminate the dangers of bulging nuclear arsenals and, as outlined at the 27th party congress, ultimately to abolish nuclear weapons altogether. Gorbachev's achievement was to invest the traditional Soviet struggle for peace, which in the old view amounted to the same thing as the struggle against war-mongering imperialism, with a less partisan content and broadened it to include new aims and a new constituency, to move from confrontation to international collaboration.

Gorbachev not only tamed the rest of the world in Soviet perceptions, but was also able to 'normalise' the Soviet Union in the eyes of the West. His impact on Soviet standing led to the triumph of equilateralism, the view that East and West are equally good or, depending on one's view, equally bad, and equally responsible for an arms race that has encompassed the globe. Above all, equilateralism suggested that there was a moral equivalence between the two superpowers. With the beginning of the overt deideologisation of Soviet foreign policy and the return to something akin to the 'normal' great power relationships of the nineteenth century, equilateralism has triumphed.

The onset of reform Communism seemed to have demonstrated the validity of the major argument of the convergence thesis, namely that industrial societies of whatever political colour share a basic commonality in social and political processes, above all focusing on economic and political pluralism. The corollary of this was that the socialist and capitalist systems were seen as moving towards each other in some form of welfare democracy. The East would accept a growing role for the market and a degree of political pluralisation, while the West would move towards a greater scope for government intervention in regulating the economy and the provision of welfare services. The triumph of the radical Right in Britain and the United States in the 1980s suggested that the West had stopped the move towards social democracy, while the Soviet Union since 1985 has come to accept some of the basic tenets of convergence and de-ideologised welfarism. Vadim Medvedev's new conception of socialism argued that the old Soviet view that capitalism and socialism would develop on diverging paths was obsolete, but rather than talking of the convergence he insisted that the two systems would develop on close but parallel lines. Both were part of human civilisation bound together by the same threats of nuclear annihilation and ecological catastrophe (_P_, 5 October 1988: 5). By this he meant that the Soviet Union would become an integral part of the world economy and society but would retain its specific political and ideological forms. The deideologisation of interstate relations had at its core the belief that universal human values take precedence over the conflict between socialism and capitalism.

One of the elements guaranteeing the irreversibility of democratic reform was the influence of world society. The international implications of the re-establishment of some sort of authoritarian regime in the USSR would be horrendous: the West, however ambivalently, supported Gorbachev's democratic revolution. There is no doubt that _perestroika_ represented a response, if a rather belated one, to changes in the world economy and society. It became clear to the reformers that in the modern world there could no longer be discrete social systems: all states were part of an international system and Soviet-type systems could not even aspire to political, let alone economic, autarky. In the late twentieth century the elements of world economy and world society have prevailed over national economic, and to a degree even national political, sovereignty. The functional imperative of co-operation and interdependence became a well-nigh irresistible force. Notions of discrete capitalist and socialist systems have been undermined, and indeed in the advanced industrial societies capitalism and socialism as ideas, notably in the social democratic welfare states of Austria and Sweden, have merged. The scope for a third model in a world where even the second model, Soviet-type socialism, is losing its identity cannot be considered bright. Rather than seeking to destroy the developing global society, the limit of Soviet aspirations was to play a part in shaping the pattern of the emerging united world.

The element of 'catching up' with the West was perhaps one of the strongest inspiring _perestroika_. In a crude way _perestroika_ can be defined as making up lost time to reach Western technological, economic and social levels. Just as under Stalin, the standard of economic achievement was set in the West, but the major difference with earlier years is that Gorbachev recognised the political and cultural context in which economic and technological progess is situated. The aim earlier was to defeat the West's capitalism by using Western economic and technological means, to borrow Western technology but to keep out the Western culture in which it was located and which gave it meaning. Traditional Soviet policy has been a curious blend of engagement and isolation. _Perestroika_ represented a solid period of engagement, and indeed the Westernisation of Soviet politics and ideas governing international relations. However, some of the old ambivalence remained, to a degree mediated by the great power status of the country. By no means can *perestroika* be taken as the 'victory' of the West over Russia, but the triumph of suppressed elements of European civilisation in the Soviet Union itself. These elements have been liberated to the greatest extent in the Baltic and western USSR.

Indeed, the Europeanisation of the USSR can be taken as the theme of *perestroika*. As Djilas pointed out, 'Changes in the USSR are either not going to happen at all, or will happen in close interaction with Western civilisation, founded, in our opinion, on human rights in the modern interpretation of the concept, and on a rational non-ideological economic system' (Djilas, *Glasnost*, 12/1987: 4). Gorbachev has striven for the USSR to adapt to the norms of 'civilisation' set by the cultural and political aims of the West (defined as a political rather than a geographical entity). This standard of 'civilisation' includes basic human rights, the right to life, dignity and property, freedom to travel, to practise religion as seen fit, and the rule of law (Gong, 1984). *Perestroika* can add little to this agenda, but what it can do is generalise them as a programme to be implemented on its own territory and the world in the coming century. This will be a natural development of the Helsinki process, perhaps confirmed by the human rights conference in Moscow in 1991.

The Soviet Union thereby will rejoin a developing global society and global culture, having failed in its aspirations born of the October Revolution of developing and spreading its own global counter-culture. It will not only rejoin world society, but will no doubt play a part in shaping its development. The return of the USSR to the European fold marks yet another step in the transition of the 'international system' into an 'international society' (cf. Gong, 1984: 10). The Soviet Union has long been an active member of the international system, with a stable state machinery, reasonable adherence to precepts of international law and treaties, patterns of diplomatic life and so on. The norms of 'international society', however, reflect more specifically the values of liberal democratic society, above all with the emphasis of individual rights of men and women to 'life, liberty and property'. This normative and rather prescriptive agenda is intrinsic to the Helsinki process, confirmed by the Vienna conference, and is one which Gorbachev accepted. The standard of 'civilisation' in this context is one where there is a civil society sheltering in the lee of a regulated, ordered and law-governed state.

Despite much criticism of the concept of a common European home as lacking content, it did provide a foundation on which a house could be built. Gorbachev's vision in Italy in December 1989 of a 'commonwealth of independent states' is the only practicable way forward, and confirmed the renunciation of Soviet regional hegemony in Eastern Europe. The status of the European Community as a post-national regional association, however, is left ambiguous in Gorbachev's thinking. There is a need, as Manfred Woerner, Secretary-General of NATO, observed in October 1989, for a new political order in Europe. This was in many ways the central theme of the Malta summit in December 1989 and the 'London declaration' marking the formal end of the cold war at the NATO summit of 5–6 July 1990. What would be the political structures that could manage the momentous changes on the Continent? In the short term the answer was the transformation of NATO and the Warsaw Pact into military–political alliances, and ultimately into purely political structures, followed, finally by the dissolution of the blocs altogether.

The outlines of a Eurasian community from the Atlantic to the Pacific are beginning to emerge in which the resources of Western Europe help develop the East as part of an expanding community of world civilisation. The first step was for the division of Europe to be overcome, not by the victory of one side over the other but through the prevailing of common human values. Communism, socialism and capitalism can never be defeated but they can be transmuted. The new unit need not necessarily be the nightmare Eurasia of Orwell's *1984*, but a society that works for common economic and social goals, and with a deeper appreciation of the potential of the democratisation of human society. Each country retains its own identity, but comes to terms positively with the growing interdependence of the world and gives it structured political and economic life.

Francis Fukuyama has generalised the process of the Soviet Union's 'Westernisation' to encompass a global process. The end of the cold war has inaugurated the 'end of history' as such in Europe, the final point of humanity's ideological evolution and the 'universalisation of Western liberal democracy as the final form of human government', the victory of economic and political liberalism. The West in this view triumphed in the cold war and demonstrated the bankruptcy of Marxism–Leninism as an effective organising principle for society, with no alternative all-embracing ideology available to take its place. Fascism has been defeated and nationalism does not offer such an organising principle (Fukuyama, 1989). In this view there can be no 'third way', a form of democratic socialism or co-operative capitalism, between Communism and capitalism, or indeed, and this is the subtext, to the American way of life. The argument is more than wishful thinking and tries to come to terms with important developments. Absent, however, is an understanding of the very complex ideas and processes that have always governed the development of Soviet society, let alone generated the radical challenges, of which socialism is only one, to liberal democracy. These challenges, at their best, encompass environmentalism, democratic feminism and anti-racism, among many others. Ultimately, the challenge facing *both* the West and the Soviet Union into the twenty-first century is not only to find effective rather than plebiscitary forms of democracy, with extended accountability and participation, but also to find new principles of community that, while developing individual rights and choice, can provide a framework for the fulfilment of the human potential of the entire society.

Once again, as under Peter the Great, the civilising or modernisation of Russia is taking the form of its 'Westernisation', evoking the same debates between the 'Westernisers' and the 'Slavophiles'. During *perestroika* the latter have been represented by Russophiles, the original term used until the mid-nineteenth century for those who cherished Russia's native traditions as opposed to the Westernisers' alleged indiscriminate supping at the foreign table. While the Soviet government has retreated from its messianic exceptionalism, Russian thinkers, who cannot be labelled nationalists in any simple sense, have stressed the exceptionalism of Russia's destiny and its communitarian traditions.

Fears that *perestroika* might open the Soviet Union to alleged pernicious Western influence strengthened the position of the more isolationist conservatives. This conservatism, based on a sense of Russia's uniqueness, has taken both a political and a cultural form. On the cultural level, there have been bitter struggles in the Writers' Union, and in effect the body has split in two. The reformist wing formed the Committee of Writers for Perestroika, endorsing Gorbachev's policies, while a more nationalist group, called Comradeship of Russian Artists led by the Siberian author Valentin Rasputin, voiced concern that the opening to the West may undermine traditional Russian values.

Soviet reforms may well have weakened the dominance of historicism and Soviet uniqueness, but there remain distinctive features. Gorbachev's thought is still imbued with a nineteenth-century view of progress. While Western Europe has lost all confidence in a *mission civilisatrice* to the rest of the world, and a demotic version haunts the American imagination, the Soviet Union still retains a strong commitment to its mission in the world. Under Gorbachev this is no longer defined in class terms but in the language of a universal humanitarianism. It is for this reason that the ideas coming from Moscow have had the power to capture the Western imagination and to fill the vacuum left by the decline of empire and any general sense of purpose and direction. The problem, of course, is that as a once great power the Soviet Union is contaminated by the poisoned chalice of imperial ambition, which is difficult to dissociate from the attractive ideas of the new thinking.

The Gorbachevite new model of socialism raised critical questions for the Western Left, including the reappraisal of the market, forms of ownership, the value to be placed on political liberty over social justice, the role of the individual and concepts of equality. The Western Left responded to the challenge provoked by Gorbachev's agenda for domestic reform and by the international system as bequeathed by Yalta with broad-ranging and critical debates and has, at its best, been enriched by the analyses being developed in the Soviet Union itself.

Western responses to *perestroika* have been varied and have changed over time. There have been few serious divisions between America and Europe, though the latter was more willing to commit itself to supporting Gorbachev and increasing economic contacts. In a paradoxical way, given her cold war past, Thatcher was one of the first to understand the implications of a more intelligent and flexible leadership in the Soviet Union. At her first meeting with President-elect Bush, Thatcher indeed noted the global implications of *perestroika*, arguing that Soviet reform had enabled humanity 'to begin the world over again' (*ST*, 20 November 1988). She perhaps exaggerated when arguing that Western policies had forced onto the Soviet Union its dramatic change of course, which prepared the way for Soviet withdrawal from Afghanistan, arms reduction talks and the INF treaty, and the settlement of regional issues but there is no doubt that a firm and united Western response to the provocative deployment of SS-20 missiles, the invasion of Afghanistan and other instances of late Brezhnevite adventurism had played its part in creating the conditions for a change in Soviet policy. President Mitterand's critique of these actions in particular was noteworthy for its principled and intelligent stance. The most dangerous policy would be one which adopted a tone of triumphalism or which tried to force the pace of change, and the West ultimately could do little more than react to Gorbachev's initiatives. The democratic revolution emerging from the womb of *perestroika* is capable of influencing the world, but at the same time the world is changing the Soviet Union. In particular, Western support for the development of a strong independent movement and the consolidation of civil rights is one way of ensuring the irreversibility of the reforms.

The new political thinking allowed the consolidation of stable and peaceful relations between East and West. The Soviet Union declared its aim to be a nuclear-free world, cut its military expenditure in line with the doctrine of reasonable sufficiency and accepted that the notion of interdependence means the primacy of politics over force in international relations. With the end of the familiar, if dangerous, post-war pattern of cold war international relations a new pattern had to be found. Indeed in September 1989 Lawrence Eagleburger, the deputy US Secretary of State, warned of 'the danger that change in the East will prove too destabilising to be sustained', and looked back to the 'stable and predictable' patterns of the cold war. Henry Kissinger sought to re-establish such a stability by urging a condominium of the great powers to regulate world affairs, and a conference to discuss the fate of Eastern Europe, both ideas which are precisely contrary to the trend towards the pluralisation of international relations.

The dilemma facing the West's leadership, however, was how to encourage Gorbachev's reforms while not making themselves hostages to fortune in the event of the defeat of Gorbachev and his reforms. Western declarations of willingness to help Gorbachev were, albeit slowly, translated into concrete policies. The most enthusiastic pro-tagonist of increased support was Hans-Dietrich Genscher, and this evolved into a variety of West German loans and increased trade. The experience of *détente* demonstrated that uncontrolled Western loans could actually exacerbate economic problems by adding a burden of debt to already overstretched economies, tending to delay the required economic restructuring and consolidating the position of an unreformed bureaucracy. A more targeted response was the development of joint ventures which acted as a conduit for the introduction of Western marketing, and technological and managerial know-how into the Soviet economy. Debt rescheduling, food relief, capital investment guarantees and much else could all facilitate the reform process.

The West could offer practical assistance in four related ways. The first was by co-operation in disarmament, the so-called 'peace dividend', so that resources could be speedily diverted to domestic reconstruction. The second was by economic assistance of all types, including co-operation to accelerate the Soviet Union's reintegration into the world economy. The third was by providing a stable political context and ways of managing the transition in Eastern Europe and the Soviet Union. The fourth was by providing commitment to the European process, in particular CSCE and its human rights agenda.

The notion of a common European home is beginning to make redundant the categories of East and West. The Hungarians and the Czechs, together with the Austrians and the Slovenes, have once again been able to consider themselves part of a common central European culture transcending the political divisions that used to separate them. However, as the USSR fell so Germany rose. The unification of Germany created an economic and political giant which could threaten Poland, in particular over Slansk (Silesia) and East Prussia, but it also created an enormous force for the economic development of Eastern Europe and the USSR. The German domination of Europe can be avoided only by strengthening the institutions of the European Community and common security, and developing a strategy for the common marketisation of Europe as a whole.

The *peredyshka* (breathing space) element in East–West relations is clearly a false analogy. If the current changes mean anything they must be based on a sense of irreversibility and on a long-term qualitative change in domestic and international Soviet affairs. Yet the transitional nature of *perestroika* added an element of uncertainty to international relations. Despite Gorbachev's great leadership skills it became clear that his ability to master events, used to such good effect in the management of foreign policy, tended to desert him in domestic affairs. The reformist drive in respect to nationalities, for example, often gave the appearance of crisis management rather than a mastery over events. Only when the fate of Russia has been decided one way or another, either a democratic Russia allied or united voluntarily with the former republics of the USSR, or the continued uncertainty and turmoil of *perestroika*, can the uncertainty in international relations be resolved.

The advent of Gorbachev filled a vacuum in the leadership of the world. His dynamic awareness and responsiveness to the problems facing humanity – nuclear annihilation, ecological disaster, the growing gap between the North and the South – and his bold initiatives to deal not only with the Soviet Union's own problems but his explicit setting of a global agenda, all suggested that at last a pilot for spaceship earth had been found (cf. Tucker, 1981). Gorbachev's consistent popularity in public opinion polls, *Time* man of the year and similar accolades clearly showed that he had struck a receptive chord in the global audience. His leadership was indeed visionary, in the sense that he saw the potential of present realities to be transformed into future possibilities. No citizen of the twentieth century need be warned of the dangers of charismatic leadership, yet Gorbachev's undoubted charisma was tempered by a severe pragmatism in considering how visionary policies could realist-ically be implemented. Gorbachev showed leadership qualities far beyond the concerns of the average national leader.

Perhaps the greatest achievement of Gorbachev and his reforms is that they set the USSR and its peoples on the path of 'normal' development, renouncing Utopianism and messianism. The curtain of fear began to be removed, *glasnost* allowed the Press to scour and probe, foreign travel became easier, thousands of informal groups agitated for all manner of causes, economic initiative began to be rewarded, nationality groups pursued their cultural and national paths, historical memory was returned to the people, and the country re-engaged with the rest of the world. The concept of change itself was now restored to social consciousness after years in which the core value was stability and controlled development. Gorbachev was a man of history and his reforms represented the recovery of history by the Soviet people and their ability effectively to shape politics. History did not end under Gorbachev but turned a new page. Yet after five years of *perestroika* an even greater challenge faced Gorbachev: to allow the transformation of the Soviet Union into a democratic community of free peoples.

Appendix 1

CHRONOLOGY OF MAIN EVENTS OF GORBACHEV'S LIFE AND RULE

2 March 1931	Mikhail Sergeevich Gorbachev born in Privolnoe, in Stavropol *krai*.
1950–5	Studied at the Faculty of Law of Moscow State University. Komsomol activist, party member from 1952.
1956	Appointed Komsomol First Secretary for the town of Stavropol.
1958	Second Secretary of Komsomol in Stavropol *krai*.
Dec. 1960	Becomes First Secretary of Komsomol in Stavropol *krai*.
Dec. 1962	Appointed party organiser for Stavropol *krai*.
Sept. 1966	Party First Secretary for the town of Stavropol.
Aug. 1968	Party Second Secretary for Stavropol *krai*.
April 1970	Party First Secretary for Stavropol *krai*.
June 1970	Elected deputy to the USSR Supreme Soviet.
April 1971	Elected voting member of the Central Committee of the CPSU missing the candidate stage.
Nov. 1978	Becomes Central Committee Secretary responsible for agriculture.
Nov. 1979	Becomes candidate member of the Politburo.
Oct. 1980	Becomes full member of the Politburo.
10 Nov. 1982	Brezhnev dies, Andropov appointed General Secretary 2 days later.
9 Feb. 1984	Andropov dies, Chernenko appointed General Secretary 4 days later.

1985

10 March	Chernenko dies; Politburo meeting selects Gorbachev as General Secretary; confirmed by meeting of Central Committee 11 March.
23 April	Central Committee plenum launches programme of restructuring and acceleration.
May	Anti-alcohol campaign launched.
1 July	Gromyko becomes Chair of the Presidium of the Supreme Soviet (President); Shevardnadze appointed foreign minister in his place.
October	Ryzhkov replaces the 80-year-old Tikhonov as Chair of the Council of Ministers; new state committee for agriculture and allied industries created, called Gosagroprom, out of five ministries and a state committee.
19–21 November	Geneva summit between Gorbachev and Reagan.

1986

January	Boris Eltsin replaces Viktor Grishin as head of the Moscow party organisation.
25 February– 6 March	Twenty-seventh party congress; political report by Gorbachev on reform; new Central Committee elected but many conservatives remain, slowing process of reform for next five years.
26 April	Chernobyl nuclear disaster, thirty-one immediate deaths, thousands in years to come, thousands evacuated and rich agricultural land lost.
June	Eighth congress of Writers' Union signals onset of cultural *glasnost*; censorship functions of Glavlit restricted.
July	Law on Unearned Income restricts unofficial economic activity.
28 July	'Vladivostok initiative' for 'the Pacific, our common home'.
31 July	Speech to Khabarovsk party activists insisting on need for 'little short of a revolution in the Soviet Union'.
18 September	Speech in Krasnodar condemning bureaucracy and calling for democratisation.

October	Reykjavik summit with Reagan, bold proposals for complete nuclear disarmament and door opened to INF treaty.
November	Law on Individual Labour Activity passed by Supreme Soviet; State Quality Inspectorate (*Gospriëmka*) created.
December	Sakharov released from internal exile in Gorky after telephone call from Gorbachev; riots in Alma Ata following replacement of Kazakhstan party leader, D. Kunaev, by a Russian, Gennadi Kolbin.

1987

27–8 January	Central Committee plenum launches programme of democratisation including multi-candidate secret elections for state and party posts and agrees to convocation of a special party conference.
February	A number of dissidents released.
April	Gorbachev visits Prague, calls for elimination of all nuclear weapons from Europe.
May	Law on Individual Labour Activity comes into effect; Matthias Rust lands aircraft in Red Square, leading to sacking of defence minister Sokolov and replacement by Yazov.
June	First multi-candidate elections held in about 5 per cent of constituencies in local soviet elections.
25–6 June	Central Committee plenum adopts radical economic reform programme, including Law on State Enterprises.
August	Gorbachev speaks in favour of leasehold in agriculture; rallies in the Baltic republics protest against their forcible incorporation into the USSR by the terms of the Nazi–Soviet Pact of 23 August 1939; Crimean Tatars hold demonstration in Red Square; first conference of independent political activists in Moscow, the Federation of Socialist Clubs; *perestroika* transformed by all these from reform from above to a slow-burning revolution from below.
23 October	Eltsin speaks against Gorbachev at Central Committee plenum.
2 November	Gorbachev's speech for seventieth anniversary of the Revolution opens door to historical re-evaluation of

the Soviet past but disappoints radicals. A period of conservative counter-attack.

November
Eltsin dropped from Politburo and relieved of his post as head of Moscow party organisation, replaced by Lev Zaikov.

December
Gorbachev visits Washington for first time and signs INF treaty whereby all intermediate-range nuclear weapons to be destroyed within three years.

1988

February
Bukharin legally rehabilitated; Talyzin sacked as head of Gosplan.

20 February
Supreme Soviet of Nagorno-Karabakh votes to leave Azerbaidzhan and to reunite the territory with Armenia; massacre of Armenians in Azerbaidzhanian town of Sumgait; countdown to civil war begins.

March
Mass demonstrations in Erevan in support of Nagorno-Karabakh, party authority withers away in the Armenian republic.

13 March
Nina Andreeva letter published in *Sovetskaya rossiya*, condemns liberalisation and defends the Stalinist past.

April
Agreement at United Nations on phased withdrawal of Soviet troops from Afghanistan.

5 April
Pravda responds to Andreeva after several weeks of official silence.

May
Gorbachev meets Orthodox leaders for first time; Reagan visits Moscow for first time; Gorbachev admits to the 'turmoil' caused by *perestroika*; the Democratic Union, the first independent party since the 1920s, established; creation of Popular Front for the Defence of Perestroika.

13 May
Central Committee conference on agricultural reform, Gorbachev again talks of leasehold.

June
Millenium of Russian Christianity; Kamenev and Zinoviev legally rehabilitated, while Suslov criticised.

28 June–1 July
Nineteenth party conference confirms process of democratisation and ratifies the course of Gorbachev's reforms.

July
Armenian Supreme Soviet and mass movement press for transfer of Nagorno-Karabakh, but Azerbaidzhan Supreme Soviet votes to keep the territory; Supreme

	Soviet in Moscow votes to maintain the status quo and against redrawing boundaries, while Gorbachev bitterly denounces Armenian activists; countdown to civil war accelerates.
August	Nationalist agitation in Baltic demanding economic and political sovereignty, and recognition of the illegality of 1940 incorporation of the republics; calls for return of inter-war flags and citizen rights.
September	Gorbachev's visit to Krasnoyarsk brings home popular anger at lack of material results of *perestroika*.
29 September	Central Committee plenum reorganises the Secretariat into six policy commissions; major personnel changes including demotion of Ligachev from responsibility for ideology to agriculture.
October	Popular fronts established in the three Baltic republics.
1 October	Meeting of Supreme Soviet, Gromyko resigns as its President, replaced by Gorbachev.
1 December	Constitutional amendments adopted by Supreme Soviet creating a new Congress of People's Deputies to meet biannually and a smaller semi-permanent Supreme Soviet; newly elected Congress to elect an executive President for a five-year term, renewable only once.
7 December	Gorbachev speech to the United Nations heralds new era of international co-operation, promises unilateral Soviet forces cuts of 500,000 (20 per cent of total), including withdrawal of 50,000 from Eastern Europe, and writes off some Third World debts.
8 December	Earthquake in Armenia.

1989

February	Nomination meetings to the new Congress of People's Deputies amid bureaucratic obstructionism against radicals.
15 February	Last Soviet troops leave Afghanistan.
15 March	Central Committee plenum devoted to agriculture.
26 March	First general multi-candidate elections deal a severe blow to conservative *apparatchiks*.
25 April	'Plenum of the long knives' purge of Central Committe old guard.
25 May	Gorbachev elected President of the Supreme Soviet.

25 May–9 June	First session of new Congress of People's Deputies, most televised live, showing vigorous political debate and unprecedented admissions of Soviet economic problems and historical distortions; Gorbachev elected President in unopposed vote; creation of the interregional group of radical deputies.
Summer	Miners' strikes in Kuzbass, Donbass and Vorkuta, voicing radical political and economic demands including the abolition of Article 6 of the 1977 constitution, ensuring the party's leading role in society.
19 September	Central Committee plenum adopts theses on nationality policy.
December	Sakharov and interregional group call for two-hour token strike on 11 December for abolition of Article 6 to be discussed at Congress; Sakharov dies 14 December.
2–3 December	Malta summit between Bush and Gorbachev against background of East European revolutions and breaching of the Berlin wall.
12–24 December	Second convocation of Congress of People's Deputies; Committee of Constitutional Review created and other laws passed, but Congress fails to resolve the key problems facing the country.
19 December	Lithuanian Communist Party declares independence from the CPSU.

1990

January	Civil war erupts in Azerbaidzhan and Armenia, Soviet power dissolves, military intervention in Azerbaidzhan; nomination meetings for local elections continue; Gorbachev visits Lithuania and concedes possibility of secession.
4 February	Massive pro-democracy demonstrations in Moscow and elsewhere.
5–7 February	Central Committee plenum adopts programme for multi-party democracy and strengthened presidency.
25 February	Second pro-democracy demonstrations urging the radicalisation of *perestroika*.
27 February	Supreme Soviet approves draft bill establishing American-style presidency.

March	Fifth anniversary of Gorbachev's leadership as country faces unprecedented difficulties and the end of *perestroika* as a reform process guided by the Communist Party as presidential power is consolidated; social, national and political struggles can no longer be contained by the old principles of rule within the terms of the one-party state, a new principle of consensus and democratic rule required; the Communist Party begins to disintegrate as it prepares for its 28th party congress.
4 March	Local and republic elections in the Russian federation and some other republics see victory of independent democratic candidates.
11 March	Lithuania adopts unilateral declaration of independence.
12 March	Third (extraordinary) convocation of Congress of People's Deputies opens.
14 March	Article 6 of the 1977 constitution amended to remove the Communist Party's guaranteed 'leading role'; strong executive presidency of the republic created together with a Presidential Council and a Federative Council.
15 March	Gorbachev elected President of the USSR.
30 March	Estonian Supreme Soviet suspends Soviet constitution on its territory thus setting it on the path of independence.
11 April	Central Committee open letter calling for purge of radicals in the party.
4 May	Latvian Supreme Soviet declares *de jure* independence but allows a period of negotiation to achieve *de facto* independence.
16 May–22 June	Eltsin elected president of the RSFSR; declaration on state sovereignty of the RSFSR. The Decree on Power stipulates the separation of the Communist Party from government.
1–3 June	Summit between Bush and Gorbachev in Washington.
12 June	Federative Council begins process of drafting new union treaty for the USSR.
20–3 June	Founding congress of the Communist Party of the RSFSR.
2–13 July	Twenty-eighth Communist Party congress in Moscow. Despite organisational and programmatic changes, no clear direction for future policy given. Eltsin

announces his resignation from the Communist Party on 12 July, followed by Gavriil Popov, Anatolii Sobchak and other members of the Democratic Platform.

11 July	Warning strike by miners.
15 July	Third major pro-democracy demonstration in Moscow.
16 July	Ukrainian parliament declares state sovereignty of the republic.

Appendix 2

POLITBURO MEMBERSHIP UNDER GORBACHEV

Full members

Name	Responsibility	Date of birth	Date joined		Date left
			cand.	full	
Gorbachev, Mikhail Sergeevich	General Secretary from 11.3.85; from 1.10.88 Chair of the Presidium of the Supreme Soviet (President)	2.3 1931	Nov. 1979	21.10 1980	
Aliev, Geidar Alievich	First Deputy Chair USSR Council of Ministers, Transport Minister	1923	1976	1982	21.10 1987
Chebrikov, Viktor Mikhailovich	Chair of KGB from 1982; from 30.9.88 to 20.9.89 head of CC Legal Policy Commission	1923	1983	23.4 1985	20.9 1989
Grishin, Viktor Vasilevich	First Secretary of Moscow party organisation	1915		1971	18.2 1986
Gromyko, Andrei Andreevich	Chair, Presidium of Supreme Soviet; up to June 1985 Foreign Minister	1909	never	27.4 1973	30.9 1988
Kryuchkov, Vladimir Aleksandrovich	Chair of KGB from Oct. 1988	1924	never	20.9 1989	July 1990
Kunaev, Dinmukhamed Akhmedovich	First Secretary of Kazakhstan party organisation	1912	1966	1971	28.1 1987

412

Name	Responsibility	Date of birth	Date joined cand.	full	Date left
Ligachev, Egor Kuz'mich	CC Secretary for ideology and party cadres; foreign policy; from 30.9.88 chair of CC Commission for Agriculture	1921	never	23.4 1985	July 1990
Maslyukov, Yurii Dmitrievich	Chair of Gosplan from 6.2.88; also First Deputy Prime Minister	1937	30.9 1988	20.9 1989	July 1990
Medvedev, Vadim Andreevich	From 30.9.88 chair of CC Ideology Commission	1929		30.9 1988	13.7 1990
Nikonov, Viktor Petrovich	CC Secretary responsible for agriculture from April 1985 to 20.9.89	1929	never	26.7 1987	20.9 1989
Romanov, Grigorii Vasil'evich	First Secretary of Leningrad party organisation	1923	1973	1976	1.7 1985
Ryzhkov, Nikolai Ivanovich	Chair, USSR Council of Ministers (Prime Minister) from Sept. 1985	1929	never	23.4 1985	July 1990
Shcherbitskii, Vladimir Vasil'evich	First Secretary of Ukraine party organisation 1972 to Sept. 1989	1918	1961–3 1965	9.4 1971	20.9 1989
Shevardnadze, Eduard Amvrosievich	Minister of Foreign Affairs	1928	1978	1.7 1985	July 1990
Slyunkov, Nikolai Nikitovich	Economics secretary; First Secretary of Belorussia party organisation; from 30.9.88 chair of CC Economy and Social Policy Commission	1929	1986	26.6 1987	July 1990
Solomentsev, Mikhail Sergeevich	Chair of Party Control Commission	1913	1971	26.12 1983	30.9 1988
Tikhonov, Nikolai Aleksandrovich	Chair of USSR Council of Ministers to Sept. 1985; earlier Gosplan	1905	1978	1979	15.10 1985

Name	Responsibility	Date of birth	Date joined cand.	Date joined full	Date left
Vorotnikov, Vitalii Ivanovich	Chair RSFSR Council of Ministers; from 3.10.88 Chair of RSFSR Supreme Soviet Presidium	1926	1983	26.12 1983	July 1990
Yakovlev, Aleksandr Nikolaevich	CC Secretary for propaganda (ideology); from 30.9.88 head of CC International Affairs Commission	1923	1987	26.6 1987	July 1990
Zaikov, Lev Nikolaevich	CC Secretary for defence industry; from Nov. 1987 First Secretary of Moscow party organisation	1923	never	6.3 1986	July 1990

Candidate members

Name	Responsibility	Date of birth	Date joined	Date left
Biryukova, Aleksandra Pavlovna	CC Secretary for consumer goods; from 1.10.88 Deputy Chair USSR Council of Ministers and Chair of Council of Ministers Bureau for Social Development	1929	30.9 1988	July 1990
Demichev, Petr Nilovich	USSR Minister of Culture; Deputy Chair of Presidium of Supreme Soviet	1918	16.11 1964	30.9 1988
Dolgikh, Vladimir Ivanovich	CC Secretary for heavy industry, energy and transport	1924	24.5 1982	30.9 1988
Eltsin, Boris Nikolaevich	First Secretary Moscow party organisation	1931	1986	Oct. 1987
Luk'yanov, Anatolii Ivanovich	General Department of CC; from 1.10.88 First Deputy Chair of USSR Supreme Soviet Presidium (Vice-President); from May 1989 Vice-President of CPD; from March 1990 Chair of Supreme Soviet	1930	30.9 1988	July 1990

Name	Responsibility	Date of birth	Date joined	Date left
Ponomarëv, Boris N.	CC Secretary, Department for Liaison with Socialist Countries	1900	19.5 1900	6.3 1986
Primakov, Evgenii	Chair of USSR Supreme Soviet's Soviet of the Union from May 1989	1929	20.9 1989	July 1990
Pugo, Boris Karlovich	Chair of CC Party Control Committee	1937	20.9 1989	July 1990
Razumovsky, Georgii Petrovich	CC Secretary for party cadres; from 30.9.88 Chair of CC Party Construction and Personnel Policy Commission	1936	18.2 1988	July 1990
Sokolov, Sergei Leonidovich	Minister of Defence	1911	1985	1987
Solov'ëv, Yuri Filippovich	First Secretary of Leningrad *oblast* party organisation to July 1989	1925	6.3 1986	20.9 1989
Talyzin, Nikolai Vladimirovich	Chair of Gosplan from Oct. 1985; 1988–9 a Deputy Prime Minister responsible for housing and consumer goods	1929	15.10 1985	20.9 1989
Vlasov, Aleksandr Vladimirovich	Minister of Internal Affairs; from 3.10.88 Chair of RSFSR Council of Ministers	1932	30.9 1988	July 1990
Yazov, Dmitrii Timofeevich	Minister of Defence	1923	26.6 1987	July 1990

Members elected July 1990

Name	Responsibility	Date of birth
Gorbachev, Mikhail Sergeevich	Re-elected General Secretary of the CPSU on 11 July 1990; from October 1988 Chair of the Presidium of the USSR Supreme Soviet, from May 1989 Chair of the USSR Supreme Soviet, and from March 1990 President of the USSR	1931
Burakevicius, Mikolas Martinovich	From 1990 First Secretary of the provisional Central Committee of the Communist Party of Lithuania (CPSU platform)	1927

Name	Responsibility	Date of birth
Dzasokhov, Aleksandr Sergeevich	In 1988 elected First Secretary of the North Ossetian *oblast* CPSU committee. From February 1990 Chair of the USSR Supreme Soviet international affairs committee. In July 1990 elected a Central Committee secretary	
Frolov, Ivan Timofeevich	From 1968 editor of *Voprosy filosofy (Problems of Philosophy)*, worked in the Academy of Sciences from 1979, and from 1986 was editor of *Kommunist*. From 1987 he was an adviser to Gorbachev. From 1989 editor of *Pravda*. In 1989–90 he was a Central Committee secretary	1929
Gumbaridze, Givi Grigorevich	From 1988 Chair of the KGB in Georgia; from 1989 First Secretary of Georgian Communist Party, Chair of the Presidium of the Georgian Supreme Soviet	1945
Gurenko, Stanislav Ivanovich	From 1987 Second Secretary of Ukrainian Communist Party, in June 1990 elected First Secretary	1936
Ivashko Vladimir Antonovich	From 1988 Second Secretary of Ukrainian Communist Party, and in September 1989 elected First Secretary. From June 1990 Chair of the Ukrainian Supreme Soviet. On 11 July 1990 elected deputy General Secretary of the CPSU	1932
Karimov, Islam Abduganievich	From 1989 First Secretary of the Communist Party of Uzbekistan. President of Uzbekistan	1938
Luchinskii, Petr Kirillovich	Between 1986 and 1989 Second Secretary of the Tadzhikistan Communist Party. From 1989 First Secretary of the Moldavian Communist Party	1940
Makkhamov, Kakhar	From 1985 First Secretary of the Communist Party of Tadzhikistan. Chair of the Tadzhik Supreme Soviet	1932
Masaliev, Absamat Masalievich	From November 1985 First Secretary of the Kirghiz Communist Party. Chair of the Kirghiz Supreme Soviet	1933
Movsisyan, Vladimir Migranovich	In April 1990 elected First Secretary of the Armenian Communist Party	1933

Name	Responsibility	Date of birth
Mutalibov, Ayaz Niyazi ogly	In January 1990 elected First Secretary of the Communist Party of Azerbaidzhan. President of Azerbaidzhan	1938
Nazarbaev, Nursultan Abishevich	From 1989 First Secretary of the Communist Party of Kazakhstan. President of Kazakhstan	1940
Niyazov, Saparmurad Ataevich	From 1985 First Secretary of the Communist Party of Turkmenistan. Chair of the Supreme Soviet of Turkmenistan	1940
Polozkov, Ivan Kuzmich	Worked in the apparatus of the CPSU Central Committee. From 1985 First Secretary of the Krasnodar regional party organisation, and from 1990 chair of the Krasnodar *krai* soviet. From June 1990 First Secretary of the Communist Party of the RSFSR	1935
Prokofiev, Yurii Anatolevich	In 1988 elected Second Secretary of the Moscow City Party organisation, and in 1989 First Secretary	1939
Rubiks Alfreds Petrovich	In April 1990 elected First Secretary of the Communist Party of Latvia	1935
Semenova, Galina Vladimirovna	Worked as editor of the paper, *Komsomol Life*, and from January 1981 edited *Krestyanka (Female Peasant)*. In July 1990 elected a Central Committee secretary	1937
Sillari, Enn-Arno Augustovich	In 1990 elected First Secretary of the Communist Party of Estonia	1944
Sokolov, Efrem Evseevich	Since 1987 First Secretary of the Communist Party of Belorussia	1926
Stroev, Egor Semenovich	From 1985 First Secretary of the Orël regional party organisation. Since 1989 a secretary of the Central Committee	1937
Shenin, Oleg Semonovich	Since 1987 First Secretary of Krasnoyarsk *krai* party committee, and from 1990 chair of Krasnoyarsk *krai* soviet	1937

Name	Responsibility	Date of birth
Yanaev, Gennadi Ivanovich	In 1990 appointed chair of VTsSPS (All-Union Central Council of Trade Unions); in July 1990 elected a Central Committee secretary and resigned as head of trade unions	1937

Appendix 3

CENTRAL COMMITTEE SECRETARIES

Name	Responsibility	Date of birth	Date joined	Date left
Gorbachev, Mikhail Sergeevich	Secretary General of the CPSU	1931	1978	
Baklanov, Oleg Dmitrievich	Defence industries	1932	18.2 1988	
Biryukova, Alexandra Pavlovna	Light industry, consumer goods	1929	6.3 1986	30.9 1988
Chebrikov, Victor Mikhailovich	Chair, CC Commission for Legal Policy to Sept. 1989	1923	30.9 1988	20.9 1989
Dobrynin, Anatolii Fedorovich	Foreign affairs, head of International Department	1919	6.3 1986	30.9 1988
Dolgikh, Vladimir Ivanovich	Heavy industry, energy and transport	1924	18.12 1972	1986
Eltsin, Boris Nikolaevich		1931	July 1985	1986
Girenko, Andrei	First Secretary of Crimean *oblast* party committee; legal affairs	1936	20.9 1989	
Ligachev, Egor Kuz'mich	Party cadres, ideology, foreign policy; up to 30.9.87 acted as 'Second Secretary'	1921	26.12 1983	July 1990
Luk'yanov, Anatolii Ivanovich	General	1930	28.1 1987	30.9 1988
Manaenkov, Yurii Alekseevich	First Secretary of Lipetsk *oblast* party committee; RSFSR affairs	1936	20.9 1989	
Medvedev, Vadim Andreevich	Relations with socialist countries	1929	6.3 1986	July 1990
Nikonov, Viktor Petrovich	Minister of Agriculture to Sept. 1989	1929	23.4 1985	20.9 1989

419

Name	Responsibility	Date of birth	Date joined	Date left
Razumovsky, Georgii Petrovich	Party cadres and organisation	1936	6.3 1986	July 1990
Ryzhkov, Nikolai Ivanovich	Industry	1929	Nov. 1982	Apr. 1985
Slyunkov, Nikolai Nikitovich	First Secretary of Belorussia party organisation; social and economic policy	1929	28.1 1987	July 1990
Stroev, Egor Semenovich	First Secretary of Orël *oblast* party committee; agriculture	1937	20.9 1989	
Usmanov, Gumer Ismailovich	First Secretary of Tatar *oblast* party committee; nationality policy	1932	20.9 1989	July 1990
Yakovlev, Aleksandr Nikolaevich	Ideology, propaganda and culture; international policy	1923	6.3 1986	
Zaikov, Lev Nikolaevich	First Secretary of Moscow party organisation; military industrial complex	1923	1.7 1985	1988
Zimyanin, Mikhail	Culture and propaganda	1914		1986

Central Committee Secretaries: elected 14 July 1990

Baklanov, O. D
Dzasokhov, A. S.
Falin, V. M.
Gidaspov, B. V.
Girenko, A. N.
Kuptsov, V. A.

Manaenkov, Yu. A.
Semenova, G. V.
Shenin, O. S.
Stroev, E. S.
Yanaev, G. I.

Members of the Secretariat: elected 14 July 1990

Aninskii, V. V.
Gaivoronskii, V. A.
Melnikov, I. I.

Teplenichev, A. I.
Turgunova, G.

BIBLIOGRAPHY

Abalkin, L. (1988) *Perestroika, puti i problemy: intervyu s akademikom*, Moscow, Ekonomika.

Abalkin, L. (1989) 'Kakim byt' novomu pyatiletnemu planu?', *Kommunist*, 6 (April): 10–19.

Action Programme of the Czechoslovak Communist Party (1968) Spokesman Pamphlet 8, Nottingham.

Adamovich, A. (1988) ' "Chestnoe slovo, bol'she ne vzorvetsya", ili mnenie nespetsialista', and responses, *Novyi mir* (September): 164–79.

Adams, M. B. (1989) ' "Red Star". Another look at Aleksandr Bogdanov', *Slavic Review*, 48, 1 (Spring): 1–15.

Aganbegyan, A. (1987) 'Pourquoi fabriquons-nous quatre fois plus de tracteurs que les USA pour une production agricole moindre?' from *Literaturnaya gazeta*, in *Les Temps Modernes*, 492–4 (July–September): 232–50.

Aganbegyan, A. (1988a) *The Challenge: Economics of perestroika*, Hutchinson.

Aganbegyan, A. (1988b) 'New directions in Soviet economics', *New Left Review*, 169 (May–June): 89–95.

Aganbegyan, A. (1989) *Moving the Mountain: Inside the perestroika revolution*, Bantam Books.

Albright, D. E. (1989) 'The USSR and the Third World in the 1980s', *Problems of Communism*, 38, 2–3 (March–June): 50–70.

Ali, T. (1988) *Revolution from Above: Where is the Soviet Union going?*, Hutchinson.

Almond, G. A. and G. B. Powell (1966) *Comparative Politics: A Developmental Approach*, Little, Brown & Company.

Almond, G. A. and S. Verba (1963) *The Civic Culture*, Princeton University Press.

Andreev, S. (1989) 'Struktura vlasti i zadachi obshchestva', *Neva*, 1 (January): 144–73.

Andropov, Y. V. (1983) *Speeches and Writings*, Pergamon.

Anishchenko, G. A. (1987) 'Human rights in the USSR', *Glasnost*, 12: 7–15.

Anishchenko, G. A. (1988) 'On the Pamyat Society, Russians, and other peoples of the Soviet Union: who is guilty?', *Glasnost*, 15.

Antonian, A. (1987) *Towards a Theory of Eurocommunism: The relationship of Eurocommunism to Eurosocialism*, Greenwood Press.

Arbatov, G. and E. Batalov (1989) 'Politicheskaya reforma i evolyutsiya sovetskogo gosudarstva', *Kommunist*, 4 (March): 35–46.

Ash, T. G. (1988a) 'The empire in decay', *New York Review of Books*, 29 September: 53–60.

Ash, T. G. (1988b) 'Central Europe: the opposition', *New York Review of Books*, 13 October: 3–6.

Ash, T. G. (1989) *The Uses of Adversity: Essays on the fate of Central Europe*, Penguin.

Aslund, A. (1989) *Gorbachev's Struggle for Economic Reform*, Pinter.

Auzan, A. (1989) 'Politicheskaya ekonomiya sotsializma: perestroika stavit problemy', *Kommunist*, 1 (January): 4–20.

Aves, J. (1988) 'The Democratic Union – a Soviet opposition party?', *Slovo*, 1, 2 (November): 92–8.

Baglai, M. (1989) 'Pravovoe gosudarstvo: ot idei k praktike', *Kommunist*, 6 (April): 38–47.

Bahro, R. (1974) *From Red to Green*, Verso.

Barry, D. D. *et al.* (eds.) (1988) *Law and the Gorbachev Era: Essays in honor of Dietrich Andre Loeber*, Nijhoff.

Batt, J. (1988) *Economic Reform and Political Change in Eastern Europe: A comparison of the Czechoslovak and Hungarian experiences*, Macmillan.

Belov, V. (1988) 'Remeslo otchuzhdeniya', *Novyi mir*, 6 (June): 152–81.

Benewick, R. and P. Wingrove (eds.) *Reforming the Revolution: China in transition*, Macmillan.

Benn, D. W. (1987) '*Glasnost* in the Soviet media: liberalization or public relations', *The Journal of Communist Studies*, 3, 3 (September): 267–76.

Berezkin, A. V., V. A. Kolosov, M. E. Pavlovskaya, N. V. Petrov and L. V. Smirnyagin (1989) 'The geography of the 1989 elections of People's Deputies of the USSR (preliminary results)', *Soviet Geography*, 30, 8 (October): 607–34.

Berliner, J. S. (1957) *Factory and Management in the USSR*, Harvard University Press.

Berliner, J. S. (1988) *Soviet Industry from Stalin to Gorbachev: Essays on management and innovation*, Edward Elgar.

Bialer, S. (1980) *Stalin's Successors: Leadership, stability and change in the Soviet Union*, Cambridge University Press.

Bialer, S. (1986) *The Soviet Paradox: External expansion, internal decline*, I. B. Tauris.

Bialer, S. (1988) ' "New Thinking" and Soviet foreign policy', *Survival*, 30, 4 (July–August): 291–309.

Bialer, S. (ed.) (1989) *Politics, Society and Nationality Inside Gorbachev's Russia*, Westview.

Bialer, S. and J. Afferica (1986) 'The genesis of Gorbachev's world', *Foreign Affairs*, 64, 3: 605–44.

Bleaney, M. (1988) *Do Socialist Economies Work?*, Basil Blackwell.

Bluch, C. (1988) 'The evolution of Soviet military doctrine', *Survival*, 30, 2 (March–April): 149–61.

Bogomolov, O. (1989) 'Menyayushchiisya oblik sotsializma', *Kommunist*, 11 (July): 33–42.

Bondarev, A. (1989) 'Vneshneekonomikicheskii mekhanism – nereshennye problemy', *Kommunist*, 12 (August): 16–27.

Bova, R. (1987) 'The role of workplace participation', *Problems of Communism*, 36, 4 (July–August): 76–86.

Breslauer, G. W. (1978) *Five Images of the Soviet Future: A critical review and synthesis*, Berkeley: Institute of International Studies, University of California.

Breslauer, G. W. (1982) *Khrushchev and Brezhnev as Leaders: Building authority in Soviet politics*, Allen & Unwin.

Breslauer, G. W. (1984) 'On the adaptability of Soviet welfare-state authoritarianism' in E. P. Hoffmann and R. F. Laird (eds.), *The Soviet Polity in the Modern Era*, Aldine.

Brezhnev, L. I. (1968) *Leninskom kursom*, vol. 2, Politizdat.

Brezhnev, L. I. (1976) *Report of the CPSU Central Committee, 25th Congress of the CPSU*, Progress.

Brezhnev: The Period of Stagnation (1989) Novosti.

Bromley, Y. (1988) *Major Ethnosocial Trends in the USSR*, Progress.

Brown, A. (1985) 'Gorbachev: new man in the Kremlin', *Problems of Communism*, 34, 3 (May–June): 1–23.

Brown, A. (1986) 'Change in the Soviet Union', *Foreign Affairs*, 64, 5: 1048–65.

Brown, A. (1987a) 'Soviet political developments and prospects', *World Policy Journal*, 4, 1 (Winter): 55–87.

Brown, A. (1987b) 'Gorbachev and the reform of the Soviet system', *Political Quarterly*, 58, 2 (April–June): 139–51.

Brown, A. (1988) 'Comment Gorbatchev a pris le pouvoir, 1978–1988', *Pouvoirs*, 45 (Avril): 17–30.

Brown, D. M. (1988) *Towards a Radical Democracy: The political economy of the Budapest School*, Unwin Hyman.

Brumberg, A. (1989) 'Moscow: the struggle for reform', *New York Review of Books*, 30 March: 37–42.

Brus, W. (1972) *The Market in a Socialist Economy*, Routledge & Kegan Paul.

Brus, W. (1973) *The Economics and Politics of Socialism*, Routledge & Kegan Paul.

Brus, W. (1983) 'Political pluralism and markets in Communist systems' in S. Solomon (ed.), *Pluralism in the Soviet Union*, Macmillan.

Brus, W. and K. Laski (1989) *From Marx to the Market: Socialism in search of an economic system*, Clarendon Press.

Brzezinski, Z. (1966) 'The Soviet political system: transformation or degeneration', *Problems of Communism*, 15, 1 (January–February): 1–15.

Bugajski, J. (1986) 'The Soviet Union and the Third World', *The Washington Quarterly*, 9, 4: 141–5.

Bull, H. (1979) *The Anarchical Society*, Macmillan.

Burlatsky, F. (1988a) *New Thinking: Dialogues and judgements on the technological revolution and Soviet reforms*, Progress.

Burlatsky, F. (1988b), 'Kakoi sotsializm narodu nuzhen', *Literaturnaya gazeta*, 16 (20 April): 2.

Burlatsky, F. (1988c), 'Posle stalina', *Novyi mir*, 10: 153–97.

Butenko, A. P. (1982) 'Protivorechiya sotsializma kak obshchestvennogo stroya', *Voprosy filosofii*, 10: 6–29.

Butenko, A. P. (1984) 'Eshche raz o protivorechiyakh sotsializma', *Voprosy filosofii*, 2: 116–23.

Butenko, A. P. (1988) 'Theoretical problems of the new society's improvement: social-economic nature of socialism' in *Soviet Society: Philosophy of development*, Progress.

Butenko, A. P. (1989) *Sovremennyi sotsializm: voprosy teorii*, Politicheskaya literatura.

Butler, W. E. (1987) 'Law and reform' in McCauley (ed.), 1987: 59–72.

Carillo, S. (1970) *Problems of Socialism Today*, Lawrence & Wishart.

Carillo, S. (1977) *'Eurocommunism' and the State*, Lawrence & Wishart.

Cassen, R. (ed.) (1985) *Soviet Interests in the Third World*, Sage.

Channon, J. (1989) 'The fall and rise of the Soviet peasantry: some observations on Gorbachev's recent agricultural reforms', *Slovo*, 2, 1 (May): 14–32.

Chebrikov, V. (1989) 'Pravovaya politika – aktivnoe zveno perestroiki', *Kommunist*, 8 (May): 3–17.

Cheng, J. Y. S. (1989) 'Whither China's reform?', *Journal of Communist Studies*, 5, 1 (March): 32–49.

Cheshko, S. (1989) 'Ekonomicheskii suverenitet i national'nyi vopros', *Kommunist*, 2: 97–105.

Chomsky, N. (1984) *Super Powers in Collision*, Penguin.

Churchward, L. G. (1987) *Soviet Socialism: Social and political essays*, Routledge & Kegan Paul.

Clemens, W. R. (1990) *Can Russia Change? The USSR confronts global interdependence*, Unwin Hyman.

Cockburn, P. (1989) 'Dateline USSR: ethnic tremors', *Foreign Policy*, 74 (Spring): 168–84.

Cohen, S. F. (1985) *Rethinking the Soviet Experience: Politics and history since 1917*, Oxford University Press.

Cohen, S. F. and K. V. Heuvel (1989) *Voices of Glasnost: Interviews with Gorbachev's reformers*, W. W. Norton.

Colton, T. (1986) *The Dilemma of Reform in the Soviet Union*, revised edn, Council on Foreign Relations.

Connor, W. D. (1986) 'Social policy under Gorbachev', *Problems of Communism*, 35, 4 (July–August): 31–46.

Connor, W. D. (1988) *Socialism's Dilemmas: State and society in the Soviet bloc*, Columbia University Press.

Conquest, R. (1971) *The Great Terror: Stalin's purge of the thirties*, Pelican.

Conquest, R. (1986) *The Harvest of Sorrow: Soviet collectivisation and the terror famine*, Hutchinson.

Cooper, J. (1989) 'Prospects for the socialist economy', *Journal of Communist Studies*, 4, 4 (December): 64–82.

Cox, T. (1989) 'The private sector and policy change in the Soviet Union', *Slovo*, 2, 2 (November): 35–48.

Crouch, M. (1989) *Revolution and Evolution: Gorbachev and Soviet politics*, Philip Allan.

Cynkin, T. M. (1988) '*Glasnost, perestroika* and Eastern Europe', *Survival*, 30, 4 (July–August): 310–31.

D'Agostino, A. (1988) *Soviet Succession Struggles: Kremlinology and the Russian question from Lenin to Gorbachev*, Allen & Unwin.

Dahm, H. (1986) 'Ideology as a key to politics' in *The Soviet Union 1984/85*, Westview.

Dallin, A. (1988) 'Gorbachev's foreign policy and the "New Political Thinking" in the Soviet Union' in P. Juviler and H. Kimura (eds.), *Gorbachev's Reforms: US and Japanese assessments*, Aldine.

Davies, R. W. (1989a) *Soviet History in the Gorbachev Revolution*, Macmillan.

Davies, R. W. (1989b) 'Soviet historians and collectivisation: recent publications', unpublished SIPS paper, CREES, University of Birmingham, 6 December.

Davies, R. W. (1990) 'Gorbachev's socialism in historical perspective', *New Left Review*, 179 (January–February): 5–27.

Dawisha, K. (1990) *Eastern Europe, Gorbachev and Reform: The great challenge*, 2nd edn, Cambridge University Press.

Dellenbrant, J. A. (1988) 'The Central Asian challenge: Soviet decision-making on regional stability under Brezhnev and Gorbachev', *Journal of Communist Studies*, 4, 1 (March): 54–77.

Desai, P. (1989) *Perestroika in Perspective*, Princeton University Press.

Deutscher, I. (1967) *The Unfinished Revolution*, Oxford University Press.

XIX vsesoyuznaya konferentsiya kommunisticheskoi partii sovetskogo soyuza, 28 iyunya–1 iyulya 1988 goda: stenograficheskii otchet (1988), 2 vols., Politicheskaya literatura.

Djilas, M. (1957) *The New Class: An analysis of the Communist system*, Praeger.

Djilas, M. and G. Urban In conversation (1988) 'Djilas on Gorbachev', *Encounter*, 71, 3 (September–October): 3–19; 71, 4 (November): 21–31.

Documents: Why Restructuring? (1987) *Survey*, 29, 4 (August): 123–43.

Doder, D. (1987) *Shadows and Whispers: Power politics inside the Kremlin from Brezhnev to Gorbachev*, Harrap.

Dreifelds, J. (1989) 'Latvian national rebirth', *Problems of Communism*, 38, 4 (July–August): 77–95.

Duncan, W. R. (1986) 'Castro and Gorbachev', *Problems of Communism*, 35, 2 (March–April): 45–57.

Dunlop, J. B. (1989) 'Gorbachev and Russian Orthodoxy', *Problems of Communism*, 38, 4 (July–August): 96–116.

Dunn, T. B. (1987) *Religion and Nationalism in Eastern Europe and the Soviet Union*, Lynne Riener.

XXV s"ezd KPSS: stenograficheskii otchet (1976) vol. 1, Politizdat.

Dyker, D. A. (ed.) (1987) *The Soviet Union Under Gorbachev: Prospects for reform*, Croom Helm.

Dyker, D. A. (1988) 'The power of the industrial ministries' in D. Lane (ed.), *Elites and Political Power in the USSR*, Edward Elgar.

Eklof, B. (1989) *Soviet Briefing: Gorbachev and the reform period*, Westview.

Elliot, I. (1985) 'And now Gorbachev, the great reformer', *Survey*: 1–11.

Elliot, I. (1988) 'How open is "openness"?', *Survey*, 30, 3 (October): 1–22.

Eltsin, B. (1990) *Against the Grain: An autobiography*, Jonathan Cape.

Enteen, G. M. (1989) 'Problems of CPSU historiography', *Problems of Communism*, 38, 5 (September–October): 72–80.

Evseev, V. E. (1989) 'Vo-pervykh, polnaya glasnost', *Voprosy istorii KPSS*, 3 (March): 3–18.

Fang Lizhi (1989) 'China's despair and China's hope', *New York Review of Books*, 2 February: 3–4.

Falk, A. (1971) *This Endangered Planet*, Random House.

Feher, F. and A. Arato (eds.) (1989) *Gorbachev: The debate*, Polity Press.

Frank, P. (1988) 'Can the centre hold?', *Détente*, 13: 12–13.

Frankland, M. (1987) *The Sixth Continent: Russia and Mikhail Gorbachev*, Hamish Hamilton.

Friedberg, M. and H. Isham (eds.) 1988) *Soviet Society Under Gorbachev: Current trends and the prospects for reform*, M. E. Sharpe.

Fukuyama, F. (1986) 'Gorbachev and the Third World', *Foreign Affairs*, 64, 4: 715–31.

Fukuyama, F. (1989) 'The end of history?', *The National Interest* (Summer): 3–18.

Gagnon, V. P. (1987) 'Gorbachev and the collective contract brigade', *Soviet Studies*, 39, 1: 1–23.

Gati, C. (1989) 'Eastern Europe on its own', *Foreign Affairs*, 68, 1: 99–119.

Gellner, E. (1988) *State and Society in Soviet Thought*, Basil Blackwell.

Gerner, K. and S. Hedlund (1989) *Ideology and Rationality in the Soviet Model: A legacy for Gorbachev*, Routledge.

Gill, G. (1987) 'The programmatic documents of the 27th congress', in R. F. Miller, J. H. Miller and T. H. Rigby, *Gorbachev at the Helm: A new era in Soviet politics*, Croom Helm.

Gill, G. (1988) *The Rules of the Communist Party of the Soviet Union*, M. E. Sharpe.

Gladkov, P. (1989) 'Mezhdunarodnoe obshchestvo: utopiya ili real'naya perspektiva?' *Mirovaya ekonomika i mezhdunarodnye otnosheniya*, 6: 60–8.

Gleisner, J. (1989) 'The empire fights back', *Détente*, 15: 19–24.

Glickham, C. (1986) 'New directions for Soviet foreign policy', *Radio Liberty Research Bulletin*, Supplement 2/86, 6 September.

Goble, P. (1989) 'Ethnic politics in the USSR', *Problems of Communism*, 38, 4 (July–August): 1–14.

Goldman, M. I. (1985) 'Gorbachev and economic reform', *Foreign Affairs*, 64, 1 (Fall): 59–75.

Goldman, M. I. (1987) *Gorbachev's Challenge: Economic reform in the age of high technology*, Norton.

Goldman, M. I. and M. Goldman (1988) 'Soviet and Chinese economic reform', *Foreign Affairs*, 66, 3: 551–73.

Gong, G. W. (1984) *The Standard of 'Civilisation' in International Society*, Clarendon Press.

Gooding, J. (1990) 'Gorbachev and democracy', *Soviet Studies*, 42, 2 (April): 195–231.

Gorbachev, M. S. (1987a) *Perestroika: Our hopes for our country and the world*, Collins.

Gorbachev, M. S., *Izbrannye rechi i stat'i*, vol. 1 (1987b); vol. 2 (1987c); vol. 3 (1987d); vol. 4 (1987e); vol. 5 (1988); vol. 6 (1989), Politizdat.

Gorbachev's Economic Plans (1987a) Study Papers Submitted to the Joint Economic Committee, Congress of the United States, 23 November 1987, vol. 1.

Gorbachev's Economic Plans (1987b) Study Papers Submitted to the Joint Economic Committee, Congress of the United States, 23 November 1987, vol. 2.

Gordon, L. and A. Nazimova (1989) 'Perestroika: vozmozhnye varianty?', *Kommunist*, 13 (September): 34–44.

Gouldner, A. W. (1980) *The Two Marxisms: Contradictions and anomalies in the development of theory*, Macmillan.

Gramsci, A. (1971) *Selections from Prison Notebooks*, Lawrence & Wishart.

Gryazin, I. (1988) 'Pravovoe gosudarstvo', *Novyi mir*, 8: 266–71.

Gunlicks, A. B. and J. D. Treadway (eds.) (1988) *The Soviet Union Under Gorbachev: Assessing the first year*, Greenwood Press.

Gustafson, T. (1986) 'Will Soviet foreign policy change under Gorbachev?', *The Washington Quarterly*, 9, 4: 153–7.

Gustafson, T. and D. Mann (1986) 'Gorbachev's first year: building power and authority', *Problems of Communism*, 35, 3 (May–June): 1–19.

Gustafson, T. and D. Mann (1987) 'Gorbachev's next gamble', *Problems of Communism*, 36, 4 (July–August): 1–20.

Gustafson, T. and D. Mann (1988) 'Gorbachev and the circular flow of power' in D. Lane (ed.), *Elites and Political Power in the USSR*, Edward Elgar.

Habermas, J. (1985) 'Modernity: an incomplete project' in Hal Foster (ed.), *Post-Modern Culture*, London.

Hagen, M. von (1988) *History and Politics Under Gorbachev: Professional autonomy and democratization*, The Harriman Institute Forum, 1, 11 (November).

Hahn, J. (1988a) *Soviet Grassroots*, Tauris.

Hahn, J. (1988b) 'An experiment in competition: the 1987 elections to the local soviet', *Slavic Review*, 47, 2 (Fall): 434–47.

Hahn, J. (1989) 'Power to the soviets', *Problems of Communism*, 38, 1 (January–February): 34–46.

Hahn, W. G. (1987) 'Electoral "choice" in the Soviet bloc', *Problems of Communism*, 36, 2 (March–April): 29–39.

Hamman, H. (1989) 'Soviet defector on origins of the New Thinking', *Report on the USSR*, 1, 42 (October): 14–16.

Hammer, D. P. (1987) 'Alternative visions of the Russian future: religious and nationalist alternatives', *Studies in Comparative Communism*, 20, 3/4 (Autumn/Winter): 265–75.

Hanson, P. (1989) 'Socialism or capitalism?', *Détente*, 16 (December): 3–6.

Harrington, M. (1989) 'Markets and plans: is the market necessarily capitalist?', *Dissent* (Winter): 56–70.

Hasegawa, T. (1986) 'Soviets on nuclear-war fighting', *Problems of Communism*, 35, 4 (July–August): 68–79.

Hasegawa, T. (1988) 'Gorbachev, the New Thinking of Soviet foreign-security policy and the military: recent trends and implications' in P. Juviler and H. Kimura (eds.), *Gorbachev's Reforms: US and Japanese assessments*, Aldine.

Hauslohner, P. (1988). Democratization "From the Middle Out": Soviet trade unions and perestroika, *The Harriman Institute Forum*, 1, 10 (October).

Hauslohner, P. (1988). 'Democratization "From the Middle Out": Soviet trade unions and perestroika', *The Harriman Institute Forum*, 1, 10 (October).

Hazan, B. A. (1985) *The Eastern European Political Systems: Instruments of power*, Westview.

Hazan, B. A. (1987) *From Brezhnev to Gorbachev: Infighting in the Kremlin*, Westview/Praeger.

Hazan, B. A. (1990) *Gorbachev's Gamble: The 19th All-Union Party Conference*, Westview.

Heller, A. and F. Feher (1988) 'Gorbachev and Eastern Europe: perestroika and historical compromise?', *Dissent* (Fall): 415–21.

Heller, M. (1988) *Cogs in the Soviet Wheel*, Collins.

Hewett, E. A. (1988) *Reforming the Soviet Economy: Equality vs efficiency*, Brookings.

Hill, R. J. (1980) *Soviet Politics, Political Science and Reform*, Martin Robertson.

Hill, R. J. (1986) 'Soviet political development and the culture of the apparatchiki', *Studies in Comparative Communism*, 19, 1 (Spring): 25–39.

Hill, R. J. (1988) 'Gorbachev and the CPSU', *Journal of Communist Studies*, 4, 4 (December): 18–30.

Hill, R. J. and P. Frank (1986) 'Gorbachev's cabinet building', *Journal of Communist Studies*, 2, 2: 168–81.

Hill, R. J. and A. Rahr (1988) 'The General Secretary, the Central Party Secretariat and the apparat' in D. Lane (ed.), *Elites and Political Power in the USSR*, Edward Elgar.

Hill, R. J. and J. A. Dellenbrant (eds.) (1989) *Gorbachev and Perestroika: Towards a new socialism?*, Edward Elgar.

Hoffman, S. (1988) 'Coming down from the summit', *New York Review of Books*, 21 January.

Hofheinz, P. (1987a) 'Gorbachev's double burden: economic reform and growth acceleration', *Millenium*, 16, 1: 21–53.

Hofheinz, P. (1987b) 'Piecing together the Gorbachev puzzle', *Journal of Communist Studies*, 3, 2 (June): 161–77.

Höhmann, H.-H. (1989) 'Soviet *perestroika*, economic reform and integration problems in Eastern Europe', *Journal of Communist Studies*, 5, 1 (March): 18–31.

Holloway, D. (1989) 'Gorbachev's New Thinking', *Foreign Affairs*, 68, 1 (1989): 66–81.

Hosking, G. (1988) 'Informal associations in the USSR', *Slovo*, 1, 1 (May): 7–10.

Hosking, G. (1990) *The Awakening of the Soviet Union*, Heinemann.

Hough, J. F. (1969) *The Soviet Prefects: The local party organs in industrial decision-making*, Harvard University Press.

Hough, J. F. (1985) 'Gorbachev's strategy', *Foreign Affairs*, 64, 1 (Fall): 33–55.

Hough, J. F. (1986) *The Struggle for the Third World: Soviet debates and American options*, Brookings.

Hough, J. F. (1987) 'Gorbachev consolidating power', *Problems of Communism*, 36, 4 (July–August): 21–43.

Hough, J. F. and M. Fainsod (1979) *How the Soviet Union is governed*, Harvard University Press.

Hyland, W. G. (1985) 'The Gorbachev succession', *Foreign Affairs*, 63, 2 (Spring).

Inogo ne dano: sud'by perestroiki, vglyadyvayas' v proshloe, vozvrashchenie k budushchemu (1988) ed. Y. N. Afanas'ev, Progress.

Istoriki sporyat: trinadtsat' besed (1988) ed. V. S. Lel'chuk, Politizdat.

Jacobson, J. (1987) 'Glasnost and the cult of Gorbachev', *New Politics*, 1, 3 (Summer): 140–50.

Jacques, M. and F. Mulhern (eds.) (1981) *The Forward March of Labour Halted*, Verso.

Johnson, C. (ed.) (1970) *Change in Communist Systems*, Stanford University Press.

Jones, A. and W. Moskoff (1989) 'New co-operatives in the USSR', *Problems of Communism*, 38, 6 (November–December): 27–39.

Jones, T. A. (1976) 'Modernization theory and socialist development' in M. G. Field, *Social Consequences of Modernization in Communist Societies*, Johns Hopkins.

Jowitt, K. (1975) 'Inclusion and mobilization in European Leninist regimes', *World Politics*, 28, 1 (October): 69–96.

Jukes, G. (1987) 'Foreign policy and defence' in R. F. Miller, J H Miller and T. H Rigby, *Gorbachev at the Helm: A new era in Soviet politics*, Croom Helm.

Juviler, P. and H. Kimura (eds.) (1988) *Gorbachev's Reforms: US and Japanese assessments*, Aldine.

Kagarlitsky, B. (1987) 'The intelligentsia and the changes', *New Left Review*, 164 (July–August): 5–26.

Kagarlitsky, B. (1988a) 'Perestroika: the dialectics of change', *New Left Review*, 169 (May–June): 63–83.

Kagarlitsky, B. (1988b) *The Thinking Reed: Intellectuals and the Soviet state from 1917 to the present*, Verso.

Kagarlitsky, B. (1989a) *Dialectic of Change*, Verso.

Kagarlitsky, B. (1989b) 'The importance of being Marxist', *New Left Review*, 178 (November–December): 29–36.

Kaiser, R. G. (1988/9) 'The USSR in decline', *Foreign Affairs*, 67, 2 (Winter): 97–113.

Kaldor, M. (1979) *The Disintegrating West*, Penguin.

Kautsky, J. H. (1972) *The Political Consequences of Modernisation*, John Wiley.

Kautsky, J. H. (1973) 'Comparative Communism versus comparative politics', *Studies in Comparative Communism*, 6, 1–2 (Spring–Summer): 135–70.

Kautsky, K. (1919/64) *The Dictatorship of the Proletariat*, Ann Arbor.

Keane, J. (1984) *Public Life and Late Capitalism: Towards a socialist theory of democracy*, Cambridge University Press.

Keane, J. (ed.) (1988) *Civil Society and the State*, Verso.

Kelley, D. R. (1986) *Politics of Developed Socialism*, Greenwood.

Kennedy, P. (1988) *The Rise and Fall of the Great Powers: Economic change and military conflict from 1500 to 2000*, Unwin Hyman.

Kennedy, P. (1989) 'Can the US remain number one?', *New York Review of Books*, 16 March: 36–42.

Keohane, R. O. and J. S. Nye (1977) *Power and Interdependence: World politics in transition*, Little, Brown.

Kessler, M. (1988) 'The paradox of perestroika', *World Policy Journal*, 5, 4 (Fall): 651–76.

Kirkpatrick, J. (1979) 'Dictatorship and double standards', *Commentary*.

Kittrie, N. N. and I. Volgyes (eds.) (1988) *The Uncertain Future: Gorbachev's Eastern bloc*, New York, Professors World Peace Academy.

Klyamkin, I. (1987) 'Kakaya ulitsa vedet k khramu?', *Novyi mir*, 11: 150–88.

Klyamkin, I. (1989) 'Pochemu trudno govorit' pravdu', *Novyi mir*, 2: 204–38.

Kolakowski, L. (1978) *Main Currents of Marxism*, vol. 3, *The Breakdown*, Oxford University Press.

Kowalski, R. (1990) *Left Communism in 1918*, Macmillan.

Komarov, B. (1978) *The Destruction of Nature in the Soviet Union*, Pluto Press.

Kooperatsiya i arenda: sbornik dokumentov i materialov (1989) 2 vols., ed. V. I. Akulinin and G. D. Golubov, Politicheskoi literatury.

KPSS o perestroike: sbornik dokumentov (1988), Politicheskaya literatura.

Krasnov, V. (1987) 'Lev Timofeev and soul-searching within the Soviet elite', *Studies in Comparative Communism*, 20, 3/4 (Autumn/Winter): 253–64.

Krukhmalev, A. E. (1989) 'Nekotorye voprosy leninskoi teorii sotsializma', *Voprosy istorii KPSS*, 1 (January): 18–35.

Kudryavtsev, V. (1989) 'Reforma politicheskoi sistemy i obshchestvennaya nauka', *Kommunist*, 3: 3–13.

Kuritsyn, V. (1983/87) *The Development of Rights and Freedoms in the Soviet State*, Progress.

Kusin, V. V. (1986) 'Gorbachev and Eastern Europe', *Problems of Communism*, 35, 1 (January–February): 39–53.

Kutafin, O. E. (1985) *Konstitutsionnye osnovy obshchestvennogo stroya i politiki SSSR*, Moscow University.

Lampert, N. (1988) 'The dilemmas of glasnost', *Journal of Communist Studies*, 4, 4 (December): 48–63.

Lane, D. (1988) 'Ruling class and political elites: paradigms of socialist societies' in D. Lane (ed.), *Elites and Political Power in the USSR*, Edward Elgar.

Lane, D. (1990) *Soviet Society under Perestroika*, Unwin Hyman.

Lapidus, G. W. (1987) 'KAL 007 and Chernobyl: the Soviet management of crises', *Survival*, 29, 3 (May–June): 215–23.

Larabee, F. S. (1988) 'Gorbachev and the Soviet military', *Foreign Affairs* 66, 5 (Summer): 1002–26.

Latsis, O. (1988) 'Perelom', *Znamya*, 6: 124–78.

Lebedinskaya, L. N. (1988) *O knige V. I. Lenina 'Gosudarstvo i revolyutsiya'*, Politicheskaya literatura.

Lenin, V. I. (1977) *Gosudarstvo i revolyutsiya (State and Revolution)*, Polnoe sobranie sochinenii, 5th edn, Politicheskoi literatury, vol. 33.

Levada, Y. (1989) 'Dinamika sotsial'nogo pereloma: vozmozhnosti analiza', *Kommunist*, 2 (January): 34–45.

Levgold, R. (1989) 'The revolution in Soviet foreign policy', *Foreign Affairs*, 68, 1: 82–98.

Lewin, M. (1988) *The Gorbachev Phenomenon: A historical interpretation*, Hutchinson Radius.

Lewin, M. (1989) *Marx, Engels and Liberal Democracy*, Macmillan.

Ligachev, E. K. (1989) *Izbrannye rechi i stat'i*, Politicheskoi literatury.

Light, M. (1987a) 'Foreign policy' in M. McCauley (ed.), *The Soviet Union Under Gorbachev*, Macmillan.

Light, M. (1987b) 'The study of international relations in the Soviet Union', *Millenium: Journal of International Studies*, 16, 2: 287–96.

Light, M. (1988) *The Soviet Theory of International Relations*, Harvester Wheatsheaf.

Likhachev, D. S. (1981) *Zametki o russkom*, Sovetskaya rossiya.

Lipitskii, V. S. (1989) 'O dialektike vzaimodeistviya sotsializma i kapitalizma', *Voprosy istorii KPSS*, 7 (July): 3–17.

Lisichkin, G. (1988) 'Mify i real'nost', *Novyi mir*, 11: 160–87.

Litvin, V. (1987) 'Reforming economic management', *Problems of Communism*, 36, 4 (July–August): 87–92.

Litwak, R. S. and S. N. Macfarlane (1987) 'Soviet activism in the Third World', *Survival*, 29, 1 (January–February): 21–39.

Loone, E. (1988) *Marxism and the Contemporary Philosophy of History: A Soviet view*, Verso.

Lowenthal, R. (1976) 'The ruling party in a mature society' in M. G. Field, *Social Consequences of Modernization in Communist Societies*, Johns Hopkins.

Luxemburg, R. (1919/1961) *The Russian Revolution*; and *Leninism or Marxism*, Ann Arbor.

Lynch, A. (1987) *The Soviet Study of International Relations*, Cambridge University Press.

Lyubomirova, N. V. *et al.* (1989) 'Perestroika soznaniya ili soznatel'naya perestroika', *Voprosy filosofii*, 4: 28–48.

McAdams, A. J. (1987) 'Crisis in the Soviet empire', *Comparative Politics*, 20, 1 (October): 107–18.

McCauley, M. (ed.) (1987) *The Soviet Union Under Gorbachev*, Macmillan.

McCauley, M. (ed.) (1990) *Gorbachev and Perestroika*, Macmillan.

MacDonald, O. (1986) 'New directions in Soviet "Westpolitik"', *Labour Focus on Eastern Europe*, 8, 2: 10–12.

Makarenko, V. (forthcoming) *Bureaucracy and Stalinism*, Progress, Moscow.

Malcolm, N. (1984) *Soviet Political Scientists and American Politics*, Macmillan.

Malcolm, N. (1989) *Soviet Policy Perspectives on Western Europe*, Routledge/RIIA.

Mandel, E. (1989) *Beyond Perestroika: The future of Gorbachev's USSR*, Verso.

Mandelbaum, M. and S. Talbott (1987) *Reagan and Gorbachev*, Vintage.

Man'kovskii, L. A. (1989) 'K voprosu o psikhologii kul'ta Stalina', *Voprosy filosofii*, 1: 162–6.

Manning, R. A. (1987/8) 'Moscow's Pacific future: Gorbachev rediscovers Asia', *World Policy Journal*, 5, 1 (Winter): 55–78.

Marsh, D. (ed.) (1983) *Pressure Politics: Interest groups in Britain*, Junction Books.

Marx, K. (1968) *The Civil War in France* in K. Marx and F. Engels, *Selected Works*, Lawrence & Wishart.

Mastny, V. (1988) 'Europe in US–USSR relations: a topical legacy', *Problems of Communism*, 37, 1 (January-February): 16–29.

Materialy XXVII s"ezda kommunisticheskoi partii sovetskogo soyuza (1986), Politicheskaya literatura.

Medvedev, R. (1977) *On Socialist Democracy*, Spokesman Books.

Medvedev V. (1988) 'K poznaniyu sotsializma', *Kommunist*, 17: 3–18.

Medvedev, Z. (1986a) *Gorbachev*, Basil Blackwell.

Medvedev, Z. (1986b) 'Innovation and conservatism in the new Soviet leadership', *New Left Review*, 157: 5–26.

Medvedev, Z. (1986c) 'New leaders, old problems, new solutions?', *Labour Focus on Eastern Europe*, 8, 2: 3–9.

Mekhanizm tormozheniya: istoki, deistvie, puti preodeleniya (1988) ed. V. V. Zhuravlev and Y. S. Aksenov, Moscow, Politizdat.

Men'shikov, S. (1989) 'Ekonomicheskaya struktura sotsializma: chto vperedi?', *Novyi mir*, 3: 190–212.

Michnik, A. (1985) 'A new evolutionism' in *Letters from Prison and Other Essays*, University of California Press.

Michnik, A. (1987) 'Gorbachev – as seen from Warsaw', *East European Reporter*, 2, 4: 32–4.

Michnik, A. (1988) interview with Erica Blair, *Times Literary Supplement*, 19–25 February: 188, 198–9.

Mickiewicz, E. (1988) 'Changes in the media under Gorbachev: the case of television', *Journal of Communist Studies*, 4, 4 (December): 35–47.

Mickiewicz, E. (1989) *Split Signals: Television and politics in the Soviet Union*, Oxford University Press.

Migranyan, A. M. (1987) 'Vzaimootnosheniya individa, obshchestva i gosudarstva v politicheskoi teorii marksizma i problemy demokratizatsii sotsialisticheskogo obshchestva', *Voprosy filosofii*, 8: 75–91.

Migranyan, A. M. (1989a) 'Dolgii put' k evropeiskomu domu', *Novyi mir*, 7: 166–84.

Migranyan, A. M. (1989b) 'Populizm', *Sovetskaya kul'tura*, 24 June.

Migranyan, A. M. (1990) 'Demokratiya v teorii i istoricheskoi praktike', *Kommunist*, 1 (January): 33–42.

Millar, J. R. (ed.) (1987) *Politics, Work and Daily Life in the USSR*, Cambridge University Press.

Miller, R. F., J. H. Miller and T. H. Rigby (1987) *Gorbachev at the Helm: A new era in Soviet politics*, Croom Helm.

Miller, W. G. (ed.) (1989) *Towards a More Civil Society?: The USSR under Mikhail Sergeevich Gorbachev; an assessment by the American Committee on US–Soviet Relations*, Harper & Row.

Minaev, L. M. (1989) 'Demokratiya, politika i plyuralizm mnenii: leninskie uroki', *Voprosy istorii KPSS*, 1 (January): 3–17.

Mitrany, D. (1946) *A Working Peace System: An argument for the functional development of international organisation*, National Peace Council.

Moiseev, N. N. (1988) 'Oblik rukovoditelya', *Novyi mir*, 4: 176–88.

Moiseev, N. N. (1989a) 'Ekologiya, nravstvennost' i politika', *Voprosy filosofii*, 5: 3–25.

Moiseev, N. N. (1989b) 'Natsional'nye problemy v kontekste obshchikh zakonov razvitiya', *Kommunist*, 8 (May): 56–78.

Morrison, D. (ed.) (1988) *Mikhail S. Gorbachev: An intimate biography*, introduced by S. Talbott, compiled by the editors of *Time* magazine, Time Books.

Murarka, D. (1987) *Gorbatchev*, Paris, Ramsay.

Nation, The (1987) special issue on Gorbachev's reforms, 13 June.

Nekipelov, A. (1989) '*Iz* plena mifov i dogm, *Kommunist*, 7 (May): 15–22.

Nersesyanits, V. S. (1989) 'Pravovoe gosudarstvo: istoriya i sovremennost', *Voprosy filosofii*, 2: 3–16.

Niiseki, K. (1987) *The Soviet Union in Transition*, Avebury.

Nove, A. (1983) *The Economics of Feasible Socialism*, Allen & Unwin.

Nove, A. (1987) ' "Radical reform": problems and prospects', *Soviet Studies*, 3 (July): 452–67.

Odom, W. E. (1988/9) 'Soviet military doctrine', *Foreign Affairs*, 67, 2 (Winter): 114–34.

Ol'sevich, Y. (1989) 'Paradoksy ili novye tendentsii?: o edinstve i plyuralizme industrial'nykh form', *Kommunist*, 6 (April): 48–57.

Osmyslit' kul't Stalina (1989) ed. K. Kobo, Progress.

Panarin, A. (1989) 'Dielektika gumanizma', *Kommunist*, 5 (March): 40–51.

Parrott, B. (1988) 'Soviet national security under Gorbachev', *Problems of Communism*, 37, 6 (November–December): 1–36.

Perestroika in Action (1988) a collection of press articles and interviews, ed. V. Mezhenkov and E. Skelley, Collets.

Perestroika i sovremennyi mir (1989) ed. T. T. Timofeev, Mezhdunarodnye otnosheniya.

Ploss, S. L. (1986) 'A new Soviet era?', *Foreign Policy*, 62 (Spring): 46–60.

Polan, A. J. (1984) *Lenin and the End of Politics*, Methuen.

Politicheskie sistemy sovremennosti: ocherki (1978), Nauka.

Popkova, A. (1987) 'Gde pyshnee pirogi?', *Novyi mir*, 5 (May): 239–41.

Popov, G. (1985) 'O sovershenstvovanii tsentralizovannogo khozyaistvennogo rukovodstva', *Voprosy ekonomiki*, 5: 82–92.

Popov, G. (1988) 'From an economist's point of view', in *The Stalin Phenomenon*, Novosti: 11–24.

Postizhenie (1989) ed. F. M. Borodkin, L. Y. Kosals and R. V. Ryvkina, Progress.

Pozdnyakov, E. and I. Shadrina (1989) 'O gumanizatsii i demokratizatsii mezhdunarodnykh otnoshenii', *Mirovaya ekonomika i mezhdunarodnye otnosheniya*, 4: 18–30.

Pravda, A. (1988a) *Soviet Foreign Policy Priorities Under Gorbachev*, Routledge/RIIA.

Pravda, A. (1988b) 'Is there a Gorbachev foreign policy?', *Journal of Communist Studies*, 4, 4 (December): 100–19.

Primakov, E. *et al.* (1989) 'Nekotorye problemy novogo myshleniya', *Mirovaya ekonomika i mezhdunarodnye otnosheniya*, 6: 5–18.

Programme of the Communist Party of the Soviet Union: New edition (1986), Novosti.

Razumov, A. (1989) 'Novoe myshlenie i 'staraya' filosofiya?', *Kommunist*, 2 (January): 65–76.

Razumovskii, G. (1989) 'Vozglavlyat' perestroiku, generirovat' energiyu obnovleniya', *Kommunist*, 4 (March): 3–14.

Reddaway, P. (1983) 'Dissent in the Soviet Union', *Problems of Communism*, 6 (November–December): 1–15.

Reddaway, P. (1985) 'Waiting for Gorbachev', *New York Review of Books*, 10 October: 5–10.

Reddaway, P. (1987) 'Gorbachev the bold', *New York Review of Books*, 28 May: 21–8.

Reddaway, P. (1988) 'Resisting Gorbachev', *New York Review of Books*, 18 August: 36–41.

Rules of the Communist Party of the Soviet Union (1986), Novosti.

Rumer, B. (1986) 'Realities of Gorbachev's economic program', *Problems of Communism*, 35, 3 (May–June): 20–31.

Rupnik, J. (1988) 'La contrainte de l'Europe de l'Est', *Pouvoirs*, 45 (Avril): 89–102.

Ryzhkov, N. (1986) *Guidelines for the Economic and Social Development of the USSR for 1986–1990 and for the Period Ending in 2000*, Novosti.

Sakharov, A. (1989) 'All power to the soviets' and his 'Decree on Power', *XX Century and Peace*, 8: 9–12.

Sakwa, R. (1986) *The Party and Opposition in Moscow, 1920–Early 1921*, University of Essex, Russian and Soviet Studies Centre Discussion Paper Series, no. 7 (January).

Sakwa, R. (1987) 'The commune state in Moscow in 1918', *Slavic Review*, 46, 3/4 (Fall/Winter): 429–49.

Sakwa, R. (1988a) *Soviet Communists in Power: A study of Moscow during the civil war, 1918–21*, Macmillan.

Sakwa, R. (1988b) 'Gorbachev and the new Soviet foreign policy', *Paradigms: The Kent Journal of International Relations*, 2, 1 (June): 18–29.

Sakwa, R. (1989a) *Soviet Politics: An introduction*, Routledge.

Sakwa, R. (1989b) 'Commune democracy and Gorbachev's reforms', *Political Studies*, 37, 2 (June): 224–43.

Sakwa, R. (1989c) 'The *perestroika* of the party in 1921–22: the case of Moscow', *Revolutionary Russia*, 2, 1 (June): 5–30.

Scanlan, J. P. (1988a) 'Reforms and civil society in the USSR', *Problems of Communism*, 37, 2 (March–April): 41–6.

Scanlan, J. P. (1988b) 'Ideology and reform' in P. Juviler and H. Kimura (eds.), *Gorbachev's Reforms: US and Japanese assessments*, Aldine.

Schmidt-Häuer, C. (1986) *Gorbachev: The path to power*, I. B. Tauris.

Schöpflin, G. (1988a) 'Reform in Eastern Europe', *Slovo*, 1, 1 (May): 1–6.

Schöpflin, G. (1988b) 'The Stalinist experience in Eastern Europe', *Survey*, 30, 3 (October): 124–47.

Schroeder, G. (1979) 'The Soviet economy on the treadmill of "reforms" ' in US Congress Joint Economic Committee, *Soviet Economy in a Time of Change*, US Government Printing Office, Washington, DC, vol. 1.

Schumpeter, J. A. (1943/1987) *Capitalism, Socialism and Democracy*, Unwin Hyman.

Selyunin, V. (1988) 'Istoki', *Novyi mir*, 5: 162–89.

Selyunin, V. and G. Khanin (1987a) 'Lukavaya tsifra', *Novyi mir*, 2 (February): 181–201.

Selyunin, V. and G. Khanin (1987b) 'Statistika znaet vse?', *Novyi mir*, 12 (December): 255–7.

Service, R. (1987) 'Gorbachev's political reforms: the future in the past', *Journal of Communist Studies*, 3, 3 (September): 277–85.

Sestanovich, S. (1988) 'Gorbachev's foreign policy: a diplomacy of decline', *Problems of Communism*, 37, 1 (January–February): 1–15.

Shafarevich, I. (1989) 'Dve dorogi – k odnomu obryvu', *Novyi mir*, 7: 147–65.

Shapiro, J. (1989) 'The perestroika of history in the Soviet Union', *Slovo*, 2, 1 (May): 5–13.

Shaw, M. (1988) 'The end of regimentation – socialism's second chance', *Détente*, 13: 14–16.

Shearman, P. (1987) 'Gorbachev and the Third World: an era of reform', *Third World Quarterly*, 9, 4 (October): 1083–117.

Sherlock, T. (1988) 'Politics and history under Gorbachev', *Problems of Communism*, 37, 3–4 (May–August): 16–42.

Shlapentokh, V. (1990) 'The XXVII Congress – a case study of the shaping of a new party ideology', *Soviet Studies*, 40, 1 (January): 1–20.

Shmelëv, N. (1987) 'Avansy i dolgi', *Novyi mir*, 6 (June): 142–58.

Shmelëv, N. (1988) 'Novye trevogi', *Novyi mir*, 4 (April): 163–75.

Shtromas, A. (1981) *Political Change and Social Development: The case of the Soviet Union*, Peter Lang.

Shtromas, A. (1987) 'Dissent, nationalism and the Soviet future', *Studies in Comparative Communism*, 20, 3/4 (Autumn/Winter): 277–86.

Shtromas, A. and M. A. Kaplan (1988) *The Soviet Union and the Challenge of the Future*, vol. 1, *Stasis and Change*, Paragon House.

Shubkin, V. (1988) 'Bureaucracy: a sociologist's point of view', in *Soviet Society: Philosophy of development*, Moscow, Progress: 201–30.

Shubkin, V. (1989) 'Trudnoe proshchanie', *Novyi mir*, 4: 165–84.

Simes, D. K. (1987) 'Gorbachev: a new foreign policy?', *Foreign Affairs*, 65, 3: 477–500.

Simis, K. (1985) 'The Gorbachev generation', *Foreign Policy*, 59: 3–21.

Smith, K. (ed.) (1986) *Soviet Industrialisation and Soviet Maturity*, Routledge & Kegan Paul.

Sochor, Z. A. (1988) *Revolution and Culture: The Bogdanov–Lenin controversy*, Cornell University Press.

Solodukhin, Y. (1989) 'Demokraticheskii potentsial sotsializma', *Partiinaya zhizn'*, 1: 7–15.

Sotsialisticheskoe pravovoe gosudarstvo: problemy i suzhdeniya (1989), Institut gosudarstva i prava AN SSSR.

Staniszkis, J. (1984) *Poland's Self-Limiting Revolution*, Princeton University Press.

Starr, S. F. (1988) 'Soviet Union: a civil society', *Foreign Policy*, 70 (Spring): 26–41.

Stent, A. (1989) 'The Soviet Union and Western Europe: divided continent or common house?', *The Harriman Institute Forum*, 2, 9 (September).

Stites, R. (1989a) *Revolutionary Dreams: Utopian vision and experimental life in the Russian Revolution*, Oxford University Press.

Stites, R. (1989b) 'Soviet popular culture in the Gorbachev era', *The Harriman Institute Forum*, 2, 3 (March).

Stranitsy istorii KPSS: fakty, problemy, uroki (1988) ed. V. I. Kuptsov, Vysshaya shkola.

Stranitsy istorii sovetskogo obshchestva: fakty, problemy, lyudi, (1989) ed. A. T. Kinkul'kina, Politizdat.

Stupishin, V. (1989) 'U kogo vlast' v pravovom gosudarstve?', *Mezhdunarodnaya zhizn'*, 11 (November): 29–43.

Sundquist, J. L. (1986) *Constitutional Reform and Effective Government*, Brookings.

Suny, R. G. (1987) 'Gorbachev and Soviet history', *Tikkun*, 2, 4.

Svec, M. (1988) 'The Prague Spring: 20 years later', *Foreign Affairs*, 66, 5 (Summer): 981–1001.

Szawlowski, R. (1988) 'A Polish introduction to the theory of civil law', *Review of Socialist Law*, 14, 4: 363–86.

Szporluk, R. (1989) 'Dilemmas of Russian nationalism', *Problems of Communism*, 38, 4 (July–August): 15–35.

Szulc, T. (1988) 'Poland's path', *Foreign Policy*, 72 (Fall): 210–29.

Taagepera, R. (1989) 'Estonia's road to independence', *Problems of Communism*, 38, 6 (November–December): 11–26.

Tatu, M. (1987) *Gorbatchev: l'URSS va-t-elle changer?*, Paris, Le Centurion.

Tatu, M. (1988) '19th party conference', *Problems of Communism*, 38, 3–4 (May–August): 1–15.

Taubman, W. (1974) 'The change to change in Communist systems: modernization, postmodernization, and Soviet politics' in H. W. Morton and R. L. Tokes (eds.), *Soviet Politics and Society in the 1970s*, Free Press.

Teague, E. (1988) 'Perestroika: the Polish influence', *Survey*, 30, 3 (October): 39–57.

Thom, F. (1989) *The Gorbachev Phenomenon: A history of perestroika*, Pinter.

Thompson, E. P. (1982) *Exterminism and the Cold War*, New Left Books.

Ticktin, H. (1986) 'The year after the three General Secretaries: change without change', *Critique*, 17: 113–35.

Ticktin, H. (1988) 'The contradictions of Gorbachev', *Journal of Communist Studies*, 4, 4 (December): 83–99.

Time magazine (1988) *Mikhail S. Gorbachev: An intimate biography*, ed. D. Morrison, introduced by S. Talbott, Time Books.

Timmermann, H. (1987) *The Decline of the World Communist Movement: Moscow, Beijing, and Communist parties in the West*, Westview.

Timmermann, H. (1989a) 'Is Gorbachev a Bukharinist? Moscow's reappraisal of the NEP period', *Journal of Communist Studies*, 5, 1 (March): 1–17.

Timmermann, H. (1989b) 'The Communist Party of the Soviet Union's reassessment of international social democracy: dimensions and trends', *Journal of Communist Studies*, 5, 2 (June): 173–83.

Timmermann, H. (1989c) 'The CPSU and the international Communist Party system: a change of paradigms in Moscow', *Studies in Comparative Communism*, 22, 2/3 (Summer/Autumn): 265–77.

Timofeev, L. (1985) *Poslednyaya nadezhda vyzhit'*, Hermitage.

Tishkov, V. (1989) 'Narody i gosudarstvo', *Kommunist*, 1: 49–59.

Tismancanu, V. (1987a), 'Pitfalls of détente', *Problems of Communism*, 36, 3 (May–June): 78–84.

Tismaneanu, V. (1987b) 'The nature of Marxist regimes', *Studies in Comparative Communism*, 20, 2 (Summer).

Tismaneanu, V. (1988) *The Crisis of Marxist Ideology in Eastern Europe*, Routledge.

Tolz, V. (1989a) 'The united front of workers of Russia: further consolidation of antireform forces', *Report on the USSR*, 1, 39: 11–13.

Tolz, V. (1989b) 'The Soviet Union retreats from Marxism–Leninism', *Report on the USSR*, 1, 42: 9–14.

Tsipko, A. S. (1988) 'Philosophy and uniformity in the context of perestroika' in *Soviet Society: Philosophy of development*, Progress.

Tsipko, A. S. (1988–9) 'Istoki stalinizma', *Nauka i zhizn'*, 11–12 (1988); 1–2 (1989).

Tucker, R. C. (1981) *Politics as Leadership*, University of Missouri Press.

Tucker, R. C. (1987) *Political Culture and Leadership in Soviet Russia: From Lenin to Gorbachev*, Harvester Wheatsheaf.

Ulam, A. B. (1985) 'Forty years of troubled coexistence', *Foreign Affairs*, 64, 1 (Fall): 12–32.

Urok daet istoriya (1989), Politicheskaya literatura.

USSR: A time of change (1987), Progress.

Valkenier, E. (1983) *The Soviet Union and the Third World: The economic bind*, Praeger.

Vardys, V. S. (1989) 'Lithuanian national politics', *Problems of Communism*, 38, 4 (July–August): 53–76.

Veen, H-J. (1987) *From Brezhnev to Gorbachev: Domestic affairs and Soviet foreign policy*, Berg Publishers.

Volkogonov, D. (1988) 'The Stalin phenomenon' in *The Stalin Phenomenon*, Novosti: 34–52.

Volkogonov, D. (1989) *Triumf i tragedii*, Moscow, Novosti.

Volobuev, O. and S. Kuleshov (1989) *Ochishchenie: istoriya i perestroika, publitsisticheskie zametki*, Novosti.

Vozvrashchennye imena (1989), 2 vols., ed. A. Proskurin, Novosti.

Walicki, A. (1987) *Legal Philosophers of Russian Liberalism*, Clarendon Press.

Walker, R. (1989) 'The psychology of perestroika', *Détente*, 16: 7–11.

Waller, M. (1981) *Democratic Centralism: An historical commentary*, Manchester University Press.

Weickhardt, G. (1985) 'Gorbachev's record on economic reform', *Soviet Union/ Union Soviétique*, 12, 3: 251–76.

Wettig, G. (1988) ' "New Thinking" on security and East–West relations', *Problems of Communism*, 37, 2 (March–April): 1–14.

White, S. (1978) 'Communist systems and the iron law of political pluralism', *British Journal of Political Science*, 8 (January): 101–17.

White. S. (1985) 'Noncompetitive elections and national politics: the USSR Supreme Soviet elections of 1984', *Electoral Studies*, 4, 3: 215–29.

White, S. (1988a) 'Gorbachev, Gorbachevism and the party conference', *Journal of Communist Studies*, 4, 4 (December): 127–60.

White, S. (1988b) 'Reforming the electoral system', *Journal of Communist Studies*, 4, 4 (December): 1–17.

White, S. (1990a) ' "Democratisation" in the USSR', *Soviet Studies*, 42, 1 (January): 3–24.

White, S. (1990b) *Gorbachev in Power*, Cambridge University Press.

White, S. and A. Pravda (eds.) (1988) *Ideology and Soviet Politics*, Macmillan.

Wilson, A. and N. Bachkatov (1988) *Living with Glasnost: Youth and society in a changing Russia*, Penguin.

Winiecki, J. (1988) *The Distorted World of Soviet-type Economies*, Routledge.

Winning the Human Race (1988), Geneva, Independent Commission on International Humanitarian Issues.

Wishnevsky, J. (1988) 'The origins of Pamyat', *Survey*, 30, 3 (October): 79–91.

Wishnevsky, J. (1989) '*Nash Sovremennik* provides focus for "Opposition Party" ', *Report on the USSR*, 1, 3: 1–6.

Woll, J. (1989) 'Glasnost and Soviet culture', *Problems of Communism*, 38, 6 (November–December): 40–50.

Yakovlev, A. N. (1990) *Realizm – zemlya perestroika: Izbrannye vystuplenie i stat'i*, Moscow, Politicheskay a literatura.

Yanov, A. (1987) *The Russian Challenge and the Year 2000*, Oxford University Press.

Yasin, E. (1989) 'Sotsialisticheskii rynok ili yarmarka illyuzii?' *Kommunist*, 15 (October): 53–62.

Z (1990) 'To the Stalin Mausoleum', *Daedalus*, 169, 1 (Winter): 295–344.

Zagoria, D. S. (1989) 'Soviet policy in East Asia: a new beginning?', *Foreign Affairs*, 68, 1: 120–38.

Zakharova, N., A. Posadskaya and N. Rimashevskaya (1989) 'Kak my reshaem zhenskii vopros', *Kommunist*, 4 (March): 56–65.

Zaprudnik, J. (1989) 'Belorussian reawakening', *Problems of Communism*, 38, 4 (July–August): 36–52.

Zaslavskaya, T. (1984) 'The Novosibirsk Report', introduced by P. Hanson, *Survey*, 28, 1 (Spring): 83–108.

Zaslavskaya, T. (1986) 'Chelovecheskii faktor razvitiya ekonomiki i sotsial'naya spravedlivost' ', *Kommunist*, 13: 61–73.

Zaslavskaya, T. (1987) 'Remettre l'économie sur ses pieds', *Les Temps modernes*, 492–4 (July–September): 202–31.

Zaslavskaya, T. (1989a) 'Restructuring as a social revolution', *Izvestiya*, 24 December 1988 in *Current Digest of the Soviet Press*, 40, 51: 1–4.

Zaslavskaya, T. (1989b) ' "Zhit' s otkrytymi glazami" ', *Kommunist*, 8 (May): 45–54.

Zaslavskaya, T. (1989c) *A Voice of Reform: Essays by Tatyana Zaslavskaya*, M. E. Sharpe.

Zaslavskaya, T. (1990) *The Second Socialist Revolution*, I. B. Tauris.

Zaslavskaya, T. and R. V. Ryvkina (eds.) (1989) *Ekonomicheskaya sotsiologiya i perestroika*, Progress.

Zaslavsky, V. (1982) *The Neo-Stalinist State: Class, ethnicity and consensus in Soviet society*, Harvester Wheatsheaf.

Zemtsov, I. and J. Farrar (1989) *Gorbachev, the Man and the System*, Transaction Books.

Zharikov, A. (1989) 'Natsional'noe samoopredelenie v zamysle i realizatsii', *Kommunist*, 9 (June): 58–67.

Zinoviev, A. (1984) *The Reality of Communism*, Victor Gollancz.

INDEX